RERUM BRITANNICARUM MEDII ÆVI
SCRIPTORES,

OR

CHRONICLES AND MEMORIALS OF GREAT BRITAIN
AND IRELAND

DURING

THE MIDDLE AGES.

THE CHRONICLES AND MEMORIALS

OF

GREAT BRITAIN AND IRELAND

DURING THE MIDDLE AGES.

PUBLISHED BY THE AUTHORITY OF HER MAJESTY'S TREASURY, UNDER THE DIRECTION OF THE MASTER OF THE ROLLS.

On the 26th of January 1857, the Master of the Rolls submitted to the Treasury a proposal for the publication of materials for the History of this Country from the Invasion of the Romans to the reign of Henry VIII.

The Master of the Rolls suggested that these materials should be selected for publication under competent editors without reference to periodical or chronological arrangement, without mutilation or abridgment, preference being given, in the first instance, to such materials as were most scarce and valuable.

He proposed that each chronicle or historical document to be edited should be treated in the same way as if the editor were engaged on an Editio Princeps; and for this purpose the most correct text should be formed from an accurate collation of the best MSS.

To render the work more generally useful, the Master of the Rolls suggested that the editor should give an account of the MSS. employed by him, of their age and their peculiarities; that he should add to the work a brief account of the life and times of the author, and any remarks necessary to explain the chronology; but no other note or comment was to be allowed, except what might be necessary to establish the correctness of the text.

The works to be published in octavo, separately, as they were finished; the whole responsibility of the task resting upon the editors, who were to be chosen by the Master of the Rolls with the sanction of the Treasury.

The Lords of Her Majesty's Treasury, after a careful consideration of the subject, expressed their opinion in a Treasury Minute, dated February 9, 1857, that the plan recommended by the Master of the Rolls "was well calculated for the accomplishment of this important national object, in an effectual and satisfactory manner, within a reasonable time, and provided proper attention be paid to economy, in making the detailed arrangements, without unnecessary expense."

They expressed their approbation of the proposal that each Chronicle and historical document should be edited in such a manner as to represent with all possible correctness the text of each writer, derived from a collation of the best MSS., and that no notes should be added, except such as were illustrative of the various readings. They suggested, however, that the preface to each work should contain, in addition to the particulars proposed by the Master of the Rolls, a biographical account of the author, so far as authentic materials existed for that purpose, and an estimate of his historical credibility and value.

Rolls House,
  December 1857.

WILLELMI MALMESBIRIENSIS MONACHI

DE GESTIS REGUM ANGLORUM.

[*All Rights Reserved.*]

WILLELMI MALMESBIRIENSIS MONACHI

DE GESTIS REGUM ANGLORUM.

LIBRI QUINQUE;

HISTORIÆ NOVELLÆ

LIBRI TRES.

EDITED FROM MANUSCRIPTS

BY

WILLIAM STUBBS, D.D.,

BISHOP OF OXFORD, AND HONORARY STUDENT OF CHRIST CHURCH.

VOL. II.

PUBLISHED BY THE AUTHORITY OF THE LORDS COMMISSIONERS OF HER MAJESTY'S TREASURY, UNDER THE DIRECTION OF THE MASTER OF THE ROLLS.

LONDON:
PRINTED FOR HER MAJESTY'S STATIONERY OFFICE,
BY EYRE AND SPOTTISWOODE,
PRINTERS TO THE QUEEN'S MOST EXCELLENT MAJESTY.

And to be purchased, either directly or through any Bookseller, from
EYRE AND SPOTTISWOODE, EAST HARDING STREET, FLEET STREET, E.C.; or
ADAM AND CHARLES BLACK, 6, NORTH BRIDGE, EDINBURGH; or
HODGES, FIGGIS, & Co., 104, GRAFTON STREET, DUBLIN.

1889.

Printed by
EYRE and SPOTTISWOODE, Her Majesty's Printers.
For Her Majesty's Stationery Office.

CONTENTS OF THE PREFACE.

	Page.
INTRODUCTION; PURPOSE OF THE PREFACE	xv

I. Materials of the first book:
    1. Variations from Bede on Helena — xviii
    2. On Constantine — xix
    3. Citations from Nennius — xix
    4. The ancient genealogies and *dicta Alfredi* — xxi
    5. The history of Kent — xxii
    6. The West Saxons — xxiii
    7. The victories of Kenwalch — xxiv
    8. Caedwalla and the tithe of the spoil — xxv
    9. Northumbria — xxv
    10. Mercia — xxvi
    11. The letters of Alcuin — xxvii
    12. The letters of Boniface — xxviii
    13. Letters of Kenulf and Leo — xxix
    14. The East Saxons and East Angles — xxx

II. Materials for early continental history:
    1. Chronicle of Hariulf of Centoul or S. Riquier, and the continuation of Ado in the Chronicle of Fontanelles — xxxi
    2. The successors of Charles the Great — xxxii
    3. The Visio Karoli — xxxiii
    4. The siege of Chartres — xxxiii
    5. The origin of Hugh Capet — xxxiv
    6. Isambard — xxxv
    7. Robert of Montdidier — xxxvi
    8. Death of duke William of Normandy — xxxvii

III. Materials for the second book:
    1. Egbert and Ethelwulf — xxxviii
    2. Asser's Life of Alfred :—Ethelwulf's donation and will — xxxix
    3. Alfred's age — xli

CONTENTS OF THE PREFACE.

	Page.
4. His visits to Rome	xlii
5. History of Grimbald	xliv
6. John, the Old Saxon	xlviii
7. The vision of Saint Cuthbert, and other additions to Asser	xlix
8. The family of Edward the elder	li
9. The sub-division of the West Saxon dioceses, and pope Formosus	liv
10. The ancient life of Ethelstan, its form and age	lx
11. Its historical interest	lxiii
12. Edmund and Edred, Edwy and Edgar	lxv
13. The stories about Gerbert	lxvi
14. Stories about Henry III., and German kings and bishops: the dancers at Colovize	lxxiv
The ugly priest made archbishop	lxxvii
15. The marriage of Gunhilda	lxxviii
16. The Conquests of Henry III.	lxxx
17. The lady and lover in the snow	lxxxi
18. The unchaste deacon	lxxxi
19. The devil in church	lxxxii
20. The sold bishopric	lxxxii
21. The tragedy of Gregory VI.	lxxxiii
22. The witch of Berkeley	lxxxv
23. The ring and statue, and the discovery of the body of Pallas	lxxxv / lxxxvi
24. The woman with two bodies	lxxxvi
25. The two clerks of Nantes	lxxxvii
26. The history of Hildebrand	lxxxvii
27. Berengarius	lxxxviii
28. Sir Gawain	lxxxix
29. Marianus Scotus and Walcher prior of Malvern	lxxxix
30. General result	xc
31. The Anglo-Saxon Hagiology	xci
32. S. Oswald the king	xciii
33. The Royal Martyrs of Kent	xciv
34. S. Ethelbert of East Anglia	xciv
35. S. Kenelm	xcv
36. S. Wistan	xcvi
37. S. Edmund of East Anglia	xcvii
38. The Royal ladies	xcvii
39. Edward the Confessor	c
40. Domestic history; reign of Ethelred	cvi

	Page.
41. Canute and his sons	cviii
42. Reign of Edward	cix

III. The reign of the Conqueror:

1. His early reign in Normandy	cxi
2. The Conquest and battle of Hastings	cxiii
3. The latter part of the reign	cxiv

IV. Reign of William Rufus:

1. Domestic history and incidental jottings	cxvi
2. The history of the first crusade	cxviii
3. Fulcher of Chartres	cxix
4. Council of Clermont	cxx
5. The outset of the expedition	cxx
6. Arrival at Rome	cxxi
7. Journey to Constantinople	cxxii
8. By Antioch to Jerusalem	cxxiii
9. Variations from Fulcher; history of Godfrey	cxxiv
10. History of Bohemond	cxxvi
11. Raymond of S. Gilles	cxxvii
12. Robert of Normandy	cxxvii
13. Summary; as to Chronicle	cxxvii
14. As to Florence of Worcester	cxxviii
The kings on the Dee	cxxix
15. Godwin's ship	cxxx

V. General estimate of the author:

1. For early history	cxxxii
2. For his own days	cxxxiii
3. The fifth book of the Gesta up to the year 1105	cxxxiv
4. Later history in book V.	cxxxvi
5. The Historia Novella, first book	cxxxviii
6. The second book	cxxxix
7. The third book	cxl
8. Conclusion	cxli

PREFACE.

PREFACE.

IN the Preface to the first volume of this work I attempted to collect the particulars, to be gathered from record, tradition or inference, which could be made to throw light on the personal history of William of Malmesbury, and on the external evidences which illustrate the fortunes of the book before us. I propose in the following pages to discuss, more or less discursively, some of the chief points which a careful analysis of materials forces upon an editor in the course of preparation, and which suggest, not infrequently, interesting questions as to the value and relation of the sources of information used by the author. Having done this, I shall venture very briefly to present my conclusions on the independent value of the portions of the Gesta Regum and Historia Novella which we owe to him as a direct and contemporaneous authority. *Purpose of Preface.*

For making a *primâ facie* analysis of our author's materials we have considerable facilities in the account which he himself gives us, in the Preface to the first book, of the labours of his predecessors. We know from this that he used the Historia Ecclesiastica of the Venerable Bede, the native Chronicles, the abstract of national History furnished by Ethelwerd, and the Historia Novorum of his own contemporary Eadmer. The first reading of the book itself reveals a large number of additional sources; the early hagiographies, for instance, and the Chronicles of the Frank kings. Our acquaintance with the other works of our author, and with his educational equipment for the task he undertook, enables *Analysis of the author's materials; authorities acknowledged; sources used without citation; and incidental illustrations.*

us to supplement this list, at least conjecturally, with a long array of theological, moral, and legal books, which we may confidently affirm were familiar to him, both as student and as librarian, and to which we should naturally look for the identification of any purple patch, or appropriate quotation, imbedded among the commonplace details of the narrative.

<small>Our author seldom makes verbal extracts.</small>
As a counterbalance to this advantage in the way of inquiry, we must set the fact that our author, even when following most closely the material details which he found in the books that he was using, does so for the most part in his own language. There are some important exceptions, as we shall see, to this rule; but it is the principle on which he wrote, and on which no doubt he prided himself, when he declared himself the successor of Bede, as an original writer of English History. His own mastery of Latin,—a mastery, which, whatever we may think of the style and taste of his composition, is a fact which we ought not to under-

<small>Paraphrase or abstract.</small>
value,—tempted him continually to paraphrase, or modify in other ways, the language of his authority, and that to such a degree as occasionally to suggest that he had still more recondite materials before him, which a chance turn of words, or a casual expression, ought to enable

<small>Question as to undiscovered sources and lost texts.</small>
us to identify. Out of this uncertainty arises a further question which, although it does not affect a large number of books, is not by itself unimportant; whether the text of the books which he certainly used has reached us in the same form as that in which he used them; whether, for instance, he possessed more perfect copies of the Life of Alfred, or other recensions of the Chronicles. And further than this, the question of lost materials opens a very tempting region for theory: we

<small>Possible recovery of texts.</small>
ask what has become of the poetical life of Ethelstan; whence were drawn the anecdotes of the age of the emperor Henry III., and the copy of his epitaph: a few years ago the same point might have been raised with

reference to the materials for his account of Edward the Confessor; and indeed such a question cannot even yet be regarded as completely answered, although the labours of Dr. Luard and the research of Sir Thomas Hardy have, perhaps, led us as far as we are ever likely to get in the direction of solution. Possibly the Vatican Library may be found to contain relics of other books which may come into competition, as objects of literary interest, with Historia Britonum or the Draco Normannicus, or the poem of Ambrose, which is the foundation of the Itinerarium Regis Ricardi;[1] but we have scarcely fathomed as yet the depth of our own treasures conserved in public libraries and in the muniment rooms of our Great Houses.

For anything like an exhaustive treatment of these questions, a running commentary on the text of the book would have been indispensably necessary. The adoption, however, of such a plan would have been foreign to the scheme on which the publications of the series have been arranged; and indeed, however high we might be inclined to place the value of the work, it is questionable whether it is worth the time and toil which such a commentary would involve. Still at the risk of some waste of labour and some repetition of argument and statement, some such method of consecutive discussion is called for, in reference to a work of

Use of a running commentary.

---

[1] I take this opportunity of stating that I fully recognise the fact that the poem of Ambrose must be the French book from which a large part of the Itinerarium was not so much translated as paraphrased. Ambrose was, I believe, the clerk who is mentioned in the Account Rolls of 2 John as receiving a fee of 25s. for singing the "Christus vincit" at the king's second coronation: "Rex, &c., W " Thesaurario et camerariis de scac- " cario, &c. Liberate de thesauro " nostro xxv. solidos Eustacio ca- " pellano et Ambrosio clericis nos- " tris, qui cantaverunt *Christus vincit* " ad secundam coronationem nos- " tram et ad unctionem et corona- " tionem I. reginæ uxoris nostræ. " T. me ipso apud Westmonasterium " x. die Octobris." Rot. Contrabrev. Normanniæ, 2 Joh. m. 2; Madox, Hist. Exch., p. 119. A large portion of this poetical history is printed in the twenty-seventh volume of the Monumenta Historica Germaniæ, pp. 533–546.

xviii   PREFACE.

Plan adopted here. such importance; and I shall adopt it, with more or less minuteness of examination, in this portion of the preface, endeavouring to supplement the marginal references and textual variants of this edition, with such remarks as the investigations, which I have made however imperfectly, suggest; especially with reference to the relation of ascertained and unascertained sources, and to the interpretation of facts and dates, rather than the transmission of special views of events and speculations on their causes.

Sources of the first book of the Gesta Regum. I. The first book of the Gesta is based on the Historia Ecclesiastica of Bede, and the Anglo-Saxon Chronicles. It comprises the history of the country and nation up to the end of the eighth century and until the consolidation of the West Saxon power under Egbert. It is the portion of the work on which the author bestowed the most pains in revision, and for the illustration of which he went furthest afield in search of good authorities. On the whole he adhered very closely to his prototypes, so closely in fact that the few places, in which he diverges from their line or authority, invite especial notice.

Variations from Bede about S. Helena. 1. In the account of Roman Britain which fills the first three sections of the book, there are two distinct variations from the narrative of Bede; and both significant. Saint Helena, the mother of Constantine,[1] is described as *stabularia*, not *concubina* as Bede calls her. The substitution has a double importance. It shows that William of Malmesbury knew the tradition, embodied in the well-known panegyric by Saint Ambrose, "de obitu Theodosii,"[2] that the wife of Constantius

---

[1] Above, page 6.

[2] " Stabulariam hanc primo fuisse " asserunt, sic cognitam Constantio " seniori qui postea regnum adeptus " est. Bona stabularia, quæ tam " diligenter præsepe Domini quæ- " sivisset. Bona stabularia, quæ " stabularium non ignoravit illum " qui vulnera curavit a latronibus " vulnerati. Bona stabularia, quæ " maluit existimari stercora ut " Christum lucrifaceret." Ambros., Orat. de obitu Theodosii imperatoris; Surius, AA. SS. May 3; tom. v. f. 17.

was the daughter of an innkeeper; it suggests that he knew also the claim which she possessed to the position of a lawful wife, proved by the fact that her husband had to divorce her before he could marry the stepdaughter of Maximian; and, what is incidentally more important, it proves that our author either disbelieved, or was altogether ignorant of, the fable that she was the daughter of the British king Coel, a story which was being already ventilated by his contemporary the Archdeacon of Huntingdon as well as by Geoffrey of Monmouth.[1] Our author ignores the story of her British origin.

2. A second divergence occurs in the brief notice of Constantine himself. The planting of the Briton colonies in Armorica is ascribed to him. Bede himself is silent on the subject: Nennius, however, to whom, as we shall see, our author owes several minute particulars of British history, assigns the measure to the tyrant Maximus.[2] Whether the error is due to a confusion between Maximus and Constantine, whose first attempts were somewhat alike; or to a misreading of the text of Nennius; or to the writer's own impression about the fitness of things, we cannot say. But a very careful examination of the extant sources from which the narrative may be supposed to have been illustrated, has failed to discover any immediate authority from which this statement was derived. Constantine's colonies in Armorica.

3. The Historia Britonum, cited by our author himself as Gesta Britonum, and known to us under the name of Nennius, supplies all the incidents which are incorporated with Bede's materials in the account of the Anglo-Saxon Conquest. The slender embroidery added, by way of detail of character and policy, is an expansion of the language of Bede and possibly of the invective of Gildas. The particular illustrations which the Chronicles afforded in the matter of dated battles are summed up Use of Nennius.

---

[1] Hen. Hunt., Mon. Hist. Brit., p. 702; Galf. Mon., lib. v. c. 6. [2] Nennius, Mon. Hist. Brit., p. 61.

in a single line, much as Milton afterwards designates them as battles of the kites and crows. The words, however, in which Arthur is described have some significance. Our author gives him the credit of being a historical and national hero; but with an indication that he knew more than he chose to tell of the development of the Arthurian Mythology: "hic est Artur de " quo Britonum nugæ hodieque delirant;"[1] an expression which may be interpreted as showing more than a historian's contempt for the composition of the Welsh or Breton legends; and his language is not less critically contemptuous when, in describing the discovery of the tomb of Sir Gawain, he refers to the superstition of the Welsh about the return of Arthur.[2]

Our author's estimate of Arthurian legends.

It may be observed further that in preserving the name of the ruler of Kent at the time of Vortigern's surrender,[3] "sub cujusdam Guorongi laborabat regimine," our author shows that he regarded the designation as a personal, not an official, name. He found it in Nennius as "Guoirangono rege."[4] In the extreme dearth of intelligible nomenclature which marks these semi-historical details, it is a little hard to be told, as Camden will have it, that "Guorongus" simply means a viceroy.[5] Nennius, who must have known his native tongue, uses the name as a personal one, and the fact that one of the twenty-eight cities of Britain was commemorated as Caer Guoeirangon,[6] would certainly seem to favour such an explanation. Whether or no the city so named can be identified with Worcester, and, if that is the case, whether the time at which the list was elaborated was late enough to allow for an Anglo-Saxon element in the construction of this particular name, are questions that for the present are claimed for local archæologists.

The name Guorongus.

---

[1] Page 11.
[2] " unde antiquitas næniarum ad-" huc eum venturum fabulatur " p. 342.
[3] Page 10.
[4] Nennius, Mon.Hist. Brit., p. 65.
[5] Camden, Britannia (ed. 1600), p. 283; " Guorongum præfecit, id " est, proregem, sive libertum."
[6] Nennius, Mon. Hist. Brit., p. 77.

4. I do not propose to dwell upon the minute points in which, by using Nennius, our author is enabled to fill in an occasional date or name that is omitted by Bede or in the Chronicles; nor to go into any analysis of the particulars in which he may be supposed to have wavered between the two last-named authorities. In most points, except the numeration of regnal years and the naming of battle-fields, the Chronicle follows the Historia Ecclesiastica until its close, and the close of the Historia Ecclesiastica only precedes by about seventy years the consolidation of the West Saxon hegemony, with which the first book of the Gesta ends. From the year 449 accordingly to the year 731, Bede, supplemented by the Chronicle, supplies the main material of the work; and the important variants of the text of the Chronicle during this period are not so numerous as to force upon us the question, which arises later, what copy of the Anglo-Saxon Chronicle did William use, or did he use at all the Latin Chronicle which possibly underlies the *Chronicon ex Chronicis* of Florence of Worcester. It is hardly possible to avoid the conclusion that he was acquainted with the ancient genealogies which are added as appendices to Florence's work; the coincidences in language and detail are too close to be accidental: and it may be questioned whether the whole of them may not have been incorporated by the Worcester historian from some more ancient source, such as the " Narratio de " sanctis qui in Anglorum regione quiescunt,"[1] or the " dicta regis Aelfredi," which are cited in one place as authority for West Saxon chronology.[2]

Relation of our author's narrative to Bede and the Chronicles.

His acquaintance with the genealogies.

---

[1] Printed by Hickes, *Dissertatio Epistolaris*, pp. 115 sq.: and carefully edited by Dr. Liebermann, *Die Heiligen Englands*, Hannover, 1889.

[2] "Deinde Kenfus duobus annis " secundum dicta regis Alfredi, " juxta vero Chronicam Anglicam " filius ejus Æscwinus fere tribus " annis regnavit," Mon. Hist. Brit., p. 641. The " Fragmentum Historiæ Regum West-Saxoniæ," printed from Wheloc's Bede, as Appendix IV. to the University College edition of Spelman's life of Alfred, does not contain this par-

I will mention a few of the places in which our author seems to have outrun or added to his authorities for this portion of the work.

The Royal martyrs of Kent.

5. In the history of the kings of Kent he preserves the tradition of the martyrdom of the two sons of Eormenred, which is not derived from Bede, and appears as an addition or interpolation only in the Canterbury MS. of the Chronicle.[1] As in the second book this tradition is referred to, with a more probable relation to Goscelin's life of S. Mildred,[2] it is unnecessary to suppose that the insertion in this place was suggested by the perusal of the Chronicle.

Obscure Kentish chronology.

The confused chronology of the last years of the Kentish kingdom has seriously affected the close of the section on the subject.[3] When Bede completed his work Wihtred had lately died, leaving his three sons Ethelbert, Eadbert, and Alric his heirs. The Chronicle preserved the name of no successor, except perhaps the West Saxon Ealhmund, before Eadbert Præn in 794. Although William recognised both the obscurity of the chronology and the extinction of the house of Hengist, he could not resist the temptation of assigning to these three princes reigns long enough to fill the intervening space. He gives to Eadbert twenty-three years, to Ethelbert eleven, and to Alric thirty-four. For the first number he has the authority of five of the existing copies

---

ticular point, although it is a careful list of the regnal years of the West Saxon kings down to Alfred's accession. It is, however, there ascribed to Alfred as the possible author. It is referred to by Hickes in the Grammatica Anglo-Saxonica (Thesaurus, p. 66, and in the first edition, p. 134), but in the Index is ascribed to Alfric. However, the whole matter is disposed of by Sir Thomas D. Hardy in the Cat. Mat., i. 575, where it is shown that in the earliest MS., Tiberius, A. 3, the list is continued as far as Edward the Martyr. Cf. also Thorpe, Anglo-Saxon Chronicle, p. 1. The MS. from which Wheloc printed was probably the MS. Otho, B. xi., now destroyed.

[1] Page 16.
[2] Page 267.
[3] See note on p. 18; cf. Councils and Ecclesiastical Documents, iii. 397, and the article on the Kings of Kent in Smith's Dictionary of Christian Biography, vol. iii.

of the Chronicle; for the second that of six; for the third none at all; but thirty-four years were required to fill up the interval between 760 and 794. If this were historical, king Alric must have survived his father for seventy years. But, although no doubt the computation is erroneous, our author's generalisation about the condition of Kent, after the decline of the royal house, is fully borne out by the evidence of charters. These show that the kingdom during the latter half of the eighth century was broken up amongst a number of small and dependent princes, attached to Mercia, Wessex, or Essex, at different points, and that the only continuous ruling power in the land itself was that of the archbishop, himself very much at the mercy of Offa and his successor Kenulf.

It may be noted finally that, in calculating the continuance of the Kentish kingdom, from A.D. 444 onwards for 375 years, the author varies a little from his own computation.[1] If Eadbert Præn has two years from 794, Cuthred eight from 796, and Baldred eighteen from 804, the end of the kingdom comes in 822 and not in 819. As a matter of history, it may be fixed to A.D. 824 or 825.[2]

6. The history of Kent is followed by that of the West Saxons, for which the Chronicle, as might be expected, furnishes more abundant and satisfactory data. And to the Chronicle, supplemented by the Glastonbury and Malmesbury additions, the narrative adheres with fair faithfulness. I have said so much about these additions in the preface to the first volume that it is needless to do more than mention them here. They are mostly fabulous; the utmost that can be said for the most probable of them is that it may be traditionary.

West Saxon history.

Sources in Glastonbury and Malmesbury legends.

---

[1] See page 19.
[2] See Councils and Ecclesiastical Documents, iii. 557. The Chronicle places it in 823, which being corrected by two years, a correction necessitated by the miscalculation of Egbert's accession, should be 825. On this, see Hoveden, vol. i., præf., pp. xci. sq.

Our author's relation to these fables.
It is not for a moment to be supposed that our author fabricated either the Glastonbury or the Malmesbury legends. The age that concocted the British history of Geoffrey was quite competent to create a history for Avalon. It would seem most probable that William of Malmesbury allowed his pleasure at discovering a new mine of history at Glastonbury to overbalance his critical acuteness. Yet he had misgivings: he thought it worth while to examine into the date of pope Eleutherus;[1] he cited Freculfus for the preaching of S. Philip in Gaul;[2] Gildas was an authority worth referring to:[3] he had seen with his own eyes the inscribed pyramids, and did not venture to determine the meaning of the inscriptions.[4] In the book on Glastonbury he produces a charter granted by Kenulf of Mercia to a certain Kenelm, whom he professes himself unable to identify, and whom therefore he did not himself invent.[5] Yet his identification of abbot Berhtwald with the archbishop who succeeded Theodore is a mistake of grievous rashness;[6] and the whole of the monastic details, unluckily inserted in the later additions to the Gesta, have had a fatal influence on his character for conscientious and critical veracity. His treatment of the history of his own monastery in this respect is entitled to more indulgence: it is less uncritical, and based on traditions for which something may be said. The memory of Aldhelm was itself a monument with which Glastonbury had, even with its memories of Dunstan, little or nothing to compare; and there is no attempt at Malmesbury to overlay the stratum of truth with wanton invention.

The battles of King Kenwalch.
7. Setting all this on one side, we have only two points to notice in the West Saxon history. In the

---

[1] Vol. i. p. 24.
[2] Vol. i. p. 23.
[3] Vol. i. p. 24.
[4] Ib., p. 25.

[5] Antt. Glaston., ed. Gale, pp. 314–316; ed. Hearne, Adam of Domerham, i. 64–68.
[6] Vol. i. p. 29.

account of Kenwalch, our author mentions two great victories over the Britons, one at Wirtgernesburg, the other at the hill called Penn.[1] In the Chronicle the battle of Penn is dated A.D. 658. The only other battle that can be supposed to be intended, that of A.D. 652, is fixed in the Chronicles at Bradford-on-Avon. I know of no reason why Bradford should be supposed to have been the city of Vortigern. But if it were not, our author must have had some other information than we can now trace: possibly local tradition, possibly another form of the Chronicle. This particular fact is one of the additions of the later issues of the Gesta.

8. The other point is this: the story that Caedwalla, before his baptism, was so pious as to tithe his spoils, won, it is true, by predatory warfare, for the service of God. The expression "decimaret"[2] is not warranted by Bede or the Chronicle. Bede[3] describes him as vowing a fourth part of the Conquest of the Isle of Wight, to be given to Wilfrid; and Eddius, in his account of the same transaction,[4] uses hyperbolical language respecting the gift: our author must have supplied the technical word on his own authority, or have had other information on the point which, in the absence of any charters, is extremely improbable. This would be hardly worth notice had not the mention of tithe, at this particular juncture, a certain amount of critical importance.

Caedwalla and the tithe.

9. In the history of Northumbria William of Malmesbury had no temptation to leave the beaten track. Bede's information was ample:[5] the Chronicle supplied missing links of pedigree. The translation of S. Oswald's relics to Gloucester, and that of S. Hilda, Aidan, and Ceolfrith

Sources of Northumbrian history.

---

[1] Vol. i. p. 23.
[2] Vol. i. p. 33.
[3] Bede, H. E., iv. 16; Eadmer follows Bede; V. Wilf., ed. Raine, York Historians, i. 205.
[4] Eddius, ed. Gale, p. 73; ed. Raine, York Historians, i. 59.

[5] Professor Freeman remarks the intelligence which our author displays in his account of the origin of the Northumbrian kingship. Norman Conquest, i. 25.

xxvi   PREFACE.

to Glastonbury, are almost the only noteworthy contributions of our author.[1] But he drew heavily on the other resources within his reach. The Vitæ Abbatum of Bede, the account of the last illness and death of the historian, the letter of pope Sergius to abbot Ceolfrith, and the valuable extracts from the letters of Alcuin, furnish illustrations of the intelligence and industry of the compiler. And these, with the dates derived from the Chronicle, enabled him to furnish a more consecutive account of Northumbria than he has done for the other kingdoms.[2] With the more abundant supply of material comes the stronger temptation to digression. In connexion with the history of Alcuin we are led off to the Frank kingdom, the pedigree and exploits of Charles the Great. Deferring the few comments which can be made on our author's sources of information on Frank and French history,[3] until they can be considered all together and consecutively, I will proceed with the examination of the remaining sections of this book.

Sources of Mercian history.

10. The Mercian kings are treated by our author very much as those of Northumbria had been: the basis of the history is Bede and the Chronicles; there are several particulars extracted from the Royal Genealogies appended to Florence of Worcester; outside these authorities, with the exception of a slight notice about the dedication of the monastic church of Winchcomb abbey, the martyrdom of Saint Kenelm,[4] and the remark that Offa was the founder of S. Alban's abbey,[5] the whole of the additional information is extracted from the letters of Alcuin and Boniface, and the correspondence of Pope Leo and King Kenulf, respecting the foundation and abolition of the archbishopric of Lichfield. Upon these additions some observations may be with advantage made in this place.

---

[1] Vol. i. p. 54; cf. for Aidan, Liebermann, Heiligen, &c., p. 18.
[2] Vol. i. p. 56.
[3] See below, p. xxxi.
[4] Vol. i. pp. 94, 95.
[5] Vol. i. p. 85.

PREFACE.   xxvii

11. It may seem Quixotic, seven hundred years after William of Malmesbury wrote, to attempt to trace the exact manuscript which he used in making the extracts from the letters of Alcuin, a writer whose compositions were so famous and authoritative as to be copied and codified more extensively perhaps than any other's of the period. But it is a matter of some interest to ascertain, if possible, the class of edition which he had before him, and with the help of the research of Dr. Jaffé, completed and edited by Wattenbach and Dümmler, in the Monumenta Alcuiniana, some measure of probability may be obtained. All the letters of Alcuin from which the extracts are taken are to be found in MSS. still existing in English libraries, and some of them are found nowhere else. Thirteen letters are quoted, four of which are not known to exist except in the Cotton MS., Tiberius A. 15, from which in all probability our author took the letter of pope Sergius to abbot Ceolfrith supposed to relate to Bede. These letters are numbers 57 and 58, 79 and 190, in Dümmler's notation; six others in this MS. are found in other places.[1] Six more are found in MS. Vespasian A. 14, four of which are common to these two MSS., and three of them found nowhere else; one, the interesting letter quoted in illustration of the

The use of Alcuin's letters.

Manuscripts of Alcuin's letters still extant.

---

[1] It may be more intelligible to give these notes in a tabular form. V. denotes the Vespasian A. 14; A., Tiberius A. 15. The numbers are from Dümmler's notation. The letters cited are—

14	-	-	from V.A.
16	-	-	,, V.A.
22	-	-	,, V.A.
27	-	-	,, V. and many other MSS.
28	-	-	,, V. and many other MSS.
35	-	-	,, V.A. and other MSS.
57	-	-	from A.
58	-	-	,, A.
72	-	-	,, A. and one other MS.
78	-	-	,, the Royal MS.
79	-	-	,, A.
171	-	-	,, A. and a Harleian MS.
190	-	-	,, A.

It is unnecessary to give more detailed references to Dümmler's pagination, as the letters can be identified by their numbers.

history of the York Library (No. 78), occurs only among English MSS. in the Royal MS. 8 E. 15; but may not improbably have been included in the Tiberius MS. which has been much damaged by fire. It is on the fact that so many of the letters that our author quotes occur only in these MSS., that our conclusion must depend that he used those identical volumes. But the bibliography of Alcuin is not yet completely settled, unless the recent criticisms of the scholars of Vienna have led to some results which are not yet known to me. With the exception of clerical errors, which may easily have occurred in the process of transcription, there is nothing in the readings of these MSS. which would lead one to suppose that our author had other copies before him.

<small>Manuscripts of the letters of S. Boniface.</small>

12. It does not appear that our libraries possess any collection of the letters of S. Boniface so ancient as to make it probable that William of Malmesbury used it. None such was known to Sir T. Duffus Hardy,[1] or is mentioned by the indefatigable Jaffé in his prolegomena to the Monumenta Moguntina, in which all relics of the Apostle of Germany are brought together. Under these circumstances we must be content to remain in the dark as to the source from which our author derived the strange addition relative to the fate of Charles Martel which occurs in his copy of the letter to Ethelbald. I have nothing to add to the notes and references which I have given on this point at pp. 81 and 256, except that it seems to me more likely that the passage in question should have been expunged from the copies of the letter made in the Frank kingdom, under the eye of Charles's descendants, than that it should have been

<small>The paragraph about the fate of Charles Martel.</small>

---

[1] Catalogue of Materials, i. 483. There is a collection of extracts from the letters of Boniface in the MS. Additional 8873; see Neues Archiv, vol. v. pp. 286, 287, but it does not include the portion of the letter to Ethelbald about Charles Martel, referred to in the text further on. See also, Neues Archiv, vii. 356, an article on the lost MSS. of Boniface, by A. Nürnberger.

foisted into a letter copied in England from an original directed to an English king. With regard to the extant MSS. of the letters of Boniface at Munich and Vienna[1], it may be observed that the incorporation with them of the letters and *opuscula* of Aldhelm, which seems to connect them to some extent with England and Malmesbury, must have taken place long before the date of William, perhaps as early as the eighth century. We must regret that the volume used by him has disappeared, and with it probably the life of S. Goar in which he found the history of Lullus and discovered the meaning of the sing-song verses which he had learned as a child.[2] It is clear from the account of Frideric of Utrecht, in the Gesta Pontificum,[3] that he had other sources of information about the history of the German church. MSS. in Germany.

13. The letters of Kenulf to Leo III., and of Leo III. to Kenulf,[4] were found by our author in some collection which is now lost. A letter, which must have formed part of the correspondence, is preserved in the Cotton MS., Vespasian A. 14, which has been already mentioned. These three, with some details derived from Alcuin, enable us to reconstruct satisfactorily the history of the archbishopric of Lichfield, which our author has, by his mistakes of names and dates, helped seriously to obscure. I will refer the reader on this well-trodden subject to the notes at pp. 85, 86, and 89, and to what has been said further on the point, not connected with our author's misunderstandings, in the *Councils and* The correspondence of Leo III. and Kenulf.

---

[1] Monumenta Moguntina, præf., pp. 8 sq.

[2] Vol. i. p. 84. There is no reason to doubt that the life of S. Goar, to which he refers, is that by Wandalbert, printed by Mabillon in the Acta Sanctorum O.S.B., sec. ii., in which Lullus is described, p. 276.

[3] Gesta Pontiff., ed. Hamilton, pp. 12-15. Another version of the history of Frideric, sufficiently akin to that of our author to be derived from it, is given by John de Beka in his Chronicle, pp. 23, 24. I do not know whether either account has ever been traced to an ancient source.

[4] Vol. i. pp. 86-91.

Ecclesiastical Documents relating to Great Britain and Ireland, vol. iii. pp. 467, 521 sq., 542. The archbishopric of Lichfield was founded in 787, and came to an end in 803; its only archbishop was Higbert; the list of bishops whom our author represents as subject to it,[1] is wrongly taken from the synodical act which abolished it.[2] The critical examination of the details belongs rather to the Gesta Pontificum than to the Gesta Regum.

The archbishopric of Lichfield.

14. The remaining sections of the first book, containing a scanty sketch of the East Saxon and East Anglian kingdoms, with a general view of the ecclesiastical and political geography of England during the period, present little or nothing for comment here. The historic data are from Bede. Where our author quits his authority, he is unlucky. If Offa of Essex was a suitor in 709 to Kinesuitha, the daughter of Penda, a lady who must have been fifty-four at the lowest computation, and he had a wife of his own,[3] as Bede specially records, such an event might help to explain some of the anomalous matrimonial adventures of our early kings; but the story is incredible, and the historian must have been dreaming when he made the assertion. The survey of provinces and dioceses is useful. We learn from it that the ancient Cornish see was in the twelfth century supposed to be at S. Germans, that Whithern was regarded as a suffragan see to York, and that the creation of the see of Carlisle was not yet treated as an accomplished fact.[4]

The concluding sections of the first book.

---

[1] Vol. i. p. 85.
[2] Kemble, Cod. Dipl., i. 226, v. 65, 66.
[3] Above, p. 99.
[4] A bishop of Carlisle was consecrated in 1133, but after his death the see was vacant to all intents and purposes until the reign of Henry III., being held for a time in commendam by Bernard, bishop of Ragusa, and before his appointment in 1203, vacant, notwithstanding the attempts of Henry II. to nominate a bishop. Whithern, which was revived at the same time, 1133, had its succession continued without serious break.

PREFACE. xxxi

II. Before proceeding to the consideration of the sources from which, in the second book, our author supplements and expands the scanty data of the Chronicles, it may be as well to attempt the identification of the books which, in this and the following portion of the Gesta, furnish him with the materials for French and imperial history in general. I will reserve for more special elucidation the particular portions or episodes which he inserts rather " pro utilitate legentium, " than as necessary to his comprehensive view of his subject and historical method. Authorities on French and German history in the early books.

1. One whole section of the first book, § 68, is given to the Franks, and traces their history from its beginning to the reign of the emperor Otto the First. The section is composed in our author's own words; it contains nothing very distinctive, and we are only guided to its original sources by the fuller extracts given in the second book to known writers from whom he may be supposed to have obtained the materials here paraphrased. Following this clue we infer that his chief guide was the Chronicle of Centoul or S. Riquier,[1] composed by Hariulf, and that he had before him the Chronicle of Ado of Vienne with the continuation contained in the Chronicle of Fontanelles. The more substantial part of the section is from Hariulf; the mention of Faramund is from Ado,[2] who likewise furnishes the tradition of the origin of the name of Franks, and mentions Valentinian and the Conquest of the Alani; the genealogy of the mayors of the palace is from the Commemoratio prefixed to the Chronicle of Fontanelles[3]; the short continuation of imperial history, comprised in half a dozen lines, does not need to be accounted for. The early history of the Franks from Ado, Hariulf, and the Chronicle of Fontanelles.

2. Another entire section, in the second book, § 110, contains an account of the successors of Charles the The successors of Charles the Great, from

---

[1] Chronicon Centulense, or S. Richarii; D'Achery, Spicileg. (ed. 1665) vol. ii., pp. 291-356.

[2] Ado, *ad ann.* 364, ed. Migne, Patrologia, vol. cxxiii. c. 95.

[3] Chron.Fontanell.,ed.D'Achery, Spicileg., ii. 263, 264.

Great. After a few lines the material of which is from Ado, the whole of the section is a transcript of the continuation of Ado, contained in the Commemoratio in the Chronicle of Fontanelles, and published, as such continuation, from several MSS. in the Monumenta by Pertz, vol. ii. pp. 324–329.

The Visio Karoli from Hariulf.

3. Section 111, the Visio Karoli, is taken verbatim from Hariulf; it may be questioned whether our text does not exhibit a more original recension than that printed by D'Achery, Spicilegium, ii. 323,[1] for the ungrammatical declension of the word *glomus* which our author faithfully reproduces,[2] is corrected in the edition. There need, however, I think, be no doubt as to the source from which it is taken. This completes, or nearly completes, our author's direct debt to these writers; the later references to Norman and Frank history are mostly to be traced to other sources.

Dates of these authorities.

Hariulf, it may be as well to say, completed his work in the year 1088;[3] Centoul or S. Riquier, his monastery, was situated in Picardy, a little north-west of Abbeville. His book which is said to be an expansion or completion of an earlier Chronicle by Saxowalus,[4] is printed by D'Achery in the Spicilegium, and in detached portions by Bouquet. The Chronicle of Fontanelles is likewise printed by D'Achery in the same volume; the best text of the portion which forms the continuation of Ado, is that printed by Pertz, already cited. The monastery to which it belongs, that of S. Wandrille, was in Normandy, not far from Caudebec.

The introduction to Norman history.

4. The two sections on Norman and French history, which are numbered 127 and 128, are of no special importance in themselves, but are interesting as presenting to us our author in his most uncritical and inaccurate

---

[1] Chron.S.Richarii, ed.D'Achery, Spicileg., ii. 323, 324.
[2] Above, pp. 112–116; p. 116, note 3.
[3] Chron. Centul., ed. D'Achery, Spicileg., ii. 356.
[4] Potthast, Wegweiser, p. 359.

form. The first, which is intended as a sketch of the Norman invasions to the submission of Rollo, seems to be a confused abridgment from William of Jumieges. To the brief account given by that writer of the siege of Chartres by Rollo, and the preservation of the city by the miraculous "camisia" of the Blessed Virgin,[1] he adds the particular that that relic had been brought from Constantinople by Charles the Bald.[2] This he derived, it would seem, from some other source which was drawn upon by the monastic writers of Anjou and Touraine, unless they obtained it from our author himself. However, he certainly errs in placing the siege before the year 876; it is sometimes dated in 898,[3] but the accepted date seems to be 911. The incident of the homage done to Charles the Simple is from William of Jumieges.

The siege of Chartres.

5. Having begun to blunder in § 127, our author becomes quite reckless in § 128: in his account of Lewis d'Outremer, the son of Charles the Simple by his English wife. The extreme intricacies of the Karolingian pedigree, and the upgrowth of romance about the origin of the house of Hugh Capet, are too much for him. He concentrates in Lewis (1) the legend about Isambard, which other writers attach to Lewis the Pious, but which, as a historical fact, belongs to Lewis

Blunders about the origin of Hugh Capet.

---

[1] Cf. Dudo, de Gestis Normanniæ ducum, lib. ii. (ed. Migne, c. 645), where the garment is called *tunica*; cf. Annales Uticenses, Ord. Vit., ed. Prevost, v. 154. The word in William of Jumieges (ii. 15) is *supparum*. *Camisiu*, which is the guiding word of the sentence, is used by William of Malmesbury; in the Chronicon Turonense, Martene and Durand, Ampl. Coll., v. 978, and in the Liber de Castro Ambasiæ, D'Achery, Spicileg., iii. 272, Chron. Andegav., Mart. and Dur. Thesaurus, iii. 1379; Duchesne, Scriptt., iii. 360.

[2] " Quam Carolus Calvus a Bysantio attulerat": Liber de Castro Amb., p. 272. " Hanc camisiam attulit Carolus Calvus a Bizantio": Chron. Turon., c. 978; Bouquet, Recueil, &c., ix. 40; Duchesne, iii. 360.

[3] See the Annals of S. Edmund, printed by Liebermann, in the Anglo-Normannische Geschichtsquellen, p. 124; Annales Rotomagenses, ibid. p. 42, &c.

III.; (2) the victory of Saucourt, which also belongs to Lewis III.; and (3) the defeasance of the house of Charles the Great, which, resulting in the promotion of Hugh Capet, must be presumed to be completed in the person of Lewis V. We might have noted a similar confusion between the emperor Lewis of Arles, and the king of the Germans, Lewis the Child, which occurs in the section on the "Visio Karoli;"[1] but that was an easy mistake, and nothing of importance depends upon it. The confusion of the two or three Lewises in the section before us leads to some more interesting questions.

The story of the traitor Isambard.

6. The apostasy and treachery of Isambard is referred to by Geoffrey of Monmouth,[2] in his chapter on the reign of the British king Careticus. Isambard, the nephew of Lewis, king of France, allies himself with Gormund, king of the pagan Africans, and, in conjunction with him, besieges Cirencester. This is, of course, rank fable, and the work in which it occurs is somewhat later than our author, who, however, may have heard the same story. Walter Map, who wrote some few years later still, describes a battle fought in Ponthieu by Lewis, son of Charles the Great,[3] against Gormund and Isembard whom he does not call the king's nephew, although he mentions "Radulfus Cambrensis," by whose pride the French army had been weakened, as standing in such a

---

[1] Above, p. 116. The Lewis who succeeded Arnulf was his son Lewis the Child; but Lewis the Blind, son of Boso, and titular emperor, also may be said to have succeeded him as emperor. But the Lewis whose death made way for Conrad (p. 117) was Lewis the Child, not Lewis the Blind. The mistake was of course a very easy one. On the marriage of Lewis the Blind, who, as well as Lewis the Child, was of Karolingian descent, see below, p. lii.

[2] Galf. Mon., lib. xi. c. 8; page 206.

[3] De Nugis Curialium (ed. Wright), p. 211:—"Lodovicus filius Karoli Magni jacturam omnium optimatum Franciæ fere totiusque militiæ Francorum apud Evore per stultam superbiam Radulfi Cambrensis nepotis sui pertulit; satis ægre rexit ab illa die regnum Francorum ad adventum usque Gurmundi cum Ysembardo contra quos cum residuis Francorum bellum in Pontivo commisit."

relation to Lewis.¹ This also belongs to legend. As for fact—Lewis III., son of Lewis the Stammerer, who reigned from 879 to 882, had to contend with an invasion of the Norsemen, under a king to whom Hariulf gives the name of Guaramund. Lewis defeated Guaramund in the battle of Saucourt,² and was celebrated in a song of triumph which is still extant among the most ancient relics of German poetry.³ Guaramund was assisted by a French traitor, Esimbard, whose name is preserved by the author of the Chronicle of S. Riquier.⁴ Hariulf describes the incidents as commemorated not only in histories, but in the memories and songs of the country people. Isambard must have been a second Ganelon; but he seems to have been an historical personage and lord of la Ferté in Ponthieu.

7. But who is Hugh, the son of count Robert of Mont Didier, whose services in the campaign of Ponthieu were rewarded by recognition as heir to the perishing Karolings? The Hugh who married the daughter of Edward the Elder, and was father of king Robert? How many Hughs are combined in this personality? To reverse in

About the origin of Hugh Capet.

---

¹ Schulz (San Marte), in his edition of Geoffrey of Monmouth (p. 441), has an interesting note on this chapter; he refers to the passages in Warton's History of English poetry in which the lay of Isenbras or Isenbard is mentioned: i. 128, where the name occurs in the Cursor Mundi; cf. ii. 173. And there is some information about the literary history in Reiffenberg, Introduction to Philip de Mouskes, vol. ii., pp. vii., cccxxiii.

² On the battle of Saucourt see the authorities printed by Richter: Annalen der Deutschen Geschichte, pp. 470, 471.

³ See the poem, the *Ludwigslied*, in Langebek, Scriptores Rerum Danicarum, ii. 72–76; also in Max Müller's German Classics, pp. 37 sq.

⁴ Chron. Centul., D'Achery, Spicileg., ii. 322: " persuadente id fieri " quodam Esimbardo Francigena " nobili, qui regis Hlugdogvici ani- " mos offenderat, quique genitalis " soli proditor gentium barbariem " nostros fines visere hortabatur. " Sed quia quomodo sit factum " non solum historiis sed etiam " patriensium memoria recolitur " et cantatur, nos pauca memoran- " tes cetera omittamus." The story is told more fully in Alberic of Trois Fontaines from Guido: Accessiones Historicæ, p. 211.

answer the order of the questions :—The father of king Robert was Hugh Capet, who did succeed when the Karolings ended. But it was not he who married the daughter of Edward; she was the first wife of his father, Hugh the Great, duke of France. But could Hugh the Great be the hero of the duel with Isambard? Scarcely, for he died in 956, seventy-five years after the battle of Saucourt. His father was indeed named Robert, but he was scarcely to be described as count of Montdidier, being duke and king. But his brother Eudes, duke and king before him, might in time be a possible champion against Isambard; his father was Robert the Strong, and if we could follow the authors of the Art de Vérifier les Dates,[1] we might maintain that Robert the Strong was a son of Theotbert, count of Madrie; can Robert the Strong be our author's count of Montdidier? True Montdidier is in Picardy; Madrie is in Normandy; the pagus Madricensis was one of the ancient divisions of Neustria, and the sphere of an imperial Missus.[2] If Montdidier could be confounded with Madrie, and Eudes with Hugh; the first king of the house from which Hugh Capet sprang, with his great nephew the first king of the house of Capet; and further if the whole incident be drawn down a century later from Lewis the grandson of Charles the Bald, to Lewis the great grandson of Charles the Simple; and if the latter Lewis can be identified with his own grandfather Lewis d'Outremer, we can begin to realise the maze in which our author has involved himself. But M. Barthelemy,[3] the latest inves-

---

[1] Art de V. les Dates, v. 496–499; ix. 208.

[2] Stapleton, Rotuli Scaccarii Normanniæ, i. pp. xlviii, xlix.

[3] Revue des Questions Historiques, 1878, pp. 114 sq. M. Barthelemy suggests that Robert the Strong was son, as he was heir, of William, count of Blois; but here again, according to the Art de Vérifier les Dates, the count Theotbert of Madrie crops up (vol. xi. p. 349) as father of count William. However, the question is about Montdidier, not Madrie. Montdidier was a lordship in the house of Crepy, and Ralph, lord or count of Montdidier, was a well-known person in the eleventh century and married the widow of Henry I. of

tigator of the antiquities of the family, discards almost contemptuously the descent from the count of Madrie, and it is impossible by a mere guess to clear up the confusion. It becomes an insignificant question whether the bewilderment were original, or derived from oral teaching, or poetic history. Making all possible allowances for the confusion of Lewises, Hughs, and Roberts, we are obliged to allow that this section is wantonly careless and uncritical.

8. In connexion with this subject it is as well to refer to the chapter on the death of duke William of Normandy,[1] § 145, which is the last episode of French history that needs to be accounted for here. Our author gives two accounts of the event; the latter, which he describes as derived from " veraciores litteræ," is an abridgment of the narrative of William of Jumieges, itself an abstract from Dudo.[2] The former bears every mark of an origin in poetic legend, but probably contains some traditional germs of truth. Perhaps the relation between the two stories is the not uncommon one, history commemorating the obvious facts, the general results, the great names; legend having something to tell us of subordinate causes, local colour, and the smaller names of the instruments by whom the great men were able to compass their ends. It is unnecessary to analyse the details: the whole of the subject is carefully treated by Mr. Freeman[3] in an appendix in the first volume of the History of the Norman Conquest. The direct source of the romantic account of the murder

The two versions of the tragedy of duke William of Normandy.

France. He was of the house of Vermandois, from which sprang the first line of the counts of Blois. It is curious to see how many lines of inquiry lead to the conclusion that our author had some lost source of information about the matter, even though his information may have been quite erroneous. The statement in question is flatly contradicted by Alberic of Trois Fontaines (ii. 27.), and is not noticed, I think, at all by M. Barthelemy.

[1] Above, pp. 160–162.
[2] Will Gemet., ii. 11, 12; Dudo, lib. iii. (ed. Migne, c. 680).
[3] Freeman, Norman Conquest, i. 616–621.

must be sought for among the poetic and probably oral traditions which seem to have been current among the Normans of the eleventh century, many of the relics of which are embodied by Sir Francis Palgrave in his History of Normandy and England, occasionally with a disturbing effect on the sequence and consistency of the story.

Account of king Robert of France.

All that is material in § 187 about the character of king Robert of France and the difficulties of the succession on his death seems to be derived in a careless and inaccurate way from Ralph Glaber, with a possible reference to William of Jumieges.[1]

The second book of the Gesta Regum.

III. I now proceed to an examination of the materials used by our author in the composition of the second book of the Gesta: the portion of the work for which we owe him on the whole the most special gratitude, not so much perhaps for its actual value as history, as for its conservation of traditions and relics of popular beliefs which are to be found nowhere else. The first book has pre-eminently the character of research: the author's power as a student of character and commentator on events is shown in the books with whose history he was familiar as a contemporary, or as removed only by a single generation from the events themselves. The second book is a congeries of relics which but for him might have been lost.

The reigns of Egbert and Ethelwulf.

1. The history of the reigns of Egbert and Ethelwulf, sections 106–109, is almost entirely taken from the Chronicle. Our author has, perhaps pardonably, followed his authority in placing the accession of Egbert in the year 800, although, by giving the regnal year of

---

[1] See the note in Freeman's Norman Conquest, i. 466, where the Chronicle of Tours, Duchesne, iii. 361, is mentioned as using similar language: "Odo erat major sed quia stultus erat non fuit rex," Bouquet, x. 225. There are other coincidences between the two works, but as the Tours Chronicle ends in 1137, I am inclined to think that the author may have seen the Gesta rather than that William cited him.

PREFACE. xxxix

Charles, he has helped us to correct the mistake, which runs through his chronology of the reign. His additions to the Chronicle are mainly his comment on the political education of Egbert at Charles's court, a very natural inference from the fact of his exile; the notice of Swithun and Ealhstan as ministers of Ethelwulf, for which he had ample authority in the charters and records of his own monastery; and his statement that the last-mentioned king, during his visit to Rome, repaired the Schola Anglorum,[1] a most probable event, but the chief evidence for which seems to rest on some questionable charters. After the episode on the Frank history which is introduced in connexion with Ethelwulf's second marriage, he takes up the life of Alfred by Asser, and makes it the chief source of all information as long as it lasts. For the sections 113 to 123, Asser is the chief and primary authority.

Slight additions to the Chronicle.

2. The present is not the place for any critical examination of this celebrated work; and if I say that, in my opinion, the present state of the text is such as to inspire some dangerous doubts, I do not wish to be understood as questioning the general truth of the work as history, or as throwing suspicion on its genuineness and authenticity. Of the particular difficulties to which I refer the most important are those which affect Asser himself and his relation to Alfred, points which do not come into consideration in the work before us. It is sufficient for the occasion to accept the hypothesis that our author had in his hands the book which we possess as the

Authority of Asser's life of Alfred.

---

[1] Anastasius who mentions Ethelwulf's other benefactions at Rome does not notice this, but as the Schola Anglorum had been burned a few years before, it is probable that the king's visit would be made to help towards the restoration. The charter in which the statement is made is one granted to Winchester, which is regarded as spurious; Kemble, Cod. Dipl., No. 1057; Cartularium Saxonicum, ii. p. 96. This charter likewise mentions the consecration of Alfred as king, at Rome, as if it had taken place during his father's visit. Se below, p. xlii.

"Vita Alfredi." It is from the text, as nearly as possible in its existing form, that he seems to have taken his extracts. These extracts, or abstracts, for the remainder of the reign of Ethelwulf and his elder sons, do not suggest further comment except on the much-controverted question of the donation of Ethelwulf, which has so long been associated with the History of Tithe. Into the common misapprehension as to the nature of the donation, a misapprehension for which our author, I fear, is largely responsible, it would be useless to go; the emancipation of every tenth hide from secular service, which is the gist of the Malmesbury charter given in § 114, is not a gift of tithe, and, if genuine, was issued several years before the king's death.[1] Such charters are numerous, and have a special, as well as a general, history. But the account given by our author of the king's will is a different thing. It is taken from Asser, and our author's association of it with the charter of donation is quite arbitrary. It is quite possible that the writer of the Vita Alfredi had seen the original will by which, after providing for the succession,[2] for the devolution of his hereditary estate and for the dowry of his

Donations of Ethelwulf to the churches.

The will of Ethelwulf.

---

[1] See Councils and Ecclesiastical Documents, iii. 680, for the first charter of the kind in 844; for the documents concerning the bestowal of the tenth part of the king's private estate on churches, &c., pp. 636–644; and the Chilcomb charter already referred to, pp. 646–648, which Kemble declares to bear marks of forgery in every line: Saxons in England, ii. 487. It is obvious enough, as it refers to pope Leo as the reigning pope during Ethelwulf's visit.

[2] Our author (p. 108) mentions the fact stated in the Chronicle that Ethelwulf on his accession made over his father's conquests to Ethelstan, including Kent, Essex and Sussex. Ethelstan is called his son, Egbert's, or Ethelwulf's. If he were Ethelwulf's son, and was old enough to be set in such a place at his father's accession, he must have been grown up ten years before Alfred's birth; which, even considering the early age at which these princes began active life, would seem improbable. If he were Egbert's son, it is most curious that so very little more should be heard of him. The point is of some importance, because Thorpe in his translation of Lappenberg has inserted in his account of this will of Ethelwulf's, a statement which is not in Lappen-

daughter, he directed that on every tenth hide of his hereditary lands a poor man or a stranger should be fed and clothed, and that an annual sum of 300 mancuses should be sent to Rome, to be equally divided between the lights of S. Peter and S. Paul and the charities of the pope.

3. There are a few points in the history of Alfred on which the present examination gives me the opportunity of commenting. One of these is his mission to Rome in his infancy. This event is placed in the Chronicle, which was drawn up under his own eye, in the year 853; and in the same year by Asser, who in the extant text describes it as the eleventh year of the boy's age.[1] If, however, Alfred was born in 849, he was sent to Rome when he was only four. The years of his age are, indeed, calculated very confusedly: from 851 to 869 from 848; from 870 to 876 from 849; and from 878 to 887 from 851. This confusion might tempt us to disregard the calculation of age altogether, and so to throw the year of the great king's birth back to a date which would make it at least credible that he was sent to Rome for education at an age at which he would be likely to profit by it. And this, again, has a bearing on the story told by Asser about his learning to read. His mother promised a book to the son who should first

Obscure points in the life of Alfred.

Alfred's age at his first visit to Rome.

Who was the mother who taught him to read?

---

berg, that "by this instrument the "king of Kent was excluded from "all hereditary claim on the king-"dom of Wessex" (ii. 27). He is not mentioned either by Asser or by Alfred in the charter in which he describes his father's settlement. But three of the Chronicles make him distinctly Egbert's second son, and he is found in command in Kent in 851. Ethelwerd calls him (p. 511) the son of Ethelwulf, and the same statement is interpolated into the text of Asser (p. 469). His name as Ethelstan rex occurs in Kemble, C. D., No. 241; 252 (A.D. 841); Cartularium Saxonicum, ii. 17; No. 442 (A.D. 843); K., C. D., No, 255; 259; 264 (A.D. 850); never, I think, as *filius regis* except by mistake, Cart. Sax., ii. 26. He disappears after the battle of 851.

[1] Asser, M. H. B., p. 469.

learn to read; Alfred was the successful competitor; and this appears to be fixed to the boy's twelfth year.[1] But his own mother, although in legend she appears as late as the year 872,[2] must be thought to have died before 856, in which year Ethelwulf married Judith, the daughter of Charles the Bald.[3] Judith was only twelve years old at the time, and is scarcely likely to have posed as the mother of a boy of seven or eight; nor was her conduct in after life such that Alfred was likely, in talking to Asser, to describe her as his mother. If, however, the year 853 were indeed his eleventh year, the story might be credible. Such an adjustment of dates is only possible on the hypothesis that the author of the Vita was altogether at sea about the matter; yet it is to his calculation of his hero's age that we owe our knowledge of the date of his writing; he wrote in the forty-fifth year, as he computed it, of Alfred's life, and the sequence of events, as well as the computation on which he was working, fixes that epoch to the year 894 or thereabouts. And all calculations of the king's age at his death are based on the statement that he was born in 849.

Complications of the chronological data.

4. That he was sent to Rome in 853 is beyond doubt. There is a letter of pope Leo IV. extant,[4] in which he writes to Ethelwulf announcing Alfred's arrival, and telling him that he had invested him as his spiritual son with the girdle and vestments of consulship, whatever

Letter of Leo IV. on Alfred's visit to Rome.

---

[1] Asser, M. H. B., pp. 473, 474.
[2] Above, p. 125.
[3] Oct. 1, 856, Ann. Bertin., Pertz., Monumenta, i. 450. Charles the Bald was married Dec. 14, 842; so that Judith, if she was the eldest child, would scarcely be thirteen at the time of her marriage.
[4] Epistolæ Leonis IV., in MS. Add. 8873, No. 31: *Edelvulfo regi Anglorum.* — "Filium vestrum Erfred quem hoc tempore ad sanctorum apostolorum limina destinare curastis, benigne suscepimus et quasi spiritalem filium consulatus cingulo, honore, vestimentisque, ut mos est Romanis consulibus, decoravimus, eo quod in nostris se tradidit manibus."

that may mean.¹ By the English a few years later, and perhaps by Alfred himself, it was regarded as an anticipation of coronation, and the unction, which might be that of confirmation,² as that of royal consecration. It is in connexion with the expedition to Rome that, according to our author, the boy made the acquaintance with Grimbald, who many years later came and settled under his patronage at Winchester. Asser proceeds to assign to Alfred, in the year 855, a second journey to Rome : in his seventh year he accompanied his father to the Eternal City ; ³ Ethelwulf's visit certainly belongs to the pontificate of Benedict III., which began in July 855 ; so that there is no possibility that a single visit of Alfred has been broken into two ; on their return it was that Ethelwulf married his second wife. If we accept the whole story as it stands, Alfred's development must have been very slow ; two journeys to Rome had been taken before he was eight years old, and yet he did not learn to read until he was twelve, that is in the year 861, when his father had been dead for three years, and the young bride after she had been given, unlawfully— even supposing that her union with Ethelwulf were only formal,— as wife to Ethelbald, and was about in her widowhood, at the mature age of eighteen, to elope with Baldwin the Forester.⁴

_{A second journey.}

_{Legend of Alfred's learning to read.}

---

¹ See Neues Archiv., v. 389 ; Wattenbach, Regesta Pontiff., No. 2645.

² The expression "quasi spiritalem filium" seems to indicate that confirmation was a part of the function, and if there was confirmation there would be unction. The investiture might mean the bestowal of the prætexta or some similar ceremony, which the child might misunderstand, or the grown-up man regard, as a solemn designation for the office afterwards reached. On the continuance of the title and office of consul during the early middle ages, see Gregorovius, Gesch. d. Stadt Roms. ii. 478 ; iii. 277, 478.

³ Asser, M. H. B., p. 470. Ethelwulf had a year at Rome according to the Chr., p. 348. The boy's name occurs among the attestations to charters of 854, Easter, Cart. Sax., 469, 470, 473, 475, 476, 478 ; and of 855, ibid. 486.

⁴ Genealogia Comitum Flandrensium, Mart. and Dur., Thesaurus, iii. 379.

Further confusion about Alfred.

5. The foolish and dishonest attempt which, as early as the fourteenth century, was made to associate Alfred with the history of the University of Oxford, has helped to increase the confusion of the chronology and to throw doubt on the genuine portions of the "Vita Alfredi." I have mentioned Grimbald already, and it is in connexion with him that our author makes one of his most distinct additions to the authority he is following. Grimbald, according to William of Malmesbury, was sent at Alfred's invitation to England by archbishop Folco of Rheims. The transcriber or editor of one version of the present work adds that Grimbald was a monk, chanter, and hostiller of the abbey of Saint Bertin.[1] By Alfred he was placed as abbot in the new monastery which was building at Winchester,[2] and by the Oxford writers, as is well known, he was adopted and foisted into the fabulous history of the University. Into this once burning question it is unnecessary for me to go; the history of the development of the fable has even now to be traced to its beginnings. But with Grimbald's identification we are more closely concerned.

History of Grimbald.

Letter of archbishop Folco introducing Grimbald to Alfred.

The letter of archbishop Folco referred to by our author is still extant, and in manuscripts so ancient as to free it from the taint of forgery.[3] In that letter Grimbald is described as a priest and monk. Folco himself had been abbot of S. Bertin, and his strong recommendation of Grimbald was evidently based upon

---

[1] This is peculiar to the Aa. text of the Gesta; see vol. i., pref., p. l.

[2] He is mentioned by Alfred in a charter of 895, which I fear is a forgery, K., C. D., 322. His death in 903 is noted in all the MSS. of the Chronicle, ed. Thorpe, pp. 180, 181; and in one the day is given, July 8. Mabillon mentions a biography of him by Goscelin, which is lost; AA. O.S.B., Sæc. v., pp. 3–6, and on this authority apparently, he was eighty-three at the time. Cf. Hardy, Cat. Mat., i. 555.

[3] The letter is printed by Wise in the Appendix to Asser, p. 128, from the MS. Evangelia, now at Crowcombe Court; 2nd Report of Hist. MSS. Commission, App., p. 75; Alford, Annales, A.D. 885, § 7; Edwards, Liber de Hyda, pp. 31–35; Cartularium Saxonicum, iii. 190.

long personal acquaintance. And the historians of S. Bertin have something to say about him. According to the local history he was dedicated in the monastery at the age of seven during the abbacy of Hugh, son of Charles the Great, who was killed in the year 844.[1] He grew up there and in time became chancellor or prior; in that capacity he wrote several charters which are preserved in the Cartularium Sithiense: in 867 he attests a document "Ego Grim-"baldus diaconus et monachus scripsi et subscripsi,"[2] and in 883 writes "Grimbaldus sacerdos et monachus "scripsi et subscripsi."[3] In this very year Folco, who had been abbot from 877, became archbishop of Rheims. Rudolf, his successor, died in 892,[4] and thereupon count Baldwin of Flanders, who it will be remembered afterwards became Alfred's son-in-law, attempted to obtain the abbacy to be held by himself. In order to prevent this the monks sent Grimbald, whom they wished to have for abbot, to the king of France. The king gave the office to Folco, who held it with his archiepiscopal see until the year 900, when he was killed by Baldwin.[5] If this much be true, we should find a date for Grimbald's mission to England between 892 and 900, whilst Folco was ruling at S. Bertin; and this may be narrowed still further if we hold that the writer of the life of Alfred was writing in 894,[6] as he speaks of Grimbald as already settled at court. Here, however, we are met with a difficulty, for Iperius, who

History of Grimbald at S. Bertin.

---

[1] Chron. Bertin. (Joh. Iper.). Mart. and Dur., iii. 510.

[2] Cartularium Sithiense (Documents Inédits), p. 114.

[3] Cart. Sith., *ut s.*, p. 129.

[4] Cart. Sith., *ut s.*, p. 133. Baldwin's marriage with Alfred's daughter must have taken place after the year 894. The Vita describes her as still being educated at her father's court, p. 485. Yet her son Arnulf is made to die in 965, aged 92, which would throw her marriage back to the year 873; whereas her father was only married in 868. All this is very puzzling. See Art de V. 1. D., xiii. 285.

[5] Chron. Bertin., *ut supra*, c. 533, 534; cf. Mabillon, AA. SS. O.S.B., Sæc. v., 1, 2.

[6] Asser, M. H. B., p. 492.

codified the history of S. Bertin in the fourteenth century, fixes Grimbald's visit to England after Folco's death. The older writer in the Cartulary does not mention this, but Mabillon[1] accepts it, and misled by the statement in the interpolated copy of Asser, which settles Grimbald at Oxford before 886, comes to the conclusion that there were two persons of the name, one who came before 886, and a second who fled to England in 900.[2] The great Benedictine writer does not seem to have considered the letter of Folco, or to have suspected the interpolation of Asser.

Possible adjustment of Grimbald's date. Now in the genuine text of the Vita Alfredi, there is nothing that necessitates our fixing the arrival of Grimbald earlier than 892 : Alfred's revival of learning seems distinctly to have begun under archbishop Plegmund[3] who attained the primacy in 890 or 891. And the name of Asser, who places his own arrival in England about the same time as Grimbald's, does not appear in the charters for some years later.[4] If we suppose that Folco, on resuming his rule at S. Bertin, thought it prudent to send Grimbald away, either to save him from the vengeance of count Baldwin, or to console him for the loss of the abbacy, the story becomes coherent and consistent; Folco's letter belongs to the year 893 or a little later. Grimbald was settled at Winchester, and there, according to the Chronicle, he died in 903, three years after his master and friend.[5]

Statements in the Book of Hyde. It must, however, be stated that the Liber de Hyda, the Chronicle of Alfred's New Minster,[6] places Folco's

---

[1] Chron. Bertin., *ut supra*, c. 537, 538.

[2] Mabillon, Ann. O.S.B., iii. 240; Gallia Christiana, iii. 490 : ix. 45–47.

[3] See Asser, M. H. B., p. 487.

[4] I do not think that Asser's name appears in charters before 901; K., C. D., 331; but he is named as bishop in Alfred's preface to S. Gregory on the Pastoral Care, together with archbishop Plegmund and the mass priests Grimbald and John.

[5] See note, p. xliv., above. So also the Chron. Bert., c. 537.

[6] Ed. Edwards, pp. 31, 35 ; and cf. præf., pp. xcvii, xcviii.

letter in the pontificate of archbishop Ethered, Plegmund's predecessor, and describes a council held at London for the purpose of welcoming Grimbald. If this is not, as I believe it to be, entirely apocryphal and inextricably connected with the Oxford forgeries, it might be conjectured that Grimbald had returned between 886 and 892 to Saint Bertin's, and only settled permanently after his return to England in 892. But this is unnecessary. There is a letter of Folco to archbishop Plegmund, complimenting him on his studies,[1] and another to Alfred, congratulating him on the appointment to Canterbury,[2] either of which might have been expected to mention Grimbald, if he had come to England before the arch-

_{Other letters of Folco.}

---

[1] Flodoard, Hist. Eccl. Remensis, lib. iv. c. 6; ed. Sirmond, p. 334; Bibl. Max. Patr., ed. Lugd., xvii. 600; cf. Alford, Annales, iii. 162.

[2] Flodoard, lib. iv., c. 5, p. 331; Bibl. Max., xvii. 599. Folco seems to have been specially interested in England: there was a letter from pope Stephen VI. to him about English travellers; see Flodoard, p. 312. Reg. Pontiff. ed. Jaffé-Wattenbach, No. 3424.

[2] Flodoard (lib. iv. c. 5) gives the following abstract of the letter from Folco to Alfred just referred to:—
"Albrado regi transmarino amica-
"biles litteras mittens, grates refert
"quia tam bonum virum et devo-
"tum ecclesiasticisque regulis
"congruentem destinaverit episco-
"pum in civitate Cantaburg nomine.
"Audierat enim quod perversissi-
"mam sectam paganicis erroribus
"exortam, et in illa gente tunc us-
"que relictam, verbi mucrone sa-
"tageret amputare. Quæ secta
"suggerere videbatur episcopis et
"presbiteris subintroductas habere
"mulieres, ad propinquas quoque
"generis sui quisque vellet acce-
"dere, insuper et sacratas Deo
"feminas incestare et uxorem ha-
"bens concubinam simul habere.
"Quæ omnia, quam sanæ fidei sint
"adversa documentis manifestat
"evidentissimis ex sanctorum pat-
"rum probatis auctoritatibus." To Plegmund also he wrote:—"Pleo-
"nico archiepiscopo transmarino
"congratulans bonis ejus studiis
"quibus eum laborare compererat,
"pro abscindendis et exstirpandis in-
"cestuosis luxuriæ fomentis, supra
"in hiis litteris quas Albrado regi
"scripserat commemoratis, quæ in
"ea gente videbantur inoluisse;
"sacris eum instruens et armans
"auctoritatibus censuræ canonicæ,
"particeps nimirum piis ipsius la-
"boribus cupiens existere"; ib. c. 6. Letters on the same subject had been written by pope John VIII., to Burhred, king of Mercia: Ivo, Decr., part 8, c. 130; and to Ethered, archbishop of Canterbury, in 878: Wilkins, Conc., i. 195; Reg. Pontiff., No. 3125.

bishop's accession, but says nothing about him. Here, however, we must close a discussion which has its interest, considerable if adventitious, in the history of the Alfredian revival. I may add that Grimbald is mentioned in Alfred's preface to his version of S. Gregory's book of the pastoral care, but in connexion with Plegmund as archbishop and Asser as bishop. The latter prelate succeeded, at Sherborne, bishop Wulfsige whose name appears in the charters as late as 892. Of the extant or known copies of S. Gregory's book, one was addressed to bishop Werefrith of Worcester, 873-915 ;[1] one to Heahstan of London, who died in 898 ;[2] another to Swithulf of Rochester,[3] 880-897 ; and another to Wulfsige, who may have been the bishop of London,[4] or removed from Sherborne to London about the year 892. There is nothing in this that would serve to throw back the date of Grimbald.

John, the Old Saxon.

6. Another of the learned company, John, the Old Saxon, has afforded ground for a good deal of conjecture. This I do not wish to traverse, only remarking that it was a curious mistake, or worse, on the part of our author to transfer the tragic history of John's end from Athelney to Malmesbury.[5] After confounding him with John Scotus Erigena,[6] it was a slight matter to make him a martyr. But the two stories of the murder are not identical, and, if the epitaph preserved by our author is genuine, there must have been two abbots John, both murdered. The name was not a common one then in the west, but there are traces of a Johannes[7] among the attestations of the charters of the next reign, which may denote the abbot of Malmesbury.

---

[1] MS. Hatton, in the Bodleian, 20.

[2] MS. Cotton, Otho B. 2.

[3] The burnt MS. Cotton, Tib. B. 11, contained a statement, "Pleg-" munde Arcebisc. is agifen his boe, " and Swithulfe bisc. and Werfer-" the bisc." See Wanley's Catalogue in Hickes, Thesaurus, pp. 70, 71, 114, 153, 168, 217.

[4] MS. C.C.C. xii.

[5] Above, p. 131; and vol. i., pref. pp. cxliv. sq.

[6] Above, pp. 131, 132, and notes.

[7] See the Cartularium Saxonicum, ii. pp. 232, 273, 275.

7. Of the few important passages in which our author adds to or varies from the book of Asser, the following are worth noting:—(*a.*) The miraculous appearance of S. Cuthbert to Alfred, when he was hiding in the isle of Athelney, is an ancient story, and possibly the key to the dedication of many churches in Southern England, especially that at Wells, in honour of the Northumbrian saint. It is given, in its earliest form, by a writer of the eleventh century, in the "Historia de Sancto Cuthberto," and with considerable expansions in the "Historia de Translationibus et Miraculis Sancti "Cuthberti," a tract drawn up by one who witnessed the translation of S. Cuthbert in the year 1104.[1] Either of these may have been in our author's hands when he wrote: or possibly he had it from a similar source with Simeon of Durham, who mentions it in his Annal of 877.[2] The story, however, is very differently told in the three writers: our author's most peculiar departure from historical probability is that he makes Alfred's mother the companion of his wanderings.[3] Both the earlier writers speak of his wife; the variation may be one of simple carelessness. William of Malmesbury knew that Osburga must have been long dead. But the story is told so differently by the several writers that a minute comparison would be useless and tedious.

(*b.*) The story of the translation of S. Martin, in the same section, was, with some abridgment and expansion, taken from the tract of Odo of Cluny, entitled "Narratio in reversione Sancti Martini Turonensis de

The appearance of S. Cuthbert to Alfred.

Miracle of S. Martin.

---

[1] The most ancient form is that printed by Twysden, Scriptt., cc. 67 sq., in the Surtees Society's edition of Simeon of Durham, i., pp. 138 sq.; and in the Rolls edition, ed. Arnold, i. 196 sq. The second is in Mabillon, AA. SS. O.S.B., Sæc. iv., part 2, pp. 291 sq.; and in the Surtees edition of Simeon, pp. 158 sq.; and in the Rolls edition, ii. 229 sq., ii. 333 sq. Cf. preface to Surtees edition, pp. xxxvi sq.

[2] Sim. Dun., M. H. B., 681.

[3] Above, page 125.

PREFACE.

"Burgundia," the fifth section of which contains the essential parts of the story.[1]

Alfred's daughters.

(c.) The list of Alfred's daughters given in the Gesta varies from that of Asser in the persistent denomination of the daughter who married count Baldwin of Flanders as Ethelswitha instead of Elftbritha.[2] In this our author stands alone, but he is consistent wherever the name occurs, and must have been misled by some authority which he trusted. The mother's name was Ethelswitha, and, as I have suggested in the note on page 129, one of the children who died in infancy may have been called after her. But this does not, if true, account for the mistake in the name of the countess of Flanders. It will be observed, however, that our author mentions four daughters, Asser only three, and only three are named in the ancient genealogies.

Mission of Sighelm to India.

(d.) In the account of the mission sent by Alfred to India, our author has given to Sighelm, one of the two envoys, the title of Bishop of Sherborne; and in the Gesta Pontificum he makes him successor to Asser in that see.[3] He is mentioned without any such title in the Chronicle under the year 883, and if he succeeded Asser it must have been after the year 910. The name does not occur in the more ancient lists of the bishops of Sherborne until three successors of Asser had lived and died, and is not found in the attestations of genuine charters before the year 926. It is scarcely possible that the two Sighelms were identical.[4]

---

[1] Above, page 127. The tract of Odo is printed from the Bibliotheca Cluniacensis, in Migne's Patrologia, vol. 133, coll. 815 sq.

[2] Above, pp. 129, 133, 150. In the last place she is called the daughter of Edward, not of Alfred. In the Vita Dunstani, p. 285, she is still called Ethelsuitha; and her son count Arnulf, "pronepos" of Alfred.

[3] Above, p. 130. G. P., lib. iv. § 80.

[4] Sighelm's name was entered at S. Gallen in or about 928, with those of Ethelstan's other bishops and ealdormen. See Goldast. Alamann. Antiq., tom. ii. p. 157.

(*e*.) The account of Alfred's literary labours, so far as it is an expansion of Asser's, is sound and useful, and shows that our author, as librarian, had not neglected his opportunities of studying the native bibliography.[1]

(*f*.) The story of Alfred's burial, in § 124,[2] and of the removal of the New Minster from the neighbourhood of the cathedral to the outside of the walls, do not call for more than cursory notice. The latter was an event which our author himself might have witnessed, as it took place in the year 1110.

<small>Alfred's burial.</small>

(*g*.) Into the passage in which the organisation of England in hundreds and tithings[3] is described, and the typical peace of the country exemplified, it is unnecessary to examine. It is without historical foundation, and finds its way into the Gesta only as similar fables have found their way into like works; the name of a great national hero gathers around itself all the glories of the national history, and after a few generations he becomes the creator of all effective institutions, whether as a matter of fact they are more ancient or more modern, and whether or no he had time to institute any organisation at all.

<small>The institution of hundreds and tithings.</small>

8. For the reign of Edward, the son of Alfred, the Chronicle furnished William of Malmesbury with all his historical material, for the story of the birth of Ethelstan came from a disreputable and too common body of legend. For our present purpose there are only two points of importance to be considered. One of these is the family pedigree, which comes into prominence in two sections, § 126 and § 135. It stands in the Gesta as follows:[4] Edward had, (1) by Egwinna his first wife, Ethelstan who succeed him, and a daughter who was married to Sihtric, king of the Northumbrians; (2) by Elfleda, the daughter of Ethelm, he had two sons, Ethel-

<small>The reign of Edward, son of Alfred.</small>

<small>The family of Edward.</small>

---

[1] Above, pp. 130–132.
[2] Above, p. 134.
[3] Above, p. 129.
[4] Above, pp. 137, 150.

lii   PREFACE.

werd and Edwin, and six daughters, Edfleda, Edgiva, Ethelhilda, Ethilda, Edgitha, and Elfgiva; and by his third wife, Edgiva, two sons, Edmund and Edred, and two daughters, Edburga and a second Edgiva. The history of the sons is well ascertained, Ethelstan, Edmund and Edred were kings; Edwin perished as a pretender, Ethelwerd died so soon after his father that he escaped the risks of his position. Of the nine daughters, the wife of Sihtric, Edgiva the wife of Charles the Simple, Ethild the wife of Hugh the Great,[1] and Elfgiva, or rather Eadgitha, the wife of Otto I., are at once accounted for. Two others, Edfleda, a nun, and Ethelhilda, a lay recluse, were buried at Wilton; and Eadburga, a daughter of the third marriage, who attained the honours of sanctity, was buried at Winchester. Of the two daughters who remain, one, Edgiva, was married to Lewis of Aquitaine, the titular emperor and king of Burgundy, the son of Ermengarde and grandson of the emperor Lewis II., who died in 928; the other, Edgitha, to a prince or duke who reigned in the neighbourhood of the Alps: this last match has been the subject of much discussion, and has finally been assigned by Dr. Dümmler to Alberic, a Burgundian duke whom it is still difficult to identify.[2]

Marriages and destinies of the daughters.

---

[1] In § 126, p. 137, Ethild (Eadhild) is given to Hugh simply; unluckily, in § 135, he is called king of the Franks; and in § 129, apparently the two, Hugh the Great and Hugh Capet, are still further confounded; but see above, p. xxxvi.

[2] See Dümmler, Otto der Grosse, in the Jahrbücher series, pp. 8, 9. The inference is from a charter printed by Mabillon, AA. SS. O.S.B., Sæc. v., p. 244, granted by king Lothar in 958 to a certain Burchard, son of the duke Alberic, confirming the foundation of a monastery at Bray in the diocese of Sens, built to receive the body of SS. Paternus and Pavatus, which last, along with certain monks, had been sent from Pershore, by Burchard's uncle, king Eadred. Alberic must, therefore, have married a daughter of Edward, who could be none other than the lost Eadgiva. She is mentioned by Hrotswitha in the Panegyris Oddonum (Meibomius, Scr., i. 713), as sent with Eadgitha to Otto I., under the name *Adiva*, which is sufficient to identify her in our author's list: "Necnon germanam "secum transmisit Adivam, quæ "fuit ætatis meriti pariterque

The paucity or perhaps too close similarity of the names of Anglo-Saxon ladies is very puzzling; we have already seen how our author was confused by the names of the daughters of Alfred. And the confusion extended to foreigners. In the continental histories the married daughters of Edward appear under very different names: Edgiva, the wife of Charles the Simple,[1] is called Eadgifu by Ethelwerd; she is named Ogiva by the French historians; Odgieva, in the Chronicle of S. Bertin. Ethilda, the wife of Hugh the Great, Eadhild, in Ethelwerd, is elsewhere described as Hedwiga. Edgitha, whom our author calls Elfgiva, the wife of Otto the Great,[2] is Edgid in the Continuation of Regino of Prüm, Edith in the Saxon Chronographer; Ethelwerd calls her Eadgyde, and possibly our author may have made a mistake between her and the other daughter whom Athelstan sent to Germany.

Edgiva, the wife of Lewis of Arles,[3] appears under her proper designation, an advantage due perhaps to the fact that but for the English writers her name would be altogether unknown.

Edgitha (or Edgiva),[4] the wife of Alberic, who is

" minoris." Burchard's wife was named Hildegardis, his brother was Theobaldus dominus de Centumliis, and he had a cousin, Adelelm, who was a benefactor of Fleury in 975. Cf. Mab., AA. SS., Sæc. iii., pt. 1, p. 444; Bouquet ix. 622; Gallia Christiana, xii. 30; Chron. S. Petri Vivi Senenensis; D'Achery, Sp. ii. 719.

Waitz, Heinrich I., p. 138, gives up the point in despair, and I cannot, as yet, at all identify *Albericus dux* as an historic person; or his duchy either; there was a count of Macon named Alberic at the time, but his wife is called Bertha.

[1] Chron. Bert., c. 536. Eadgiva married, after the death of Charles, Herbert, count of Troyes.

[2] Edgidh in Otto's charter, Meibomius, Scr., i. 741. Waitz, Heinrich I., p. 138, gives Edgyde, Edgid, Eaditha, Eadit, Edith, Otgith, and Etheid as forms of her name.

[3] See above, p. xxxiv, note 1.

[4] According to the Art de V. les Dates, Ebles, count of Poictiers, 902–932, married a daughter of Edward named Adela or Alaine, who, however, is said, by Adhemar of Chabannais, to be daughter of the count of Rouen; Labbe, Bibl. MSS., ii. 165. Chron. S. Maxent., ib. 199–201. Art de V. l. D., x. 93.

scarcely to be recognised under the name, is Adiva in Hrotswitha, and I do not know that any other writer identifies her at all.

I think that we may fairly distribute the names thus: Eadgifu, the wife of Charles the Simple; Eadhild, of Hugh the Great; Eadgith, of Otto; Elfgifu, of Lewis; and the second Eadgifu, of the Alpine nobleman Alberic.

<small>Evidence of the genealogies.</small>

In conclusion it may be noted that the ancient genealogies,[1] appended to Florence of Worcester, give the names differently: Egwinna is the mother of Ethelstan; Edgiva has three sons, Edwin, Edmund and Edred, and four daughters, of whom Eadburga was one, the other three being the wives of Charles the Simple, Otto, and Hugh. But the virgin daughters are known from the places of their burial, and the whole detail seems to be slovenly and incomplete. As far as with our present materials we can argue, our author's account is the most perfect and most probable; he may well have drawn it, so far as it is not copied from Ethelwerd,[2] from the calendars or local muniments of the West Saxon monasteries, Wilton or perhaps Malmesbury itself.

<small>Rearrangement of the West Saxon dioceses.</small>

9. The second of the salient points in our discussion on this reign is the question about the subdivision of the great West Saxon dioceses. This, which is the great ecclesiastical event of the reign of Edward, is one of those incidents which owe their obscurity not so much to the paucity of authorities, as to the unfortunate attempts to fill up and harmonise accounts which, if they could have been harmonised, would not have been so imperfect as to require filling up. The main features

---

[1] Mon. Hist. Brit., pp. 641, 642.

[2] Ethelwerd, who possibly is the best authority, names them Eadgyfu, wife of Charles; Eadhild, wife of Hugh; and Eadgythe, the ancestress of the lady Matilda, to whom he was writing; and another married to the king near the Jupitereos montes, probably Lewis the Blind. Matilda herself is believed to be the daughter of Liudolf, son of Otto I., by Eadgith; Waitz, Heinrich, p. 459; Dümmler, Otto der Grosse, p. 9. Cf. Meibomius, Scriptt., i. 699. Ann. Quedlinburg, ad ann. 955; Lappenberg i., pf., p. lvii.

of the controversy are well known; the remonstrance of pope Formosus as to the condition of the Anglo-Saxon Church, the division of the diocese of Winchester, and rearrangement of the less coherent jurisdiction of the western shires of Wessex; the consecration of the seven bishops at Canterbury, and the identification of the seven, in the event of its being proved that that consecration is historical. Each of these points is beset with inconsistencies and anachronistic statements. *Points in debate.*

Our author, in § 129,[1] gives an abstract of a statement which is found in fuller detail in the most ancient records of at least three of the cathedrals; in the Missal of Leofric of Exeter,[2] now in the Bodleian Library, in the Codex Wintoniensis, now in the British Museum,[3] and in the Register of John Cranbourne at Canterbury, which contains transcripts of the early documents of the metropolitan see as they existed in the fourteenth century, many of the originals of which are still extant. According to this document, which is dated A.D. 905,[4] pope Formosus, having learned that the West Saxon Church was in danger of being left without a due and adequate episcopate, seven years having elapsed since the sees were vacated, remonstrated strongly with king Edward, who in consequence, with the assistance of archbishop Plegmund, appointed a bishop for each of the tribes of the West Saxons, and instead of two bishoprics constituted five. Plegmund then went to Rome, and there obtained the papal approbation for the rearrangement. To the five sees, subsequently, at Canterbury, five clerks were consecrated, Frithstan to Winchester, Æthel- *Original records on the subject.*

---

[1] Above, pages 140, 141.
[2] Edited by Mr. Warren, at the Clarendon Press, in 1883.
[3] MS. Additional 15,350; the Codex Wintoniensis purchased by the trustees of the British Museum in 1845.
[4] The best accounts of the MSS of this document will be found in the Cartularium Saxonicum, vol. ii, pp. 276–278. They are the Codex Wintoniensis (12th cent.); Cotton, Cleopatra E. 1 (also 12th cent.); Leofric's Missal (probably 11th cent.); and Reg. Cant. A. (14th cent.).

lvi   PREFACE.

stan to Ramsbury in Wiltshire, Werstan to Sherborne, Æthelhelm to Wells, Eadwulf to Crediton. And the same day were consecrated Beorneh to Selsey, and Ceolwulf to the Mercian Dorchester.

Such is the completed record of the conflicting traditions, which must, I think, have acquired its present form soon after the middle of the eleventh century, although, if it could be thrown forty years later, we might be enabled to speculate with some plausibility as to the method of its development. We mark first the portions of the documents which are *primâ facie* irreconcileable with chronology. The pontificate of Formosus[1] ended four years before the reign of Edward began; in the year 905 Formosus had been dead for nine years; and his acts had been rescinded by his successor Stephen VI. in 897, were reinstated by Theodore II. the same year, and by John IX. in 898;[2] and were in 904 again condemned by Sergius III. The year 905[3] is thus a date at which nothing could have been done by Formosus, and at which it was extremely unlikely that anything should be done on his authority, especially as the validity of ordinations performed by him was one of the matters most vehemently disputed.

Secondly, we may mark the points, connected with the subject, that are beyond reasonable dispute. The diocese of Winchester is known from the charters of Edward to have been divided into two in the year 909.[4] The ancient list of sees and bishops, which was drawn up at the latest within 80 years of this date,[5] states that

Points irreconcileable with chronology.

Date of Formosus.

Points which are fairly clear.

---

[1] Reg. Pontiff., Jaffé-Wattenbach pp. 384, 439, 440.
[2] Ib., pp. 441, 442.
[3] Ib., p. 445.
[4] See Kemble, Cod. Dipl., numbers 342, 1090-1096; and Birch, Cartularium Saxonicum, numbers 620-629; of which n. 620 is from an original tenth-century charter.

[5] The ancient list in MS. Tiberius B. 5, is of the age of archbishop Sigeric, 990-995; it is printed in the Mon. Hist. Brit., p. 620; and conveniently, as being freed from various readings, in Wright and Halliwell's Reliquiæ Antiquæ, ii. 69.

this division of the diocese of Winchester was accomplished in the time of bishop Frithestan,[1] his fellow-bishop being Æthelstan, the predecessor of Odo, both of whom we know to have been bishops of Ramsbury, in Wiltshire; and that subsequently the Wiltshire bishopric was divided between Wilts, Wells, and Crediton; Ethelhelm is the first bishop of Wells, and Eadulf the first bishop of Crediton; no date is assigned to this second, if it were a second, act of subdivision; but the occurrence of some of the names in the charters may help us to a decision about it. Further, we are able on the authority of Ethelwerd to fix the year 908 as the date of a visit of archbishop Plegmund to Rome;[2] in that year he consecrated the New Minster at Winchester and carried the alms of king Edward to the apostolic see.

Thirdly, we may conjecture some of the reasons that may have created or suggested a complication at the time. Formosus became pope in 891; archbishop Plegmund obtained the primacy that year or the year before, and, according to the tradition of the Church of Canterbury, received[3] from Formosus the pallium, which in that age, as long after, was the type and vehicle of the metropolitan jurisdiction. In the year 897 the acts of Formosus, and especially his ordinations, were annulled, and that annulment was confirmed, after bitter controversy in 904. Accordingly, in the year 905, the validity of the acts of Plegmund and of all the bishops whom he had consecrated, was more than disputable, and, I may

Possible causes of the complication of tradition.

Invalidity of the acts of Formosus.

---

[1] "Tempore quo diucesim Wentanæ ecclesiæ in duas divisi parochias, obnixe rogatus fui a Frithestano quem tunc prædictæ ecclesiæ episcopum constitueram": Birch, Cart. Sax., ii. 283. The attesting bishops to these charters are Plegmund, Frithstan (as bishop), Wulfsige, Wighelm, Ceolmund; in No. 627, three witnesses, who in the other charters are described as "filius regis," are called "episcopus": Ethelstan, Ethelweard, and Elfweard, probably by clerical error. Of the three bishops, Wulfsige is probably the bishop of London.

[2] Ethelwerd, Mon. Hist. Brit., p. 519.

[3] Anglia Sacra, i. 87; Gervase, Opp., ii. 350.

add, it is only very tentatively that we are able to assign any dates of consecration of bishops in England to the intervening years.[1] It is then far from improbable that the paucity of bishops which, in the current record, is said to have called for the remonstrance of Formosus, may have been caused by the doubt felt about the validity of his own acts.[2] Further, it may have been known or believed, at the time at which that record was framed, that Formosus had interested himself in the affairs of the English Church; at all events, during the controversy between Canterbury and York, which was going on in the year 1070 and onwards, a letter of Formosus was produced by archbishop Lanfranc,[3] in which he remarks severely on the continued existence of pagan rites in England, and urges the more expeditious filling-up of vacant sees, although not with the vehement threat inserted in the record of 905. The authenticity of this letter is open to doubt, as it contains the too convenient assertion of the primacy of Canterbury, the doctrine in support of which the other letters in the series are suspected to have been fabricated; but supposing it to have existed when the record of 905 was drawn up, it would account for the position asserted for Formosus in that document.

Supposing for the moment that this was a genuine letter, or even dispensing with it altogether, and accounting for the introduction of the name of Formosus on other

---

[1] See Wattenbach, Regesta Pontificum, i. 440, 441, 442, 445; Dümmler, Auxilius und Vulgarius, pp. 72 sq., 78; Auxilius, de OrdinationibusFormosi: in Mabillon, Analecta, pp. 28, 32, 39 sq., Morinus, de Sacris Ecclesiæ Ordinationibus, part 3, p. 85 (ed. 1655).

[2] Formosus's bishops were reordained according to Sigebert quoting Luitprand, ad ann. 900, 902, 907.

[3] W. Malmesb., Gesta Pontiff., pp. 59-61; MS. Cotton, Cleopatra E. 1. This letter is not marked as suspicious by Jaffé or Wattenbach, Reg. Pontiff., p. 438. Although it comes to us through an awkward channel, I do not feel inclined to reject it wholly, especially as it contains matter which is not at all necessary to the purpose of a forger; and it would be cruel to regard Lanfranc as being art and part with a mere invention.

grounds, we may well suppose that the situation had by the year 905 become critical; and that, after drifting on until 908, Plegmund found it necessary to go to Rome. It had been necessary, even under Benedict IV. who had himself been ordained by Formosus, for Arngrin bishop of Langres, to have the pall which that pope had granted him recognised and confirmed by the pontiff in synod. Still more was it needed under Sergius.[1] The carrying of king Edward's alms would be a very plausible cover for a visit really intended to secure the recognition of the validity of his own position. The acts and ordinations [2] of Formosus were still matters of dispute, and pope Sergius III. might be inclined, out of consideration for Plegmund's visit and the accompanying compliment, to agree to the proposals made to him. The king and archbishop had divided the sees; the proper confirmation was granted; on the archbishop's return, the vacant churches were filled up.

Attempt at a theory of explanation.

But were the seven bishops consecrated together, and, if so, who were they? It is just possible that the two acts of subdivision were transacted in the same council at Winchester, or wherever it may have been, and that the five West Saxon prelates, Frithstan, Ethelstan, Ethelhelm and Eadulf, and the new bishop of Sherborne, were consecrated together, the sees of Selsey and Dorchester, which were not within the purview of the acts of subdivision, being filled up at the same time. If we look for the successor of Asser, whose death is fixed in the same year,[3] we shall find that the bishop of

Consecration of the seven bishops.

---

[1] See the references in Reg. Pontiff., Jaffé-Wattenbach, nn. 3527, 3528.

[2] The controversy about them lasted for at least seventeen years; see Morinus, de Sacris Ecclesiæ Ordinationibus, part 3, page 85, ed. 1655.

[3] Chron. Sax., 910, "and after that," possibly after the nomination and before consecration of Frithstan

"bishop Asser died." Mon. H. B., p. 374; ed. Thorpe, pp. 182, 183. The name of his successor is given as Æthelwerd both in the tenth century Cotton MS., Tiberius B. 5, and in the splendid Sherborne pontifical, called Dunstan's, now in the National Library at Paris; Memorials of S. Dunstan, pref., p. cxiii.

Sherborne was named Ethelweard; Beorneh may have been appointed to Selsey at this time, but his name in the charters occurs first in 926; the history of the Mercian episcopate just now is very dark; there may have been a Ceolwulf, who is otherwise unrecorded. The matter must be left in a certain shade of obscurity still; and the conjectural adjustment which I have proposed lies under the objection that nothing is said about the doubtfulness of the ordinations of Formosus by the English historians. In answer to that, it may be said that, on the much later, and possibly more critical events which marked the substitution of Roger Walden for archbishop Arundel in 1398, the records of the see of Canterbury are absolutely silent. Time in the one case, policy as well as time in the other, is " edax rerum," at all events, of all such things as inconvenient documents. The consecration of the seven bishops is not a very important point, although it interested the ecclesiastical writers of the twelfth century as being a sort of parallel with Saint Anselm's consecration of five at Canterbury in 1107; but it was not invented for the occasion.[1] The date of the subdivisions of the dioceses is more important, but perhaps the most interesting point in the whole discussion is the reference of the action to pope Formosus, who, unless there were some traditionary interest attached to his name at Canterbury, was a most unlikely person to be intruded into the ecclesiastical history of England.

10. The history of the reign of Ethelstan is written by William with peculiar care.[2] The very jejune notices of the Chronicle seem to have suggested to our author the need of more diligent research, and he had recourse to oral tradition as well as to written authorities. The legendary history of the king's birth and of the

The reign of Ethelstan.

---

[1] Flor. Wig., ad ann. ed. Thorpe, ii. 57.

[2] See Freeman, Norman Conquest, i. 60.

PREFACE. lxi

difficulties which attended his succession, the opposition of the ealdorman Elfred, and the fate of Edwin, the king's half-brother and rival, are given, for what they are worth, as traditions preserved in ballads, not in books.[1] They have, he allows, a certain verisimilitude, but he is not disposed to defend them as true, and inserts them lest his critics should charge him with suppressing matter derogatory to the character of his hero. It is impossible for us to test their value, but they cannot be said to rest upon ballad testimony only. The story of Elfred's conspiracy, exile and forfeiture, has some sort of confirmation from the charter which our author produces from the treasury at Malmesbury.[2] The cruel exposure of Edwin, and Ethelstan's remorse and penance, found their way into other chronicles besides William's,[3] and the place of the king's retirement was traditionally fixed at Lamport.[4] The Chronicle furnished a few data of marriages and conquests, and the poetical account of the battle of Brunanburh, to be amplified with a few traditionary or imaginary details. But the chief interest centres in our author's use of a poetical life or panegyric on Ethelstan, which he found in an ancient volume that no later writer has ever been able to trace or identify. The fragments of this work, which he has incorporated in his own, serve to prove that this century was not so barren of learning in England as the extremely scanty remains now extant would seem to imply. William of Malmesbury, although he criticises the style of the poem rather superciliously,[5] still shows that he thought that he had found a treasure, and that it was worth his while to retrace his way over some part at

The poetical life of Ethelstan.

---

[1] Above, pp. 142, 155, 157.
[2] Above, p. 153; Kemble, Cod. Dipl., No. 1092; Cartularium Saxonicum, ii. 426.
[3] Chron. Bertin., Joh. Iperius, cap. 22, pars 4; Mart. and Durand, Thesaurus, iii. 547.
[4] Rad. Dic. Opp., ii. 235; Gervas. Opp., ii. 48.
[5] Above, p. 144. The volume was *vetustum*, the style what Tully called, in the Rhetoric, suffult or stilted.

least of the history of the reign which he had already written.

Its versification. The versification of the poem is worth notice, although, from the fact that we have only fragments which may be disconnected, it is difficult to be quite certain that the arrangement was symmetrical. There is an alternation of single or double-rhymed distichs, running in pairs or triplets, with similar pairs of single-rhymed lines, in which the rhyme, as was common in ecclesiastical sequences, turned on a single syllable only: of the rhymed distichs an example is

> Regia progenies produxit nobile stemma
> Cum tenebris nostris illuxit splendida gemma;

of the single-rhymed lines,

> Et potans avidis doctrinæ mella medullis,

in which only an experienced eye detects any coincidence at all. I do not know that it would be difficult to find analogies among the fantastical metres of the period, nor perhaps among the remains of the Anglo-Saxon poets expressions that might guide conjecturally to the authorship.

Question of the date of the poem. The style of the work does not afford much of a clue to the date of its author. William describes the book in which he found the poem as an ancient volume, and the composition as that of a writer who wrestled with the difficulty of his material, being evidently unable to express as well as he wished what was in his mind. He certainly chose a very awkward vehicle for the expression of his sentiments, so awkward that we must be grateful indeed that we are able to understand him at all. The combination of the "versus leoninus" with the "versus caudatus" is not calculated to fix the attention of either writer or reader on the substance of the argument. So far however as touches the date, there is no objection, I believe, in the structure of the verse, to referring it to the tenth century. The tendency in regard to such fragments has of late years been to minimise their claims to antiquity. But the judgment of one of the most authoritative of the rhythmical critics of the present day, Wilhelm Meyer, is that rhymed hexameters may be found as early as the eighth century, whilst in compositions of the ninth, especially within the Irish and Anglo-Saxon area, may be found examples of middle and end rhymes, as well as of what he calls the "Tiraden-reim" in which the burden rests on the repetition of a single final vowel. He has not, so far as I am aware, passed judgment on these verses, but judging from incidental expressions, I conclude that he would incline to refer them to the eleventh, rather than to the tenth century. I think that our author's description of the book would apply best to a late tenth, or early eleventh century date. But it is an obscure subject.[1]

11. The great value of the poem, however, consists in the particular details which, either in extracts, or in abstracts clothed in his own language in his review of the work, our author preserves for us. Such especially are the facts that Ethelstan had as a child received knightly arms, or analogous investiture from his grandfather Alfred, the scarlet cloak, the jewelled belt, and the Saxon sword with golden scabbard, an honour that recalls the king's own inauguration by pope Leo;[2] that he was educated by Ethelfleda his aunt and Ethered her husband; the description of the coronation festival; the submission of the Scots at Dacor;[3] the details of the

Particulars preserved in the poem.

---

[1] There are some verses addressed to Ebbo, archbishop of Rheims (816-841), printed in Dümmler's first volume of medieval poets, in the Monumenta series, pp. 623 and 624, which furnish analogies, but not very sufficient ones. But the subject is carefully worked out in the two articles in the Sitzungsberichte of the Munich Academy, for 1873, vol. i., and 1882, vol. i. pp. 1-192. The rhymes in the life of Ethelstan may well be compared with those attached to one of the letters among the relics of Dunstan; Memorials, &c., pp. 373, 374.

[2] Above, page 145; and cf. p. xliii, note 2.

[3] See above, § 134, page 147. I am not aware that this submission at Dacor is mentioned by any other writer.

expedition to the north, which serve to account, among other things, for the king's traditionary interest in the Yorkshire churches;[1] his relations with Wales and Cornwall; the negotiations for the marriage of the king's sisters, and the description of the treasures, the sword of Constantine, with a nail of the true cross in its hilt, the lance of Charles, and the standard of S. Maurice; the deaths of the two sons of Ethelweard, grandsons of Alfred; all which particulars, we are given to understand, were excerpted from this precious book. The second extract which contains the account of the return and defeat of Anlaf, has so much of the "suffult" tone of which our author complains, that we wonder how he had abstracted, from a book of such obscure and enigmatic style, anything so definite as the account of the court which entertained count Adulf of Boulogne at Abingdon, as ambassador from Hugh the Great.[2] It is very possible that the poet drew on his imagination for some of the details on which our author dwells with pleasant hyperbole: it is possible that count Adulf drew on a store of relics capable of much reduplication and indefinite multiplication. The perfumes such as had never been seen before in England; the emeralds whose colour in the sunlight was so refreshing to the eyes; the gallant coursers; the onyx vase carved so as to present the waving cornfields, the budding vines, and the moving figures of men; were all so capable of poetic embellishment, that here and there we can detect in our author's prose paraphrase the echoes of the original

---

[1] Especially with Ripon and Beverley, the connexion with which foundations is apparently matter of continuous tradition, although the documents that illustrate it are fabricated. Mon. Angl., ii. 127, 129; vi. 307, &c.

[2] The two mistakes of our author already noted, by which he makes Hugh the Great, king of the Franks, and Adulf, the son of Baldwin, by the daughter instead of the sister of Edward, and calls her Ethelswitha instead of Elfthritha, may possibly have been caught from his book. Further Henry I. of Germany was not son of Conrad, his predecessor (p. 149).

rhymes. But, whether true or false, imbedded in the prosaic narrative where we find them, these details have a literary value of singular interest. It is too late now to anticipate any rediscovery of the curious volume which our author was so pleased and so fortunate as to find; but it is by no means certain that the whole interest of the reign of Ethelstan has been as yet explored. In the search for relics of the history of Dunstan, it was my good fortune many years ago to collect a number of fragments of letters, which have a good deal to tell to those who have patience to read them.[1] The foreign relations of England, monastic and literary, as well as diplomatic and dynastic, have for this period been very incompletely examined, and a careful investigation of foreign cartularies may yet discover to us relics as precious in their way as the banner of S. Maurice, or the lance of Charles the Great.[2]

12. Ethelstan was succeeded by Edmund, and Edmund by Edred. On the history of these two reigns as he found it in the Chronicles, our author sheds no new light. He does indeed insert a Glastonbury charter in his later editions, but he does not seem to have cared to avail himself of the materials which the history of Dunstan would have afforded him. He reserved them no doubt for the Gesta Pontificum, which he had already in hand. The reigns of Edwy and Edgar, however, are illustrated from Osbern's life of Dunstan, which he cites by name as well as Wulfstan's life of S. Ethelwold.[3] Under these reigns as under

Reigns of Edmund, Edred, Edwy, and Edgar.

---

[1] Memorials of Saint Dunstan, pp. 354 sq.

[2] It is worth while to compare with the description of the lance, sword, and standard, Turpin's account of the sword of Roland (V· Caroli, ap. Reuber, p. 82); the lance of S. Maurice was the palladium of the kingdom of Burgundy: Chron. Virdun., Labbe, Bibliotheca, i. 182.

[3] Above, page 166; the encomium here bestowed on Osbern is very much modified in our author's own life of Dunstan, in which he is very severe on both his historical and his doctrinal accuracy, as Eadmer also was. See Memorials of Saint Dunstan, pp. 162, 163, 250–252, &c.

previous ones, long episodes and charters of Glastonbury history are inserted, together with a letter of the pope to the Ealdorman Elfric, and a charter of Edgar to Malmesbury.[1] The remaining sections that belong to Edgar's reign contain the legend of his vision, a panegyric on his administration, the story of the tribute of wolves' heads, of Kenneth's insult and apology, the tragedy of Ethelwold and Elfrida, Edgar's sin and penance, his late coronation and death.[2] Beyond a few incidental notes in the Chronicles, the whole of this is drawn either from the lives of Dunstan, or from popular legend, of which Malmesbury is the first exponent. The same remark applies to the history of Edward the Martyr and the early days of Ethelred. The narrative is beginning to flag very seriously just where it ought to become most interesting.[3] Accordingly, apropos of Ethelred's marriage with Emma, our author inserts a letter of pope John XV.,[4] and then strikes off at a tangent on the history of Gerbert whom he has confounded with his predecessor.

The legendary history of Gerbert. 13. The legend or mythical history of pope Sylvester II. fills six sections of the Gesta. Of all the entertaining episodes with which our author diversifies his narrative, or fills up the gaps in the scantier parts of the history, this is perhaps the most famous, for in it are summed up, with a few genuine data, the floating traditions of the previous century relating to one of its most famous men.[5] It is possible to glean from earlier writers glimpses of the growing myths; it is to William of Malmesbury, first of extant writers, that we owe the collective presentation of them. Some brief analysis of the sections may be taken here, as serving to indicate possible sources from which our author derived

---

[1] Above, page 167.
[2] See Freeman, Norman Conquest, i. 65, 265.
[3] See Freeman, Norman Conquest, i. 626 sq.
[4] See Freeman, Norman Conquest, i. 286, 643.
[5] Pages 195-203.

his information, besides that popular and oral authority to which he refers, and which in all probability he derived from the Aquitanian friend, the monk of Malmesbury who preserved the story of the treasures of Octavian.[1]

The episode is introduced in connexion with the letter of pope John XV., on the peace between Ethelred and duke Richard. Our author, in his first edition, and possibly in the later ones, for the MSS. in which the correction is supplied are too late to be regarded as contemporary authority,[2] confounded this pope John with Sylvester II., and it is only by a somewhat violent correction of the text in two places that the true computation is vindicated. The name of Sylvester is not in this connexion assigned at all to the hero of the legend; he is Gerbert throughout, and his reign as pope is limited, as was John XVI.'s, to ten months. He was born in Gaul and educated at Fleury.[3] Having fled from Fleury, actuated either by weariness or by ambition, he studied in Spain under Saracen teachers, and learned from them not only arithmetic, music, astronomy, and geometry, but, augury, necromancy and magic generally. He finished his career in Spain by stealing a book of magic, and was only saved from the vengeance of its owner by making a compact with the enemy of mankind. On his return to his own country he became a professor in the schools of Gaul, and had amongst his pupils Constantine, abbot of S. Maximin of Orleans, Adelbold of Utrecht, Robert, afterwards king of the French, and the emperor Otto III. Hugh Capet, father of king Robert, made him archbishop of Rheims;

Our author mistaken in his identification of Gerbert with pope John.

His account of Gerbert's career.

---

[1] Pages 198, 202.
[2] See vol. i., pref., p. li; pp. 193, 195.
[3] Gerbert's connexion with Fleury seems to be accepted by scholars; but, although his friend Constantine was scholasticus at Fleury, he himself is always described as a pupil at Aurillac. His letter to the monks of Fleury (ep. 95; Opp., ed. Migne, c. 225) reads as if the tie was honorary, but it is written in the name of the abbots of Rheims.

Otto gave him Ravenna, and procured his appointment to the papacy. Having by magic ascertained that he was not to die until he had said mass at Jerusalem, he was undeceived by finding himself seized with illness in the church used for the "statio ad Jerusalem,"[1] and, having collected the cardinals and expressed his penitence, ordered that his body should be torn in pieces so as to evade, if possible, the compact which he had made with the devil when he escaped from Spain.[2]

Germs of truth in the legend.

How much of this was floating rumour, how much historic truth, how much the tribute which superstitious ignorance pays to genius or unexpected success in life? The three are curiously intermixed. Gerbert was probably an Aquitanian; he was educated at Aurillac in Auvergne, and after he became famous was claimed as belonging to a noble family in that province. According to the Chronicle of Adhemar which ends in the year 1029,[3] he was a man of low birth, was educated at Aurillac, afterwards travelled through France "causa

---

[1] "Ecclesia Sanctæ Crucis, quæ est "Jerusalem ubi statio fieri debet." Ordo Romanus, Mabillon, Museum Italicum, ii. 102 : the proper days for visiting this church were the second Sunday in Advent, the fourth in Lent, and Good Friday, ib., pp. 544, 546, also 366, &c. This church was visited by archbishop Sigeric in 990 (Memorials of S. Dunstan, p. 392), between the Lateran and S. Maria Maggiore. See also Urlichs, Codex Urbis Romæ Topographicus, pp. 167, 174; Montfaucon, Diarium Italicum, p. 111.

[2] The history of Gerbert has been well worked out in the Histoire Littéraire de la France, vol. vi., as well as by the ecclesiastical historians. There is a dissertation on him by J. C. Spoerl, of Nürnberg, Altdorf, 1720; and another by C. F. Hock, Vienna, 1837; translated by the Abbé J. M. Axinger, Paris, 1842, in which most of the extant material is brought together. The letters of Gerbert were first edited in 1611, with those of John of Salisbury, from the library of Papirius Masson, and will be found in the several Bibliothecæ Patrum; also in Migne's Patrologia, vol. 139, where his other works are collected.

[3] Chron. Ademari monachi S. Eparchii; Labbe, Bibl. MSS., ii. 169; Chron. S. Maxentii, ibid., ii. 20; cf. Rad. Glaber, ed. Pith., p. 7; Chron. Aureliac., Mabillon, Vet. Analecta (ed. 1723) p. 350. The two first named chronicles place his studies at Cordova; modern writers, perhaps referring to our author's account, place them at Seville.

PREFACE.   lxix

"sophiæ," and studied at Cordova. Hugh of Flavigny whose Chronicle closes in 1102, describes him as banished from Aurillac for the insolence of his manners, and sent by his abbot to the duke of Hither Spain, by whom he was intrusted to a bishop named Hayto to learn mathematics.[1] The historian Thietmar of Merseburg, who died in 1018, says that he was promoted unjustly to Rheims;[2] Hugh of Flavigny that it was by "quibusdam præstigiis"[3] that he obtained the see of Ravenna. The story of his compact with the devil, his disappointment and miserable death, is first told by cardinal Benno in his life of Hildebrand,[4] but with so much difference of detail that we can hardly suppose William of Malmesbury to have taken his account from him. Sigebert of Gemblours, writing not later than 1112, regards the bargain with Satan, not as true but as a part of current history;[5] and Ordericus Vitalis, who was compiling his history almost at the same time with our author, expresses in somewhat more reticent terms his acquaintance with the same scandal.[6]

Early suspicion about him.

---

[1] Hugo Flaviniac., Chron. Virdunense, Labbe. Bibl. MSS., i. 157, 158; cf., Chron. Aureliac., ut s. "quia ingenio erat vafer præclarus in litteris evasit."

[2] Thietmar, lib. vi. c. 61.

[3] H. Flav., i. 157.

[4] Vita et Gesta Hildebrandi; Fascic. Rerum Expetend., &c., vol. ii. p. 83; cf. the enlarged version of the story by Joh. Stella, ibid. p. 88.

[5] Sigebert's words are worth quoting, as helping to show the growth of the myth : "A.D. 995. Ger-"bertus qui et Silvester . . . "qui et ipse inter scientia littera-"rum claros egregie claruit . . . "is enim Silvester non per ostium "intrasse dicitur, quippe qui a qui-"busdam etiam nichromantiæ ar-"guitur; de morte quoque ejus non "recte tractatur; a diabolo enim "percussus dicitur obisse, quam "rem nos in medio relinquimus," ed. Migne, Patrol, vol. 160, c. 197.

[6] Ord. Vit., lib. i. c. 24:—"Fer-"tur de illo quod dum scholasticus "esset cum dæmone locutus fuerit "et quid sibi futurum immineret "inquisierit," ed. Prevost, i. 175. The prophetic verse cited by Orderic and so many other writers as the oracle of the familiar spirit, "Scan-"dit ab R. Gerbertus ad R.", post "papa viget R."; is given by Helgald, who lived about 1050, as Gerbert's own playful saying (ed. Pithœus, p. 63).

Gerbert's scientific accomplishments.

Perhaps, however, the most interesting parts of the story are those connected with Gerbert's accomplishments, and the very curious terms in which his scientific achievements are recorded. Whilst in Spain, we are told, he surpassed Ptolemy in his knowledge of the astrolabe,[1] Alandreus[2] in his acquaintance with the distances of the stars, Julius Firmicus in astrological anticipations of the future. The first and third of these names were doubtless well known and typical; Alandreus seems to be the Arabian astronomer, magician, and philosopher, Alkendi, who flourished under the Calif Almamon, son of Haroun al Raschid. From the Saracen enchanter, from whom he stole the fatal book of magic, he learned the arithmetic lore which enabled him to lay down rules scarcely understood by the perspiring abacists of Gaul, even Constantine and Adelbold.[3] These accomplishments are amply attested by the extant works of Gerbert: William of Malmesbury had seen in all probability the " Libellus de numerorum divisione " dedicated to Constantine of S. Maximin, and fairly described as " regulæ de abaco."[4] If he had not, his friend Walcher of Malvern no doubt knew it. We possess a letter to Adelbold on the cause of diversity of areas in the equilateral triangle, and another to Constantine on the construction of the sphere.[5] Other epistles exhibit Gerbert as a collector and corrector of Latin texts,[6] as a moral

---

[1] His work on the Astrolabe is mentioned by Fabricius, Bibl. Lat. (ed. 1858), tom. ii. p. 44.

[2] Jacoub ben Ishak Al Kendi; d'Herbelot, Dictionnaire, p. 469; or AbouYoussouf ben Ishak Al Kendi, ibid. 956; called Alkindus, Arcandam, Arcandum, Alcandrinus (Moreri, s.v.); he translated into Arabic the Spheres of Autolycus, and wrote also on astrology; cf. Lewis, Astronomy of the Ancients, pp. 184, 185.

[3] The work on the Abacus was dedicated to his master " S." or "J." or possibly Joseph; Opp.,ed.Migne, Patr., vol. 139, c. 63.

[4] Above, pp. 195, 196.

[5] Pez, Anecdota, tom. iii. pt. 2, pp. 82–84; Gerb. Opp., ed. Migne, cc. 151–154.

[6] Mabillon, Vet. Analecta (ed. 1723), pp. 102,103; Opp.,ed. Migne cc. 155, 156.

philosopher,[1] a logician,[2] and an ecclesiastical legislator. A man of so many accomplishments and so many political rivalries might well in his lifetime obtain the repute of an enchanter; the story of the Satanic compact would follow as soon as his name began to be bandied about in controversy.

If the curious diagrams which fill the pages of his geometrical and arithmetical books were liable to be interpreted as magical, much more must his mechanical contrivances have astonished the vulgar among his contemporaries: they have in fact puzzled also the historians of inventions in later times. Thietmar mentions as existing at Magdeburg, made for the emperor Otto, an "oralogium" constructed "considerata per fistulam quadam "stella nautarum duce."[3] Whether the "fistula" was an anticipation of the telescope or no, is a matter of dispute among antiquaries, as may well be the relation between the oralogium and the pole star, unless the point of the invention was the exact orientation of a sun-dial. But what our author had heard of as kept at Rheims was more astonishing by far; there also was a "horologium arte mechanica compositum," but there were also hydraulic organs,[4] in which, after a wonderful

His mechanical contrivances.

The dial at Magdeburg.

The water organ at Rheims.

---

[1] See the "de rationali et ratione "uti," Pez, Anecd., i. p. ii. c. 147; Opp., ed. Migne, cc. 154 sq.

[2] See the letter to the emperor Otto on a passage in Porphyry, Mab., Vet. Anal., p. 106.

[3] "In Magdaburg oralogium fecit, "illud recte constituens considerata "per fistulam quadam stella nauta- "rum duce;" Thietmar, Chron., lib. vi. c. 61, ed. Migne, c. 1360; ed. Leibnitz, Scr. Bruns, i. 399.

[4] Ammianus Marcellinus, xiv. 5 (ed. Ernesti, p. 15): "organa fa- "bricantur hydraulica et lyræ "speciem carpentorum ingentes." Hydraulic organs are also mentioned by Eginhard, if he be the author of the book on the Translation of S. Marcellinus. It is the steam agency that characterises Gerbert's. Above, p. 196, I have translated "barbiton" simply as "instrument," properly, of course, it is a stringed instrument. I do not see how the "multifora- "tiles tractus" can be made to harmonise with the stringed construction of the lyre; but, however unintelligible or the reverse, the passage certainly implies the use of steam; the barbitos may have been something like an Æolian harp, but the description has baffled many critics.

fashion, by the violence of heated water, the wind emerging fills the concavity of the instrument, and brazen pipes emit modulated sounds through surfaces perforated with many holes. How the result, which may have combined the railway whistle with the hydraulic, or steam engine, working of the organ, and possibly the mechanism of a stringed instrument to boot, would have struck modern ears, we can scarcely conjecture. But whatever modern discovery Gerbert may have had the credit of anticipating, it is certain that there was a curious and perhaps original effort of inventive power, which we have no right to discredit. If the description is false, the language in which it is clothed is as unaccountable as the event itself. It is at least as curious that Malmesbury should have described it as that Gerbert should have invented it.

The supplementary legends added to Gerbert's history.

The three stories that illustrate Gerbert's reputation as an enchanter are clearly derived from oral tradition and through the Aquitanian monk, and they are of a sort which, whether found current in Spain or in Italy; in reference to Gerbert, or Virgil, or Michael Scott; in the Gesta Romanorum, or in the Arabian Nights; belong to a common treasury of entertainments meant for the diversion of uncritical listeners. The Aquitanian monk was the son of a native of Barcelona; he had been in Spain and Italy, and had himself witnessed wonderful adventures in search of the treasures of Octavian. Unluckily he had seen too much, and neither the quotation from S. Clement nor the authority of Peter Damian,[1] could justify our author in treating his travellers' tales as true. He breathes, however, no word of doubt as to this part of the story. The greater scandal, the history of Gerbert's engagement with the devil, he thinks, will be believed, vulgar fiction as it is, because people are wont to disparage the character of

---

[1] Above, page 202. The story is given by the author of the Eulogium, i. 398, with a marginal note " Gesta Romanorum;" it is not, however, in that collection.

learned men, saying of any one who is excellent in a particular department of work, that he has had a talk with the devil. Even Boetius had not escaped that. And yet he has misgivings that there is a germ of truth in it; or why should the pope have ordered his corpse to be dismembered, and why should the chronologist who gave the length of his pontificate have added " hic tur- " piter vitam suam finivit." [1] *Gerbert's dying command about his body.*

And this point is still open. Benno had described him as a necromancer who had heard from his familiar spirit that he should not die until he had said mass in Jerusalem. In the agony of his sudden seizure in the church which bore the name he had ordered his hands to be amputated and his tongue to be cut out.[2] But our author gives a more picturesque and impressive version in which the Aquitanian monk had scarcely drawn merely on his own imagination. The invention of the metallic statue, with its astronomical or astrological framework, and its automatic power of answering "yes" or "no," is not without parallel in legend:[3] the oracular quibble about Jerusalem is familiar to us in the history of our own king Henry IV. Still the section reads as if it were an extract from some more ancient written source, from which Benno may have borrowed as much as it was convenient for him to tell. The work of Benno is scarcely likely to have fallen into the hands of William of Malmesbury, nor is William likely, even on the authority of his marvel-loving friend, to have elaborated the pious and speculative details with which his story is embellished. *The complete form of this part of the legend.*

But is any explanation possible? Was the confusion between Sylvester II. and John XVI. at the bottom of the whole story? John XVI. was made pope by Crescentius in 997, and had a nominal reign of ten months. In March 998 he was seized by the partizans of Otto III. *Possible confusion connected with the mutilation of pope John.*

---

[1] Page 195.
[2] See above, page 52, note 5.
[3] See above, page 202.

and Gregory V., and was mutilated; his eyes were put out and his nose and tongue cut off. It is true that he survived for many years; and no confusion could have arisen between him and Gerbert during the life of either.[1] There is no indication that Benno confounded the two; yet he knew the story of the pope who was a magician and was mutilated. Our author brings us, perhaps, a step nearer to the solution, but he does not solve the mystery, and he did not invent the fable. If this conjecture is tenable, it will serve as a clue also to the confusion of persons and events which makes the later German stories retailed in the Gesta, so curiously puzzling.

The legends of the treasure. Of the three legends told in connexion with the history of Gerbert, I need say no more than has been said already, as to their origin and transmission through the Aquitanian story-teller. The first of them, the legend of the treasure discovered by Gerbert with the help of the statue in the Campus Martius, was thought worthy to find a place and an exposition in the Gesta Romanorum.[2] It appears there, however, with so much expansion and embellishment as to suggest that at the time of its incorporation in the series it was current in a much more elaborate form than it takes in the Gesta Regum Anglorum.

The legends from German history. 14. From the review of the Gerbert legends I pass on to the consideration of the other stories, inserted by our author among the sober and obscure details of the events of the eleventh century. These are scattered through divers sections from § 174 to § 293; they have one common element, their relation to German history and tradition, and especially connect themselves with the reign of the emperor Henry III. A very few

---

[1] See the authorities cited in Wattenbach's Regesta Pontificum, pp. 495, 496.

[2] Gesta Romanorum, No. 107; ed. Osterley, p. 439; cf. Warton, History of English Poetry, vol. iii. pp. xlii–xliv, xlvii.

pages will suffice to tell all that I am able to put together on this subject.

The story of the miracle of the dancers in Saxony is fixed to the year 1012, and the pontificate of archbishop Herbert of Rothenburg, who presided over Cologne from the year 999 to the year 1021; it is placed in a village the church of which was dedicated to S. Magnus the Martyr, and the truth of the story is vouched by a sort of affidavit of an eye-witness, Otbert, certified by Piligrinus, the archbishop who succeeded Herbert. The statement, copied by our author, that the certificate was delivered by Piligrinus in 1013, is a mistake arising no doubt from a confusion between the date of the record and that of the miracle.[1]

The dancers in Saxony.

This curious legend comes to us on other authority besides our author's, or perhaps it is safer to say, on authority which, it would be difficult to suppose, was based upon his report. In a Brussels MS. of the twelfth century, described by Pertz in the Archiv,[2] which contains copies of the crusading historians Fulcher and Robert, is found a " relatio miraculi in regione Saxonum " facti tempore Heriberti Coloniensis archiepiscopi, anno " 1021, indictione 4ta, regnante Henrico II." This runs on the same lines as the letter in the Gesta, but with

Other accounts of the portent.

---

[1] Above, page 203.

[2] The MSS. are described by Pertz, in the Archiv, vii. 431, in connexion with the materials for the life of S. Heribert of Cologne. The story in the Hague MS. (Haag, No. 906) begins " Ego peccator no- " mine Stephanus, etsi vellem tegere " peccatum meum... Eramus octo- " decim.. in villa Colovize regionis " Saxonicæ ubi Sanctus Magnus mar- " tyrium consummavit... anne In- " carnationis 1021, indict. 4ta reg- " nante Henrico secundo." The Brussels MS. reads " peccator Ot- " bertus... xv. viri et tres mu- " lieres," &c., as in the text : " Pres- " biter vero nomine Robertus jam " primam missam inchoaverat, set " hæc ita nostra cantilena impedie- " batur ut ipsum inter sacra verba " personaret.... Erat vero una " trium mulierum filia dicti presbi- " teri nomine Mersent." The other MSS. are Paris, 5129; and Leipzig, Rathsbibliothek, Rep., ii. 64 Pertz, Archiv, vi. 208; vii. 56. *See also* Annales Albiani, Langebek, I. 201.

important additions. The peccator Otbertus is the writer, but the locality of the miracle is fixed "in villa " Colovize regionis Saxonicæ ubi Sanctus Magnus mar- " tyrium consummavit;" the hour is fixed more definitely, " in sanctissima Nativitate Domini expletis matu- " tinis." The evil inspiration of the dancers is identified, " suadente diabulo choros in cimiterio duximus;" the lady who led the dance is named " erat vero una trium " mulierum filia dicti presbiteri nomine Mersent." In another MS., also described by Pertz as "Haag, No. 906," containing the Annals of Fontanelles, the same letter appears as the work of "Ego peccator nomine Stephanus" and with minor variations, but preserving the name Colovize, and mentioning the martyrdom of Saint Magnus. There is also a Paris MS. of Robertus Monachus in which the same occurs; there is another MS. in the Leipzig town library, where it is found appended to a life of Henry II. and Cunegunda; and it may, I believe, be traced elsewhere. The matter is certainly obscure, and some of the details may be fabulous; the date also appears to have shifted. But the special identification of the place in which it occurred is a point which seems to indicate that the writers of these accounts wrote on independent information, and that our author accordingly took his story at second hand. As he used the Annals of Fontanelles, he may even have used a copy corresponding with the Paris MS. and abridged the letter of Otbert from it. The error in date, which is obvious, must likewise be ascribed to him. Where Colovize was, and who S. Magnus the Martyr may have been, I am not able to say. The author of the Eulogium,[1] who, in one section of his work, abridges the story direct from our author, notes it in two other places as occurring in the pontificate of Gregory V., and with a date A.D. 1005; so that possibly he had found

The legend of the dancers.

---

[1] Eulogium, i. 255, 379, 399.

another version of it in some other work. Higden took it direct from the Gesta.¹

The story, however, was evidently derived by William of Malmesbury from a written authority and not from the mere gossip of a German friend. It is possible that the two anecdotes contained in the next section, the story of the ugly priest who was made archbishop, and of the prophecy of the same on his deathbed, may have been derived from the same source.² It is, I think, impossible to fix them to any probable date or persons, although in their general tone they resemble the stories about the emperor Henry III. which follow later; and, indeed, the first of the two is referred to that sovereign by Ralph de Diceto, who places it under the year 1036.³ If we could think that Ralph derived his information from any other source than the Gesta Regum, this might be an indication of importance; but, although I was at one time inclined to think it possible, I am now convinced that mediately or immediately the dean of S. Paul's extracted the whole series from the work of William of Malmesbury. Neither of the prelates nominated by Henry III. to Cologne could by any possibility be described as an unknown rustic priest before his promotion. It is, however, possible that, under the "presbyter agrestis, " deformis sane et pene portentum naturæ,"⁴ may be discovered the canon of Goslar, "homo pusillus, vultu " despicabilis, genere obscurus," who was appointed by Henry IV. in the year 1076. This person, archbishop Hildulf, was assailed by the canons, "tanquam " aliquod monstrum antiquitatis," but, notwithstanding their opposition, was maintained by Henry until his death in 1079. The description of the person of the archbishop is, perhaps, insufficient ground for identifying him with the hero of Malmesbury's story, but, taken

The story of the ugly priest who was made archbishop.

The story may belong to the reign of Henry IV.

---

¹ Polychron., vii. 112, 113.
² Above, pp. 204–206.
³ R. de Diceto, Opp., i. 178.
⁴ Above, p. 203.

lxxviii   PREFACE.

Theory of a confusion of Henries. with what follows, it serves to strengthen the presumption that our author has confounded the traditions and characters of the two Henries in an unintelligent manner, and possibly combined with them legends of the earlier emperor of the same name, the Sainted Henry of Bavaria, in whose history he might have found some parallels for that of the Confessor, had he thought of looking for them.[1]

The marriage of Gunhilda. 15. The legends distinctly assigned by our author to Henry III.[2] follow on the story of his marriage with Gunhilda, the daughter of Canute and Emma, and the curious fable of her trial and vindication. Historically the facts are these: Gunhilda, who, as the daughter of Emma, could not have been born before the year 1018, was betrothed, perhaps as early as 1027, to Henry, son of Conrad the Salic, the match being probably a condition of the surrender of the territory beyond the Eydor, by Conrad to Canute. In the year 1035, the bride being seventeen, and her spouse, now king and heir of the empire, a year older, the solemnities of the marriage took place at Bamberg.[3] Gunhilda bore the young king a daughter, and died on the 17th of July 1038.[4] Her actual marriage falls thus within the reign of Harold Harefoot; but, as Hardicanute was at Bruges during these years, and certainly would be regarded as his sister's guardian, our author's assertion that he gave Gunhilda to Henry may pass as true.[5]

---

[1] See Lambert of Hersfeld, ad ann. 1076; Scriptores, Pistor., ed. Struve, i. 402, 403.

[2] In the following paragraphs I have used Steindorff's Excursus on "Heinrich III. in Sage und Legende," appended to his "Jahrbücher des Deutscher Reichs unter "Heinrich III.," Leipzig, 1874, with such other illustrations as I could find in other books. But I have no doubt that the subject is one capable of much development in the realms of comparative mythology and folk-lore.

[3] Ann. Hildesheim, ad ann. 1035; Steindorff, i. 33, 34. Steindorff suggests that Hardicanute was older than Gunhilda.

[4] Wippo, Vita Conradi, c. 37; Steindorff, i. 42, 575.

[5] Above, p. 230.

It is a strange thing that her pitiful little story, closing before she was twenty, should have become a text for a baseless legend; it must have been so perverted before our author wrote. His account, however, is brief enough. After telling of her beauty, her numerous suitors and the magnificent ceremonial of her marriage, the subject, still we are told, of popular songs, "in triviis cantitata;" he brings her to her husband; for a long time they are happy together; then she is accused of adultery. She is tried by combat; her champion is the little page whom she has brought from England, "the groom of the starling";[1] her adversary is represented by a giant. The English boy cuts the hamstring of the giant: Gunhilda triumphs, divorces the emperor, retires to a monastery, and "grows "old in placid ease." From Ralph de Diceto we learn that the page's name was Mimicon, and that the giant was called Rodingar;[2] both names, perhaps, belong to the original song abridged by our author To a later date no doubt belongs the invention of Gunhilda's retirement to Bruges, and the burial record there on the monument in the Church of S. Donatian, with the date, August 21, 1042.[3]

Legend of her trial and vindication.

---

[1] "Sturni sui alumpnum," p. 230. I have remarked in the note the peculiarity of this expression; but I am convinced that it has no other meaning than that given above. The word alumnus is used by our author actively in another place: Tarsus is described as "Sancti Pauli alumpnam," § 374. And the usage has some ancient authority; cf. Isidor Orig., i. 10: "qui alit et alitur, alumnus dici potest;" "cana veritas Atticæ philosophiæ alumna," M. T. Varron. Sat. Menipp. (ed. Riese, 1865), p. 135. Nonius, 86, 26: "Alumnos consuetudo quos alas vel educes "... . vel eos qui aluntdici vult," ibid. 242, 26,

[2] R. de Diceto, Opp., i. 174. Matthew Paris is sometimes cited as the first authority for Mimicon (Chron. Maj., i. 515), and Bromton (ap. Twysden, c.933) for Rodingar; but Ralph gives both names. They are, however, omitted in Twysden's edition, c. 468. It is perhaps worth noting that Mimican was a Norman surname; see Stapleton, Rot. Scacc. I. clxix., &c.

[3] This inscription, recording the fabulous calamity of Gunhilda, "post acceptam gravissimam a marito injuriam," is of course a late fabrication. It may be found in Ellis's Introduction to Domesday, ii. 137.

lxxx PREFACE.

Prevalence of such legends.

What is the origin of this strange perversion? The eleventh century was no stranger to legends turning on the ordeal as vindicating the purity of queens maligned. The great empress Cunigunda[1] herself, whose relations with Henry II. were analogous to those of Edward the Confessor and his wife Eadgitha, had not escaped without trial. Westminster was to the Confessor what Bamberg was to Henry II.; if there was no doubt of the chastity of queen Eadgith, the historians repeated the adventure of Cunegunda in reference to queen Emma.[2] The ordeal of the red-hot plough-shares was an element of myth common to England and Germany. It is possible that the idea of the story was in the air of the age, and, unluckily for the credit of the inventor, he appropriated his sentiment and zeal to a mistaken object. Whatever may have been the truth about Cunegunda, the legend about Gunhilda is an unidyllic fable.

Character of Henry III.;

16. The character of the great emperor, with which William follows up the legend of Gunhilda, is somewhat spoiled by the account which he gives of the Conquest of the Vindelici and Leuticii, the last pagan races of Europe, and the curious serjeanty by which he made

his treatment of subject Kings.

their kings do him honour. Edgar had been rowed by seven kings on the Dee, Henry made the four tributaries, whom he had subdued, carry the cauldron in which his meat was boiled, slung on poles by four rings, upon their royal shoulders. The German historians decline to own the story.[3]

---

[1] Vita S. Henrici, Canisius, Lectiones, tom. iii. p. 2, p. 29; Vita Kunegundæ; Ludewig, Scr. Bamberg. i. 346. Steindorff gives other authorities, pp. 515 sq., to Pertz, Scr., iv. 789, 819, and xvi. 65.

[2] This story appears in its full growth in Rudborne's Historia Major Wintoniensis, Anglia Sacra, i. 235; in R. Cirencester, Sp. Hist. ii. 254; in Knighton, c. 2329; and in Bromton (Twysden), c. 941. But these writers are much too late to prove even the existence of such a tradition. It appears, however, in the C. C. C. MS. 339, which Sir Thomas Hardy assigns to the thirteenth century: Cat. Mat., ii. 201; Ann. Winton, ed. Luard, p. 21. See Freeman, Norman Conquest, ii. 569.

[3] Above, pp. 230, 231: "auf " grund einer schlechten, mit fa" beln durchsetzen, quelle," Steindorff, i. 286.

PREFACE.   lxxxi

17. The character of Henry stood sufficiently high **The lady and her lover in the snow.** without these embellishments; he was a king who could indulge in a jest. Unluckily, the illustration given is a very old story; it is the reproduction of the adventure in the snow, of the daughter of Charles the Great and her clerical lover.[1] Here she becomes the emperor's sister, the clerk becomes a bishop, the lady an abbess. As the whole anecdote would seem to be a transfer from the Frankish period, there is no need to localise either abbey or see.

18. The following story, of the unchaste deacon, promoted to a bishopric because he had declined to sing the **The unchaste deacon.** Gospel after spending the night with his paramour, is by no means appropriate to the character of either Henry III. or Henry IV. Matthew Paris repeats it as belonging to the emperor Henry V.,[2] naming the deacon Arnulf, and his bishopric Ravenna. But no Arnulf **Possibility of identification.** ruled Ravenna in the reign of Henry V.; and the story so far falls back into the reign of Henry II., when Arnold presided from 1014 to 1019;[3] but this Arnulf or

---

[1] I do not know how old the story, as belonging to Charles and Einhard, may be, but it must be older than William of Malmesbury. It occurs in the Annals of Lauresham, ed. Freher, vol. i. pp. 102, 103; Pertz, Scriptt., xxi. 357, 358. As belonging to Henry III., it occurs in John de Beka's Chronicles of Utrecht, where it is said to have taken place during an expedition against the Slaves. If John's account is more than a paraphrase of William of Malmesbury's, he must have had fuller information. But the story is easy of adaptation and may be true of neither emperor. Cf. Steindorff, Henry III., p. 517, who thinks it not impossible that the Lorsch annalist took it from William of Malmesbury; and it may have been quite arbitrarily connected with the marriage of Bertha, Charles's daughter, and Angilbert, or with that of Einhard and Imma. See also Wattenbach, Geschichtsquelle, i. 133–135; ii. 283, 284. The Magnum Chronicum Belgicum (Pistorius, ed. Struve, iii. 115) has the story assigned to Henry III., but with the note of the editor, " Falsa illa in hunc locum, " et vera de Carolo Magno, nisi " fortassis repetita." It should be observed that all these compilations are later in date than our author. See further Abel, Gesch. d. Deutsch. Volk. ix. Jahrh., i. 56.

[2] M. Paris, Hist. Angl., ed. Madden, i. 236, 237.

[3] Hieron. Rub. Hist. Ravenn. (ed. Venice, 1590), pp. 274, 275, 894; cf. Ann. Quedlinburg, ad ann. 1014.

Arnold was the emperor's half-brother,[1] and the pious Henry is scarcely likely to have promoted him solely on such grounds as the story indicates.

The devil in church.

19. The next anecdote has some indications of time and place. As our author tells it, the event happened at Mainz at Whitsuntide.[2] There was a quarrel about precedence between the servants of the archbishop and those of the abbot of Fulda, and blood was shed. As the choir sang the sequence, "Thou hast made this a " day of glory," a voice in the air was heard, "I have " made it a day of warfare"; the emperor addressed the evil spirit to whom the voice was attributed, "We will " make it a day of grace." Whatever is the truth about the voice and answer, it is certain that in a court held

The story belongs to Henry IV.

at Goslar in 1063 [3] under Henry IV., there was such a quarrel between the servants of the bishop of Hildesheim and the abbot of Fulda. The story then belongs to Henry IV., and not to Henry III. In relation to this it is as well to note that in the MSS. of the sections printed by Commelin, and described in the preface to our

Variation of MSS.

first volume, the monastery of Fulda is described as situated, not "in Saxonia," but "in Bochovia," the Bochonia or Buochunna of Spruner; and its fame as due to S. Boniface, not, as our author has it, to S. Gall.[4] This may be an indication of a collation of Malmesbury's story with some other authority, or it may be a mere assertion of the transcriber's geographical knowledge. Why our author should so especially connect Fulda with S. Gall is not clear. Walafrid Strabo, the biographer of the saint,

---

[1] Richter, Zeittafeln, p. 48; Steindorff, i. 536.

[2] Above, p. 233.

[3] Lambert. Hersfeld, Scriptt. Pistor., ed. Struve, i. 327, 328; Pertz., Scriptt., v. 163; Steindorff, i. 518.

[4] Commelin, Scriptores, p. 310: " Fuldense coenobium est in Bocho- " via, Sancti Bonifacii archiepi- " scopi et martyris corpore insigni- " tum." This is almost the only various reading worth notice in the whole mass of the sections. The site of Fulda is "in loco qui voca- " tur Boconia," epp. Bonif. 82. Jaffé, Mon. Mogunt., p. 298; "ad " introitum silvæ Bochoniæ," ib. 480.

was a pupil at Fulda, but it seems probable that S. Boniface rather than S. Gall should have been in the writer's mind.

20. The next story, beginning with the promise of a bishopric, said to have been made by Henry during his father's reign, in return for a silver squirt, is extremely unlikely to belong to Henry III.[1] His son Henry IV. might have been guilty of such levity, but the incidental mention of S. Laurence as an agent in the imperial vision, has been thought to connect the tradition, if such it be, with the church of Merseburg, which was dedicated to S. Laurence and restored by Henry II. *The story of the sold bishopric.*

Our author takes leave of Henry III. with a reference to other legends of which he was the hero, particularly that of the hind which carried him over an impassable river, when flying from his enemies; and finally gives a poetical epitaph which we must suppose to have been placed on his tomb at Speyer. Whether it ever was there, is uncertain; there is no trace of any such memorial now. Our author is mistaken in making pope Leo IX. bishop of Speyer before he became pope. *Other legends concerning Henry III.*

21. After following up the national history until he reaches the exile of Tostig, our author breaks off with a new series of stories, this time starting with the much-controverted history of pope Gregory VI.[3] It is impossible to go into any detailed criticism on this peculiar episode, on which the minds of modern writers are as much in conflict as those of contemporaries. Gregory VI. was, before his purchase of the pontificate, known as an austere and honest reformer; justifying the means by the end, he forced himself into the chair of S. Peter by simony, and from the 1st of May 1045 to the 20th of *The legend about pope Gregory VI.*

---

[1] Steindorff, Henry III., i. 536.
[2] Steindorff, ii. 357: "in dem "schwungvollen, aber historisch "wenig ausgiebigen epitaphium."
Another epitaph, beginning "con-"cidit Henricus lux orbis," is in the Neues Archiv, i. 176.
[3] Above, p. 246.

December 1046 he appears to have been the most respectable of the three rival popes.[1] According to Bonitho, he was seduced by the devil;[2] according to Ralph Glaber, he was a man of conspicuous sanctity.[3] Anyhow he was the pope of a faction; his reign was one series of strifes and struggles; to make peace the emperor was brought down into Italy, and at the synod of Sutri, Gregory was deposed. He was taken away by Henry into Germany, and died on the banks of the Rhine.[4] It was to be expected that there would be at least two readings of such a career; one by those who would vindicate the imperial interference, another by those who, in their antipathy to the German reform, would justify the most factious and irreligious policy at Rome. Between such views we are not now to arbitrate. William of Malmesbury, however, leant an ear to some advocate of Gregory who knew more of the theory of advocacy than of the facts of the history. The result is a presentment of character and events which is, to say the least, apocryphal, and ends with a complete displacement of facts and dates. Whatever the true story may have been, whether the pope was forcibly deposed, resigned in order to avoid deposition, or in a solemn way as judge of the world passed sentence on himself as unworthy, it is certain that he ceased to reign and died far from Rome. Our author's story of his being warned that he should not be buried in S. Peter's, of his death-bed defence, and demand of a miraculous sign in vindication; the granting of the prayer and the portent of the doors of S. Peter's opening of their own accord to admit his coffin—all falls to the ground, or

Difficulties about our author's representation of the events.

---

[1] Reg. Pontiff., Wattenbach pp., 524, 525.

[2] Bonitho, ed. Jaffé, Mon. Gregoriana, p. 626.

[3] Rad. Glaber, v. 5; cf. Robertson, Church History (590-1122), p. 416.

[4] Bonitho, ed. Jaffé, p. 630: he seems, however, to have survived his successor pope Clement II. Gesta Epp. Leod. c. 62; Martene and Durand, Ampliss. Coll., iv. 902.

takes rank as a mere academic speculation on what might have been.[1]

22. The story of the miracle, however, suggested to our author a local prodigy of which he had heard from an eye-witness, and by a somewhat ludicrous transition he passes from the great crisis of the eleventh-century reformation to the episode of the witch of Berkeley. She, like Gregory VI., was anxious about the disposal of her remains; unlike the pope, she was drawn from her coffin, bound as it was with leather, lead, and iron, and carried off on a proud black horse, to which she was fixed with iron hooks. The story may have been indigenous, for Berkeley is situate in the county next to our author's native Somerset, and he at all events is the primary authority for it; but he cites the Dialogue of S. Gregory and the strange tradition of the fate of Charles Martel in support of its probability.[2] The latter story seems to have taken a strong hold on his imagination; he had mentioned it already in connexion with the history of Saint Boniface; now he bolsters it up with a reference to the evidence of S. Eucherius of Orleans, who, however, died before the hero whose doom he was supposed to have attested.[3] *The witch of Berkeley.*

23. Once, however, having got into the realm of wonder, our author finds it hard to leave it. The story of the witch of Berkeley leads on to that of the ring and the statue, which must either at the time or a little later have been known as the story of Lucian and *The story of the ring and statue.*

---

[1] If the contention of Gfrörer (Robertson, ut s., p. 414 note), that Gregory VI. was supported by a reforming party directed from Cluny, we may infer that our author derived his information on the period from Cluny, whence certainly some of his other stories came. Steindorff, however, inclines to the belief that, somehow or other, some part of the history of Gregory VII. has got mixed with that of Gregory VI. This is very unlikely. On the abdication of Gregory VI., see Jaffé, Mon. Greg., pp. 594 sq.

[2] Above, p. 253.

[3] Above, p. 256, note 1, and of Mabillon, AA. SS. O. S. B., Sæc. iii., pt. 1, p. 554.

lxxxvi   PREFACE.

Eugenia. For this our author is the earliest extant authority, and from him it has filtered down to us, by divers media, in Burton's Anatomy of Melancholy, and last in Mr. Morris's poem.[1] Unfortunately we find no indication of the source from which the most picturesque of his stories is derived, or it would have been a most pleasing task to seek for more. At Rome, however, anything might be expected and everything would be found: for had not the body of Pallas, the son of Evander, been found there, in such preservation too that the wound which Turnus had inflicted was still to be traced in the gigantic form, a wound four feet and a half in breadth;[2] the epitaph, too, in Latin, for which even Turnus might have blushed. Our author doubts whether it could have been contemporary, although the nymph Carmentis, the mother of Evander, invented Latin letters; perhaps it was the work of Ennius. But as the never-dying lamp in the tomb was extinguished, when the air was admitted, so the gigantic corpse which was as high as the city wall against which it was made to lean, recognised the common law of mortality and disappeared under atmospheric influences.[3]

The discovery of the body of Pallas.

24. Our credulity thus tasked may well accept the portentous story of the woman with two bodies, the predecessor of the Siamese twins of later times; a story which, however, has the merit of a suggestive capacity for interpretation, and so brings us round into genuine history. The "mulier biformis" perhaps meant England and Normandy, the union of which our author very skilfully parallels with the freak of nature which he records. He is coming to the history of the Norman

The woman with two bodies.

---

[1] See above, vol. i., pref. pp. li, lxxv, xciii.
[2] Above, p. 258.
[3] This story of the discovery of the body of Pallas was embodied among the Gesta Romanorum, No. 158; ed. Osterley, p. 538. Warton, Hist. of English Poetry, iii. p. lxvi.

Conquest. But again he draws back as if he disliked to face the subject; and prefers to lead up to the history of the Confessor by a *resumé* of Anglo-Saxon hagiography of which the Saintly King was the crown and consummation.[1]

I will postpone comment on these details and complete our survey of the miraculous stories of less edifying origin which are interspersed in the later books, in special connexion with the foreign history of the time.

25. The story of the two clerks of Nantes, § 237, is introduced for the curious reason that the author wished to make amends for his apparent neglect to say anything interesting about Brittany. It has nothing whatever to do with the history of the period, and is a mere well-told ghost-story, such as might be derived from a repertory of local miracles. We may suppose that it was found in some such record as may have existed at Rennes, where the church of S. Melanius was celebrated for such events. There is among the Bollandist Acta a letter from archbishop Gervase of Rheims, on the miracles of S. Melanius, addressed to abbot Evelinus, before year 1072, but it contains no reference to this story.[2] It was in the church of the same saint that the clerk to whom the vision of his deceased friend was vouchsafed proved his repentance by works of charity and devotion. Our author leaves the subject as rapidly as he has entered upon it, with the complacent intimation that he is not bored with the attempt to benefit his readers.

The two clerks of Nantes.

26. The next series starts from a higher and nobler point, the history of Hildebrand.[3] It contains three characteristic stories and one chapter of historical detail, all derived from the conversation of a friend, who, in

The history of Hildebrand.

---

[1] See page 295.
[2] AA. SS. Boll. January, vol. i. p. 333.
[3] Page 322.

his time, had heard them from abbot Hugh of Cluny.[1] Abbot Hugh died in 1109, and unfortunately our author forgets to tell us who the common acquaintance was. The anecdotes themselves are of little interest.

27. The history of Berengarius, § 284,[2] suggests a more attractive digression, to which the writer is drawn by his theological as well as by his historical instincts. After illustrating the career of the heresiarch, as he calls him, by a long quotation from Hildebert of le Mans, and a prophecy by Fulbert of Chartres,[3] he gives his opinion on the doctrinal question, and on this cites a story told by Paschasius Radbert of a miraculous vision seen by the Englishman Plegild in Alemannia,[4]

The history of Berengarius.

---

[1] The life of Hugh of Cluny was written by Hildebert of le Mans and Tours (AA. SS. Boll. April, iii. pp. 634–648), with whose works, so far as they were published in his time, our author was well acquainted. Here, however, he distinctly tells us that the stories were orally conveyed to him. A story about the vision of the Saviour is told by Hildebert (ap. Surium, iv. 278) of the same class, but with altogether different details from that in § 264. These stories, and much else connected with them, are abridged by the author of the Eulogium, i. 383. The anecdote about the simoniacal archbishop who could not invoke the Holy Ghost, is as old as Peter Damiani, who tells it "in opusc. 19, tom. iii. c. 6;" Concilia, Labbe and Cossart, vol. ix. col. 1080.

[2] See pages 338–340.

[3] Page 341. William of Malmesbury is cited as primary authority for the particulars about Fulbert, given here and above, p. 226. See literary notices in the edition of his work in Migne's Patrologia, vol. cxli, cc. 163 sq.

[4] Page 341: "Sicut illud in ges- tis Anglorum, quod quidam pres- byter fuerit religiosus valde, Plecgils nomine, frequenter Mis- sarum solemnia celebrans ad Corpus Sancti Niniæ episcopi et confessoris," &c. Pasch. Radb., de Corpore et Sanguine Domini, Mart. and Dur., Ampl. Coll., ix. 436, Alemannia is not mentioned by Paschasius as the locality of the vision, and although our author certainly knew the works of Pas- chasius, he may be quoting here at second hand, especially as he gives Berengarius's comment on the story. Paschasius lived about the year 840; the Gesta Anglorum must have been either Bede or some early life of some English saint; the story is not in Bede, or, so far as I can find, in any work of Al- cuin. Mabillon, in his disquisition on the Confessio fidei ascribed to Al- cuin, mentions the story of Plegils, which he says Paschasius must have taken out of some ancient author (ed. Migne, ii. 1014), as a proof that such miraculous events are on record before the age of Alcuin, but he does not guide us any further in the search.

PREFACE. lxxxix

How Paschasius got hold of the story, or what were the Gesta Anglorum to which he refers as his authority, is not, so far as I am aware, now known. Nor does it concern us here to conjecture, as the question does not arise from the text of our author.

28. But the merest contact with the miraculous seems to have the effect of starting him off at a tangent; the miraculous vision of the Eucharist may have suggested some thought of the Sangreal; anyhow, he turns off to tell of the discovery of the tomb of Sir Gawain, and has a little sneer at the fables about king Arthur.[1] Then, after a lamentation over the miseries of the empire under Henry IV. and Henry V., he finds an opening for the last group of stories; one of the enemies of the emperor was torn to pieces by mice;[2] a still more distressing tradition follows of the fate of those who are bitten by leopards, attested by an eye-witness who had brought the report from Asia.[3] *The discovery of the tomb of Sir Gawain.*

29. The same reign was made illustrious by the existence of the historian and annalist Marianus Scotus, at Fulda,[4] and the mention of Fulda recalls one more story, told by prior Walcher of Malvern, of the way in which the funeral expenses of the monks were met in the time of the plague. The story is edifying enough, but the interest turns chiefly on the name of the narrator who may not improbably have been our author's informant for all his stories about Fulda. Walcher, like so many other ecclesiastics promoted in England during the period, was a Lorrainer and a man of mark. His epitaph is preserved as follows:[5] *Marianus Scotus. Prior Walcher of Malvern.*

---

[1] Page 342. Walwyn's castle, or, in Welsh, Castell Gwalchmai, a strong earthwork encampment, one of a chain running across the promontory of Roos from Little Haven to Sandyhaven, between Walton and Robeston; Fenton's Pembrokeshire, p. 160.

[2] Page 344.

[3] Pages 344, 345.

[4] Page 345.

[5] Antiquitates M. M. Maiverne; Errata, before page 1. The inscription was discovered in November 1719, according to Hearne, Antiquities of Glastonbury, pref., p. xlvi. The death of prior Walcher is dated 1135.

xc   PREFACE.

" Philosophus dignus, bonus astrologus, Lotharingus,
". Vir pius ac humilis monachus, prior hujus ovilis,
" Hic jacet in cista, geometricus ac abacista,
" Doctor Walcherus ; flet plebs dolet undique clerus ;
" Huic lux prima mori dedit Octobris seniori ;
" Vivat ut in cælis, exoret quisque fidelis."

It is so seldom that our author introduces us personally to any of his friends, that we are tempted to make the most of one whom he does mention especially with the high encomium, " cujus verbis qui non " credit injuriam religioni facit." Yet even in this compliment there is a suggestion of a doubt that occasionally Walcher may have told travellers' tales. If so, may he not have been the authority for the adventures of Gerbert in pursuit of mathematical knowledge? Himself an abacist, and an ally doubtless of the Lotharingian bishop of Hereford [1] who abridged Marianus's work on the cycle, he would have a special interest in the great scholar who wrested the knowledge of the abacus from the Saracens, and laid down the rules for the perspiring abacists to follow. But the indications are too slight to furnish a trustworthy theory. Walcher was, however, an Arabic scholar, and his translation of Peter the Hebrew "de dracone" is preserved among the Hatton MSS. in the Bodleian.[2]

His possible interest in Gerbert.

Comment on the purpose of the stories introduced by our author.

30. Here, I think, our author ceases to attempt the entertainment of his readers with stories not directly connected with the serious history that he is trying to make acceptable. The attempt was not thrown away; trifling as many of them are, they are suggestive, as we have seen, of investigations as to matters of far more importance than themselves, the existence

---

[1] W.Malmesb., Gesta Pontificum ed. Hamilton, pp. 300, 301.

[2] " Sententia Petri Ebrei cognomento Amphus de dracone, quam dominus Walcerus prior Malvernensis ecclesiæ in Latinam transtulit linguam." MS. Hatton, No. 112, folio 96 ; Bernard's Catalogue, p. 186. Tanner, Bibliotheca, p. 745.

of traditions, superstitions, and forms of thinking that throw some light on the mental and moral history as well as the literary life of the times in which they were told. They answered their purpose at the time, and helped to make William of Malmesbury a popular historian. It would be most ungrateful to be hypercritical about them. But although, as direct digressions, they cease in the course of the third book of the Gesta, somewhat of the spirit that induced the author to insert them is traceable further on; the commentaries on the Crusades, and on the adventures of the Crusaders in the East, abound with glimpses of the marvellous not less illustrative in themselves of the mind of the writer and his expected readers. Into these, however, it will hardly be necessary to go with any detail for the purpose of literary inquiry; most of them bear distinct marks of the sources from which they were derived.

31. Returning now to the string of English History, we find ourselves on the eve of the Conquest. We have reached the accession of the Confessor; the writer seems conscious that he has to make a plunge into troubled waters. He has hung back with the long stories of Gerbert and the German kings. But he hangs back still. He must approach the history of the Royal Saint through an avenue of other royal saints, his predecessors; and with this view carries us through a rapid abridgment of the lives of the native kings and queens, who had not lacked biographers to celebrate them.[1] It might be pardonable for Lanfranc or Anselm to question the merits of heroes who bore such uncouth names as the English saints had made famous at home. William of Malmesbury, as patriot and antiquary, was free from such fanciful prejudice; he would have been a most unworthy pretender to the succession of Bede if he had not been careful to commemorate the long line

The English History in the second book of the Gesta, still delayed.

History of the royal saints of England.

---

[1] Sections 207–219.

xcii   PREFACE.

of holy men and holy women to whom England owed so much. So he does, in a somewhat desultory and discursive way, reproduce the series of portraits that he found sketched in the works of Osbern and Goscelin. These sketches fill the sections 208-219, after which the narrative takes up the miraculous history of king Edward.

The saints celebrated in these sections are S. Oswald of Northumbria, the royal martyrs of Kent, Ethelbert of East Anglia, Kenelm of Mercia, Wistan, also of Mercia, and Edmund of East Anglia; the royal ladies follow: Etheldreda, Ethelburga, Sexburga, Ercongota, Ermenhilda, Werburga, Mildred, Milburga, Eadburga, and Eadgitha. A very few words, taken in connexion with what has been already said on their secular history, will complete our commentary on these great names and their literature.

Difficulties of the literary history of Anglo-Saxon hagiology.

The literary history of Anglo-Saxon hagiology is as yet unwritten, and it may be questioned whether it ever will be. There are peculiar difficulties about it, arising in some measure from the destruction of ancient manuscripts at the Reformation, but chiefly from the fact that the compilers of martyrologies and hagiologies, in most cases used the labours of their predecessors without acknowledgment. We know the names of certain biographers of the saints, and we know the biographies which are extant either entire or abridged, and edited in Capgrave's Vitæ Sanctorum, or in fragments such as are to be found in Leland's Collectanea. But we are often at a loss to connect the biography, as it now appears, with the reputed or possible author. Goscelin, for instance, wrote a life, say of S. Milburga: a life of S. Milburga appears among the collections of John of Tynemouth and Capgrave; the basis of it may be Goscelin's, or it may be the work of a competitor; and, without any ancient and authenticated copy, it is absolutely impossible to say what it may have lost or gained in the mill of transmission. The labour of collecting and collating the numerous notices and fragments of these lives, would no doubt be far beyond the value of the results; but greater labour has often been spent on less interesting and less worthy material; and a collection of " Acta Genuina " of the Anglo-Saxon saints would have a literary, if not an historical, value. In default of anything like an adequate work of reference on this subject, it is impossible with any certainty to trace the particular paragraphs or expressions used by William of Malmesbury in this connexion, to authorities which he may conceivably have laid under contribution.[1] A coincidence of expression may be used with as much probability to show that the extant biographies were indebted to him, as that he was indebted to them. Indeed, his common practice of paraphrasing, rather than of transcribing, the words of the books which we know him to have used, might be thought to indicate that he in such cases was the lender rather than the borrower. Under such circumstances criticism must be very tentative.

32. About S. Oswald of Northumbria, however, there is not much room for question. In the first book of the Gesta,[2] as well as in the second, it is obvious that the authority is Bede: and Bede used not uncritically; William of Malmesbury was aware that, in certain copies of the Ecclesiastical History, a portion of the miraculous acts of Oswald was contained: " secundum quædam exem-" plaria."[3] The limitation shows that he knew of a copy or copies which omitted it. The Cotton MS., Tiberius C. 2, omits the chapter, the fourteenth of the fourth book.[4] And it is, of course, absent from the transcripts of that ancient copy, and from the Anglo-Saxon translation of

S. Oswald of Northumbria.

---

[1] See, in particular, what is said about Osbert of Clare, pp. cii, ciii.
[2] Above, pp. 50 sq.
[3] Above, p. 260.
[4] Hardy, Cat. Mat., i. 434, where the MS. Hatton 43, is mentioned as omitting the chapter. See also Mon. Hist. Brit., i. 924.

the book. At Glastonbury, if not at Malmesbury itself, our author might have found such a copy. The remark furnishes an interesting illustration of his care in working. The contents of the omitted section are of no special importance, and its omission from the ancient text was as likely as not accidental.

The royal martyrs of Kent.

33. The history of Ethelred and Ethelbert, the murdered sons of Ercombert, was probably taken direct from Goscelin's life of S. Mildred. How old the story is it is hard to say: it seems to have found its way into one copy of the Chronicle during the twelfth century;[1] but if we may credit the history of Ramsey, which places the translation of the martyrs, mentioned by our author, in the days of the ealdorman Ethelwin, it must have been known as early as the days of archbishop Oswald; and it is recorded in the "Narratio de Sanctis," which dates from the beginning of the eleventh century.[2] It is not very clear, from this record, that Ethelwin knew whom he was translating from Wakering to Ramsey; but the identification may have followed the revival of a local tradition, which again may have been incorporated into the Kentish hagiology, and so found a place in the Anglo-Saxon life of S. Mildred, from which Goscelin may have taken the materials for his own work.[3]

S. Ethelbert of East Anglia.

34. The reference made by our author to S. Ethelbert of East Anglia goes scarcely beyond his own comment on the subject in the first book. The extant remains of more detailed biography, whether written by Osbert

---

[1] Chron. Sax., M. H. B. i., 340; ad ann. 640. Simeon Dun., M. H. B., i. 645, and note; Hardy, Cat. Mat., i. 376.

[2] Ed. Liebermann, page 4. Mr. Cockayne printed an Anglo-Saxon account of the martyrdom from MS. Caligula A. 14; in the Saxon Leechdoms, iii. 422-428. Sir T. D. Hardy regarded this as the authority for Goscelin's account; Cat. Mat. I. 381, 382, and earlier than the Narratio.

[3] Chron. Abb. Ramesiæ, ed. Macray, pp. 55, 191. The martyrs are merely described as "duo gemelli " fratres," and " ex ingenuo anti- " quorum regum stemmate oriundi, " et post obitum patris, . . . edaci " cujusdam nebulonis livore inno- " center jugulati."

of Clare¹ or some S. Alban's writer, would seem to be later than the date of William of Malmesbury. The recognition, however, of Ethelbert's sanctity is much earlier, and he must have been regarded as the patron of Hereford long before the eleventh century. That there was some doubt as to how he acquired the position, may be inferred from our author's words in the Gesta Pontificum, " Could the blessed Dunstan, full as he " was of the knowledge of letters and of the grace of " God, have suffered Kenelm, Ethelbert, or Wistan to be " honoured as martyrs, unless it was quite clear to him " that he was welcome among the citizens of heaven ? " ² There was very little historical material forthcoming about him, but it was not necessary, as was the case with the royal martyrs of Kent, to investigate the question of his identity.

35. The collocation of the three names Ethelbert, Kenelm, and Wistan in this place is not fortuitous. I should remark, however, that I have substituted the last name for that of Wlstan, which is found in the printed copies of the Gesta Pontificum; for the saint of that name was not obscure, was not a martyr, and lived long after S. Dunstan. In the place we are now examining the three occur in succession : from Ethelbert our author goes on to Kenelm.³ Kenelm was the patron saint of Winchelcomb, and his biography may have formed a part of the Chartulary from which our author extracted his notice of the dedication of the abbey in the first book of the Gesta.⁴ Whether it was the work of Goscelin may be questioned; it has scarcely any claim to historical truth, and its quaintness seems to border on wantonness of invention scarcely serious enough for Goscelin. Our author's notes agree with the fragments

_{The legend of S. Wistan, and S. Kenelm.}

_{Kenelm at Winchcombe.}

---

¹ Hardy, Cat. Mat., i. 494.
² G. P., ed. Hamilton, p. 305. Cf. Narratio, etc., ed. Liebermann, p. 12.

³ Page 262.
⁴ Above, p. 95 ; Mon. Angl., ii. 300, 301.

of the biography given by Leland ;[1] and in substance, if not in language, with the Vita printed by the Bollandists from the MS. of the Canonesses Regular of Rubea Vallis, near Brussels.[2]

The legend of S. Wistan.

36. The fame of S. Wistan was much less widespread than that of Kenelm; and Evesham, which claimed to possess his relics, had greater names to show. His life, however, had been written,[3] and some abstract of it appears in the Chronicle of Florence of Worcester,[4] who was working up his Chronicle a few years before our author. The best extant life is that written by prior Thomas of Marlborough, and printed by Mr. Macray in an appendix to his edition of the Chronicle of the abbey of Evesham.[5] Thomas was a contemporary of archbishop Baldwin of Canterbury, and must have written long after Florence, with whom he coincides in a few verbal

Biographies of him.

expressions.[6] His work, however, seems to have been based on one by prior Dominick, who was living in the year 1125,[7] and from whose book, or from personal acquaintance with him, both these earlier writers may have derived their knowledge of the saint. If it be ascertained that Canute translated Wistan from Repton to Evesham, the cultus was much more ancient. But the reputed translations from Repton, as for instance that of S. Werburg to Chester, are not well authenticated.[8]

---

[1] Leland, Collectanea, i. 391 (314).
[2] AA. SS. Boll. July, tom. iv. p. 300. Rubea Vallis is Raucloistre in the diocese of Mechlin.
[3] Hardy, Cat. Mat., i. 472, 473.
[4] Fl. Wig., ad ann. 850; ed. Thorpe, p. 72.
[5] Chron. Evesham, pp. 325–337.
[6] In particular the column of light that guided the discoverers to the body of Wistan is called by Florence, and in Thomas's life, "columna " lucis usque ad cœlum porrecta ;" our author calls it " cœlo demissa " columpna lucifera," p. 263 ; but, in point of fact, prior Thomas's life quotes Florence in the idea that he is quoting Bede: Chron., App., p. 333.
[7] See Macray's preface, p. xi.; and the Chronicle itself, p. 27.
[8] See page 264; and Chron. Evesham, pp. 326–332. The translation of S. Werburg to Chester was from Hanbury, five miles off Repton, and is assigned to a much earlier date, the days of king Burhred. See Higden, Polychr., vi. 126, 176, 366 ; and Cf. Liebermann, Die Heiligen Englands, pp. 10, 12.

The more direct interest of the life of Wistan, if it be at all authentic, would consist in its addition of two generations to the obscure genealogy of the Royal House of Mercia.[1]

37. The chapter on S. Edmund of East Anglia is mainly derived from Abbo of Fleury,[2] whose authority approaches sufficiently near the time of his hero, to make itself worth consideration as matter of tradition. It is unnecessary to pursue the search further. This completes our author's tale of Ancient Saints among the kings of the Anglo-Saxons. He goes next to the Royal Ladies, of whom our early Christianity furnished so many. *S. Edmund of East Anglia.*

38. The first group mentioned is that of the three daughters of Anna, king of the East Angles:[3] nothing is here added to the notices of Bede respecting them. For the history of Ercongota the reader is simply referred to the Historia Ecclesiastica. The observations on Eormenhild[4] and Werburga do not go beyond the particulars given in the ancient genealogies appended to Florence of Worcester, further than to enlarge slightly on the miracles by which the latter saint was rendering her shrine at Chester already famous, in the church which earl Hugh had founded within the memory of living men.[5] *The saintly daughters of king Anna.*

The second cluster, including the two daughters of Merewald and Eormenberga, the famous Mildred and

---

[1] This is elaborated in the ancient genealogies appended to Florence of Worcester, M. H. B., p. 638, and may be more historical than would be inferred from the general obscurity of contemporary details.

[2] Page 264; and see Memorials of Saint Dunstan, pp. xxvii, xxviii, 378–380.

[3] Page 266. Cf. Narratio, &c., p. 6.

[4] Leland has extracts from a life of Eormenhild which he supposes to be by Goscelin: Coll., ii. 155; also of Sexburga, ib. p. 152.

[5] Above, page 267. Leland quotes also a life of S. Werburga, which he conjecturally assigns to Goscelin, Coll., ii. 154. This life is printed from a MS. of Camden, in the Bollandist Acts, February, tom. i., pp. 384 sq.; and in Migne's Patrologia, vol. 155, cc. 93 sq.

the scarcely less famous Milburga, were not, it would seem, known to Bede. They appear, however, in the genealogies,[1] and in the Anglo-Saxon "Narratio de Sanctis," where the brief enumeration of the burial-places of the saints is about a century older than the work of Goscelin.[2] It was certainly to the last-named writer that these ladies owed their restored and current celebrity.[3] S. Mildred had long flourished in Thanet; S. Milburga had, under the influence of a Cluniac colony, recently recovered her fame at Wenlock. Of the third sister, Milgitha, our author is silent;[4] it would seem, from another place where he mentions the saintly family, that he did not know her name correctly;[5] at p. 78, he describes the three as Milburga, Mildritha, and a second Mildritha. Savile has a various reading: Milgitha for this last, but I have not seen any manuscript in which the form occurs, and he probably made the correction from the genealogies which our author was using in that place.

S. Eadburga, daughter of Edward.

The next step takes him on more familiar ground and period: Eadburga, the daughter of Edward the Elder.[6] Her miracles were wrought at Winchester and Pershore.[7] Her life was written by Osbert of Clare, and, in the fragments of it which Leland has preserved, there are expressions used in common by him and our author.[8] They were so nearly contemporaries that either might have borrowed of the other; it is, perhaps, more likely that both used a more ancient source of

---

[1] Flor. Wig., App , M. H. B., 6.
[2] Ed. Liebermann, Hanover, 1889. Hickes, Dissertatio Epistolaris, p. 120.
[3] Mon. Angl., v. 75; Leland, Collectanea, ii. 156 (iii. 169). Leland supposes the life of S. Milburga to be the work of Goscelin.
[4] Mabillon, AA. SS. O. S. B., Sæc. iii., pt. 1, pp. 420, 421.
[5] Scriptores, fo. 14 v°.

[6] Mabillon, AA. SS. O. S. B., Sæc. v., pp. 626, 697.
[7] Hickes Diss. Epist., p. 120.
[8] Leland. Coll., i. 337 (i. 277):
" Edwardus rex obtulit Eadburgæ
" cum trima esset hinc ornamenta
" regalia hinc ecclesiastica; sed
" puella data electione manum ec-
" clesiasticis apposuit." Cf. above, p. 268.

information, of which we have no other trace. The story of the child of three years old foreshowing her monastic destination by preferring the chalice and Gospels to the necklaces and bracelets, is simply told by our author in both his historical works, and in nearly the same words.

The last of the list is S. Eadgitha, great niece of S. Eadburga and aunt of the Confessor, the nun of Wilton. Her life had been written by Goscelin and dedicated to Lanfranc.[1] Both the stories told by William are found in Goscelin, but our author seems to have improved upon the language of his precursor. It seems not impossible that Goscelin may have written a life of S. Eadburga also.[2] S. Eadgith, daughter of Edgar.

It is curious how little is really known of these holy women, for such they must have been to have left their names so long, as the usual Christian names of their countrywomen. Edith and Mildred are common enough in the present day, and that, probably, without much break. Etheldreda is a revival. Eadburga, under the forms of Edbora and Edborough, lingered, with Frisworth and Syth, long after the Reformation, and long after the more ancient masculine names excepting Edward,—for Alfred is in that form a revival—had disappeared before the names of the Apostles and others taken out of Holy Scripture.

As our author himself refers to Goscelin, we cannot be very far wrong in supposing that he may have seen other of his works, besides that on the Translation of S. Augustine, which he distinctly quotes.[3] He was, he tells us, a monk of St. Bertin, a link in that long chain Goscelin the biographer of the Anglo-Saxon saints.

---

[1] Acta Sanctor., O. S. B., Sæc. v., pp. 622 sq. See, however, Leland, Coll., ii. 156, for some verses on Edward the Martyr which he found in Goscelin's life, which are not in Mabillon, nor in the reprint in Migne's Patrologia, vol. 155, cc. 109 sq.

[2] Memorials of Saint Dunstan, pp. 316, 317.

[3] Above, p. 389. Cf. Tanner, Bibliotheca, pp. 334, 335; Wharton, Anglia Sacra, vol. ii., pref., p. vi.

which connected a certain phase of English monachism with the monasteries of Flanders. As a biographer he came next to Bede, as a musician next to Osbern, the precentor of Canterbury, who likewise had written lives of saints and bishops, to which William of Malmesbury was indebted. He had, we are told, explored and done honour to many monasteries, and had written or revised innumerable lives of the saints. It is quite possible that the whole of this section of the Gesta Regum was derived, paraphrased, from works which " lost by the hostility of the ancients, or edited in un- " scholar-like fashion, he had restored in the more elegant " and modern style of composition." So wide a description would cover all the separate biographies that Leland conjecturally ascribes to Goscelin.

It must be observed that these sections are devoted to the royal saints exclusively, the episcopal and monastic saints proper being reserved for the Gesta Pontificum. In this way the images of the Holy Ancestors lead us up to the shrine of the Confessor.

The hagiography of Edward the Confessor.

39. The history of the development of the hagiography of Edward the Confessor is in itself a matter of some interest, but I shall not attempt to investigate it further than is necessary for the illustration of our author's position in regard to it. So far as we are at present informed, the basis of the whole fabric is found in the early biography contained in the Harleian MS. 526, which, after having been forgotten since the days of Stow, was restored to light by Mr. Luard in his volume of the Lives published in the present series in the year 1858. That our author was largely indebted to this work is proved by the many passages, noted in the margin of the present edition,[1] in which, on a plan which he very seldom adopts, he copies the authority with almost verbal accuracy. It is not by any means im-

The biography contained in the Harleian MS. 526.

---

[1] Above, pp. 236, 239 sq.

probable that he used this book at first hand; but it is quite possible that he came upon it in connexion with a mass of later materials, out of which, unless, indeed, he found them in a more complete copy of the ancient biography itself, he must have culled the miraculous stories with which he follows up his account of the king's life. And it is this portion of the subject to which I have already referred as obscure, and affording openings for future research. For our author is the earliest extant authority for several of the so-called miracles, and, unless they can be referred with some verisimilitude to such an older source, he must be regarded as the first propounder of them. They appear in a somewhat developed form, but practically identically, in the life written by Ailred of Rievaulx, and dedicated to king Henry II. But Ailred worked on materials collected by Osbert of Clare, who himself wrote later than William of Malmesbury, although not so much later as absolutely to preclude the supposition that William may have seen his collections before they were given to the world.[1]

Osbert of Clare and Ailred of Rievaulx.

---

[1] Very little is known about Osbert, and even the proper form of his name is questionable. In the C. C. C. MS. he is called Osbern; in his letters the form is Osbertus; the identity of the person being indisputable, as the occurrence of the letter cited above shows. Hence there are two articles about him in Tanner's Bibliotheca, pp. 564 and 565. It would seem fairly certain that he was the monk Osbert whom Ailred of Rievaulx describes as cured of a quartan fever by the relics of the Confessor (Twysden, cc. 410, 411). There was another Osbert prior of Daventry in 1135 (Mon. Angl., v. 176), who is quoted by him as an authority on the history of Saint Etheldreda (Ep. 34, ed. Anstruther p. 173). Osbert himself was of Stoke Clare in Suffolk, and was prior of Westminster (ib. pp. 110, 114), and was sent by bishop Henry of Winchester to Innocent II. to obtain the canonization of Edward (ib. p. 118), with letters also from king Stephen, ib. p. 120, in which he is described as having been prior for five years at the time of writing, that is 1140–1142 (p. 121). The letters, although containing nothing of any value, are worthy of some attempt at illustration, for a few allusions to contemporary events and persons. See, besides Tanner, Leland, Coll., i. 337; Wharton, Ang. Sac., ii., pref., p. xiv. He must not be confounded with Osbern of Canterbury.

PREFACE.

Our author's debt to the ancient biography.

The Gesta Regum was issued not later than 1125; all the stories of the Confessor's miracles appear in the first edition; and the author certainly uses language derived from the anonymous biographer which is not to be traced in Ailred or his prototype. It is sufficient to adduce in illustration of this the application of the surname "Digera" to earl Siward, at p. 312. In the same way the mention of Wulfwin Spillecorn as the hero of the miracle, at p. 273, seems to show that our author's account of the event is drawn from material more circumstantial than that furnished by the later writers. We are led thus to the inference that there was at Westminster a growing store of traditions, possibly even a codified and arranged record, of which the old biography may have been a part, and the earlier miracles an extension. To this our author may have had recourse before Osbert of Clare, the prior of the Abbey, took his work in hand. But it is not absolutely necessary to suppose that he had any more recondite source than a perfect copy of the Vita.

The work of Osbert known only in the abridgment.

The original work of Osbert, which is not known to exist, was completed in or about the year 1139; and professes to be based on certain "schedulæ" or manuscript collections kept in the Abbey, but not yet reduced to order. It was dedicated to Alberic, cardinal bishop of Ostia, who visited England as legate in the year just mentioned, in a letter preserved among the other epistles of Osbert, and printed by Anstruther in his volume of Scriptores Monastici, from the Gale MS. in the Library of Trinity College, Cambridge.[1] He describes his materials thus: "Ex diversis namque opus hoc fratrum
" imperio collectum est schedulis, quas sancti patres
" nostri nobis reliquerunt scriptas, qui eas viderunt et
" audierunt sicut referimus perpetratas. Tuæ itaque
" celsitudini novum regis opus sacrandum dirigitur,
" quia inspirante Spiritu veritatis sic retexere ordimur

Osbert's dedication to cardinal Alberic.

---

[1] The Gale MS. is a copy from the Cotton MS., Vitellius A. 17.

" historiam, ne mens officiosa lectoris eam sentiat impo-
" litam."[1] The letter is preserved in a series, a great part
of which is devoted to an attempt to secure the canonization of the Confessor by Innocent II. The attempt failed
at the time, but was repeated twenty years later and was
then successful. Although Osbert's work itself is lost,
an abridgment of it made almost contemporaneously
occurs in the Corpus Christi MS. 161, described by Mr.
Luard in his preface to the Lives. This abridgment is
appended in the MS. to the still later work of Ailred,
and is prefaced by an extract from the letter to Alberic:
" Incipit excerptum epistolæ domini Osberni prioris West-
" monasterii ad Albericum legatum in vitam Sancti
" Eadwardi regis." The extract closes with the words
cited above, stopping at *dirigitur*. Mr. Luard has given
a table of the sections. The colophon is: " Explicit vita
" et miracula Sancti Eadwardi regis et Confessoris ab-
" breviata ex tractatu domini Osberni Westmonasterii
" prioris." It is not clear whether Ailred worked
from the abridgment or from the original,[2] but neither
Osbert nor Ailred contains all that William has extracted
from the biography, and we may safely infer from the
miracles recorded by our author that they treated the
miracles in the same way. One instance already
referred to will suffice to show this: the restoration
of sight to a blind man is recorded by William, p. 273.
The name is given, Wulfwin Spillecorn, son of Wulmar
of Nutegareshale, who had lost his sight whilst cutting
wood in the forest at Brill (Bruelle). Ailred and possibly Osbert were ignorant where Brill was; Ailred,

The miracle of Wulfwin Spillecorn.

---

[1] Anstruther, Epistolæ Herberti de Losinga, &c., Brussels, 1846, pp. 110–114.

[2] Ailred's words unquestionably refer to Osbert's book, although he does not name the author; writing to abbot Laurence he says, "in-
" spexi codicem quem mihi tua
" dignatio tradidit transferendum .
" . . . A sensu sano illius codicis
" non recedens, pauca quæ vel ex
" Chronicis veracissimis transtuli,
" vel ex veterum certa et vera re-
" latione didici, non inutiliter ut
" mihi videtur apposui;" (Twysden, col. 371).

as printed by Twysden, gives the name Bruheham, and mentions neither the surname, parentage, nor home of Wulfwin. This story, which in the Gesta immediately follows the miracle performed on the citizen of Lincoln, most probably occurred on the missing page of the ancient life as transcribed in the Harleian MS.[1] On the other hand, it must be admitted that, whilst our author extracted from the most ancient life as much as was necessary for his portraiture of the person and character of the king, he omitted much that is of historical interest, in particular the details about the appointment of archbishop Robert of Canterbury, which are not found elsewhere, and which in a remarkable way illustrate the process, possible under the Confessor, for election and appointment of bishops. These considerations justify us in assigning to our author a greater proximity to original authority on the life of the Confessor than can be attributed to the other works specially written on the subject, and in supposing that he directly used the schedules preserved at Westminster, some fifteen years before they were brought forward in support of the proposal of canonization.

Possibly existed in the ancient biography which is mutilated.

In connexion, however, with the revival of the design, I must recur to a point only briefly touched in the introduction to the first volume. A letter addressed to pope Alexander III., and printed from the Vatican MS. 6024 in the Spicilegium Liberianum, p. 672, is not unnaturally but with some diffidence ascribed by the editor to William of Malmesbury.[2] If this ascription is warranted, our author must have lived on to the year 1163, or thereabouts. It is quite conceivable that our author might in 1140 have written such a letter, and, that having been found among the letters addressed to Innocent II., it might be re-addressed to his successor. The purport of the

The letter to Alexander III. from the abbot of Malmesbury.

---

[1] Ed. Luard, pp. 339, 400.

[2] The conjecture is, indeed, very tentative, " si idem fuisset."

letter might belong to either date. But against this compound hypothesis may be alleged two objections. The writer describes himself as "humilis minister " Malmesburiensis ecclesiæ," a title which would scarcely be taken by one of lower rank than an abbot; and further on claims for himself, " utpote peculiaris hujus " gloriosissimi alumnus," a special title to be listened to as advocating the canonization. It is impossible to suppose that, if our author had lived to become abbot of so important a monastery as Malmesbury, no notice whatever of the fact should have been preserved by historians or bibliographers, or in the Fasti of the house, and it is scarcely likely that William, although, as a Somersetshire man, he might affiliate himself to Glastonbury, could with any show of sincerity describe himself as a special votary of the saint of Westminster.[1] I have accordingly suggested that the letter really was written by Gregory who became abbot of Malmesbury about the year 1159, and that the initial G., by which he may be supposed to have denoted himself in his original letter, has been by a too clever transcriber expanded into Guillelmus. Whether Gregory had any especial tie to Westminster, I have not been able to discover.

Not to be assigned to our author.

I have been led into this review by a wish to correct the misapprehension which appears in my note in vol. i. p. 237, where I have supposed that William may have used Osbert's compilation. It is clear that the latter was not published until at least fourteen years after our author had completed his history of the Confessor.

Correction of note.

In the foregoing examination of the authorities used by, or within reach of, our author, I have confined my remarks, so far as they are critical, to the points of facts, dates, and style, and have not commented on our author's modifications of the language of his predecessors

---

[1] See vol. i., pref., p. xliii. Gregory, as abbot, was contemporary with pope Alexander III., who addresses to him a bull, dated July 13, 1163; Reg. Malmesb., i. 352.

where they concern his political views or interpretations of facts. In the early books of the Gesta there was little temptation to partizan views, or even to patriotic expressions of sympathy or antipathy. But as he approached his own date, scarcely sixty years after the great struggle between the two nationalities which claimed a share in him, we could not expect the same serenity. And, although I must recur to the point again, his treatment of the Vita Edwardi necessitates the remark here. The tract was written by an admirer of Godwin and Harold, and for the reading of queen Eadgith the widow of the Confessor. It contained, as was necessary and indeed inevitable, much of the language of panegyric. This our author has either omitted or so seriously retrenched as to put another colour on almost all the questionable details. Probably sympathy as well as self-preservation made this the most ingenuous and the wisest course; but the result is not inspiriting.

Our author's presentation of the facts recorded in the ancient biography.

40. After this long digression we must return to the reign of Ethelred, and take up the slender string of the national history from which we have been diverted. The notices are contained in sections 176–186, 188, 196–200, and 228.

Return to the string of the history.

It is, I believe, tolerably certain that for a great deal of this history we must choose between two theories. Our author had before him the Chronicles which we possess, and the lives of one or two of the saints which are still extant. A portion of his facts and dates are taken from the Chronicle, a tinge of pious vindictiveness from such writers as Osbern. What there is beyond he must have got from books or traditions which are now lost, or else have worked his own critical faculty into misinterpretations and confusions of his own. His treatment of the great earl Thurkill is partly coloured by Osbern's misunderstandings,[1] but his statements

The author's general treatment of his sources.

---

[1] See Freeman, Norman Conquest, i. 359, 653.

PREFACE. cvii

about him are either inventions or extracts from lost books. Thurkill was not involved in the murder of S. Elfege, nor did Sweyn return to England by his persuasion.[1] The picture of the decapitation and dying prophecy of Gunhilda rests on no other authority than our author's.[2] The leading points of Sweyn's invasion, the submission of earls Uhtred and Ethelmer, the mission of Emma and her children to Normandy, are from the Chronicle; the sentiments of Ethelred and his address to the witan are not. The sketch of Norman history that follows is perhaps mainly from William of Jumieges, although the verbal coincidences are so rare as hardly to be recognizable; eked out with the story of the pious exercises[3] and edifying death of duke Richard and the pilgrimage and death of duke Robert.[4] For the anecdote of duke Richard, and the name of the man who was accused of poisoning duke Robert, we know no earlier source.[5] For the death of Sweyn, the accession of Canute, the slaying of the hostages, the witenagemote of Oxford, the murder of Sigeferth and Morcar, the Chronicle is the authority. The burning of the tower of S. Frideswide's church, about which William of Malmesbury read an account among the archives of

Points to be noticed.

Debt to William of Jumieges.

The fire at S. Frideswide's at Oxford.

---

[1] Canute's return to England by Thurkill's invitation is described in the Encomium Emmæ, ed. Pertz, p. 13.

[2] Freeman, Norman Conquest, i. 306, 634, 638.

[3] Freeman, Norman Conquest. iv. 89, Cf. W. Gemet. (additament), ed. Camden, p. 691.

[4] The expressions descriptive of duke Robert's pilgrimage are very like those in the Chron. Turonense, Duchesne, iii. 360, and the words of our author, p. 211, imply a real suspicion, as well as a rumour that he had helped to poison duke Richard. In the Tours Chronicle the statement is stronger (Duchesne, iii. 360) : " Hic dicitur veneno necasse " Ricardum fratrem suum. Quare " vii° anno ducatus sui nudipes " Hierosolimam abiit et Bithiniæ " obiit." I think that this writer is later than our author.

[5] Radulfus Mowinus, p. 212. Is this a form of the name Moyon, Mohun, or Moon ? See Stapleton, Norman Exchequer, i. pp. lxxxii, lxxxiii. Is it not possible that this is Ralph of Wacey, son of archbishop Robert, who might have a hereditary claim, "spe ducatus," and who afterwards killed Gilbert of Eu.

the house, belongs probably to the year 1004 and not to 1013.[1] The charter, anyhow, which our author says that he has seen, is identified with an existing one of the earlier date. The events of the year 1016 are from the Chronicle; the manner of Edmund's death belongs to tradition.[2] The history of his children and the account of Robert's intended expedition to England are from the ordinary sources;[3] William himself had seen at Rouen the remains of the transports which had been driven back by a providential storm.

The reign of Canute.

41. The reign of Canute is treated in the same way. The one important addition to the Chronicle being the letter of the king giving an account of his pilgrimage to Rome.[4] As this epistle is preserved by Florence of Worcester in identical wording, we must infer either that Latin was the original language in which it is written, or that it was translated and circulated in the monasteries in the existing form. The historical difficulty about the date is well known. Canute's visit to Rome is certainly known to belong to the year 1027; our author assigns it to the fifteenth year of his reign.[5] Even if his years be calculated from his father's death there is a serious anachronism. Probably the letter was entered in the monastic chronicles, under the year of its publication or reception. Florence dates it in the year 1031 which agrees with our author's computation.

Historical difficulty about the king's visit to Rome.

---

[1] The history of this "casualty" is carefully worked out by Mr. Parker in his volume on the Early History of Oxford (Oxford Historical Society), pp. 142 sq. In the Gesta Pontificum, p. 315, the burning of the tower is connected with the massacre of 1004, and that is certainly the date to which the charter, which our author saw, refers. The charter is printed by Kemble, C. D., No. 709, vol. v. p. 327, with the mark of doubtfulness; the attestations in the better copies are all right: cf. Parker, ut s., pp. 320, 321; and Mr. Freeman, Norman Conquest (Third Edition), i. 648, is inclined to accept it as genuine. It has suffered, however, at the hands of transcribers.

[2] See Freeman, Norman Conq., i. (3rd ed.), pp. 711-716.

[3] Freeman, Norman Conquest, i. 473, 474.

[4] Above, pp. 221-224.

[5] Page 221.

A section of the church history of the reign, the translation of S. Elfege, the purchase of the arm of S. Augustine at Pavia, and the glories of the Glastonbury saints follow. In the later editions a charter of Glastonbury is inserted; and a notice of the correspondence of the king with Fulbert of Chartres,[1] with the mention of his death and burial, completes the record. The whole of the history of Harold, son of Canute, is from the Chronicle.[2] The reign of Hardicanute is embellished with a single purple patch, the account of earl Godwin's splendid peace-offering, and then the marriage of Gunhilda launches us at once on the full tide of German legend already examined.

Fulbert of Chartres.

Harold and Hardicanute.

42. Two or three lines will be enough to characterize the history of the reign of the Confessor and to close our survey of this book. All is derived from the Vita Edwardi and the Chronicle, except a few particulars about earl Leofric, queen Emma, and the family of Godwin. To the latter our author is apparently unjust; and although, after he has given his account of the Conquest, he seems to retain some remains of English feeling, there is little appearance of it in this portion of the work. I have already remarked[3] that he contrives, in his extracts from the Vita Edwardi, to omit anything that redounded to the glories of the house, and in his account of Harold's succession seems half inclined to treat him as an usurper. The extremely balanced wording of the sentence in which he introduces Harold to us testifies perhaps as much as anything in the whole work to his consciousness that he was only half an Englishman. On the day of the Epiphany, we are told,[4] Harold seized the crown, having extorted fealty from the witan; the English say that the crown was given him by Edward, " but " I think it is alleged rather out of kindness than

The reign of Edward the Confessor.

The author's attitude towards Harold.

---

[1] See above, page lxxxviii, note 3.
[2] See below.
[3] Above, page cvi.
[4] See above, page 280.

PREFACE.

"of judgment," more kindly than wisely, "that he should transfer his inheritance to him whose power he had always suspected"; although, that the truth may not be concealed, considering the character he assumed, he might govern the realm with prudence and bravery had he only succeeded to it legally; and, *His wavering judgment.* in fine, during Edward's life, whatever wars were kindled against him he put an end to by his own valour, desiring to display himself to the people of the country, doubtless aspiring, with itching hope, to the kingdom.[1] All throughout the desire to assert some sort of worthiness on the national hero, is weighted with some disparaging word:—"itching hope" is an uncomplimentary synonym for patriotic ambition. And so throughout: Harold refused his fellow-warriors a share of the spoils at Stamford bridge; hence they refused to follow him to Hastings. Yet with Harold all the strength of England fell; but he paid the penalty of his perfidy, through the inertness of the nation; yet again, was the nation so inert that the Normans won no glory by their victory? far from it, in the eyes of one who is proud to regard himself as a Norman. Yet again, surely it is a mistake to exaggerate the numbers of the English, and to disparage their bravery: to do this is to damn the Normans with awkward praise; it would be a strange glory to a nation which had never been conquered, to have conquered an army encumbered with its numbers and embarrassed by its own incapacity. Verily they were few and most ready men of their hands who there laid *Judicial see-saw.* down their lives for their country. Our good author, trying to sum up merits and demerits equitably, only exhibits himself on a judicial see-saw. The same propensity, to go two ways, appears in the comments

---

[1] I am sorry to have to note that the word "transfunderet," in line 20, is printed "transfunderent," which makes the passage unintelligible.

on the same crisis contained in the third book, and even the interesting and doubtless sincere reflexions on the Conquest itself, which furnished one of the best illustrations of our author's best qualities, are to some extent shaded with this neutral tint. But I do not wish to anticipate here any general conclusions, and, leaving some literary points to be summed up later on, I proceed to the examination of the third and fourth books.

III. The third book of the Gesta is entirely devoted to the History of the Conqueror. In our analysis of its composition we are not tempted to look for recondite elements; and almost every detail that cannot be traced in the contemporaneous writers on the period may, without much temerity, be referred to our author's personal authority. Considering, however, that he must have been acquainted with many to whom the main events of the Conquest were matters of personal recollection, we might expect much more than we find of original information. The result of the analysis may be very briefly stated. *The history of William the Conqueror.*

1. The early history of William of Normandy, sections 229–238, is derived entirely from William of Poictiers,[1] who, however, is never cited by name. Our author has added here and there a little verbal embroidery, and has very largely retrenched the material details as well as the inflated language of his prototype, but he has carefully followed the string of the narrative, and has added nothing material. I have not thought it necessary to mark, either by marginal reference or by variety of type, the coincidences in matter and language, but the most superficial view of the two writers proves the fact. One or two added particulars may be noted. Our author fixes the place of the council at which *The early history is from William of Poictiers.* *Our author's additions.*

---

[1] Edited by Baron Maseres in 1783. On the character of his history, see Freeman, Norman Conquest, 3rd edition, ii. 4, 163, 164, &c.

duke Robert declared William his son and heir, at Fécamp.¹ This fact is not mentioned by earlier writers, but it is likely enough that it was derived from the copy of William of Poictiers which our author used, and which would be complete; our extant copy is only a fragment. Possibly the same source may have furnished the story of the adventure at the Conqueror's birth, the child's grasping at the rushes on the floor;² although that, like the corresponding scene at the landing at Pevensey, may seem to be an outgrowth of later tradition. The marriage of Herleva with Herlewin is placed before the death of duke Robert, not after it, as William of Jumieges states.³ The rumour of the poisoning of duke Robert by Ralph Mowin, which is introduced in an earlier section in the second book, is not repeated in the third.⁴ William of Poictiers is not accessible as a possible authority; William of Jumieges does not mention the story, which occurs, however, in the Roman de Rou. The count of Ponthieu, who was beheaded at the siege of Arques, is called Isembard,⁵ instead of Ingelram or Enguerrand, as William of Poictiers named him; this may be a mere clerical error, but on the authority of our author, or rather of the extracts current in Commelin's collection as a continuation of Bede, Isembard is given as an *alias* or surname to Ingelram in the French lists of the counts of Ponthieu. In his account of the deposition of archbishop Malger of Rouen, which occurs in a later section (§ 267), our author has followed the same authority, adding from his own information the circumstances of the archbishop's opposition to the Conqueror's marriage;⁶ and a legend

Ralph Mowin.

Isembard of Ponthieu.

Archbishop Malger.

---

¹ Cf. Will. Gemet., vi. 12.
² Page 286. On these and the like myths, see Freeman, Norman Conquest, ii. 180, and Appendix U, pp. 628 sq.
³ Page 333; W. Gemet., vi. 3.
⁴ See above, p. 91.

⁵ Page 289. See W. Pict., p. 54. Of course Isembard may have been a surname, or even a nickname, after the traitor of 881.
⁶ See Freeman, Norman Conquest, iii. 94–96.

of the vision vouchsafed to Maurilius, the successor of Malger, before his death. His description of Maurilius as a monk of Fécamp seems to be taken from William of Jumieges;[1] for the story of the vision our author is, as Mabillon has remarked, the "antiquissimus "auctor." I am unable to refer the account of Fulk Nerra, count of Anjou, and his pilgrimage to Jerusalem, to any earlier source, so far as concerns the minute particulars related by our author.[2] The story of the two clerks of Nantes, which he inserts "pro utilitate "legentium," as well as for the purpose of saying something about Brittany, must take its place with the episodes on Gerbert and Henry III.[3]

Maurilius of Rouen.

Fulk of Anjou.

2. The influence of William of Poictiers may be traced here and there in the account of the Conquest. This, including the preparation for the expedition, the negotiations with Harold, the battle of Hastings, and the subsequent settlement and pacification occupies sections 238–247. It is chiefly derived from domestic sources, the Chronicles and our author's own knowledge. The fixing of Lillebonne as the place of rendezvous seems to be original;[4] the refusal of the ransom of Harold's body, offered by his mother, is from William of Poictiers;[5] the burial at Waltham, although the fact does not rest on our author's testimony, is first attested by him.[6] But it would be tedious, and under present

The account of the Norman Conquest.

Additional particulars furnished by our author.

---

[1] W. Gemet., vi. 24. Here, as before, we note our author's special indications of interest in Fécamp. He seems to be the "antiquissimus "auctor" of the stories about duke Richard's actions there; above, p. 178.

[2] See Freeman, Norman Conquest, ii. 279. Some of the material is common to the Gesta Consulum Andegavensium (D'Achery, Spicilegium, iii. 234–266), which was abridged later on by Ralph de Diceto, Opp., i. 162–164; but the relations of the authors are scarcely definite enough to allow a decision as to the originality of the treatment. The Gesta Consulum is, in its present form, much later than William of Malmesbury, and dedicated to Henry II.

[3] See above, p. lxxxvii.

[4] Page 299. See Freeman, Norman Conquest, ii. 291.

[5] Page 306; Will. Pict., p. 134.

[6] Pages 306, 307.

circumstances useless, to dwell upon the minor particulars in which William of Malmesbury agrees with or differs from the other narrators of the great crisis. The careful analysis to which the history of the Conquest has during the last few years been subjected by Professor Freeman absolves the editor of any one of the principal authorities from the obligation to retraverse the same ground. The result of that analysis may, I think, be held to be the placing of our author in the distinguished place of a primary, and honest, if not always absolutely trustworthy authority for the period.[1]

The later history of the Conqueror.

3. The same general conclusion applies to the remainder of the third book, and its illustrations of the reign and character of the Conqueror. It is really rather a *resumé*, and commentary on the narrative, of the Chronicle than an attempt at connected history. And it is little more. Our author's reflexions are, of course, his own. The more trifling incidents with which he varies the narration are oral anecdotes. His mention of Edgar Atheling as still alive at the time of writing is an interesting memorandum;[2] the denomination of earl Siward as "Digera" is a reminiscence, as I have already noted, of the "Vita Eadwardi;[3]" the recognition of the laws of William FitzOsbern as still in force in Herefordshire is a remark of importance in legal history;[4] the account of the Danish and Norwegian succession is a contribution of some secondary importance in European chronology which, so far as its form is concerned, it would be difficult

---

[1] Mr. Freeman's general opinions about our author's tone, powers, and credibility, which are quite different things, may be gathered from several passages in his books: especially Norman Conquest, ii. 4; iii. 588; v. 578.

[2] Page 278. The Edgar Ætheling, who, in the 4th year of Henry II., rendered account of 20 marks in Northumberland (Rot. Pip., p. 177), must, of course, be another Edgar Atheling. But supposing the original Edgar to be alive in 1126, he must either have been extremely old, or else was a mere child in 1066, which is most probable.

[3] Page 312. Digr; stout, big; Vigfusson, Icelandic Dictionary, p. 99. Cf. Langebek, Scriptores Rer. Danic., iii. 288, note *k*.

[4] Page 314.

to refer to older authority.¹ The account of Hildebrand as I have already noted, seems to be derived from Cluny. The praises of Lanfranc are natural and original enough in the mouth of a Benedictine. The tragedy of bishop Walcher of Durham was too critical and notorious an event to be the monopoly of a single story-teller.² The lying story of the Conqueror's ill-treatment of his wife seems to owe its survival to our author's vehement contradiction.³ The ill-timed jests of king Philip at the Conqueror's obesity are conserved with a sure instinct that they are the sort of stories that catch the fancies of light readers.⁴ The statement of the decision of the controversy between York and Canterbury, drawn from sources carefully circulated at the time, was meant for more serious students, and such as would welcome the account of the rearrangement of the bishoprics derived from the same sources. When I have mentioned the episode of Berengarius and the supplementary jottings of papal and imperial history, I have traversed with sufficient minuteness the materials of this book. Taken altogether it is, as a piece of literary work, perhaps the most presentable portion of the Gesta; it furnishes the best illustrations of our author's industry and carefulness, as well as of his wit and wisdom, his ingenuousness and discretion, but there is little of

Scraps and anecdotes about the Conqueror.

General character of the third book.

---

¹ Pages 317–320. A great deal of the history of Svend Estrithson, in sections 259 and 261, may be worked out of the Anglo-Saxon Chronicles; but the particulars about the dedication of S. Laurence's Eve, page 318, and the succession secured to the fourteen sons (cf. Langebek, Scriptores, iii. 336; iv. 258), require adjudication. The particulars about S. Canute, not derived from the Chronicle, must be from the legend of the saint. The history of Magnus and his successors in Norway may be similarly accounted for; the points being S. Olaf, Harold Hardrada, and Sigurd the Crusader, all prominent in external history.

² Page 330. It is told by Florence and Simeon, but in different language, and with no special coincidences.

³ Page 331.

⁴ Page 332. There is another story at p. 479, which reads as if either Philip himself or William of Malmesbury saw in the ringing of the church bells on his departure the ground of the pun "bella quo-" "modo nos effugant."

recondite character about it, and the sources of its information are obvious enough. Its weak features I have already pointed out. The original information which it contains, relating to the early history of the counts of Anjou, § 236; Edgar Atheling and Robert FitzGodwin, § 251; the expedition of William FitzOsbern to Flanders, § 256; and the succession to the Scandinavian kingdoms, is a distinct element of importance, an abundant illustration of the author's research, and a tempting field for investigation or speculation on the part of future editors. I am unable, as I have shown, to indicate any probable source from which these details can have been borrowed.

<small>The fourth book; the history of William Rufus.</small>

IV. In proceeding to the examination of the fourth book, we find that we have already reached the ground on which we have no occasion to search for authorities earlier or more independent than the writer himself. However late we place the year of his birth, he must have been old enough at the time of the death of William Rufus, to understand and remember the stories which were told and which he, with some slight reticence, perhaps, is contented to record. For the main events he had still the Chronicle before him in that edition to which we have reason to believe he had chiefly trusted, now represented by the Laudian or E. Manuscript. The variations are rather of view and opinion than of incident.

<small>Characteristic details.</small>

Still here and there we have an additional point; the Conqueror's reply to Lanfranc's intercession for Odo;[1] the characteristic stories of the conduct of William and Robert at Mont S. Michel;[2] the general sketch of the king's conduct and court;[3] his extortions; his dealings with the Jews at Rouen and London,[4] and the description of his personal peculiarities; these are

---

[1] Page 361. See the other versions of the story in Freeman, Norman Conquest, iv. 681.
[2] Pages 363–366.
[3] Page 366–370.
[4] Pages 370, 371. Cf. Eadmer, ed. Rule, pp. 99–101; Freeman, William Rufus, i. 162.

matters which could scarcely come into the Chronicle, but would be amusing enough in conversation when, twenty years after, the royal oppressions, cruelties, and other abominations were beginning to be forgotten. After refreshing himself with general reflexions, our author, in the dearth of recollections, turns back to the Chronicle and gives, under the dates of the regnal years, the physical and political incidents that seemed most important from the year 1089 to 1100.[1] Amongst these he notes the descent of Magnus and Harold on Anglesey in 1098,[2] in language so much more circumstantial than that of the Peterborough Chronicle, and so nearly akin to that of Florence of Worcester, as to suggest either a suspicion that he was not entirely unacquainted with the Chronicon ex Chronicis, or that he had another copy of the Anglo-Saxon Chronicle which is now lost. The history of the last days and death of Rufus, on which our author is a primary authority, brings the domestic history to a close. The chapters on the Cistercians and on the Bishops of the time come in, I grieve to say, as padding, but with no small interest. The account of the Cistercians was, perhaps, derived from Stephen Harding, himself a pupil of Sherborne and possibly an acquaintance of our author. He became abbot of Cîteaux in 1109, and was alive when the Gesta was written. He died in 1134.[3] The stories of the Bishops[4] are original anecdotes, and tinged with the feeling so common in the monastic writers whose jealousy of all administration but their own so frequently colours their view of character and events. They ought, however, to have been relegated to their proper place in the Gesta Pontificum. Incidentally our author adds a notice of Goscelin the hagiographer[5] which is really valuable,

Recourse to the Chronicle.

The chapters on the Cistercians.

On the bishops of the time.

---

[1] Pages 375, 376.
[2] Page 376; Freeman, William Rufus, ii. 134, 619.
[3] Pages 380-385. See Acta Sanctorum, Boll. April, vol. ii. pp. 496-501.
[4] Pages 385 sq.
[5] Page 389.

but seems to come in fortuitously, although not before it was called for by the gratitude which the author ought to have felt for the services of so important a predecessor in his historical work.

<small>The history of the first Crusade.</small>

2. The second half of the fourth book, §§ 343–389, is almost entirely devoted to the History of the first Crusade, and the personal and geographical details which our author had collected for the illustration of that great crisis in European development. On this subject, even at so early a date, a compiler had an embarrassing quantity of material before him. The expedition itself was the central point of the interests of warriors and churchmen throughout the West; its particular details were collected and diversified under the hands of the very men who had witnessed them; the curiosity of the pilgrims and the enthusiasm of the men who stayed at home combined to swell the mass of anecdote, and at the same time to consolidate the chronological and geographical consistency of the story. William of Malmesbury must have conversed with many of the heroes who returned from the Crusade, and here and there we may trace in his narration vestiges of oral information. But the whole of this episode as he has treated it is disappointing; it is a work of art rather than a proper chronicle, and the Gesta Regum would have been as complete without it as it is with it. In other words, the historical material which it contains is not the result of a comparison of authorities, but a simple paraphrase of one particular account of the Crusade, with a very few variations and additions; and the general reflexions on the subject wear the look of an academic exercise, and have their chief value as illustrating our author's epigrammatic style. The additional illustrations, however, geographical and other, have a certain value of their own, and the concluding particulars in which the author tries to trace the later History of his heroes have likewise the merit of some

<small>Materials for the history abundant.</small>

originality of information. Valuable as the whole section of the work undoubtedly is, it is less valuable than at first sight it might appear to be when we consider the era and the opportunities of the author.

He begins with a fair account of his intention. He is going to record what other men have witnessed, but in his own words: he will add from the writings of the ancients what it is good to know about Constantinople, Antioch, and Jerusalem.[1] No slight task he seems to think it, and accordingly as an epic poet he invokes divine assistance for his attempt.

The author's plan of treatment.

3. It is clear from the very beginning of the narration that Fulcher of Chartres was to be the text book.[2] Fulcher was himself a Crusader; he had attended Robert of Normandy in the expedition and was chaplain to the first two Baldwins of Jerusalem. William of Malmesbury follows him certainly down to the year 1113, and possibly down to the very year of writing; for he mentions the capture of Baldwin II. and his return after a year's obscurity, which occurred in the year 1123, as happening "anno præterito."[3] It is with the year 1124 that Fulcher's work in its first form terminates; possibly the few final details may have been derived by our author from other sources, but the coincidence is worth notice, and if we conclude that our author took these particulars from Fulcher, this portion of the Gesta must have been composed within a year of the completion of the whole work. Our marginal references will enable the reader to follow up the relations of the two writers

Fulcher of Chartres the main authority used.

---

[1] Page 390.

[2] It is possible that he knew Fulcher through the abridgment which, under the name Gesta Francorum Obsidentium Jerusalem, is printed by Bongars in the same volume with the original, pp. 361 sq.; some few exceptional expressions occur which suggest the suspicion; *e.g.*, the war cry "Deus "Vult," in the battle that follows the capture of Nicea (page 414; Gesta Francorum, p. 564). On the other hand, the note of the devastation of Asia, which follows (page 415), is from Fulcher and not from the Gesta.

[3] Page 452.

when and where they coincide. It will be sufficient now to point out the more important additions which William of Malmesbury contributes, and the few significant variations in which he seems to be indebted to other sources of information.

The council of Clermont.

4. Starting with Fulcher he brings Urban II. over the Alps to Clermont, and then diverges into an account of the great council of 1095.[1] The summary of the canons of this assembly he might take from public documents; the papal oration on the occasion is unquestionably an effort of his own rhetorical genius; from those who heard it he received a general account of its purport; he preserves the sense but is unable to conserve the vigour of the eloquence with which it was enunciated. Other writers did the same:[2] Robert the Monk, Fulcher himself, William of Tyre and others, elaborated the allocution which in their minds the pope ought to have given; perhaps our author's comes as near to the truth as theirs: whatever were the arguments the application was the same, war for the recovery of the East.

The excitement attending the crusading movement.

5. The general description of the turmoil that followed, the often-quoted characteristics of the Welshman, the Scot, the Dane, and the Norseman; the crowding of the highways, the family flittings, the enormous forces of volunteers, and what is far the most striking feature of the movement, its general and concentrated enthusiasm, all this is given surely in our author's own words.[3]

---

[1] Pages 391 sq.

[2] A reference to the several authorities will be enough to show that they all treated the speech as an exercise of their own: Robertus Monachus, ap. Bongars, p. 31; Baldric, ibid. p. 86; Fulcher, ibid. p. 382; Guibert of Nogent, ibid. p. 478; and the Acts of the Council in the Concilia of Labbe and Cossart.

[3] There is something like this in Guibert of Nogent (ed. D'Achery, p. 380) to whom we owe the touching illustration:—" Videres mirum " quiddam et plane joco aptissi- " mum, pauperes videlicet quosdam " bobus biroto applicitis, eisdem- " que in modum equorum ferratis, " substantiolas cum parvulis in car- " ruca convehere, et ipsos infantu- " los, dum obviam haberent quæli- " bet castella vel urbes, si hæc esset " Jerusalem ad quam tenderent " rogitare."

Abbot Guibert of Nogent describes the same scenes in even more picturesque terms, but the opportunities were such as no literary man could possibly overlook, and the coincidences between the two writers are not significant.[1] The description of the outset of the Crusade under its several leaders and by their several routes is floridly told, but all the facts are, I think, discoverable in Fulcher.[2]

6. Fulcher, followed by our author, takes duke Robert to Lucca; the return of the pope to Rome, which Fulcher himself witnessed, gives William of Malmesbury his opportunity for digression. He introduces the poem of Hildebert on the Eternal City, and adds a catalogue of the " gates and holy places " of Rome. The poem requires no remark.[3] The catalogue is a valuable document, and partakes so far of the character of a primary authority that it is incorporated by Professor Urlichs among the original materials for Roman topography in the Codex Topographicus Urbis Romæ.[4] In that collection it follows the Einsiedeln Itinerary of the eighth century, and the Würzburg one of the ninth; coinciding almost in date with the Ordo Romanus under Innocent II., and forming the fourth of the itineraries that the professor has thought worth collation. This is not the place to inquire into its exact relations with the other kindred catalogues; and the more pertinent question as to the source from which our author obtained it, I am unable to answer. Judging, however, from the existence of

Our author's topography of Rome.

---

[1] Pages 398, 399.
[2] Pages 400-401. The details about the manœuvres of Alexius are perhaps expanded from some other source, as well as the notices of William of Poictou; which, however, is discoverable further on in Fulcher's notice of the year 1102, c. xxvii.
[3] Except, perhaps, that it may have been communicated by Hildebert himself to our author, who seems to be the original proprietor of it. See page 403.
[4] Codex Topographicus Urbis Romæ; Würzburg, 1871. Compare the *Descriptio regionum* with Mabillon's notes, in the Prolegomena to Anastasius, Migne's Patrologia, cc. 347 sq.

such memoranda as those of archbishop Sigeric's visit to Rome, still extant among the Cotton manuscripts,[1] I should be inclined to think that our author would have had no difficulty in finding similar details among the treasures of English libraries, especially among the compilations of chronological data such as the lists of emperors, kings, and patriarchs, which he furnishes in other parts of his work. Whencesoever it comes, it has the prerogative right of first appearance.

The journey to Constantinople.

7. We accompany Fulcher to Constantinople, pausing, however, to lament over the loss of the pilgrims drowned at the devil's ford on their way through Bulgaria. Whether the "vadum demonis" of Fulcher, or "diaboli" of William, is the origin of the Divalus,[2] Divol or Devol, of medieval and modern geography, or there is a play on some earlier local name, I cannot say; the point has its importance to us as showing that our author steadily follows his guide. At Constantinople, however, he has another opportunity. His patron Saint Aldhelm, in his book on the praises of virginity, had told the legend of the foundation of the city;[3] that book was certainly in the Malmesbury library. The account which follows is not from Fulcher, but contains nothing special; the list of the emperors and the note of the relics required no recondite research. The geographical expressions are taken, as Du Cange has observed, from Sidonius Apollinaris.[4] In the account of the embellishment of

The account of Constantinople and list of the patriarchs.

---

[1] See Memorials of Saint Dunstan, pp. 391 sq.

[2] "Pervenit ad quemdam cui nomen Divalus amnem"; Guillelmus Appulus, de Normannis, ap. Leibnitz, Scr. Rer. Brunswic., i. 619.

[3] For Constantine's Vision, compare Rob. Monach. (Bongars), p. 38.

[4] Du Cange, Constantinopolis Christiana, page 3. The passage from Sidonius is so important that I transcribe it here, italicizing the words borrowed by our author:—

At tu, *circumflua ponto*
Europæ atque Asiæ commissam
carpis utrinque
Temperiem, nam Bistonios *Aquilonis hiatus*
Proxima Chalcidici sensim tuba
temperat *Euri*.
* * * *

the city the Greek historian Socrates furnishes the authority, and, through the translation of the Historia Tripartita, the very words which our author borrows.[1] The notice of the visit of the emperor Constans to Rome in the following section (§356) is from Anastasius the Librarian, or possibly, through his compilation, from Paulus Diaconus.

8. Partly abridging and partly paraphrasing his authority, our author takes us on to Nice, Antioch, and Jerusalem. Antioch he characterizes very briefly, referring as a general repertory of information to the Pseudo-Ambrosian Hegesippus.[2] For Jerusalem he used the Itinerary of Bernard the Monk,[3] supplementing his account, however, with incidental references of no very recondite character, and with a list of the patriarchs of Jerusalem from S. James, the brother of our Lord, to Simeon in whose time it was taken by the Crusaders. The Cotton MS., Tiberius B. 5, contains two ancient lists; one of them ends with S. Cyril; the other, which, until I saw it, I thought that our author might have used, is a mere fabrication, being a farrago of New Testament names

Notes on Antioch and Jerusalem.

Bernard the Monk.

List of patriarchs.

Porrigis ingentem spatiosis mœnibus urbem
Quam tamen *angustam populus* facit, itur in æquor
Molibus et *veteres tellus nova contrahit undas.*
Namque Dicarcheæ translatus pulvis arenæ
Intratis solidatur aquis, durataque massa
Sustinet advectos *peregrino in gurgite campos.*
Sic te dispositam, spectantemque undique portus
Vallatam pelago *terrarum commoda cingunt,*
Fortunata satis, Romæ partita triumphos.

[1] Hist. Tripart., lib. ii. c. 18 (Cassiodor, Opp., i. 232) :—" In hac " quoque civitate duas quidem " ædificavit ecclesias, quarum " unam nominavit Irenem aliam " vero appellavit Apostolorum. " Non solum autem, sicut dixi, " auxit Constantinus Christianorum " dogmata, sed etiam paganorum " templa destruxit. Simulacra " namque ornata publice in Con-" stantinopolitana urbe proposuit, " et tripodas Delphicos in Circo, " ad spectaculum dedit, qui cum " ipso videantur aspectu, referun-" tur." Vita Vitaliani, in Conc., Labbe and Cossart, vi. 444; Paul., Hist. Langobard., lib. v. c. 11 (ed. Waitz, p. 150).

[2] Page 415.

[3] Page 423; Mabillon, AA. SS. O.S.B., sæc. iii., pt. 2, pp. 472-475.

ranged without regard to age or order. But it is certain, from the occurrence of this and similar lists, in the works of the contemporary and crusading historians that a careful collector like our author would have had, perhaps, even less difficulty than we have, even with the help of Le Quien, in laying his hands on such a catalogue as he wanted. The authoritative catalogues, that of Papebroch[1] in the Bollandist Acts, and that of Le Quien in the third volume of his "Oriens Christianus,"[2] refer constantly to Catalogi Latini, but without much indication of date or locality of MSS. In one of these references Le Quien quotes words almost exactly agreeing with those of William of Malmesbury, as occurring in a Latin catalogue, but he does not say enough to make it clear whether or no he is quoting from the Gesta.

Detailed accounts of the heroes of the Crusade.

9. Up to the capture of Jerusalem (§ 372) our author continues to follow Fulcher with more or less fidelity. He then gives a more detailed and elaborate account of the heroes, Godfrey, Baldwin, Bohemond, Raymond, and Robert of Normandy.[3] The history of Baldwin, comprising that of the Frank kingdom of Palestine

---

[1] AA. SS. Bolland. May, tom. iii. pp. i-lxxii.

[2] Le Quien, Oriens Christianus, iii., 475 :—" In Latino Catalogo " lego 'tempore cujus Achim sol- " ' danus nepos ejus Hierosolimam " ' veniens, ecclesias destruxit, et " ' quatuor milia hominum avuncu- " ' lumque suum patriarcham duxit " ' in Babilonem et occidit.' " Compare page 425.

[3] The following minor points are worth notice : the verse, "nec " prius abstiterunt ferro exercere " dolorem," page 413, line 30. Aoxianus, the governor of Antioch, is called in the printed text of Fulcher, Gratianus, and in the Gesta Francorum, Capsianus (p. 565); Darsianus in Albert of Aix, p. 234; Cassianus in Guibert, p. 408. The connexion of Seleucus with Antioch, p. 415, is not mentioned by Fulcher, but does occur in Guibert of Nogent, p. 422. The appearance of S. George and S. Demetrius is noted in Guibert, p. 418 (below, p. 420). The notices about Robert, son of Godwin, at pp. 310, 318, and 449, are a contribution by our author. See Freeman, William Rufus, ii. 122, 128, 616, 617. The curious mode of concealing coins by the people of Cæsarea, p. 445 : Fulcher, c. 25, is also remarked on by Guibert, p. 452.

onwards to the year 1124, is almost entirely from Fulcher. The other biographies are more independent in style and originality; and that of duke Robert is of course our author's own contribution. Before deserting Fulcher, I may note two or three particulars of detail in which the hand of some other authority may be traced, even when and where the line of his narrative is most closely followed. Such are these:— the assertion that count Robert of Flanders refused to do homage to the emperor Alexius;[1] that Hugh the Great deserted the Crusade after the capture of Antioch on the plea of a chronic pain in the bowels;[2] the appearance of S. George and S. Demetrius in the final battle;[3] the story of the cannibalism into which the besiegers of the city were compelled by famine;[4] the curious use of the word "nothos"[5] for the crusading army; and the quotations from Lucan's Pharsalia with which the trying story is here and there embellished. A careful scrutiny of the contemporary historians of the first Crusade might possibly help us to discover sources from which these details and others like them are derived; but our author is sure to have had communication with the travellers who were so weak or

Divergences from Fulcher of Chartres.

---

[1] "Comes vero Flandriæ, sic sicut "alii jusjurandum fecit"; Fulcher, ed. Bongars, p. 386; cf. Guibert, ibid. p. 490; Baldric, p. 91; R. de Agiles, p. 140; Rob. Monach., p. 38; Gesta Francorum, p. 5. Raymond of S. Gilles refused both oath and homage; possibly count Robert took the oath and refused the homage. *See* below, p. 401.

[2] Page 421.

[3] Page 420. See Gesta Francorum, ap. Bongars, p. 21.

[4] The story of cannibalism appears also in the Gesta Francorum Expugnantium Jerusalem (Bongars, p. 565), a work chiefly extracted from Fulcher; and that the pilgrims at Antioch were nearly driven to it, is stated in the "Epistola Cru-"ciferorum," in Dodechin's Auctarium of Marianus, Scriptt. Pistorius, i. 665, which our author may have seen. See also Guibert of Nogent, p. 414; Albert of Aix, p. 250.

[5] The word is not in Fulcher or in the Gesta Francorum; but it may be intended for a concentration of Fulcher's words:—"Quosdam "luxuria polluebat, quosdam vero "avaritia vel superbia vitiabat;" if so, it is rather hard.

Stories of eye-witnesses.

so fortunate as to return home, and to have had many such stories at first hand. He had heard from an eye-witness, how Godfrey of Bouillon had slain a lion during the siege of Jerusalem;[1] the story of his exploit at Antioch, when he cut the Turk in two from head to groin, was current in other channels besides the Chronicle of Robert the Monk;[2] and his escape and perils during the siege of Rome, which led to his vow of Crusade,[3] were doubtless the burden of many legends such as our author loved to collect. The hero had indeed begun in earnest his pilgrimage into the land of fable, and for the stories that are here told it is common to find the Gesta Regum Anglorum cited as the first authority.

Story of Bohemond.

10. This is the case more or less with Bohemond also. The few distinct particulars stated about him in § 387 are taken from Fulcher; the story of his vow, made in his captivity, that he would hang up his chains in the shrine of S. Leonard, is told by Ralph of Caen in the Gesta Tancredi,[4] and may have been told elsewhere. According to Geoffrey of Vigeois his offering was silver of the same weight as the chains of Danischemend. The jest about Durandus and Dyrrhachium is repeated by later writers with some variation of phrase from our author's,[5] but he is the most ancient story-teller who records it, and yet the circumstantial way in which the brief sketch is arranged indicates that he had some other authority beyond oral tradition. The tragic end of the regent of Antioch, Roger fitz Richard, with which

---

[1] Page 433. Cf. Guibert of Nogent, who makes the combatant a bear, p. 433; as does Albert of Aix, p. 716.

[2] Page 433. Cf. Guibert of Nogent, p. 433; Robert. Mon., p. 50.

[3] Page 482. There is a very good and comprehensive sketch of Godfrey's whole career in the Histoire Littéraire de la France, vol. viii. pp. 598 sq., which is reprinted in Migne's Patrologia, vol. clv. cc. 369 sq.

[4] Rad. Cadom., Mart. and Dur., Thesaurus, iii. 207; Gauf. Vosion., Labbe, Bibl. MSS., ii. 297.

[5] See Alberic of Trois Fontaines, Leibnitz, Acc. Hist., p. 125.

the chapter on Bohemond closes,[1] must have been recent news when our author was writing, and, as it is not described by Fulcher, may have been told in a letter or by a returning pilgrim.

11. The career of count Raymond of S. Gilles is told with much more care and unity of treatment. It begins with a mistake as to his parentage: his father was Pontius, not William, count of Toulouse; the William whom he succeeded was his elder brother.[2] His ambitions and disappointments, however, are carefully traced; his successive concessions at Antioch, Jerusalem, Ascalon, and Laodicea, are chronicled as if they were meritorious acts, and not, as they were usually regarded, frustrated attempts at self-aggrandisement. At last he wins Tripoli, and, just as he is going to take possession of it, dies. His infant child, Alfonso Jordan, the offspring of his Spanish wife, called by our author William,[3] is sent to Europe to be educated, and ultimately to succeed to Toulouse. The conquest of Tripoli is completed by Bertram, who again is succeeded by Pontius, count of Tripoli at the time of writing.[4] In all this our author must have had before him an authority more circumstantial and more encomiastic than Fulcher, but the general outline of the section is common to the two writers.

History of Raymond of S. Gilles.

12. For the account of Robert of Normandy we may accept the Gesta as being so nearly a primary authority that there is no need to seek for outside sources of information.

Robert of Normandy.

13. And this brings down our investigation to the time at which William of Malmesbury becomes distinctly

Concluding questions.

---

[1] Page 455. This occurred in 1119. The story is told by Gautier the Chancellor, in Bongars, p. 455, but quite differently.

[2] Page 455 sq. Art de Vérifier les Dates, ix. 374.

[3] Page 458. Art de V. les D., ix. 379.

[4] Art de V. les D., ix 379; Mas Latrie, Trésor de Chronologie, c. 2213.

a contemporary writer. Before, however, we attempt to estimate the importance of his direct contributions to our national history, it will be as well to dismiss or to sum up two or three questions which have from time to time suggested themselves in our inquiry. This can be done very briefly.

What Chronicle did our author use? Our author used the Chronicles; certainly he used that which we know as the Peterborough version, which comes down to us in the Laud MS. 636. Possibly he had other editions and continuations which we have not. There is one place in which he seems to have used the Abingdon book: the account of the champion at Stamford bridge, which occurs in that copy only. But in that copy this particular episode is said to be inserted in a different hand and in another dialect from that of the bulk of the Chronicle.[1] It may be questioned accordingly whether both writers may not have taken it from some legend or heroic story current so long after the event. That William used the Chronicle in its native form he tells us himself; but it is a point on which I confess myself to have long had some questionings whether it is not possible, and even probable, that there was a Latin version of the Chronicle, which formed the basis of the work of Florence of Worcester and Simeon of Durham.

Did our author know the work of Florence of Worcester? 14. Was William of Malmesbury acquainted with the Chronicle of Florence? So far as time affects the question he might well have been so: Fulcher of Chartres and Eadmer of Canterbury, both continue their work after the date at which Florence finished his; and our author plundered both. He does not, however, mention Florence, as his generosity and vanity would have led to do, if he had used his book. But there are two or three passages in which the language of the two is very similar. In particular the account of Edgar's being

---

[1] Two of the Saxon Chronicles, ed. Earle, pp. 201, xxxviii; Freeman, Norman Conquest, iii. 371.

rowed on the Dee by the tributary kings, and the account of the magnificent peace-offering of earl Godwin to king Hardicanute. All the other coincidences may, I think, be more easily accounted for when we remember the common material which lay before both writers in the pages of Ethelwerd, the Vita Alfredi, the ancient genealogies, and the treasure of charters in the great monasteries. The two passages I have referred to may be exhibited in parallel columns :— *Two passages to be collated.*

| Regem Scottorum Kinadium, Cumbrorum Malcolmum, archipiratam Mascusium, omnesque reges Walensium quorum nomina fuere Dufnal, Giferth, Hunal, Jacob, Judetthil, ad curiam coactos, uno et perpetuo sacramento sibi obligavit, adeo ut apud civitatem Legionum sibi occurrentes in pompam triumphi per fluvium De illos deduceret. Una enim navi impositos, ipse ad proram sedens remigare cogebat; per hoc ostentans regalem magnificentiam qui subjectam haberet tot regum potentiam. Denique fertur dixisse tunc demum posse successores suos gloriari se reges Anglorum esse cum tanta honorum prærogativa fruerentur.[1] | Interjecto deinde tempore, ille cum ingenti classe septentrionali Britannia circumnavigata ad Legionum civitatem appulit, cui subreguli ejus octo, Kynath scilicet rex Scottorum, Malcolmus rex Cumbrorum, Maccus plurimarum rex insularum, et alii quinque Dufnal, Siferth, Huwal, Jacob, Juchil, ut mandarat occurrerunt, et quod sibi fideles et terra et mari cooperatores esse vellent juraverunt: cum quibus die quadam scapham ascendit, ilisque ad remos locatis, ipse clavum gubernaculi arripiens, eam per cursum Deæ perite gubernavit, omnique turba ducum et procerum simili navigio comitante, a palatio ad monasterium S. Johannis Baptistæ navigavit; ubi facta oratione eadem pompa ad palatium remeavit; quod dum intraret optimatibus fertur dixisse tunc demum quemque suorum successorum suorum se gloriari posse regem Anglorum fore cum tot regibus sibi obsequentibus potiretur pompa talium honorum.[2] |

[1] Above, page 165. [2] Flor. Wig., M. H. B. p. 578.

Comparison of William of Malmesbury with Florence of Worcester.

This coincidence cannot be accidental. The Chronicle gives the fact, but without detail, names, or comment. The names of the kings are indeed found together in a very suspicious charter of Canterbury, dated at Bath at Whitsuntide, 966 : " Ego Kinath rex Scotorum—Ego " Maccus rex Insularum—Ego Malcolm rex Cumbrorum " —Ego Dufnal—Ego Jacob subregulus—Ego Jukil sub- " regulus—Ego Sifred subregulus." [1] Florence may have seen the charter ; or the writer of the charter may have borrowed the list from Florence. And again, in a Glastonbury charter which our author knew and quotes, we have : " Ego Kinadius rex Albaniæ—Ego Mascusius " archipirata." [2] If the variations in the list of names are sufficient to acquit either of our historians of having copied from the other, the curiously exact tenour of the whole passage in the two books points clearly to a common source, some lost panegyric on the reign of the peaceable king, about whom so many less pleasant stories were in circulation.[3]

The ship of Earl Godwin.

The other passage is less significant, and perhaps the coincidence in the language used may be capable of a similar explanation.

Apposuit ille fidei juratæ xenium ut gratiam plenam redimeret, locupletissimum sane et pulcherrimum, ratem auro rostratam, habentem octoginta milites qui haberent in brachiis singulis armillas duas, unamquamque sedecim unciarum auri, in capitibus cassides deauratas, securim Danicam in humero sinistro, hastile ferreum dextra manu gestantes, et ne singula enumerem armis omnibus instructos in quibus	Godwinus autem regi pro sua amicitia dedit trierem fabrefactam caput deauratum habentem, armamentis optimis instructam, decoris armis electisque lxxx militibus decoratam quorum unusquisque habebat duas in suis brachiis aureas armillas sexdecim uncias pendentes, loricam tricilem indutam, in capite cassidem ex parte deauratum, gladium deauratis capulis renibus accinctum, Danicam securim

---

[1] Kemble, C. D. No. 519.
[2] Kemble, C. D., No. 567.
[3] On the possibility that William of Malmesbury had seen the notice of S. Wistan in the Chronicle of Florence, see above, p. xcvi, note 6.

fulgor cum terrore certans sub auro ferrum occuleret.[2]	auro argentoque redimitam in sinistro humero pendentem, in manu sinistra clypeum cujus umbo claviquo erant deaurati, in dextra lanceam, quæ lingua Anglorum ategar appellatur.[1]

There is nothing corresponding with this in any of the Chronicles; there must have been some account of the magnificent present in some book of which now we have no other recognisable relic. And here I must apologise for the curious mistake which I have made in the note on page 229 of the first volume, saying that two of the MSS. of the Chronicle contain this story in a shorter form; what they do contain under the year 1040, is not an account of Godwin's ship, but of the exaction made for Hardicanute's fleet. {Correction of a mistake in Vol. I.}

If, on examination of these two passages, we can acquit our author of a plagiarism, which by itself would be venial, but, taken in conjunction with his absolute silence about the work of an industrious contemporary, would be in the highest degree offensive, all the other incidental concurrences of words and sequences of events in the two writers may be accounted for by their use, and necessary use, of all the common material to which they could have access.

It is hardly necessary to add that amongst the other earlier and contemporary writers whose works our author might have used, and did not, must be counted the earliest lives of Dunstan, and Oswald, the Encomium Emmæ, and the works of Turgot of Durham. To these, I think, no distinct reference either in word or matter occurs in the Gesta, and although these books as well as the Chronicle of Florence, and the Historia Novorum of Eadmer, must have been at least as accessible to him {Authors no used by William of Malmesbury.}

---

[1] Flor. Wig., M. H. B., p. 600.

[2] Above, page 229; and compare the account of a similar offering made by Godwin to king Edward: Vita Edwardi, ed. Luard, p. 327.

as the works of Fulcher of Chartres and William of Poictiers, he seems at the time of writing the book never to have heard of them. His hagiology, moreover, does not appears to have included the lives of Swithun of Winchester, or Odo of Canterbury, or of the other Canterbury saints whose lives were hammered out by Osbern.

That he has made so little use of the life of Wulfstan which he himself translated and expanded from the Anglo-Saxon, may perhaps be explained by the date at which he may be supposed to have edited it. But it is of little use to speculate on the limits of his resources, or his own reticence in quoting the works of his contemporaries. On the whole, perhaps, the writer with whose details he has most in common, for their joint contemporary portion, is Ordericus Vitalis. The two were working at the same material, and at the same time. William of Malmesbury's books must have been largely known and indefinitely copied before Ordericus ceased to write. Neither seems to have had any knowledge of the other, or of his writings. From Guibert of Nogent, too, our author might have drawn some curious augmentations of his own stores. Sigebert of Gemblours finished his work in 1112, and was certainly accessible. But our author's ambition of originality was most probably even greater than his passion for research.

Our author's contributions as an original writer and thinker.

V.— 1. In attempting to define the amount and character of the debt which English history owes to William of Malmesbury as an independent writer and thinker, we are obliged to recur to the earlier portions of the work; but on those portions a word must suffice. In the collection and arrangement of his materials he has shown a real historical, or perhaps rather antiquarian instinct. In the first two books, certainly, he has brought together all that he could find, and, where he was able to balance conflicting accounts of the same event, has shown discrimination in doing so. He was

safe for the most part in his criticisms, and his sympa- As a recorder of early history.
thies, although divided, were not torn very widely
asunder. But if his remarks were intelligent, and his
personal likings and dislikings on the whole harmless, he
has added little or nothing to the stores of the writers
who preceded him; the utmost that can be said for his
arrangement is that it is convenient, his treatment is
frequently confused, his "padding" is occasionally tan-
talising. We have most, if not all, the books he used;
his independent contributions are infinitesimal.

2. When we reach his own days, we have occasion to As a contemporary observer.
modify both our praise and our blame; the third and
fourth books cover a period about which he might, even
at second hand, have told us much and told it fairly, as
he might have told it safely. But in these books the
English spirit which, although gradually vanishing as he
approached the Conquest, breaks out occasionally and
unconsciously in the earlier books, seems to fall into
abeyance; of independent chronicle work we have very
little indeed; the sequence of events and much of the
detail are taken from the works of other writers which
are still extant. There are well-told stories, interesting
anecdotes, and illustrations of character, some small
generalisations and comparisons that are more suggestive
than they appear to be at first sight, but few real remi-
niscences even of what might have been learned from
eye-witnesses. And now the arrangement of such facts
as are recorded is puzzling, so puzzling and so desultory
that the only possible defence of it must be that our
author was resolutely determined that his work should
be read not as a book of reference, but as a literary production that would not allow skipping. I know no book
that stands more in need of a perfect index, and, whilst
I may honestly say that none of my indexes in the
works which I have edited in this series has cost me half
as much trouble as that contained in the present volume,
I confess that it is far from satisfactory. But this by
the way.

3. The fifth book and the Historia Novella remain, as being principal contributions to contemporary history. Between these we must make a distinction. The epideictic character of the first four books affects the fifth book and part of the Historia Novella; the latter parts of the Historia Novella, which alone in the whole work have a proper chronicle or annal character, are really little more than notes which the author must have meant to work up later in better form. At least this is the inference which I am obliged to draw from both their omissions and the proportions of their parts.

The fifth book in this edition contains fifty-two pages. Of these, fourteen or fifteen are almost direct extracts from Eadmer, or from documents which may be supposed to have been collected by David the Scot,[1] connected with the ecclesiastical controversies of the reign;[2] some ten are panegyrics, to a great degree secondhand, of the holy men of the time;[3] there are two or three of compliment to Robert of Gloucester,[4] which have a value of their own. Of the remainder, which is supposed to contain the chief incidents of from twenty to twenty-five years of the reign of king Henry I., more than half is concerned with events arranged in the Peterborough Chronicle,[5] and only scantily illustrated here and there with independent additions. It may be said, and truly, that everyone of these independent contributions has its value, the great fault is that there are so few of them. The imprisonment of Henry at Rouen in the reign of William Rufus,[6] his murder of

---

[1] See pages 498–509.
[2] Pages 489–493, 498.
[3] Peter of Poictiers, pp. 510, 511; the founders of Tiron, p. 512; abbot Serlo of Gloucester, p. 513; Lanzo of Lewes, pp. 513–516; Godfrey of Winchester, p. 516; and the Translation of S Cuthbert, pp. 517, 518.
[4] Pages 518–522.
[5] See especially § 391. Cf. Chron. 1087. §§ 393, 394; Chron. 1100. § 395; Chron. 1101. § 396; Chron. 1102. § 398; for the battle of Tenchebrai, Chr. 1105. § 400; Chr. 1107.
[6] Page 469.

Conan;[1] the use made by the Norman malcontents of his English marriage;[2] the details of the surrender of Shrewsbury,[3] of the fate of the Montgomeries,[4] of the battle of Tenchebrai, of the Scottish succession in the sons of Malcolm and Margaret;[5] the planting of the Flemings in Roos,[6] the relations between England and Flanders;[7] the stories about Philip I. and Lewis VI.;[8] the sketch of count Robert of Meulan, and bishop Roger of Salisbury, whom he knew personally;[9] the comprehensive note about Ireland and the Irish;[10] and that on Siward of Norway, are all valuable in themselves,[11] and, even when and where they can be traced to other authorities, occurring where they do, they are illustrations of history not to be despised. The notices of Henry's character and administration are still more important. Yet on reviewing the whole, and considering that the twenty-five years so briefly and discursively treated are the portion of our national history, during which the coercive influences of positive government, as distinct from the disciplinary lessons of civil war and its

The general result disappointing.

---

[1] Page 469. Cf. Freeman, William Rufus, i. 257; ii. 517.

[2] Page 471. Cf. Freeman, William Rufus, i. 382, 389.

[3] Page 472. The appearance of Ralph of Seez, afterwards archbishop of Canterbury, at the siege of Shrewsbury, and in the rebel camp, has yet to be accounted for; see Will. Ruf., i. 430.

[4] Page 473. Cf. Freeman, Norman Conquest, i. 449, 450.

[5] Pages 476, 477. Cf. Freeman, William Rufus, ii. 22.

[6] Page 477.

[7] Pages 479–482

[8] Page 482; and especially the story of the two clever sons of the count who exhibited their scholarship and acuteness before pope Calixtus when he visited the north of France in 1119, and met Henry at Gisors. Hermann of Laon mentions two sons of Ranulf, Henry's Chancellor, studying in the school of Anselm of Laon, under William of Corbeuil, afterwards archbishop; Guibert, Opp., p. 536. So little is known of Ranulf the Chancellor, whose daughter was married to Ralph, son of Hugh of Montpinçon, Ord. Vit., v. 17, and who was, probably, a layman, that one is tempted to ask whether there is any confusion between the two families in Hermann's story. The pope was at Laon the same year: see Jaffé-Wattenbach, p. 790; and probably the same week.

[9] Pages 483, 484.

[10] Page 485.

[11] Page 486.

experiences of misery, were working upon our forefathers to make them one nation, we are obliged to conclude that a great opportunity was lost, and that the result is disappointing. We should not expect too much, but our author had capacity and he had opportunity. Without him we should be much poorer than we are. We had no right to expect that he should unite the qualities of Thucydides with those of Herodotus, or combine the merits of Hallam with those of Hume, and we are not ungrateful. But he himself would probably answer that he was an historian of events, not of influences or of tendencies, much less of influences and tendencies that were in his time altogether below the surface; that the years were years of peace and the events few and uninteresting, an illustration of the saying, "Happy is the nation that has no history." Still he might have given us dates and told us where the king spent his Christmas, Easter, and Whitsuntide. In justification of the censure I need only observe that, although, between the first and second recensions of the fifth book, the writer seems to indicate, that seven or eight years had elapsed,[1] he adds nothing whatever to fill up the gap; in fact, to his mind the history of the reign of Henry I. was as complete when it was brought down to the year 1120 as when it was re-edited up to the year 1128. As a literary production it was, like the account of the siege of Malta in Vertot, complete when the author had finished it.[2]

Note of omissions. 4. A comparison of the portions of the work of Florence and his continuator, and of Henry of Huntingdon, with the corresponding portions of the Gesta, will prove at a glance the weakness of our author's position, and to prove this in detail would be tedious and out of place. Taking, however, a few prominent facts,—and

---

[1] See page 518, note; and vol. i., pref., pp. xxxi sq.

[2] Sutherland, Achievements of the Knights of Malta, i. p. xi.

the important incidents are prominent because they are few,—we may leave the conclusion to the reader.

In the fifth book, after the description of the battle of Tenchebrai, there is no attempt at consecutive narration. The only events that are in their places are the war with Lewis VI.,[1] the death of queen Matilda,[2] the catastrophe of the white ship,[3] and the second marriage of the king.[4] The affairs of the English Church are designedly relegated to the Gesta Pontificum; the episodes on foreign history crowd out the little domestic history that the other writers thought worth commemorating. The marriage of the king's daughter with the emperor Henry V. comes in merely as a peg on which to hang the story of the investiture controversy, and yet it was an event which must have been seen, even at the earliest date at which the composition of the Gesta can be supposed to have been undertaken, to be a leading influence in the immediate distance. The clustering together of events under the several heads of foreign affairs, dealings with France and Flanders,[5] is illustrated with no dates to make their sequence intelligible. The movements of the king in England or between England and Normandy, which generally are noted in the Chronicle faithfully, and as faithfully followed by Florence and Henry of Huntingdon, are, as a rule, unnoticed. The great constitutional question about the election and consecration of archbishop Thurstan, far too important to be consigned to the Gesta Pontificum, is not even mentioned. It is true, as I have already remarked, that the period was, for internal history, dull and uneventful; and it is also true that our author aimed at being an historian, not a chronicler or an annalist; but it is no

Want of consecutive arrangement.

Important omissions.

---

[1] Pages 480, 481.
[2] Page 493.
[3] Pages 496, 497.
[4] Page 495.
[5] The notes on pp. 478, 479, &c., on the pension paid by the kings to the counts of Flanders, should be compared with the copies of the treaties printed by Hearne in the Liber Niger Scaccarii, i. 7-23.

part of the intrinsic character of an historian, or even of a monastic historian, to shut his eyes to the movements of the world around him, or, contenting himself with generalisations of causes and consequences, to neglect his duty of trying to get contemporary events into their proper places. And our author's great merits exemplified in other aspects of his work, his insight into character, his epigrammatic power, the really philosophic perspicacity which he occasionally displays, only make this negligence more provoking.

The Historia Novella; first book.

5. In the first book of the Historia Novella some attempts are made to fill up the blanks; but nothing is done to illustrate the history and fate of William, son of Robert of Normandy, which assuredly had its direct bearing on the complications of the time; and the last five years of the reign are absolutely blank. There was, perhaps, little to tell; Henry of Huntingdon tells it all in a couple of pages, and the Peterborough Chronicle in three.[1] The five years may have been years of misery, or of recovery; they were years of peace; they must, to all appearance, have been years of stagnation. Still we need not have been left to find it out for ourselves. The facts which have been adduced in illustration of our author's biography must account for much. He had dropped the study of history; he was too busy reading and transcribing to watch the things that wanted watching; then were no sounds loud enough to pierce the walls of the Malmesbury library, or if there were, the librarian was too busy to heed them. There is one section which may be regarded as an exception to this generalisation; a summary of annals from the thirty-first year of the king, into which are crowded a cattle plague, an ecclesiastical law suit, and a note of the acceptance of the legation by the archbishop of Canter-

Our author engaged in other pursuits during the period.

---

[1] Vol. i. pp. xxiv sq.

bury. Of these one at least, the last, is misplaced by four or five years.¹

The history of the measures taken to secure the succession is all that the writer considers important,² and the incidents of the death of Henry, and accession and coronation of Stephen, are told in a straightforward way. It is probable that we owe to our author the exact date for the last event. Stephen was, he tells us, crowned on the 22nd of December 1135.³ The Chronicle says on Midwinter day. Our author adds that the day was Sunday, which fixes it to the 22nd; and, having exerted himself so far as to give us a date, leaves us to make out the sequence of events for ourselves. And the year 1136 was a very eventful year. Immediately after the funeral of Henry I., Stephen had to go into the north; at Easter he was in London; soon after Easter Robert of Gloucester arrives and makes his terms, then follows the council at Oxford and the publication of the charter.⁴ All this is told briefly but consecutively; the troubles that fill up the second half of the year, the revolts in Eastern and Western England, which are described by Henry of Huntingdon and in the Gesta Stephani, are not so much as mentioned, although our author was writing within three years of the events. For the year 1137 we have no detail of domestic history; the theatre of politics was Normandy, and the omission is so far forth accounted for. But it is an astounding fact that the great struggle with the Scots in the following year is altogether ignored; there is not a single word about the invasion or about the battle of the Standard.

Valuable particulars touching the succession.

Coronation of Stephen.

Scantiness of events in 1136 and 1137.

Omission of note on the Scottish invasion.

6. The second book begins well with the series of events that led to the break-up of the king's government; his attempt to get hold of the castles of the bishops, the council of Oxford, the arrest of Roger of

The second book of the Historia Novella.

---

¹ Pages 534, 535; compare Florence and Henry of Huntingdon for the facts and dates.
² Pages 527–537.
³ Page 538.
⁴ Pages 539–542.

PREFACE.

Its value.

Salisbury and his kinsmen, and the council of Winchester, the arrival and reception of the empress; the capture and recovery of the castle of Malmesbury, and a very few points of the military history of the autumn. The year ends with the death of bishop Roger. Although we miss in these details the guidance which we might have expected, to secure us through the puzzling incidents recorded in the Gesta Stephani, we have otherwise no reason to complain. The narrative of the year 1140,

Anarchic character of the year 1140.

on the contrary, is as confused as might be expected from the anarchical condition of things in general and our author's position at Malmesbury. The events whatever they were, and we are bound to say that Henry of Huntingdon has as little to say about them as our author himself, had not, at the time of writing, fallen into their places either as to sequence or as to relative importance. The notice of the seizure of Devizes by Robert Fitz Hubert, and of the negotiations between Henry of Blois, the archbishop, and the queen at Whitsuntide, are, however, important contributions to the history of the struggle. And this brings us to the end of the book.

Events of 1141.

7. The great crisis of the year 1141, the siege of Lincoln, the battle there and capture of the king; the triumph of the empress; her reception as sovereign; the

Our author at the council of Winchester.

great council of Winchester which our author witnessed himself; the recoil of the wheel of fortune, in the capture of the earl of Gloucester; the negotiations for exchange of prisoners, and the deliberations which ended practically in the recognition of Stephen: these are the contents of the third book. They are told by our author in his best manner, and complemented with an argued panegyric on the earl of Gloucester, his patron.

Close of the work.

The year 1142 closes the history. Our author watches, but has little to tell that lies beneath the surface. It was a year of exhaustion; of armistice and uneasy negotiation between parties who neither trusted nor had reason to trust one another. The empress's party, although strong in the influence of her brother and his great ability, was not strong enough to conquer the party of Stephen and his queen without help from Normandy and Anjou; and count Geoffrey, who did not care much about his wife, but was desirous, on his own behalf and his son's, to keep hold on Normandy, was by no means ready to sacrifice the hereditary policy of his fathers for the very uncertain prospects of his children. Earl Robert was sent to fetch him; Stephen took advantage of his absence to renew active hostilities. The earl returns and recovers his position; the empress is besieged in Oxford, the earl collects forces to relieve the castle, but before they arrive she escapes, and her escape is the last thing that William of Malmesbury has recorded. He does it with a promise to clear up matters in a fourth book. That fourth book, so far as we know, was never even begun. Promises of a fourth book.

8. It would be wrong to base any serious judgment of our author's character as an historian on the scanty and scrambling notes of the Historia Novella; they are so obviously imperfect, and, to a great extent, disorderly in their arrangement. Yet they are in themselves very valuable, and we cannot help feeling that if he had lived to digest them into the order, and plan and style, of the five books of the Gesta, we might have lost rather than gained. We should, no doubt, have had some clever stories and neat hits at character and person, some instructive generalities, and some suggestive lights, but in all probability the sequence would have become more irregular, and the details more confused and confusing. The Historia Novella little more than a collection of notes.

We lay down our pen with a mixed feeling. Our author has great claims on our equitable consideration. He was a very learned man and an apt, well-furnished, universal scholar. The ideal he set for himself was a very high ideal; we are not to disparage it because it may not be our own. His personal character was not General conclusion.

that of an earnest partisan; nor was his judicial faculty that of a judge; he wrote for the ear of great men, not simply for the love of his subject, yet he is not a flatterer; he is not an impartial critic; he is not an unsympathising cosmopolitan. He has a distinct personality; he is not the able editor, although not a few of his more ambitious sections have a little of the look of leading articles. He is careful to guard himself wherever he suspects suspiciousness. He is ingenuous enough where he is not forced by his position or his pretension to be on his guard. So the value of his book varies on every page, and any minute estimate of our debt to him would involve a criticism on every section. But we may fairly conclude that, considering his character; his aim in writing; his learning and sincerity; his position in the development of historical study, and the interest which his works have from the first inspired—an interest to which the most glaring of his weaknesses contributed in no small proportion, —the history, the literature, and the culture of the English race would have been much poorer without him.

I have to mention that the poem "Frequenter cogi-" tans," which, as occurring in MSS. in connexion with the extracts from the Gesta, was printed, as I supposed, for the first time, in the preface to the first volume, had been edited from a Notre Dame MS. as long ago as 1847, by Edelstand Duméril, in Poésies populaires Latines du Moyen-Age, pp. 128-136; and again, in 1854, among the Poésies inédites du Moyen-Age, pp. 313-326, by the same editor from a Douai MS., with a very large number of additional stanzas.

Cuddesdon, August 1, 1889.

WILLELMI MONACHI MALMESBIRIENSIS
DE GESTIS REGUM ANGLORUM
LIBRI QUINQUE.

PROLOGUS

IN LIBRUM TERTIUM.

Incipit Prologus Libri Tertii.

DE WILLELMO rege scripserunt, diversis incitati causis, et Normanni et Angli: illi ad nimias efferati sunt laudes, bona malaque juxta in cælum prædicantes; isti, pro gentilibus inimicitiis, fœdis dominum suum proscidere convitiis. Ego autem, quia utriusque gentis sanguinem traho, dicendi tale temperamentum servabo: bene gesta, quantum cognoscere potui, sine fuco palam efferam;[1] perperam acta, quantum sufficiat scientiæ, leviter et quasi[2] transeunter attingam; ut nec mendax culpetur historia, nec illum nota inuram censoria cujus cuncta pene, etsi non laudari, excusari certe possunt opera. Itaque de illo talia narrabo libenter et morose quæ sint inertibus incitamento, promptis exemplo, usui præsentibus, jocunditati sequentibus. Verum in his protrahendis non multum temporis expendam impendium, quæ nulli emolumentum, immo legenti fastidium, scribenti pariant odium. Satis superque sufficiunt qui genuino molari facta

Norman and English estimates of William.

Our author, akin to both races, will treat impartially about him.

He will not devote much time to trifles.

---

[1] *efferam*] proferam, Bc. | [2] *quasi*] om. Ce.

bonorum lacerent. Mihi hæc placet provincia, ut mala, quantum queo, sine veritatis dispendio extenuem; bona non nimis ventose collaudem. De qua moderatione, ut æstimo, veri qui erunt arbitri me nec timidum nec inelegantem pronuntiabunt. Hoc itaque non solum de Willelmo, sed et de duobus filiis ejus stylus observabit, ut nihil nimie, nihil nisi vere dicatur: quorum primus parum quod laudetur egit, præter primos regni dies; tota vita dampno provincialium comparans favorem militum. Secundus, patri quam fratri morigeratior, invictum animum inter adversa et prospera rexit: cujus si expeditiones attendas, ignores cautior an audacior fuerit; si fortunas aspicias, hæsites beatior, aut boni eventus indigentior, fuerit. Sed de talibus tempus erit cum lector arbitretur. Nunc, tertium volumen incepturus, satis reor egisse ut attentum et docilem facerem; ipse sibi benigne persuadebit ut benivolus sit.

The same method will be observed for the three Norman reigns.

EXPLICIT PROLOGUS.

WILLELMI MALMESBIRIENSIS
DE GESTIS REGUM ANGLORUM
LIBER TERTIUS.

Incipit Liber Tertius de Adventu Normannorum in Angliam.

§ 229. ROBERTUS,[1] alter filius Ricardi secundi, post-quam septem annis gloriose ducatum Normanniæ tenuit, Jerosolimam pergere mentem appulit. Habebat tunc filium septennem, ex concubina susceptum, cujus speciem in choreis saltitantis forte conspicatus, non abstinuit quin sibi nocte conjungeret; deinceps unice dilexit, et aliquamdiu justæ uxoris loco habuit. Puer ex ea editus, Willelmus a nomine abavi dictus: cujus magnitudinem futuram matris sompnium portendebat, quo intestina sua per totam Normanniam et Angliam extendi et dilatari viderat; ipso quoque momento quo, partu laxato, in vitam effusus pusio humum attigit, ambas manus junco, quo pavimenti pulvis cavebatur, implevit, stricte quod corripuerat compugnans. Ostensum visum mulierculis, læto plausu gannientibus; obstetrix quoque fausto omine acclamat puerum regem futurum. *Duke Robert goes to Jerusalem. His son William. His mother's dream. His adventure at his birth.*

§ 230. Paratis ergo omnibus quæ Jerosolimitani itineris viaticum informarent, apud Fiscannum concilium proceribus indicitur. Ibi, jubente patre, in nomen et fidem Willelmi ab omnibus juratur: Gislebertus comes tutor pupilli constituitur; tutela tutoris regi Francorum Henrico assignatur. Roberto cœptam *Council at Fecamp. Oaths sworn to William.*

---

[1] *Robertus*] Rodbertus, At. Bc.¹ Bq. Cd. Cm.; Rotbertus, Al. Bc.²

viam expediente, Normanni omnes communi umbone patriam per sua quisque munimenta tutari, parvum herum ex amore venerari. Stetit hæc fides usque ad famam obitus ejus; qua ubique gentium disseminata, cum fato mutatus amor: mox quisque sua munire oppida, turres agere, frumenta comportare, causas aucupari quibus quamprimum a puero discidium meditarentur. Inter hæc ille, haud equidem reor sine Dei auxilio qui eum tanto principaturum præviderat imperio, tutus adolescebat; cum solus pene Gislebertus æquum et bonum armis defensitaret suis. Ceteri studiis partium agebantur. Jam vero interfecto Gisleberto a Radulfo patruele suo, ubique cædes, ubique ignes versabantur. Clarissima olim patria, intestinis dissensionibus exulcerata, pro latronum libito dividebatur, ut merito posset querimoniam facere, "Væ terræ cujus rex puer est!" At ille, ubi primum per ætatem potuit, militiæ insignia a rege Francorum accipiens, provinciales in spem quietis erexit. Sator discordiarum erat Guido quidam, Burgundus a patre, nepos Ricardi secundi e filia; infantiam cum Willelmo cucurrerat, tunc quoque januas adolescentiæ pariter urgebant. Convictus familiaritatem, familiaritas amicitias paraverat. Huc accedebat quod ei Brionium et Vernonium castella dederat, nihil pro consanguinitate negandum putans. Horum Burgundus immemor, afflictis criminibus quibus id merito facere videretur, abalienavit se a comite. Longum est et non necessarium si persequar quæ hinc inde acta, quæ castella capta: repererat enim perfidia socios Nigellum vicecomitem Constantini, Rannulfum vicecomitem Bajocensem, Haimonem dentatum, avum Roberti qui nostro tempore in Anglia multarum possessionum incubator extitit.[1] Cum his per totam Normanniam grassabatur prædo improbissimus, inani spe ad comitatum illectus. Ne-

---

[1] Robert FitzHamon, lord of Glamorgan, and father-in-law of earl Robert of Gloucester.

cessitas regem tutorem excivit ut desperatis partibus pupilli succurreret. Itaque paternæ benivolentiæ recordatus, quod eum favore suo in regnum sublimaverat, apud Walesdunes in defectores irruit: cæsa illic multa eorum milia; multi fluminis Olnæ rapacitate intercepti, quod, in arcto locati, equos ad transvadandos vortices instimularent. Gwido, vix elapsus, Brionio se recepit: inde per Willelmum expulsus, non ferens probri famam, ultro Burgundiam, nativum scilicet solum, contendit. Nec ibi inquietus animus quietem invenit: nam a comite illius provinciæ, fratre suo Willelmo, quem insidiis impetiverat, fugatus, incompertum quem finem habuit. Nigellus et Radulfus in fidem recepti: Haimo in acie cæsus, cujus insignis violentia laudatur quod ipsum regem equo dejecerit; quare a concurrentibus stipatoribus interemptus, pro fortitudinis miraculo regis jussu tumulatus est egregie. Tulit hujus gratiæ stipendium rex Henricus, a Normanno domino contra Gaufredum Martellum apud Molendinum Herle, quod castrum in Andegavensi regione est, summa vi adjutus; nam jam in virile robur excreverat, majoribus natu et pluribus solus metuendus, solus caput discriminibus inferre, solus vel [1] cum paucis in confertissimos diversæ partis insilire: quapropter ab illa expeditione laudatæ fortitudinis specimen, et amicitiarum apud regem culmen, retulit; adeo ut quasi paterno consilio sæpe admoneret ne ad pericula promptus vitam suam despiceret, quæ esset Francis decori, Normanniæ tutamento, utrisque exemplo.

§ 231. Eo tempore erat comes Andegavorum Gaufredus cognomento Martellus, quod ipse sibi [2] usurpaverat quia videbatur sibi felicitate quadam omnes obsistentes contundere. Denique dominum suum, comitem Pictavensem, aperto marte cepit, ferreisque vin-

---

[1] *vel*] om. Cd. Ce.¹ | [2] *sibi*] nomen, ins. Cd.

culis innodatum ad ignobiles pacis conditiones adduxit; Burdegala et confinibus urbibus cederet, de ceteris annuum vectigal pensitaret: sed ille, ut creditur, pro ferri injuria et ciborum inedia, beneficio opportunæ mortis post triduum perpetuæ ignominiæ exemptus est. Tum Martellus, ne quid deesset impudentiæ, novercam defuncti matrimonio sibi copulavit, fratres in tutelam recipiens quoad possent principatui regendo sufficere. Mox Teodbaldi Blesiensis comitis ingressus limites, urbem Turonicam obsedit: ipsum, civibus suis auxilium ferre volentem, consortio ærumnæ implicuit; siquidem captus Teodbaldus, et in ergastulo reclusus, urbem sibi omnibusque suis heredibus in posterum abjuravit. Pudendam miseriam hominis quis dixerit? ut, pro ambitione quantulæcunque vitæ, tantæ urbis dominio successores suos perpetuo fraudaret; licet severiores plerumque aliorum arbitri simus, quam ipsi nobis consulere noverimus si forte in talibus deprehensi fuerimus. Ita Martellus, tantarum virium augmento turgidus, etiam Normannum comitem Alentii castelli possessione vellicavit, pronis in perfidiam habitatoribus. Qua is irritatus injuria, par pari retulit; et Danfruntum, quod erat tunc comitis Andegavorum, obsidione coronavit. Nec mora, obsessorum querelis commonitus Gaufredus, non segnis advolat innumero stipatus milite. Nuntio advenientis accepto, Willelmus Rogerium de Monte Gomerico, et Willelmum filium Osberni, exploratum mittit: illi, pro alacritate juventæ, brevi multa miliaria progressi, equitantemque Martellum conspicati, certiorem de domini sui audacia faciunt. Ille contra fremere, immania minari, postridie[1] se illuc venturum, ostensurum mundo quam præstet in armis Andegavensis Normanno; simul, eximia arrogantia, colorem equi sui, et armorum insignia, quæ habiturus sit, insinuat. At exploratores,

---

[1] *postridie*] post triduum, Aa. Cd.

non minori fastu eadem de Willelmo denunciantes, regrediuntur, et suos in certamen accendunt. Hæc ideo seriatim retuli, ut Martelli tumor legentibus elucesceret. Ceterum, nihil tunc de solita magnanimitate ausus, antequam in manus veniretur terga ostendit. Quo audito, Alentini se dedidere, pacti membrorum salutem : post etiam Danfrontini feliciora signa secuti.

Boasts of the two parties.

Geoffrey retires.

§ 232. Posterioribus annis rebellavit Willelmus comes de Archis, patruus ejus sed nothus, a primis auspiciis ducatus infidus et versipellis ; nam et in obsidione Danfronti clam profugerat, et multis sæpe animi sui latebras aperuerat. Quapropter Willelmus quibusdam, quos fideles falso arbitrabatur, firmitatem castelli commiserat ; verum ille astu quo callebat, multa largiendo, plura pollicendo, in suas partes eosdem traduxit. Munitione igitur potitus, bellum domino suo denuntiavit. Ille solito more alacerrime Archas obsedit, dissuadentibus amicis ; palam professus, nihil latrones ausuros si in conspectum ejus venissent. Nec promissio fide caruit ; namque plusquam trecenti milites, qui pabulatum et populatum processerant, eo pene solo conspecto, intra munitiones refugere. Dux sine sanguine rem peragere volens, obfirmato contra Archas castello, ad alia quæ magis urgebant bella conversus est : simul quia sciebat regem Francorum, jam pridem, nescio qua simultate, sibi infensum, ad opem obsesso ferendam adventare ; namque prædicandi moderaminis consilio, quamvis justiorem causam habere videretur, cum eo decernere ferro cavebat, cui et pro sacramento et pro suffragio obnoxius erat. Reliquit tamen primates aliquos qui impetum regium tardarent ; quorum astutia insidiis exceptus, Isembardum Pontivi comitem coram se obtruncari, Hugonem Pardulfum capi, merito ingemuit. Nec multo post, eo dulcem Franciam, quia res male cesserat, repetente, comes Arcensis, fame tabidus et vix ossibus hærens, deditioni consensit, ad exemplum clementiæ, ad indicium in-

Rebellion of the Count of Arques.

William besieges Arques.

The king of the French threatens him.

Fall of the Count of Ponthieu and capture of Hugh Bardulf.

Retreat of the king and surrender of Arques.

dustriæ, vitæ et membris reservatus. Hujusce obsidionis intervallo populus castri quod Molendinis dicitur, exolescens, ad partes regis incentore quodam Galterio transiit. Imponitur ibi non segnis militum manus, præfecto Guidone fratre comitis Pictavensis. Is aliquantis diebus sedulo militiæ munia executus est; verum crebrescente fama Arcensis victoriæ, Franciam elapsus, non leve incrementum accessit ducalis gloriæ.

§ 233. Nec rex Henricus otio indulsit, quin gruniret exercitus suos ludibrio fuisse Willelmo: coactis itaque omnibus viribus, et copiis bipartitis, totam inundavit Normanniam: ipse de parte Galliæ[1] Celticæ, quæ inter Garumnam et Sequanam fluvios jacet, quicquid militum erat suo ductu trahens; Odonem fratrem populo Galliæ Belgicæ, quæ est inter Renum et Sequanam, præficiens. Eodem modo Willelmus suos, qua poterat animositate, divisit, juxta regis castra sensim obambulans, quæ jam in Ebroicensi pago metabatur, ut nec cominus pugnandi[2] copiam faceret, nec provinciam coram se vastari sineret. Duces ejus, Robertus comes Aucensis, Hugo Gornacensis, Hugo Montis fortis, Willelmus Crispinus, ad castellum quod Mortuum mare vocatur, infestis signis contra Odonem constitere. Nec ille pro numero militum, quo tumebat, moram pugnæ fecit, sed parumper resistere ausus, mox impetum Normannorum non ferens, terga nudavit, omen fugæ primus auspicatus: ibi dum Guido Pontivi comes studiosius ultioni fratris intendit, captus, fatalem familiæ suæ manum exhorruit; præterea plures alii, præcellentes opibus,[3] turgentes majorum natalibus. Hunc successum, ex advenientibus[4] cognitum, Willelmus circum regis tentoria nocte intempesta præ-

---

[1] *Galliæ*] Galliciæ, Aa. At.
[2] *pugnandi*] pugnando, Ce.¹
[3] *opibus*] operibus, Cd. Ce.¹ Bk. Bq.
[4] *advenientibus*] adventantibus, Aa. Al.

conari curavit; quo audito, post aliquot dies quos in Normannia egit, refugit in Franciam: nec multo post tempore, discurrentibus utrobique nuntiis, pacifice conventum ut regii captivi absolverentur, comes erepta vel eripienda Martello jure vendicaret legitimo. *Terms of peace.*

§ 234. Longum est et non necessarium referre quantae inter eos contentiones versatae sint, quomodo Willelmus semper superiorem manum retulerit. Quid quod inaestimabili praesumptione fortitudinis, nunquam subito, nec nisi praenuntiata die, illum aggredi dignatus, nostri temporis morem animi magnitudine contempserit? Illud quoque praetereo, quod, iterum ruptis amicitiis, rex Henricus Normanniam ingressus, per pagum Oximensem [1] usque ad fluvium Divae pervenerit, jactitans solum oceanum progressioni suae esse obstaculum: verum Willelmus, qui se videret propter fidei dissimulationem immoderate premi, tunc tandem consciae virtutis arma concutiens, regias copias, quae circa flumen erant, nam pars paulo ante, ejus adventu audito, transvadaverat, tanta internicie cecidit ut nihil postea Francia plus metueret [2] quam Normannorum ferociam irritare. Terminum discordiarum fecit properata mors Henrici, nec multo post Martelli. Rex moriens Baldewino comiti Flandriae tutelam admodum parvuli Philippi filii delegavit. Is erat fide et sapientia aeque mirandus, praeviridantibus membris incanus, praeterea regiae sororis connubio sublimis: filia ejus Matildis Willelmo jamdudum nupserat; foemina nostro tempore singulare prudentiae [3] speculum, pudoris culmen. Hinc factum est, ut pupilli et generi mediator tumores ducum et provincialium salubri proposito compesceret. *Constant success of William. Henry's third attempt on Normandy; Defeated by William. Death of the king and of Geoffrey Martel. Baldwin of Flanders guardian to the young king Philip.*

§ 235. Sed, quia totiens Martelli se occasio ingessit, genealogiam comitum Andegavensium, quantum [4] relatoris *Descent of the counts of Anjou.*

---

[1] *Oximensem*] Eximensem, Ao. Bc. By.; Exiomensem, Al.
[2] *metueret*] metuerat, Cd. Ce.¹
[3] *prudentiae*] om. Ce.¹
[4] *quantum*] quam, Ce.

nostri memoria attigit, transcurram, præfata diverti-
culi venia. Fulco antiquior, pluribus annis, usque ad
senium, illum moderatus comitatum, multa fecit industrie, multa egregie. Unum omnino est quo eum notari
audierim, quod Herbertum comitem Cenomannensem,
Sanctonas sponsione urbis illectum, in medio colloquio
ab apparitoribus arctari, et quibus placuit conditionibus irretiri fecit. Cetera[1] sanctus et integer, extremis
fere annis filio sæpe dicto Gaufredo principatu vivens
cessit. Ille in provinciales immane quam dure, in
ipsum collatorem honoris quam superbe actitans, jussusque magistratum et fasces deponere, adeo sibi arro-
gavit ut contra patrem arma sumeret. Tunc senis
frigidus jam et effœtus sanguis ira incaluit, filiumque
juveniliter insultantem paucis diebus maturiori consilio
adeo infregit, ut, per aliquot miliaria sellam dorso
vehens,[2] pronum se cum sarcina ante pedes patris
exponeret. Ille, cui vetus animositas adhuc palpitaret,
assurgens, et pede jacentem pulsans, "Victus es, tan-
"dem victus," ter quaterque ingeminat: superfuit
victo spiritus, et quidem egregius, ut responderet,
"Tibi pater soli, quia pater[3] es, victus; ceteris om-
"nibus invictus sum." Hoc relatu tumentis animus
emollitus, patriaque pietate verecundiam prolis con-
solatus, principatui restituit, monitum ut maturius
se ageret, provincialium fortunas et pacem suum
esse decus ad extraneos, commodum ad domesticos.
Eodem anno veteranus, et secularibus stipendiis emeritus, jam de animæ viatico cogitans, Jerosolimam
adiit: ibi a duobus servis, sacramento adactis ut quod
juberet facerent, per publicum ad sepulcrum Domini
nudus, inspectantibus Turchis, tractus est; alter restem[4]
lineam[5] collo ejus intorserat, alter flagris terga expo-
liati urgebat. Inter hæc ille clamabat, "Accipe, Do-

Fulk the father of Geoffrey Martel.

Rebellion of the son.

His humilia-tion.

His boast.

Fulk's pil-grimage to Jerusalem, and penance there.

---

[1] *cetera*] ceterum, Aa.
[2] *vehens*] evehens, Aa. Al. Cd.
[3] *pater*] meus, ins. Cd.
[4] *restem*] vectem, Bc. Bk. Bq.; rastem, Al.
[5] *lineam*] ligneum, Bc. Bk. Bq.

"mine, miserum Fulconem, perjurum tuum, fugitivum
"tuum; confessam dignare animam, Domine Jesu
"Christe." Nec tamen quod desiderabat tunc impetravit; sed, domum placide regressus, post aliquot annos obiit. Filii ejus Gaufredi præruptam audaciam superior narratio patefecit. Is moriens Gaufredo, sororis filio, hereditatem suam contradidit, sed industriam seculi transfundere non potuit: nam ille, simplicium morum juvenis, magis in ecclesiis orare quam arma tractare consuetus, homines regionis illius, qui quiete victitare nescirent, in contemptum sui excitavit; quare, tota terra prædonibus exposita, Fulco frater illius ultro ducatum corripuit. Fulco, Rechin dictus, quod, germani simplicitati[1] crebro infrendens, ad ultimum honore spoliatum perpetua custodia coercuerit, habuit uxorem quæ, pruritu altioris nominis allecta, illo relicto, Philippo regi Francorum nupsit; quam is, immemor dicti,

Ovid, Met. ii. 846.

"Non bene conveniunt, nec in una sede morantur,
"Majestas et amor,"

tanta venere ardebat, ut, cum imperare aliis omnibus cuperet, ab ea sibi imperari æquanimiter ferret. Denique omnium digitis quasi fatuus notari, ab omni orbe Christiano excommunicari, propter ejus libidinem, aliquantis annis sustinuit. Filii Fulconis fuerunt Gesfridus,[2] et Fulco: Gesfridus, cognomen Martelli hereditarium sortitus, suis sudoribus ampliavit; tanta pace et quiete per terras illas parta, quantam nemo[3] viderit, nemo visurus sit; quapropter suorum insidiis necatus, egregiæ probitatis decus luit. Fulco, in regimine succedens, adhuc[4] in rebus humanis versatur; de quo forsitan tempore regis Henrici dicturus, nunc de Willelmo explanabo quod restat.

---

[1] *simplicitati*] supplicitati, Ce.¹
[2] *Gesfridus*] Gelfridus, Cd.; Gosfridus, Bc.
[3] *nemo viderit*] om. Bc. Bk. Bq. Ce.
[4] *adhuc*] Fulk surrendered Anjou to his son Geoffrey in 1129, became king of Jerusalem in 1131, and died in 1143.

§ 236. Ille, ubi civile discidium multo exercitio composuit, rem majoris gloriæ animo sequens, terras olim Normanniæ appendices, quæ longo usu insoleverant, restituere intendit; Cenomannicum dico comitatum et Brittanniam. Quorum Cenomannis, dudum[1] a Martello succensa, et domino suo Hugone[2] privata, tunc nuper aliquantulum sub Herberto Hugonis filio respiraverat: qui, ut tutior contra Andegavensem esset, Willelmo se manibus dederat, in ejus fidelitatem sacramento juratus; præterea filiam ipsius petierat et desponderat, quæ priusquam nubilibus annis matura conjugio fieret, ille morbo decessit, heredem sibi Willelmum pronuntians, adjuratis civibus ne alium susciperent: habituri, si vellent, lenem et probum dominum; si nollent, recti sui exactorem immodicum. Quo defuncto, Cenomannenses magis ad Gualterium Medantinum declinantes, cui soror Hugonis nupserat, sero tandem ut Willelmum susciperent resipuere, gravibus sæpe dampnis admoniti. Illud fuit tempus quo Haroldus invitus Normanniam importuna sibi aura evectus est: quem, sicut supra Above § 228. dictum est, Willelmus in Britannicum expeditionem duxit, volens ejus manum explorare; simul et strictiori consilio apparatum ostentans suum, conspicaturo quantum præstaret Anglicis bipennibus ensis Normannicus. Alanus tunc ibi comes, viridis juventa et præcellens robore, Eudonem patruum vinxerat, multa egregie fecerat: Willelmum non solum non timebat, sed et irritabat: at ille Britanniam ut hereditarium solum calumpnians, quod eam Carolus Rolloni cum filia[3] Gisla dederat, brevi effecit ut, ultro Alanus adveniens, suppliciter se suaque dederet. Sed, quia de Brittannia parum alias dicturus sum, hic quoddam miraculum, quod illis ferme diebus in Namnetis civitate contigit, paucis inseram.

---

[1] *dudum*] olim, Bc. By.
[2] *Hugone*] om. Ce.¹
[3] *filia*] sua, ins. Aa. Al.

De duobus clericis sociis.

§ 237. Erant in urbe illa duo clerici, nondum patientibus annis, presbyteri; id officium magis precario quam bonæ vitæ merito ab episcopo loci exegerant: denique alterius miserandus exitus superstitem instruxit quam fuerint antea in inferni lapsum ambo præcipites. Ceterum quod ad scientiam litterarum tendit ita edocti, ut aut parum aut nihil ipsis deberent artibus; a reptantibus infantiæ rudimentis adeo jocundis amicitiæ officiis æmuli, ut, juxta Comici dictum, "Manibus "pedibusque conando, periculum etiam, si necesse esset, "capitis pro invicem facerent." Quare die quadam liberiorem animum[1] a curis forinsecis nacti, in secreto conclavi hujusmodi sententias fudere: Pluribus se annis nunc litteris, nunc seculi lucris, mentes exercuisse, nec satiasse, magis ad distortum quam ad rectum intentas: inter hæc, illum acerbum diem sensim appropinquare qui societatis suæ inextricabile in vita vinculum dirumperet; unde præveniendum mature, ut fides, quæ conglutinarat viventes, primo mortuum comitaretur ad manes. Paciscuntur ergo ut quisquis eorum ante obiret, superstiti, vel dormienti vel vigilanti, appareret infra triginta proculdubio dies: si fiat, edocturus quod, secundum Platonicos, mors spiritum non extinguat, sed ad principium sui Deum tanquam e carcere emittat; sin minus, Epicureorum sectæ concedendum, qui opinantur animam corpore solutam in aerem evanescere, in auras effluere. Ita data acceptaque fide, cotidianis colloquiis sacramentum frequentabant. Nec multum in medio, et ecce, mors repentine imminens indignantem halitum uni eorum violenter extraxit. Remansit alter, et serio de socii sponsione cogitans, et jam jamque affuturum præstolans cassa opinione triginta diebus ventos pavit; quibus elapsis, cum desperans aliis negotiis avocasset

---

[1] *animum*] om. Ce.¹

otium, astitit subito vigilanti, et quiddam operis molienti, vultu, qualis solet esse morientium anima fugiente, exsanguis. Tum tacentem vivum prior mortuus compellans, "Agnoscis me?" inquit: "Agnosco," respondit; "et non tantum de insolita tua turbor præ"sentia, quantum de diuturna miror absentia." At ille, ubi tarditatem adventus excusavit, tandem ait, " Tandem, expeditis morarum nexibus, venio: sed " adventus iste tibi, si voles, amice, erit commodus, " mihi omnino infructuosus; quippe qui, pronun- " tiata et acclamata sententia, sempiternis sim depu- " tatus suppliciis." Cumque vivus, ad ereptionem mortui, omnia sua monasteriis et egenis expensurum, seque dies et noctes jejuniis et orationibus continuaturum, promitteret; "Fixum est," inquit, "quod dixi, " quia sine pœnitentia sunt judicia Dei, quibus in " sulphuream voraginem inferni demersus sum: ibi " 'dum rotat astra polus, dum pulsat littora pontus,' " pro criminibus meis volvar; inflexibilis sententiæ " manet rigor, æterna et innumera pœnarum genera " comminiscens, totus modo mundus valitura remedia " exquirat. Et ut aliquam experiaris ex meis innu- " merabilibus pœnis," protendit manum sanioso ulcere stillantem, et "en," ait, "unam ex minimis, videturne " tibi levis?" Cum levem sibi videri referret, ille, " curvatis in volam digitis, tres guttas defluentis tabi super eum jaculatus est; quarum duæ tempora, una frontem contingentes, cutem et carnem sicut ignito cauterio penetrarunt, foramen nucis capax efficientes. Illo magnitudinem doloris clamore testante, "Hoc," inquit mortuus, "erit in te[1] quantum vixeris, et " pœnarum mearum grave documentum, et, nisi neg- " lexeris, salutis tuæ singulare monimentum. Qua- " propter dum licet, dum nutat ira, dum pendula " Deus[2] operitur clementia, muta habitum, muta an-

---

[1] *in te*] tibi, Aa. Al. Bc. Cd.
[2] *Deus*] te, ins. Aa. Al. Cd.

"imum Redonis monachus effectus apud sanctum Me-
"lanium." Ad hæc verba vivo respondere nolente,
alter eum oculi vigore perstringens, "Si dubitas,"
inquit, "converti, miser, lege litteras istas;" et simul
cum dicto manum expandit tetricis notis inscriptam,
in quibus Sathanas et omne inferorum satellitium
gratias omni ecclesiastico cœtui de Tartaro emittebant,
quod cum ipsi in nullo suis voluptatibus deessent,
tum tantum numerum subditarum animarum paterentur ad inferna descendere prædicationis incuria, quantum nunquam retroacta viderunt secula. His dictis loquentis aspectus disparuit; et audiens, omnibus suis per ecclesias et egenos distributis, sanctum Melanium adiit, omnes audientes et videntes de subita conversione[1] admonens ut dicerent "Hæc est mutatio dexteræ Excelsi."

§ 238. Ista pro utilitate legentium me inseruisse non piguit; nunc de Willelmo loquar. Nam quia breviter, nec ut puto inutiliter, res ejus, quas duntaxat comes in Normannia annis triginta actiavit, percurri; modo aliud narrandi exordium ordo temporum flagitat, ut de regno ejus quantum nostra sciscitatio penetrare potuit, mendacium arguam, veritatem pronuntiem. Rex Edwardus fato functus fuerat: Anglia dubio favore nutabat, cui se rectori committeret incerta, an Haroldo, an Willelmo, an Edgaro: nam et illum, pro genere proximum regno, proceribus rex commendaverat, tacito scilicet mentis judicio, sed prono in clementiam animo. Quare, ut prædixi, Angli diversis votis ferebantur, quamvis palam cuncti bona Haroldo imprecarentur: et ille quidem, diademate fastigatus, nihil de pactis inter se et Willelmum cogitabat; liberatum se sacramento asserens, quod filia ejus quam desponderat citra nubiles annos obierat. Fertur enim vir ille, non paucis virtutibus præditus,

---

[1] *conversione*] et illustri conversatione, add An. A₁. By.

His rash confidence against William.

parum adversus perfidiam sibi consuluisse dummodo posset quibuscunque præstigiis hominum ratiocinationes suspendere: præterea, qui putaret minas Willelmi nunquam ad factum erupturas, quod ille conterminorum ducum bellis implicaretur, totum animum otio cum subjectis indulserat; nam profecto, nisi quod Noricorum regem adventare didicit, nec militem convocare nec aciem dirigere dignatus fuisset. Alter interea illum per nuntios leniter convenire, de rupto fœdere expostulare, precibus minas insuere; sciret se ante annum emensum ferro debitum vindicaturum, illuc iturum quo Haroldus tutiores se pedes habere putaret. Contra, ille, quæ dixi de puellæ nuptiis referens, de regno addidit, præsumptuosum fuisse quod, absque generali senatus et populi conventu et edicto, alienam illi hereditatem juraverit; proinde stultum sacramentum frangendum. Nam si jusjurandum vel votum quod puella in domo patris, nesciis parentibus, de suo corpore volens fecerit, judicatur irritum; quanto magis quod ille, sub regis virga constitutus, nesciente omni Anglia, de toto regno, necessitate temporis coactus, impegerit, videatur[1] non esse ratum: præterea iniquum postulat ut imperio decedat, quod tanto favore civium regendum susceperit; hoc nec provincialibus gratum, nec militibus tutum. Ita revertebantur inanes nuntii, vel veris vel verisimilibus argumentis præstricti. Sed comes toto illo anno bello necessaria expediebat, largis sumptibus milites suos continebat, alienos invitabat: ordines aciesque ita instituebat, ut milites proceri corpore, præcellentes robore, essent; duces et antesignani, præter scientiam rei militaris, etiam consilii et ætatis maturitate pollerent; ut, si singulos vel in acie vel alibi cerneres, non proceres sed reges putares. Ita episcopi et abbates illius temporis religione, ita optimates[2] magnanima

William's remonstrances and threats.

Above § 228.

Harold's argument in reply.

---

[1] *videatur*] judicatur, Aa. Bc. | [2] *optimates*] primates, Bc.

liberalitate certabant, ut mirum sit quod, paucissimis [1] annis evolutis, pleraque et pene omnia in utrisque ordinibus mutata videas: illi in quibusdam hebetiores, sed largiores; isti in omnibus prudentiores, sed tenaciores; utrique tamen in defensanda patria manu validi, consilio providi, fortunas suas evehere, inimicorum deprimere parati.[2] Verum tunc Willelmi industria, cum providentia Dei consentiens, jam spe Angliam invadebat; et, ne justam causam temeritas decoloraret, ad apostolicum, qui ex Anselmo Lucensi episcopo Alexander dicebatur, misit, justitiam suscepti belli quantis poterat facundiæ nervis allegans. Haroldus id facere supersedit; vel quod turgidus natura esset, vel quod causæ diffideret, vel quod nuntios suos a Willelmo et ejus complicibus, qui omnes portus obsidebant, impediri timeret. Quare, perpensis apud se utrinque partibus, papa vexillum in omen regni Willelmo contradidit; quo ille accepto, conventum magnatum apud Lillebona fecit, super negotio singulorum sententias sciscitatus. Cumque omnes, ejus voluntatem plausibus excipientes, magnificis promissis animasset,[3] commeatum navium omnibus, pro quantitate possessionum, indixit. Ita tunc discessum, et mense Augusto ad sanctum Walericum in commune ventum: portus ita [4] per metonymiam dicitur. Congregatis undecunque navibus, felix exspectabatur aura

Sympathy of nobles and prelates.

The pope's support of his cause.

Council at Lillebonne.

Rendezvous at S. Valery.

---

[1] The following passage *paucissimis—parati* is one of the best passages for illustrating the relation of the MSS. It is found as in the text in MSS. Bc. Bk. Bq. By. Cd. Ce. Cf. The MSS. Aa. Ag. Aah. Al. Ao. Ap. At. (of the first recension) have the reading given in the next note. MSS. Cd. Cm. have both, but omit *paucissimis annis* after *emendicantes*. The A recension was written before A.D. 1126.

[2] *paucissimis—parati*] nondum sexaginta annis evolutis, utraque turba abortivum bonitatis effecti, jurata bella contra justitiam susciperent: illi, pro ambitione sacrorum, magis distortum quam æquum et bonum amplectentes; isti rejecto pudore, undecumque captatis occasionibus, compendia pecuniarum velut quotidianam stipem emendicantes, Aa. Aah. Ag. Al. Ao. Ap. At.

[3] *animasset*] animassent, Aa. Al. Bc. Cd. Ce.

[4] *ita*] ille, Bc.

quæ illas ad destinatum locum[1] eveheret. Qua multis diebus remorante, vulgus militum, ut fieri solet, per tabernacula mussitabat: insanire hominem qui vellet alienum solum in jus suum refundere; Deum contra tendere, qui ventum arceret; idem patrem voluisse eodemque modo inhibitum; fatale illi familiæ esse, ut, altiora viribus spirans, Deum adversantem experiatur. Ista per publicum serebantur, quæ possent fortium robur enervare. Dux itaque, facto cum senioribus concilio, corpus sancti Walerici foras efferri, et, pro vento deprecando, sub divo exponi jussit; nec mora intercessit quin prosper flatus carbasa impleret. Tunc lætus clamor exortus omnes ad naves invitavit: comes ipse, a continenti primus ad[2] altum provectus, ceteros in medio fere mari anchoris jactis sustinuit. Omnibus itaque ad prætoriæ puppis vermiculatum velum convolantibus, post cibum sumptum placido cursu Hastingas appulerunt. In egressu navis pede lapsus, eventum in melius commutavit, acclamante sibi proximo milite, "Tenes," inquit, "Angliam, comes, " rex futurus!" Omnem exercitum a præda continuit, parcendum rebus quæ suæ forent prælocutus; continuisque quindecim diebus adeo se quiete agens, ut nihil minus quam bellum cogitare videretur.

§ 239. Interea Haroldus de pugna Noricorum revertebatur, sua æstimatione felix quod vicerat; meo judicio contra, quod parricidio victoriam compararat: allatoque ad se nuntio adventus Normannici, sicut erat cruentus in armis, paucissimo stipatus milite Hastingas protendit. Præcipitabant eum nimirum fata, ut nec auxilia convocare vellet, nec, si vellet, multos parituros inveniret; ita, ut ante dixi, omnes illi erant Above § 228. infensi, quod solus manubiis borealibus incubuerat. Præmisit tamen qui numerum hostium et vires specularentur; quos intra castra deprehensos Willelmus

---

[1] *locum*] om. Aa. Al. Bc.   [2] *ad*] in, Aa. Al.

circum tentoria duci, moxque, largis eduliis pastos, domino incolumes remitti jubet. Redeuntes percunctatur Haroldus quid rerum apportent: illi, verbis amplissimis ductoris magnificam confidentiam prosecuti, serio addiderunt, pene omnes in exercitu illo presbyteros videri, quod totam faciem cum utroque labio rasam haberent; Angli enim superius labrum pilis incessanter fructicantibus intonsum dimittunt, quod etiam gentilitium antiquis Britonibus fuisse Julius Cæsar asseverat in libro Belli Gallici. Subrisit rex fatuitatem referentium, lepido insecutus cachinno, quia non essent presbyteri, sed milites armis validi, animis invicti. Rapuit ergo ex ore ipsius sermonem Gurtha frater, plus puero adultus, et magnæ ultra ætatem virtutis et scientiæ. "Cum," inquit, "tantam fortitudinem Normanni præ-
" dices, indeliberatum æstimo cum illo confligere, quo [1]
" inferior robore et merito habearis. Nec enim ibis
" in inficias quin illi sacramentum vel invitus vel
" voluntarius feceris; proinde consultius ages si, in-
" stanti necessitati te subtrahens, nostro periculo collu-
" dium pugnæ temptaveris: nos, omni juramento expe-
" diti, juste ferrum pro patria stringemus. Timendum
" ne, si ipse decernas, vel fugam vel mortem oppetas:
" sed, nobis solis præliantibus, causa tua utrobique in
" portu navigabit; quia et fugientes restituere, et
mortuos ulcisci, poteris."

§ 240. Noluit effrænata temeritas aurem placidam monenti commodare, existimans inglorium et anteactæ vitæ opprobrium cuicunque discrimini terga nudare: eademque impudentia, vel, ut indulgentius dicam, imprudentia, monachum, Willelmi legatum, nec bono vultu dignatus turbide abegit; hoc tantum imprecans, ut Deus inter eum et Willelmum judicaret. Afferebat ille tria: ut vel regno secundum conditiones descenderet; vel sub eo regnaturus teneret: vel certe, spec-

---

[1] *quo*] qui, Bc. Bk.

tante utroque exercitu, gladio rem ventilarent. Calumpniabatur enim Willelmus regnum, quod rex illi Edwardus concesserat, consilio Stigandi archiepiscopi, et Godwini et Siwardi comitum; ejusque doni obsides filium et nepotem Godwini Normanniam miserat. Si id negare velit Haroldus, judicio se sedis apostolicæ vel prælio acturum: quibus omnibus solo, quod dixi, nuntius frustratus responso discessit, suisque ad dimicandum vivaciores animos dedit.

His claim of the crown and appeal.

§ 241. Itaque utrinque animosi duces disponunt acies, patrio quisque ritu: Angli, ut accepimus, totam noctem insompnem cantibus potibusque ducentes, mane incunctanter in hostem procedunt: pedites omnes cum bipennibus, conserta ante se scutorum testudine, impenetrabilem cuneum faciunt; quod profecto illis ea [1] die saluti fuisset, nisi Normanni simulata fuga more suo confertos manipulos laxassent. Rex ipse pedes juxta vexillum stabat cum fratribus, ut, in commune periculo æquato, nemo de fuga cogitaret. Vexillum illud post victoriam papæ misit Willelmus, quod erat in hominis pugnantis figura, auro et lapidibus arte sumptuosa intextum.[2]

The eve of the battle.

Craft of the Normans.

Harold fights on foot.

His standard.

§ 242. Contra Normanni, nocte tota confessioni peccatorum vacantes, mane Dominico corpore communicarunt. Pedites cum arcubus et sagittis primam frontem muniunt, equites retro divisis alis consistunt. Comes vultu serenus, et clara voce suæ parti utpote justiori Deum affuturum pronuntians, arma poposcit; moxque ministrorum tumultu loricam inversam indutus, casum risu correxit, "Vertetur," inquiens, "fortitudo comitatus mei in regnum." Tunc cantilena Rollandi inchoata, ut martium viri exemplum pugnaturos[3] accenderet, inclamatoque Dei auxilio, prælium[3] consertum, bellatumque acriter, neutris in

Pious preparation of the Normans.

Incident of William's arming.

Song of Roland.

---

[1] *ea*] illa, Bc. Cd. By.
[2] *intextum*] contextum, An. Al.
[3] *pugnaturos*] pugnatores, Ce.¹
[4] *prælium*] utrinque, ins. An.

multam diei horam cedentibus. Quo comperto, Willelmus innuit suis ut, ficta fuga, campo se subtraherent. Hoc commento Anglorum cuneus solutus, quasi palantes hostes a tergo cæsurus, exitium sibi maturavit; Normanni enim, conversis ordinibus reversi, dispersos adoriuntur, et in fugam cogunt. Ita ingenio circumventi, pulchram mortem pro patriæ ultione meruere : nec tamen ultioni suæ defuere, quin, crebro consistentes, de insequentibus insignes cladis acervos facerent; nam, occupato tumulo, Normannos, calore successus[1] acriter ad superiora nitentes, in vallem dejiciunt, levique negotio in subjectos tela torquentes, lapides rotantes, omnes ad unum fundunt. Item fossatum quoddam præruptum compendiario et noto sibi transitu evadentes, tot ibi inimicorum conculcavere, ut cumulo cadaverum planitiem campi æquarent. Valuit hæc vicissitudo, modo illis, modo istis vincentibus, quantum Haroldi[2] vita moram fecit; at ubi jactu sagittæ violato cerebro procubuit, fuga Anglorum perennis in nocte fuit.

Onset and feigned flight of the Normans.

Rout of the English.

Harold's death.

§ 243. Emicuit ibi virtus amborum ducum. Haroldus, non contentus munere imperatorio ut hortaretur alios, militis officium sedulo exequebatur; sæpe hostem cominus venientem ferire, ut nullus impune accederet quin statim uno ictu equus et eques prociderent : quapropter, ut dixi, eminus lethali arundine ictus mortem implevit. Jacentis femur unus militum gladio proscidit; unde a Willelmo ignominiæ notatus, quod rem ignavam et pudendam fecisset, militia pulsus est.

His behaviour in battle.

William degrades a knight who stabbed him when down.

§ 244. Item Willelmus suos clamore et præsentia hortari, ipse primus procurrere, confertos hostes invadere : ideo dum ubique sævit, ubique infrendet, tres equos lectissimos sub se confossos ea die amisit. Perstitit tamen magnanimi ducis et corpus et animus, quamvis familiari susurro a custodibus corporis revo-

Conduct of the Conqueror.

---

[1] *successus*] succensus, Al.; succensos, Edd.
[2] *Haroldi*] Haroldo, Bc.; Heroldi, Bk.

caretur; perstitit, inquam, donec victoriam plenam superveniens nox infunderet. Et proculdubio divina illum manus protexit, ut nihil sanguinis ex ejus corpore hostis[1] hauriret, quamquam illum tot jaculis impeteret.

<small>A memorable and fatal day for England.</small>

§ 245. Illa fuit dies fatalis Angliæ, funestum excidium dulcis patriæ, pro novorum dominorum commutatione. Jam enim pridem moribus Anglorum insueverat, qui varii admodum pro temporibus fuere: nam, primis adventus sui annis, vultu et gestu barbarico, usu bellico, ritu fanatico vivebant; sed postmodum, Christi fide suscepta, paulatim et per incrementa temporis, pro otio quod actitabant, exercitium armorum in secundis ponentes, omnem in religione operam insump-

<small>Characteristics of the early history of the nation.</small>

sere. Taceo de pauperibus, quos fortunarum tenuitas plerumque continet ne cancellos justitiæ transgrediantur: prætermitto graduum ecclesiasticorum viros, quos nonnunquam professionis contuitus, sed et infamiæ metus, a vero deviare non sinit. De regibus dico, qui pro amplitudine potestatis licenter indulgere voluptatibus possent: quorum quidam in patria, quidam

<small>The pious kings and prelates.</small>

Romæ, mutato habitu, cæleste lucrati sunt regnum, beatum nacti commercium; multi specie tenus tota vita mundum amplexi, ut thesauros egenis effunderent, monasteriis dividerent. Quid dicam de tot episcopis, heremitis, abbatibus? nonne tota insula tantis reliquiis indigenarum fulgurat, ut vix aliquem vicum insignem prætereas ubi novi sancti nomen non audias? quam multorum etiam periit memoria, pro scriptorum inopia!

<small>Extinction of literary culture.</small>

Veruntamen litterarum et religionis studia ætate procedente obsoleverunt, non paucis ante adventum Normannorum annis. Clerici litteratura tumultuaria contenti, vix sacramentorum verba balbutiebant: stupori erat et miraculo ceteris qui grammaticam nosset.

<small>Depression of monastic discipline.</small>

Monachi, subtilibus indumentis et indifferenti genere

---

[1] *hostis*] om. Ce.[1]

ciborum, regulam ludificabant. Optimates, gulæ et veneri dediti, ecclesiam more Christiano mane non adibant; sed in cubiculo, et inter uxorios amplexus, matutinarum sollempnia et missarum a festinante presbytero auribus tantum libabant. Vulgus, in medio expositum, præda erat potentioribus, ut, vel eorum substantiis exhaustis, vel etiam corporibus in longinquas terras distractis, acervos thesaurorum congererent, quanquam magis ingenitum sit illi genti commessationibus quam opibus inhiare. Illud erat a natura abhorrens, quod multi ancillas suas ex se gravidas, ubi libidini satisfecissent, aut ad publicum prostibulum aut ad externum[1] obsequium venditabant.[2] Potabatur in commune ab omnibus, in hoc studio noctes perinde ut dies perpetuantibus. Parvis et abjectis domibus totos absumebant[3] sumptus, Francis et Normannis absimiles, qui amplis et superbis ædificiis modicas expensas agunt. Sequebantur vitia ebrietatis socia, quæ virorum animos effœminant. Hinc factum est, ut, magis temeritate et furore præcipiti quam scientia militari Willelmo congressi, uno prælio, et ipso perfacili, servituti se patriamque pessundederint. Nihil enim temeritate levius; sed quicquid cum impetu inchoat, cito desinit vel compescitur. Ad summam, tunc erant Angli vestibus ad medium genu expediti, crines tonsi, barbas rasi, armillis aureis brachia onerati, picturatis stigmatibus cutem insigniti; in cibis urgentes crapulam, in potibus[4] irritantes vomicam. Et hæc quidem extrema jam[5] victoribus suis participarunt, de ceteris in eorum mores transeuntes. Sed hæc mala de omnibus generaliter Anglis dicta intelligi nolim: scio clericos multos tunc temporis simplici via semitam sanctitatis trivisse; scio multos laicos omnis generis et conditionis Deo in eadem gente placuisse: facessat ab hac relatione in-

Luxury among the nobles.

Oppression of the people; especially of the women.

Drunkenness, and extravagance in mean houses.

Rashness led to defeat.

Dress and habits.

Many exceptions to the description here given.

---

[1] *externum*] æternum, Aa.; extremum, By.
[2] *venditabant*] vendicabant, Aa.
[3] *absumebant*] abliguricbant, Al.
[4] *potibus*] poculis, Bc.
[5] *jam*] om. Aa. Bc.

vidia, non cunctos pariter hæc involvit calumpnia; verum sicut in tranquillitate malos cum bonis fovet plerumque Dei serenitas, ita in captivitate bonos cum malis nonnunquam ejusdem constringit severitas.

De moribus Normannorum.

Manners of the Normans.

§ 246. Porro Normanni, ut de eis quoque dicamus, erant tunc, et sunt adhuc, vestibus ad invidiam culti, cibis citra ullam nimietatem delicati: gens militiæ assueta, et sine bello pene vivere nescia; in hostem impigre procurrere, et ubi vires non successissent, non *Their fine houses and economy.* minus dolo et pecunia corrumpere. Domi ingentia, ut dixi, ædificia moderatos sumptus moliri, paribus invidere, superiores prætergredi velle, subjectos sibi[1] velli- *Their levity and readiness to receive strangers.* cantes ab alienis tutari; dominis fideles, moxque levi offensa infideles. Cum fato ponderare perfidiam, cum nummo mutare sententiam. Ceterum, omnium gentium benignissimi advenas æquali secum honore colunt; matrimonia quoque cum subditis jungunt; religionis normam, usquequaque in Anglia emortuam, adventu *Revival of monachism after the conquest.* suo suscitarunt; videas ubique in villis ecclesias, in vicis et urbibus monasteria, novo[2] ædificandi genere consurgere; recenti ritu patriam florere, ita ut sibi perisse diem quisque opulentus existimet quem non aliqua præclara[3] magnificentia illustret. Sed, quia de his satis dictum, Willelmi gesta prosequamur.

Quomodo Willelmus ab Anglis susceptus est.

Burial of Harold at Waltham.

§ 247. Ille, ubi perfecta victoria potitus est, suos sepeliendos mirifice curavit; hostibus quoque si qui vellent, idem exequendi licentiam præbuit. Corpus Haroldi matri repetenti sine pretio misit, licet illa multum per legatos obtulisset; acceptum itaque apud Waltham sepelivit, quam ipse ecclesiam, ex

---

[1] *sibi*] ipsi, Aa. Al. Bc. Cd. By.
[2] *novo*] nova, Ce.¹
[3] *præclara*] om. Ce.¹

proprio constructam in honore sanctæ Crucis, canonicis impleverat. Sensim ergo Willelmus, ut triumphatorem decebat, cum exercitu non hostili sed regali modo progrediens, urbem regni maximam Londoniam petit; moxque cum gratulatione cives omnes effusi obviam vadunt. Prorupit omnibus portis unda salutantium, auctoribus magnatibus, præcipue Stigando archiepiscopo Cantuariensi et Aldredo Eboracensi: nam præcedentibus diebus, Edwinus et Morcardus, amplæ spei fratres, apud Londoniam audito interitus Haroldi nuntio, urbanos sollicitaverant ut alterutrum in regnum sublevarent; quod frustra conati, Northanhimbriam discesserant, ex suo conjectantes ingenio nunquam illuc Willelmum esse venturum. Ceteri proceres Edgarum eligerent si episcopos assertores haberent; sed proximo urgente periculo, et domesticæ litis discidio, nec illud quidem [1] effectum: ita Angli, qui, in unam coeuntes sententiam, potuissent patriæ reformare ruinam, dum nullum ex suis volunt, alienum induxerunt. Tunc ille, haud dubie rex conclamatus, die Natalis Domini coronatus est ab Aldredo archiepiscopo; cavebat enim id munus a Stigando suscipere, quod esset is archiepiscopus non legitime.

Summa bellorum Willelmi in Anglia.

§ 248. Omnium deinde bellorum quæ gessit, hæc summa est. Urbem Exoniam [2] rebellantem leviter subegit, divino scilicet jutus auxilio, quod pars muralis ultro decidens ingressum illi patefecerit: nam et ipse audacius eam assilierat, protestans homines irreverentes Dei destituendos suffragio; quia unus eorum, supra murum stans, nudato inguine auras sonitu inferioris partis turbaverat, pro contemptu videlicet Normannorum. Eboracum,[3] unicum rebellionum suffugium,

---

[1] *quidem*] om. Ce.[1]

[2] *Exoniam*] so Aa. Ag. Al. Bc. Bk. Bq. By. Cc. Cd. Cm. Savile reads *Oxoniam.*

[3] *Eboracum*] civitatem, add Aa. Al. Bc. By. Cd.

civibus pene delevit, fame et ferro necatis: ibi enim rex Scottorum Malcolmus cum suis, ibi Edgarus et Marcherius et Weldeofus cum Anglis et Danis, nidum tyrannidis sæpe fovebant; sæpe duces illius trucidabant, quorum singillatim exitus si commemoravero, fortasse superfluus non ero, licet fastidii discrimen immineat, dum relatori, si forte secundum dictores suos mentiatur, difficilis sit regressus ad veniam.

Quomodo Eboracum ceperit, et totam provinciam vastaverit.

Policy of Malcolm.

§ 249. Malcolmus omnes Anglorum perfugas libenter recipiebat, tutamentum singulis quantum poterat impendens; Edgarum præcipue, cujus sororem, pro antiqua memoria nobilitatis, jugalem sibi fecerat. Ejus causa conterminas Angliæ provincias rapinis et incendiis infestabat; non quod aliquid ad regnum illi profuturum arbitraretur, sed ut Willelmi animum contristaret, qui Scotticis prædis terras suas obnoxias indignaretur. Quapropter Willelmus, coacta peditum

William's expedition to the north.

et militum [1] manu, aquilonales [2] insulæ partes petiit: et primo urbem metropolim, quam Angli cum Danis et Scottis obstinate tenebant, in deditionem accepit, civibus longa inedia consumptis; maximum quoque hostium numerum, qui obsessis in auxilium convenerant, ingenti et gravi prælio fudit, non incruenta sibi victoria multos suorum amittens. Tunc totius regionis

Devastation of the coast on the alarm of a Danish invasion.

vicos et agros corrumpi, fructus et fruges igne vel aqua labefactari jubet; maritima maxime, tum propter recentem iram, tum quia Cnutonem Danorum regem, filium Swani, adventare rumor sparserat: ea præcepti ratio, ut nihil circa oram maritimam prædo piraticus inveniret secum asportaturus, si citius remeandum, vel fami consulturus, si diutius manendum putaret. Itaque provinciæ quondam fertilis, et tyrannorum

---

[1] *militum*] equitum, Aah.   [2] *aquilonales*] aquilonalis, Ce.

nutriculæ, incendio, præda, sanguine, nervi succisi; humus, per sexaginta et eo amplius miliaria, omnifariam inculta; nudum omnium solum usque ad hoc etiam tempus: urbes olim præclaras, turres proceritate sua in cælum minantes, agros lætos pascuis, irriguos fluviis, si quis modo videt peregrinus, ingemit; si quis superest vetus incola, non agnoscit.

General destruction of Yorkshire.

De Malcolmo Rege Scottorum.

§ 250. Malcolmus, antequam ad manus veniretur, se dedidit, totoque Willelmi tempore incertis et sæpe fractis fœderibus ævum egit; sed, filio Willelmi Willelmo regnante, simili modo impetitus, falso sacramento insequentem abegit. Nec multo post, dum fidei immemor superbius provinciam inequitaret, a Roberto de Molbreia, comite Northanhimbriæ, cum filio cæsus est; humatusque multis annis apud Tinemuthe, nuper ab Alexandro filio Scotiam ad Dunfermelin portatus est.

Malcolm submits and revolts.

He is killed in the next reign.

De Edgaro.

§ 251. Edgarus, cum Stigando et Aldredo archiepiscopis regis dedititius,[1] sequenti anno, facto ad Scottum[2] transfugio, jusjurandum maculavit; sed cum ibi aliquot annis degens, nihil ad præsens commodi, nihil ad futurum spei, præter cotidianam stipem nactus esset, Normanni liberalitatem experiri pergens, ad eum, tunc ultra mare degentem, navigavit. Quod regi gratissimum fuisse ferunt, ut incentore bellorum Anglia vacaret; nam et ultro solitus erat quoscunque Anglos suspectos habebat, quasi honoris causa, Normanniam ducere, ne quicquam se absente in regno turbarent. Receptus ergo Edgarus, et magno donativo donatus est; pluribusque annis in curia manens, pedetemptim pro ignavia, et, ut mitius dictum sit, pro sim-

Flight of Edgar Atheling to the Scots.

His indolence or simplicity.

---

[1] *dedititius*] deditius, Ce.   [2] *Scottum*] Scottiam, Bc. Cd.

plicitate, contemptui haberi cœpit. Quantula enim simplicitas, ut libram argenti, quam cotidie in stipendio accipiebat, regi pro uno equo perdonaret? Subsequenti tempore cum Roberto filio Godwini, milite audacissimo, Jerosolimam pertendit. Illud fuit tempus quo Turchi Baldwinum regem apud Ramas obsederunt; qui, cum obsidionis[1] injuriam ferre nequiret, per medias hostium acies effugit, solius Roberti opera liberatus præeuntis, et evaginato gladio dextra lævaque Turchos cædentis: sed cum, successu ipso truculentior, alacritate nimia procurreret, ensis manu excidit; ad quem recolligendum cum se inclinasset, omnium incursu oppressus, vinculis palmas dedit. Inde Babilonem ut aiunt ductus, cum Christum abnegare nollet, in medio foro ad signum positus, et sagittis terebratus, martyrium sacravit. Edgarus amisso milite regressus, multaque beneficia ab imperatoribus Græcorum et Alamannorum adeptus, quippe qui etiam cum retinere pro generis amplitudine temptassent, omnia pro natalis soli desiderio sprevit; quosdam enim profecto fallit amor patriæ, ut nihil eis videatur jocundum nisi consuetum hauserint cælum. Unde Edgarus, fatua cupidine illusus, Angliam rediit, unde,[2] ut superius dixi, diverso fortunæ ludicro rotatus, nunc remotus et tacitus canos suos in agro consumit.

De Edwino et Morcardo fratribus.

§ 252. Edwinus et Morcardus erant fratres, filii Elfgari filii Leofrici. Hi comitatum Northanhimbrorum susceperant, et communi umbone pacifice tuebantur; nam, ut prædixi, paucis diebus ante mortem regis Edwardi, provinciales aquilonis in rebellionem surrexerant, et Tostinum comitem suum expulerant, petierantque et acceperant unum e fratribus dominum, annitente Haroldo. Fiebant ista, ut a consciis accepi-

---

[1] *obsidionis*] om. Ce.¹ | [2] *unde*] ubi, Aa. Al. Cd.

mus, infenso rege, quia Tostinum diligeret: sed morbo invalidus, senio gravis, pene jam despectui omnibus[1] haberi cœperat, ut dilecto auxiliari non posset; quare ex animi ægritudine majorem valitudinem corporis contrahens, non multo post decessit. Perstitit in incepto Haroldus ut fratrem exlegaret: quocirca ille, prius piraticis excursibus avitos triumphos polluens, mox cum rege Noricorum, ut supra scripsi, cæsus est. Cadaver ejus, indicio verrucæ inter duas scapulas agnitum, sepulturam Eboraci meruit. Tunc Edwinus et Morcardus, Haroldo jubente, manubiales prædas Londoniam tulere; nam ipse ad Hastingensem pugnam festinabat, unde[2] jam partam victoriam falso præsagus sompniabat. At, eo interempto, germani, ad terras suæ potestatis perfugientes, aliquot annis pacem Willelmi turbaverunt, clandestinis latrociniis sylvas infestantes, nec unquam cominus et aperte martem agentes; sæpe etiam capti plerumque se dedidere, sed miseratione juvenilis decoris, et gratia nobilitatis, impune dimissi. Postremo nec vi nec dolo hostium, sed suorum perfidia trucidati, regem ad lacrymas flexere; quibus ipse et conjugia cognatarum et amicitiæ dignationem jam pridem indulsisset, si quieti adquiescere vellent.

Tostig slain in battle and buried at York.

Edwin and Morcar, after the battle of Hastings, stir up rebellion.

De Weldeofo Comite.

§ 253. Weldeofus, amplæ prosapiæ comes, multam familiaritatem novi regis nactus fuerat, quod ille, præteritarum offensarum immemor, magis illas virtuti quam perfidiæ attribuebat. Siquidem Weldeofus in Eboracensi pugna plures Normannorum solus obtruncaverat, unos et unos per portam egredientes decapitans: nervosus lacertis, thorosus pectore, robustus et procerus toto corpore, filius Siwardi magnificentissimi

Earl Waltheof;

his prowess and origin.

---

[1] *omnibus*] om. Al. Bc. Cc.
[2] *unde*] inde, Al.; indeque, Aa. Aah.

comitis, quem "Digera" Danico vocabulo, id est fortem, cognominabant. Postmodum vero, victis partibus, sese sponte dedens, et Judithæ neptis regis connubio privataque amicitia donatus, non permansit in fide, pravum ingenium cohibere impotens: compatriotis enim omnibus, qui existimarant resistendum, cæsis vel subjectis, etiam in Radulfi de Waher perfidia se immiscuit, sed conjuratione detecta, comprehensus diuque in vinculis tentus, ultimo spoliatus capite, Crolando sepultus est; quamvis quidam dicant, necessitate interceptum, non voluntate addictum, infidelitatis sacramentum agitasse. Anglorum est ista excusatio; nam cetera Normanni afferunt,[1] Anglorum qui plurimum præstent. Quorum astipulationi Divinitas suffragari videtur, miracula multa, et ea permaxima, ad tumbam illius ostendens. Aiunt enim, in catenas conjectum, quotidianis singultibus perperam commissa diluisse.

§ 254. Inde propositum regis fortassis merito excusatur, si aliquanto[2] durior in Anglos fuerit, quod pene nullum eorum fidelem invenerit. Quæ res ita ferocem animum exasperabant, ut potentiores primum pecuniis, mox terris, nonnullos etiam vita exueret: quin etiam Cæsarianum secutus ingenium, qui Germanos in Ardenna maxima sylva abditos, et inde crebris eruptionibus exercitum suum affligentes, non per Romanos suos sed per Gallos fœderatos expulit; ut, dum alienigenæ alterutros transfoderent, ipse sine sanguine triumphum duceret. Idem, inquam, Willelmus in Anglos egit: nam contra quosdam, qui post primam infelicis ominis pugnam Danemarchiam et Hiberniam profugerant, et valida congregata manu tertio anno redierant, Angligenam exercitum et ducem objecit, Normannos feriari permittens; ingens sibi levamen providens, utrilibet vincerent. Nec eum cogitatio lusit; nam utrique Angli, aliquamdiu digladiati inter

---

[1] *afferunt*] asserunt, Aa.　　[2] *aliquanto*] aliquando, Al.

se, palmam otiosam regi refudere: advenæ Hiberniam fugati; regii, maxima sui clade, nomen inane victoriæ, amisso duce, mercati. Vocabatur is Ednodus, domi belloque Anglorum temporibus juxta insignis, pater Herdingi qui adhuc superest, magis consuetus linguam in lites acuere, quam arma in bello concutere. Ita laicorum potentia subruta, stabili quoque obfirmavit edicto ut nullum ejus gentis, monachum vel clericum, ad aliquam dignitatem conari pateretur: a Cnutonis quondam regis facilitate immaniter abhorrens, qui victis honores integros exhibuit; unde factum est, ut, eo defuncto, indigenæ advenas leviter expellerent, sibique antiquum jus vendicarent. At iste certis de causis viventes quosdam canonice deposuit, et in locum illorum qui morerentur, cujuscunque gentis industrium,[1] præter Angligenam, imposuit. Exigebat hoc, nisi fallor, indurata in regem pervicacia; cum sint Normanni, ut ante dixi, in conviventes advenas naturali benignitate proclives.

§ 255. Radulfus, de quo prius tetigi, erat per donum regis comes Northfolki et Suthfolki; Brito ex patre, distorti ad omne bonum animi. Is, quod cognatam regis, filiam Willelmi filii Osberni, desponderat, majora justo mente metiens, tyrannidem adoriri meditabatur. Itaque ipso nuptiarum die magnis apparatibus convivium agitatum, quod Normannorum gulæ jam Anglorum luxus influxerat, ebriis convivis, et vino tumentibus, amplo verborum ambitu propositum suum aperit: illi, quia in eorum animo pro potu omnis ratio caligabat, ingenti plausu dicenti acclamant. Ibi Rogerius comes Herefordensis, uxoris Radulfi frater, ibi Weldeofus, ibi præterea quamplurimi, in necem regis conjurant; sed postero die, cum, digesto calore vini, temperatior aura corda quorundam afflasset, major pars facti pœnitens a convivio dilapsa. Unus eorum

---

[1] *industrium*] hominem, ins. Aa. Al. Cd.

Weldeof fertur, qui consilio Lanfranci archiepiscopi Normanniam ultro enavigans,[1] rem regi, causa sua duntaxat celata, detulit: at comites in incepto persistere, provinciales suos quisque in tumultum excitare; sed obsistebat eis Deus, omnes conatus eorum in irritum deducens. Mox enim re comperta, duces regis, qui custodiam prætendebant, Radulfum ad hoc calamitatis compulere, ut, arrepta nave apud Norwic, mari se committeret: uxor ejus, pacta membrorum salute, traditoque castello, maritum secuta. Rogerius, a rege vinculis irretitus, tota vita carcerem frequentavit vel potius incoluit; detestandæ perfidiæ juvenis, nec moribus patrissans.

§ 256. Siquidem genitor ejus, Willelmus filius Osberni, principibus[2] optimis comparandus fuerit haud scio an etiam præponendus. Ejus consilio rex Willelmus primo animatus ad invadendam Angliam; mox, virtute adjutus, ad manutenendam. Erat in eo mentis animositas quam commendabat manus pene prodiga liberalitas: unde factum est, ut militum multitudine, quibus larga stipendia dabat, hostium aviditatem arceret, civium sedulitatem haberet; quare pro effusis sumptibus asperrimam regis offensam incurrit, quod gazas suas improvide dilapidaret. Manet ad hanc diem, in comitatu ejus apud Herefordum, legum quas statuit inconcussa firmitas, ut nullus miles pro qualicunque commisso plus septem solidis solvat; cum in aliis provinciis, ob parvam occasiunculam in transgressione præcepti herilis, viginti vel viginti quinque pendantur. Sed tam secundos eventus turpi fine fortuna conclusit, dum tanti regni sustentator, Angliæ et Normanniæ consiliarius, pro fœminea cupidine Flandriam pergens, ab insidiatoribus impetitus interiit. Nam Baldwinus antiquus ille, de quo superius dixi, pater Matildis, duos habuit filios: Robertum, qui, patre superstite comitissam Frisiæ uxorem nactus,

---

[1] *enavigans*] navigans, Ce.[1]   [2] *principibus*] principis, Al.

Frisonis cognomen accepit: Baldwinum, qui post patrem aliquot annis Flandriæ præfuit, immatureque fato functus est; superstitibus duobus liberis Arnulfo et Baldwino, de Richilde uxore, quorum tutelam regi Francorum Philippo, cujus amitæ filius erat, et Willelmo filio Osberni, commendaverat. Libens id munus suscepit Willelmus, ut, fœderatis cum Richilde nuptiis, altius nomen sibi pararet. At illa, fœmineo fastu ampliora¹ sexu spirans, novaque a provincialibus tributa exigens, in perfidiam illos excitavit; misso quippe propter Robertum Frisonem nuntio, ut supplicantis patriæ habenas acciperet, omnem fidelitatem Arnulfo, qui jam comes dicebatur, abjurant.² Nec vero defuere qui pupilli partes fulcirent. Ita multis diebus Flandria intestinis dissensionibus conturbata; id filius Osberni, qui totus in amorem mulieris concesserat, pati nequivit, quin, militari manu coacta, Flandriam intraret; susceptusque primo ab his quos tutari venerat, post paucos dies securus de castello in aliud equitabat, expeditus cum paucis: contra, Friso, quem hujusmodi fatuitas non latebat, occultatis insidiis inopinum excepit, et nequicquam fortiter agentem ipsum et nepotem suum Arnulfum cecidit.

§ 257. Ita Flandria potitus, sæpe Willelmum regem Normannicis prædis irritavit. Filia ejus Cnutoni regi Danorum nupsit, de qua genitus est Carolus, qui modo³ principatur in Flandria. Pacem cum Philippo rege comparavit, data sibi in uxorem privigna, de qua ille Lodowicum tulit qui modo regnat in Francia; nec multo post, pertæsus connubii, quod illa præpinguis corpulentiæ esset, a lecto removit, uxoremque Andegavensis comitis contra fas et jus sibi conjunxit. Eorum affinitate tutus, Robertus nihil quod deploraret

---

¹ *ampliora*] altiora, Aa. Al.; altiora vel ampliora, interl. Ce.
² *abjurant*] abjuravit, Bc. By.

³ *modo*] Charles was killed in 1127, before which date this portion of the work received its present form.

suo tempore vidit; licet Baldwinus frater Arnulfi, qui in Hanoea provincia et castello Valentianis comitatum habuit, regis Willelmi auxilio plures assultus faceret. Tribus ante mortem annis, jam canis sparsus caput, Jerosolimam contendit pro peccatorum alleviamento; regressus mundanis involucris renuntiavit, finem vitæ quietus a negotiis Christiana sollicitudine operiens. Filius ejus Robertus ille fuit qui in expeditione Asiatica quam nostris diebus Europa contra Turchos movit, mirandus innotuit; sed nescio quo infortunio, postquam domum reversus est, nobilem illum laborem decoloravit, in quodam quod vocant torniamento ad mortem læsus. Nec filium ejus Baldwinum fortuna excepit felicior, qui, ultro in Normannia regis Anglorum Henrici vires lacessens, juvenilis audaciæ temeritatem luit; namque conto in capite percussus, multorumque medicorum promissis illusus, metam vitæ abrupit, Carolo illi de quo supra diximus principatu tradito.

§ 258. At vero rex Willelmus in subjectos leniter, turbide in rebelles agens, feliciter omni Anglia potiebatur, Walenses omnes tributarios habens. Jam vero trans mare, nunquam otiosus, Cenomannico solo pene exterminium indixit, ducta expeditione illuc de Anglis, qui sicut facile in solo suo potuerunt opprimi, ita in alieno semper apparuere invicti. Apud Dolum, castellum transmarinæ Britanniæ, dum nescio qua simultate irritatus manum illuc militarem duxisset, innumeros ex suis desideravit. Philippum regem Francorum, cujus amitæ filiam uxorem duxerat, semper infidum habuit, quod scilicet ille tantam gloriam viro invideret quem et patris sui et suum hominem[1] esse constaret: sed Willelmus nihilo secius[2] ejus conatibus improbe obviabat, quamvis primogenitus filius ejus Robertus fatuo consilio conatibus ejus[3]

---

[1] *hominem*] om. Bc.
[2] *secius*] segnius, Cd.
[3] *conatibus ejus*] contra patrem illi, Aa. Aah.

assisteret; unde contigit, ut in quodam assultu apud Gibboracum filius patri resultans, eo vulnerato, equum ipsius confoderet, Willelmus medius filiorum saucius abiret, multi ex regiis caderent. Ceterum tota vita ita fortunatus fuit, ut exteræ et remotæ gentes nihil magis quam nomen ejus timerent. Provinciales adeo nutui suo substraverat, ut sine ulla contradictione primus censum omnium capitum ageret, omnium prædiorum redditus in tota Anglia notitiæ suæ per scriptum adjiceret, omnes liberos homines, cujuscunque essent, suæ fidelitati sacramento adigeret. Solus ejus majestatem concutiebat Cnuto[1] rex Danorum, qui et affinitate Roberti Frisonis et suapte potentia in immensum extollebatur; rumore in populos sato quod Angliam invaderet, debitum sibi pro affinitate antiqui Cnutonis solum: et profecto fecisset nisi Deus ejus audaciam vento contrario infirmasset. Quæ res admonuit ut genealogiam regum Danorum qui post nostrum Cnutonem fuere seriatim[2] abbreviem, de Noricis quoque pauca inserturus.

§ 259. Ei, ut ante dictum est, successit Haroldus in Anglia, Hardecnutus in Danemarchia, filii ejus; nam Noricam, quam subegerat, recuperavit Magnus, filius Olavi quem in gestis Cnutonis dixi a provincialibus suis necatum fuisse. Haroldo in Anglia defuncto, ambo regna tenuit Hardecnutus pauco tempore: quo mortuo successit Edwardus simplex, avitoque regno contentus, transmarinum imperium ut laboriosum et barbarum despuit. Tunc rex Danorum levatus est Swanus quidam, haud dubie nobilissimus; cujus cum regnum aliquot annis prosperaretur, Magnus rex Noricorum, consentientibus Danis quibusdam, illum vi bellica expellens, suo animo terram subjecit. Ejectus Swanus regem Suevorum adiit, ejusque auxilio, cum Suevos et Windelicos et Gothos corrasisset, rediit ut

---

[1] *Cnuto*] om. Ce.¹
[2] *seriatim*] strictim, Aa. Al. Bc. Cd. Ce.²

regnum reformaret ; sed conspirantibus Danis, qui potestatem Magni diligerent, prioris fortunæ calamitatem expertus est. Ingens illud et memorabile in ea barbarie prælium fuit, quod nunquam vel discrimen formidabilius vel omen lætius Dani viderunt. Denique ad hoc tempus votum illibatum custodiunt, quo se ante pugnam[1] constrinxerunt, ut vigiliam sancti Laurentii cunctis in posterum seculis jejunio et eleemosynis sacrarent.[2] Eo enim die certatum, et tunc quidem Swanus fugit : sed non multo post, mortuo Magno, regnum suum integre recepit.

§ 260. Successit Magno in Norica Swanus quidam, Herdhand cognominatus, non de regia progenie, sed manu et calliditate provectus : illi Olavus, patruus Magni, quem sanctum ferunt : Olavo Haroldus Harvagra, frater Olavi, qui etiam imperatori Constantinopolitano dudum juvenis militaverat ; cujus jussu pro stupro illustris fœminæ leoni objectus, beluam immanem nudo lacertorum nisu suffocavit. Hic in Anglia ab Haroldo filio Godwini[3] cæsus.[4] Filii ejus, Olavus et Magnus, regnum paternum partiti ; sed, Magno præmature mortuo, Olavus totum occupavit. Illi successit filius Magnus, qui nuper in Hibernia, dum temere illuc appulisset, miserabiliter occisus est. Ferunt Magnum superiorem, filium Haroldi, post mortem patris ab Haroldo rege Angliæ clementer domum dimissum, illius beneficii memoria, Haroldum filium Haroldi, post victoriam Willelmi ad se venientem, benigne tractasse ; eundemque in expeditione socium habuisse quam in Angliam tempore Willelmi junioris duxit, quando et Orchadas et Mevanias insulas sibi subjecit, et occurrentes comites, Hugonem Cestrensem et Hugonem Salopesbiriensem, priorem fugit,[5] secundum interemit. Filii ultimi Magni, Hasten et

---

[1] *pugnam*] om. Ce.[1]
[2] *sacrarent*] consecrarent, Bc. Bk.
[3] *Godwini*] om. Bc.
[4] *cæsus*] est, ins. Aa. Al. Cd.
[5] *fugit*] fugavit, Aa. Cd.

Siwardus, regno adhuc diviso imperitant; quorum posterior, adolescens speciosus et audax, non multum est[1] quod Jerosolimam per Angliam navigavit, innumera et præclara facinora contra Saracenos consummans, præsertim in obsessione[2] Sidonis, quæ pro conscientia Turchorum immania in Christianos fremebat.

Present kings of Norway.

§ 261. Sed Swanus in regno Danorum ut dixi restitutus, ægre quietem ferens, in Angliam bis Cnutonem filium misit; primo cum trecentis, secundo cum ducentis navibus. Prioris classis socius fuit Osbernus frater Swani, sequentis Hacco: utrique accepta pecunia conatus adolescentis fregere, domum sine effectu repatriantes; quare a Swano rege gravi contumelia inusti, quod fidem pecunia læsissent, in exilium acti sunt. Swanus, ad mortem veniens, omnes juramento provinciales constrinxit ut, quia quatuordecim filios habebat, omnibus per ordinem regnum delegarent, quantum ipsa soboles[3] durare posset. Eo ergo defuncto, successit filius[4] Haroldus annis tribus; illi Cnuto, quem pater in Angliam miserat. Is, veteris repulsæ memor, classem, ut accepimus, mille et eo amplius navium in Angliam parat; auxilio ei erat socer Robertus Friso secentarum ratium dominus: sed duobus pene annis venti adversitate coercitus, voluntatem mutavit, pronuntians non sine Dei nutu esse quod transfretare nequiret. Verum post modicum[5] quorundam coloquiis depravatus, qui difficultatem transitus anicularum maleficiis imputabant, optimatibus quarum fœminæ de hoc insimulabantur, pensiones importabiles indixit; Olavum quoque fratrem, factionis ejusdem principem accusatum, vinculis irretivit, et

Sweyn of Denmark sends two fleets to England.

Succession of Harold and Canute.

Canute's preparation for invading England.

He banishes his brother Olaf.

---

[1] The crusade of Siward took place in 1107, when he wintered in England; the siege of Sidon in 1110

[2] *obsessione*] obsidione, Aa.

[3] *soboles*] progenies, Bc.

[4] *filius*] ejus, ins. Cd.

[5] *post modicum*] postmodum Aa, Al.

socero in exilium misit: quapropter barbari, libertatis suæ injuriam non ferentes, intra ecclesiam quandam altare amplexum, et emendationem facti promittentem, trucidarunt. Aiunt eo loci multa miracula cælitus ostensa, quod fuerit vir ille jejuniis et eleemosynis deditus, et qui in legum transgressores magis divinas quam suas persequeretur contumelias; unde et ei martyris honor consecratus est a papa Romano. Post eum homicidæ, ut invidiam facti aliquo bono compensarent, Olavum a vinculis decem milibus marcarum argenti redemerunt. Hic, octo annis ignave imperitans, regnum fratri Henrico reliquit. Is, viginti et novem annis modeste vivens, Jerosolimam abiit, medioque mari spiritum evomuit. Quintus nunc Nicolaus in regno subsistit.[1]

§ 262. Rex igitur Danorum, ut dixi, solus erat obstaculum ne Willelmus continua feriaretur lætitia, cujus respectu tantam multitudinem stipendiariorum conducebat militum ex omni quæ citra montes est provincia, ut eorum copia regnum gravaret; sed ipse, pro magnanimitate sua, dispendium expensarum non sentiens, etiam Hugonem Magnum, regis Francorum fratrem, cum illius commilitio, inter militares numeros sibi serviturum redegerat. Animabat et excitabat ipse virtutem suam propter Roberti Guiscardi memoriam, pronuntians pudendum si illi fortitudine cederet quem nobilitate præiret; siquidem Robertus, mediocri parentela in Normannia ortus, quæ nec humi reperet nec altum quid tumeret, paucis ante adventum Willelmi in Angliam annis, cum quindecim militibus abierat Apuliam, penuriam necessariorum gentis illius ignavæ stipendiis correcturus. Nec multi fluxerunt anni quod, stupendo Dei munere, totam terram[2] in potestatem accepit: nam ubi viribus destituebatur, ingenio callebat; oppida primo, mox civitates, suæ ditioni associans.

---

[1] Nicolas was killed in 1135. | [2] *terram*] illam, ins. Bc.

Ita ergo profecit ut se ducem Apuliæ et Calabriæ, *His brothers and son.*
fratrem Ricardum principem Capuæ, alterum Rogerum
comitem Siciliæ, faceret. Postremo, data Apulia filio
Rogero, cum altero filio Boamundo Adriaticum pelagus
transivit; statimque Dirachio capto, super Alexium *Siege of Durazzo.*
imperatorem Constantinopolitanum ulterius progrediebatur: sævientem retinuit nuncius Hildebrandi apostolici. Imperator enim Alamannorum Henricus, filius *Henry IV. besieges*
Henrici de quo supra memoravimus, iratus contra *Rome and expels the*
papam quod excommunicationem in eum propter in- *pope.*
vestituras ecclesiarum promulgaverat, cum exercitu
veniens, Romam obsedit, Hildebrandum expulit, Guibertum Ravennatem introduxit. Quo per litteras
expulsi Guiscardus audito, relicto filio Boamundo cum
militibus ut inchoata paterna persequeretur, Apuliam *Robert Wiscard restores*
rediit: contracta velociter Apulorum et Normannorum *the pope.*
manu, Romam tendebat. Nec sustinuit nuntium advenientis Henricus, quin cum falso papa, sola fama
territus, terga daret.[1] Vacua ab obsessoribus, Roma
legitimum præsulem accepit; sed non multo post,
eadem violentia qua prius, amisit. Tunc quoque
Alexius, audiens Robertum ad sua necessario revocatum, summamque manum bello imponere sperans, supra
Boamundum, qui partes relictas tuebatur, irruit;[2] sed *Bohemond his son*
Normannus, gentilitii roboris tenax adolescens, arie- *defeats the Greeks.*
tantes Græcos, et ceteras quæ convenerant gentes, usu
militari, quamvis multum numero inferior, fugæ tradidit. Eodem quoque tempore Veneti, gens mari *Robert beats the*
assueta, Guiscardum, propter quæ venerat sedatis, *Venetians.*
transfretare volentem aggressi, superiorem calamitatem
sensere; pars mersi et cæsi, pars fugati. Ille, cœptam
enavigans viam, multas civitates Alexii suæ voluntati
applicuit. Sustulit imperator maleficio quem virtute *Craft of the emperor*
nequibat,[3] uxori ipsius conubium augustale mentitus: *Alexius.*

---

[1] *daret*] dumpnaret, Aa. Aah. Al. Bc. Bk. Bq. Ce.
[2] *irruit*] venit, Bc.
[3] *nequibat*] non poterat, Bc.

cujus insidiis elaboratum virus hauriens interiit, meliorem exitum, si Deus voluisset, emeritus; invincibilis hostili ferro, et domestico obnoxius veneno. Sepultus est apud Venusam Apuliæ,[1] habens epitaphium :

Death and burial of Robert Wiscard.

" Hic terror mundi Guiscardus; hic expulit urbe
" Quem Ligures regem, Roma, Lemannus, habent.
" Parthus, Arabs, Macedumque phalanx non texit Alexin,
" At fuga; sed Venetum nec fuga nec pelagus."

De Hildebrando Papa.

Account of Hildebrand.

§ 263. Verum, quia Hildebrandi mentio se ingessit, de eo dicam quæ non frivolo auditu hausi, sed seria relatione ejus audivi qui se illa ex ore Hugonis abbatis Cluniacensis audisse juraret. Quæ[2] ideo admiror et prædico, quia cogitationes aliorum prophetico mentis intuitu pronuntiabat. Alexander eum[3] papa efficax, ipsius studium conspicatus, cancellis apostolorum præfecerat. Circumibat ergo pro sui contuitu officii provincias, ut perperam acta corrigeret. Accurrebatur ab omnium[4] ordinum hominibus, decisiones diversorum negotiorum postulantibus. Cuncta ei[5] submittebatur secularis[6] potentia, tum pro sanctitatis, tum pro ministerii ipsius reverentia. Unde die quadam, cum solito major adequitantum[7] esset turma, abbas prædictus in extremo agmine cum monachis suis sensim progrediebatur; visoque eminus tanto viri honore, quod tot mundanæ potestates nutum illius præstolarentur, hujuscemodi sententias ventilabat animo: Homuncionem exilis staturæ, despicabilis parentelæ, quo Dei judicio tot divitum sepiri famulitio? tumere illum proculdubio, et metiri

He is archdeacon and chancellor under Alexander II.

---

[1] *Apuliæ*] hoc, ins. Cd.
[2] *Quæ*] Quem, Cc.¹
[3] *eum*] enim, Bc.; om. Aa. Al. Cd.
[4] *omnium*] omnibus, Aa. Al.
[5] *ei*] eis, Al.
[6] *secularis*] secularibus, A_t.
[7] *adequitantum*] ad equitandum, Aa. Al. Bc.

altiora merito, pro tot obambulatorum obsequio. Vix hæc ut, dixi, mente versarat, cum archidiaconus, reflexo equo et calcaribus incito, a longe clamans et abbatem obuncans, "Tu, tu," inquit, "male cogitasti, falso in-
"famans hujusce duntaxat rei innocentem; non enim
"mihi hanc gloriam, si gloria dici potest quæ cito
"transit, vel ego imputo vel ab aliis imputari volo,
"sed beatis apostolis, quorum exhibetur privilegio."
Suffusus ille pudore, nec quicquam inficiari ausus, hoc solum retulit: "Quæso, domine, quomodo nosti cogi-
"tatum meum, quem nulli communicavi?" "Ab ore,"
ait, "tuo, quasi per fistulas, ad aures meas omnis illa
"cogitatio deducta est." *He detects the thoughts of the Abbot of Cluny.*

§ 264. Item in eadem provincia ecclesiam urbanam ingressi, ante aram continuatis et junctis lateribus se prostraverant. In multam horam protracta oratione, respexit archidiaconus abbatem, turbulento rictu infrendens: ille, cum diutius oratum esset, fores egressus, causamque commotionis percunctatus, responsum accepit: "Si me amare vis, cave ne ulterius hac me
"injuria expungas. Dominus meus Jesus, speciosus
"ille præ filiis hominum, postulationibus meis visi-
"biliter astabat, intendens dictis, et serenis favens
"oculis; sed, tuæ orationis addictus violentia, me
"deseruit, ad te conversus: puto quod tu ipse non
"diffiteberis esse genus injuriæ si amico eripias
"auctorem salutis suæ. Præterea prænoveris mortali-
"tatem hominum, et huic loco imminere excidium;
"cujus conjecturæ signum habeo, quod angelum
"Domini super altare stantem vidi evaginatum gla-
"dium stringere, et huc illucque rotare. Futuræ
"cladis notabilius habeo indicium, quod jam spissus
"et nebulosus aer provinciam istam circumvolat, ut
"vides. Maturemus ergo profugium, nisi cum aliis
"velimus subire exitium." His dictis introeuntes diversorium, ad curam corporis assedere; continuoque dapibus appositis, exortus in domo luctus aviditatem *Another story of the Abbot.*

esurientium repressit, siquidem unus et alter, et mox plures e familia, dubium qua pernicie intercepti, animas subito amisere. Tum eadem peste per vicinas ædes grassante, ascensis mulis diffugiunt, festinationem viæ stimulis timoris [1] accelerantes.

De Episcopo per Simoniam introducto.

§ 265. In Gallia vicepapa [2] præsederat concilio; ibi plures episcopi, olim per simoniam in ecclesias introducti, degradati, potioribus locum dedere. Unus erat quem suspicio istius apostasiæ insimulabat, sed nullis testibus argui, nullis argumentis confutari poterat: quem cum putares constrictum maxime, more anguis lubrici elapsum mirareris; ita dicendi arte callebat ut omnes eluderet. Tunc archidiaconus: " Cesset homi-
" num eloquium, producatur in medium divinum
" oraculum: scimus profecto quod episcopalis gratia
" Sancti Spiritus munus est; et quisquis episcopatum
" mercatur, Spiritus Sancti donum posse comparari
" pecunia opinatur. Coram nobis ergo, qui judicio
" Sancti Spiritus congregati sumus, dicat iste, 'Gloria
" 'Patri, et Filio, et Spiritui Sancto;' quod si ex-
" presse et sine titubantia dixerit, constabit apud me
" non illum venaliter, sed legitime, præsulatu functum."
Libens hanc conditionem ille accepit, nihil minus quam horum verborum difficultatem ratus; et certe " Gloria Patri, et Filio," integre protulit, sed in " Spiritu Sancto" hæsit. Suscitato cunctorum strepitu, nullo conatu, vel tunc vel in vitæ reliquo spatio, Spiritum Sanctum nominare potuit. Hujus miraculi testis fuit abbas sæpe nominatus, qui, dejectum episcopum per loca secum ducens, illius rei experimentum sæpe risit; de cujus verborum certitudine dubitantem omnis Europa confutat, quæ religionis Cluniacensis numerum per eum augmentatum non nescit.

---

[1] *timoris*] om. Ce.¹
[2] *vicepapa*] vice papæ, An. Al. By. Cd. Cm.

§ 266. Alexandro ergo defuncto, successit Hildebrandus, Gregorius septimus dictus. Hic quod alii mussitaverant palam extulit, excommunicans electos qui investituras ecclesiarum de manu laici per anulum et baculum acciperent; unde Henricus imperator Alamannorum fremens, quod sine sua conscientia electus[1] talia praesumeret, illum, ut praedixi, post undecim annos Roma deturbavit, Guiberto inducto. Nec multo post lethali papa morbo ictus, quo se moriturum non ambigeret, rogatus est a cardinalibus ut papam constitueret, beati Petri exemplum referentibus, qui, lactentis ecclesiae rudimentis vivens Clementem praefecerat. Negavit ille id se[2] exemplum secuturum, quod ab antiquo conciliis esset vetitum; consilium vero daturum: si vellent hominem in seculo potentem, eligerent Desiderium abbatem Cassinensem,[3] qui salubriter et in tempore numero militari violentiam Guiberti infringeret; sin ecclesiasticum et eloquentem, acciperent episcopum Hostiensem Odonem. Ita obiit vir apud Deum felicis gratiae, et apud homines austeritatis fortassis nimiae. Denique fertur quod, inter eum et imperatorem primi tumultus initio, illum nudipedem, et forcipes cum scopis portantem, nec etiam foribus admiserit; abominatus hominem sacrilegum,[4] et sororii incesti reum. Abscessit Caesar exclusus, repulsam illam multorum necis causam protestans. Statimque quaecunque posset incommoda Romanae sedi infligens, e diverso fautores papae in tyrannidem excitavit; siquidem rebellante quodam Radulfo, jussu ipsius apostolici, qui ei coronam ex parte apostolorum miserat, bellorum fragoribus undique conflictatus est: sed ille, semper adversis superior, et illum et ceteros improbe assurgentes tandem oppressit. Postremo non aliorum impetu, sed domestico filii odio extrusus im-

---

[1] *electus*] om. Aa.
[2] *id se*] idem, Aa.
[3] *Cassinensem*] Cassiorensem, Bc.
[4] *sacrilegum*] ut ferebatur, ins. Cd.

perio, miserabilem vitæ terminum habuit. Successit Hildebrando Desiderius, Victor appellatus; sed ad primam missam, incertum quo discrimine, cecidit exanimatus, calice, si dignum est credere, veneno infecto. Tunc in Odonem declinavit electio: is natione Gallus, primum Remensis archidiaconus, inde prior Cluniacensis, mox episcopus Hostiæ, ultimo papa Romæ, Urbanus vocatus est.

§ 267. Hactenus circumvagari licuerit, dum occasione gestorum Willelmi quædam succurrebant quæ prætermittenda non putabam: nunc familiarem ejus vitam, et mores interiores, lector qui volet audiet. Inprimis, Dei[1] famulis humilis, subjectis facilis, in rebelles inexorabilis erat. Religionem Christianam, quantum secularis poterat,[2] ita frequentabat, ut cotidie[3] missæ assisteret, cotidie[4] vespertinos et matutinos hymnos audiret. Monasteria, unum in Anglia, alterum in Normannia, construxit. Primum Cadomis, quod sancto Stephano consecravit, opportunis prædiis et magnificentissimis donariis insignitum, ubi et Lanfrancum abbatem, post etiam Cantuariæ archiepiscopum instituit: virum antiquis scientia et religione comparandum, de quo serio dici potest, "Tertius e cælo cecidit Cato;" adeo cælestis sapor pectus ejus et palatum infecerat; adeo Latinitas omnis in liberalium artium scientiam, per doctrinam ejus, se incitabat; adeo, ipsius exemplo vel metu, professio monastica in religione sudabat. Non tunc episcoporum ambitus, non tunc abbatum venalitas proficiebat: ille majoris gloriæ, amplioris gratiæ, apud regem et archiepiscopum erat, qui tenacioris sanctitudinis opinionem habebat. Alterum monasterium Hastingis ædificavit[5] sancto Martino, quod cognominatur De Bello, quia in eo loco principalis ecclesia cernitur ubi inter consertos cada-

Juvenal,
Sat. ii. 40.

---

[1] *Dei*] om. Bc. Bk.
[2] *poterat*] potentiæ, Bc.
[3] *cotidie*] cotidianæ, Aah.
[4] *cotidie*] om. Aa.
[5] *ædificavit*] construxit, Bc. Bk. Bq. By.

verum acervos Haroldus inventus fuisse memoratur. Pene puer, et maturiora [1] ætate sapiens, patruum suum Malgerium ab archiepiscopatu Rotomagensi removit. Is erat litteris quidem non mediocriter cultus; sed, pro natalium conscientia professionis oblitus, venationibus et avium certaminibus sæpius justo intendebat,[2] et gazas ecclesiasticas conviviis profusioribus insumebat: cujus rei fama crebrescente, tota vita pallii usu caruit, quod negaret sedes apostolica honoris hujusce privilegium homini qui sacratum negligebat officium. Unde crebro conventus, expostulante nepote patruelis offensas, cum nihilo reverentius se ageret, cogente ultima necessitate degradatus est. Ferunt quidam esse arcanam depositionis causam; Matildem, quam Willelmus acceperat, proximam sibi sanguine fuisse; id, Christianæ fidei zelo, Malgerium non tulisse, ut consanguineo cubili fruerentur; sed in nepotem et comparem excommunicationis jaculum intentasse; ita cum iræ adolescentis uxoriæ querelæ accederent, excogitatas occasiones quibus persecutor peccati sede pelleretur: sed postmodum provectioribus annis, pro expiatione sceleris, illum sancto Stephano Cadomis monasterium ædificasse, illam beatæ Trinitati in eodem vico idem fecisse; utroque pro sexu suo personas inhabitantium eligente.

§ 268. Malgerio successit Maurilius, Fiscannensis monachus, multis virtutibus sed maxime abstinentia laudatus. Is post bene et sancte actam vitam, cum ad extremum Deo vocante venisset, vitali privatus halitu[3] ferme dimidia die jacuit defunctus; veruntamen, cum jam pararetur in ecclesiam ferri, anima resumpta circumstantes lacrymabili gaudio perfudit. Stupentes hoc sermone corroborat: "Attenti animo estote, ultima

---

[1] *maturiora*] maturi, Cd.
[2] *intendebat*] incumbebat, Bc. By.
[3] *halitu*] anhelitu, Cd.

328   GESTA REGUM ANGLORUM.   [LIB. III.

"pastoris vestri verba excipientes. Naturali morte
"resolutus fui, sed, ut vobis intimarem quæ vidi, re-
"ductus sum; nec aliquanto diutius subsistam, quia
"in Domino soporari delectat. Ductores spiritus mei
"vultibus et vestibus ad omnem elegantiam erant
"compositi; concordabat verborum lenitas cum nitore
"vestium, ut nihil desiderarem præter talium viro-
"rum obsequium. Itaque blandis assentationibus ga-
"visus, ibam, ut vere mihi videbatur, versus orien-
"tem: promittebatur mihi sedes paradisiaca, non multo
"post intranda. In momento præterita Europa, in-
"gressi Asiam, venimus Jerosolimam; ibi sanctis
"adoratis, Jordanem pertendimus; citerioris ripæ ac-
"colæ, ductorum meorum contubernio mixti, lætum
"cœtum fecere. Ego, visendi ulteriora studio, tran-
"situm maturabam. Tunc comites Deum præcepisse
"referunt ut ante dæmonum visione terrificarer, qua-
"tenus veniales culpæ, quas confessione non dilueram,
"pavore horrendarum formarum purgarentur. Cum
"dicto astitit alteri parti tanta dæmonum vis, hastilia
"acuta vibrantium, ignes efflantium, ut ager ferreus,
"aer flammeus videretur. Eorum horrore[1] ita sum
"affectus, ut si terra dehisceret, si cælum patesceret,
"tuto mihi utrobique refugiendum non æstimarem.
"Ita meticulosus, dum quo evadam dubito, repente,
"ut hæc dicens vestræ saluti nisi negligitis consu-
"lerem, halitum[2] recepi, confestim effusurus." Dixit,
et cum verbo pene spiritum emisit. Corpus, in ecclesia sanctæ Mariæ tunc humi defossum, miraculo
modo, ut aiunt, divino altius tribus pedibus super terram elevatum est.

§ 269. Porro Willelmus, propositi quod in Normannia cœperat tenax, Stigandum, perperam et falso
archiepiscopum, per cardinales Romanos, et Ermen-
fredum episcopum Sedunensem, deponi passus est.

---

[1] *horrore*] horrorum, Aa. Al. | [2] *halitum*] anhelitum, Cd.

Successit ei in Wintonia Walkelinus;[1] cujus bona opera, famam vincentia, vetustatem oblivionis a se repellent quamdiu ibi sedes episcopalis durabit: in Cantia Lanfrancus, de quo supra dixi, qui talis Angliæ Dei dono emicuit,[2] *Praises of Walkelin and Lanfranc.*

"Qualis discutiens fugientia Lucifer astra,
"Cum roseo clarum provehit ore diem;"

ita ipsius industria monasticum germen effloruit, ita eo vivente vigor pontificalis induruit. Ejus consilio rex pronum se fecerat, ut nihil negandum duceret quod is faciendum diceret. Ipsius etiam impulsu ambitum nebulonum fregerat, qui consueto more mancipia sua Hiberniam venditabant: cujus facti præconium cui potius imputem, Lanfranco an Wulstano Wigorniæ antistiti, pro vero non discerno, qui regem, pro commodo venalitatis quod sibi pensitabatur, renitentem vix ad hoc coegerint, nisi quod Lanfrancus laudaverit Wulstanus præceperit, auctoritate episcopali pro conscientia sanctitatis abunde exuberans; homo quo nullus unquam justior, nullus nostro seculo par illi apparuerit miraculorum potentia et prophetali gratia, quorum aliqua intendo dicere posterius si tamen sanctissimis illius placuerit sensibus. *Abolition of the slave trade, by advice of Lanfranc, or of Wulfstan.*

§ 270. Veruntamen, quia alea fortunæ incertis jactibus volvitur, multa tunc tempore adversa pervenere. Fœda inter abbatem Glastoniæ et monachos ejus discordia, ita ut post verborum lites ad arma ventum sit. Coacti ergo intra ecclesiam monachi sancto altari miserias suas ingemebant;[3] sed irrumpentibus militibus, duo ex eis interfecti, quatuordecim vulnerati, ceteri repulsi, nam et furor militum etiam crucifixum sagittis inhorrere fecerat. Hujus noxæ crimine infama- *Disgraceful riot at Glastonbury.*

---

[1] *Walkelinus*] Here MS. Al. has the following late gloss: "Walke- "linus, de quo alibi scribitur quod "abstulit monachis trescentas libra- "tas terræ, et eas tam usibus suis "quam successorum suorum damp- "nabiliter applicuit."

[2] *emicuit*] apparuit, Bc. By.

[3] *ingemebant*] applorabant, Aa. Al.

tus abbas, tota vita regis exilio deportatus est; eoque defuncto, pro redemptione peccati auxiliaribus annumerata pecunia, honori restitutus est.

Tragedy of bishop Walcher of Durham.

§ 271. Miserabilis et infanda caedes Walkerii[1] Dunelmensis episcopi, quem Northanhimbri populus, semper rebellioni deditus, abjecto sacrorum ordinum respectu, multis impetitum convitiis trucidarunt. Fusus ibi non paucus numerus Lotharingorum, quod praesul ipse nationis ejus erat. Causa caedis haec fuit: erat episcopus praeter pontificatum custos totius comitatus; praefeceratque rebus forensibus Gislebertum cognatum, interioribus Leobinum clericum, ambos in rebus commissis strenuos sed effraenes. Tolerabat episcopus eorum immodestiam, gratia strenuitatis inductus; et, quia eos elevarat, cumulum benignitatis augebat. Indulget enim natura sibi, placidoque favore suis arridet ipsa muneribus. Is Leobinus Liulfum, beatissimi Cuthberti ministrum, adeo dilectum ut ipse sanctus coram vigilanti assistens placita imperaret,—hunc, inquam, Liulfum per Gislebertum obtruncari fecit, livore ictus quod amplioris amicitiae locum apud pontificem, pro conscientia et aequitate judiciorum, haberet. Perculsus nuntio Walkerius, furenti parentelae defuncti legalis placiti judicium opposuit,[2] protestatus Leobinum suae suorumque necis auctorem. Ubi ventum ad placitum, nullis effera gens rationibus emolliri potuit quin in episcopum referret culpam, quod ambos homicidas in curia ejus post necem Liulfi familiariter diversatos vidissent. Surrectum ergo in clamores et iras; et Gislebertus de ecclesia, in qua cum episcopo sederat, ultro egrediens, ut suo periculo vitam domini mercaretur, impie occisus. Tum praesul, prae januis pacem praetento ramo offerens, rabiem vulgi explevit interemptus: fomes etiam mali Leobinus semiustulatus, quod nisi ecclesia cremata exire nolebat, exiliens mille

---

[1] The following tragedy is told in nearly the same words in the Gesta Pontificum, lib. iii. § 132.

[2] *opposuit*] apposuit, Bc. Cd. Ce.

lanceis exceptus est. Prædictum id ab Edgitha relicta regis Edwardi; nam cum olim Walkerium vidisset Wintoniæ ad consecrandum duci, cæsarie lacteolum, vultu roseum, statura prægrandem, "Pulchrum hic," ait, "martyrem habemus," conjectura videlicet immodestæ nationis ad præsagiendum inducta. Successit ei Willelmus abbas sancti Carilefi, qui monachos in Dunelmo posuit.

Saying of queen Edith about him.

§ 272. Præterea, anno antequam moreretur proximo, mortalitas hominum et jumentorum, vis tempestatum frequens, violentia fulgurum, quantam nemo viderat, nemo audierat. Illo quoque anno quo obiit, promiscua febris plusquam dimidiam partem plebis depasta, adeo ut plures incommoditas morbi extingueret; deinde, pro intemperie aeris, fames subsecuta vulgo irrepsit, ut quod febribus erat reliquum ipsa corriperet.

Portents of the year before the Conqueror's death.

§ 273. Præter ceteras virtutes, præcipue in prima adolescentia castitatem suspexit, in tantum ut publice sereretur nihil illum in fœmina posse; veruntamen, ex procerum sententia matrimonio addictus, ita se egit ut pluribus annis nullius probri suspicione notaretur. Tulit ex Matilde liberos multos, quæ, et marito morigera et prole fœcunda, nobilis viri animum in sui amoris incitabat aculeum: quanquam non desint qui ganniant eum cælibatui antiquo renuntiasse cum regia potestas accrevisset, volutatum cum cujusdam presbyteri filia, quam per satellitem succiso poplite Matildis sustulerit; quapropter illum exheredatum, illam ad mortem fræno equi cæsam. Sed hæc de tanto rege credere dementiæ ascribo; hoc constanter asseverans, quod aliquantula simultas inter eos innata extremis annis fuerit pro Roberto filio, cui mater militarem manum ex fisci redditibus sufficere dicebatur: verum propter hoc nihil conjugalis gratiæ diminutum ipse ostendit, dum quatuor annis ante se defunctam et magnificentissimis inferiis extulit, et lacrymis per multos dies ubertim prosecutus, amissæ caritatem

Chastity of William the Conqueror.

False legend about his treatment of his wife.

His grief at her death.

desideraverit; quin et ex eo tempore, si credimus, ab omni voluptate descivit. Sepulta est regina Cadomis in monasterio sanctæ Trinitatis. Ejusdem pietatis indicium in Edgithæ reginæ funere curando non minus fuit, quæ, apud Westmonasterium studio ejus prope conjugem locata, habet tumbam argenti aurique expensis operosam.

Burial of Queen Edith.

§ 274. Filios habuit, Robertum, Ricardum, Willelmum, Henricum. Posteriores duo post eum successione continua in Anglia[1] regnavere. Robertus, patre adhuc vivente, Normanniam sibi negari ægre ferens, in Italiam obstinatus abiit, ut, filia Bonefacii marchionis sumpta, patri partibus illis adjutus adversaretur: sed, petitionis hujusce cassus, Philippum Francorum regem contra patriam[2] excitavit; quare et genitoris benedictione et hereditate frustratus, Anglia post mortem ejus caruit, comitatu Normanniæ vix retento. Ea quoque post novem annos fratri Willelmo pro pecunia invadata, Asiaticam expeditionem cum ceteris Christianis aggressus est; inde, transactis quatuor annis, clarus militiæ gestis regressus, Normanniæ sine difficultate immersit, quod, germano Willelmo nuper defuncto, Henricus rex, novitate tener, Angliam in fide tenere satis habuit: sed quia de hoc alias dicendum, nunc cœptam de filiis Willelmi magni narrationem terminabo.

The Conqueror's sons.

Robert: his rebellion.

His mortgage of Normandy.

His crusade and return.

§ 275. Ricardus magnanimo parenti spem laudis alebat, puer delicatus; ut id ætatulæ pusio, altum quid spirans. Sed tantam primævi floris indolem mors acerba cito depasta corrupit; tradunt cervos in Nova Foresta terebrantem, tabidi aeris nebula morbum incurrisse. Locus est quem Willelmus pater, subrutis ecclesiis,[3] desertis villis, per triginta et eo amplius miliaria in saltus et lustra ferarum redegerat.

Richard: his death.

Story of the New Forest.

---

[1] *in Anglia*] om. Ce.
[2] *patriam*] patrem, Cd.
[3] *subrutis ecclesiis*] om. Bc. Bk. Ce.

Ibi libenter ævum exigere, ibi plurimis, omitto diebus, certe mensibus, venationes exercere gaudebat. Ibi multa regio generi contigere infortunia, quæ habitatorum præsens audire volentibus suggerit memoria: nam postmodum[1] in eadem silva Willelmus filius ejus, et nepos Ricardus filius Roberti comitis Normanniæ, mortem offenderunt; severo Dei judicio, ille sagitta pectus, iste collum trajectus, vel, ut quidam dicunt, arboris ramusculo equo pertranseunte fauces appensus. *Fatalities there.*

§ 276. Filiæ ipsius fuerunt quinque.[2] Cecilia, Cadomensis abbatissa, vivit;[3] altera, Constantia, comiti Brittanniæ Alano Fergant in conjugium data, austeritate justitiæ provinciales in mortiferam sibi potionem exacuit; tertia, Adala, Stephani Blesensis comitis uxor, laudatæ in seculo potentiæ virago, noviter apud Marcenniacum sanctimonialis habitum sumpsit. Duarum nomina exciderunt: unius, quæ Haroldo, ut diximus, promissa, infra maturos conjugio annos obiit; alterius, quæ, Aldefonso Galliciæ regi per nuntios jurata, virgineam mortem impetravit a Deo. Repertus in defunctæ genibus callus crebrarum ejus orationum index est. *The Conqueror's daughters, Cecilia, Constance, and Adela. Two, whose names are forgotten.*

§ 277. Patris memoriam quantis poterat occasionibus extollens, ossa,[4] olim Niceæ condita, sub extremo vitæ tempore per legatum transferebat; sed ille prospere rediens, audita morte Willelmi, apud Apuliam resedit, sepultis ibi illustris viri exuviis. Matrem quantum vixit insigni indulgentia dignatus est; quæ, ante patris obitum, cuidam Herlewino de Comitisvilla, mediocrium *Removal of duke Robert's remains. Marriage of the Conqueror's mother.*

---

[1] *Ibi libenter—postmodum*] instead of this the MSS. of the A recension (Aa. Aah. Al. Ag. At.) read: Infando prorsus spectaculo, ut ubi ante vel humana conversatio vel divina veneratio fervebat, nunc ibi cervi et capreoli, et ceteræ illud genus bestiæ petulanter discursitent, nec illæ quidem mortalium usibus communiter expositæ. Unde pro vero asseritur quod —.

[2] *quinque*] prima, Aa. Aah.

[3] *vivit*] quæ vivit, Aa. Cd. Cecilia died in 1127.

[4] *ossa*] om. Ce.[1]; Willelmus ossa patris sui, Cd.

opum viro, nupserat. Ex eo Willelmus fratres habuit: Robertum, quem comitem Moritonii fecit, crassi et hebetis ingenii hominem; Odonem, quem ad episcopatum Bajocensem provexit comes, comitem Cantiæ rex instituit. Callidioris pectoris ille totius Angliæ vicedominus sub rege fuit, post necem Willelmi filii Osberni. Itaque in aggerandis thesauris mirus, tergiversari miræ astutiæ,[1] pene papatum Romanum absens a civibus mercatus fuerat; peras peregrinorum epistolis et nummis infarciens. Cujus futuri itineris opinione cum certatim ex toto regno ad eum milites concurrerent, rex indigne ferens, compedibus irretivit; præfatus non se Bajocarum episcopum sed comitem Cantiæ prendere. Clientes ejus, minis impulsi, tantam auri copiam prodidere, ut nostri seculi æstimationem superaret fulvi congeries metalli; denique et cullei plures e fluviis extracti, quos per certa loca, sublatis consciis, infoderat, plenos auro molito. Post mortem fratris absolutus, nepotique Willelmo adversatus, partem Roberti fovebat; sed tunc quoque male cedente fortuna, extorris Anglia, Normannico nepoti et episcopatui insistebat. Deinde cum eodem Jerosolimitanam viam ingressus, Antiochiæ, in obsidione Christianorum, finem habuit.

§ 278. Exterarum nationum homines dignanter ad amicitiam admisit, indifferenter honoribus extulit: eleemosynæ curam habuit: transmarinis ecclesiis multas possessiones in Anglia largitus; nec ullum fere monasterium, præsertim in Normannia, vel ejus vel ducum munificentia pertransiit, ut Angliæ copia tenuitas illorum sustentaretur. Ita ejus tempore ultro citroque coenobialis grex excrevit, monasteria surgebant religione vetera, ædificiis recentia. Sed hic animadverto mussitationem dicentium, melius fuisse ut antiqua in suo statu conservarentur, quam, illis semimutilatis, de rapina nova construerentur.

---

[1] *astutiæ*] abstinentiæ, Aa. Al. At.

§ 279. Justæ fuit staturæ, immensæ corpulentiæ, facie fera, fronte capillis nuda, roboris ingentis in lacertis, ut magno sæpe spectaculo fuerit quod nemo ejus arcum tenderet, quem ipse admisso equo pedibus nervo extento sinuaret; magnæ dignitatis sedens et stans, quanquam obesitas ventris nimis protensa corpus regium deformaret; commodæ valitudinis, ut qui nunquam aliquo morbo periculoso præter in extremo decubuerit; exercitio nemorum adeo deditus, ut, sicut prædixi, multa milia ejectis habitatoribus silvescere juberet, in quibus, a ceteris negotiis avocatus, animum remitteret. Convivia in præcipuis festivitatibus sumptuosa et magnifica inibat; Natale Domini apud Gloecestram, Pascha apud Wintoniam, Pentecosten apud Westmonasterium agens quotannis quibus in Anglia morari liceret: omnes eo cujuscunque professionis magnates regium edictum accersiebat, ut exterarum gentium legati speciem multitudinis apparatumque deliciarum mirarentur. Nec ullo tempore comior aut indulgendi facilior erat, ut qui advenerant largitatem ejus cum divitiis conquadrare ubique gentium jactitarent. Quem morem convivandi primus successor obstinate tenuit, secundus omisit.

William's personal appearance and strength.

His three annual court days.

Later neglect of the custom of court days.

§ 280. Sola est de qua nonnihil[1] culpetur pecuniæ aggestio,[2] quam undecunque captatis occasionibus, honestas modo et regia dignitate non inferiores posset dicere, congregabat. Sed excusabitur facile, quia novum regnum sine magna pecunia non posset regere.[3] Non est hic aliquid aliud[4] excusationis quod afferam nisi quod quidam dixit, "Necesse est ut multos timeat, " quem multi timent." Nam ille, pro timore in-

William's avarice.

A palliation.

---

[1] *nonnihil*] merito, Aa. Al.
[2] *aggestio*] cupiditas, Aa. Al.
[3] *honestas—regere*]. For this clause the MSS. of the A recension read "nihil unquam pensi habuit, " quin corraderet; faceret, diceret, " nonnulla et pene omnia, tanta majestate indigniora, ubi spes nummi " effulsisset;" Aa. Aah. Ag. Al. At. Ap.
[4] *aliud*] om. Aa, Al.

imicorum, provincias suas pecunia emungebat, qua impetus eorum vel tardaret vel etiam propelleret, persæpe ut fit in rebus humanis viribus cassatis, fidem hostilem præmio pigneratus: regnat adhuc et indies augetur hujusce dedecoris calamitas, ut et villæ et ecclesiæ pensionibus supponantur; et ne hoc quidem perpetua exactorum fide, sed quicunque plus obtulerit, statim, pactis irritis prioribus, palmam habeat.

Insolent saying of king Philip on William's illness.

§ 281. Extremo vitæ tempore in Normannia habitans, contractis inimicitiis cum rege Francorum, aliquantisper se continuit; cujus abutens patientia, Philippus fertur dixisse, "Rex Angliæ jacet Rotomagi, more absolutarum partu fœminarum cubile fovens," jocatus in ejus ventrem quem potione alleviarat. Quo præstrictus convitio, respondit, "Cum ad missam post *The Conqueror's rejoinder.* "partum iero, centum milia candelas ei libabo;" talia "per resurrectionem et splendorem Dei" pronuntians, quod soleret ex industria talia sacramenta facere, quæ ipso hiatu[1] oris terrificum quiddam auditorum mentibus insonarent.

He ravages the French border.

§ 282. Nec multo post, Augusto mense declinante, quando et segetes in agris, et botri in vineis, et poma in viridariis, copiam sui volentibus faciunt, exercitu coacto, Franciam infestus ingreditur. Omnia proterit, cuncta populatur; nihil erat quod furentis animum mitigaret, ut injuriam insolenter acceptam multorum *He burns Mantes.* dispendio ulcisceretur. Postremo Medantum civitatem injectis ignibus cremavit, combusta illic ecclesia sanctæ Mariæ; reclusa una ustulata, quæ spelæum suum nec in tali necessitate deserendum putavit; fortunæ omnes civium pessundatæ. Quo successu exhilaratus, dum suos audacius incitat ut igni adjiciant pabula, propius flammas succedens, foci calore et autumnalis æstus *Fatal accident.* inæqualitate morbum nactus est. Dicunt quidam quod

---

[1] *hiatu*] halitu, Al. At.; rictu, Aa. Aah.

præruptam fossam sonipes transsiliens interanea sessoris disruperit,[1] quod in anteriori parte sellæ venter protuberabat. Hoc dolore affectus receptui suis cecinit; Rotomagumque reversus, crescente indies incommodo, lecto excipitur. Consulti medici inspectione urinæ certam mortem prædixere. Quo audito querimonia domum replevit, quod eum præoccuparet mors emendationem vitæ jamdudum meditantem. Resumpto animo, quæ Christiani sunt executus est in confessione et viatico. Normanniam invitus et coactus Roberto, Angliam Willelmo, possessiones maternas Henrico delegavit. Vinctos suos omnes educi et solvi, thesauros efferri et ecclesiis dispergi, præcepit. Certum numerum pecuniæ ad reparationem ecclesiæ nuper crematæ ipse indixit. Ordinatis ergo bene rebus, octavo idus Septembris decessit, anno regni vicesimo primo,[2] comitatus quinquagesimo secundo, vitæ quinquagesimo nono, Dominicæ incarnationis millesimo octogesimo septimo. Ille fuit annus quo Cnuto rex Danorum, ut supra diximus, interemptus est; quo Sarraceni Hispani in Christianos efferati, mox ab Aldefonso rege Galliciæ ad sua redire coacti, etiam urbibus quas olim tenuerant inviti cessere.

His preparation for death and disposal of his possessions.

He dies Sept. 6, 1087.

Above § 261.

Contemporary events.

§ 283. Corpus, regio sollempni curatum, per Sequanam Cadomum delatum; ibi magna frequentia ordinatorum, laicorum pauca, humi traditum. Varietatis humanæ tunc fuit videre miseriam, quod homo ille totius olim Europæ honor, antecessorumque suorum omnium potentior, sedem æternæ requietionis sine calumpnia impetrare non potuit: namque miles quidam, ad cujus patrimonium locus ille pertinuerat, clara contestans voce rapinam, sepulturam inhibuit, dicens, avito jure solum suum esse, nec illum in loco quem violenter invaserat pausare debere. Quocirca volente Henrico

The Conqueror's body brought to Caen.

A knight claims the grave ground.

Henry pays the price.

---

[1] *disruperit*] ruperit, Ce.[1] | [2] *primo*] secundo, At,

filio, qui solus ex liberis aderat, centum libræ argenti litigatori persolutæ audacem calumpniam compescuere: nam tunc Robertus primogenitus in Francia contra patriam bellabat; Willelmus, antequam plane pater exspiraret, Angliam enavigaverat, utilius ducens suis in posterum commodis prospicere, quam obsequiis[1] paterni corporis interesse. Porro, in dispertienda pecunia nec segnis nec parcus, omnem illum thesaurum Wintoniæ totis annis regni cumulatum ab arcanis sacrariis eruit in lucem; monasteriis aurum, ecclesiis agrestibus solidos quinque argenti, unicuique pago centum libras viritim egenis dividendas, largitus. Patris etiam memoriam ingenti congerie argenti et auri, cum gemmarum luce, conspicue adornavit.

William, at Winchester, seizes the treasure.

His expenditure on his father's memory.

De Berengario.

§ 284. Fuit hoc tempore Berengarius, Turonensis hæresiarcha, qui panem et vinum in altari apposita, post consecrationem sacerdotis, verum et substantiale corpus Domini, sicut sancta ecclesia prædicat, esse denegabat. Jamque scatebat omnis Gallia ejus doctrina, per egenos scholares, quos ipse cotidiana stipe sollicitabat, disseminata. Unde soliditati catholicæ timens, sanctissimæ[2] memoriæ Leo papa, Vercellis contra eum instituto concilio, tenebras nebulosi erroris evangelicorum testimoniorum fulgure depulit; sed cum post obitum ejus virus hæreseos, diu in sinibus quorundam nebulonum confotum, iterum erumperet, Hildebrandus cum archidiaconus esset Turonis, mox papa Romæ, adunatis conciliis, convictum ad dogmatis sui anathema compulit: quæ scripta suis locis qui desiderat inveniet. Responderunt ei libris Lanfrancus archiepiscopus, sed præcipue et fortiter Guimundus, prius monachus de sancto Leufredo Normanniæ, postea

History of Berengarius of Tours.

Council of Vercelli.

Lanfranc and Guimund answer Berengarius.

---

[1] *obsequiis*] exsequiis, Aa. Cd. | [2] *sanctissimæ*] sanctæ, Cc.

episcopus Aversanus Apuliæ, nostri temporis eloquentissimus. Porro, licet Berengarius primum calorem juventutis aliquarum hæresium defensione infamaverit, ævo austeriore ita resipuit ut sine retractatione a quibusdam sanctus habeatur, innumeris bonis, maximeque humilitate et eleemosynis, approbatus; largarum possessionum dispertiendo dominus, non abscondendo et adorando famulus; fœmineæ venustatis adeo parcus, ut nullam conspectui suo pateretur admitti, ne formam videretur delibasse oculo quam non pruriebat animo. Non aspernari pauperem, non adulari divitem; secundum naturam vivere; habens victum et vestitum, juxta apostolum, his contentus esse. Unde eum laudat Cenomannensis pontifex Hildebertus, inprimis versificator eximius; cujus verba propterea inserui, ut prædicabilis episcopi affectum in magistrum ostendam, simul et doctrina ejus erit exemplo posteris qua[1] quomodo vivi debeat instituit, etsi fortasse metas veræ laudis amore incitatus transsilierit.

Marginalia: 1 Tim. vi. 8. Character of Berengarius. Verses of Hildebert of le Mans, about him.

> " Quem modo miratur, semper mirabitur orbis,
>   " Ille Berengarius non obiturus obit.
> " Quem, sacræ fidei fastigia summa tenentem,
>   " Jani quinta dies abstulit, ausa nefas.
> " Illa dies damnosa dies, et perfida mundo,
>   " Qua dolor et rerum summa ruina fuit;
> " Qua status ecclesiæ, qua spes, qua gloria cleri,
>   " Qua cultor juris, jure ruente, ruit.
> " Quicquid philosophi, quicquid cecinere poetæ,
>   " Ingenio cessit eloquioque suo.
> " Sanctior et major sapientia, majus adorta,
>   " Implevit sacrum pectus et ora Deo.
> " Pectus eum voluit, vox protulit, actio prompsit,
>   " Singula Factori sic studuere suo.
> " Vir sacer et sapiens, cui nomen crescit in horas;
>   " Quo minor est quisquis maximus est hominum.
> " Cui sensus peperit, partos servavit honores;
>   " Cui potior pauper divite, jusque lucro.

Marginalia: His death, Jan. 5.

---

[1] qua] quo, Ce¹.

Poem of Hildebert on Berengarius.

"Cui nec desidiam nec luxum res dedit ampla,
"Nec tumidum fecit multus et altus honos.
"Qui nec ad argentum nec ad aurum lumina flexit;
"Sed doluit quotiens, cui daret hæc, aberat.
"Qui non cessavit inopum fulcire ruinas,
"Donec inops dando pauper et ipse fuit.
"Cujus cura sequi naturam, legibus uti,
"Et mentem vitiis, ora negare dolis;
"Virtutes opibus, verum præponere falso;
"Nil vacuum sensu dicere vel facere;
"Lædere nec quenquam, cunctis prodesse; favorem
"Et populare lucrum pellere mente, manu.
"Cui vestis textura rudis; cui non fuit unquam
"Ante sitim potus, nec cibus ante famem.
"Quem pudor hospitium statuit sibi; quamque libido
"Incestos superat, tam superavit eam.
"Quem natura parens cum mundo contulit inquit,
"'Degenerant alii, nascitur iste mihi.'
"Quæque vagabatur, et pene reliquerat orbem
"Inclusit sacro pectore justitiam.
"Vir sacer a puero, qui quantum præminet orbi
"Fama, tam famæ præminet ipse suæ.
"Fama, minor meritis, cum totum pervolet orbem,
"Cum semper crescat, non erit æqua tamen.
"Vir pius atque gravis; vir sic in utroque modestus,
"Ut livor neutro rodere possit eum.
"Livor enim deflet quem carpserat antea; nec tam
"Carpsit et odit eum, quam modo laudat, amat.
"Quam prius ex vita, tam nunc ex morte gemiscit,
"Et queritur celeres hujus abisse dies.
"Vir vere sapiens, et parte beatus ab omni;
"Qui cælos anima, corpore ditat humum.
"Post obitum vivam secum, secum requiescam,
"Nec fiat melior sors mea sorte sua."[1]

§ 285. Videas in his versibus quod laudis excesserit modum episcopus; sed sic se ostentat eloquentia, tali gestu procedit aureus lepos, eo modo

"Purpureos flores fundit facundia dives."

Berengarius, plane quamvis ipse sententiam correxerit,

---

[1] Hildeberti Turonensis, *Opera*, ed. Beaugendre, p. 1323; ed. Migne, col. 1396.

omnes quos ex totis terris depravaverat convertere nequivit; adeo pessimum est alios exemplo vel verbo a bono infirmare, quia fortassis peccatum te gravabit alienum, cum deletum fuerit tuum. Quod episcopum Carnotensem Fulbertum, quem Domini mater Maria olim ægrotum lacte mamillarum suarum visa fuerat sanare, prædixisse aiunt: nam cum in extremis positum multi visitarent, et ædium capacitas vix confluentibus sufficeret, ille inter oppositas catervas oculo longe rimatus, Berengarium nisu quo valuit expellendum censuit, protestatus immanem dæmonem propter eum consistere, multosque ad eum sequendum blandiente manu et illice anhelitu corrumpere; quin et ipse die Epiphaniorum moriens, gemituque producto recordatus quot miseros quondam adolescens primo erroris calore secta sua infecerit, "Hodie," inquit, "in die "apparitionis suæ apparebit mihi Dominus meus Jesus "Christus, propter pœnitentiam, ut spero, ad gloriam; "vel propter alios, ut timeo, ad pœnam."

Prophecy of Fulbert of Chartres about Berengarius.

§ 286. Nos sane credimus, post benedictionem ecclesiasticam, illa mysteria esse verum corpus et sanguinem Salvatoris; adducti et veteris ecclesiæ auctoritate, et multis noviter ostensis miraculis. Quale fuit illud quod beatus Gregorius exhibuit Romæ.[1] Quale quod Paschasius narrat contigisse Alamanniæ:[2] presbyterum Plegildum visibiliter speciem pueri in altare contrectasse et, post libata oscula, in panis similitudinem conversum ecclesiastico more sumpsisse: quod arroganti cavillatione ferunt Berengarium carpere solitum, et dicere, "Speciosa certe pax nebulonis, ut, cui oris "præbuerat basium, dentium inferret exitium." Quale de pusione Judaico; quod, in ecclesiam cum æquævo[3]

Our author's opinion on the doctrinal question.

Illustrations.

Berengar's levity.

---

[1] The story is given by Paschasius, as cited in the next note, col. 434.

[2] Paschasius Radbertus, de Corpore et Sanguine Domini, cap. 14. (Martene & Durand, *Amplissima Collectio*, ix. 437. Plegils is described as a votary of S. Ninian, and the story is taken from the "Gesta Angiorum."

[3] æquævo] cœquævo, Bc. Bk.

Christiano forte et ludibunde ingressus, vidit puerum in ara membratim discerpi, et viritim populo dividi. Id cum innocentia puerili parentibus pro vero assereret, in rogum detrusum ubi occluso ostio æstuabat incendium, multis post horis sine jactura corporis exuviarumque et etiam crinium, a Christianis extractum; interrogatusque quomodo voraces ignium globos evaserit, respondit, "Illa pulchra fœmina quam vidi "sedere in cathedra, cujus filius populo dividebatur, "semper mihi in camino ad dexteram astitit, flam- "meas minas et fumea volumina peplo suo summo- "vens."[1]

§ 287. Tunc in provincia Walarum, quæ Ros vocatur, inventum est sepulchrum Walwen, qui fuit haud degener Arturis ex sorore nepos. Regnavit in ea parte Britanniæ quæ adhuc Walweitha vocatur: miles virtute nominatissimus, sed a fratre et nepote Hengestii, de quibus in primo libro dixi, regno expulsus, prius multo eorum detrimento exilium compensans suum; communicans merito laudi avunculi, quod ruentis patriæ casum in plures annos distulerint. Sed Arturis sepulcrum nusquam visitur, unde antiquitas næniarum adhuc eum venturum fabulatur. Ceterum, alterius bustum, ut præmisi, tempore Willelmi regis repertum est super oram maris, quatuordecim pedes longum; ubi a quibusdam asseritur ab hostibus vulneratus, et naufragio ejectus; a quibusdam dicitur a civibus in publico epulo interfectus. Veritatis ergo notitia labat in dubio, licet neuter eorum defuerit famæ suæ patrocinio.

§ 288. Illa fuit tempestas qua Henrici, de quo inter gesta Willelmi locutus sum, miserabile et pene funestum per quinquaginta annos Alamannia ingemuit imperium. Erat is neque ineruditus neque ignavus, sed fato quodam ab omnibus ita impetitus, ut rem reli-

---

[1] *See* Pasch. Radb. (as cited above), cap. 9, col. 414.

gionis tractare sibi videretur quisquis in illum arma produceret. Habebat filios duos, Conradum et Henricum : prior nihil impium contra parentem ausus, subjugata Italia, apud Aretium civitatem Tusciæ dies expleverat: alter patrem, aliquantulum ab externis feriatum, primo ævi tirocinio aggressus, cedere imperio compulit ; nec multo post, defunctum imperialibus inferiis extulit. Vivit adhuc, ejusdem sententiæ pertinaciter sequax pro qua patrem persequendum putaverat: nam et investituram ecclesiarum per baculum et anulum donat, et sine suo arbitratu papam electum non legitimum æstimat; licet Calixtus,[1] qui modo apostolicæ sedi præsidet, immodicam viri aviditatem egregie inhibuerit. Verum de his plura me dicturum lector præstoletur, cum series narrationis expetierit.

Rebellion of his sons.

Henry V. and his controversy with Calixtus.

§ 289. Porro Hildebrando papa, ut dixi, mortuo, et Urbano a cardinalibus electo, imperator hæsit in proposito ut Wibertum præferret et papam dictitaret, Romæque, altero expulso, inferret: sed aequiori, ut videbatur, causæ affuit militia Matildis Marcisæ, quæ oblita sexus, nec dispar antiquis Amazonibus, ferrata virorum agmina in bellum agebat fœmina ; ejus suffragio Urbanus, posteriori tempore thronum indeptus apostolicum, securum per undecim annos actitavit otium. Post eum Paschalis, consputa Henrici scientia, a Romanis institutus est. Gravabat superas adhuc vivendo Wibertus auras, unicus schismatis sator, nec unquam quoad vixit pervicaciam deposuit ut justitiæ manus daret; imperatoris judicium pronuntians sequendum, non lanistarum vel pellificum Romanorum : quare ambo, ab Urbano sequentibus[2] conciliis excommunicati, arguto sententiam suspendebant ludibrio. Inter hæc erant multa quæ in Cæsare probares ; quod esset ore facundus, acer ingenio, multa eruditus lectione, impiger eleemosynis ; prorsus in eo [3]

The antipope Wibert of Ravenna.

The Marchioness Matilda.

Succession of popes.

Wibert's persistence.

Good points in the emperor.

---

[1] Henry V. died May 22, 1125 ; Calixtus, Dec. 12, 1124.
[2] *sequentibus*] frequentibus, Aa. Al. Ce.
[3] *eo*] ea, Ce.

bona animi corporisque cerneres; ad arma prompte concurrere, ut qui sexagies et bis acie collata dimicarit; juste lites componere; cum res non successisset, querelis in cælum conversis inde opem expectare. Plures inimicorum ejus vitam exitu miserando conclusere.

De homine a muribus dilacerato.

Story of the sad fate of one of his enemies.

§ 290. Audivi virum veracissimum referentem quod quidam ex adversariis ejus, homo impotens et factiosus, dum resupinatis cervicibus in convivio resideret, ita a muribus repente circumvallatus est ut nusquam esset effugium; tantus erat numerus bestiolarum ut in quamlibet ampla provincia tot esse non putarentur. Itaque fustibus, et subselliorum quæ ad manum occurrissent fragminibus, diu in eas sævitum, nec quicquam profectum; et quamvis a cunctis repellerentur, nulli tamen noxam vicariam referebant; illum solum dentibus, illum terribili quodam occentu persequebantur. Quapropter a famulis ultra jactum sagittæ in pelagus provectus, nec sic violentiam evasit; continuo enim tanta vis murium ponto inundavit ut marmor paleis *He was torn to pieces by mice.* constratum jurares. Sed cum jam tabulata navis corroderent, et naufragium indubitatum aqua per rimulas ingrediens minaretur, servientes puppem ad littus retorquent. Tum vero animalia, juxta carinam annavigantia, priora ad terram perveniunt; ita miser ille in aridam expositus, moxque totus dilaceratus, horrendam murium famem explevit.

Quod quem leopardus mordicus attigerit mures commingant.

Another story about mice.

§ 291. Id eo minus mirum judico, quia certum est in Asiaticis regionibus si leopardus aliquem mordicus attigerit, confestim murium copiam adventare, ut vulneratum commingant, immundum urinæ diluvium comitari hominis exitium; sin vero sedulitate arcentium ministrorum intra novem dies vitata fuerit pernicies, advocari medicorum industriam profecto valituram. Conspicatus est relator meus quendam ejusmodi saucium, cum desperaret in terra salutem, in altum jactis anchoris processisse; nec mora, plures illo[1] mures annasse, corticibus malorum granatorum quorum medullas exederant inclusos, mirabile dictu, sed obstrepentibus nautis demersos. Nihil enim ille Parens rerum creatum destituit ingenio, nihil porro noxium sine remedio.

De Mariniano Scotto.

§ 292. Sub isto imperatore regnante floruit Marinianus Scottus, qui primo Fuldensis monachus, post apud Magontiacum inclusus, contemptu praesentis vitae, gratiam futurae demerebatur. Is, longo vitae otio chronographos scrutatus, dissonantiam cyclorum Dionysii exigui ab evangelica veritate deprehendit; itaque, ab initio seculi annos singulos recensens, viginti duos annos qui circulis praedictis deerant superaddidit, sed paucos aut nullos sententiae suae sectatores habuit. Quare saepe mirari soleo cur nostri temporis doctos hoc respergat infortunium, ut in tanto numero discentium, in tam tristi pallore lucubrantium, vix aliquis plenam scientiae laudem referat. Adeo inveteratus usus placet; adeo fere nullus novis, licet probabiliter inventis, serenitatem assensus pro merito indulget; totis conatibus in sententiam veterum reptatur, omne recens sordet: ita, quia solus favor alit ingenia, cessante favor obtorpuerunt[2] omnia.

De miraculo quod accidit in Fuldensi coenobio.

§ 293. Sed quia Fuldense coenobium[3] nominavi, dicam quod ibidem accidisse vir reverendus mihi nar-

---

[1] *plures illo*] plus mille, Aa. Al.
[2] *obtorpuerunt*] torpent, Bc. By.
[3] *coenobium*] semel, ins. Bc. By.

ravit, Walkerius prior Malverni;[1] cujus verbis qui non credit, injuriam religioni facit. "Non," ait, "plus-
"quam quindecim anni sunt quod in eodem loco
"exitialis lues grassata prius abbatem corripuit, mox
"multos monachorum exstinxit. Superstites primo
"quisque sibi timere, orationes et eleemosynas lar-
"giores facere: sed processu temporis, ut est omnium
"natura hominum, pedetemptim, metu dempto, omit-
"tere; cellararius præsertim, qui palam et ridicule
"clamitaret non posse penum tot expensis sufficere;
"sperasse se nuper aliquod alleviamentum, pro tot
"elationibus funerum; nihil ultra spei esse, si quod
"vivi nequissent mortui consumerent. Itaque cum
"quadam nocte, pro re necessaria soporem diu distu-
"lisset, tandem elaqueatis morarum retibus in dor-
"mitorium ire pergebat; et ecce rem miram auditurus
"es, videt in capitulo abbatem, et omnes qui obierant
"illo anno, eo quo excesserant ordine sedere. Timi-
"dus et effugere gestiens, vi retractus est; increpitus,
"et monastico more flagellis coercitus, audivit verba
"abbatis in hanc omnino sententiam: stultum esse
"de alterius morte emolumento inhiare, cum sors
"cujusque sub eodem pendeat fato; impium esse,
"cum monachus omnem vitam in ecclesiæ consump-
"serit obsequio, ut careat unius saltem anni post
"mortem stipendio: illum citissime obiturum, sed
"quicquid pro eo fieret, ad aliorum quibus abstulerat
"refundendum commodum; iret modo, et alios corri-
"geret exemplo quos corruperat verbo. Abiit ille;
"et nihil se vanum vidisse, tam recentibus plagis
"quam proximo sui obitu, monstravit."

Dispute between Canterbury and York.

§ 294. Interea, dum alia agimus, irrepsit materia, et voluntas accessit, ut quid tempore Willelmi regis diffinitum sit de controversia quæ adhuc inter archiepiscopos Cantuariensem et Eboracensem volutatur,

---

[1] Walcher, prior of Malvern, died Oct. 1, 1135; Antiqq. Malv. p. xciii.

describam. De qua re, ut plane norint posteri, quid inde antiqui patres senserint apponam.

Quod omnes episcopi totius Britanniæ Archiepiscopo Doroberniæ subjiciantur.

§ 295. *Gregorius papa Augustino primo Anglorum archiepiscopo Dorobernæ.*—" Tua fraternitas non solum eos episcopos
" quos ordinaverit, neque hos tantummodo qui per Eboracensem[1] episcopum fuerint ordinati, sed etiam omnes Brittanniæ sacerdotes, habeat, Deo Domino nostro Jesu Christo
" auctore, subjectos."

§ 295. *Bonefacius Justo archiepiscopo Dorobernæ.*[2]—" Absit
" ab omni Christiano ut ex illa civitate Dorobernia aliquid
" minuatur, aut in aliud mutetur, nunc vel futuris tem" poribus, quæ a prædecessore nostro domino papa Gre" gorio statuta sunt, quoquo modo res humanæ quassantur:
" sed magis ex auctoritate beati Petri apostolorum principis
" id ipsum præcipientes firmamus, ut in Dorobernia civitate
" semper in posterum metropolitanus totius Britanniæ locus
" habeatur; omnesque provinciæ regni Anglorum, ut præ" fati loci metropolitanæ ecclesiæ subjiciantur, immutilata
" et perpetua stabilitate decernimus. Hanc autem ecclesiam,
" utpote specialiter consistentem sub potestate et tuitione sanc" tæ Romanæ ecclesiæ, si quis conatus fuerit imminuere, eique
" de concessæ potestatis jure quicquid abstulerit, auferat eum
" Deus de libro vitæ, sciatque se sub anathematis vinculis
" esse nodatum."

§ 297. *Alexander Willelmo regi Anglorum.*[3]—" Causam Alricii,
" qui olim Cicestrensis ecclesiæ dictus est episcopus, dili" genter retractandam et diffiniendam, fratri nostro episcopo
" Lanfranco commisimus. Item sibi negotium, de dis" cernenda lite quæ inter archiepiscopum Eboracensem et
" episcopum Dorcacestrensem de pertinentia[4] diocesis eorum

---

[1] *Eboracensem*] Eborac æ. Al. Bc. Cd.; Eboracem, Bk.

[2] This extract is from one of the spurious or questionable letters adduced in the controversy, and given in full by our author in the Gesta Pontificum (ed. Hamilton, p. 49), lib. i., § 31.

[3] See the whole letter in Wilkins, Conc. i. 326; Rymer, Fœd. i. 1; Lanfranc, Opp. (ed. Giles i., 30); Mansi xix., 950.

[4] *pertinentia*] pertinacia, Bc. Bk. Bq. Ce.; obtinentia, Aa.

"est, firmiter injungendo commendavimus, ut hanc causam diligentissima perquisitione pertractet, et justo fine determinet. In causis autem pertractandis et diffiniendis ita sibi nostræ et apostolicæ auctoritatis vicem dedimus, ut quicquid in eis justitia dictante determinaverit, quasi in nostra præsentia diffinitum, deinceps firmum et indissolubile teneatur."[1]

---

[1] Here the MS. Al. has this note: "Explicit de Willelmo Magno. Desunt leges ejusdem continentes fere unum folium." MSS. Aa. Aah, contain the following version of the Conqueror's "Carta de Appellatis" (cf. Ancient Laws, ed. Thorpe, p. 210; ed. Schmid, p. 358) :—

"EXPLICIT DE WILLELMO MAGNO, NORMANNIÆ COMITE ET REGE ANGLORUM.

"INCIPIUNT LEGES EJUSDEM.

"Willelmus rex Anglorum, omnibus ad quos scriptum hoc perveniet per totam Angliam, salutem et amicitiam. Mando et præcipio per totam Angliæ nationem custodiri: Si Anglicus homo compellet aliquem Francigenam per bellum de furto, vel homicidio, vel aliqua re pro qua bellum fieri debeat, vel judicium inter duos homines, habeat plenam licentiam hoc faciendi. Et si Anglicus bellum nolit, Francigena compellatus allegiet se jurejurando contra eum per testes suos secundum legem Normanniæ.

"Item; si Francigena compellet Anglicum per bellum de eisdem rebus, Anglicus plena licentia defendat se per bellum, vel per judicium si magis ei placeat. Et si *untrum* sit, id est, invalidus, et nolit bellum, vel non possit, quærat sibi legalem defensorem. Si Francigena victus fuerit, persolvat regi sexaginta solidos. Et si Anglicus nolit se defendere per bellum vel per testimonium, allegiet se per Dei judicium.

"De omnibus uthlagii rebus rex instituit ut Anglicus purget se ad judicium. Et si Anglicus appellat Francigenam de uthlagaria, et hoc super eum inveritare velit, defendat se Francigena per bellum. Et si Anglicus non audeat eum probare per bellum, defendat se Francigena plano juramento, non in verborum observantiis."

The same MSS. proceed with the following paragraph, which contains the greater part of the "Præfatio super decretales emendationes Henrici Regis," prefixed in the MS. Cotton Titus A. 27 to the so-called Leges Henrici I. Here it appears in a fragmentary state. The whole is printed by Liebermann in the Zeitschrift of the Savigny-Stiftung for 1883, page 132. "Item. Regem Angliæ, singulari majestate, regni sui dominum esse manifeste veritatis intuitus et singulorum denique cognovit effectus. Quod cum inclita benignitate regis et jure, debita subditorum fidelitate proveniat, situs quoque patriæ confidenter adjuvat, naturæ beneficiis et maris vicinitate conclusus, ut sine gratuita dominorum

Quod Eboracensis Archiepiscopus et omnes sibi subjecti Archiepiscopo Doroberniæ subjiciantur.

§ 298. *Generale concilium regni Anglorum de jure et primatu Dorobernensis sive Cantuariensis ecclesiæ.*—" Anno ab incarnatione Domini nostri Jesu Christi millesimo septuagesimo

" licentia nullus exitus, nulli relinquatur ingressus. Unde tanta genti
" securitas, tanta bonorum omnium copia successit, ut, si veræ rationis
" honestate regeretur, ætatis aureæ pristina tempora conformaret. Sed
" hoc tantis eam promotionibus elicit, quod cum omni forinseca per-
" turbatione sit libera, tantis gaudiorum voluptatibus evehatur, sicut
" miseranda mortalium conditio est, malo scilicet acclinis et lapsui
" prona, intestinis animi seditionibus et cæco novorum molimine semper
" infrendit. Hinc a primævo mundi nascentis exordio, quos rerum
" Deus Artifex æqua libertate ditaverat, inobedientiæ motus inflam-
" mantis ejecit. Et qui cæli Dominum ferre non poterant, hominum
" serviunt pravitate distincti, continuis malorum persecutionibus, in
" deteriora quæque projecti. Et licet immeritos divina miseratio tanta
" prosequitur, et tali dominos informatione componit, ne vilis aliquos
" servitus adnichilet, aut impunita securitas elata præcipitet, reges
" quoque qui perfunctoria ceteros pompa præveniunt, ne potentatibus
" insolescant, carnis infirmitatibus et humanis admodum necessitatibus
" expositos utili penitus sollicitudine frequentat. Regem quippe non
" faciunt vulgi de fascibus fabulosa commenta, vel furentis insaniæ,
" vel infinita jugera, vel amica putredinis ingeniosa crapula, vel de
" lamentis pauperum convulsa pecunia. Regem non faciunt vestes
" Tyriæ, non auro nitidiæ trabes, non color frontis vel vota regia.
" Sed rex est qui posuit metus et diri mala pectoris, quem non am-
" bitio impotens et numquam stabilis favor vulgi præcipitis movet.
" Rex est qui se diri pectoris fœtoribus evacuat, et prodesse singulis
" sollerter invigilat, quales nuper ad fastigium hujus culminis non am-
" bitio popularis, sed spectata inter bonos moderatio, provexit. Neces-
" saria siquidem est mansuetudo prælatis, et disciplina subjectis. Post-
" quam enim ad singula quæque sagax hominum penetravit intentio,
" et nichil ad pecuniam visum est incommodum, crevit opulentia,
" crevit invidia, ex invidia odium, ex odio bellum, nulli fides, nulli
" profuit eleemosyna. Si qua tamen nativæ bonitatis remanserant
" monimenta, sanxere leges et vivendi jura, constituerunt urbes et fida
" receptacula quo tuta fieret inter improbos innocentia, et quos ipsa
" probitatis hortamenta non excitant, saltem conquiescant ad pœnæ
" formidinem. Lex, alia naturalis, quæ apud omnes eadem est; alia
" consuetudinis, in qua habet unaquæque patria suum aliquid pro-
" prium."

The MS. Titus A. 27 completes this document as follows :—" viven-
" dique vernaculum. Sed legem placite dicimus quicquid potius eligitur

350 GESTA REGUM ANGLORUM. [LIB. III.

touching the primacy of Canterbury.

"secundo, pontificatus autem domini Alexandri papæ unde-
"cimo, regni vero Willelmi gloriosi regis Anglorum et ducis
"Normannorum sexto, ex præcepto ejusdem Alexandri papæ,
"annuente eodem rege, in præsentia ipsius et episcoporum
"atque abbatum, ventilata est causa de primatu quem
"Lanfrancus Dorobernensis archiepiscopus super Eboracen-
"sem ecclesiam jure suæ ecclesiæ proclamabat; et de ordi-
"nationibus quorundam episcoporum, de quibus ad quem
"specialiter pertinerent certum minime constabat: et tan-
"dem aliquando diversis diversarum scripturarum auctori-
"tatibus probatum atque ostensum est quod Eboracensis
"ecclesia Cantuariensi debeat subjacere, ejusque archiepis-
"copi, ut primatis totius Britanniæ, dispositionibus, in iis
"quæ ad Christianam religionem pertinent, in omnibus obe-

Durham is subject to York.

"dire. Subjectionem vero Dunelmensis, hoc est, Lindisfar-
"nensis episcopi, atque omnium regionum a terminis Lici-
"feldensis episcopii, et Humbræ magni fluvii, usque ad
"extremos Scotiæ fines, et quicquid ex hac parte prædicti
"fluminis ad parochiam Eboracensis ecclesiæ jure competit,
"Cantuariensis metropolitanus Eboracensi archiepiscopo ejus-
"que successoribus obtinere concessit. Ita ut si Cantuari-
"ensis archiepiscopus concilium cogere voluerit, ubicunque

Rules for attendance at councils.

"visum ei fuerit, Eboracensis archiepiscopus sui præsentiam
"cum omnibus sibi subjectis ad nutum ejus exhibeat, et
"ejus canonicis dispositionibus obediens existat. Quod au-
"tem Eboracensis archiepiscopus professionem Cantuariensi
"archiepiscopo etiam cum sacramento facere debeat, Lan-
"francus Dorobernensis archiepiscopus ex antiqua anteces-

Lanfranc excuses archbishop Thomas from the oath, not from the profession.

"sorum consuetudine ostendit; sed, ob amorem regis, Thomæ
"Eboracensi archiepiscopo sacramentum relaxavit, scriptam-
"que tantum professionem recepit, non præjudicans succes-

"dum religioni consonet, disciplinæ conveniat, saluti proficiat. Hoc enim
"est emendatio Willelmi regis in Legibus Anglicis, quicquid honestum
"et utile circumquaque probaveris, quod beatissimus rex et dominus
"noster cotidianis laudibus illustrare non desinit. Unde librum istum
"quem nostri temporis argumento constitui, solo principio non fine con-
"veni, velut in horto delitiarum inter omnia voluptatis odora pigmenta
"florem unum carpserim, siciensque Tantalus non fugientia sed gratis
"accommoda fluenta laudaverim; successus vero bellicos et prolis suæ
"gloriam musis doccioribus invitavi pro voto suscipiens si merum pacis
"rivulum nostro simposio propinavi. Hæc sunt denique," etc., as in
Thorpe, p. 215.

[1] *etiam cum sacramento*] om. Cc.[1]

"soribus suis qui sacramentum cum professione a successoribus Thomæ exigere voluerint. Si archiepiscopus Cantuariensis vitam finierit, Eboracensis archiepiscopus Doroberniam veniet; et eum qui electus fuerit, cum ceteris præfatæ ecclesiæ episcopis, ut primatem proprium jure consecrabit. Quod si Eboracensis archiepiscopus obierit, is qui ei successurus eligitur, accepto a rege archiepiscopatus dono, Cantuariam, vel ubi Cantuariensi archiepiscopo placuerit, accedet, et ab ipso ordinationem canonico more suscipiet. Huic constitutioni consenserunt præfatus rex, et archiepiscopi Lanfrancus Cantuariensis et Thomas Eboracensis, et Hubertus, sanctæ Romanæ ecclesiæ subdiaconus et præfati Alexandri papæ legatus, et ceteri qui interfuerunt episcopi et abbates. Ventilata est autem hæc causa prius apud Wentanam civitatem in Paschali sollempnitate,[1] in capella regia quæ sita est in castello; postea in villa regia quæ vocatur Windlesor, ubi et finem accepit in præsentia regis, episcoporum, abbatum diversorum ordinum, qui congregati erant apud curiam in festivitate Pentecostes. Signum Willelmi regis. Signum Matildis reginæ. Ego Hubertus, sanctæ Romanæ ecclesiæ lector et domini Alexandri papæ legatus, subscripsi. Ego[2] Lanfrancus Dorobernensis archiepiscopus subscripsi. Ego Thomas Eboracensis archiepiscopus subscripsi. Ego Willelmus Londoniensis episcopus consensi. Ego Hermannus Scirburnensis episcopus subscripsi. Ego Wulstanus Wigornensis episcopus subscripsi. Ego Walterus Herefordensis episcopus subscripsi.[3] Ego Giso Wellensis episcopus consensi. Ego Remigius Dorcacensis episcopus subscripsi. Ego Walkelinus Wentanus episcopus subscripsi. Ego Herfastus Helmeanensis episcopus subscripsi. Ego Stigandus Cicestrensis episcopus consensi. Ego Siwardus Rofensis episcopus consensi. Ego Osbernus Exoniensis episcopus consensi. Ego Odo Bajocensis episcopus, et comes Cantiæ, consensi. Ego Godefridus Constantiensis episcopus, et unus de primatibus Anglorum, consensi. Ego Scotlandus abbas cœnobii sancti Augustini consensi. Ego Elfwinus, abbas cœnobii quod Ramasege dicitur, consensi. Ego Elnothus Glestoniensis abbas consensi. Ego Turstanus, abbas cœnobii quod in insula quæ dicitur Heli situm est, consensi. Ego Wlnothus, abbas cœnobii quod Certesei dici-

---

[1] *sollempnitate*] festivitate, Bc. By.
[2] *Ego—subscripsi*] om. Bc.
[3] *subscripsi*] consensi, Cc.[2] Al.; concessi, Bk.

"tur, consensi. Ego Elfwinus abbas cœnobii Evesandi consensi. Ego Fridericus abbas sancti Albani consensi. Ego Gosfridus abbas cœnobii sancti Petri, quod non longe a Londonia situm est, consensi. Ego Baldewinus abbas cœnobii sancti Edmundi consensi. Ego Turoldus abbas de Burgo consensi. Ego Adelelmus abbas Abbendoniæ consensi. Ego Rualdus abbas Novi Monasterii Wintoniæ consensi."[1]

<small>Profession of archbishop Thomas to the archbishop and see of Canterbury.</small>

§ 299. *Professio Thomæ Eboracensis archiepiscopi.*—" Decet Christianum quemque Christianis legibus subjacere, nec iis quæ a sanctis patribus salubriter instituta sunt quibuslibet rationibus contraire. Hinc namque iræ, dissensiones, invidiæ, contentiones, ceteraque procedunt, quæ amatores suos in pœnas æternas[2] demergunt. Et quanto quisque altioris est ordinis, tanto impensius debet obtemperare præceptis. Propterea ego Thomas ordinatus jam Eboracensis ecclesiæ metropolitanus antistes, auditis cognitisque rationibus, absolutam tibi Lanfrance, Doroberuensis archiepiscope, tuisque successoribus, de canonica obedientia professionem facio; et quicquid a te vel ab eis juste et canonice mihi injunctum fuerit, servaturum me esse promitto. De hac autem re, dum a te adhuc ordinandus essem, dubius fui; ideoque tibi quidem sine conditione, successoribus vero tuis conditionaliter, obtemperaturum me esse promisi."[3]

<small>Ancient arrangement of sees under Canterbury:</small>

§ 300. Habebat autem ex antiquo, sicut in libro <small>Above § 99.</small> primo dixisse me memini, Cantuariensis archiepiscopus hos episcopos; Londoniensem, Wintoniensem, Rofensem, Scireburnensem, Wigornensem, Herefordensem, Lichetfeldensem, Selesiensem, Legacestrensem, Elmanensem, Sidnacestrensem, Dommuccensem : additi sunt, tempore regis Edwardi senioris, Cornubiensis, Cridiensis, Wellensis in West-Saxonia, et in Merciis Dorcestrensis, <small>Above § 129.</small> ut secundo libro dixi. Eboracensis autem archiepiscopus habebat omnes trans Humbram episcopos suæ

---

[1] This important document is printed in the Concilia, Wilkins, i., 324, from MS. Cotton Domitian A. 5, and other sources. It occurs without the attestations in the Gesta Pontificum, lib. i., § 27.

[2] *æternas*] om. Bc. Cd. Ce.

[3] This document is given here from the collection of Professions preserved at Canterbury, possibly from the copy now existing in the MS. Cotton, Cleopatra E. 1. It is found also in Gesta Pontificum, lib. i., § 26.

ditioni subjectos, Ripensem, Haugustaldensem, Lindis- *under York* farnensem, illum de Candida Casa quæ nunc Witerne dicitur, et omnes episcopos Scotiæ et Orcadum ; sicut Cantuariensis habet episcopos Hiberniæ et Walarum. Perierunt autem jamdudum episcopatus Ripensis et *Extinct and removed* Haugustaldensis vi hostilitatis ; et Legacestrensis, et *sees.* Sidnacestrensis et Dommuccensis, quo nescio modo. Porro autem, tempore regis Edwardi simplicis, Cornubiensis et Cridiensis uniti sunt, et translatus est episcopatus in Exoniam. Sub rege Willelmo, in isto eodem concilio pronuntiatum est, secundum scita canonum, ut episcopi transeuntes de villis constituerent[1] *Removal from villages to* sedes suas in urbibus diocesium suarum: Licitfeldensis *cities under* ergo migravit[2] in Cestram, quæ olim Civitatis Le- *the Conqueror.* gionum dicebatur; Selesiensis in Cicestram ; Elmanensis in Tethford primo, nunc ab Herberto episcopo in Norwic ; Scirburnensis in Salesbiriam ; Dorcestrensis in Lincoliam. Nam Lindisfarnensis pridem veteri tempore transierat in Dunelmum, et nuper Wellensis in Bathoniam.

§ 301. In hoc conventu Lanfrancus, qui erat adhuc *Places of the bishops* rudis Anglus, quæsivit a senioribus episcopis qui esset *in councils.* ordo sedendi in concilio, antiquo more statutus: illi vero, excusata difficultate responsi, in diem distulerunt posterum. Et tunc, diligentissime advocata memoria, hunc se vidisse morem asseruere ; ut Cantuariæ archiepiscopus, concilio præsidens, habeat a dextro latere archiepiscopum Eboraci, et juxta eum episcopum Wintoniæ, a sinistro autem Londoniensem : quod si, ut contingit, pro aliqua necessitate Cantuariensis primas adventum suum negaverit,[3] vel obitu defuerit, Eboracensis archiepiscopus, concilio præsidens, habeat a dextra Londoniensem episcopum, a sinistra Wintoniensem ; ceteri secundum tempora ordinationum sedilia sua agnoscant.

---

[1] *constituerent*] construerent, Bc.
[2] *migravit*] transiit, Bc. By.
[3] *negaverit*] excusaverit, Aa. Al. At.

§ 302. Tunc quoque querela archiepiscopi Eboracensis de clamore in Wigornensem et Dorcacestrensem episcopos decisa et sopita est, namque dicebat eos suæ ditioni subjacere debere; quod, cum jamdudum muto silentio ruminasset, Romam cum Lanfranco profectus, ut pallia sua ab apostolico reciperent, palam audiente senatu Romano extulit. Tunc vero Lanfrancus, quamvis ad omnes injurias inconcussæ soliditatis esset, nonnihil tamen tam proterva et ante sibi inaudita postulatione turbatus, iræ motum vultu prodidit, verbis aliquamdiu intra fauces devoratis: at Alexander papa, qui gravaretur Lanfrancum contristare, nam et venienti dignanter assurrexerat, professus illud insigne reverentiæ non se detulisse honori archiepiscopii, sed amori magisterii, tunc quoque judicandi invidiam a se rejecit,[1] litis arbitrium trajiciens in Anglorum concilium. Quapropter, ut dixi, res, multum diuque ventilata in hoc concilio, hunc sortita est terminum; ut, quia citra Humbram essent, hi episcopi Cantuariensi applicarentur, omnes vero Transhumbranos Eboracensis obtineret.

§ 303. Hic sancta simplicitas beati Wulstani Wigornensis episcopi, immo magnanima in Deo confidentia, laudanda et plausu excipienda est. Cum enim et de hac re, et de parva scientia litterarum pulsatus, foras exisset ut a strictiori consilio responsum comeret suum, a tumultibus remoto animo, "Crede mihi," inquit, " nondum cantavimus horam sextam; cantemus ergo." Tum sociis referentibus ut prius propter quod venerant expedirent, quod satis superque sufficeret cantibus tempus; regem et proceres, si hæc audierint, risui se haberi opinaturos; "Prius, crede mihi," dixit, " faciemus Dei " servitium, et post agitabimus hominum litigium." Hora igitur cantata, nulla excogitata falsi tergiversatione, nullo commentato veri splendore, confestim aulam

---

[1] *rejecit*], removit, Bc. By.

concilii ingredi pergebat. Suis cum retinere temptantibus persuaderi non potuit; quin potius timentibus causæ: "Pro certo," ait, "noveritis visibiliter me hic "videre beatos archiepiscopos Dunstanum Cantuariensem et Oswaldum Eboracensem, qui hodie, suis me "precibus tuentes, falsiloquorum acumen hebetabunt." Ita data benedictione monacho, minimæ facundiæ viro, sed Normannicæ linguæ sciolo, rem perorans obtinuit, ut qui suæ diocesis ante indignus putabatur regimine, ab archiepiscopo Eboraci suppliciter rogaretur ut suas dignaretur lustrare partes, quo ipse pro timore hostium vel sermonis ignorantia cavebat accedere.

§ 304. Verum ego non ulterius lectorum expectationem macerabo, qui hæc forsitan non libenter intuentur, quia gesta Willelmi successorum præstolantur; quamvis, nisi me nimius amor mei fallit, nulli varietatem relationum displicituram opinor, nisi si quis tam nubilus est ut Catonis supercilium æmuletur. Sed alia in quarto et quinto libro qui volet experietur, nam tertius debitum agnoscit modum. *Conclusion of the Book.*

DOMINO venerabili et famoso Comiti Roberto,[2] filio regis, Willelmus Malmesbiriæ monachus salutes, et, si quas valet, orationes. Virtus clarorum virorum illud vel maxime laudandum in se commendat, quod etiam longe positorum animos ad se diligendum invitat; unde inferiores superiorum virtutes faciunt suas, dum earum adorant vestigia, ad quarum aspirare non valent exempla. Porro totum ad majorum redundat gloriam, quod ipsi et bonum faciunt, et minores ad se amandum accendunt. Vestrum est igitur, O duces, si quid boni facimus; vestrum profecto si quid dignum me- *Dedicatory letter to earl Robert.*[1]

---

[1] This letter occurs in this place in MSS. Ce. Cd.[1] Cd.[2] Cm. Cf.; it is found at the beginning of the first book in MSS. Bc.[1] Bc.[2] Bk. Bq. and does not appear at all in MSS. Aa.[1] Aa.[2] Aah. Ag. Al. Ap. Ao. Ar. By.; MS. At. has it inserted on a flyleaf, in a sixteenth century hand.

[2] *Roberto*] Rodberto, Bk.

moria scribimus; vestra industria nobis est incitamento ut, quia pericula vestra paci nostræ impenditis, vos vicissim per labores nostros omni ævo inclarescatis. Hinc est quod Gesta Regum Anglorum, quæ nuper edidi, vobis potissimum consecranda[1] credidi, domine Comes venerabilis et merito amabilis. Nullum enim magis decet bonarum artium fautorem esse quam te, cui adhæsit magnanimitas avi, munificentia patrui, prudentia patris; quos cum æmulus industriæ liniamentis repræsentes, illud peculiare gloriæ tuæ facis quod litteris insistis. Quid quod etiam notitia tua dignaris litteratos, quos vel invidia famæ vel tenuitas fortunæ fecit obscuros. Quia enim natura indulget sibi, quod quis probat in se ipso non improbat in altero, consentaneos igitur sibi mores experiuntur in te litterati, quos citra intellectum ullius acrimoniæ benignus aspicis, jocundus admittis, invitus[2] dimittis. Nihil plane in te mutavit fortunæ amplitudo, nisi ut pene tantum benefacere posses quantum velles. Suscipe ergo, virorum clarissime, opus, in quo te quasi ex speculo videas; dum intelliget tuæ serenitatis assensus ante te summorum procerum imitatum facta quam audires nomina. Continentiam autem[3] operis prologus primi libri exponit; quem si placuerit legere, materiam totam poteris de compendio colligere. Illud a vestra dignitate impetratum velim, ut non mihi vertatur vitio quod sæpe per excessum alias quam in Anglia[4] peregrinatur narratio; volo enim hoc opus esse multarum historiarum breviarium, quamvis a majori parte vocaverim Gesta Regum Anglorum.

---

[1] *consecranda*] consectanda, Bc. Bk. Bq.
[2] *invitus*] munus, Bc. Bq.
[3] *autem*] hujus, ins. Bc.
[4] *Anglia*] Grecia, Bc.[2] Bk. Bq.; vel gente nostra, interl. Bc.

PROLOGUS
IN LIBRUM QUARTUM.

Incipit prologus Willelmi Malmesbiriensis in Libro Quarto de Gestis Regum Anglorum.

SCIO plerisque ineptum videri quod gestis nostri temporis regum scribendis stylum applicuerim; dicentibus quod in ejusmodi scriptis sæpe naufragatur veritas et suffragatur falsitas, quippe præsentium mala periculose, bona plausibiliter dicuntur. Eo fit, inquiunt, ut, quia modo[1] omnia magis ad pejus quam ad melius sint proclivia, scriptor obvia mala propter metum[2] prætereat, et, bona si non sunt, propter plausum confingat. Sunt alii qui, nos ex segnitie sua metientes, impares tanto muneri existimant, et hoc studium prava suggillatione contaminant. Quapropter jam pridem, vel illorum ratiocinio vel istorum fastidio perculsus, in otium concesseram, silentio libenter adquiescens; sed dum aliquamdiu solutus inertia vacassem, rursus solitus amor studiorum aurem vellit et manum injecit, propterea quod nec nil agere possem, et istis forensibus et homine litterato indignis curis me tradere non nossem. Accessere amicorum meorum stimuli, quorum vel tacitæ suggestioni deesse non debui; et illi quidem modeste jam prurientem impulere ut cœptum prosequerer.[3] Illorum itaque, quos penitus reposito amore diligo, hortatibus animatus assurgo, ut ex pectoris nostri promptuario victurum apud se amicitiæ[4]

The author meets objections to his writing of the recent history.

These have had weight with him, but he now resumes the work;

at the instigation of friends.

---

[1] *modo*] pene, ins. Aa. Aah. Aq. Al. At.
[2] *propter metum*] om. Bc.
[3] *prosequerer*] persequerer, Al. Ce. Cd.
[4] *amicitiæ*] amicitiarum, Bc.

pignus contineant. Quocirca illorum, qui mihi timent ut aut odiar aut mentiar, benivolentiæ gratus, ita sub ope Christi satisfaciam, ut nec falsarius nec odiosus inveniar: sic enim bene et secus acta perstrin;am, ut, quasi inter Scyllam et Charibdim illæso volante navigio, nihil desit sententiæ, etsi aliquid deesse putetur historiæ Porro illis, qui alieni laboris onus sua æstimatione premunt, hoc respondeo quod olim sanctus Jeronimus canibus suis objecit, "Si placet, legant; si "non placet, abjiciant:" quia et ego hæc non tædiosis ingero, sed studiosis, si qui dignentur, consecro; quod et isti juri concinere pronuntiabunt, si non de his sunt de quibus dicitur "Stulti facile possunt convinci, "difficile compesci." Dicam igitur in hoc libro, qui hujus operis est quartus, quicquid de Willelmo filio Willelmi magni dici poterit; ut nec veritas rerum titubet, nec principalis decoloretur majestas. Ibunt et in istas paginas quædam quæ sub eo, vel in hac terra tristia, vel alias gloriosa, acciderunt,[1] quantum duntaxat nostra scientia attingere potuerit; præsertim de peregrinatione Christianorum in Jerusalem, quam hic apponere non erit injurium, quia tam famosam his diebus expeditionem audire sit operæ pretium et virtutis incitamentum. Neque vero confido quod hæc a me, quam ab aliis qui scripserunt, dicantur commodius; sed ut, quod a multis scribitur, a multis legatur. Verum, ne tam diu procemiari lecturo generet nausiam, jam nunc quod intendo incipiam.

---

[1] *acciderunt*] contigere, Bc. By.

EXPLICIT PROLOGUS.

WILLELMI MALMESBIRIENSIS
DE GESTIS REGUM ANGLORUM.

LIBER QUARTUS.

Incipit liber quartus de Willelmo Rege Rufo, filio regis Willelmi Primi.

§ 305. WILLELMUS igitur filius Willelmi natus est Normanniæ, pluribus annis antequam pater Angliam adiret. Ingenti cura parentum altus, cum et illi naturaliter inesset ingentia parturiens animus, ad culmen supremæ dignitatis evasit. Incomparabilis proculdubio nostro tempore princeps, si non eum magnitudo patris obrueret, nec ejus juventutem fata præcipitassent, ne per ætatem maturiorem aboleret errores licentia potestatis et impetu juvenili contractos. Emensa pueritia, in militari exercitio adolescentiam egit; equitari, jaculari, certare cum primævis obsequio, cum æquævis officio. Jacturam virtutis putare si forte in militari tumultu alter eo prior arma corriperet, et nisi primus ex adverso provocaret, vel provocantem dejiceret. Genitori in omnibus obsequelam gerens, ejus se oculis in bello ostentans, ejus lateri in pace obambulans. Spe sensim scaturiente, jam successioni inhians, maxime post abdicationem fratris majoris, cum et tirocinium minoris nonnihil suspiceret. Ita a patre, ultima valitudine decumbente, in successorem adoptatus, antequam ille extremum efflasset ad occupandum regnum contendit: moxque volentibus animis provincialium exceptus, et claves thesaurorum nactus est; quibus fretus totam Angliam animo subjecit suo.

Accessit etiam favori ejus, maximum rerum momentum, archiepiscopus Lanfrancus, eo quod eum nutrierat et militem fecerat: quo auctore et annitente, die sanctorum Cosmæ et Damiani coronatus, reliquo hyemis quiete et favorabiliter vixit.

He is crowned, Sept. 27, 1087.

Quomodo adversarios rex Rufus vicerit.

Revolt of bishop Odo.

§ 306. Qua exacta, mox in initio veris primus illi conflictus contra Odonem patruum, episcopum Bajocensem, fuit. Namque, cum ille, ut dixi, solutus a vinculis, Robertum nepotem in comitatu Normanniæ confirmasset, Angliam venit, recepitque[1] a rege comitatum Cantiæ; sed cum omnia non suo arbitratu ut olim in regno disponi videret, nam Willelmo Dunelmensi episcopo commendata erat administratio rerum publicarum, livore ictus, a rege et ipse descivit, et multos eodem susurro infecit: Roberto regnum competere, qui sit et remissioris animi, et juveniles stultitias multis jam laboribus decoxerit; hunc delicate nutritum, animi ferocia, quam vultus ipse demonstret, prætumidum, omnia contra fas et jus ausurum; brevi futurum ut honores jamdudum plurimis sudoribus partos amittant; nihil actum morte patris, si quos ille vinxerit iste trucidet. Hæc ipse, hæc Rogerius de Monte Gomerico, hæc Gaufridus Constantiensis episcopus cum nepote Roberto comite Humbrensium, et cum reliquis, primo clam fremebant; post etiam palam, per veredarios missis epistolis, frequentabant. Quin etiam Willelmus Dunelmensis episcopus, quem rex a secretis habuerat, in eorum perfidiam concesserat: quod graviter regem tulisse ferunt, quia, cum amissæ caritatis dispendio, remotarum provinciarum frustrabatur compendio. Itaque Odo prædam omnem Rovecestram comportabat, regios fiscos in Cantia devastans, maxime terras archiepiscopi; immortale in eum odium anhelans,

He puts forth the claim of Robert.

Roger Montgomery, Geoffrey of Coutances, and Robert Mowbray join him.

Conduct of the bishop of Durham.

Odo ravages Kent out of hatred to Lanfranc.

---

[1] *recepitque*] recepit, Cc.

quod ejus consilio a fratre se in vincula conjectum asserebat. Sed nec fides verborum vacillabat: nam cum olim Willelmus senior apud Lanfrancum quereretur se a fratre deseri, "Tu," inquit, "prende eum et "vinci." "Et quid," respondit ille, "quia clericus "est?". Tunc archiepiscopus, lepida hilaritate, ut Persius ait, "crimina rasis librans in antithetis," "Non," dixit, "episcopum Bajocarum capies, sed co"mitem Cantiæ custodies." Gaufridus episcopus, cum nepote, Bathoniam et Bercheleiam partemque pagi Wiltensis depopulans, manubias apud Bristou collocabat. Rogerius de Monte Gomerico, exercitum suum a Scrobesbiria cum Walensibus mittens, coloniam Wigorniensem prædabatur: jamque Wigorniam infestus advenerat, cum regii milites qui prætendebant, freti benedictione Wulstani episcopi cui custodia castelli commissa erat, pauci multos effugarunt, pluribusque sauciis et cæsis, quosdam abduxerunt. Præterea Rogerius Bigot apud Northwic, et Hugo de Grentemesnil apud Legecestram, suis quisque partibus rapinas urgebant. Ita totis defectionis viribus in eum, cui nec prudentia nec fortuna deerat, frustra sæviebatur. Namque ille, videns Normannos pene omnes in una rabie conspiratos, Anglos probos et fortes viros, qui adhuc residui erant, invitatoriis scriptis accersiit; quibus super injuriis suis querimoniam faciens, bonasque leges, et tributorum levamen, liberasque venationes pollicens, fidelitati suæ obligavit. Nec minori astutia Rogerium de Monte Gomerico, secum dissimulata perfidia equitantem, circumvenit. Seorsum enim ducto magnam ingessit invidiam; dicens, libenter se imperio cessurum, si illi et aliis videatur quos pater tutores reliquerat. Non se intelligere quid ita effrænes sint: si velint, pecunias accipiant pro libito; si augmentum patrimoniorum, eodem modo; prorsus, quæ velint, habeant. Tantum videant ne judicium genitoris periclitetur: quod si de se putaverint aspernandum, de se ipsis caveant exemplum; idem enim se regem, qui illos duces fecerit. His verbis comes et pollicitationibus incensus, qui primus factionis post Odonem signifer fuit, primus defecit. Continuo ergo in desertores profectus, castella patrui sui Tunebrige et Pevenesel effregit; ipso in posteriori intercepto: captum ad quod libuit jusjurandum impulit, ut Anglia discederet et Rovecestram traderet.[1] Ad quod implendum eum cum fidelibus suis præmisit, lento pede præeuntes subsecutus. Erat tunc apud Rovecestram omnis pene juventutis ex Anglia et Normannia[2] nobilitas; tres filii Rogerii comitis, et Eustachius Bononiæ junior, multique alii quos infra curam nostram existimo. Regii cum episcopo pauci et inermes, quis enim eo præsente insidias timeret? circa muros desiliunt, clamantes oppidanis ut portas aperiant; hoc episcopum præsentem velle, hoc regem absentem jubere. At illi, de muro conspicati quod vultus episcopi cum verbis oratorum non conveniret, raptim apertis portis ruunt, equos involant, omnesque cum episcopo vinctos abducunt. Rumor facti ad regem cito perlabitur. Severior ille malis, iramque intra conscientiam resorbens, Anglos suos appellat; jubet ut compatriotas advocent ad obsidionem venire, nisi si qui velint sub nomine Niðing, quod nequam sonat, remanere. Angli, qui nihil miserius putarent quam hujusce vocabuli dedecore aduri,[3] catervatim ad regem confluunt, et invincibilem exercitum faciunt. Nec diutius potuere pati oppidani quin se traderent; experti quamlibet nobilem, quamlibet consertam manum, nihil adversus regem Angliæ posse proficere. Odo, secundo captus, perpetuo Angliam abjuravit. Dunelmensis episcopus ultro mare transivit; quem rex, verecundia præteritæ amicitiæ, indempnem passus est effugere. Ceteri omnes in fidem recepti. Inter has obsidionis moras, homines regis mare custo-

---

[1] *et—traderet*] om. Bc. By.
[2] *et Normannia*] om. Bc.
[3] *aduri*] notari, Bc. By.

dientes, quosdam quos comes Normanniæ in auxilium perfidorum miserat, partim cæde, partim naufragio oppressere: reliqui fugam intendentes et suspendere carbasa conati, moxque vento cessante destituti, ludibrio nostris, sibi exitio fuere; nam, ne[1] vivi caperentur, e transtris se in mare præcipitarunt.

De pace inter Willelmum et Robertum.

§ 307. Postero anno, ut dolor semper retractatione acescit, magno scrutinio rex agere cœpit quo modo injurias suas ultum iret, et vicariam fratri contumeliam referret. Itaque castrum sancti Walerici, et portum vicinum, et oppidum quod Albamarla vocatur, sollertia sua adquisivit, pecunia custodes corrumpens. Nec fuit animus comiti ut resisteret; sed domino suo regi Franciæ per nuntios violentiam fratris exposuit, suppetias orans. Et ille quidem iners, et cotidianam crapulam ructans, ad bellum singultiens ingluvie veniebat: sed occurrerunt magna pollicenti nummi regis Angliæ; quibus infractus, cingulum solvit et convivium repetiit. Ita bello intestino diu laboravit Normannia; modo illis, modo istis vincentibus: proceres utriusque furorem incitabant, homines levissimi, in neutra parte fidem habentes. Pauci quibus sanius consilium, consulentes suis commodis quod utrobique possessiones haberent, mediatores pacis fuere; ut comiti rex Cinomannis adquireret, comes regi castella quæ habebat et Fiscannum cœnobium concederet. Juratum est hoc pactum, et ab utrorumque hominibus sacramento firmatum.

Quomodo Willelmus et Robertus obsederint Henricum fratrem suum apud montem Sancti Michaelis.

§ 308. Nec multo post rex mare transiit, ut fidem promissorum expleret. Ergo uterque dux ingentes

---

[1] *ne*] cum, Bc. By.

moliebantur conatus ut Cinomannis invaderent: sed obstitit jam paratis, jamque profecturis, Henrici fratris minoris animositas, qui frenderet propter fratrum avaritiam, quod uterque possessiones paternas dividerent, et se omnium pene expertem non erubescerent. Itaque montem sancti Michaelis armatus insedit, et crebris excursibus obsidentem militiam germanorum contristavit. In ea obsidione præcluum specimen morum in rege et comite apparuit; in altero mansuetudinis, in altero magnanimitatis. Utriusque exempli notas pro legentium notitia affigam.[1]

Exploits.

De magnanimitate Willelmi.

Magnanimity of the king.

§ 309. Egressus rex tabernaculo, vidensque eminus hostes superbum inequitantes, solus in multos irruit, alacritate virtutis impatiens, simulque confidens nullum sibi ausurum obsistere: moxque occiso sub feminibus deturbatus equo, quem eo die quindecim marcis argenti emerat, etiam per pedem diu tractus est; sed fides loricæ obstitit ne læderetur. Jamque miles qui dejecerat manum ad capulum aptabat ut feriret, cum ille, periculo extremo territus, exclamat, "Tolle, nebulo! "rex Angliæ sum!" Tremuit, nota voce jacentis, vulgus militum; statimque reverenter de terra levato equum alterum adducunt. Ille, non expectato ascensorio, sonipedem insiliens, omnesque circumstantes vivido perstringens oculo, "Quis," inquit, "me dejecit?" Mussitantibus cunctis, miles audacis facti conscius non defuit patrocinio suo, dicens: "Ego, qui te non pu- "tarem esse regem, sed militem." Tum vero rex placidus, vultuque serenus, "Per vultum," ait, "de Luca," sic enim jurabat, "meus a modo eris, et meo "albo insertus laudabilis militiæ præmia reportabis." Macte animi amplissime rex, quod tibi præconium super hoc dicto rependam? A magni quondam Alex-

He is unhorsed in battle and rewards the knight, who attacked him, for his brave confession.

---

[1] *affigam*] infigam, Bc.; affingam, By.

andri non degener gloria, qui Persam militem se a tergo ferire conatum, sed pro perfidia ensis spe sua frustratum, incolumem pro admiratione fortitudinis conservavit.

De mansuetudine Comitis Roberti.

§ 310. Jam vero ut de mansuetudine comitis dicam. Cum obsidio eo usque processisset ut aqua deesset obsessis, misit Henricus nuntios comiti, qui eum de siti sua conveniant; impium esse ut eum aqua arceant, quæ esset communis mortalibus: aliter, si velit, virtutem experiatur; nec pugnet violentia elementorum, sed virtute militum. Tum ille, genuina mentis mollitie flexus, suos qua prætendebant laxius habere se jussit, ne frater siticulosus potu careret: quod cum relatum regi esset, ut semper calori pronus erat, comiti dixit, "Belle scis actitare guerram, qui "hostibus præbes aquæ copiam; et quomodo eos do- "mabimus si eis in pastu et in potu indulserimus?" At ille renidens illud come et merito famosum verbum emisit: "Papæ, dimitterem fratrem nostrum mori siti? "et quem alium habebimus si eum amiserimus?" Ita rex, deridens mansueti hominis ingenium, resolvit prælium; infectaque re quam intenderat, quod eum Scottorum et Walensium tumultus vocabant, in regnum se cum ambobus fratribus recepit.

§ 311. Statimque primo contra Walenses, post in Scottos expeditionem movens, nihil magnificentia sua dignum exhibuit; militibus multis desideratis, jumentis interceptis. Nec tunc solum, sed multotiens, parva illi in Walenses fortuna fuit; quod cuivis mirum videatur, cum ei alias semper alea bellorum felicissime arriscrit. Sed ego intelligo, pro soli inæqualitate et cæli inclementia, sicut rebellionem eorum adjutam, ita ejus virtutem impeditam. Porro rex Henricus, excellentis ingenii vir, qui modo regnat, invenit qua commenta illorum labefactaret arte, Flandritis in patria illorum collocatis, qui eis pro claustro sint et eos perpetuo coerceant. At vero tunc satagente Roberto comite, qui familiarem jam dudum apud Scottum locaverat gratiam, inter Malcolmum et Willelmum concordia inita: veruntamen multis controversiis utrobique habitis, et fluctuante propter utrorumque animositatem justitia, Malcolmus ultro Gloecestram venit, æquis duntaxat conditionibus, multus pro pace precator; nec quicquam obtinuit, nisi ut in regnum indempnis rediret,[1] dedignante rege dolo capere quem virtute subegisset. Idemque proxima hyeme, ab hominibus Roberti comitis Humbrensium, magis fraude quam viribus occubuit. Cujus interitus accepto nuntio, uxor Margarita, eleemosynis et pudicitia insignis, fastidiens hujus lucis moram, mortem precario exegit a Deo: ambo cultu pietatis insignes, illa præcipue. Namque toto vitæ tempore viginti quatuor pauperes habebat, ubicunque locorum erat, quos cibis et vestibus reficiebat. Ceterum, sacerdotum cantum in Quadragesima præveniens, noctibus in templo excubabat, triplicibus matutinis ipsa insistens, de Trinitate, de Cruce, de sancta Maria; inde psalterium, cum lacrymis vestem infundentibus, pectus succutientibus. Templo digrediens pascebat pauperes, primo tres, mox novem, inde viginti quatuor, postremo trecentos; ipsa cum rege assistens, et manibus aquam infundens. Eadgarum filium ejus, expulsum a patruo, Willelmus reformavit solio, egregia plane et quæ tantum virum decebat pietate, ut, paternarum injuriarum immemor, filium supplicem restitueret regno.

§ 312. Excellebat in eo magnanimitas, quam ipse processu temporis nimia severitate obfuscavit; ita in ejus furtim pectus vitia pro virtutibus serpebant ut discernere nequiret. Diu dubitavit mundus quo tandem

---

[1] *rediret*] abiret, Bc.

vergeret, quo se inclinaret, indoles illius. Inter initia, *Under Lanfranc's influence he behaves well; but his later life was bad.* vivente Lanfranco archiepiscopo, ab omni crimine abhorrebat, ut unicum fore regum speculum speraretur; quo defuncto, aliquamdiu varium se præstitit æquali lance vitiorum atque virtutum: jam vero, postremis annis bonorum gelante studio, incommodorum seges[1] succrescens incaluit.[2] Et erat ita liberalis quod prodigus, ita magnanimus quod superbus, ita severus quod sævus. Liceat enim mihi, pace majestatis regiæ, verum non occuluisse; quia iste parum Deum reverebatur, nihil homines: quod indiscretum si quis dixerit *He feared God too little, man not at all.* non peccabit, quia a sapientibus tenenda sit moderatio, ut Deus timeatur omni tempore, homo pro tempore. Erat is foris et in conventu hominum tumido vultu erectus, minaci oculo astantem defigens, et affectato *His terrible aspect to the outside world.* rigore feroci voce colloquentem reverberans; quantum conjectari datur, metu inopiæ et aliorum perfidiæ plus justo lucris et severitati deditus. Intus et in triclinio *He was merry enough in private.* cum privatis, omni lenitate[3] accommodus, multa joco transigebat; facetissimus quoque de aliquo suo perperam facto cavillator, ut invidiam facti dilueret et ad sales transferret. Sed de liberalitate ejus qua se ipsum fallebat, post etiam de ceteris, sermo prolixior erit, ut ostendam quanta vitia in eo sub prætextu virtutum pullularint.

§ 313. Sunt enim duo omnino genera largorum; *Prodigality as contrasted with liberality.* alteri prodigi, alteri liberales dicuntur. Prodigi sunt, qui in ea pecunias suas effundunt quorum memoriam aut brevem aut nullam omnino sunt relicturi in seculo, nec eleemosynam habituri in Deo: liberales sunt, qui captos a prædonibus redimunt, aut inopes sublevant, aut æs alienum amicorum suscipiunt. Est ergo largiendum, sed diligenter et moderate; plures enim

---

[1] *seges*] vel segnities, ins. Cd.
[2] *bonorum—incaluit*] omni gelante studio virtutum, vitiorum in eo calor efferbuit, Aa. Ag. Al. At. Ap.
[3] *lenitate*] lenitati, Bc.

patrimonia sua effudere inconsulte largiendo: quid vero est stultius quam, quod libenter facias, curare ne diutius facere possis? Itaque quidam, cum non habeant quod dent, ad rapinas convertuntur; majusque odium assequuntur ab hiis quibus auferunt, quam beneficium ab hiis quibus contulerunt: quod huic regi accidisse dolemus. Namque cum primis initiis regni metu turbarum milites congregasset, nihil illis denegandum putabat, majora in futurum pollicitus. Itaque quia paternos thesauros evacuarat impigre,[1] et modicæ ei tunc pensiones numerabantur, jam substantia defecerat; sed animus largiendi non deerat, quod usu donandi pene in naturam verterat: homo qui nesciret cujuscunque rei effringere pretium vel æstimare commercium, sed cui pro libito venditor distraheret mercimonium, et miles pacisceretur stipendium. Vestium suarum pretium in immensum extolli volebat, dedignans si quis allevasset. Denique quodam mane, cum[2] calciaretur novas caligas, interrogavit cubicularium quanti constitissent: cum ille respondisset tres solidos, indignabundus et fremens, "Fili," ait, "meretricis! ex quo " habet rex caligas tam exilis pretii? vade, et affer " mihi emptas marca argenti." Ivit ille, et multo viliores afferens, quanti præceperat emptas ementitus est. "Atqui," inquit rex, "istæ regiæ conveniunt majestati." Ita cubicularius ex eo pretium vestimentorum ejus pro voluntate numerabat, multa perinde suis utilitatibus nundinatus.

§ 314. Excitabat ergo totum occidentem fama largitatis ejus, orientem usque pertendens: veniebant ad eum milites ex omni quæ citra montes est provincia, quos ipse profusissimis expensis munerabat; itaque cum defecisset quod daret, inops et exhaustus ad lucra[3] convertit animum. Accessit regiæ[4] menti, fomes cupiditatum, Rannulfus clericus, ex infimo genere hominum

---

[1] *impigre*] om. Bc. Ce.
[2] *cum*] pro libito, ins. Aa. Cd.
[3] *lucra*] rapinas, Aa. Al. At.
[4] *regiæ*] avidæ, Aa. Al. Cd.

lingua et calliditate[1] provectus ad summum. Is, si quando edictum regium processisset ut nominatum tributum Anglia penderet, duplum adjiciebat, expilator divitum, exterminator pauperum, confiscator alienarum hereditatum. Invictus causidicus, et tum verbis tum rebus immodicus, juxta in supplices ut in rebelles furens: subinde cachinnantibus quibusdam ac dicentibus,[2] solum esse hominem qui sciret sic agitare ingenium, nec aliorum curaret odium dummodo complacaret dominum. Hoc auctore sacri ecclesiarum honores, mortuis pastoribus, venum locati; namque audita morte cujuslibet episcopi vel abbatis, confestim clericus regis eo mittebatur, qui omnia inventa scripto exciperet, omnesque in posterum redditus fisco regio inferret. Interea quaerebatur quis in loco defuncti idoneus substitueretur, non pro morum sed pro nummorum experimento; dabaturque tandem honor, ut ita dicam, nudus, magno tamen emptus. Haec eo indigniora videbantur, quod, tempore patris, post decessum episcopi vel abbatis omnes redditus integre custodiebantur, substituendo pastori resignandi, eligebanturque personae religionis merito laudabiles; at vero, pauculis annis intercedentibus, omnia immutata. Nullus dives nisi nummularius, nullus clericus nisi causidicus, nullus presbyter nisi, ut verbo parum Latino utar, firmarius. Cujuscunque conditionis homunculus, cujuscunque criminis reus, statim ut de lucro regis appellasset, audiebatur: ab ipsis latronis faucibus resolvebatur laqueus si promisisset regale commodum. Soluta militari disciplina, curiales rusticorum substantias depascebantur, insumebant fortunas, a buccis miserorum cibos abstrahentes. Tunc fluxus crinium, tunc luxus vestium, tunc usus calceorum cum arcuatis aculeis inventus:

---

[1] *calliditate*] assiduitate, Bc.
[2] *cachinnantibus—dicentibus*] cachinnante rege ac dicente, Al. Al At. By.

Extravagance and effeminacy.

mollitie corporis certare cum fœminis, gressum frangere gestu soluto et latere nudo incedere, adolescentium specimen erat. Enerves, emolliti, quod nati fuerant inviti manebant; expugnatores alienæ pudicitiæ, prodigi suæ. Sequebantur curiam effœminatorum manus et ganearum greges, ut non temere a quodam sapiente dictum sit, felicem fore Angliam si Henricus regnaret; talia conjectans quod is ab adolescentia obscœnitates execraretur.[1]

Persecution of Anselm.

§ 315. Adjicerem his, si esset necesse,[2] quod Anselmus archiepiscopus ista corrigere conatus, sed societate suffraganeorum suorum[3] destitutus, sponte discesserit, duritiæ[4] temporis cedens. Anselmus, quo nemo unquam justi tenacior, nemo hoc tempore tam anxie doctus, nemo tam penitus spiritualis fuerit, pater patriæ, mundi speculum.[5] Hic cum, jamjamque navigaturus, in portu ventos expectaret, ut prædo publicus[6]

Eadmer the authority on this.

expilatus est, manticis omnibus et bulgis in medium prolatis et exquisitis: de cujus injuriis plura dicerem si quicquam hoc solo sol vidisset indignius; simul et supersedendum est in historia, quam reverendissimi Edmeri præoccupavit facundia.

Moral reflexion.

§ 316. Vides quantus e liberalitate quam putabat fomes malorum[7] eruperit. In quibus corrigendis quia ipse non tam exhibuit diligentiam quam prætendit negligentiam, magnam et vix abolendam incurrit infamiam; immerito credo, quia nunquam se tali supponeret probro qui se tanto meminisset prælatum imperio. Hæc igitur ideo inelaborato et celeri sermone

---

[1] *felicem—execraretur*] curia regis Angliæ non est majestatis diversorium sed exoletorum prostibulum, Aa. Aah. Ag. Al. At. Ap.—MS. At. has both clauses, adding "qua propter" before "felicem;" the second clause is added in a 13th century hand.

[2] *Adjicerem—necesse*] Ad dedecus temporum illorum pertinet, Aa. Al. Ap.

[3] *suorum*] om. Ce.[1]

[4] *duritiæ*] nequitiæ, Aa. Al.

[5] *speculum*] fuit, ins. Ce.[1]

[6] *publicus*] jussu regis, Al. By.

[7] *fomes malorum*] gurges vitiorum, Aa. Al.

convolvo, quia de tanto rege mala dicere erubesco; in dejiciendis et extenuandis malis[1] laborans.

§ 317. Insolentiæ in Deum Judæi suo tempore dedere indicium: semel apud Rothomagum, ut quosdam ab errore suo refugas ad Judaismum revocarent, muneribus inflectere conati; alia vice apud Londoniam, contra episcopos nostros in certamen animati, quia ille ludibundus, credo, dixisset, quod si vicissent Christianos, apertis argumentationibus confutatos, in eorum sectam transiret.[2] Magno igitur timore episcoporum et clericorum res acta est, pia sollicitudine fidei Christianæ timentium. Et de hoc quidem certamine nihil Judæi præter confusionem retulerunt, quamvis multotiens jactarint se non ratione sed factione superatos.

§ 318. Posteriori tempore, id est anno regni ejus ferme nono,[3] cum Robertus comes Normannorum Jerosolimam eundi, monitionibus Urbani papæ, ut posterius dicetur, impetum cepisset, Normanniam fratri suo pro pecunia decem milium marcarum invadatus est. Itaque importabilis pensionis edictum per totam Angliam cucurrit. Tunc episcopi et abbates frequentes curiam[4] adeunt, super violentia querimoniam facientes, non se posse ad tantum vectigal sufficere, nisi si miseros agricolas omnino effugarent.[5] Quibus curiales[6] turbido, ut solebant,[7] vultu, "Non habetis," inquiunt,[8] "scrinia auro et argento composita, ossibus mortuorum

---

[1] *malis*] criminibus, Al.

[2] *Insolentiæ — transiret*]. The MSS. of the A recension read: "Insolentiæ vel potius inscientiæ contra Deum hoc fuit signum. Judæi qui Lundoniæ habitabant, quos pater e Rothomago illuc traduxerat, eum in quadam sollempnitate adierunt xenia offerentes; quibus delinitus, etiam ausus est animare ad conflictum contra Christianos. 'Per vultum,' ait, ''de Luca!' pronuntians quod, si vicissent, in eorum sectam transiret" Aa. Aah. Ag. Al. At. Ap.

[3] *Posteriori—nono*] Paris arrogantiæ altera vice dedit indicium, nam, Aa. Ag. Al.

[4] *curiam*] regem, Aa. Al.

[5] *effugarent*] effugerent, Bc.[1] At.; effugent, Bc.[2] Bk. Ce.[1] Al.; effugaret, Aa.; effugient, Ce.[2]

[6] *curiales*] ille, Al. Al.

[7] *solebant*] solebat, Aa. Al.

[8] *inquiunt*] inquit, Aa. Al.

"plena:" nullo alio responso obsecrantes dignati.[1] Ita illi, intelligentes quo responsio tenderet, capsas sanctorum nudaverunt, crucifixos despoliaverunt, calices conflarunt, non in usum pauperum, sed in fiscum regium: quicquid enim pene sancta servavit avorum[2] parcitas illorum grassatorum[3] absumsit aviditas.

§ 319. Nihilo secius in homines grassabantur;[4] primo pecuniam, deinde terras auferentes. Non pauperem tenuitas, non opulentum copia tuebatur: venationes, quas rex primo indulserat, adeo prohibuit ut capitale esset supplicium prendisse cervum. Quapropter multa severitate, quam nulla condiebat dulcedo, factum est[5] ut sæpe contra ejus salutem a ducibus conjuraretur: quorum unus, Robertus de Molbrei comes Humbronensium, orta inter eum et regem non modica controversia verborum, in provinciam juris sui abiit, ingentia contra dominum suum molimina conaturus; sed subsequente illo captus et æternis vinculis irretitus est. Alter, Willelmus de Ou, proditionis apud regem accusatus, delatoremque ad duellum provocans, dum se segniter expurgat, cæcatus et extesticulatus est. Plures illa delatio involvit, innocentes plane[6] et probos viros. Ex his fuit Willelmus de Alderia, speciosæ personæ homo et compater regis. Is patibulo affigi jussus, Osmundo episcopo Salesbiriæ confessus, et per omnes ecclesias oppidi flagellatus est. Itaque, dispersis ad inopes vestibus, ad suspendium nudus ibat; delicatam carnem frequentibus super lapides genuflexionibus cruentans. Episcopo et populo sequente ad locum supplicii ita satisfecit: "Sic," inquit, "adjuvet Deus animam meam " et a malis liberet,[7] ut de re de[8] qua accusor im" munis sum, et quidem sententia de me prolata non

---

[1] *dignati*] dignatus, Aa. Al.
[2] *avorum*] aliorum, Ce¹.
[3] *illorum grassatorum*] hominis unius, Aa. Ag. Al.
[4] *grassabantur*] grassabatur, Aa. Ag. Al.
[5] *Quapropter—factum est*] Quibus artibus ita amorem provincialium a se effugaverat, Al. Ag. Bd. Ap.
[6] *plane*] om. Bc.
[7] *liberet*] eruat, Bc.
[8] *de*] om. Aa. Al. Bc.

" revocabitur, sed volo omnes homines innocentiæ
" meæ esse conscios." Tunc dicta commendatione
animæ, et aspersa aqua benedicta, episcopus discessit.
Ille appensus est admirando fortitudinis spectaculo,
ut nec moriturus gemitum, nec moriens produceret
suspirium.

§ 320. Veruntamen sunt quædam de rege præclaræ *Illustrations of the king's greatness of spirit.*
magnanimitatis exempla, quæ posteris non invidebo.
Venationi in quadam silva intentum nuntius detinuit
ex transmarinis partibus, obsessam esse civitatem
Cenomannis; quam nuper fratre profecto suæ potestati
adjecerat. Statim ergo ut expeditus erat retorsit
equum, iter ad mare convertens. Admonentibus duci- *He sets out from a hunting field to recover le Mans.*
bus exercitum advocandum, paratos componendos, " Vi-
" debo," ait,[1] " quis me sequetur; putatis me non habi-
" turum homines? si cognovi juventutem meam, etiam
" naufragio ad me venisse volet." Hoc igitur modo
pene solus ad mare pervenit. Erat tunc nubilus aer
et ventus contrarius; flatus violentia terga maris
verrebat. Illum statim transfretare volentem nautæ
exorant ut pacem pelagi et ventorum clementiam ope-
riatur. "Atqui," inquit rex, "nunquam audivi regem *He insists on sailing in a storm.*
" naufragio interiisse. Quin potius solvite retinacula
" navium, videbitis elementa jam conspirata in meum
" obsequium." Ponto transito obsessores, ejus audita
fama, dissiliunt. Auctor turbarum, Helias quidam,
capitur; cui ante se adducto rex ludibundus, " Habeo
" te, magister!" dixit. At vero illius alta nobilitas, *His treatment of the leader of the revolt.*
quæ [2] nesciret in tanto etiam periculo humilia sapere,
humilia loqui: "Fortuitu," inquit, "me cepisti; sed
" si possem evadere, novi quid facerem." Tum
Willelmus, præ furore fere extra se positus, et obuncans Heliam, "Tu," inquit, "nebulo! tu, quid faceres?
" Discede, abi, fuge! concedo tibi ut facias quicquid
" poteris: et, per vultum de Luca! nihil, si me viceris,

---

[1] *ait*] inquit, Bc.
[2] *At—quæ*] At ille cujus alta nobilitas, Bc. By.

"pro hac venia tecum paciscar." Nec inferius factum verbo fuit, sed continuo dimisit evadere, miratus potius quam insectatus fugientem. Quis talia de illitterato homine crederet? Et fortassis erit aliquis qui, Lucanum legens, falso opinetur Willelmum hæc exempla de Julio Cæsare mutuatum esse: sed non erat ei tantum studii vel otii ut litteras unquam audiret; immo calor mentis[1] ingenitus, et conscia virtus, eum talia exprimere cogebant. Et profecto, si Christianitas nostra pateretur, sicut olim anima Euforbii transisse dicta est in Pythagoram Samium, ita possit dici quod anima Julii Cæsaris transierit in regem Willelmum.

§ 321. Unum ædificium, et ipsum permaximum, domum in Londonia incepit et perfecit, non parcens expensis dummodo liberalitatis suæ magnificentiam exhiberet; et mores quidem ejus ex his, quæ diximus, animadvertere poterit lector. Si quis vero desiderat scire corporis ejus qualitatem, noverit eum fuisse corpore quadrato, colore rufo, crine subflavo, fronte fenestrata, oculo vario, quibusdam intermicantibus guttis distincto; præcipuo robore, quanquam non magnæ staturæ, et ventre paulo projectiore. Eloquentiæ nullæ, sed titubantia linguæ notabilis, maxime cum ira succresceret. Plura sub eo subita et tristia acciderunt, quæ singulatim per annos ejus digeremus, veritati maxime secundum chronicorum fidem inservientes.

§ 322. Secundo anno regni ejus terræ motus ingens totam Angliam exterruit tertio idus Augusti, horrendo miraculo, ut ædificia omnia eminus resilirent, et mox pristino more residerent. Secuta est inopia omnium[2] fructuum; tarda maturitas frugum, ut vix ad festum sancti Andreæ messes reconderentur.

§ 323. Quarto anno tumultus fulgurum, motus turbinum; denique idus Octobris apud Winchelcumbam

---

[1] *mentis*] om. Ce.¹   [2] *omnium*] om. Ce.¹

ictus de cælo emissus latus turris impulit tanta vi, ut, debilitata maceria in confinio tecti, ingens foramen ad modum humanæ grossitudinis aperiretur. Ibi ingressus trabem maximam perculit, ut fragmina in tota[1] spargerentur ecclesia, quin et crucifixi caput cum dextra tibia, et imaginem sanctæ Mariæ dejecit. Secutus est odor teterrimus, hominum importabilis naribus. Tandem monachi, felici ausu irrumpentes, benedictæ aquæ aspergine præstigias inimici effugarunt.

§ 324. Quid illud omnibus incognitum seculis? discordia ventorum inter se dissidentium, ab euro-austro veniens, decimo sexto kalendas Novembris Londoniæ plusquam secentas domos effregit. Cumulabantur ecclesiæ cum domibus, maceriæ cum parietibus. Majus quoque scelus furor ventorum ausus, tectum ecclesiæ sanctæ Mariæ quæ "ad Arcus" dicitur pariter sublevavit, et duos homines ibi obruit. Ferebanturque tigna cum trabibus per inane, spectaculo a longe visentibus, timori prope stantibus ne obruerentur. Quatuor tigna, sex et viginti pedes longa, tanta vi in humum impacta sunt ut vix quatuor pedes exstarent; notabili visu quomodo duritiem stratæ publicæ perruperint, eo ibi ordine posita quo in tecto manu artificis fuerant locata, quoad ob impedimenta transeuntium ad planitiem terræ sunt desecta, quod aliter erui nequirent.

Oct. 17. Great storm at London.

The roof of Bow church blown away.

§ 325. Quinto anno eadem violentia fulminis apud Salesbiriam tectum turris ecclesiæ omnino disjecit, multumque maceriam labefactavit, quinta sane die postquam eam dedicaverat Osmundus, præclaræ memoriæ episcopus.

A.D. 1092. The tower of Salisbury cathedral struck by lightning.

§ 326. Sexto anno tantum fuit pluviarum diluvium, tanta tempestas imbrium, quantum nullus meminerat. Mox, accedente hyeme, fluvii ita sunt congelati ut essent pervii equitantibus et plaustra ducentibus; nec

A.D. 1093. Floods and ice.

---

[1] *in tota*] per totam, Bc. | [2] *ecclesia*] ecclesiam, Bc.

mora, resoluto gelu, impetu glacialium crustarum pontes effracti.

A.D. 1094. Dearth, famine, and plague.

§ 327. Septimo anno, propter tributa quæ rex in Normannia positus edixerat, agricultura defecit: qua fatiscente, fames e vestigio; ea quoque invalescente, mortalitas hominum subsecuta, adeo crebra ut deesset morituris cura, mortuis sepultura. Tunc etiam Walenses in Normannos efferati, Cestrensem pagum et partem Scrobesbiriensis depopulati, Anglesiam armis obtinuere.

A.D. 1097. Oct. 1. A comet.

§ 328. Decimo anno kalendis Octobris apparuit cometes, quindecim diebus, majorem crinem emittens ad orientem, minorem versus euro-austrum: apparuerunt et aliæ stellæ, quasi jacula inter se emittentes. *Chron. A.D. 1097.*

Anselm goes to Rome.

Ille fuit annus quo Anselmus lux Angliæ, ultro tenebras erroneorum effugiens, Romam ivit.

A.D. 1098. Invasion by Harold son of Harold.

§ 329. Undecimo anno rex Noricorum Magnus, cum Haroldo filio Haroldi regis quondam Angliæ, Orcadas insulas et Mevanias, et si quæ aliæ in oceano jacent, armis subegit; jamque Angliam per Anglesiam obstinatus petebat: sed occurrerunt ei comites, Hugo Cestrensis, et Hugo Scrobesbiriensis; et, antequam continentem ingrederetur armis, eum expulerunt. Cecidit ibi Hugo Scrobesbiriensis, eminus ferreo hastili perfossus.

Hugh of Shrewsbury killed.

A.D. 1099. Flood in the Thames.

§ 330. Duodecimo anno fluctus marinus per Tamesim fluvium ascendit, et villas multas cum hominibus mersit. *Chron. A.D. 1099.*

A.D. 1100. Appearance of the devil.

§ 331. Tertiodecimo anno, qui et extremus fuit vitæ, multa adversa: hoc quoque maxime horrendum, quod visibiliter diabolus apparuit hominibus in saltibus et deviis, transeuntes allocutus. Præterea in pago Berrucscire, in villa Hamstede, continuis quindecim diebus fons sanguinem tam ubertim manavit ut vicinum vadum inficeret. Audiebat ille hæc, et ridebat;[1] nec sua sompnia de se, nec aliorum visa, curans. *Chron. A.D. 1100.*

---

[1] *ridebat*] garriebat, Aa. Al.; irridebat, By.

§ 332. Multa de ipsius nece¹ et prævisa et prædicta homines ferunt, quorum tria probabilium relatorum testimonio lecturis communicabo. Edmerus, nostrorum temporum historicus sinceritate veritatis laudandus, dicit nobilem illum exulem Anselmum, cum quo pariter omnis religio exulabat, Marcenniacum venisse, ut Hugonis abbatis Cluniacensis conscientiæ querelas curarum suarum ingereret; ibi, cum de rege Willelmo sermo volutaretur, abbatem prædictum dixisse, proxima nocte regem illum ante Deum ductum, et adjudicatum librato judicio, tristem dampnationis² subiisse sententiam. Id quo modo nosset, nec ipse tunc exposuit, nec aliquis audientium requisivit: veruntamen, pro contuitu religionis ejus, nulli præsentium de fide dictorum inhæsit ambiguum. Ejus erat vitæ Hugo, ejus famæ, ut omnes ejus suspicerent eloquium, mirarentur consilium, quasi ex cælesti adyto insonuisset oraculum. Nec multo post occiso, ut dicemus, rege, venit nuntius ut sedem suam dignaretur archiepiscopus.

§ 333. Pridie quam excederet vita,³ vidit per quietem se phlebotomi ictu sanguinem emittere; radium cruoris in cælum usque protentum lucem obnubilare, diem interpolare. Ita, inclamata sancta Maria, sompno excussus, lumen inferri præcepit, et cubicularios a se discedere vetuit. Tunc aliquot horis antelucanis⁴ nonnihil vigilatum. Paulo post, cum jam Aurora diem invehere meditaretur, monachus quidam transmarinus retulit Roberto filio Hamonis, viro magnatum principi, sompnium quod eadem nocte de rege viderat, mirum et horrendum: quod in quandam ecclesiam venerat, superbo gestu et insolenti, ut solebat, circumstantes despiciens; tunc, crucifixum mordicus apprehendens, brachia illi corroserit, crura pene truncaverit; crucifixum diu tolerasse, sed tandem pede ita regem depu-

---

¹ nece] interitu, Aa. Al.
² dampnationis] om. Ce.¹
³ excederet vita] periret, Aa. Aah. Al. At.
⁴ antelucanis] antelucanum, Ce¹.

lisse ut supinus caderet: ex ore jacentis tam effusam flammam exisse, ut fumeorum voluminum orbes etiam sidera lamberent.[1] Hoc sompnium Robertus non negligendum arbitratus, regi confestim, quod ei a secretis erat, intulit: at ille cachinnos ingeminans, "Mona- "chus," inquit, "est, et causa nummorum monachiliter " sompniat; date ei centum solidos." Multum tamen motus, diu cunctatus est an in silvam sicut intenderat iret, suadentibus amicis ne suo dispendio veritatem sompniorum experiretur. Itaque ante cibum venatu abstinuit, seriis negotiis cruditatem [2] indomitae mentis eructuans; ferunt, ea die largiter epulatum, crebrioribus quam consueverat poculis frontem serenasse. Mox igitur post cibum in saltum contendit, paucis comitatus; quorum familiarissimus erat Walterius cognomento Tirel, qui de Francia, liberalitate regis adductus, venerat. Is, ceteris per moram venationis, quo quemque casus tulerat, dispersis, solus cum eo remanserat. Jamque[3] Phœbo in oceanum proclivi, rex cervo ante se transeunti, extento nervo et emissa sagitta, non adeo sævum vulnus inflixit; diutile[4] adhuc fugitantem vivacitate oculorum prosecutus, opposita contra violentiam solarium radiorum manu. Tunc Walterius pulchrum facinus animo parturiens, ut, rege alias interim intento, ipse alterum cervum qui forte propter transibat prosterneret, inscius et impotens regium pectus, Deus bone! lethali arundine trajecit. Saucius ille nullum verbum emisit; sed ligno sagittæ quantum extra corpus exstabat effracto, moxque supra vulnus cadens, mortem acceleravit. Accurrit Walterius; sed, quia nec sensum nec vocem hausit, perniciter cornipedem insiliens, beneficio calcarium probe evàsit. Nec vero fuit qui persequeretur, illis coniventibus, istis

---

[1] *ut—lamberent*] ut fumi magnitudo etiam sidera obnubilaret, Aa.
[2] *cruditatem*] crudelitatem, Bc. By.
[3] *Jamque*] Itaque, Ce.¹
[4] *diutile*] diutine, Aa.

miserantibus, omnibus postremo alia molientibus; pars receptacula sua munire, pars furtivas praedas agere, pars regem novum jamjamque circumspicere. Pauci rusticanorum cadaver, in rheda caballaria compositum, Wintoniam in episcopatum devexere, cruore undatim per totam viam stillante. Ibi infra ambitum turris, multorum procerum conventu, paucorum planctu, terrae traditum. Secuta est posteriori anno ruina turris: de qua re quae opiniones fuerint parco dicere, ne videar nugis credere; praesertim cum, pro instabilitate operis, machina ruinam fecisse potuisset etiamsi nunquam ipse ibi sepultus fuisset.[1] Obiit anno Dominicae incarnationis millesimo centesimo, regni tertio decimo, nonas Augusti quarto, major quadragenario, ingentia praesumens, et ingentia, si pensa Parcarum evolvere vel violentiam fortunae abrumpere et eluctari potuisset, facturus. Tanta vis erat animi, ut quodlibet sibi regnum promittere auderet. Denique ante proximam diem mortis interrogatus ubi festum suum in Natali teneret,[2] respondit Pictavis, quod comes Pictavensis, Jerosolimam ire gestiens, ei terram suam pro pecunia invadaturus dicebatur. Ita paternis possessionibus non contentus, majorisque gloriae spe raptatus, indebitis incubabat honoribus. Vir sacrati ordinis hominibus pro dampno animae, cujus salutem revocare laborent,[3] maxime miserandus; stipendiariis militibus pro copia donativorum mirandus; provincialibus, quod eorum substantias abradi sinebat,[4] non desiderandus. Nullum suo tempore concilium fieri memini,[5] in quo, delictis ener-

---

[1] *Secuta—fuisset*] Neque defuere opiniones quorundam, dicentium ruinam turris, quae posterioribus annis accidit, peccatis illius contigisse, quod injuria fuerit illum sacrato tumulari loco, qui tota vita petulans et lubricus moriens etiam Christiano caruerit viatico, Aa. Ag. Aah. Al. At. Ap.

[2] *teneret*] celebraret, Al.

[3] *laborent*] nequeant, Aa. Ag. Al. Ap. Cd.

[4] *abradi sinebat*] abradebat, Aa. Ag. Al.

[5] *memini*] permisit, Aa. Ag. Al.

vatis, vigor ecclesiasticus confirmaretur. Ecclesiasticos honores diu antequam daret deliberabat, sive pro commodo sive pro trutinando merito,[1] utpote qui, eo die quo excessit, tres episcopatus et duodecim [2] abbatias desolatas pastoribus in manu sua teneret. Quin et accepta occasione qua inter se dissiderent Urbanus in Roma, Gwibertus in Ravenna, tributum Romanæ sedi negavit; pronior tamen in Gwiberti gratiam, quod fomes et incentivum inter eum et Anselmum fuerat discordiæ quod [3] ille vir Deo dilectus Urbanum apostolicum, alterum apostatam, pronuntiaret.

De Cisterciensibus.

§ 334. Ejus diebus religio Cistellensis [4] coepit, quæ nunc optima via summi in cælum processus et creditur et dicitur. De qua hic loqui suscepti operis [5] non videtur esse contrarium, quod ad Angliæ gloriam pertineat, quæ talem virum produxerit qui hujusce religionis fuerit et auctor et mediator. Noster ille, et nostra puer in palæstra primi ævi tirocinium cucurrit. Quapropter, si non invidi sumus, eo illius bona complectimur gratiosius quo agnoscimus propinquius; simul et laudes ejus attollere mihi est animus, quia ingenua mens est si bonum in alio probes quod in te non esse suspires. Is fuit Hardingus [6] nomine apud Anglos, non ita reconditis natalibus procreatus. A puero Scireburniæ monachus; sed cum adolescentem seculi urtica sollicitaret, pannos illos perosus, primo Scottiam, mox Franciam contendit. Ibi aliquot annis litteris liberalibus exercitus, divini amoris stimulos accepit:

Juvenal, Sat. i., 38.

---

[1] *Ecclesiasticos—merito*] Sed quia in præceps pecuniæ aviditate ferebatur, sacros honores sui juris esse dictitabat, An. Ag. Al.

[2] *duodecim*] quatuordecim, An.

[3] *quod*] quo, Ce.

[4] *Cistellensis*] Cisterciensis, An. Aah.

[5] *suscepti operis*] suscepto operi, An. Aah. Al. Ap.

[6] Stephen Harding, the third abbot of Citeaux, died in 1134.

namque cum pueriles ineptias robustior ætas excluderet, Romam, cum consorte studiorum clerico, profectus est; nec illos continuatio et difficultas itineris, et facultatum penuria, unquam cohibere potuit quin cotidie totum psalterium et euntes et redeuntes cantitarent. Profecto jam prædicabilis viri spirabat animus quod non multo post, per Dei gratiam, est adorsus: nam Burgundiam regressus, in Molesmo, novo et magno monasterio, crinem abjecit, et prima quidem elementa regulæ olim visa facile recognovit; cum vero ei alia proponerentur observanda, quæ nec in regula legerat nec usquam viderat, rationem eorum efflagitare cœpit, modeste sane et ut monachum decet: "Ratione," inquiens, "supremus rerum Auctor omnia fecit, ratione
" omnia regit; ratione rotatur poli fabrica, ratione ipsa
" etiam quæ dicuntur errantia torquentur sidera, ra-
" tione moventur elementa; ratione et æquilibritate
" debet nostra subsistere natura. Sed quia per de-
" sidiam sæpe a[1] ratione decidit, leges quondam mul-
" tæ latæ; novissime per beatum Benedictum regula
" divinitus processit quæ fluxum naturæ ad rationem
" revocaret; in qua etsi habentur quædam quorum
" rationem penetrare non sufficio,[2] auctoritati tamen
" adquiescendum censeo. Ratio enim et auctoritas
" divinorum scriptorum, quamvis dissonare videantur,
" unum idemque sunt: namque cum Deus nihil sine
" ratione creaverit, et recreaverit; qui fieri potest ut
" credam sanctos patres, sequaces scilicet Dei, quic-
" quam præter rationem edicere, quasi soli auctoritati
" fidem debeamus adhibere? Itaque illorum, quæ
" procuditis, aut rationem aut auctoritatem afferte.
" Quamvis non multum debeat credi, si quid humanæ
" rationis possit allegari, quod æquipollentibus argu-
" mentis valeat enervari. Quapropter ex regula quæ
" ratione et auctoritate nixa, utpote omnium justorum

Receive tonsure a Molesme.

His argument on monastic rule.

[1] a] om. Cc¹. | [2] *sufficio*] valeo, Bc. By.

" spiritu dictata est, date exempla; quod si non potes-
" tis, frustra profitemini illius praerogativam cujus con-
" tempnitis sequi doctrinam."

Result of his words in the reform of the Order.

§ 335. Hujusmodi sententia, ab uno, ut fit, serpens in alios, merito movit corda Deum timentium ne forte in vacuum currerent aut cucurrissent. Frequent- Gal. ii. 2. ibus ergo capitulis disputatio agitata hunc finem habuit, ut ipse abbas sententiam probaret, supersedendum superfluis, solam medullam regulae vestigandam. Ita duo fratres electi, in quibus scientia litterarum cum religione quadraret, qui, vicaria collatione, auctoris regulae voluntatem inquirerent, inquisitam aliis proponerent. Abbas sedulo agere ut totus conventus assentiretur: sed, quia difficile a mentibus hominum avellitur quod ex antiquo insederit, quia inviti exspuunt quod prima saliva combiberint, pene omnes suscipere[1] recusarunt res novas, quia antiquas diligebant.[2] Soli decem et octo, in quibus Hardingus, qui et Stephanus, sancta obstinatione pervicaces, cum abbate suo coenobium derelinquunt; pronuntiantes non posse regulae puritatem custodiri in loco ubi et opum congeries et ciborum indigeries etiam reluctantem animum offocarent. Igitur Cistellas venere, locum prius saltuosum, nunc ita frequenti religione monachorum perspicuum, ut divinitatis ipsius conscius non immerito aestimetur. Ibi suffragio archiepiscopi Viennensis, qui nunc apostolicus[3] est, memorabile et omni seculo venerabile opus coeptarunt.

Eighteen monks follow the abbot to Citeaux.

Patronage of the archbishop of Vienne.

§ 336. Et plura certe videntur aspera, sed haec praecipue: nihil pellicium aut lineum vestiunt, nec illud quod subtiliter texitur laneum, quod nos staminium vocamus; nunquam femoralia, nisi in itinere directi, habent, quae revertentes lota restituunt. Duas tunicas cum cucullis habentes, hyeme augmentum non

Usages of the brethren as to dress;

---

[1] *suscipere*] recipere, Bc. By.
[2] *diligebant*] om. Aa. Ag. Bc. By. Cd. Ce.
[3] Calixtus II. A.D. 1119-1124.

assumunt; sed æstate, si volunt, levamen accipiunt. Vestiti dormiunt et cincti, nec ullo[1] tempore post matutinas ad lectos redeunt: sed ita horam matutinarum temperant, ut ante laudes lucescat; ita regulæ incubantes, ut nec iota unum nec apicem prætereundum putent. Statim post laudes primam canunt, post *devotions* primam in opera horis constitutis exeunt; quicquid faciendum vel cantandum est die sine aliena lucerna consummant. Nullus ex horis diurnis, nullus ex completorio unquam deest, præter infirmos: cellararius et *service,* hospitarius post auditum completorium serviunt hospitibus, summo tamen studio servantes silentium. Ab- *silence.* bas nihil sibi, nisi quod aliis, licere permittit; ubique præsens, ubique gregis sui curam circumferens: solummodo edentibus non adest, quia mensa ejus cum peregrinis et pauperibus est semper. Nihilominus, ubi- *Conduct of the abbot.* cunque sit, verborum et obsoniorum abstemius; quia nec ipsi nec aliis unquam nisi duo fercula apponuntur, sagimen et carnes nunquam nisi infirmis. Ab idibus *Moderation in food.* Septembris usque ad Pascha nullius festivitatis contuitu, præter dies Dominicos, nisi semel in die jejunium solvunt. Nunquam claustrum nisi causa operandi egrediuntur; nec ibi, nec usquam, nisi abbati aut *Simplicity* priori invicem colloquentes. Horas canonicas indefesse *of worship.* continuant, nulla appenditia[2] extrinsecus adjicientes, præter vigiliam pro defunctis. Cantus et hymnos Ambrosianos, quantum ex Mediolano addiscere[3] potuerunt, frequentant in divinis officiis. Hospitum et infirmorum curam habentes, importabiles corporibus suis pro animarum remedio comminiscuntur cruces.

§ 337. Hæc abbas ille primo ingenti impetu et ipse *The monks of Molesme* faciebat et alios compellebat,[4] sed temporis intercessu *recall the abbot.* pœnituit homo delicate nutritus, et ægre ferens tam diutinam ciborum parsimoniam. Cujus voluntatem

---

[1] *nec ullo*] nullo, Cc¹.
[2] *appenditia*] appendentia, Bc.Cd.
[3] *addiscere*] addicere, Cc¹.
[4] *compellebat*] facere compellebat, Aa. Aah. Al.

monachi apud Molesmum residui cognoscentes, verbis quibusdam incertum an et epistolis, per obedientiam papæ astu quodam ad monasterium retrahunt,[1] volentem cogentes. Quasi enim diffatigatus improbitate supplicum, angustos parietes reliquit pauperum, augustiorem repetens thronum. Secuti eum ex Cistellis omnes qui cum eo venerant, præter octo. Illi pauci numero, sed multi merito, abbatem Albericum quendam ex suis, priorem Stephanum constituunt. Nec ille in vita moratus plus octennio, supremo feliciter conventus est arbitrio. Tum, haud dubie nutu divino, Stephanus absens etiam in abbatem eligitur, dux olim facti totius, speciale et insigne nostrorum dierum decus; cujus quanti sit meritum testantur abbatiæ sexdecim jam per eum factæ, septem cœptæ. Ita ipse, resona Dei tuba, circumpositos tum verbo, tum exemplo, in cælum dirigit, nihil infra præceptum faciens: sermone comis, facie jocundus, animo semper in Domino lætus. Hinc palam præclari vultus gaudium, hinc clam, illud desuper veniens iriguum; quia, incolatum istum fastidiens, patriam continuo amore desideret. Per hæc favorabilis cunctis habetur, quia Deus amorem viri quem diligit in animos hominum dignanter refudit. Quocirca beatum se computat terræ illius indigena quisquis per illius manum pecunias suas transmittit ad Deum.[2] Plura quidem ille accipit; sed, paucis in suos suorumque usus expensis, cetera in egenos et monasteriorum ædificationem confestim dispertit. Est enim Stephani marsupium omnium egentium publicum ærarium. Abstinentiæ illius est indicium, quod nihil ibi, sicut in ceteris cœnobiis, videas fulgurare auro, renidere gemma, micare argento; nam, ut Gentilis ait, "in sancto quid facit aurum?" Nos in sacratis vasis parum putamus actum nisi crassi crustam metalli obumbret honor lapidum, vel topazior-

---

[1] *retrahunt*] eum retrahunt, Aa. Al.
[2] *Deum*] eum, Bc. Ce. Cd. Cm.

um flamma, vel ametistorum viola, vel smaragdorum lux herbida; nisi tunicæ sacerdotales auro ludant; nisi multicoloribus parietes picturis renideant, et solem ad lacunar sollicitent. At vero illi, ea quæ prima mortales falso æstimant in secundis habentes, omne studium in ornandis moribus ponunt, magisque amant splendidas mentes quam auratas vestes; scientes quod benefactorum retributio optima est munda frui conscientia. Quin etiam laudabilis abbatis clementia cum vel vult, vel velle se simulat, aliquid de jugo regulæ inflectere, illi contra nituntur: non multum superesse vitæ suæ dicentes, nec tam diu se victuros quam vixere: sperare se duraturos in proposito, et successuris futuros exemplo, qui si flexi fuerint peccabunt. Et profecto fiet pro humana debilitate; cujus perpetua lex est, ut nihil maximis laboribus partum diu possit consistere. Sed ut omnia quæ de illis dicta sunt, vel dici possunt, in summam conferam, sunt hodie monachi Cistellenses omnium monachorum exercitium, studiosorum speculum, desidiosorum œstrum.

De Translatione trium Episcopatuum, Wellensis, Cestrensis, et Thetfordensis.

§ 338. His temporibus in Anglia tres episcopatus ex antiquis sedibus transiere alias; Wellensis per Johannem in Bathoniam, Cestrensis per Robertum in Coventreiam, Thetfordensis per Herbertum in Norwic: omnes majori ambitu quam ut tantorum virorum debuisset interesse studio.[1] Denique, ut primum de postremo dicam, Herbertus cognomento Losinga, quod ei ars adulationis impegerat, ex abbate Ramesiensi emit episcopatum Thetfordensem; patre quoque suo Roberto, ejusdem cognominis, in abbatiam Wintoniæ intruso. Fuit ergo vir ille magnus in Anglia simoniæ fomes,

---

[1] *omnes—studio*] omnes nummorum maleficio, omnes venalitatis ambitu et sacrilegio, Aa. Aah. Al. Ag. Ao. Ap. At.

His history. abbatiam episcopatumque nummis aucupatus; pecunia scilicet regiam sollicitudinem inviscans, et principum favori non leves promissiones assibilans; unde quidam egregie tunc temporis versificus ait:

His reputation for simony.
" Surgit in ecclesia monstrum, genitore Losinga,
" Simonidum secta, canonum virtute resecta.
" Petre, nimis tardas, nam Simon ad ardua temptat;
" Si præsens esses, non Simon ad alta volaret.
" Proh dolor! Ecclesiæ nummis venduntur et ære."

Et infra:

" Filius est præsul, pater abbas, Simon uterque.
" Quid non speremus si nummos possideamus?
" Omnia nummus habet; quod vult facit, addit, et
" aufert.
" Res nimis injusta, nummis fit præsul et abba."

De Herberto Losinga.[1]

His repentance and pardon.
§ 339. Veruntamen erroneum impetum juventutis abolevit pœnitentia, Romam profectus severioribus annis; ubi loci, simonicum et baculum et anulum deponens, indulgentia clementissimæ sedis iterum recipere meruit; quod Romani sanctius et ordinatius censeant, ut ecclesiarum omnium sumptus suis potius marsupiis serviant, quam quorumlibet regum usibus militent. Ita Herbertus, domum reversus, sedem episcopalem quæ quondam fuerat in Helmam, et tunc *His see twice removed.* erat apud Thetford, ad insignem mercimoniis et populorum frequentia vicum transtulit, nomine Norwic. Ibi monachorum congregationem numero et religione percelebrem instituit, omnia eis necessaria ex nummis *Monastery at Norwich.* mercatus domesticis: providens scilicet successorum querelæ, nullas episcopii terras monachis largitus est; ne illi Dei famulos fraudarent victualibus, si quid donatum offendissent quod suis competeret rebus.

---

[1] The history of Herbert Losinga occurs, in nearly the same words, in the Gesta Pontificum, lib. ii. § 74.

Præterea apud Thetford monachos Cluniacenses instituit, quod sint illius cœnobii professores, ubique pene gentium dispersi, locupletes in seculo et splendidissimæ religionis in Deo. Ingenti ergo et numerosa virtutum gratia præteritarum offensarum molem obumbravit; disertitudinis et litterarum copia, nec minus secularium rerum peritia, Romanæ quoque celsitudini suspiciendus. Fuitque Herbertus mutatus, ut Lucanus de Curione dixit, "momentum et mutatio rerum:" sicut tempore istius regis simoniæ causidicus, ita posterius propulsator invictus, neque ab aliis fieri voluit quod a se præsumptum quondam juvenili fervore indoluit; præ se semper, ut aiunt, ferens Jeronimi dictum, " Erravimus juvenes, emendemus senes." Postremo quis in illius facti laudem digne pergat, quod tam nobile monasterium episcopus non multum pecuniosus fecerit; in quo nihil frustra desideres, vel in ædificiorum sublimium specie, vel in ornamentorum pulchritudine vel in monachorum religione, et ad omnes sedula caritate? Hæc et vivum spe felici palpabant; et defunctum, si non vana fides pœnitentiæ, super æthera tulerunt.

De Johanne Episcopo primo Bathoniæ.

§ 340. Johannes erat Wellensis episcopus, natione Turonicus; usu, non litteris, medicus probatus. Is, defuncto abbate Bathoniensi, abbatiam a rege non gravante[1] obtinuit, eo quod et in curia omnia venum agebantur, et aviditatem videbatur palliare ratio ut urbs tam insignis nomen celebrius acciperet ex episcopio. Itaque primo in monachos severitatem exercere, quod essent et hebetes et sua æstimatione bar-

---

[1] *gravante*] gravate, Aa. Al. Bc. Cd. Ce². This section occurs with some important variations in the Gesta Pontificum, lib. ii. § 90.

bari; omnes terras victualium ministras subtrahens,[1] pauculumque victum per laicos[2] exiliter inferens: sed procedentibus annis factis monachis novis, mitius se agere, aliquantulum terrarum quo[3] se hospitesque suos quomodocunque sustentarent indulgens priori. Et quamvis primo coepisset austerius,[4] multa per eum ibi nobiliter coepta et consummata in ornamentis et libris; maximeque monachorum congregatione, qui sunt scientia litterarum et sedulitate officii[5] praedicabiles. Ceterum nunquam, nec etiam moriens, emendare[6] voluit[7] ut plena manu terrarum servitium manumitteret; successoribus suis non imitandum praebens[8] exemplum.

His great works.

A fault.

De Roberto Episcopo Cestrensi.

§ 341. [9] Erat in Cestrensi diocesi coenobium Coventreia nomine, quod comes magnificentissimus Lefricus, ut supra fatus sum, cum uxore Godiva, constituerat; tanto auri et argenti spectaculo, ut ipsi parietes ecclesiae angusti viderentur thesaurorum receptaculis,[10] miraculo porro magno visentium oculis. Hoc Robertus, ejusdem episcopus provinciae, inhians, non episcopaliter[11] involavit; ex ipsis ecclesiae gazis surripiens unde datoris[12] manum suppleret, unde papae occupationes falleret, unde aviditati Romanorum irreperet; pluresque ibi annos moratus nihil probitatis exhibuit. Adeo tecta ruinam minitantia nunquam periculo exemit, adeo sacras opes dilapidans peculatus crimen incurrit, repetundarum reus futurus episcopus,

The monastery of Coventry founded by Leofric and Godiva.

Above, § 196.

Oppressions of bishop Robert.

---

[1] *subtrahens*] auferens, Al. Ag.
[2] *laicos*] suos, ins. Aa. Al. Ag.
[3] *quo*] qua, Cd. Ce.
[4] *Et—austerius*] Et quamvis pene in omnibus insulsi esset animi et parum stabilis, Ag. Al. At. Ap.
[5] *officii*] officiorum, Aa. Al.; juxta, add. Aa. Al.
[6] *emendare*] emolliri, Aa. Al.
[7] *voluit*] potuit, Aa. Al.; potuit vel voluit, Bk. Bq.
[8] *praebens*] relinquens, Aa. Al.
[9] This section is wanting in Cd. Cm.
[10] *receptaculis*] spectaculis, Bc.
[11] *non episcopaliter*] more praedonis, Al. Ag.
[12] *datoris*] regis, Al. Ag.

si esset, accusator paratus. Monachos miserabili stipe cibans, nec ad regularis ordinis amorem curavit accendere, nec nisi ad popularem litteraturam passus est aspirare; ne vel ciborum affluentia delicatos, vel regulæ rigor et scientiæ vigor contra se faceret elatos. Agresti igitur victu et triviali litteratura contenti, satis habebant si vel saltem quieti vivere possent. Quin etiam moriturus, parvi faciens scita canonum quibus edicitur pontifices in suis sedibus sepeliri debere, non apud Cestram, sed apud Coventreiam se tumulatum iri præcepit; sua opinione relinquens successuris non indebitum calumpniandi, sed quasi jus legitimum vindicandi.[1]

He directs that he should be buried at Coventry.

§ 342. Hic occasio temporum Willelmi translationem Augustini præcellentissimi Anglorum apostoli cum sociis suis exponi animaret, nisi peritissimi Goscelini præcurrisset ingenium; Goscelini, qui, monachus de sancto Bertino, cum Heremanno episcopo Salesbiriæ quondam Angliam venerat, insignis litterarum et cantuum peritia. Is, multo episcopatus et abbatias perlustrans tempore, præclaræ scientiæ multis[2] locis monumenta dedit, in laudibus sanctorum Angliæ nulli[3] post Bedam secundus; musicæ porro palmam post Osbernum adeptus. Denique innumeras sanctorum vitas recentium stylo extulit; veterum vel hostilitate amissas, vel informiter editas, comptius renovavit. Hujus quoque translationis seriem ita expolivit,[4] ut eam præsentibus monstrasse digito, futurorumque videatur subjecisse oculo. Felix lingua quæ tot sanctis servierit, felix pectus quod tot vocales melodias emiserit, præsertim cum in ejus conversatione certaret honestas doctrinæ! Veruntamen quia de quibusdam episcopis parum laudanda huc usque contexui, aliquos alterius modi disparisque vitæ, sed contemporaneos, introducam

Account of Goscelin.

His hagiographics.

His musical ability.

His account of the translation of S. Augustine.

---

[1] *vindicandi*] the whole of this section occurs in the Gesta Pontificum, lib. iv. § 173.
[2] *multis*] pluribus, Al.
[3] *nulli*] om. Al.
[4] It is printed by Mabillon, *A A. SS. O.S.B.* sæc. vi. pt. 2, pp. 748–765.

episcopos; ne ita videatur nostrum obtorpuisse seculum, quod non aliquem producat sanctum. Sed hanc sponsionem sequenti libro, post enarrata gesta Henrici regis, cui placuerit experietur.

Quædam præfatio sequentis narrationis.

Our author proceeds to the story of the crusade.

§ 343. Nunc iter Jerosolimitanum scripto expediam, aliorum visa et sensa meis verbis allegans. Proinde,[1] sicut se occasio ingesserit, de situ et divitiis Constantinopoleos, Antiochiæ, Jerusalem, ex scriptis majorum deflorata subtexam; ut qui ea ignorat, et hæc forte invenerit, in promptu habeat quæ aliis cognoscenda ipse proponat: sed ad hæc enarranda ferventiore opus est spiritu, ut consummem efficaciter quod incipio tam hilariter. Appellata igitur in auxilium,[2] ut mos est, Divinitate, tale aucupabor exordium.

De Itinere Christianorum in Jerusalem.

A.D. 1095. Urban II. visits Gaul.

§ 344. Anno ab incarnatione Domini millesimo nonagesimo quinto, papa Urbanus secundus, qui præsidebat apostolico culmini, evasis Alpibus venit in Gallias: adventus causa ferebatur perspicua, quod, violentia Guiberti Roma extrusus, citramontanas ad sui reverentiam sollicitaret ecclesias. Illud repositius

His purpose of a crusade by counsel of Bohemond.

propositum non ita vulgabatur, quod Boamundi consilio pene totam Europam in Asiaticam expeditionem moveret; ut, in tanto tumultu omnium provinciarum facile obæratis auxiliaribus, et Urbanus Romam, et Boamundus Illyricum et Macedoniam, pervaderent: nam eas terras, et quicquid præterea a Dirachio usque in Tessalonicam protenditur, Guiscardus pater super Alexium adquisierat, iccirco illas Boamundus juri suo competere clamitabat; inops hereditatis Appulæ, quam

---

[1] *Proinde*] Porro inde, Al.   [2] *in auxilium*] om. Bc. By.

genitor Rogero comiti¹ filio delegaverat. Veruntamen, quæcunque transeundi fuerit occasio, magno et illustri adventus ejus fuit emolumento Christianis. Coactum ergo est apud Clarum Montem concilium, quæ clarissima est urbs Arvernorum; numerus² episcoporum et abbatum trecenti decem; ubi aliquot diebus primo de catholica fide, et inter se dissidentium³ pace, tractatus prolixe habitus. Nam præter flagitia quibus singuli licenter incubabant, ad hæc calamitatis omnes Cisalpini devenerant, ut nullis vel minimis causis exstantibus quisque alium caperet, nec nisi magno redemptum abire sineret. Præterea simonicus anguis ita lubricum caput erexerat, ita venenato fœtu mortiferi germinis ova vaporaverat, ut totus orbis lethali sibilo infectus ecclesiasticos honores corrumperet. Tum enim non dicam episcopi ad ecclesias, sed nec quislibet ad quoscunque ordines, nisi per pecunias aspirabat. Tunc, legitimis uxoribus exclusis, multi contrahebant divortium, alienum expugnantes matrimonium; quare, quia in his et illis erat confusa criminum sylva, ad pœnam quorundam potentiorum designata sunt nomina. Unde, ne longum faciam, totius actionem concilii subnectam; quædam meis sermonibus pro compendio brevians.⁴

Council of Clermont.

Points to be reformed.

De Concilio Clari Montis.

§ 345. In concilio apud Clarum Montem, sub præsentia domini Urbani papæ, hæc capitula finita sunt:—Quod ecclesia catholica sit in fide casta,⁵ libera ab omni servitute;⁶ ut episcopi, vel abbates, vel aliquis de clero, aliquam ecclesiasticam dignitatem de manu principum vel quorumlibet laicorum non accipiant.

Proceedings of the Council.

---

¹ *comiti*] minori, Aa. Al.
² *numerus*] fuit congregatorum, Al.
³ *inter se dissidentium*] eorum qui inter se dissidebant, Al.
⁴ *See* Concilia, Labbe and Cossart, x. 506; Mansi, xx. 815 sq.
⁵ *casta*] pudicitia, add. Al. Ag.
⁶ *servitute*] seculari, ins. Ag. Al.

Enactments of the council of Clermont. Quod clerici in duabus ecclesiis vel civitatibus præbendas non habeant. Quod aliquis simul episcopus et abbas esse non possit. Quod ecclesiasticæ dignitates a nullo emantur vel vendantur. Quod nullus cujuslibet sacri ordinis carnali commercio utatur. Quod eis qui, ignorantes canonum prohibitionem, canonias emerunt, ignoscatur. Quod eis, qui scienter emptas a se vel a parentibus suis possederunt,[1] auferantur. Quod nemo laicorum a capite jejunii, nemo clericorum a Quadragesima usque in Pascha, carnes comedat. Quod omni tempore primum jejunium quatuor temporum prima hebdomada Quadragesimæ fiat. Quod ordines omni tempore vel in vespere Sabbati, vel, perseverante jejunio, in Dominica celebrentur: ut in Sabbato Paschæ, non nisi post horam nonam officium celebretur; ut jejunium secundum in hebdomada Pentecostes celebretur.[2] Quod ab Adventu Domini usque ad octavas Epiphaniæ, et a Septuagesima usque ad octavas Paschæ, et a prima die Rogationum usque ad octavas Pentecostes, et a quarta feria occidente sole omni tempore usque ad secundam feriam oriente sole trevia Dei custodiatur. Quod episcopum qui ceperit, omnino exlex habeatur. Quod qui sacri ordinis viros vel eorum famulos ceperit, anathema sit. Quod qui episcoporum vel clericorum morientium bona ceperit, anathema sit. Quod qui usque ad septimam generationem consanguinitati se copulaverit, anathema sit. Quod nemo in episcopum eligatur, nisi presbyter, aut diaconus, aut subdiaconus, et cui natalium dignitas suffragatur, nisi maxima necessitate et licentia papæ. Quod filii presbyterorum vel concubinarum ad presbyteratum non promoveantur, nisi prius ad religiosam vitam transierint. Quod qui ad ecclesiam vel ad crucem confugerint, data membrorum impunitate, justitiæ tradantur, vel innocentes liberentur. Quod una-

---

[1] *possederunt*] habuerunt, Al.
[2] *Pentecostes celebretur*] fiat Pentecostes, Al.

quæque ecclesia decimas suas habeat, nec ad aliam transeat. Quod laicus decimam[1] nec emat, nec vendat.[2] Quod pro sepultura mortuorum pretium non recipiatur.[3] In eo concilio excommunicavit dominus papa Philippum regem Francorum, et omnes qui eum vel regem vel dominum suum vocaverint, et ei obedierint, et ei locuti fuerint, nisi quod pertinet ad eum corrigendum. Similiter et illam maledictam conjugem ejus, et omnes qui eam reginam vel dominam nominaverint, quousque ad emendationem venerint, ita ut alter ab altero discedat. Similiter Guibertum Ravennatem, qui se papam appellat; et Henricum imperatorem Alamannorum, qui eum manutenet.

§ 346. Posteris diebus processit sermo ad populum sane luculentus et efficax, qualem decet sacerdotis[4] esse, de Christianorum expeditione in Turchos; quem, sicut ab auditoribus accepi, placuit posteris transmittere, integro verborum sensu custodito: illius enim facundiæ vigorem servare quis poterit? Nobiscum agetur feliciter si, propinquam terentes orbitam, per aliquod diverticulum redeamus[5] ad sententiam.

Sermo Urbani Papæ.

§ 347. "Multa," inquit, "fratres[6] carissimi, his
" diebus vobis dicta recolitis; quædam in concilio
" nostro jussa, quædam inhibita. Inconditum et con-
" fusum scelerum chaos exigebat dierum multorum
" interstitium; veternus morbus volebat cauterium.
" Dum enim indulgenti fune clementiæ dimittimus
" lineam, multa modo apostolatus nostri offendit offi-
" cium quæ præcideret, nulla quibus parceret. Sed
" fuerit hactenus humanæ fragilitatis quod peccastis;

---

[1] *decimam*] decimas, Aa. Al.

[2] *nec—vendat*] nec vendat nec retineat, Al.

[3] *recipiatur*] exigatur, Aa. Al. By.

[4] *sacerdotis*] pontificis, Al.

[5] *redeamus*] recurramus, Aa. Aah. Al.

[6] *fratres*] om. Cc.

Great oration of Urban II. at the council of Clermont.

"quod, illecebrarum involucris sopiti, cælestem ex-
"asperastis misericordiam, suspensam parvipendendo
"iracundiam. Fuerit mundanæ temulentiæ quod,
"legitima non curantes matrimonia, alieni cubilis non
"pensastis injuriam. Fuerit aviditatis nimiæ quod
"fratres vestros, illo magno et eodem pretio emptos,
"ut quisque poterat illaqueantes, contumeliose pecu-
"niis emunxistis. Nunc vobis, inter ista peccatorum
"naufragia constitutis, portus placidæ quietis aperitur,
"nisi negligitis. Parvi laboris in Turchos compendio
"retribuetur vobis perpetuæ salutis statio. Comparate
"nunc labores quos in scelerum exercitio habuistis, et
"eos quos in itinere quod præcipio habituri estis.
"Plures vel adulterii vel homicidii meditatio dat
"timores, nihil enim timidius nequitia, ut ait Salo- Wisdom,
"mon;[1] multos labores, quid enim laboriosius injus- xvii. 10.
"titia? qui autem ambulat simpliciter, ambulat
"confidenter. Horum laborum, horum timorum, exitus
"erat peccatum; stipendium autem peccati mors, mors Rom. vi. 23.
"vero peccatorum pessima. Nunc a vobis par labor
"atque metus pretio meliore petuntur. Horum la-
"borum erit causa caritas, ut, præcepto Dominico
"admoniti, animas pro fratribus ponatis: caritatis
"stipendium erit Dei gratia, Dei gratiam sequetur
"vita æterna. Ite ergo feliciter, ite confidenter, ad
"inimicos Dei persequendos. Illi enim jam pridem,
"proh! quantus Christianorum pudor! Syriam, Ar-
"meniam, omnem postremo Asiam Minorem, cujus
"provinciæ sunt Bithinia, Frigia, Galatia, Lidia,
"Caria, Pamphilia, Isauria, Licia, Cilicia, occupa-
"verunt; nunc Illiricum et omnes inferiores terras
"insolenter inequitant, usque ad mare quod Brachium
"Sancti Georgii[2] vocatur. Quid quod Dominicum
"monumentum, unicum fidei pignus, ditioni suæ ven-
"dicant, et ejus urbis introitum peregrinis nostris

---

[1] *Salomon*] per Salomonem Sapientia, Al. Aa. Aah.

[2] *Georgii*] Gregorii, Ce.

" venditant, quæ solis Christianis patere deberet si *Great oration of*
" aliquod solitæ virtutis vestigium eis inesset: hoc, si *Urban II.*
" solum esset, frontes nostras onerare sufficeret; jam *at the council of Clermont.*
" vero quis ferat nisi multum iners, nisi Christianæ
" gloriæ invidus, quod non ex æquo divisimus orbem?
" Illi Asiam, tertiam mundi partem, ut hereditarium
" nidum inhabitant; quæ a majoribus nostris æqua
" duabus residuis partibus, et tractuum longitudine et
" provinciarum magnitudine, non immerito æstimata
" est. Ibi olim devotionis nostræ rami pullularunt;
" ibi apostoli omnes, præter duos, mortes suas conse-
" crarunt; ibi modo Christicolæ, si qui supersunt,
" pauperculo agricolatu transigentes inediam, nefandis
" illis vectigal pensitant, vel tacitis suspiriis nostræ
" libertatis desiderantes conscientiam, quia perdidere
" suam. Illi Affricam, alteram orbis partem, ducentis
" jam annis et eo amplius armis possessam tenent;
" quod ideo Christiani honoris periculum pronun-
" tio, quia fuerit terra illa olim præclarorum inge-
" niorum altrix, quæ divinis scriptis omnem vetus-
" tatis situm a se repellent quamdiu fuerit qui La-
" tinas litteras legat. Norunt litterati quod loquor.
" Tertium mundi clima restat Europa, cujus quantu-
" lam partem inhabitamus Christiani? nam omnem
" illam barbariem quæ in remotis insulis glacialem
" frequentat oceanum, quia more belluino victitat,
" Christianam quis dixerit? Hanc igitur nostri mundi
" portiunculam Turchi et Saraceni bello premunt;
" jamque a trecentis annis Hispania et Balearibus in-
" sulis subjugatis, quod reliquum est spe devorant,
" homines inertissimi, et qui, cominus pugnandi fidu-
" ciam non habentes, fugax bellum diligunt. Nun-
" quam enim Turcus pede conserto martem audet, sed
Lucan, Pharsalia, viii. 384. " pulsus loco longe tendit nervos, et permittit vulnera
" ventis; et quoniam habet tela mortifero succo ebria,
" in hominem quem percutit, non virtus sed virus
" mortem facit. Quicquid igitur agit, fortunæ, non
" fortitudini, attribuerim, quod pugnat fuga et veneno.

Great oration of Urban II. at the council of Clermont.

"Constat profecto quod omnis natio quæ in ea plaga
"nascitur, nimio solis ardore siccata, amplius quidem
"sapit, sed minus habet sanguinis; ideoque vicinam
"pugnam fugiunt, quia parum sanguinis se habere
"norunt. Contra, populus qui oritur in arctois pru-
"inis, et remotus est a solis ardoribus, inconsultior
"quidem, sed largo et luxurianti superbus sanguine
"promptissime pugnat. Vos estis gens quæ intemper-
"atioribus mundi provinciis oriunda; qui sitis et
"prodigi sanguinis ad mortis vulnerumque contemptum,
"et non careatis prudentia: namque et modestiam
"servatis in castris, et in dimicatione utimini con-
"siliis; itaque, scientia et fortitudine præditi, aggre-
"dimini memorabile iter, totis seculis prædicandi,
"si fratres vestros periculo exueritis. Præsentibus ex
"Dei nomine præcipio, absentibus mando. Ituri et
"Christianitatem propugnaturi specimen crucis vestibus
"insigniant, ut intestinæ fidei foris amorem præten-
"dant; habentes per Dei concessum, et beati Petri
"privilegium, omnium absolutionem criminum; et hac
"interim lætitia laborem itineris allevient, habituri
"post obitum felicis martyrii commercium. Pon-
"entes ergo ferias sceleribus, ut saltem in his region-
"ibus liceat Christianis pacifice vivere, vadite; illam
"fortitudinem, prudentiam illam, quam in civili
"conflictu habere consuestis, justiori effundentes
"prælio. Ite, prædicabiles per orbem milites! ite, et
"prosternite ignavas gentes! Eat famosa Francorum
"virtus, cum appenditiis sibi gentibus, solo sui no-
"minis terrore totum orbem motura. Sed quid vos
"diutius immoror, ut fortitudinem gentilium verbis
"extenuem? Immo proponite animis vestris Deificam
"sententiam, 'Angusta est via quæ ducit ad vitam.' S. Matt. vii. 14.
"Esto ergo ut sit semita itinerantium arcta, plena
"mortibus, suspecta periculis; sed hæc eadem vos
"amissam ducet ad patriam; per multas nimirum tri-
"bulationes oportet vos introire in regnum Dei. Acts, xiv. 21.

" Spectate ergo animo, si prensi fueritis, cruces;
" spectate catenas, quæcunque postremo possunt tor-
" menta infligi; operimini pro fidei vestræ robore
" horrenda supplicia, ut, si necesse fuerit, dampno
" corporum agatis animarum remedium. Mortemne
" timetis, viri fortissimi, fortitudine et audacia præ-
" stantes? Nihil certe in vos poterit comminisci
" humana nequitia, quo superna pensetur gloria; non
" enim sunt condignæ passiones hujus temporis ad
" futuram gloriam quæ revelabitur in nobis. An
" nescitis quod vivere hominibus est calamitas, mori
" felicitas? Hæc vobis doctrina, si recordamini, cum
" lacte matrum affusa est sacerdotum verbo; hanc ma-
" jores vestri martyres prætenderunt exemplo. Mors
" enim a cænulento carcere liberat animas, ad proprium
" locum pro meritis evolaturas. Mors accelerat bonis
" patriam; mors præcidit reis malitiam: per mortem
" ergo liberæ animæ vel oblectantur gaudiis, spe meliora
" præsumentes; vel fruuntur suppliciis, nihil pejus ti-
" mentes. Dum autem vinculis corporum irretiuntur,
" trahunt ab ipsis terrulenta contagia, et, quod vera-
" citer quis dicat, mortuæ sunt; nec enim luteum
" cælesti, divinum mortali, pulchre cohæret. Pluri-
" mum quidem potest anima, etiam nunc corpori
" juncta; instrumentum enim suum vivificat latenter
" id movens, et ultra mortalem naturam gestis pro-
" ducens: veruntamen cum, sarcina qua in terram
" trahitur absoluta, proprium locum receperit, beatam
" et undique liberam participat fortitudinem, quomodo-
" cunque divinæ naturæ invisibilitati communicans.
" Gemino ergo functa officio, corpori vitam ministrat
" cum adest, causam vero mutationis cum recedit.
" Videtis quam jocunde anima in dormiente corpore
" vigilet, et, a sensibus seducta pro divina cognatione
" multa futura prævideat. Cur ergo mortem timetis,
" qui sompni requiem, quæ instar mortis est, diligitis?
" Res est nimirum dementiæ, pro cupiditate brevis

Great oration of Urban II. at the council of Clermont.

Rom. viii.18.

Speech of Urban II. at Clermont.

"vitæ, invidere sibi perpetuam. Quin potius, fratres carissimi, si ita contigerit, ponite pro fratribus ani-mas vestras; vacuate ab impiis Dei sacrarium, extru-dite latrones; inducite pios. Nulla vos necessitu-dinis pietas contineat, quia prima hominis pietas in Deum. Nullum natalis soli caritas tricet, quia di-versis respectibus Christiano totus est mundus exil-ium et totus mundus patria; ita exilium patria, et patria exilium. Nullum patrimoniorum amplitudo remoretur, quia ampliora sunt quæ promittuntur; nec ea quæ inani spe miseris adulentur, vel ignavam mentem pigro rerum medicamine palpent; sed crebris exemplis exhibita, frequenti usu comprobata. Et hæc quidem sunt dulcia, sed caduca, et quæ centu-plicatum contemptoribus suis pretium important. Hæc edico, hæc mando, terminumque proximi veris affigo. Aderit Deus euntibus, ut eis bonus arrideat annus, tum copia frugum, tum serenitate temporum. Morituri cæli intrabunt triclinium, victuri videbunt sepulcrum Dominicum. Et quæ major felicitas quam ut homo, in terris agens, videat loca illa in quibus cælorum Dominus conversatus est humanitus? Felices qui ad hæc vocantur munia, ut illa nancis-cantur munera! fortunati qui meditantur ista prælia, ut illa consequantur præmia!"

Excitement caused by the speech.

§ 348. Hujusce[1] orationis tenorem scripsi, pauca prop-ter veritatem dictorum incastigato sermone depromens, plura manumittens. Hinc igitur populus auditorum accensus, judicium animi clamore testatur, favens ser-mocinationi, favens peregrinationi: statimque in con-cilio proceres nonnulli, papæ genibus affusi,[2] se suaque Dei militiæ consecrarunt; e quibus fuit Aimarus, in-signis potentiæ Podiensis episcopus, qui postea exer-citum illum rexit[3] prudentia, auxit eloquentia. Igitur

Adhemar of Puy.

---

[1] *Hujusce*] Hucusque, Bk.; Hujuscemodi, Cm.
[2] *affusi*] acclines, Aa. Ag. Al. Cd.; affusi vel acclines, interl. Cc.
[3] *rexit . . . auxit*] tr. Bc.

Novembri mense, in quo concilium actum fuit, a singulis in sua discessum. Continuoque fama boni, totum perlapsa¹ per orbem, dulci Christianorum animos ininfecit aura: qua circumquaque spirante, nulla fuit tam remota gens, tam abdita, quæ non sui partem mitteret; nam non solum mediterraneas provincias hic amor movit, sed et omnes qui vel² in penitissimis³ insulis, vel in nationibus barbaris, Christi nomen audierant. Tunc Walensis venationem saltuum, tunc Scottus familiaritatem pulicum, tunc Danus continuationem potuum, tunc Noricus cruditatem reliquit piscium. Destituebantur agri cultoribus, ædes habitatoribus, totis porro migrabatur urbibus. Nullus necessitudinum amor, affectus patriæ vilis, solus Deus præ oculis; quicquid in horreis, quicquid in tricliniis repositum, responsurum erat vel avari votis agricolæ, vel thesaurorum incubatoris, deseritur; in solum Jerosolimitanum iter esuritur. Gaudium erat euntibus, mæror remanentibus. Quid dico⁴ de remanentibus? Videres maritum cum matrona, cum omni postremo familia, euntem; rideres, carpentis impositos, totos in iter transferre penates. Angustus erat limes transeuntibus, arctus trames itinerantibus, sic ruebant agmina serie longa hærentia.⁵ Opinionem⁶ hominum vincebat numerus, quamvis æstimarentur sexagies centum milia itinerantium. Nunquam proculdubio tot gentes in unam coiere sententiam; nunquam tanta barbaries imperio uni, et pene nulli, cervicositatem substravit suam. Præcipuum enim erat videre miraculum, cum tam infinita multitudo sensim per terras Christianorum, et non prædabunda procederet, et non esset qui coerceret. Fervebat in omnibus alterutra dilectio, ut si penes aliquem quid repertum esset quod suum non esse cognosceret, per multos dies passim agnoscendum

---

¹ *perlapsa*] dilapsa, Bc. By.
² *vel*] om. Cc¹.
³ *penitissimis*] penultimis. Cd.
⁴ *dico*] dicam, Cc¹.
⁵ *hærentia*] trahentia, Bc.
⁶ *Opinionem*] omnium, ins. Bk.

proponeret: suspendebaturque interim inventoris aviditas, dum forte illius qui perdiderat corrigeretur necessitas.

De ducibus Christianorum itineris Jerusalem.

§ 349. Jamque advenerat desiderantibus mensis Martius, quando, senecta brumali deposita, mundus, vernali vestitus juventa, in plagam orientis ituros invitabat: nec illi moras nexuere, tantus ardor animos invaserat. Godefridus, dux Lotharingorum, per Pannoniam iter instituit, nulli unquam militi virtute secundus; de antiqua Caroli magni origine lineam trahens, et cui vere plurimus inerat Carolus tam sanguine quam mente: sequebantur eum Frisones, Lotharingi, Saxones, et quicquid gentium[1] inter Renum et Garumnam fluvios jacet. Per Dalmatiam iter adorti Raimundus comes de Sancto Ægidio, et Aimarus Podii episcopus, par insigne virtutis, viri armis in hostes, pietate in Deum splendidi: sub signis eorum militabant Gothi et Wascones, et quicunque populus in Pireneum et Alpes diffunditur. Prævenerat eos compendio Boamundus, loco Appulus, gente Normannus; namque is apud Brundusium navibus conscensis, Dirachioque appulsus, inde itinere pedestri Constantinopolim per notos sibi tramites contendit: ductu ejus agebat prælium Italia, et quæcunque contermina provincia a Tirreno mari in Adriaticum protenditur. Hi omnes, pariter apud Constantinopolim convenientes, nonnihil mutuæ lætitiæ habuere; ibique Hugonem magnum, Philippi regis Francorum fratrem, invenere, quod is inconsulte et cum raro milite terras imperatoris ingressus, et ab hominibus ejus captus, in libera custodia habebatur. At vero Alexius, ejus[2] civitatis imperator,[3] horum procerum adventu territus, volens, sed

---

[1] *gentium*] om. Ce¹.
[2] *ejus*] hujus, Cd.
[3] *ejus—imperator*] om. Aa. Ag. Al.

quasi precibus coactus, captionis gratiam fecit; homo tergiversatione famosus, et nihil unquam magnum nisi dolo machinatus. Ipse Guiscardum, ut superius dixi, veneno, uxoremque ejus corruperat auro; fidem conjugalem falso per nuntios pactus. Ipse denique Willelmum comitem Pictaviensem in insidias Turcorum inductum, et sexaginta milibus armatorum privatum, pene solum effugere permisit; indignatus super ejus responso, quo Græco negaverat hominium. Ipsum postremo Boamundum, posteriori tempore contra se venientem ut injurias peregrinorum ulcisceretur, bis terque insidiis impetivit; sed cum parum promoveret, Guidone fratre et toto pene spoliavit exercitu, notis artibus toxica vel fluminibus vel vestibus infundens: sed hæc postmodum. Tum vero exercitum urbe arcens, proceribusque blande collocutus, tantum Graia facundia valuit, ut a singulis hominium et sacramentum exigeret, quod illi nihil doli machinarentur; quod urbes imperio suo appendices, si adquirere possent, redderent, sanguinis sui periculo alienum mercantes commodum. Soli Raimundo visa est antiquior tuendæ libertatis gratia, ut nec ipsi suum substerneret hominium, nec profiteretur sacramentum. Itaque, coactis omnibus viribus, Nicæam urbem Bithiniæ aggrediuntur. Ipsam enim [1] primitus placuerat invadi, quod et viantibus obsisteret, et mortem peregrinorum nuper ibi occisorum ultum ire animati essent: namque Walterus quidam, miles probatus sed præceps, quia vix in homine uno sapientiam et audaciam conspicaberis, quod altera moretur, altera præcipitet, incircumspecte circa moenia cursitans, cum multa manu occubuerat. Eam manum Petrus heremita prædicationibus suis de patria pellexerat.

---

[1] *enim*] om. Ce¹.

De Roberto Normanno.

A.D. 1096, September.

Robert of Normandy sets out, with Stephen of Blois.

§ 350. Jam vero mense Septembri, Robertus Normannorum comes, frater Willelmi regis, cujus titulum hic liber gestat, iter illud adoriri gestiens, habuit socios Robertum Flandrensem, Stephanum Blesensem sororis maritum; omnes amplæ prosapiæ comites, in quibus virtus citra genus non erat. Parebant eis Angli, et Normanni, et Occidentales Franci, et Flandritæ, et omnium populorum cunei qui ab oceano Britannico usque ad Alpes mediterraneo tractu jacent.

They find the pope at Lucca.

Ita viam profecti repererunt[1] apud Lucas papam Urbanum, qui Guiberto infensus, ut dixi, auxilio Matildis Italiam et urbem circumsonabat armis. Jamque[2] tantum promoverat, ut Quirites, ad gratiam ejus versi, Guibertinos tum verbis tum verberibus lacesserent; nec erat alterutris vel in ecclesiis vel in triviis parcendi animus, donec Guibertus, viribus impar, Urbano sedem vacuefecit, Alamanniam elapsus.

Fulcher, Gest. Peregr. c. 2.

He drives the antipope from Rome.

De urbe Roma.

Contrast of ancient with modern Rome.

§ 351. De Roma,[3] quæ quondam domina orbis terrarum, nunc ad comparationem antiquitatis videtur oppidum exiguum; et de Romanis, olim rerum dominis, genteque togata, qui nunc sunt[4] hominum inertissimi, auro trutinantes justitiam, pretio venditantes canonum regulam;—de urbe, inquam, et urbicis quicquid conarer dicere prævenerunt versus Hildeberti Cenomannensis primo[5] episcopi, post etiam Turonensis archiepiscopi:[6] quos hic cum inseruero, non ideo faciam ut alieno labore partam gloriam in me transferam;

Virgil, Æneid, i., 286.

---

[1] *repererunt*] receperunt, Ce.
[2] *Jamque*] Itaque, Ce.
[3] *Roma*] nova domina, Bq.
[4] *sunt*] dicuntur, Aa. Al. Ag. Bc.
[5] *primo*] om. Aa. Al.
[6] *post—archiepiscopi*] om. Aa. Aah. Ag. Al. Ap. Hildebert was translated to Tours in 1125.

sed erit ingenuæ mentis indicium, si, ejus non invidus gloriæ, apponam testimonium venustæ[1] facundiæ.

Versus Hildeberti, de Roma.

"Par tibi Roma nihil, cum sis prope tota ruina;
  "Quam magni fueris integra, fracta doces.
"Longa tuos fastus ætas destruxit; et arces
  "Cæsaris, et superum templa, palude jacent.
"Ille labor, labor ille ruit quem dirus Araxes
  "Et stantem tremuit, et cecidisse dolet;
"Quem gladii regum, quem provida jura senatus,
  "Quem superi rerum constituere caput;
"Quem magis optavit cum crimine solus habere
  "Cæsar, quam socius et pius esse socer:
"Qui crescens studiis tribus, hostes, crimen, amicos,
  "Vi domuit, secuit legibus, emit ope;
"In quem, dum fieret, vigilavit cura priorum,
  "Juvit opus pietas, hospitis unda locum;
"Materiam, fabros, expensas, axis uterque
  "Misit; se muris obtulit ipse locus:
"Expendere duces thesauros, fata favorem,
  "Artifices studium, totus et orbis opes.
"Urbs cecidit, de qua si quicquam dicere dignum
  "Moliar, hoc potero dicere, 'Roma fuit!'
"Non tamen annorum series, non flamma, nec ensis,
  "Ad plenum potuit hoc abolere decus.
"Cura hominum potuit tantam componere Romam,
  "Quantam non potuit solvere cura deum.
"Confer opes, marmorque novum, superumque favorem,
  "Artificum vigilent in nova facta manus;
"Non tamen aut fieri par stanti machina muro,
  "Aut restaurari sola ruina potest.
"Hic superum formas superi mirantur et ipsi,
  "Et cupiunt fictis vultibus esse pares,
"Non potuit Natura deos hoc ore creare,
  "Quo miranda deum signa creavit homo.
"Vultus adest his numinibus; potiusque coluntur
  "Artificum studio, quam deitate sua.
"Urbs felix, si vel dominis urbs illa careret,
  "Vel dominis esset turpe carere fide."[2]

---

[1] *venustæ*] vetustæ, At.
[2] Hildebert, *Opp.* ed. Beaugendre, pp. 1334, 1335.

De numero portarum et Sanctis Romæ.

Rome described.

§ 352. Parvane sunt hæc ad demonstrandum in tanta urbe vel olim bonorum dignitatem, vel modo malorum majestatem? Sed, ne quid honori desit, adjiciam et portarum numerum, et multitudinem sacrorum cinerum; et, ne quis [1] obscuritate verborum se causetur a cognitione rerum rejici, erit sermo cotidianus et levis.

Prima Porta.

The Cornelian Gate.

Prima porta Cornelia, quæ modo dicitur Porta Sancti Petri, et Via Cornelia. Juxta eam ecclesia beati Petri sita est, in qua corpus ejus jacet, auro [2] et lapidibus parata; et jam nullus hominum scit numerum [3] martyrum qui in eadem ecclesia pausant. In eadem via est altera ecclesia, in qua requiescunt sanctæ virgines Rufina et Secunda. In tertia ecclesia [4] sunt Marius et Martha; etiam Audifax et Abacuc, filii eorum.

Secunda Porta.

The Flaminian Gate.

Secunda porta Flaminia, quæ modo appellatur Sancti Valentini, et Via Flaminia; et cum ad pontem Molbium pervenit, vocatur Via Ravennana quæ ad Ravennam ducit. Ibi in primo miliario foris sanctus Valentinus in sua ecclesia requiescit.

Tertia Porta.

The Pincian Gate.

Tertia porta Porciniana,[5] et via eodem modo appellata, sed cum pervenit ad Salariam nomen perdit: et ibi prope, in eo loco qui dicitur Cucumeris, requies-

---

[1] *quis*] om. Cc.
[2] *auro*] et argento, add. Aa. Al.
[3] *numerum*] sanctorum, ins. Aa. Al. Bc.
[4] *ecclesia*] basilica, Aa. Al.
[5] *Porciniana*] Portitiana, Bc.

cunt martyres Festus, Johannes, Liberalis, Diogenes, Blastus, Lucina; et in uno sepulchro ducenti sexaginta,¹ et in altero triginta.

Quarta Porta.

Quarta porta et Via Salaria, quæ modo Sancti Sil- *The gate of S. Sylvester.* vestri dicitur. Ibi juxta viam sanctus Hermes requiescit, et sancta Vasella, et Protus, et Jacinctus, Maxilianus, Herculanus, Crispus; et in altero loco prope requiescunt sancti martyres Pamphilus, Quirinus, septuaginta gradibus in imo terræ. Deinde basilica sanctæ Felicitatis, ubi requiescit illa et Silanus filius ejus, et non longe Bonefacius martyr. Ibidem in altera ecclesia sunt Crisantus, et Daria, et Saturninus, et Maurus, et Jason, et mater eorum Hilaria, et alii innumerabiles. Et in altera basilica sanctus Alexander, Vitalis, Martialis, filii sanctæ Felicitatis; et sanctæ septem virgines, Saturnina, Hilarina, Dominanda, Rogantina, Serantina,² Paulina, Donata. Deinde basilica sancti Silvestri, ubi jacet marmoreo tumulo coopertus; et martyres Celestinus, Philippus, et Felix: et ibidem martyres trecenti sexaginta quinque in uno sepulchro requiescunt; et prope Paulus, et Crescentianus, Prisca, Semetrius, Praxedis, Potentiana pausant.

Quinta Porta.

Quinta porta Numentana; ibidem³ sanctus Nicho- *The Numentan Gate.* medes, presbyter et martyr: itemque via eodem modo dicitur. Juxta viam ecclesia sanctæ Agnetis, et corpus: in altera⁴ sancta Emerentiana, et martyres Alexander, Felix, Papias. In septimo miliario ejusdem viæ sanctus papa Alexander, cum Eventio et Theodolo, pausat.

---

¹ *sexaginta*] quadraginta, Aa. Al.
² *Serantina*] Serotina, Aa. Al. Bc.
³ *ibidem*] ibi, Aa. Al. Bc.
⁴ *altera*] ecclesia, add. Aa. Al.

Sexta Porta.

The gate of S. Laurence.

Sexta porta et Via Tiburtina, quæ modo dicitur Porta Sancti Laurentii. Juxta hanc viam jacet sanctus Laurentius in sua ecclesia, et Abundius martyr. Et ibi prope in altera ecclesia pausant hi martyres, Ciriaca, Romanus, Justinus, Crescentianus. Et ibi, non longe, basilica sancti Ipoliti, ubi ipse cum familia sua pausat, id est, decem et octo. Et ibi requiescunt beata Trifena[1] uxor Decii, et filia ejus Cirilla, et Concordia nutrix ejus.[2] Et in altera parte viæ illius est ecclesia[3] Agapiti martyris.

Septima Porta.

The Greater Gate.

Septima porta modo Major dicitur, olim Sircurana[4] dicebatur, et Via Lavicana, quæ ad beatam Helenam tendit. Ibi sunt prope, Petrus, Marcellinus, Tyburtius, Genuinus, Gorgonius, et quadraginta milites, et alii innumerabiles; et non longe sancti Quatuor Coronati.

Octava Porta.

The gate of S. John.

Octava porta Sancti Johannis, quæ apud antiquos Assenarica dicitur.

Nona Porta.

The Porta Metrosi.

Nona porta Metrosi[5] dicitur, et coram istis ambabus jacet Latina.

Decima Porta.

The Latin Gate.

Decima porta et Via Latina dicitur. Juxta eam quiescunt in una ecclesia martyres Gordianus et Epi-

---

[1] *Trifena*] Trifona, Aa. Al.; Trifonia, Bc.
[2] *ejus*] Ypoliti, Aa. Al.
[3] *ecclesia*] sancti, ins. At.
[4] *Sircurana*] Siracusana, Aa. Bc. Cd.
[5] *Metrosi*] Metrosa, Bc.

machus, Sulpicius, Valerianus,¹ Quintus, Quartus, Sophia, Triphenus.² Et ibi prope, in alio loco, Tertullinus: et non longe ecclesia beatæ Eugeniæ, in qua jacet, et Claudia mater ejus; et Stephanus papa cum clero suo, numero decem et novem, et Nemesius diaconus.

Undecima Porta.

Undecima porta et Via dicitur Appia. Ibi requiescunt sanctus Sebastianus et Quirinus; et olim requieverunt ibi apostolorum corpora. Et paulo propius Romam sunt martyres Januarius, Urbanus, Xenon, Quintinus,³ Agapitus, Felicissimus. Et in altera ecclesia Tiburtius, Valerianus, Maximus. Non longe ecclesia Ceciliæ martyris, et ibi reconditi sunt Stephanus, Sixtus, Zepherinus, Eusebius, Melchiades, Marcellus, Euticianus, Dionysius, Anteros, Pontianus, Lucius papæ, Optatius, Julianus, Colocerus, Parthenius, Tarsicius, Policamus,⁴ martyres. Ibidem ecclesia sancti Cornelii, et corpus. Et in altera ecclesia,⁵ sancta⁶ Sotheris: et non longe pausant martyres Ipolitus, Adrianus, Eusebius, Maria, Martha, Paulina, Valeria, Marcellus; et prope, Marcus papa in sua ecclesia.

The Appian Gate.

De Via Ardeatina.

Inter Viam Appiam et Ostensam⁷ est Via Ardeatina, ubi sunt Marcus et Marcellianus. Et ibi jacet Damasus papa in sua ecclesia; et non longe, sancta Petronilla, et Nereus, et Achilleus,⁸ et alii plures.

Via Ardeatina.

---

¹ *Valerianus*] Servilianus, Aa. Aah. Al.; Seasserianus, Bc.; Searserianus, Bk.
² *Triphenus*] Triphonius, Aa. Al.
³ *Quintinus*] Quirinus, Aa. Al. Bc.
⁴ *Policamus*] Politanus, Bc.
⁵ *ecclesia*] om. Bc. Ce.
⁶ *sancta*] sanctæ, Cd. Ce.
⁷ *Ostensam*] viam, præf. Aa. Bc. Cd.
⁸ *Achilleus*] Anchilleus, Ce.

Duodecima Porta.

Gate of S. Paul.

Duodecima porta et Via Ostensa [1] dicitur, modo Porta Sancti Pauli vocatur, quia juxta eam requiescit in sua ecclesia. Ibidemque Timotheus martyr; et non longe, in ecclesia sanctæ Teclæ, sunt martyres Felix, et Adauctus,[2] et Nemesius. In Aqua Salina est caput Anastasii martyris.

Tertiadecima Porta.

The gate of Portus.

Tertiadecima porta et Via Portuensis dicitur. Ibi prope sunt, in una ecclesia, martyres Felix, Alexander Abdon, et Sennes, Simeon, Anastasius, Polion, Vincentius, Milex, Candida, Innocentia.[3]

Quartadecima Porta.

The Aurelian Gate.

Quartadecima porta et Via Aurelia,[4] quæ modo Porta Sancti Pancratii dicitur, quia juxta eam requiescit in ecclesia sua; et alii martyres, Paulinus, Arthemius, sancta Sapientia, cum tribus filiabus Fide, Spe, Charitate. Et in altera basilica[5] Processus et Martinianus; et in tertia Felices duo; et in quarta sanctus Calixtus et Calepodius; et in quinta sanctus Basilides. Duodecimo intra urbem miliario in monte Celio sunt martyres Johannes et Paulus in sua domo, quæ est facta ecclesia post eorum martyrium; et Crispinus et Crispinianus, et sancta Benedicta. In eodem monte est ecclesia sancti Stephani prothomartyris, et ibi reconditi sunt martyres Primus et Felicianus. In monte Aventino sanctus Bonefacius, et in monte Nola sancta Tatiana, pausant.

---

[1] *Ostensa*] The Via Ostiensis.
[2] *Adauctus*] Audactus, Cd.
[3] *Innocentia*] Annocentia, Ce.
[4] *Aurelia*] Aurea, Ce.
[5] *basilica*] martyres, add. Aa. Al.

De itinere comitum de Roma ad Constantinopolim.

§ 353. Hæc sunt Romana sanctuaria, hæc sunt in terris divina pignora; et tamen intra hoc quasi cæleste promptuarium insano furore gens ebria, tum, cum illuc peregrini venerunt, fœdo ambitu omnia turbabant, et supra ipsa sanctorum corpora civilem libabant sanguinem, dum non possent satiare pecuniarum libidinem. Urbani igitur benedictione freti, comites, transita Tuscia et Campania, per Apuliam Calabriam venere; statimque mare transissent, nisi consulti nautæ propter austrorum violentiam vetuissent. Quapropter Normannus et Blesensis comites, qua quisque poterat, hyemem fovere, apud amicos perhendinantes. Solus Flandrensis ventis vela credidit, præcipiti consilio feliciter usus: ideoque gregariorum vulgus, pars propter inopiam domum revertit, pars pro intemperie soli morbo defecit. Nec non et residui duces, ut videre pacatum classibus æquor, vernali sole redeunte, maris fidem experti, et Christi auxilio illæsi, duobus portibus excepti applicuere. Inde per Thessaliam, cujus metropolis est Thessalonica, Traciam, et hinc Constantinopolim venere. Multi pauperum illa via morbo et inedia extincti; multi in vado, quod pro rapiditate "Diaboli" dicitur, intercepti;[1] plura esque profecto perissent nisi equi emissarii, adverso amni[2] oppositi, violenti gurgitis vortices fregissent: ita quibusdam vita procurata, reliqui equis transducti. Omnis itaque multitudo, quindecim dierum spatio, præteritorum laborum indulsit solatio, positis castris in suburbano civitatis; de qua, quia locus se obtulit, pauca dicenda.

---

[1] *intercepti*] suffocati, Al.; suffocaturi, Aa.
[2] *adverso amni*] adversus amnem, Cd.; in adversum amnem, Aa. Al.; adversum amni, Bc.; adversi ampni, Bk.

Visio Constantini.

§ 354. Constantinopolis primum Bizantium dicta; formam antiqui vocabuli præferunt imperatorii nummi Bizantini vocati: hanc divinitus mutasse nomen, Sanctus Aldelmus auctor est in libro De Virginitate,[1] hujusmodi sententia. Constantino, in eadem urbe soporato, visa est astitisse vetula rugis anilibus arata frontem; mox imperiali chlamyde amicta in juvenculam refloruisse, viridisque formæ decore Constantini pellexisse oculum ut non abstineret quin porrigeret ei osculum. Tunc Helenam matrem, quæ adesset, dixisse, "Hæc tua semper erit, nec unquam morietur, nisi in "fine seculi." Hujus sompnii solutionem Augustus, extruso sopore, jejuniis et eleemosynis extrahebat e cælo. Et ecce, post octo dies iterum soporatus, visus est videre Silvestrum papam, paulo ante defunctum, qui dulci luminum risu discipulum perstringens, "Consueta," inquit, "egisti prudentia, ut quod intel-
"lectum effugeret hominis, a Deo expectares solven-
"dum nodum ænigmatis. Hæc igitur quam vidisti
"anicula est civitas ista, ævi situ decrepita; cujus
"jam vetustate quassa mœnia, et vicinam ruinam
"minantia, reparatorem desiderant. Sed tu eam
"muris reformans et opibus, vocabulo quoque in-
"signies tuo, et regnabit in ea perpetuo imperatoria
"progenies. Non tamen tuo arbitratu fundamenta
"jacies, sed ascenso sonipede, cui quondam rudis
"Christicola insidens apostolorum Romæ circuisti
"ecclesias, laxatis habenis, quo volet eundi promp-
"tum illi cedes arbitrium; habebisque in manu has-
"tam regiam, cujus cuspide in terram tracta muri
"scribentur vestigia. Consules ergo in terra cuspidis
"magisterium quo ordine disponi debeant fundamenta
"mœnium."

Aldhelm, De Laud. Virg. c. 25.

---

[1] The narrative is here abridged, in our author's own words, from the story as recorded by Aldhelm, Opp. ed. Giles, pp. 28, 29.

De urbe Constantinopolitana.

§ 355. Paruit Augustus visioni præcluæ,[1] et civitatem æquam Romæ constituit; lege[2] professus non debere imperatorem Romæ principari ubi a Christo coronati apostoli principabantur. Fecit in ea duas ecclesias, quarum una Hirenis, altera dicitur Apostolorum; invehens illuc numerosa sanctorum corpora, qui possint contra incursus hostium cælestium impetrare patrocinium. Statuas quoque triumphalium virorum a Roma deductas, et simulacra deorum ad videntium ridiculum, et tripodas Delphicos, in Circo dedit, ad spectaculum simul et ad civitatis ornamentum. Gratumque admodum fuisse ferunt imperiali animo ut illic urbem divino jussu fundaret, ubi et soli ubertas et cæli temperies mortalium saluti conveniret; quia enim in Britannia natus fuerat, ardores solis exosus erat. Est vero Tracia una[3] Europæ provincia, ut poetæ quoque canunt, Hebri fluminis glacie et Bistonio aquilone perfrigida; fœcundæ[4] vicina Mœsiæ, cujus, ut ait Virgilius, "mirantur Gargara messes." At vero Constantinopolis, circumflua Ponto, Europæ atque Asiæ carpit utrinque libratam temperiem, quod aquilonares hiatus mulceat e proximo veniens Asiaticus Eurus. Porrigitur ergo urbs ingentibus mœnibus, sed eam angustat convenarum innumerus populus; quapropter, rupium molibus et arenarum cumulis profundo injectis, longe itur in salum, et novo commento tellus inventa veteres contrahit undas. Stupet itaque mare peregrinos vitreo in gurgite campos, urbemque suam totis terrarum commodis cingit et pascit. Est enim civitas undique, præter ad aquilonem, mari magno cincta, ambitu murorum juxta situm pelagi angulosa, viginti[5] milia passuum muro complexa. Dan-

---

[1] *præcluæ*] præclaræ, Aa.
[2] *lege*] om. Aa. Al.
[3] *Tracia una*] tertia, Aa. Cd.
[4] *fœcundæ*] fœcunda, Cd., fœcundas, Al. Ce.; om. Aa. Bc.
[5] *viginti*] duodecim, Aa. Al. Cd. Bk. Bq.; MS. Ce. omits *milia*.

ubius, qui et Hister, occultis canalibus sub terra influit urbi; diebusque constitutis, ablato pessulo inductus, cænum platearum pelago importat. Certavere zelo imperiali Augusti singuli decorem addere, quisque arbitrantes aliquid se institutæ debere operæ; iste sanctorum reliquiis, ille divitiis, Constantinus omnibus.

De Imperatoribus Constantinopolis.

§ 356. Regnaverunt in ea, post Constantinum magnum, imperatores quorum hæc sunt nomina: Constantinus filius ejus, Julianus apostata, Jovinianus, Valens, Theodosius major, [Archadius,][1] Theodosius minor, Marcianus, Leo primus, [Leo minor,] Zeno, Anastasius, Justinus major, Justinianus; hic, litteris et bellis nobilis, fecit in Constantinopoli ecclesiam Divinæ Sapientiæ, id est, Domino Christo, quam Agiam Sophiam cognominavit; opus, ut ferunt, omnibus per orbem ædificiis magnificentius, quodque certa rerum facie inspectum vincat ampullata verba referentium; Justinus minor, Tiberius, Mauricius, primus Græcus, Focas, Heraclius, Heracleonas, Constans, Constantinus filius Heraclii; iste Romam veniens, et quod reliquum erat ornatus antiqui corradens, tegulis etiam æreis fastigia ecclesiarum nudavit, triumpho scilicet apud Constantinopolim de hisce manubiis inhians; sed ei infeliciter illa cessit aviditas, quia, continuo apud Siracusas extinctus, Saracenis Alexandriam deferentibus omnes illas reliquit exuvias; Constantinus, Justinianus, Leo secundus, Tiberius, iterum Justinianus, Philippicus, Anastasius, Theodosius, Leo tertius. Hi omnes regnaverunt et in Constantinopoli et in Roma; sequentes tantum in Constantinopoli: Constantinus, Leo, Constantinus, Nicephorus, Stauratius, Michael, [Leo, Michael,] Theophilus, Michael, Basilius, Leo, Alexander, Constantinus, Romani duo, Nicephorus Focas, Johannes, Basilius [et Constantinus], Romanus, Michael, Michael, Constantinus, Theodora imperatrix, Michael, Sachius,

---

[1] The names in brackets are omitted in MS. Cc. There is much confusion in all the MSS.

Constantinus, Romanus Diogenes, Nicephorus Butanius, Michael: hic, per Alexium depulsus imperio, ad Guiscardum in Apuliam clandestinam fugam composuit; traditaque illi potestate, aliquid se opinatus est fecisse quod[1] noceret Alexio. Unde Guiscardo aggrediendi magna increvit animus, ut inani spe mentiretur sibi adquiri posse per industriam quod alter amiserat per ignaviam; sed quantum istis profecerit præcedens liber patefecit. Est in ea civitate lignum Domini ab Helena de Jerosolimis delatum. Requiescunt ibi apostoli, Andreas, Jacobus frater Domini, Mathias; prophetæ, Heliseus, Samuel, Daniel, et alii plures; Lucas evangelista, martyres innumerabiles; confessores, Johannes Chrysostomus, Basilius, Gregorius Nazanzenus, Spiridion; virgines, Agatha, Lucia; omnesque postremo sancti quorum corpora illuc ex omnibus regionibus imperatores convehere potuerunt.

§ 357. Normannus itaque et Blesensis comites hominium suum Græco prostraverunt,[2] nam jam Flandrita transierat, et id facere fastidierat, quod se meminisset natum et educatum libere. Alii, data fide acceptaque, Niceam pertendunt hebdomada Junii[3] prima, quam jam ceteri a medio Maii obsederant. Ita conjunctis viribus multæ utrinque mortes actæ sunt: cum ab oppidanis facile in subjectos telorum omnia genera rotarentur, nec alicujus licet inertissimi manus in confertos frustraretur. Quin et exanimatorum cadavera Turci uncis ferreis in murum trahebant, ludibrio nostrorum excarnificanda, vel ablatis vestibus denudanda.[4] Doluerunt id Franci: nec prius abstiterunt ferro exercere dolorem, quam Turchi, extremis malis fessi, die solstitii æstivalis per clandestinos nuntios impera-

---

[1] *fecisse quod*] effecisse quo, Aa. Al.

[2] *prostraverunt*] prostituere, Aa. Al.; the word is probably intended as a play on "præstiterunt."

[3] *Junii*] jejunii, Al. Bc. Bk.

[4] *denudanda*] deicienda, Aa. Al. Bc. By.

The emperor bids the Franks depart.

tori se dedidere. Ille, qui nihil præter commodum suum pensare nosset, denuntiavit Francis ut abirent; malens urbem servari Turchorum apertæ perfidiæ, quam Francorum suspectæ potentiæ. Jussit tamen distribui argentum et aurum optimatibus, nummos æreos in-

The Turks retire from Bithynia.

ferioribus, ne se irremuneratos quererentur. Ita Turchi, qui jam a quinquaginta annis Bithiniam, quæ est pars Minoris Asiæ, quam Romaniam dicunt, Euphrate transito possederant, in superiores fuga terras conces-sere; veruntamen ausi sunt, obsidione soluta, exerci- *Fulcher, Gesta Per. c. 5.* tum ultra progredientem incessere, auctore quodam

They attack the Crusaders on their march.

Solimanno cui dominium totius Romaniæ obtigerat.[1] Is, coactis sagittariorum milibus æstimatione trecentis sexaginta, nostros, nihil minus quam bellum meditantes, tanta vi aggressus est, ut, ferreo imbre sagittarum inundante perterriti, omnes incunctanter dorsa nudarent. Et tum forte dux [2] Godefridus, et Hugo magnus, et Raimundus aliam viam invaserant, ut et inimicorum solum popularentur latius, et suis pabula

Duke Robert sends for Godfrey to help him.

compararent facilius. At vero Normannus, ancipiti discrimine permotus, adventum Turchorum, expeditis cursoribus, Godefrido et ceteris per tutos tramites intimavit. Illi, moræ nescii, signis in hostem conversis, socios eripuere periculo; namque hi jam indiscrete in tentoriis suis necabantur, nihil bello intenti, sed solis lacrymis et precibus auras implentes. Nec rimabatur hostis vulneri aditum, sed in nothos[3] fortunam emittens, nunquam pro densitate cuneorum inanem referebat manum. Sola erat mortis dilatio, quod, quia juxta quoddam arundinetum pugnabatur, equi Turchorum impediti liberis non exultabant cursibus. Sed tandem visis antesignanis optimatum venientium, nostri ex arundineto prodeunt; et acclamato signo militari, "Deus vult!" dissipatos ordines hostium invadunt, sociis ut ex altera parte feriant

---

[1] *obtigerat*] obvenerat, Bc. By.
[2] *dux*] om. Ce.
[3] *nothos*] This is the reading of the MSS. *Nostros* may be suggested as the true reading.

innuentes. Ita Turchi, cum utrinque premerentur, nescio quid dirum stridentes, ululatibus in caelum actis diffugere; nec solito more pugna fugaci usi, sed, abjectis arcubus, majus aliquid quam humanum timorem continua trium dierum fuga testati sunt. Nec erat qui eos fugaret; quia equi nostrorum, vix jejuno cespite vitam sustentantes, alacrem persecutionem negabant, lasso statim ilium pulsu defectionem suam[1] ostendentes. Erat enim[2] Asia, terra quondam frugum feracissima, ita moderno et antiquo tempore Turchis saevientibus expilata, ut vix raro exercitui alimoniam ministrare sufficeret, nedum tantae multitudini, quae totas segetes depastura, totos amnes[3] epotatura[4] videretur: aestimabantur enim cum a Nicea[5] discessere septingenta milia, pars reliqua vel ferro interempta[6] vel valitudine minuta, major domos dilapsa.

§ 358. Inde, per Antiochiam Pisidiae et Iconium urbes, Eracleam venere: ibi signum in caelo viderunt modo ensis fulminei figuratum, mucrone versus orientem protento. Jamque a kalendis Julii,[7] cum Niceam deseruerant, Octobris mensis nonae volvebantur, quando Antiochiam Syriae venere: cujus situm commemorarem, nisi aviditatem meam praeoccuparet Ambrosiana in Egesippo facundia,[8] simul et quod vereor ne mihi vertatur vitio quod tam frequenter in digressionibus peregrinatur narratio. Veruntamen quantum suscepti operis narratio postulat, dicam.

De urbe Antiochia.

§ 359. Civitas est maximo muro circumdata, montem etiam moenibus complexa;[9] a Seleuco, rege Asiae,

---

[1] *defectionem suam*] defectum suum, Al.
[2] *enim*] autem, Aa.Ah.
[3] *amnes*] se, ins. Bc.
[4] *epotatura*] epotura, Aa. Ah.
[5] *a Nicea*] antea, Bc. By.
[6] *interempta*] intercepta, Cc.
[7] *Julii*] Junii, Bc. By. Cd.
[8] *narratio*] necessitas, Aa.Al. By. The reference is to the Pseudo-Ambrosian Hegesippus, *de Bello Judaico*.
[9] *complexa*] circumplexa, Aa. Al. By.

nomine Antiochi patris cognominata; post Romam, et Constantinopolim, et Alexandriam quarto per orbem loco cunctis civitatibus praelata; moenibus tuta, montibus ardua; magis ingenio quam vi, si unquam capiatur, obtinenda. Fluvius illi proximus, quem modo Fernum, quondam Orontem vocatum intelligo, duodecimo ab urbe miliario accipitur pelago, fluentis rapacibus, et ipso impetu frigidioribus, salubris aurae temperie saluti[1] medetur civium;[2] commeatum quoque navium oppidanis invehens, perseverantiam obsidentium quantolibet tempore deridet. Ibi primum Christianismi[3] venerabile vocabulum excogitatum. Inde Paulus, hujusce religionis incentivum et fomes, ad praedicandum processit. Ibi beatus Petrus primi antistitii cathedram sedit; in cujus honore fundata illic ecclesia toto Turchorum tempore illibata permansit: nec minus altera, in honore sanctae Mariae consecrata, decore sui oculos spectantium tenebat; mirum in modum, ut cujus persequebantur fidem revererentur aedem.

De obsidione Antiochiae.

§ 360. Hanc itaque civitatem Franci ab Octobri usque ad Junium circumsedere,[4] tentoriis circum muros amne transito locatis: perspectaque difficultate expugnandi,[5] timiditati quorundam obviandum arbitrati, omnes pariter proceres sacramento fecere obsidioni non ponendas ferias quoad vel vi vel ingenio prenderetur civitas; et, ut quod intendebant facilius implerent, castra cis fluvium constituerunt multa, quibus impositi milites excubias[6] praetenderent. Aoxianus[7] quoque civitatis admiratus, videns Francos non joco et

---

[1] *saluti*] sanitati, Al.
[2] *civium*] civicae, Aa. Al. Bc.
[3] *Christianismi*] Christiani olim nominis, Aa. Ag. Aah. Al. Bc.; Christianismi olim nominis, Bc.
[4] *circumsedere*] circumdedere, Aa. Ag. Al.
[5] *expugnandi*] capiendi, Bc.
[6] *excubias*] castra, Bc. Cc. Cf.
[7] *Aoxianus*] Bagi Sejan seems to be the proper name of the emir; it is curiously distorted by the historians of the Crusade.

jejune agere, sed civitatem serio impetere, Sansadolem filium ad Soldanum imperatorem¹ misit, qui Francorum audaciam exponens, suppetias expeteret.² Soldanus apud Persas qui apud Romanos Augustus, totius orientis et omnium Saracenorum rector. Quod ideo, ut æstimo, tamdiu manet et propagatur imperium, quod gens illa parum, ut dixi, bellicosa, et vivacis sanguinis inops, semel acceptum nescit dediscere servitium ignorantque, ut Lucanus ait, ideo

Continuity of the Persian Empire.

Lucan, Pharsalia iv., 579.

"datos ne quisquam serviat enses."

At vero gens occidentalis, audax et effera, diuturnam unius populi³ dedignatur dominationem; sæpe se servitio exuens, et de uno in aliud transferens. Denique Romanum imperium prius ad Francos, post ad Teutones declinavit; orientale apud Persas semper durat.

Quare Turchi Christianos urbis indigenas occiderint.

§ 361. Ad hujus igitur imperii principem Sansadoles missus, viam studio celerabat juvenili; pater interim, in custodia urbis, imperatorio non deerat muneri. Nec contenta virtus inclusorum sua tutari, nostros ultro lacessebat; crebro illos, et subito, pabulantes et nundinantes aggressa; nam, de inventis navibus pontem facientes, nundinas ultra fluvium constituerant.⁴ Ope igitur Christi pertinaces sumptis armis hostes audacter propellere, ut nunquam eos superiorem gloriam paterentur referre: cujus contumeliæ ultionem in Syros et Armenios, civitatis indigenas, Turchi refundebant;⁵ balistis et petrariis capita interemptorum in castra Francorum emittentes, ut illos eo modo ad dolorem incenderent.

Shemsuddawla sent to Persia for aid.

Conduct of the besieged.

---

¹ *imperatorem*] Persidis, ius. Aa. Ag. Aah. Al. Ap. By.
² *expeteret*] oraret, Aa. Al.
³ *populi*] gentis, Ai.
⁴ *constituerant*] instituerant, Aa. Al. Bc.
⁵ *refundebant*] infundebant, Bc.

De fame obsidentium.

Famine among the Crusaders.

§ 362. Et jam, devastatis omnibus circa urbem quæ ad victum poterant parari, temeraria fames, quæ tuta etiam expugnare solet, exercitum incessere cœperat; adeo ut, nondum surgentibus in altam segetem culmis, quidam siliquas fabarum nondum[1] adultarum pro summis deliciis amplecterentur. Alii carnes jumentorum, alii coria aquis mollita, quidam carduos parum coctos per abrasas fauces utero demittebant; quidam vel mures, vel talium quid deliciarum, poscentibus aliis venundabant, et esurire sustinebat prolato jejunus venditor auro. Nec defuere qui cadavera cadaveribus infarcirent, humanis pasti carnibus; longe tamen et in montibus, ne nidore carnis adustæ ceteri offenderentur. Plures, spe reperiendæ alimoniæ, ignotis vagabantur semitis; et a latrunculis, viarum gnaris, trucidabantur. Sed non multo post civitas deditioni consensit.

Fulcher, Gesta Per. c. 8.

Lucan, Pharsalia, iv. 97.

Quomodo Boamundus Turchum quendam ad proditionem urbis flexit.

Bohemond bribes a Turkish officer to betray the principal tower.

§ 363. Boamundus enim, sollertis ingenii vir, ea parte qua prætendebat, principem quendam Turchum, maximæ turris custodem, promissis ingentibus ad proditionem per internuntios sollicitaverat. Ille quoque, ut infamiam proditionis insigni excusatione palliaret, Boamundo filium in obsidatum dedit; Christi edicto, quod per sompnium didicisset, id se facere professus. Suos igitur ad turrim Boamundus admovit, prius clandestino astu perpetuum a proceribus civitatis donum nactus, si possit adquirere. Ita Franci, per funeas scalas nocte intempesta in murum evecti, vexilloque Boamundi, quod vermiculatum erat, ventis in fastigio turris exposito, signum Christianum lætis fragoribus ingemi-

Fulcher, Gesta Per. c. 9.

The Franks scale the walls and set up Bohemond's standard.

---

[1] *nondum*] om. Cc.

nant, "Deus vult! Deus vult!" Turchi experrecti, et soporis penuria inertes, fugam per angiportus invadunt: districtis nostri gladiis insecuti magnas de inimicis strages acervant. In ea fuga occidit[1] Aoxianus urbis admiratus, a quodam rustico Syro decollatus: caput ejus, Francis allatum, ridiculo et gaudio fuit. *Death of the governor.*

De adventu Turchorum.

Fulcher, Gesta Per. c. 11.

§ 364. Nec diu opima victoria laetati, postero die Turchorum obsidionem extra muros ingemuere. Venerant illi a Sansadole invitati, duce Corbaguath satrapa orientali, qui ab imperatore Persidis acceperat trecenta milia cum viginti septem admiratis. Horum sexaginta milia[2] in arcem urbis per scopulos ascendere, advocantibus eos Turchis qui adhuc ibidem remanserant. Itaque illi crebris excursibus Christianos potissimum fatigabant, nec erat ulla spes nisi in Dei auxilio; cum bello infestatis cresceret inedia, inedia semper magnorum[3] comes prima malorum. Quapropter, triduano prius cum letaniis exacto jejuno, legatus Petrus heremita mittitur ad Turchos. Is familiari sibi eloquio ista prosecutus est, ut Turchi Christianorum terras, quas olim pervaserant indebite, nunc evacuent voluntarie; justum esse, ut sicut Christiani non infestant[4] Persidam, ita Turchi non urgeant[5] Asiam; proinde aut libenti discessu nativum solum repetant, aut mane futuro bellum exspectent; sortem per duos vel quatuor vel octo experiantur, ne periculum ad totum vergat exercitum. *The Turks, under Korbogha, besiege the Crusaders.*

Lucan, Phars. iv. 93.

Fulcher, Gesta Per. c. 14.

Peter the hermit sent to negotiate.

His argument.

Quomodo Christiani Turchos vicerint.

§ 365. Non erat Corbaguath ejus facilitatis ut legatum dignaretur responso; sed scacchis ludens, et *Korbogha declines to listen to him.*

---

[1] *occidit*] occiditur, Al.
[2] *milia*] om. Cd. Cc. Cf.; but see Fulcher, c. 11. MSS. Bk. Bq. read XL^{ta} for LX^{ta}.
[3] *magnorum*] om. Cc.
[4] *infestant*] urgent, Aa. Al.
[5] *urgeant*] infestent, Aa. Al.

dentibus infrendens, inanem dimisit; hoc tantum dicto, jam conclamatam esse Francorum superbiam. Ille quoque concite rediens exercitum de insolentia Turchi certiorem reddidit. Tunc omnes se alterutrum animantes, etiam per præconem clamare fecere, ut quisque nocte illa equo suo pro posse præbendam porrigeret, ne sequenti die multiformibus gyris fatigatus deficeret. Jamque mane inclaruerat, cum, per acies dispositi, vexillis in hostem infestis prodeunt. Primam turmam duxere duo Roberti, Normannus et Flandrensis, et Hugo magnus; secundam dux Godefridus; tertiam Podiensis episcopus. Boamundus in extremo agmine incedebat,[1] ceteris subsidio futurus. Raimundus in urbe remanserat, qui nostris receptui provideret, si necesse foret. Hoc Turchi eminus conspicati, primo quid esset hæsere. Mox cognito vexillo episcopi, quod eum maxime metuerent, quia illum papam Christianorum et incentorem bellorum dictitarent,[2] antequam ferirentur, videntes quod nostri tam animose et incunctanter procederent, terga dedere: alteri quoque, insperato exilientes tripudio, cedentes cecidere, quantum vel peditum ilia vel equitum calcaria sufficere potuerunt. Persuadebantque sibi videre se antiquos martyres, qui olim milites fuissent, quique mortis pretio parassent præmia vitæ, Georgium dico et Demetrium, vexillis levatis a partibus montanis accurrere, jacula in hostes, in se auxilium vibrantes. Nec diffitendum est affuisse martyres Christianis, sicut quondam angelos Macchabæis simili duntaxat causa pugnantibus. Reversi vero in prædam, tanta in castris illorum reperiunt quæ cujuslibet avidissimi[3] exercitus satietatem possent vel temperare vel exstinguere. Hoc prælium actum est anno incarnationis Dominicæ millesimo nonagesimo octavo, quarto kalendas Julii; nam pridie nonas Junii[4]

---

[1] *incedebat*] om. Bc.
[2] *dictitarent*] dicerent, Bc. Bk.
[3] *avidissimi*] avarissimi, Aa. Al.
[4] *Junii*] Julii, Bc.

capta fuerat urbs. Mox, kalendis Augusti sequentibus, Podiensis episcopus, Christianorum vexillifer, illius boni auctor præcipuus, communi mortalium conditioni feliciter manus dedit; et Hugo magnus, concessu ut aiunt heroum, Franciam rediit, causatus continuam viscerum tortionem.

Death of Adhemar and return of Hugh the Great.

§ 366. Sed cum, sex[1] mensibus Antiochiæ morati, præteritos labores tam diuturna quiete abstersissent, iter jamdudum inceptum resumere meditabantur. Primusque Raimundus, nullius unquam ignaviæ conscius, et cui semper cura primum in procinctu militari esse, et post eum Roberti et Godefridus, iter adorti;[2] solum Boamundum florentissimæ civitatis aspectus et pecuniarum fames continuit, ut interim differret. Sed latebat sub cupiditate ratio persuasibilis, qua diceret Antiochiam non sine principe Turchis exponendam continuo involaturis. Residit ergo in urbe; et Raimundi homines, qui vicum unum tenebant, improbus exactor mœnibus depulit.[3] At vero ceteri per Tripolim, et Beritum, et Tyrum, et Sydonem, et Acaronem et Caipham, et Cæsaream Palestinæ transeuntes, ibi a dextra dimittentes maritima, pervenerunt Ramulam; a quibusdam civitatibus gratanter excepti, quarundam subjectione virtutem suam insignientes. Non enim diutius moram protelari consilium erat, quod Aprilis mensis erat, et campestres fruges in maturas messes coaluerant. Ramula est civitatula, muro indiga, beati Georgii, si famæ credimus, martyrii conscia; cujus ibi ab antiquo fundatam ecclesiam Turchi nonnihil deformaverant, tunc metu Francorum, subreptis omnibus suis, in montana dilapsi. Sequenti mane, dubio adhuc diei et noctis confinio, Tancredus nepos Boamundi, præstans animi miles, sumptis armis, et quidam alii, Bethleem pertendunt, loca vicina explorare cupientes.

Fulcher, Gesta Per. c. 15, 16.

Advance on Jerusalem.

Bohemond stays at Antioch.

c. 17.

The army reaches Ramlah.

c. 18.

Tancred arrives at Bethlehem.

---

[1] *sex*] septem, Cd.
[2] *iter adorti*] viam moliti, Aa. Ag. Al. Bc. Bk. Bq. By.
[3] *depulit*] expulit, Bc.; depulsit, Bk.

Syri qui essent in loco, progressi obviam, lætitiam suam desiderio lacrymante prodebant, saluti eorum pro paucitate nimirum metuentes; nam non multo plus quam centum milites venerant. At illi, supplicibus votis sacram ædem venerati, confestim Jerosolimam intentis animis invadunt. Turchi quoque, pro fiducia virium mentibus efferati, foras exiliunt, in nostros aliquantisper arietantes; totus enim jam exercitus adventarat: sed mox, Francis annitentibus, summoti hostes claustrorum muralium objectu salutem suam tutabantur.

De Urbe Jerusalem.

§ 367. De situ et positione Jerusalem nihil me dicere copia scriptorum admonet: nec necesse est ut in hoc campo nostra[1] exultet oratio; adeo fere omnium notitiæ patet quod Josephus, quod Eucherius, quod Beda scripsere. Quis enim nesciat eam a Melchisedech Salem, a Jebuseis Jebus, a Salomone Jerosolimam vocatam? Quis non audierit quotiens, sub adverso marte cadens, cives ruinis sepelierit suis, vel Nabugodonosor, vel Tito, vel Adriano agentibus? Adrianus ille fuit qui Jerosolimam, ex suo cognomine cognominatam Heliam, orbiculato et majori murorum ambitu ædificavit, ut locum sepulcri Dominici, quod olim extra fuerat, amplecteretur; nam et mons Sion, intra urbem receptus, pro arce supereminet. Fons intra nullus, sed cisternis ad hoc præparatis colliguntur latices siti civium profuturi; quod ipsius urbis situs, supercilio ab aquilone montis Sion incipiens, ita sit molli clivo dispositus, ut pluvia ibi decidens nequaquam lutum faciat, sed instar fluviorum vel cisternis excipiatur, vel per portas defluens torrentem Cedron augeat. Ibi templum Domini et templum quod dicunt Salomonis, quibus incertum auctoribus ædificata, Tur-

---

[1] *nostra*] mea, Bc. By.

chorum celebri frequentia colebantur; templum præsertim Domini, quod cotidianis venerabantur excubiis, Christianosque ingressu arcebant, simulacro Mahumet ibidem collocato. Ibi decenti[1] opere compacta ecclesia sancti sepulcri capax, a Constantino magno ædificata, nullam unquam ab inimicis fidei tulit injuriam; metu, sicut conjicio, pro igne cælesti percussis, qui quotannis in vigilia Paschæ lampadibus serenus infulget. Quod miraculum quando cœperit, vel si ante tempora Saracenorum[2] fuerit, nullius historiæ cognitione discernitur. Legi ego in scripto Bernardi monachi,[3] quod abhinc annis ducentis quinquaginta, id est, anno incarnationis octingentesimo septuagesimo, idem, Jerosolimam profectus, ignem illum viderit; hospitatusque fuerit in xenodochio quod ibidem[4] gloriosissimus Carolus magnus construi jusserat, ubi et bibliotecam ingentis expensæ compegerat. Tantamque et Ægypti, et per id locorum, commemorat pacem Christianos sub Turchorum dominio habuisse, ut si alicui vianti in mediis forte triviis jumentum quo necessaria veheret defungeretur, ille, relictis sarcinis,[5] ad proximam urbem expeditus pro auxilio pergeret, omnia quæ dimiserat illibata proculdubio reperturus. Nullus tamen ibi Christianus alienigena secure vivere, pro exploratorum suspicione, poterat, nisi sigillo imperatoris Babilonii fretus: indigenæ pacem Turchorum tribus annuis talentis vel bizantinis redimebant. Veruntamen quia Bernardus Theodosii tunc patriarchæ nomen non tacet, ipsa me monet occasio ut omnium patriarcharum nomina proponam.

---

[1] *decenti*] tereti, An. Ag. Al. Cd.
[2] *Saracenorum*] paganorum, Al.
[3] The Itinerary of Bernard is printed by Mabillon, AA. SS. O. S. B. sæc. iii. pt. 2, pp. 472-475, but it does not contain all the matter here cited from it by our author.
[4] *ibidem*] idem, Bc. Bk.
[5] *sarcinis*] sarculis, Cc.

Nomina Patriarcharum Jerusalem.

List of the patriarchs of Jerusalem.

§ 368. Jacobus frater Domini, filius Alphei;[1] Simeon filius Cleophæ, consobrinus Christi; Cleophas autem fuit frater Joseph; Justus, Zacheus, Tobias, Benjamin, Johannes, Machabeus, Philippus, Seneca, Justus, Levi, Effrem, Justus,[2] Judas; hi quindecim circumcisi fuerunt; Marcus, Cassianus, Publius,[3] Maximus, Julianus,[4] Gaius; iste primus celebravit Pascha et Quadragesimam more Romanorum; Simacus, Gaius, Julianus, Capito, Maximus, Antonius, Valens, Docilianus, Narcissus, Dius, Germanio, Gordius, Alexander, Mazabanus, Irmeneus, Zabdas, Ermon, Macharius; hujus temporibus inventa est sancta crux ab[5] Elena; Ciriacus, Maximus, Cirillus; iste construxit ecclesiam sancti Sepulcri et montis Calvariæ, et Bethleem et vallis Josaphat. Hi omnes vocati sunt episcopi. Post hos surrexere patriarchæ: Cirillus, protus patriarcha; Johannes, Prailius,[6] Juvenalis, Johannes,[7] Zacharias, in cujus tempore venit Chosdroe[8] rex Persarum Jerusalem, et destruxit ecclesias Judeæ et Jerusalem, et occisa sunt ab exercitu suo triginta sex milia Christianorum; Modestus; iste constitutus est patriarcha ab Heraclio imperatore postquam reversus est victor de Perside; Sofronius, cujus temporibus venere Saraceni, et ejecerunt Christianos omnes de Jerusalem, excepto patriarcha, quem ob reverentiam sanctitatis ibi dimiserunt. Illud fuit tempus quo Saraceni totam Ægyptum, et Affricam, et Judæam, et Hispaniam, et Baleares insulas pervaserunt. Partem Hispaniæ abstulit eis Carolus magnus; reliquas[9] et

Discovery of the Cross.

Jerusalem taken by Chosroes.

Capture by the Saracens.

---

[1] *Alphei*] Joseph, Aa. Al.
[2] *Justus*] Jesse, Aa. Al.
[3] *Publius*] Publicus, Cd.
[4] *Julianus*] om. Bc.
[5] *ab*] a beata, Aa. Al.
[6] *Prailius*] Julius, Cd.
[7] *Johannes*] om. At. There were eleven patriarchs between Juvenal and Zacharias, of whom two bore the name of John. There are other omissions in the list.
[8] *Chosdroe*] Cosdroe, Aa. Al. Bc.
[9] *reliquas*] reliquam, Aa. Al. Bc.

omnes quas nominavi terras possident usque hodie, annis abhinc circiter quingentis; Theodorus, Ilia, Georgius, Thomas, Basilidis, Sergius, Salomontos, Theodosius: hunc Theodosium fuisse abbatem Bernardus memorat, et raptum de monasterio suo, quod distabat ab Jerusalem quindecim milibus; et factum fuisse patriarcham Jerosolimæ; tunc[1] Michaelem dicit[2] fuisse patriarcham Babilonis super Ægyptum, translato patriarchatu Alexandriæ in Babilonem: Ilia, Sergius, Leonthos, Athanasius, Christodolus, Thomas, Joseph, Orestes, in cujus tempore venit Achim Soldanus de Babilonia, nepos Orestis patriarchæ; misit exercitum suum Jerusalem, et destruxit omnes ecclesias, scilicet quatuor milia; et avunculum suum patriarcham adduci fecit Babiloniam et ibidem occidi; Theofilus, Nicefous; hic ædificavit ecclesiam[3] sancti Sepulcri quæ nunc est, favente Achim Soldano; Sofronius, in cujus tempore Turchi, Jerosolimam venientes, pugnaverunt cum Saracenis et omnes interfecerunt, et obtinuerunt civitatem; Christiani autem remanserunt ibi sub dominio Turchorum; Euthimius,[4] Simeon: hujus tempore venerunt Franci et expugnaverunt Jerosolimam, et liberaverunt eam de manibus Turcorum et regis Babiloniæ.

Visit of Bernard.

Jerusalem seized by Hakem.

Conquered by the Turks.

§ 369. Anno igitur Jerosolimitanæ peregrinationis quarto, post captam Niceam tertio, post Antiochiam secundo, obsessa est a Francis Jerusalem; urbs bellorum maxima merces, blandimentum laborum, supremæ spei viaticum. Erat tunc Junii mensis dies septimus; nec quicquam sibi obsessor verebatur in cibatu vel in potu, quod messis in agris, uvæ in vineis, maturaverant: sola jumentorum cura erat miserabilis, quæ pro qualitate loci et temporis nullo sustentabantur irriguo; nam et fontis Siloe recessus, qui horis incertis dulcibus scatet aquis, tunc calor solis ebiberat.

Fulcher, Gesta Per.' c. 18.

Jerusalem besieged by the Crusaders June 7, 1099.

---

[1] *tunc*] etiam, ins. Aa. Al. Bc.
[2] *dicit*] dicunt, Bc.
[3] *ecclesiam*] casam, Aa. Ap.Al. Bc.
[4] *Euthimius*] Eubinnus, Cd.

The water supply.

The attack on the Tower of David.

The escalade and engines.

Assault on July 14.

Fons ille, si quando pluvialibus pascitur aquis, torrentem Cedron auget, indeque undivomo impetu in vallem Josaphat decurrit; sed hoc admodum raro, quia nullus ejus augmenti vel decrementi serius[1] est terminus: quocirca nostros, ad aquationem jumentorum crebro dispersos hostes e cavernis egredientes inopine credebant. Interea duces suo quisque muneri, Raimundus vero turri Daviticæ impiger assidebat. Hæc, ab occasu solis urbem muniens, ad medium fere tabulatum quadratorum lapidum plumbo infuso compaginata, omnem metum obsidentium paucis intus defendentibus repellit. Itaque videntes urbem ad capiendum, propter præruptra montium et firmitatem mœnium et ferocitatem hostium, difficilem, machinas fieri præcepere: et prius quidem, obsessionis[2] die septimo, fortunam scalis erectis temptarunt, in resistentes volaticas moliti sagittas; sed quia erant scalæ paucæ, ascendentibus dampnosæ, quod vulneribus expositi undique nulla parte protegerentur, consilium mutarunt. Unum fuit machinamentum quod nostri suem, veteres vineam vocant; quod machina levibus lignis colligata, tecto tabulis cratibusque contexto, lateribus crudis coriis munitis,[3] protegit in se subsidentes,[4] qui, quasi more suis, ad murorum suffodienda penetrant fundamenta. Alterum fuit, pro lignorum penuria, turris non magna, in modum ædificiorum facta; Berfreid appellant, quod fastigium murorum æquaret. Hoc machinamentum, dum fieret, moram obsidioni dedit pro fabrorum inscitia et lignorum inopia.[5] Et jam quartusdecimus dies Julii volvebatur, cum hi admotis vineis murum suffodere, hi turrem promovere cœpere: quod ut opportunius fieret, membratim disjunctam ad muros tulere; ibique, prope quantum a jactu sagittæ cavere poterant, compaginatam, rotarum vo-

Fulcher. Gesta Per. c. 18.

---

[1] *serius*] certus, Cd.
[2] *obsessionis*] obsidionis, Al.
[3] *munitis*] communitis, Bc.
[4] *subsidentes*] subsistentes, Aa. Al.
[5] *inopia*] penuria, Aa. Al. At.

lubilitate muro pene conjunxere. Interea funditores lapidibus, sagittarii jaculis, arcubalistæ telis, quisque suum exercentes officium, instare, et propugnantes de muro submovere; milites quoque virtute incomparabiles turrim ascendere, æquo jam pene marte telis et lapidibus in hostes agentes. Nec illi feriis vacabant, sed, omnem virtuti salutem committentes, adipem et oleum ignitum in turrim et in milites fundibalis jaculabantur, multorum mortibus voti sui se compotes gloriantes. Ita toto illo die certatum, ut neutra pars se victam putaret. Sequenti die, qui erat quintusdecimus Julii, ad suprema ventum: namque Franci, pridiani certaminis eventu eruditiores, faces oleagino succo vividas in turrim muro proximam et ejus custodes jecerunt. At flamma, vento agente in comas erecta, primo ligna, mox[1] lapides corripiens, custodes effugavit. Quin et tigna quæ Turchi e muro pendula demiserant, ut turrim, si propius admoveretur, reducto nisu brachiorum arietando effringerent, Franci funibus desectis ad se traxere; et de machina in murum jactis, cratibusque constratis, pontem, qui turrim et mœnia continuaret, fecere. Ita perfidis versum in exitium quod paraverant ad remedium. Tum vero, et fumeis flammarum globis, et nostrorum audacia, hostes infracti fugam ineunt. Alteri[2] in murum, et inde in urbem progredientes, quantum illa exigebat animorum lætitia, manibus egere. Et hæc quidem victoria in parte Godefridi et duorum Robertorum evenit. Ignorabat hoc Raimundus donec fugitivorum clamor, et se de muro ultro præcipitantium timor, qui, dum mortem fugiunt, mortem invadunt, urbem captam prodidit. Quod intuitus, strictisque gladiis in fugitivos[3] irruens, quantum animositati suæ sufficere judicavit injurias Dei ultum ire festinabat. Quingentos quoque Æthiopas, qui, in arcem David refugi, claves portarum, pollicita membrorum impunitate,

---

[1] *mox*] postea, Bc.
[2] *Alteri*] Alii, Bc.
[3] *fugitivos*] fugientes, Aa. Al.

tradiderant, spectato pacis commodo praesentis, incolumes Ascalonem dimisit. Nec ullum erat Turchis refugium, ita et supplices et rebelles insatiabilis ira victorum consumebat. Decem milia in templo Salomonis interfecta; plura ex fastigiis templorum et arcis praecipitata. Post haec cadavera cumulata, igne immisso, in aerium resoluta sunt elementum, ne, sub divo in tabem fluentia, inerti attraherent contagia mundo. Ita caede infidelium expiata urbe, sepulcrum Domini, quod tamdiu desideraverant, pro quo tot labores tulerant, supplicibus cordibus et corporibus expetierunt. Quot ibi precum thurificatione caelum incenderint, quot lacrymis Deum in gratiam revocaverint, nullus unquam profiteor evolveret: nec si veterum pompatica eloquentia procederet; non si Orpheus, qui vocalibus fidibus auritos, ut dicitur, scopulos flexit, resurgeret. Cogitetur igitur potius quam dicatur.

§ 370. Illud insigne continentiae in omnibus optimatibus exemplum fuit, quod nec eo die, nec consequentibus, quisquam respectu praedae avocavit animum quin coeptum persequerentur triumphum. Solus Tancredus, intempestiva cupidine occupatus, quaedam pretiosissima de templo Salomonis extulit: sed postmodum, sua conscientia et aliorum conventus colloquio, vel eadem vel appretiata loco restituit. Tum quicunque egenus vel domum vel aliquas divitias invasit; nunquam ulterius ullius locupletis tulit convitium, sed semel possessa in jus adoptavit hereditarium. Nec mora, praelucidum illud Christianae nobilitatis specular, in quo velut in splendido lacunari omnium virtutum repercutiebatur jubar, Godefridus, in regem eligitur, omnibus non ignava spe conferentibus, nullo modo posse decentius prospici ecclesiae utilitatibus; dilato interim de patriarcha consilio, qui Romani papae deberet substitui judicio.

§ 371. At vero Babilonis imperator, non illius quae, a Nembroth facta, a Semiramide aucta esse asseritur;[1]

---

[1] *esse asseritur*] nunc asseritur deserta, Aa. Ág. Al. Ap. Bc. Bk. By.

sed illius quam Cambyses Cyri filius aedificavit in Ægypto, in loco ubi quondam fuerat Thaphnis,—imperator ergo Babilonis, diu conceptas in Francos iras parturiens, misit ducem militiae qui eos de regno, ut dictitabat, suo propelleret.[1] Ille, praecepta maturans munia, cum audisset captam Jerusalem, majori cura stimulavit negotium, quanquam ante nihil segnitiei admisisset. Eratque barbaro animus ut Christianos in Jerusalem obsideret; et, post victoriam quam jam mente sompniabat falso praesagus, sepulcrum Domini a fundo erutum dilapidaret. Nostri, qui nihil minus diligerent quam obsidionales aerumpnas denuo perpeti,[2] sumpta ex Dei parte audacia, ex urbe versus Ascalonem prodeunt, obvia hostibus inferentes pectora; portabantque secum partem Dominici ligni, quam quidam Syrus civis Jerosolimitanus avita successione domi custoditam propalaverat. Felix plane et fidele furtum, ut toto tempore Turchis celaretur mysterium! Ingentem ergo praedam pecorum et pecudum secus[3] Ascalonem nacti, generale proposuerunt edictum ut omnia in patulis campis relinquerent, ne postero mane pugnaturis impedimento forent: satis superque se praedam habituros si vincerent, dummodo expediti divinas ulciscerentur injurias. Itaque mane jam exercitu prodeunte,[4] videres, supero credo instinctu, cornibus erectis pecora lateribus militum obambulantia, nec ulla posse abigi violentia: quod eminus hostes intuiti, et solaribus radiis visus hebetati, animis ante praelium conciderunt, quod crederent innumeram esse adversariorum manum; quamvis ipsis non deesset militaris copia multo exercitio ad praelium praeparata. Lentius itaque procedentes, Francos, bipartito agmine et sinuatis alis, includere conati sunt; sed duces, et maxime Robertus Normannus, qui antesignanus erat, arte artem, vel potius vir-

---

[1] *propelleret*] perturbaret, Aa. Al.
[2] *perpeti*] experiri, Aa. Al.
[3] *secus*] juxta, Aa. Al.
[4] *prodeunte*] procedente, Aa. Al.

tute calliditatem eludentes, sagittariis et peditibus Fulcher, Gesta Per. deductis, medias gentilium perruperunt acies. Eques c. 19. quoque Lotharingus, qui in extremo agmine cum domino suo erat, a lateribus involitans, libertatem fugæ et campos abstulit omnes. Ita Turchi, ab anterioribus penetrati et ab exterioribus inclusi, ad voluntatem [1] victorum cæsi sunt;[2] reliqui, noctis quæ imminebat beneficio, liberati. Multum aureæ supellectilis in eorum castris inventum; multum gemmarum, quarum raritas in nostris regionibus incognita, ibi nativo decore refulgurat: nec ulla victoria lætior fuit Christianis, quod incruenti opima retulere spolia.

Slaughter and spoil.

§ 372. Jerusalem itaque reversi, cum stativa multorum dierum requie vires reformassent, quidam, suspirantes in natalis soli desiderium, marinum adornarunt reditum. Soli Godefridus et Tancredus remanserunt; prædicabiles profecto principes, et quorum titulis nullas unquam affiget metas postera, si rectum judicet, ætas: viri, qui ab extremo Europæ frigore in importabiles se Orientis calores immerserunt, vitæ suæ prodigi dummodo Christianitati laboranti concurrerent; qui, præter metum barbaricorum incursuum, semper pro incommoditate ignoti[3] poli suspecti, securitatem quietis et sanitatis in patria contempserint, et, pauculi numero, tot inimicorum urbes fama et effectu virtutum presserint; memorabili fiduciæ Dei exemplo, ut illic non dubitarent subsistere, ubi vel pestifero afflarentur aere vel Saracenica occiderentur rabie. Cedant ergo poetarum præconia; nec priscos heroas vetus attollat fabula. Nihil unquam horum laudi comparabile ulla genuere secula: nam, et si qua illorum fuit virtus, in sepulcrales favillas post mortem evanuit; quod potius in mundialis pompæ fumum quam in ullius boni solidum, effusa fuerit. Istorum

The return of the Crusaders.

Godfrey and Tancred remain in Palestine.

Praises of Godfrey and Tancred.

---

[1] *voluntatem*] satietatem, Al. Ag. Ap.
[2] *Ita—cæsi sunt*] om. Aa. Aah.; written over an erasure in Ap.
[3] *ignoti*] igniti, Aa. Al. Ap.

autem fortitudinis sentietur utilitas, et ostendetur dignitas, quamdiu orbis volubilitas et sancta vigebit Christianitas. Quid vero de disciplina et abstinentia totius exercitus dicam? Nulla ibi ventris ingluvies, nulla fuit penis illuvies, quæ non continuo vel ducum auctoritate[1] vel episcoporum sermone corrigeretur. Nulli prædandi per terras Christianorum cupido; nulla inter se controversia quæ non facile, mediatorum judicum cognitione, recideretur. Quapropter, quia tam ordinati exercitus laus ad prælatorum redundat gloriam, singulorum procerum facta et exitus scripto insigniam; nec quicquam veritati secundum relatorum meorum credulitatem subtraham. Nullus vero, cui amplior provenit gestorum notitia, me pro incurioso arguat; quia trans oceanum Britannicum abditos vix tenui murmure rerum Asianarum fama illustrat.

Discipline of the army.

De Godefrido.

§ 373. Initium laudum rex Godefridus occupat, qui Eustachii comitis Bononiensis, de quo tempore regis Edwardi dixi, filius, materno excellentior genere, ad Caroli magni spectabat lineam. Siquidem mater, Ida nomine, Godefridi antiqui Lotharingorum ducis filia, habuit fratrem, a genitoris nomine Godefridum dictum, cognomento Bocardum. Illud fuit tempus quando Robertus Friso, de quo superius locutus sum, mortuo Florentio Frisiæ duce, uxorem ejus Gertrudem duxit; privignum Theodericum in successionem ducatus provehens. Non tulit hoc Bocardus, sed, Frisonem expellens, regionem suis voluntatibus addixit: ultus se ille insidiis, qui non posset præliis, per Flandritas suos sedentem ad requisita[2] naturæ extinxit, ferro per verenda immisso. Ita privignus beneficio vitrici

History of Godfrey.
Above, §199.
§ 257.
His descent from the dukes of Lorraine.
His uncle Godfrey.

---

[1] *auctoritate*] austeritate, Ag. Al.
[2] *requisita*] secreta, Bc. By.; necessaria, Aa. Al.

successit ducatui. Uxor hujus Godefridi fuit Matildis Marcisa, quam superior liber prædicat: quæ, mortuo marito, ducatum impigre contra imperatorem retentavit, maxime intra Italiam; nam Lotharingiam et inferiores terras imperator obtinuit. Ida vero,[1] ut dicere cœperam, magnis spebus ad comitatum Lotharingorum[2] petendum filium Godefridum erexit: namque seniori filio Eustachio hereditas paterna obtigerat; minor, Baldewinus, pueriles adhuc annos terebat. Godefridus, habilem ad arma ætatem nactus, imperatori Henrico, de quo proximus liber loquitur, militiam suam consecravit. Ingentibus ergo sudoribus ejus in se transferens amicitiam, egregia liberalitate Cæsaris totam pro stipendio accepit Lotharingiam. Unde factum est, ut, orta inter papam et Henricum simultate, cum eo ad oppugnandam Romam profectus, eam partem muri[3] quæ vigiliis suis observabatur primus perrumperet, magnam fenestram irrupturis aperiens. Ita potissimum sudans, et præfervidis venis suspiriosus, cellarium subterraneum, quod forte se discursanti[4] obtulerat, ingressus est: ibi, cum nimio vini haustu intemperantiam sitis placasset, febrim quartanam iniit. Dicunt alii venenato Falerno infectum; quod soleant Romani, et illius terræ homines, totis infundere toxica tonnis. Alii, ei partem illam mœnium sorte obtigisse ubi Tiberis influens mane sævas exhalat nebulas, quarum pernicie omnes milites ejus præter decem interiisse; ipsum, amissis crinibus et unguibus, dubie convaluisse. Verumtamen, quodlibet horum fuerit, constat eum nunquam continuæ sed lentæ febris incommodo vacasse; donec, audita fama viæ Jerosolimitanæ, illuc se iturum vovit si Deus propitius ei salutem[5] largiretur: quo voto emisso, ita ducis vires refloruisse, ut nodosos integer artus, et

---

[1] *vero*] ergo, An. Al. Bc. Ce.²
[2] *Lotharingorum*] om. Ce.¹
[3] *muri*] om. Bc. By.
[4] *discursanti*] discurrenti, Al.
[5] *salutem*] sanitatem, Al.

spatioso erectus pectore, quasi squalentibus annis exutus, recenti emicaret juventa. Quare, divinis bene- ficiis in se confluentibus responsurus, Jerosolimam ivit vel primus vel cum primis, magnas in bellum trahens catervas; et quamvis durum et exercitatum militem haberet, nullus tamen eo vel prior in congressu, vel promptior in effectu, habebatur. Denique notum est, quod Turchum, in Antiochena obsidione pugnam singularem poscentem, medium a lateribus gladio Lotharingo dissecuerit; et jam palpitabat arvis medietas hominis, cum alteram cornipes volucri cursu asportavit, adeo firme nebulo insederat; alterum, æque congressum, librata in caput spatha a vertice ad inguina diffiderit; nec adhuc ictus horrendus steterit, sed sellam et spinam equi penitus disciderit.[1] Audivi veracem hominem referentem vidisse se quod subjiciam: in ipsa obsidione militem ducis pabulari progressum, et a leone invasum, objectu clypei mortem aliquamdiu distulisse;[2] indoluisse Godefridum viso, et venabulo feram transfodisse; illam sauciam, et dolore acrius sævientem, in principem irruisse, adeo ut ferro quod extabat e vulnere tibiam ejus læderet;[3] et, nisi properasset gladio beluam eviscerare, illud virtutis specimen potuisset dente ferino interire. His successibus clarus, in regem Jerosolimæ levatur; propterea quod esset genere et virtute conspicuus, nec tamen superbus. Parvum admodum et finibus angustum fuit regnum, quod, præter paucas in circuitu villas, nullas pene[4] urbes haberet: nam et infesta regis valitudo, quam statim post bellum Babilonicum incurrerat, ferias bellis dedit, ut nihil acquireretur; et divina sollertia barbaricas aviditates toto illo anno probe compescuit, ut nihil amitteretur. Fama est regem otii desuetudine febrim antiquam nactum fuisse;

---

[1] *nec adhuc—disciderit*] om. Ce[1].
[2] *distulisse*] propulsasse, Al. Ad. Aah.
[3] *læderet*] sauciaret, Al.
[4] *pene*] om. Bc.

sed ego conjicio Deum placitam sibi animam, et tot laboribus emeritam, in melius regnum transferre voluisse mature, ne malitia mutaret animam ejus,[1] aut fictio deciperet intellectum illius. Igitur, rota temporis referente annuum regni spatium, placida morte resolutus, et sub Golgothana rupe tumulatus est. Rex invicti sicut in ferrum sic in mortem animi, qui lacrymas astantium sæpe benignus coercuerit; interrogatusque de successore, neminem nominatim, sed [2] eum qui dignus foret, pronuntiaverit: nec unquam regium insigne ferre sustinuerit, professus unicam esse arrogantiam si coronaretur ipse ad gloriam in ea urbe qua Deus coronatus fuerat ad contumeliam. Obiit quintodecimo kalendas Augusti.[3]

Wisdom, iv. 11.

His burial on Golgotha.

His modesty.

De Baldewino.

Baldwin, his brother, chosen to succeed him.

§ 374. Eo defuncto Tancredus et alii proceres Baldewinum, fratrem ejus, futurum regem pronuntiant, qui tum in Mesopotamia morabatur; nam Eustachius senior, qui cum Godefrido Jerosolimam venerat, jamdudum hereditarium solum repetierat. Baldewini actus integra et brevi veritate apponentur, fidei soliditate accommodata dictis Fulkerii Carnotensis; qui, capellanus ipsius, aliquanta de ipso scripsit, stilo non quidem agresti, sed, ut dici solet, sine nitore ac palæstra, et qui alios admonere potuit ut accuratius scriberent. Baldewinus igitur, iter sanctum cum ceteris adorsus, multos milites habuit indolis suæ complices; quibus fretus, novos sibi exercitus ipse moliri, splendidas occasiones aucupari, quibus virtus enitescere posset. Denique, non contentus communi omnium laude, trium dierum ab Antiochia spatio a reliquis discedens, Tarsum, Ciliciæ urbem mobilem,

Fulcher of Chartres the authority for this history.

Fulcher, Gesta Per. c. 6.

---

[1] *ejus*] ipsius, Aa. Al.
[2] *sed*] tantummodo, ins. Aa. Al.
[3] *Obiit—Augusti*] om. Bc. Cd.

voluntate civium suscepit;[1] Tarsum, Pauli quondam apostoli alumpnam, in cujus honore ibi ecclesia episcopatus cernitur. Voluntarie Tarsenses se ejus clientelæ subdidere, quod essent Christiani, et ipsius patrocinio se sperarent a Turchis protegi. Certatim itaque Cilices in ejus jus transiere; maxime post Turbexel deditum;[2] quod est oppidum natura munitum,[3] cujus nutum inferiora spectarent castella: quo, ut dixi, dedito cetera ejus judicium secuta. Nec solum Cilicia, sed et Armenia et Mesopotamia familiaritatem ejus[4] appetivere: erant enim hæ terræ pene Turchorum dominio liberæ, sed inequitationibus infestatæ. Quare dux Edessæ urbis, qui et civium odio et hostium gladio premeretur, litteras necessitatis suæ interpretes Baldewino misit: veniret ergo quantocius, adoptionis præmio laborem veniendi consolaturus, namque ipse sexus utriusque prole carebat. Ea est urbs in Mesopotamia Syriæ ubere glebæ redditu et negotiatorum mercimoniis nominatissima, distans ab Euphrate viginti miliariis, ab Antiochia centum: Edessam Græci, Syri Rotasiam dicunt. Ita Baldewinus, exacto a legatis fidelitatis sacramento, cum octoginta solum militibus Euphratem transmeavit;[5] spectaculo mirando, seu dicere velis fortitudinis, seu temeritatis, ut inter circumfusas barbarorum nationes, quas alter haberet vel pro gente vel pro incredulitate suspectas, cum tantillo exercitu non hæsitaret procedere. Et ab Armeniis quidem et Syris grato[6] excipiebatur gaudio, et indulgenti fovebatur hospitio, cum crucibus et candelabris per tramites occurrentibus. Turchi autem, posterius agmen temptare aggressi, sollertia Baldewini omnibus frustrati sunt insidiis; Samosathenis exemplum fugæ facientibus. Samosatha est civitas ultra Euphraten, de qua fuit[7] Paulus Samosathenus, cujus hæresim confutatam in

---

[1] *suscepit*] recepit, Aa. Al.
[2] *deditum*] flexum, Aa. Al. Bc.
[3] *munitum*] invictum, Bc.
[4] *ejus*] viri, Al.
[5] *transmeavit*] transfretavit, Bc.
[6] *grato*] gratato, Ce.¹
[7] *fuit*] om. Ce.¹

historia Eusebii leget qui volet: hanc etiam, si bene occurrit memoriæ, dicit Josephus obsedisse Antonium quando ad eum Herodes venit. Hujus igitur urbis incolæ Turchi, qui primi fuissent in Francos audaciæ incentivum primi defectionis dedere auspicium. Itaque Baldewinus, tuto Edessam perveniens, nihil inferius quam sperabat invenit;[1] nam et invitatoris profuso favore susceptus, et non post multum tempus, illo a perfidis civibus dilaniato, legitimum urbis ducatum adeptus, toto tempore quo Franci apud Antiochiam et Jerosolimam laboraverunt non immunis bellorum fuit, frequentibus assultibus hostes contristans suos.

Fulcher, Gesta Per. c. 6. Eusebius, H. E. vii. 30. Josephus, xiv. 30, 16 §8.

At vero Novembri mense admonitus a Boamundo principe Antiochiæ ut iter Jerosolimæ jam tandem experirentur, profectionem composuit; propulsatisque solo candidi vexilli visu, quod insigne in prælio habebat, Turchis, qui sperato ejus discessu pacem læserant, a dextra relinquens Antiochiam, venit Laodiciam. Ibi liberalitate Raimundi comitis, qui ei civitati principabatur, tenui pretio sufficientiam stipis mercatus, Gibello transito recentibus vestigiis Boamundum insecutus est, qui eum fixis tentoriis operiebatur. Junxit se cum eis communione viæ Daibertus Pisanus archiepiscopus, qui navigio multis sibi sociatis civibus Laodiciam applicuerat; et præterea duo alii episcopi. Ita junctis agminibus computabantur, æstimatione librata, esse viginti quinque milia: quorum multi, terras Saracenorum ingressi, pro caritate mercimonii fame conclusi; multi ex equitibus in pedites mutati, equis inedia interceptis. Accedebat miseriis imbrium affluentia, quod in illis terris quasi præcipiti torrente pluvia hybernis duntaxat mensibus inundet; itaque pauperes,[2] carentes mutatoriis, algido rigore moriebantur, quampluribus diebus nulli tecto succedentes. Et hujus quidem calamitatis nullum erat remedium, quod

Fulcher, Gesta Per. c. 20.

---

[1] *nihil—invenit*] nihil minus promissis desideravit, Al.

[2] *pauperes*] pauperiores, Al.

et tentoria et ligna deficerent. At vero famem nonnihil levabant, arundines mellitas continue dentibus terentes, quas canamellas, nomine composito ex canna et melle, vocant. Sic bis[1] omnino a Tripolitanis et Cæsariensibus immenso[2] ære necessaria nacti, Jerosolimam venere solstitii brumalis die. Occurrit illis ad portas rex Godefridus cum fratre Eustachio, quem ad hoc tempus detinuerat, nihil liberalitatis et gratiæ[3] in eorum omittens obsequio. Illi, peractis in Bethleem ex more Dominicæ Nativitatis sollempnibus, Daibertum patriarcham constituere. In quo facto Urbani papæ consensum obligatum non ambigo; quod esset is et reverendus senio, et potens eloquio, et pollens marsupio. Igitur post Circumcisionem Domini sumptis[4] in Jerico palmis, quod insigne peregrinantium antiquitas instituit, sedes quisque suas raptim repetere properarunt. Causa festinationis erat putor inconditorum cadaverum, quorum ita exhalabat cænum ut ipsum violaret cælum. Quocirca tabida pestis, in auras effluens, multos ex his qui noviter venerant letho dedit; ceteri per urbes maritimas, Tiberiadem dico et Cæsaream Philippi, maturaverunt iter, quod eos tenuitas victus et hostilis metus urgebant. Sed fami, ut dixi, consuluere pedum celeritate: et trecentorum militum, qui eos de Baldac castello infestabant, furori prospexerunt militaris artis calliditate; namque simulata paulisper fuga, ut ipsi de angustiis locorum evadentes Turchos inducerent, consulto cessere, sed mox retroversi dispersos hostes pro libito fudere.[5] Putaverant illi nostros inhabiles pugnæ, quod essent clypei eorum et arcus pluviali abundantia lentati; nesciebantque quod non in armorum vel in tegminum fiducia, sed in excellenti vi animorum et crudo robore brachiorum victoria virorum consistat.

---

[1] *bis*] his, Bc. Cd.; hi., Aa. Bc.[2]
[2] *immenso*] infinito, Al.
[3] *gratiæ*] gratiarum, Aa. Al.
[4] *sumptis*] cæsis, Al.; after Fulcher.
[5] *fudere*] cecidere, Al. Ag. Ap.

§ 375. Et tum quidem Baldewinus Edessam, Boamundus vero Antiochiam, incolumes remearunt. Initio autem Julii mensis licentia famæ Baldewini auribus detulit splendidum ducum nostrorum margaritum obfuscatum, Boamundum scilicet captum, et in catenas conjectum, a quodam Danisman gentili, et in illis terris potenti. Quapropter, Edessenorum et Antiochenorum manu coacta, insignem Christianorum contumeliam ulcisci sperabat. Porro Turcus, qui magis fraude et eventu quam virtute et bellica[1] militia[2] ducem cepisset, quod cum paucis ad Mellentiniam urbem recipiendam venerat, sciens Francos pro rei pudore viribus extremis in se usuros, in sua se recepit, compositis sane ordinibus, non quasi fugam intenderet, sed quasi triumphum duceret. Tunc Baldewinus, ultra Mellentiniam duorum dierum viam progressus, cum videret hostem belli necessitatem declinare, redeundum putavit; et ante tamen urbem in suos usus, non invito præfecto Gabriele, transduxit.

§ 376. Interea perlato ad se nuntio de fratris obitu, provincialium ac ducum in ejus electionem consensu, commendata Edessa Baldewino cognato, arctissimæ necessitudinis propinquitate conjuncto, et præter hæc neque imprudenti neque ignavo, ad Jerosolimitanum regnum mentem impulit. Congregatis ergo equitibus ducentis, et peditibus septingentis, iter plenum mortis et periculorum ingressus est; unde audaciæ tantæ contuitu multi, quos falso fideles arbitrabatur, fuga clandestina dilapsi. Ipse cum reliquis Antiochiam petiit, ingens momentum desolatis futurus, consilio sagacis mentis informans ut Tancredum peterent in ducatum. Inde per Gibellum et Laodiciam venit Tripolim : cujus urbis admiratus, natione quidem Turcus, sed genio naturali clementiæ visceribus profusus, extra muros illi victui necessaria destinavit; adjecto quinetiam be-

---

[1] *bellica*] om. Bc. | [2] *militia*] justitia, Aa. Al.

<small>Fulcher, Gesta Per. c. 22.</small>

nignitatis mandato ut prudenter se ageret, quia Ducah rex Damascenorum tramitem angustum occupaverat per quem illum audierat venturum. Ille, quem puderet minis Saracenicis moveri, constanti animo, quó proposuerat, contendit; sed, ad locum veniens, fidem admirati probavit. Est enim citra civitatem Beritum, miliariis circiter quinque, locus omnino angustus juxta mare, quem et præerupta rupium et arcta callium¹ adeo coercent, ut centum viri faucibus illis potiti, quantumvis numerum itinerantium aditu prohibere queant. Locus est inevitabilis de Tripoli Jerosolimam euntibus. Huc ergo Baldewinus perveniens, speculatores misit qui situm loci et vires hostium renuntiarent. Regressi legati difficultatem faucium et adversariorum qui insederant fiduciam, vix pro timore intellecti anhelarunt: at Baldewinus, qui parum ab optimo qui unquam fuerit milite distaret, nihil perterritus, aciem dispositam in eos constanter instituit. Tunc Ducah mittit aliquos qui prælia prima lacessant, eliciantque incautos; retentans ampliores vires in locis opportunis. Itaque illi primo magno impetu venire, mox subinde subterfugere, ut nostros in angustias deducerent. Non latuit Baldewinum hujuscemodi calliditas; sed, antiquæ militiæ usu instructus, suis ut fugam simularent innuit; simul et, ut suspicionem metus urgeret, sarcinas et impedimenta quæ posuerant resumit,² et jumenta stimulis agitari, quin et ordines laxari, ut hostes incurrerent, edixit. Tum vero hoc viso Turchi exultare, et dirum frendentes, ut Eumenides exululare crederes, nostros insequi. Quidam ascensis navibus littora præoccupare; quidam equis præcurrere, et peregrinos incaute juxta mare ambulantes interimere. Nec Franci simulatam fugam omisere donec ad planitiem quam oculis destinaverant pervenirent: nullique tumultus excussere viris mentes, quinimmo necessitas qua intercepti erant aluit, et ministravit au-

<small>Description of the pass between Tripoli and Berytus, where Dokak's forces were posted.</small>

<small>Baldwin's feigned flight.</small>

---

¹ *callium*] collium, Bc.   ² *posuerant resumit*] jam deposuerant resumit, Aa. Al. Bc.

daciam; et pauci terraque marique innumeras sustinuere manus. Namque, ut visum est satis metum finxisse, confertis ordinibus et conversis signis inimicos jam jamque incursantes inclusere;[1] ita versa rerum facie, qui vicerant victi, et victi fuere victores. Turchi perniciosa clade prostrati; reliqui ad naves præcipiti studio fugientes, cum in altum plus jactu sagittæ processissent, ita navigium remis et totis pectoribus innixi propellebant, quasi manibus adversariorum ad terram retrahi possent. Et ut miraculum non sicut opinabile dubites, sed sicut visibile quodammodo palpes, solummodo quatuor Christiani milites fusi victoriam ceteris sanguine peperere suo. Quapropter confirmo quod nunquam Christicolæ a paganis vincerentur si ante bellum fortitudinem suam cælestibus fulcirent præsidiis, et in bello armis suis amicas superorum applicarent virtutes; sed quia in pace omnibus se ingurgitant flagitiis, et in pugna sola nituntur audacia, ideo, nec immerito, multotiens fortitudo eorum deviat a bona fortuna. Comes ergo pulchro triumpho exultans, cum reversus esset ad spolia cæsorum detrahenda, non paucos Turchos offendit vivos; quos dampni corporum immunes, sed pecuniis inanes, dimisit. Ipse cum suis, ne aliqua fraus lateret, retro secedens, nocte illa sub olivarum virgultis requievit: sed mox diluculo cum expeditis ad angustias accessit, fide oculata visurus loci naturam; intuitusque omnia tuta esse, nam Turchi qui pridie circa montem discursibus lascivierant, nocte intempesta, cæde suorum visa, omnes diffugerant, significatione fumi facta, sicut convenerat, sociis discessum hostium intimavit. Illi, morarum vinculis absolutis, ducem continuo secuti. Tunc Beriti admiratus victum prætereuntibus[2] misit, pro virtute tam pauci[3] exercitus stupefactus. Idem et Tyrii, et Sidonii, et Acharonitæ qui et Ptholomaitæ, fecere, tacito metu Fran-

---

[1] *inclusere*] includere, Ce.
[2] *prætereuntibus*] præcuntibus, Bc. Bk.
[3] *tam pauci*] tanti, Bc.; tam parvi, Aa.

corum fortitudinem suspicientes. Nec minus homines Tancredi, qui in Chaipha erant, liberales fuere, quamvis ipse absens esset. Castri illius nomen antiquum reperire nequeo, quia omnes mediterraneæ civitates, quæ in Josepho leguntur quondam fuisse, modo vel non sunt, vel, in viculos mutatæ, nomina perdiderunt: maritimæ integræ manent. Ita per Cæsaream Palestinæ et Azotum in Joppen ventum, ubi prima illi gratulatio regni fuit, civibus ingenti gaudio portas aperientibus.

§ 377. Igitur ab Joppitis Jerosolimam deductus, et ibi favorabiliter exceptus, dierum sex [1] spatio quieti satisfecit. Inde, ne Turchi dubitarent indolem regni ejus magno eorum malo adolescere, versus Ascalonem expeditionem movit. Cumque non longe ab urbe vires suas ostentaret, impetentes Ascalonitas facili opera depulit; opportunum tempus ad id quod mente intendebat operiens. Denique repulsionem illorum gloriæ suæ tunc sufficere arbitratus, in montana receptui cecinit, ut hostes persequeretur; nec non et inimicorum dampno necessaria suis conquisiturus, qui pro penuria terræ fame singultiebant, quia illo anno messis ægra victum negaverat, spem provinciæ sterili proventu decipiens. Itaque montana conscendit, quo habitatores terræ Turchi relictis villis concesserant, Syros secum in penitus abditos specus immergentes: sed invenere Franci quo commenta fugitivorum fallerent, fumo in ora cavernarum immisso; quo latrones fugati pertinaciam amisere, uni et uni egredientes. Ita Turchi ad unum omnes interfecti, Syri reservati. Inde digressus exercitus, Arabiamque petiturus, busta præteriit patriarcharum Abrahæ, Isaac, et Jacob, et trium matronarum Saræ, Rebeccæ, Liæ; locus est in Hebron, distans ab Jerosolimis tredecim milibus; nam corpus Joseph jacet in Neapoli, quæ olim Sichem dicta est, marmore candido tectum, omnibusque transeuntibus perspicuum;

---

[1] *sex*] septem, Cd.

ubi¹ quoque fratrum visuntur mausolea, sed inferiori gloria. Venit ergo exercitus in vallem ubi quondam Deus Sodomam et Gomorram subvertit, cælestem flammam in scelestos jaculatus. Ibi lacus per octodecim milia diffunditur, nullius viventis capax; præterea tractatu adeo horribilis, ut potantium ora torqueat, et gustu amaro rictus distendat. Valli mons prominet, per loca scrobes salsas eructans, et quasi congelato vitro totus perlucidus; ubi colligitur quod quidam nitrum, quidam salis gemmam, vocant. Evadentes ergo lacum venerunt ad villam sane locupletissimam et mellitis pomis quæ dactylos dicunt² fœcundam; quorum esu se infarcientes vix lacunas ventrium implere, vix ingluviem faucium præ dulcedine temperare valebant. Cetera timore incolarum abrasa, præter aliquantos Æthiopes, ferrugineam capillorum lanugine fuliginem prætendentes; quorum cædem nostri æstimantes infra virtutem suam, non eos ira, sed risu dignati sunt. Huic villæ subjacet vallis in qua hodieque silex cernitur quo percusso Moises mussitanti populo aquas infudit: latex adhuc tam uberi et præcipiti rivo influit, ut molendinorum vertigines impetu suo rotet. Tum in declivi montis extat ecclesia, in honore legiferi Aaron ædificata; ubi ipse, mediante et cooperante fratre, serebat cum Deo alloquia. Ibi a præviis, viarum gnaris, qui ex Saracenis Christiani essent, addiscentes inde usque ad Babilonem nihil esse nisi jejunum solum et omnium bonorum indigum, Jerosolimam reversi sunt, primitias regni tot hostilium regionum subjectione Deo consecraturi.

§ 378. Paratis igitur regiis³ insignibus, magna gloria in Bethleem die Dominicæ Nativitatis a Daiberto patriarcha coronatus est Baldewinus, fausta omnibus acclamantibus; nam ex tunc et deinceps nihil non venerationis regiæ et ipse labore suo est meritus, et aliorum

---

¹ *ubi—visuntur*] visunturque ibi fratrum ejus, Aa. Al.

² *dicunt*] vocant, Al.

³ *regiis*] regis, Al.; regalibus, Bc.

favore adeptus, quamvis minimi et pene dico pudendi regni dominus. Quare decet Christi Domini clementiam suspicere, et in potentiæ[1] illius[2] contuitu spatiari, cujus suffragio timeri Christiani possent qui officere nequirent; vix enim in tota militia[3] quadringenti milites erant, et tot pedites, qui Jerosolimam, et Ramulam, et Caipham, et Joppen custodirent. Nam qui veniebant navigio, intuto tamen inter tot hostium portus animo sanctis adoratis, statim repatriandum censebant, pedestri via penitus interclusa. Cumulabat quinimmo difficultatem quod Martio mense Tancredus discesserat Antiochiæ principaturus, et nec ipse regi, nec rex ipsi, auxilium pro viæ longitudine ferre[4] valebat;[5] adde quod, si necessitas exposceret, sine irreparabilis discriminis metu gentem suam de uno in aliud castrum non transduceret. Evidens ergo miraculum pronuntio, quod Dei solius tutum suffragio tanta barbarorum horrebat natio.

§ 379. Illo anno, qui fuit Dominicæ incarnationis millesimus centesimus primus, ignis sacratus, qui solebat vigiliam Paschæ illustrare, tardavit plus solito. Sabbato enim lectis alternatim lectionibus Græce et Latine, repetitoque ter "Kirie eleison," et clara Syrorum melodia perstrepente, cum necdum appareret ignis, et jam occiduus sol vesperam urgeret, noctem inveheret, ab omnibus cum mærore in domos discessum. Placuerat enim perpenso consilio ut illa nocte omni homine vacaret sancti Sepulcri ecclesia, ne aliquis, cui ulcerosa squalebat conscientia, Deum magis irritaret ingerendi impudentia. Jamque diluculo sensim in lucem serpente, processio Latinorum ad templum Salomonis edicitur, ut ibi oraturi Dei misericordiam invitarent: idem circa sepulcrum Domini

---

[1] *potentiæ*] om. Bc.
[2] *illius*] ipsius, Bc.
[3] *in tota militia*] inter tot milia, Aa.; in tota milia, Al. Ap.; in tota [fa- *in marg.*] milia, Ce.
[4] *ferre*] conferre, Aa. Al.
[5] *valebat*] valebant, Bc.

faciebant Syri, vi doloris barbas et capillos vellicantes. Nec diu potuere pati divina viscera, confestim igne in unam lampadem sepulcri immisso. Quem cum animadvertisset Syrus per fenestras scintillantem, plausu manuum lætitiam prodens, cursum patriarchæ acceleravit. Ille, clavibus quas gestabat aditum ædiculæ sepulcralis aperiens, cæleste munus cereo accenso extulit, omnibus ad hoc concurrentibus communicans. Mox per omnem ecclesiam ceteræ divinitus accensæ sunt lampades; mirum in modum illa, quæ proxime illuminanda[1] esset, fumo præmisso vicinam accensionem docente. Sic nimirum Christi vetus artificium novit quos amat terrere ut mulceat, et in materiam transeat laudis comminatio potestatis. Quia enim dona Dei usitata assiduitate ipsa vilescunt hominibus; plerumque assensum indulgentiæ suæ raritate[2] commendat, ut ametur gratius quod desideratum fuerat ardentius.

The fleets of Genoa and Pisa arrive at Joppa.

§ 380. Tunc stolus navium Januensium et Pisanorum Laodiciam applicuerat, et inde Joppen prospero cursu navigaverat; nautæque, tractis ad terram ratibus, Jerosolimæ cum rege Pascha exegerant. Quorum ipse virtutem pretio vadatus, tertiam partem pecuniæ pepigit de omnibus urbibus quas adquirere pariter[3] possent, et vicum unum civitatis quem eligerent: ita præcipites, aurique cupidine cæcos magis quam pro Dei amore, impulit, ut, sanguinem suum nundinantes,

Siege of Azotus.

statim Azotum obsiderent, et ad deditionem post tres dies flecterent. Nec vero difficulter oppidani se dedidere, iram regis, si vi caperentur, reveriti; quia præterito anno Godefridum idem aggressum acriter repulerant, maleficio fortunæ adjuti: siquidem cum

Fulcher, Gesta Per. c. 25.

---

[1] *proxime illuminanda*] proxima, Co¹.
[2] *raritate*] veritate, Ce².; caritate, Ce¹.
[3] *pariter*] om. Aa. Al. Bc.

ille suos ascensu scalarum in murum erigeret,[1] jam victores, jam fastigia moenium tenentes, repentinus ligneae turris casus quae forinsecus muro adjecta erat, viros victoria privavit, et plures extinxit; plures capti, et saevitia Saracenorum dilaniati. Inde Caesaream Palestinae Baldewinus totis viribus et obfirmato robore obsidens, cum videret civium pertinaciam et expugnandi difficultatem, machinas compaginari praecepit: factae ergo petrariae; facta turris ingens, viginti cubitis muri altitudinem vincens. At vero nostri, morae impatientes, et tam diutinae impotes expectationis, scalis erectis murum superare aggressi obstinatione virium ad superiora evasere; conscientia virtutis frementes, quod, jam quindecim diebus Saracenicis bellis intenti, tanti temporis spatium perdidissent. Quamvis igitur extrema vi a Caesariensibus certaretur, multos molares in ascendentes volventibus, illi, dissimulato periculo, cuneos obstantes perrumpere, brachiis exertis et strictis gladiis rem agentes. Turchi ulterius non ferentes, fugamque adorsi, vel ipsi se praecipitaverunt, vel hostili manu occubuerunt; plures servituti, pauci redemptioni servati, inter quos admiratus urbis, et episcopus, quem Archadium vocant. Eratque spectaculum quod videnti cachinnum excuteret, cum Turcus, in collo Christiani pugno percussus, bizantinos evomeret; nam miseri, extremae inopiae metu, mares intra gingivas, foeminae intra non dicenda, nummos absconderant. Vides quod aperte loqui erubescit oratio; sed intelligit profecto lector quod volo, immo quod nolo, dicere.

§ 381. Nec adhuc quievit imperator Babilonis, quin ducem et exercitum ad expugnandos Francos missitaret. Illi, navigio Ascalonem appulsi, mox juxta Ramulam cursitarunt, curis regis abutentes, qui tunc Caesariensi bello tenebatur. Agrorum igitur depopulatione ad congrediendum crebrius illum irritarunt. At

---

[1] *ascensu—erigeret*] ascensu scalarum in muros promovisset, Ag. | Al.; scalarum in murum erectione promovisset, Aa. Aah.

Advance of the Saracens to Ramlah.

ille non impari calliditate, ut calor indomitus defervesceret, vetito instantes passus languescere bello: hac effecit cunctatione, ut plerique morarum pertæsi[1] dilaberentur; reliquos, qui essent undecim milia equitum,[2] viginti unum[3] milia peditum, cum suis, ducentis quinquaginta equitibus, peditibus paulo minus septingentis, invasit. Paucaque militibus locutus, quibus, si perstarent, victoriam, si morerentur, gloriam promitteret; si fugerent, longe Franciam esse commoneret; primus in hostes irruit: productoque aliquantum certamine, cum acies suas labare cerneret, desperatis rebus occurrit. Itaque notâ sui specie Turchos proturbans, conto ducem prostravit; quo interempto, tota diffugere agmina. Nostri, qui principio pugnæ ita circumsepti fuerant ut nullus alterum videret, tunc, Dominicæ crucis vexillo prævio, adeo virtutem exercuerunt ut quinque milia trucidarent; ex Francis octoginta equites, pedites paulo plus desiderati. Porro sequens successus solatio fuit, quod quingentos equites Arabas interemerunt. Illi ante Joppen biduo cucurrerant, sed, parum explicantes, Ascalonem redibant; visoque eminus exercitu nostro, suos esse sperantes, tanquam triumphantibus congratulaturi obviam ibant: sed tandem aliquando in se jaculis emissis intelligentes Francos esse, perinde palluerunt, " sicut " nudis pressit qui calcibus anguem," ut poetæ verbo utar; itaque, ipso hebetes stupore, terga cædentibus exhibuere. Ita rex Joppen perveniens errorem epistolæ, quæ, Tancredo a Joppitis missa, falso regem cum exercitu extinctum nuntiaverat, veraciori scripto correxit: jamque Tancredus iter ad Jerosolimam paraverat, cum nuntius veniens, ostenso sigillo regio, mæstitiam depulit, lætitiam reformavit.

Attack by Baldwin.

Great loss on both sides.

Flight of the enemy.

News sent to Tancred.

Lucan, *Phars.* iv. 281.

Juvenal, Sat. i. 43.

---

[1] *morarum pertæsi*] om. Bc. Cd. Cc.
[2] *equitum*] om. Aa. Aah.
[3] *viginti unum*] om. Aa. Aah.; viginti, Ce¹.

§ 382. Longum est si velim explicare omnia ejus certamina; quomodo Tiberiadem, Sidonem, Accaronem, id est Ptholomaidem, quomodo postremo cunctas maritimas urbes, subegerit; quomodo pene omnem diem Turchorum mortibus insignierit, aut assultu clandestino aut bello publico. Ingentes operas ejusmodi desiderat oratio[1] hominis qui ampullato eloquio et curioso abundet otio; nobis utrumque deest, et, quod maxime obest, rerum expedita scientia; omnia vero indulgenti famæ credere, et facilitatem auditorum fallere, veracis historici non debet esse. Quocirca illa solummodo quæ scripto comperi apponam, quibus ad unguem comprobetur gloriosa viri devotio, et gratia victura in seculo: illudque constanter asseruerim, parva[2] manu magna illum prælia persæpe lusisse; nec unquam campum fugisse, præter apud Ramulam et apud Accaronem. Enimvero ambas fugas prædicabiles exceperunt victoriæ, quod magis inconsiderata virtute quam timore provenerint, sicut paucis insertis lector agnoscet.

§ 383. Eo Septembri cujus septimo idus prælium fuit,[3] Willelmus comes Pictavensis Jerosolimam perrexit, multa secum ducens agmina, ut æstimarentur sexaginta milia militum, et multo plura peditum. Ivit cum eo Stephanus comes Burgundiæ, et Hugo Lizianensis, frater Raimundi comitis, et Hugo magnus, et Stephanus Blesensis, antiquæ discessionis improperium nova et excogitata virtute sarcire cupientes. Ita per Constantinopolim profectus, cum insolenti responso, ut superius dixi, Alexium offendisset, illo non curante, vel potius procurante, Solimanni incurrit insidias; qui sciens exercitum fame ac siti laborare, quod aliquantis diebus errabundi per palustria et invia loca iverant, cum trecentis milibus sagittariorum occurrit. Nulla unquam luctuosior Francis pugna visa, quia nec timidum fuga, nec audacem virtus, poterat eripere discri-

---

[1] *oratio*] relatio, Aa. Aah. Al.
[2] *parva*] pauca, Aa. Aah. Al.
[3] *prælium fuit*] prædictum fuit prælium, Aa. Al.

mini; quod in arcto loco pugnaretur, et in consertos sagittarum nubes non frustraretur. Interfecta igitur plusquam centum milia, præda omnis abducta; ita Solimannus, ex manubiis Francorum claras manibus suorum nactus inferias, dispendium Niceæ ultus est. Sed quia multis tramitibus itum erat, nec omnes cæsi, nec omnia direpta; nam præter Pictavensem, qui pene ad pudenda nudatus erat, ceteri comites prompte sua defensitaverant. Omnes ergo recollectis ex fuga militibus, præter Hugonem magnum, quem mortuum Tarsensis civitatis urna excepit, Antiochiam convolarunt; in quibus Tancredus, egregiæ pietatis miles, ingentem munificentiæ suæ gratiam ostendit, cunctos quatenus poterat pecuniis sustentans; Willelmum præcipue, quem fortunæ vicissitudo eo afflictaverat invidiosius quo ante provexerat serenius, qui præter gazas, quarum dampno non adeo afficiebatur, quod caducæ sunt et reparabiles, ex tot eximiis militibus solus pene remanserat superstes. Ita recreatis animis iter moliti, undecunque belli occasiones quærebant. Sensit sitim furentium prima Tortuosa civitas; qua pervasa et direpta, non modicum præteritas ærumpnas relevarunt. Inde ad angustias de quibus superius dixi venerunt, ubi eos rex jampridem operiebatur, contra Turcos, si prohibere vellent, opem laturus. Ejus virtute defensi, et benigno apud Joppen hospitio suscepti Jerosolimam proximo Pascha contenderunt; ubi sacrosanctum ignem lætis hauserunt oculis, devotis adorarunt animis. Post hæc reversi Joppen, ascensis navibus, patriam quisque suam redire meditabatur: quorum Pictavensis, continua venti prosperitate provectus, patriam tenuit; ceteri retro violenter acti.

§ 384. Jam vero mense Maio inchoante,[1] Turchi et Arabes Ramulam obsederunt, superioris anni dampnum, novi exercitus supplemento, eodem reficientes numero.

---

[1] *inchoante*] mediante, Aa. Ag. Al. Ap.; the word used by Fulcher.

Episcopus urbis, prudenter opportunitate spectata, cavit sibi loco, Joppen latenter profectus. Jamque rex exierat, credens falso asserentibus non esse hostes plusquam quingentos: itaque nec aciem dirigere, nec pedites convocare curavit, tantum milites regem sequi cornicines monuerunt; multum amicis suadentibus ut Turcorum fraudes caveret. Stephani duo, Blesensis et Burgundus, regem equis insecuti, ne desides et inglorii, sed triumphalis pompæ conscii,[1] terras repeterent suas; sed aliam quam opinabantur gloriam, aliam victoriam, parabant fata viris. Namque rex, visa hostium multitudine, dum se frustratum opinione cognosceret, ira mentem saucius, et magnanimitatis conscientia fremens, quid faceret hæsitabat: si cederet præteritæ gloriæ ignominiam; si pugnaret, suorum mortes animo volutabat. Veruntamen vicit calor ingenitus, et terga jam dabat metus, cum, commilitonum hortatibus animatus, ut fugam in castellum per medios hostes intenderet, adquievit. Ceteri, cum clamore secuti, densissimas perruperunt acies, animas suas Deo consecrantes, et mortes impigre ulti; comites quoque, feriendo defatigati adeo ut manus gladiis obrigescerent, neci succubuerunt. Rex, in arcem lapsus, ex ducentis quos duxerat aliquantos socios habuit; quibus orantibus ut vitam dignaretur fugiendo producere, sua pericula mundo parvi ponderis esse, illius vitam ad multorum profectum valere, utpote qui omni seculo sit virtutis spectaculum, quamvis in fractis rebus ingenti animi constantia, dignum se credidit vita. Itaque quinque militibus comitatus, in montana rependo, insidiantes elusit. Militum fuit unus Robertus Anglus, ut superius dixi; ceteros notitiæ nostræ fama tam longinqua occuluit. Ille cum tribus[2] comprehensus est; unus[3] evasit cum rege. Turchi extremam vim furoris in illos qui evaserant[4] in arcem effuderunt, in quibus

---

[1] *conscii*] consocii, At.
[2] *tribus*] aliis, add. Aa. Al.
[3] *unus*] quintus, Aa. Al.
[4] *evaserant*] refugerant, Al.

fuit Hugo Lizianensis et Gaufredus Vindocinensis; tres tantum superstites Jerosolimitanis nuntii miseriarum fuere. Rex interdiu latens,[1] cornipedem cursu exhaustum stimulans, Azotum pervenit: pulchro et ad miraculum Dei prono salutis eventu, quod paulo ante Turchi discesserant, qui jam biduo circa urbem praedas egerant. Inde Joppen navigio veniens, Jerosolimitanis epistolam de vitae suae certitudine legavit. Portitor cartae fuit homuncio Syrus, qui, etsi inveniretur, habitus vilitate et sermonis noti commercio insidiantes falleret. Hic, notis sibi per devia compendiis, perfidorum pericula declinans, tertio die Jerosolimam pervenit. Tum equites qui urbem tutabantur, junctis sibi auxiliarium peditum turmis, ad Joppen profecturi, iter mari proximum direxerunt, mediterraneis devitatis: extremi tamen[2] agminis Turchis urgentibus interfecti, quod vel equis vel peditibus destituebantur. Ita congregatis ex Jerosolimis nonaginta equitibus, ex Tyberiade octoginta, quos Hugo dux strenuissimus adduxerat in subsidium, armigeri quoque pro penuria in locum militum allecti. Postera ergo die moram pugnae absolvit, Turchis jam adeo ferocibus ut paratis machinis murum Joppis aggredi meditarentur.[3] Praeventum hoc Baldewini diligentia, et, Dominica cruce praevia, qua superius bellum caruerat, totis[4] viribus in hostes alacriter itum, acriter certatum; at illi, more solito nostros circumgirantes, actum de Christianis putarunt, hilari ululatu vociferantes: sed affuit, et de caelo tandem respexit Dominus Jesus, Franciscoque animositatem ingerens inimicos campo privatos conjecit in fugam. Hoc et in anteriori praelio factum est, ut, non semel ejecti tentoriis, postea multitudine superarint: tum autem cum pedites eminus

Fulcher, *Gesta Per.* c. 28.

---

[1] *latens*] noctu per avia, Aa. Al.
[2] *tamen*] om. Ce¹.
[3] *meditarentur*] deliberarent, Aa. Aah. Al. At.
[4] *totis*] regni, ins. Al. At.; regiminibus, Aa. Aah.

sagittis, et equites lanceis cominus ferirent, omni spe pedibus commissa, fugere perseveravere.

§ 385. Altera illi pugna posterioribus annis fuit, in qua milites nostri, Turcorum copia pressi et in fugam acti, etiam salutare vexillum amisere: sed cum longiuscule fugissent, reversi sunt; pudor famae trepidos animavit ut ignominiam propulsarent. Ingens ibi pugna virorum fuit, collato pede et adverso pectore rem agentium. Nostri crucem reportarunt, fusis adversariis campum vindicantes. Ceciderunt ibi plures quos ego quoque noram; inter quos Godefridus, abnepos ejus nothus, jam inde a pueritia umbram virtutis vultu colorans, veritatem animo spirans. Ambae ergo fugae fuere in principio quasi fomentum ignominiae, sed in fine verax alimentum gloriae: illa nominatior, sed ista fructuosior. Denique ad supplementum rerum quas amiserat, simul et ad legitimum connubium, non multo post comitissa Siciliae Jerosolimam venit; tantas gazas cubiculo regis inferens, ut mirum cuivis videatur unde mulier tam infinitos pretiosae supellectilis cumulos coacervarit; et tunc quidem illam thoro recepit, sed non multo post dimisit; aiunt incommodo tactam, quo ejus genitalia cancer, morbus incurabilis, exederit.[1] Illud constat, regem prolis inopem fuisse; nec mirum si homo, cujus otium erat aegrescere, uxorios amplexus horruerit, omnem aetatem in bellis deterens. Quibus laboribus effecit, ut admirabilis et pene divina virtus ejus fuerit praesentibus stimulo, futura posteris miraculo. Obiit in expeditione Arabica mense Aprili, et publico funere Jerosolimis juxta fratrem tumulatus, cum decimo septimo anno regni[2] quartus accresceret mensis. Vir multis laboribus emeritus, et cujus gloriae nullus praetendit nubila livor, nisi quod fuerit pecuniae justo tenacior; sed hujus culpae facilis et vera erit

---

[1] *exederit*] exesit, Bc. By.; corroserit, Aa.; exedit, Bq.

[2] *cum—regni*] cum septem et decem regni annis, Aa. Aah.; Ce¹. omits regni.

excusatio, si consideretur quod necessaria in remanentes effusio munerum inhibuerit quo minus mercaretur favorem abeuntium.

Baldwin of Edessa succeeds him.

§ 386. Successit ei Baldewinus cognatus, dux Edessæ, quem moriens regem denuntiaverat, antiquis jam stipendiis laudatum. Ille multis annis[1] regnum impigre tutatus, etiam auxit Antiocheno principatu; quem *He had also governed Antioch.* occiso Rogerio filio Ricardi obtinuit. Utrasque ergo regiones egregio moderamine rexit, minori quidem præsumptionis roncho, sed majori et consultiori providentia; quamvis sint qui opinionem ejus lacerent, tenacitatis eum nimiæ arguentes. Quare, cum præterito anno non longe ab Jerosolima equitantem Turchi cepissent, paucis aut nullis gemitibus[2] sui eum desiderarunt; latuitque pene anno et incolas et rumigerulos, *His captivity.* quo terrarum abductus, si superis auris vesceretur, necne. Refutarunt porro Jerosolimitæ vel regem facere vel ordinem et ducatum militum interrumpere, quoad rei certitudo sciretur, propter ejus absentiam in nullo infractiores. Postmodum vero, cognito loco quo vinculatus fuerat, milites audacissimi speciem negotiatorum mentientes, armis sub vestibus occultatis, oppidum *His deliverance.* ingressi, regem eripuere discrimini; protestati non conferre se id ejus avaritiæ, sed Gozelini de Turbexel gratiæ, qui nihil unquam pensi fecerat quin omnia quæ posset militibus erogaret. Vixit diu[3] frugi homo, et nulli præter hanc culpam infamiæ obnoxius. Principatus Antiochenus ad Boamundi[4] spectat filium, de quo nunc dicam.

Fulcher, c. 52, 55.

De Boamundo.

History of Bohemond, son of Robert Wiscard.

§ 387. Boamundus Roberti Guiscardi ex Normanna[5] filius fuit: alter, Rogerus, ex Appula genitus, qui

---

[1] *multis annis*] ad hoc tempus, Aa. Al.
[2] *gemitibus*] ut ferunt, ins. Aa. Aah. Al.
[3] *Vixit diu*] Vivit adhuc, Aa. Aah. Al. Ap. Baldwin died Aug. 21, 1131.
[4] *Boamundi*] Boamundum, Al.
[5] *Normanna*] Normannia, Aa. Al. Bc. Cd. Ce².

cognomen Marsupii a patre meruit, quod paterno et curioso intuitu deprehendisset eum jam a tenero libenter nummos numerare; nam Boamundus ætatis majusculæ nihil erat quod retineret, sed etiam puerilia xenia dispertiret. Itaque Rogerus Apuliam, quæ sibi materno genere competere videbatur, accepit: Boamundus cum genitore ad bellum Durachinum profectus est. Cumque oppidani fiducia mœnium jactitarent ideo urbem Durachium nominatam, quod contra omnes obsidiones imperterrita duraret, "Et ego," inquit[1] "vocor Durandus; et eo usque in obsidione "durabo quo civitati nomen auferam, ut non Dura- "chium sed Mollicium amodo dicatur." Cujus responsi constantia effecit et confestim pavefacti portas aperirent. Ita tutus a tergo, ceteras urbes usque ad Tessalonicam leviore labore subegit. Jamque illuc pervenerat, jam Alexium tum per se tum per filium vinci posse docuerat, cum uxoria fraude deceptus ingens depositum[2] morte destituit. Tum vero Boamundus, Apuliam reversus, aliquot castella fraterna indulgentia tenuit, multa ipse virtute et prudentia conquisivit, nam ad fratrem specie tenus ducatus pervenerat; alterum bello meliores[3] sunt[4] secuti. Nec vero parvi momenti fuit quod, paterni propositi sequax, Guibertum repellens, Urbano validissime astitit, et cunctantem impulit ut Gallias ad concilium Clari Montis accederet, quo eum Raimundi Provincialis comitis et episcopi Caturcensis epistolæ invitabant. Concilioque celebrato, libens occasionem accepit, et in Græciam copias trajecit; subindeque promovens exercitum, modeste Raimundum et Godefridum[5] operiebatur: quibus venientibus sociatus, magnum incitamentum ceteris erat, disciplinæ militaris scientia et

His pun at Durazzo.

His conquests in Greece.

His life in Apulia.

He is at the Council of Clermont.

He sets out with Raymond and Godfrey.

---

[1] *inquit*] Guiscardus, ins. Aa. Al.
[2] *depositum*] dispositum, Al. Bc. Cd. Cc².
[3] *meliores*] meliorem, Bc.; meliore, Ce¹.
[4] *sunt*] om. Aa. Al. Bc. Cd.
[5] *Godefridum*] venturos, ins. Aa. Aab. Al.

virtute nulli secundus. Sed quia quæ cum ceteris fecit communi laudi sors attribuit, et quomodo captus fuerit anterior sermo notitiæ dedit, nunc qualiter se servitio exuerit dicendum. Danisman enim, cum videret nihil utilitatibus suis applicari quod tantum virum teneret, inflexus animo [1] de pacis conditionibus actitare cœpit: nam nec illum occidere, ne in se odia Christianorum effusa concitaret, nec, sine spebus in perpetuum valituræ pacis, dimittere volebat. Pollicitus ergo Boamundus continuam gentili concordiam, revertit Antiochiam, argenteos compedes quibus alligatus [2] fuerat secum deferens: a suis ergo exceptus plausibiliter, Laodiciam, et ceteras urbes quas Tancredus adquisierat, suscepit, ne videretur oscitare otio dum avunculus suspiraret in ergastulo. Nec multo post Gallias venit, offerens catenas sancti Leonardi honori, quæ sibi fuerant oneri. Fertur enim in primis ille sanctus absolvendorum vinculorum potens, ut, videntibus nec mutire audentibus adversariis, pondera sua captivus liber asportet. Ita ducta uxore filia regis Francorum, et altera Tancredo missa, repetiit Appuliam; sequentibus se Francorum proceribus, qui spe majoris commodi patriam deserebant, simul et spectaturi cominus quid viva virtutis species efficeret, quam tam insignis fama ubique loqueretur. Itaque ille, dispositis apud Apuliam rebus suis, denuo in Alexium efferatus est, prætendens belli causam peregrinorum injuriam, qua ille perinfamis erat; sed parum et prope nihil gessit prospere, sollertis imperatoris deceptus astutia, qui omnes duces ejus aut pecuniis obæratos ab eo alienavit, aut veneno, ut dixi,[3] sustulit. Quapropter animo dejectus Apuliam rediit; ibique post paucos dies, dum ad Antiochiam iter meditatur,[4] defungitur, ætate citra senium, prudentia infra nullum, relicto tenerioris ævi filio. Vir in adversis constans, in prosperis circumspectus; nam et, pro sus-

---

[1] *animo*] animi mollitie, Al.
[2] *alligatus*] illigatus, Al. Ap. Bc.
[3] *ut dixi*] om. Ce¹.
[4] *meditatur*] meditaretur, Aa. Al.

picione noxiæ potionis, paratum commentus erat remedium, cultellum, qui, ante ora comedentis infixus, sudore, mirum dictu, prodebat manubrii si quid tecto illatum esset veneficii. Post eum Tancredus Antiochiæ principatui præfuit, haud pudendus avunculo nepos; qui cum et ipse communem mortalium viam obitu præpropero trivisset, successit Rogerius filius Ricardi. Is, gloriæ antecessorum in bellis non impar, ignominiam tamen avaritiæ incurrit; quapropter, cum eum milites caverent, stipendiario milite pene [1] nullo et indigena raro Turchis congressus occubuit, mortem suam non ignave ultus. Nam cum ab eis [2] captus et diloricatus juberetur ensem reddere, negavit se ulli nisi duci daturum,[3] quod omnes infra dignitatis suæ deditionem aspiceret. Credidit infelix admiratus simulatis vocibus; et jam, galea caput nudatus, porrexit manum ut reciperet Rogerii gladium. Tunc vero ille infrendens, et totis fortitudinis reliquiis in ictum se cogens, Turco caput decussit; moxque perfossus, excogitato genere virtutis, dedecus servitutis effugit. Ejus mortem Baldewinus secundus rex Jerosolimorum ultus insigniter, principatum civitatis et filiam suam Boamundo filio Boamundi servavit [4] fideliter.

De Raimundo.

§ 388. Raimundus fuit filius Willelmi antiquissimi Tolosæ comitis, qui, vir acer et efficax, patriam, antecessorum suorum socordia obscuram, titulis suis reddidit illustrem. Uxor ejus Almodis, multis vicissim desponsata, multam ex omnibus sobolem tulit; insano muliercula pruritu et irreverenti, ut cum ei longo usu vir displicuisset, alias migraret novos impletura penates; denique primum Arelatensi comiti nupta, mox

---

[1] *pene*] om. Cc.
[2] *eis*] Turcis, Aa. Al.
[3] *daturum*] redditurum, Bc.
[4] *et filiam—servavit*] Boamundi filio reservat, Aa. Aah. Ag. Ao. Al. At.

illius pertæsa, huic Willelmo se conjunxit; cui cum duos peperisset filios, Barcinonensem ad connubium illexit comitem. Porro Willelmus, mortis confinis foribus, Tolosanum comitatum dedit filio æquivoco, sed moribus absono, quod esset crassioris ingenii,[1] et nihil Tolosani contra eum novarent, familiæ illius dominatui assueti. Raimundus vero, vivacioris spiritus Caturcensem accepit et non mediocriter[2] auxit; Arelatensi, et Narbonensi, et Provinciali, et Lemovicensi adjunctis. Tolosam quoque a germano emit, pluribus annis ante magni motus viam profecto Jerosolimam. Sed hæc multi temporis intercessu et ætate impensa labori. Itaque, pugnis semper assiduus legitimam uxorem non desideravit, multinubo concubinatu voluptatem exercens. Denique ex una pellicum filium natum, Bertramnum cognatione et hereditate dignatus est, quod in aliquantis patrissaret; cui uxorem conjunxit Matildis marcisæ neptem ex Longobardia natam, ut illius affinitate illas[3] provinciæ partes tutaretur. Ipse quoque extremis fere annis uxorem ascivit filiam regis Tarraconensis, splendidam dotem pactus, æternam scilicet conterminarum provinciarum pacem. Nec multo post, nivem capitis respiciens, Jerosolimitanum iter vovit, ut lassi et effœti corporis vires jam vel sero Deo deservirent; auctore præcipue Caturcensi episcopo, cujus præcipua opera ipse semper impugnatus fuerat: etiam in quodam duellio altero lumine privatus, cujus insigne calamitatis præ se ferens non solum non occultabat, sed etiam gloriabatur ultro specimen nobilis militiæ ostentans. Tunc autem mutua fœderati amicitia, ut senectutem suam divinis consumerent cultibus, Urbano jam in prædicationem prono stimulos addidere, ut, transitis Alpibus, potissimum apud Clarum Montem concilium cogeret, quod esset ea civitas et illorum

---

[1] *ingenii*] animi, Al. At.
[2] *non mediocriter*] immane quantum Ag. Al. Ao. Ap. At.; in immensum, Aa. Aah.
[3] *illas*] illius, Bc.

patriæ propinqua, et ex tota Gallia venientibus opportuna. Veruntamen, in ipso ad concilium itinere, pontifex obitu defecit. Successit curæ illius præsul[1] Podii, de quo supra diximus: cujus hortatibus animatus, et umbone protectus, Raimundus primus omnium laicorum crucem accepit; adjiciens voto ut nunquam in patriam rediret, sed potius, duraturo in Turcos labore arvinam[2] præteritarum iniquitatum extenuaret. Jam vero in itinere plura dedit indicia fortitudinis, ad laborem primus, ad quietem ultimus; plura etiam patientiæ, quod arce[3] Antiochiæ, quam occupaverat,[4] Boamundo, et turri David, Godefrido, libenter cesserit. Sed tandem, nimiis exactionibus quorundam fracta patientia, in deditione urbis Ascalonensis decidit. Siquidem in primo Francorum adventu oppidani, exploratis omnium ducum nostrorum moribus, ipsum in patronum elegere, quod multi, eo ante a Monte Pessulano[5] navigio venientes negotiatum, fidem ejus et virtutem in cælum tulerant. Itaque, traditis clavibus, sacramento ducem adegere ut nulli Christianorum potestatem urbis refunderet, si vel ipse nollet tenere vel nequiret. Tunc a proceribus mussitatum est, expostulantibus urbem regis dominio, quod parum ei valeret regnum si non haberet Ascalonem, quæ hostibus esset receptaculo, nostris obstaculo. Et rex quidem leviter, ut omnia, et vultu tranquillis conveniente moribus, rem allegabat; ceteri pervicacius. Hæc ille verba parvi pendebat, non infirmis rationibus dicta eorum cassans:[6] omnes socios suos jam sibi receptui consuluisse, partim patriam devectos, partim adquisitam inhabitantes provinciam; se solum, abjurata naturali[7] terra, nec illuc

He is the first to take the cross.

He yields his claims to Antioch and Jerusalem,

but accepts the homage of Ascalon.

His refusal to surrender it provokes hostility,

---

[1] *præsul*] pontifex, Aa. Al.
[2] *arvinam*] ruinam, An. Aah.; a ruina, Cd. Ce².
[3] *arce*] a parte, Aa. Al. Bc. Cd.
[4] *occupaverat*] præoccupaverat, Bc.
[5] *Pessulano*] Pislerio, Aa. Al.
[6] *cassans*] cassatus, Bc.²; cassa sunt, Bc¹.
[7] *naturali*] natali, Aa. Al. Bc.

posse redire, nec hic receptum habere; cessisse se in aliis: hoc modo paterentur, ut Ascalonem in fidelitatem sancti Sepulcri teneret; ceterum, ne redderet sacramento fecisse. Quo audito cuncti strepere, perfidum et cupidum vocare, ut vix manibus temperarent. Contumeliæ hujus rubore comes suffusus, ab æqui bonique viri descivit officio; inimicis Dei claves civitatis[1] contradens, et metum pejerandi multorum in posterum sanguine compensans. Neque enim ad hunc diem civitas illa capi vel vi vel ingenio potuit: quin et plures ex hominibus illius, affluenti urbis opulentia delectati, fidei transfugio civium caritatem meruere. Ita vir ille, Jerosolimam egressus, Laodiciam venit; qua subjugata, aliquantum ibi morarum nexuit: cumque Constantinopolim ivisset, obtinuit Laodiciam Tancredus, vi an amore ambiguum. Ille interea Bizantio commoratus, prudentia qua vigebat effecit ut Alexii gratiam haberet: unde contigit, ut, imperatoris benignitate per tuta deductus, societati ærumpnarum non implicaretur quas Willelmum Pictavensem et ceteros superius[2] incurrisse diximus; cum quibus Tortuosam civitatem cepit, sed, illis ultra euntibus, solus possedit. Et, ut latius vires suas spargeret, oppidum contra Tripolim, quod Castellum Peregrinorum vocant, firmavit, et ibi Herbertum episcopum ex abbate constituit; et, ut quassæ suorum vires aliquanta quiete coalescerent, cum Tripolitanis in septennium fœdus jecit. Veruntamen ante præstitutum terminum pax rupta est; deprehenso intra castellum quodam oppidano cum pugione toxicato, quem sub femore occuluerat. Tum profecto Tripolitanæ victoriæ supremam manum imposuisset, nisi prope diem mors adveniens præsentis vitæ spiritum subduxisset ingentia parturientem. Cujus morte audita, Willelmus de Monte

---

[1] *civitatis*] om. Aa. Al. Bc. | [2] *superius*] om. Ce¹.

Pessulano,¹ et ceteri duces provinciæ, Willelmum peregrinum, quem in ipsa obsidione ex Hispana susceperat,² quadrimum, patriam devehendum curarunt, sollicita omnium spe in successionem educandum. Nec invitus Bertramnus factum, quamvis se inconsulto, audivit, ut paternas adoreas instauraret. Itaque innumero succinctus milite, præcipueque Januensibus et Pisanis, qui de conjugis cognatione erant, annitentibus, Tripolim terra marique aggressus est, diuturnaque obsidione fractam in potestatem redegit. Successit ei filius Pontius ex Longobarda, adolescens majorum æmulus gloriæ; sortitusque est jugalem³ Tancredi quondam Antiocheni principis uxorem. Id enim ille moriens præceperat, protestatus adolescere⁴ in ephebo et Christianorum commodum et Turchorum omnifariam dispendium. Pontius ergo Tripoli principatur, sancti Sepulcri se profitens servum, avitum scilicet et paternum secutus exemplum.

Bertram completes the conquest.

Pontius succeeds him.

De Roberto Curta Ocrea.

§ 389. Robertus filius Willelmi Anglorum regis primi, natus in Normannia, spectatæ jam virtutis habebatur adolescens quando pater Angliam venit; fortitudinis probatæ, quanquam exilis corporis et pinguis aqualiculi. Inter bellicas patris alas excrevit primævo tirocinio, parenti morem in omnibus gerens. Veruntamen, juvenilem⁵ indutus⁶ calorem, Normanniam a patre adhuc vivente, fatuorum sodalium instinctu, impetrare se posse speravit: quod cum ille negasset, terrisonæ vocis roncho juvenem abigens, iratus abscessit Robertus, multisque assultibus patriam infestavit; primo quidem genitore cachinnos excutiente, et

Robert of Normandy.

He asks Normandy of his father, who gives him his nickname.

---

¹ *Pessulano*] Pislerio, Aa. Al.
² *susceperat*] vix, ins. Aa. Al. Bc. By.
³ *jugalem*] conjugalem, Cd.

⁴ *adolescere*] om. Bc. By. Cd. Ce.
⁵ *juvenilem*] juventæ viridem, Aa. Ag. Al.
⁶ *indutus*] inductus, Cd.

subinde dicente, "Per resurrectionem Dei! probus erit Robelinus Curta Ocrea." Hoc enim erat ejus cognomen, quod esset exiguus; ceterum nihil habens quod succenseres, quia nec illepidæ formæ, nec infaceti eloquii, nec virtutis imbecillæ, nec enervis erat consilii. Posterius vero rex adeo effera succensus est ira ut eum et benedictione ultima et hereditate fraudaret Anglica. Comitatu tamen Normanniæ ægre licet et improbe retento, post novem annos Jerosolimitanæ viæ laboribus suæ fortitudinis periculum fecit; et in multis quidem mirabilis apparuit, ut nunquam a Christiano vel pagano potuerit ex equite pedes effici.[1] Tum vero maxime in bello Antiocheno, cujus ipse victoriam pulchra experientia nobilitavit. Nam cum Turchi, ut diximus, subito terrefacti fugæ se dedissent,[2] nostrique palantes vehementius impeterent, Corbaguath dux, genuinæ virtutis memor, retento equo suos inclamat;[3] famulos ignavos et annosarum victoriarum oblitos vocans, ut victores quondam orientis paterentur se ab advena et pene inermi populo finibus excludi: quo clamore multi, resumentes animum, Francos conversi urgere et propiores cedere cœpere; Corbaguath suos animante et hostes feriente, ut imperatoris et militis probe officium exequeretur. Tum vero Normannus comes, et Philippus clericus, filius Rogerii comitis de Monte Gomerico, et Warinus de Tanea[4] castello Cenomannico, mutua se vivacitate invicem hortati, qui ante simulata fuga cedebant, convertunt cornipedes, et quisque suum comparem incessens dejiciunt. Ibi Corbaguath, quamvis comitem cognosceret, solo tamen corpore mensus, simul et fugere inglorium arbitratus, audaciam congressus morte propinqua luit, vitali statim spiritu privatus: cujus nece visa, Turchi, qui jam gloriabundi ululabant, spe recenti exinaniti,

---

[1] *effici*] fieri, Bc. By.
[2] *dedissent*] commisissent, Al.
[3] *inclamat*] inclamavit, Aa. Al.
[4] *Tanea*] Tanca, Aa. Al.

fugam iterarunt. In eo tumultu Warinus cecidit, Robertus cum Philippo palmam retulit: Philippus hac militia præcluus,[1] sed Jerosolimis, ut fertur, bono fine functus; præter exercitium equestre litteris clarus. Ita Robertus, Jerosolimam veniens, indelebili macula nobilitatem suam respersit, quod regnum, consensu omnium sibi utpote regis filio delatum, recusaret, non reverentiæ, ut fertur, contuitu, sed laborum inextricabilium metu. Veruntamen patriam regresso, in qua licenter se delicatis voluptatibus inserviturum putaverat, affuit pro hac culpa,[2] credo, Deus misericorditer ubique sæviens, et omnes ejus dulcedines amarissimis offensionibus offuscans, sicut consequenti scripto palam fiet. Uxorem filiam Willelmi de Conversana, quam rediens in Apuliam duxerat, cujus elegantissimæ speciei prodigium vix ullius disertitudinis explicabit conatus, post paucos annos morbo amisit; deceptam, ut dicunt, obstetricis[3] consilio, quæ pro affluentis lactis copia, puerperæ mammas stricta præceperat illigari fascia. Sed accessit, tantorum malorum grande solatium, filius ex conjuge susceptus;[4] qui, Willelmus dictus vaticinio nominis aviti, spem egregiæ pietatis[5] aleret in posterum. Pecuniam infinitam, quam ei socer dotis nomine annumeraverat, ut ejus commercio Normanniam exueret vadimonio, ita dilapidavit[6] ut pauculis diebus nec nummus superesset. Præcipitavit quoque infamiam ejus inconsultus adventus in Angliam, ut fratri Henrico regnum eriperet; sed, desertorum qui eum invitaverant destitutus auxilio, germani paci facile adquievit utriusque[7] partis ducum auxilio,[8] trium milium marcarum annuum do-

He declines the kingdom of Jerusalem.

His return home.

Death of his wife.

His son William.

His extravagance.

His war with Henry.

---

[1] *præcluus*] præclusus, At.

[2] *culpa*] ut, ins. Aa. Al.

[3] *obstetricis*] pellicis, Aa. Aah. Al. At.; pelicis, Ap.

[4] *susceptus*] sublatus, Aa. Al. Cd. Ce.

[5] *pietatis*] probitatis, Aa. Al.; indolis, Bc. By.

[6] *ita dilapidavit*] mimorum et nebulonum sinibus ita ingessit, Aa. Aah. Ag. Al.

[7] *utriusque*] utrique, Ce¹.

[8] *auxilio*] arbitrio, Aa. Al. By.

The pacification. — num ab Anglia verbo tenus habiturus. Nam promiserat ista rex, non daturus; sed, fratris facilitatem non nesciens, blandam credulitatem luserat dum interim calor bellicus defervesceret. Porro ille, quasi cum fortuna certaret utrum plus illa daret an ipse dispergeret, sola voluntate reginae tacite postulantis comperta, tantam massam argenti benignus in perpetuum ignovit; acclines foeminei fastus preces pro magno *Robert's gentleness of character.* exosculatus; erat enim ejus in baptismo filiola. Offensarum igitur erat immemor; culparum, quatenus non debet, remissor; omnibus pro voto respondens adeuntibus, ne tristes dimitteret; et quod dare non posset, repromittens.[1] Qua morum dulcedine, qui laudari et subjectorum amorem mercari debuerat, adeo in contemptum sui Normannos exacuit ut nullius eum momenti aestimarent.[2] Tunc enim potentum quisque sibi adversari, tunc[3] manubiae praedarum per totam regionem agi, tunc vulgus exspoliari. Quas incommoditates comiti provinciales deferentes, nullum referebant auxilium; dum ille primo commotus, mox vel munusculis, vel temporis intercessu ira languescente, leniebatur. Iccirco, extremis malis admoniti, opem regis *Henry is called in as a saviour.* Henrici censuere implorandam, ut laboranti patriae succurreret. Ille Caesarianae sententiae assistens, "Si *Cicero, De Officiis, iii. 21.* "violandum est jus, gratia civium violandum est; "aliis rebus pietatem colas," non semel in Normanniam vires trajecit, ut laboranti justitiae manum daret: tantumque postremo valuit, ut totam terram, praeter Rotomagum, et Falesium, et Cadomum, subjugaret. Jamque ad hoc Robertus venerat, ut in vicis illis pene se altero vagaretur, precarium victum a burgen- *Robert's humiliation.* sibus nundinans.[4] Quare offensi Cadomenses, non diu in fide mansere; sed, rege per nuntios admonito, portis seratis et repagulis objectis urbem clausere. Quo

---

[1] *repromittens*] compromittens, Aa. Al. Bc.

[2] *aestimarent*] aestimarant, Ce¹.
[3] *tunc*] om. Cd. Ce.
[4] *nundinans*] nundinatus, Bc.

Robertus cognito effugere gestiens, vix permissus est, armigero tamen cum cubiculi pannis retento. Inde raptim Rotomagum veniens, dominum suum regem Francorum, et cognatum comitem Flandrensem, de suffragio convenit; sed, nullo impetrato, ad bellum publicum venit, ultimam fortunam experturus. Qua illum infelici pede prosequente, captus, ad diem mortis[1] in libera tentus est[2] custodia, laudabili fratris pietate; quod nihil præter solitudinem passus sit[3] mali, si solitudo dici potest ubi et custodum diligentia et jocorum præterea et obsoniorum non deerat[4] frequentia. Tenebatur[5] ergo sociorum omnium viæ superstes, nec unquam usque obitum relaxatus.[6] Patria lingua facundus, ut sit jocundior nullus; in aliis consiliosus, ut nihil excellentius; militiæ peritus, ut si quis unquam; pro mollitie tamen animi nunquam regendæ reipublicæ idoneus judicatus. Veruntamen quia superius[7] dixi quæcunque noram de Hugone magno, et Blesensi et Flandrensi comitibus, non incongrue, ut opinor, quartum librum hac meta concludam.

Explicit liber Quartus Magistri Willelmi Malmesbiriensis de Gestis Regum Anglorum.

---

[1] *diem mortis*] hunc diem, Aa. Al. Ap.

[2] *tentus est*] tenetur, Aa. Ag. Al. Ap.

[3] *passus sit*] patiatur, Aa. Al.Ap.

[4] *deerat*] deest, Aah.; deesse, Ao.

[5] *Tenebatur*] Tenetur, Aa. Aah. Al. Ag. Ao. Ap. At.

[6] *nec—relaxatus*] et utrum aliquando sit exiturus vero vacillante in dubio, Aa. Aah. Ag. Al. At. Ap.

[7] *superius*] jam superius, Aa. Al.

PROLOGUS
IN LIBRUM QUINTUM.

Incipit prologus ejusdem in librum quintum.

ORDINE rerum vocante, tempus Henrici regis ingressi sumus: cujus gesta stili officio posteris tradere, majoris quam a nobis debeat exquiri[1] est operæ; nam et si sola quæ nostras aures attigerunt scripto mandarentur, cujuslibet eloquentissimi nervos fatigare, et grandia possent armaria gravare. Quis ergo conetur omnia illa consiliorum pondera, illa gestorum regalium molimina, enucleatim retexere? altioris sunt ista negotii et otiosioris animi. Vix hæc auderet vel Cicero in prosa, cujus adorat sales tota Latinitas, vel si quis versuum favore Mantuanum lacessit poetam. Adde quod, dum ambiguis relatoribus fidem detraho, homo procul ab aulicis mysteriis secretus, majora gesta ignorans, paucis manum appono. Quare verendum est, ne, dum litteræ distant ab animi voto, minor videatur cujus gesta multa prætereo. Veruntamen hujus culpæ, si culpa dicenda est, bona erit apud illum deprecatio qui meminerit me nec omnia ejus gesta potuisse nosse, nec omnia quæ noveram scriptum iri debuisse: alterum exegerit personæ meæ exilitas, alterum coactura sit lecturorum satietas. Pauca igitur rerum ejus liber hic quintus suo vendicabit gremio; cetera proculdubio et seret fama, et victura in posteros feret memoria. Nec vero a proposito priorum quatuor

---

[1] *exquiri*] om. Aa. Ag. Al. Bc. Bk. By.

degenerabit; sed quædam quæ hic et alias ejus acciderunt tempore procudet, quæ forsitan vel non scripta, vel multis sunt incognita. Occupabunt itaque ista magnam partem voluminis; præfata venia tam longarum digressionum et in hoc et in aliis.

Explicit Prologus.

WILLELMI MALMESBIRIENSIS
DE GESTIS REGUM ANGLORUM
Liber Quintus.

Incipit liber quintus de gestis Henrici Regis.

HENRICUS, junior filius Willelmi magni, natus est in Anglia anno tertio postquam pater eam adierat; infans jam tum omnium votis conspirantibus educatus egregie, quod solus omnium filiorum Willelmi natus esset regie, et ei regnum videretur competere. Itaque tirocinium rudimentorum in scholis egit litteralibus, et librorum[1] mella adeo avidis medullis indidit, ut nulli postea bellorum tumultus, nulli curarum motus, eas excutere illustri animo possent. Quamvis ipse nec multum palam legeret, nec nisi summisse cantitaret; fuerunt tamen, ut vere confirmo, litteræ, quamvis tumultuarie libatæ, magna supellex ad regnandum scientiæ, juxta illam[2] Platonis sententiam, qua dicit "Beatam esse rempublicam si vel philosophi regnarent, "vel reges philosopharentur." Philosophia ergo non adeo exiliter informatus, sensim discebat ut successu temporis provinciales mitius contineret, milites nonnisi diligentissime explorata necessitate committere sineret. Itaque pueritiam ad spem regni litteris muniebat; subinde, patre quoque audiente, jactitare proverbium solitus, "Rex illiteratus, asinus coronatus." Ferunt quinetiam genitorem, non præatereunter notata

Henry was born in 1068.

His education thorough and effective.

Use of literature in politics.

Benefit of philosophy.

---

[1] *librorum*] litterarum, Aa. Aah.; littera, Al. Ap. Bc.[2]; litteralia, Bc¹.; erasure in Bk.; litterea, At. Bq.

[2] *illam*] om. Ce¹.

His father's augury.

morum ejus compositione quibus vivacem prudentiam aleret, ab uno fratrum læsum, et lacrymantem his animasse, "Ne fleas, fili, quoniam et tu rex eris."

He is knighted at Westminster, May 24, 1086.

§ 391. Vicesimo ergo primo regni paterni anno, ætatis suæ nono decimo, in Pentecoste, apud Westmonasterium sumpsit arma a patre, cum quo tunc Normanniam navigans, non multo post præsens funeri ejus astitit, ceteris fratribus quo quemque spes tulerat dilapsis, ut superior sermo non occuluit. Quapropter paterna benedictione et materna hereditate, simul et multiplicibus thesauris nixus,[1] supercilium germanorum parum faciebat, utrique vel assistens vel adversans pro merito: inclinatior porro Roberto pro mansuetudine, ejus lenitatem suo rigore satagebat acuere. Contra, ille, noxia facilitate delatoribus credulus, fratrem immeritum injuriis vexabat, quas vel breviter taxare non erit incongruum.

His regard for his brother Robert.

Robert's harshness to him.

§ 392. Eo tempore, quo, frementibus adversus Willelmum secundum Angliæ proceribus, Robertus in Normannia ventum prosperum expectabat ad navigandum, Henricus in Britanniam ejus jussu abscesserat. Tum ille, occasione aucupata, omnem illam pecuniarum vim testamento patris adolescentulo legatam, quæ erat trium milium marcarum, in stipendiarios suos absumpsit. Id Henricus reversus, licet forsitan ægre tulisset, taciturna præteriit industria; enimvero, nuntiata pacis compositione in Anglia, deposita militia ferias armis dedere. Comes in sua, junior in ea quæ frater suus dederat vel promiserat, discessit; namque et in acceptum promissa referebat, custodiens turrim Rotomagi in ejus fidelitatem: sed delatione pessimorum cessit in adversum fidelitas, et nulla sua culpa in ipso eodem loco Henricus libere custoditus est, ne servatorum diligentiam effugio luderet. Post medium annum laxatus, fratri Willelmo invitanti serviturum se obtulit; at ille, nihilo modestius ephebum remunerans, plus

He spends Henry's fortune on his mercenaries.

He confines him at Rouen.

Henry joins William, but returns after a year's experience.

---

[1] *nixus*] nexus, Ce[1].

anno inanibus sponsionibus egentem distulit. Quapropter, Roberto emendationem facti per nuntios promittente, Normanniam venit, amborum fratrum expertus insidias. Nam et rex, pro repulsa iratus, ut retineretur frustra mandarat; et comes accusatorum lenociniis mutatus, voluntatem verterat, ut blanditiis attrectatum non ita facile dimitteret. Verum ille, Dei providentia et sagaci sua diligentia, cuncta evadens pericula, occupatione Abrincarum et quorundam castellorum coegit fratrem libenter paci manum dedere. Nec multo post, Willelmo veniente in Normanniam ut se de fratre Roberto ulcisceretur, comiti obsequelam suam exhibuit, Rotomagi positus. Denique regios eo interdiu venientes, qui dolo civium totam jampridem occupaverant urbem, probe expulit, admonito per nuntios comite ut ille a fronte propelleret quos ipse a tergo urgeret. Unde factum est, ut Conanum quendam, proditionis apud comitem insimulatum, quem ille vinculis irretire volebat, arbitratus nihil calamitosius posse inferri misero quam ut exosum spiritum in ergastulo traheret,—hunc ergo Conanum Henricus suæ curæ servatum iri postulavit. Quo concesso, in superiora Rotomagensis turris duxit; jussoque ut late circumposita diligenter ex arcis edito specularetur, sua per ironiam omnia futura pronuntians, inopinum ex propugnaculo deturbans in subjectum Sequanam præcipitavit, comitibus qui secum aderant pariter impellentibus: protestatus, nullam vitæ moram deberi traditori; quoquo modo alieni hominis posse tolerari injurias, illius vero, qui tibi juratus fecerit hominium, nullo modo posse[1] differri supplicium si fuerit probatus perfidiæ. Parum hic labor apud Robertum valuit, virum animi mobilis; qui, statim ad ingratitudinem flexus, bene meritum urbe cedere coegit. Illud fuit tempus quo, ut supra lectum est, apud montem sancti

---

[1] *posse*] om. Cc.

Michaelis ambobus fratribus Henricus pro sui salute, simul et gloria, restitit. Ita, cum utrique germano fuerit fidelis et efficax, illi, nullis adolescentem possessionibus dignati, ad majorem prudentiam ævi processu penuria victualium informabant.[1]

§ 393. Occiso vero rege Willelmo, ut supra dictum est, post justa funeri regio persoluta, in regem electus est, aliquantis tamen ante controversiis inter proceres agitatis atque sopitis; annitente maxime comite Warwicensi Henrico, viro integro et sancto, cujus familiari jamdudum usus fuerat contubernio. Itaque, edicto statim per Angliam misso, injustitias a fratre et Rannulfo institutas prohibuit, pensionum et vinculorum gratiam fecit: effœminatos curia propellens, lucernarum usum noctibus in curia restituit, qui fuerat tempore fratris intermissus; antiquarum moderationem legum revocavit in solidum, sacramento suo et omnium procerum, ne luderentur, corroborans. Lætus ergo dies visus est revirescere populis, cum, post tot anxietatum nubila, serenarum promissionum infulgebant lumina. Et ne quid profecto gaudio accumulato abesset, Rannulfo nequitiarum fæce tenebris ergastularibus incluso, propter Anselmum pernicibus nuntiis directum. Quapropter, certatim[2] plausu plebeio concrepante, in regem coronatus est Londoniæ nonis Augustis, quarto post obitum fratris die. Hæc eo studiosius celebrabantur, ne mentes procerum electionis quassarentur pœnitudine, quod ferebatur rumor Robertum Normanniæ comitem ex Apulia adventantem jam jamque affore. Nec multo post, suadentibus amicis, ac maxime pontificibus, ut, remota voluptate pellicum, legitimum amplecteretur connubium, die sancti Martini accepit Mathildem filiam Malcolmi regis Scottorum; cujus amori jampridem animum impulerat, parvi pendens dotales divitias, dummodo diu cupitis potiretur amplexibus. Erat enim illa, licet genere sublimis, utpote regis Edwardi

---

[1] *informabant*] reformabant, Ce¹. | [2] *certatim*] statim, Aa. Ag. Al. Bk.

ex fratre Edmundo abneptis, modicæ tamen domina supellectilis, utroque tunc parente pupilla: de qua posterius uberior erit narrandi materia.

§ 394. Robertus interea, Normanniam veniens, comitatum suum obsistente nullo recepit: quo audito, omnes pene hujus terræ optimates fidei regi juratæ transfugæ fuere; quidam nullis extantibus causis, quidam levibus occasiunculis emendicatis, quod nollet eis terras quas vellent ultro pro libito eorum impertiri. Soli Robertus filius Haimonis, Ricardus de Retvers, et Rogerius Bigot, et Robertus comes de Mellento, cum fratre Henrico, justas partes fovebant. Ceterum, omnes vel clam pro Roberto, ut rex fieret, mittere, vel palam contumeliis dominum inurere; Godricum eum, et comparem Godgivam, appellantes. Audiebat hæc ille, et formidabiles cachinnos iram differens ejiciebat; stultitias fatuorum insania objectas artificioso silentio dissolvens, blandus odii dissimulator, sed pro tempore immodicus retributor. Accessit temporum turbini versutia Rannulfi; namque ille, sollicitato per nuntios dapifero suo, funem afferri sibi impetravit: funem minister aquæ bajulus, proh dolus,[1] amphora immersum detulit; quo ille muro turris demissus, si læsit brachia, si excoriavit manus, parum curat populus. Inde Normanniam evadens, comiti jam anhelanti, et in fervorem prælii prono, addidit calcaria ut incunctanter veniret.

§ 395. Secundo ergo Henrici anno, mense Augusto, allitans[2] apud Portesmuthe, copias suas in omnem regionem exposuit, effudit, objecit. Nec vero rex segnitiei deditus fuit, sed innumeram e regione manum traxit,[3] dignitatem suam, si necesse foret, asserturus: nam, licet principibus deficientibus, partes ejus solidæ manebant; quas Anselmi archiepiscopi, cum episcopis[4]

---

[1] *dolus*] dolor, Bc. Bk.
[2] *allitans*] applicans, Aa.
[3] *traxit*] contraxit, Aa. Ag. Al. Bc. Bk. Cd.
[4] *episcopis*] coepiscopis, Aa. Al.

suis, simul et omnium Anglorum tutabatur favor. Quapropter ipse provincialium fidei gratus, et saluti providus, plerumque cuneos circuiens, docebat quomodo, militum ferociam eludentes, clypeos objectarent et ictus remitterent; quo effecit ut ultroneis votis pugnam deposcerent, in nullo Normannos metuentes. Sed satagentibus sanioris consilii hominibus, qui dicerent pietatis jus violandum si fraterna necessitudo praelio concurreret, paci animos accommodavere; reputantes quod, si alter occumberet, alter infirmior remaneret, cum nullus fratrum praeter ipsos superesset. Sed et trium milium marcarum promissio lenem comitis fallebat credulitatem, ut, procinctu soluto, de tanta pecunia menti blandiretur suae, quam ille posteriori statim anno voluntati reginae libens, quod illa peteret, condonavit.

§ 396. Posteriori anno rebellavit Robertus de Belesmo, major filiorum Rogerii de Monte Gomerico, obfirmans contra regem castella Brigas et Arundellum; comportatum eo frumentum ex omni regione Scrobesberiae, et quicquid necessarium bellum efflagitat diuturnum: nec minus castellum Scrobesberiense rebellioni consensit, Wallensibus pro motu fortunae ad malum pronis. Rex itaque animo ingens, omniaque adversa virtute premens, militia coacta Brigas obsedit, unde jam in Arundellum transierat Robertus, alimentorum copia et militum ferocia satis abundeque munitum locum praesumens; sed paucos post dies oppidani, et formidine conscientiae et fortitudine militiae regiae flexi, se dedidere. Quo audito, ab incepto tumore Arundellum destitit, regali se addicens clientelae; egregia sane conditione, ut dominus suus integra membrorum salute Normanniam permitteretur abire. Porro Scrobesberienses per Radulfum tum abbatem Sagii, postea Cantuariae archiepiscopum, regi misere castelli claves, deditionis praesentis indices, futurae devotionis obsides. Ita dissensionis incendium, quod putabatur fore magnum, paucissimis diebus in cineres consenuit; et desertorum, semper novis rebus inhiantium, aviditatem coercuit. Robertus, cum fratribus Ernulfo, qui paternum cognomen sortitus fuerat, et Rogerio Pictavensi, quod ex ea regione uxorem acceperat sic dicto, Angliam perpetuo abjuravit; sed vigorem sacramenti temperavit adjectio, nisi regi placito quandoque satisfecisset obsequio.

Robert and his brothers are banished.

§ 397. Tunc fax bellorum immissa Normanniæ, perfidorum admixtione, quasi rogalibus alimentis animata, convaluit, circumquaque posita corripiens. Est enim Normannia opportuna et patiens malorum nutricula, quamvis non multo tractu regionum diffusa; itaque diu seditiones intestinas probe tolerat, et pace reddita in fœcundiorem statum mature resurgit, turbatores suos illius provinciæ diffisos cum libuerit in Franciam liberis anfractibus emittens. Contra Anglia nec diu infestos patitur, sed semel intra sinum suum receptos vel dedit, vel exstinguit; nec, populatibus attrita, redivivum cito caput attollit. Quocirca Normanniam Belesmitanus veniens, et tunc et deinceps habuit malignitatis suæ complices, et, ne parum videretur, illices. In his erat Willelmus comes Moretolii, filius Roberti, regis patrui. Is semper a puero Henrici gloriæ invidus, tum maxime in adventu Normanni pravum animum extulit: non enim contentus duobus comitatibus, Moretolii in Normannia, Cornugalliæ in Anglia, comitatum Cantiæ, quem Odo patruus habuerat, a rege exigebat; infestus et improbus adeo, ut infami arrogantia se devotaret non induturum chlamydem nisi a patruo, ut dictitabat, sibi refusam consequeretur hereditatem. Sed tunc quidem, suspensi calliditate responsi, frustratus est rex prudentissimus hominem: discussis vero turbinibus, serenoque pacis reddito, non solum quæ petebat non annuit, verumetiam indebite retenta repetere cœpit; modeste tamen et judiciali placito, ut nihil quod faceret videretur resultare juri et calcitrare ab æquo. Tunc vero Willelmus,

The struggle revives in Normandy.

Comparison of England and Normandy.

Allies of Robert of Belesme; the count of Mortain is chief.

Reasons for his hostility.

He attacks the earl of Chester, a ward of the king.

sententia judicii expunctus, indignabundus et fremens Normanniam abiit: ibi, præter assultus quos regiis castellis irritus fecerat, in Ricardum quoque comitem Cestrensem, Hugonis filium, debacchatus, nonulla partibus ejus appenditia invasit, carpsit, abrasit. Erat ille tunc pro ætate parvulus, et regis fidei tutelæque accommodatus.

Duke Robert temporizes.

§ 398. Hi ergo duo, factionum capita, rebellionum incentiva, cum aliis quos nominare pudet, patriam populationibus late contristabant. Consumebanturque frequentes sed cassæ apud comitem querelæ provincialium de violentia clamantium: movebatur his ille; sed rebus suis timens, ne exacerbati ejus interpolarent otium, dissimulabat. At vero rex Henricus, pro fratris infamia, quam cumulabat patriæ miseria, dolorem

Henry urges him to stronger measures.

transeunter ferre nequibat: crudele et a boni principis officio longe esse permensus, quod impii homines pauperum fortunis ingluviem suam urgebant. Itaque fratrem ad se accitum in Angliam semel blande verbis, post vero in Normanniam veniens non semel dure bellis, admonuit ut comitem, non monachum, ageret; nam et incentori Willelmo omnia quæ habebat in Anglia abstulit, castella ad solum complanavit. Sed cum ad pacem nihil promoveret, diu deliberatione consilii regia sublimitas curis pectus exercuit, utrum fraternæ necessitudinis oblitus patriam discrimini eriperet, an indiscreta pietate fluctuare permitteret: et profecto commune commodum et pietas, privatæ necessitudinis intuitu, terga dedissent, nisi, ut aiunt,

Henry consults pope Paschal II.

Paschalis apostolicus dubitantem ad hoc opus epistolis impelleret; asseverans, facundia qua vigebat, non fore civile bellum, sed præclare patriæ prædicandum emo-

He overruns Normandy.

lumentum. Itaque Normanniam veniens brevi totam cepit, vel potius recepit, omnibus ad ejus dominium confluentibus, ut fessæ provinciæ, vigore quo pollebat, consuleret. Non tamen sine sanguine tantam victoriam consummans, multos ex carissimis amisit: inter quos

Rogerium de Glocestra, probatum militem, in obsessione Falesii arcubalistæ jactu in capite percussum ;[1] præterea Robertum filium Hamonis, qui conto ictus tempora, hebetatusque ingenio, non pauco [2] tempore quasi captus mente supervixit. Merito mulctatum ferunt, quod, ejus liberandi causa, rex Henricus Bajocas civitatem cum principali ecclesia ignibus absumpserit: sed utrique, ut speramus, purgabile fuit; nam et detrimenta ecclesiæ rex mirifice resarcivit, et Robertus monasterium Theochesberiæ suo favore non facile memoratu quantum exaltavit, ubi et ædificiorum decor, et monachorum caritas, adventantium rapit oculos et allicit animos. Horum dispendium ut fortuna sarciret, summam manum ingruente bello imposuit; venientemque contra se cum non contempnenda manu fratrem, et Willelmum comitem Moretolii, et Robertum Belesmi, ditioni ejus facili opera contradidit. Hoc bellum actum est apud Tenerchebrei, castellum comitis Moritoliensis, Sabbato in sancti Michaelis vigilia. Idem dies ante quadraginta circiter annos fuerat, cum Willelmus Hastingas primus appulit; provido forsitan Dei judicio, ut eo die subderetur Angliæ Normannia, quo ad eam subjugandam olim venerat Normannorum copia. Captus est ibi comes Moretolii, qui eo venerat studiosam sui operam oppidanis pollicitus, simul et injurias suas ultum iri sperans; sed, ut dixi, prensus,[3] squaloris carcerei tota vita accolatum accepit: vivacitate mentis et alacritate juventutis nonnihil laudandus, sed pro perfidia finem asperum emeritus. Et tunc quidem Belesmensis in ipso belli exordio mortem cavit effugio; sed dum postmodum clandestinis factionibus regem irritasset, et ipse captus ceterorum involutus est periculo, ad mortem perpetuo inclusus ergastulo. Vir pro incompositis moribus intolerabilis,[4] et in aliorum delicta

---

[1] *Non—percussum*] For the passage inserted here in Ms. Cs., see below, p. 521.
[2] *pauco*] parvo, Ce¹.
[3] *prensus*] pressus, Bc. Cd.
[4] *intolerabilis*] om. Bc. Cd. Ce. By.

inexorabilis; præterea sævitia notabilis, cum in aliis tum in hoc, quod puerulum ex baptismo filiolum, quem in obsidatum acceperat, pro modico delicto patris excæcarit, lumina miselli unguibus nefandis abrumpens: simulationis et argutiarum plenus, frontis sereno et sermonum affabilitate credulos decipiens, gnaros autem malitiæ exterritans, ut nullum esset majus futuræ calamitatis indicium quam prætensæ affabilitatis eloquium.

§ 399. Ita rex clarus, successibus ovans, regnum regressus est; composita pace in Normannia, qualem nulla ætas meminit, qualem nec ipse pater, magno illo rerum et verborum fastu,[1] unquam efficere potuit. In ceteris quoque genitoris æmulus, rapinas curialium, furta, stupra, edicto compescuit; deprehensis oculos cum testibus[2] evelli præcipiens. Contra trapezetas, quos vulgo monetarios vocant, præcipuam sui diligentiam exhibuit; nullum falsarium, quin pugnum perderet, impune abire permittens, qui fuisset intellectus falsitatis suæ commercio fatuos irrisisse.

§ 400. Scottorum reges lenitate sua palpavit, morem fratris æmulatus: siquidem ille Dunecanum, filium Malcolmi nothum, et militem fecit, et regem Scottorum mortuo patre constituit; sed eo patrui Duvenaldi fraude interempto, Edgarum in regnum promovit, præfato Duvenaldo astutia David junioris et viribus Willelmi extincto. Edgaro fatali sorte occumbente, Alexandrum successorem Henricus affinitate detinuit, data ei in conjugium filia notha; de qua ille viva nec sobolem, quod sciam, tulit, nec ante se mortuam multum suspiravit: defuerat enim fœminæ, ut fertur, quod desideraretur, vel in morum modestia, vel in corporis elegantia. Alexandro majoribus suis apposito, David minor[3] filiorum Malcolmi, quem rex comitem fecerat et connubio insignis fœminæ donaverat, solium Scottorum ascendit: juvenis ceteris curialior, et qui,

---

[1] *fastu*] roncho, Aa. Al.
[2] *testibus*] testiculis, Aa. Al.
[3] *minor*] junior, Aa. Al.

nostrorum convictu et familiaritate limatus a puero, omnem rubiginem Scotticæ barbariei deterserat; denique regno potitus mox omnes compatriotas triennalium tributorum[1] pensione levavit, qui vellent habitare cultius, amiciri elegantius, pasci accuratius. Neque vero unquam in acta historiarum relatum est tantæ sanctitatis tres fuisse pariter reges et fratres, maternæ pietatis nectar redolentes; namque præter victus parcitatem, eleemosynarum copiam, orationum assiduitatem, ita domesticum regibus vitium evicerunt, ut nunquam feratur in eorum thalamos nisi legitimas uxores isse, nec eorum quenquam pellicatu aliquo pudicitiam contristasse. Solus fuit Edmundus Margaretæ filius a bono degener; qui, Duvenaldi patrui nequitiæ particeps, fraternæ non inscius necis fuerit, pactus scilicet regni dimidium: sed captus, et perpetuis compedibus detentus, ingenue pœnituit; et, ad mortem veniens, cum ipsis vinculis se tumulari mandavit, professus se plexum merito pro fratricidii delicto.

§ 401. Walenses rex Henricus, semper in rebellionem surgentes, crebris expeditionibus in deditionem premebat; consilioque salubri nixus, ut eorum tumorem extenuaret, Flandrenses omnes Angliæ accolas eo traduxit. Plures enim, qui tempore patris pro materna cognatione confluxerant, occultabat Anglia, adeo ut ipsi regno pro multitudine onerosi viderentur; quapropter[2] cum substantiis et necessitudinibus apud Ros, provinciam Walliarum, velut in sentinam congessit, ut et regnum defæcaret, et hostium brutam temeritatem retunderet. Nec eo secius illuc expeditionem pro temporum opportunitate dirigebat; in quarum una, incertum cujus audacia eminus insidianti arundine impetitus probe et pulchre evasit, fideliter hamatæ thoracis adjutus beneficio, et simul perfidiam frustrante Dei consilio. Sed nec tunc auctor teli eminuit, nec unquam

---

[1] *tributorum*] cubitorum, Bc.   [2] *quapropter*] omnes, ins. Aa. Al.

postea investigari valuit, quamvis ille statim non haesitasset dicere, sagittam non a quolibet Walensi, sed a provinciali emissam, "per mortem Domini nos-" tri," talia pronuntians: quem morem jurandi, vel irae nimietas, vel rei serietas, ab ore principis extorquebat; nam et ea hora in proprio solo, non in hostica regione, progrediebatur sensim et caute exercitus, ut nihil minus quam insidias quis opinari possit. Nec tamen, intestini discriminis metu, pedem ab incepto retulit, donec Walenses, datis obsidibus nobilium suorum filiis, cum aliquanta pecunia et multo peculio, regiae magnanimitatis motum sedarent.

§ 402. Britones transmarinos, quos adolescens vicinos castellis[1] Danfronto et[2] Sancti Michaelis habuerat, pecuniis ad obsequium transducebat. Est enim illud genus hominum egens in patria, aliasque externo aere laboriosae vitae mercatur stipendia: si dederis, nec civilia, sine respectu juris et cognationis, detrectans proelia; sed pro quantitate munerum ad quascunque voles partes obnoxium. Hujus consuetudinis ille non inscius, si quando opus habuisset stipendiariis militibus, multa perdebat in Britones, fidem perfidae nationis nummis suis mutuatus.[3]

§ 403. Robertum comitem Flandriae primis regni sui temporibus offendit hac causa: Baldewinus senior, hujus Roberti avus, Willelmum in Angliam venientem, arguto quo pollebat consilio, et militum additamento, vivaciter juverat. His ille illustres crebro retributiones refuderat, omnibus, ut ferunt, annis trecentas argenti marcas pro fide et affinitate socero annumerans. Ea munificentia, in filio Baldewino non imminuta, haesit in Roberti Frisonis malitia, quam superior non praeteriit sermo. Porro iste Robertus, Frisonis filius, omissum munus a Willelmo secundo non difficulter impetraverat; quod et is cognationem

---

[1] *castellis*] suis, add. Aa. Al.
[2] *et*] Monti, ins. Aa. Al.
[3] *mutuatus*] mutuans, Ce¹.

prætenderet, et ille invictum animum in spargenda pecunia haberet. Verum Henricus majori pondere rem ventilans, ut nec indebite adunaret pecunias, nec nisi debite dilapidaret habitas, Roberto ab Jerosolima reverso, et quasi pro imperio trecentas argenti marcas exigenti, in hanc respondit sententiam: Non solitos reges Angliæ Flandritis vectigal pendere, nec se velle libertatem majorum macula suæ timiditatis fuscare: quapropter, si suo committat arbitrio, libenter se quod opportunitas siverit ut cognato et amico dare; si vero in exactione permanendum putaverit, omnino negare. Hac ille ratione dejectus, animum multo tempore in regem tumuit: sed, parum aut nihil simultatibus adjutus, mansuetudini mentem accommodavit, expertus regem posse flecti precario, non fastu tyrannico. Jam vero Baldewino filio ejus varietas temporum causas irarum in regem dedit: siquidem Willelmum filium Roberti Normanni volens hereditati intrudere, alienis se sponte negotiis immiscuit, crebroque castella regis in Normannia inopinatis fatigabat assultibus; magnum incommodum, si fata sivissent, terræ minatus: sed apud Archas majori manu militum quam timebat exceptus mortem maturavit, crebris ictibus galea quassata cerebrum violatus. Causam ferunt morbi augmentati, quod ea die allium cum auca præsumpserit, nec nocte Venere abstinuerit. Hic intuebuntur posteri eximium regalis pietatis exemplum, quod medicum peritissimum decumbenti miserit; illacrymatus, si credimus, morbo perire, quem pro admiratione fortitudinis salvari maluisset. Successor ejus Carolus nulla molestia vires regis inquietavit: primo fœdere suspenso, mox etiam consummato,[1] amicitiam ejus amplexus.

§ 404. Philippus rex Francorum regi nostro nec utilis[2] nec infestus fuit, propterea quod esset ventri magis quam negotiis deditus, nec præterea in castellis

---

[1] *consummato*] confirmato, Aa. Al. By.
[2] *utilis*] inutilis, Cc[1].

ejus collimitaneus; pauca enim, quæ tunc habebat in Normannia, magis Britanniæ quam Franciæ vicina erant: adde quod, ut superius dixi, Philippus accedente senio, libidine gravis, comitissæque Andegavensis specie lusus, illicitis ardoribus defæneratus famulabatur. Quocirca ab apostolico excommunicatus, cum in villa qua mansitabat nihil divini servitii fieret, sed, discedente eo, tinnitus signorum undique concreparent, insulsam fatuitatem cachinnis exprimebat; "Audis," inquiens, "bella quomodo nos effugant!" Adeo erat omnibus episcopis provinciæ suæ derisui, ut nullus eos desponsaret præter Willelmum archiepiscopum Rotomagensem; cujus facti temeritatem luit multis annis interdictus, et vix tandem aliquando per Anselmum archiepiscopum apostolicæ communioni redditus. Philippo interea nulla mora insanæ temulentiæ satietatem fecit, nisi quod, in extremo vitæ tactus morbo, monachicum apud Floriacum accepit habitum: pulchrius et fortunatius illa, quod ætate et sanitate integra, nec specie rugata, apud Fontem Evraldi sanctimonialium appetiit velum; nec multo post præsenti vitæ valefecit, Deo forsitan providente non posse delicatæ mulieris corpus religionis laboribus inservire.[1]

§ 405. At vero Lodowicus filius Philippi varium se præstitit, in neutra parte bene constans. Primo enim tempore plurimus in fratrem irarum auctor Henrico ad capiendam Normanniam fuit, corruptus videlicet Anglorum spoliis et multo regis obryzo. Non quod ille obtulerit, sed quod alter invitaverit, ultro adhortans ne clarissimæ olim patriæ nervos dissimulatione sua succidi sineret. Postea vero simultas inter eos exorta est pro Thetbaldo comite Blesensi, filio Stephani qui apud Ramulam occubuit, quod Thetbaldus susceptus esset Stephano ex Adala filia Willelmi magni. Diu igitur ex parte regis nostri labores viarum con-

---

[1] *inservire*] deservire, By.

sumpserunt nuntii, ut dignaretur Lodowicus satisfactionem Thetbaldi. Ille vero, parvi faciens preces Thetbaldum ab apostolico denotari[1] fecit quasi arrogantem et Deo rebellem; qui præter austeritatem morum, quæ omnibus videbatur intolerabilis, ferebatur dominum suum privare avitis possessionibus. Itaque diu[2] productis inimicitiis, cum uterque grossum tumeret, nec alter alteri pro[3] persona cederet, Lodowicus Normanniam venit, inflatiori anhelitu late omnia exhauriens. Nuntiabantur hæc regi, qui apud Rotomagum se continebat, adeo ut[4] vulgus militum aures ejus infestaret; pateretur repelli Lodowicum, hominem aqualiculi pondere olim lectum foventem, sed nunc pro dissimulatione minis auras onerantem. Ille, paterni memor exempli, fatuitatem Franci patientia extundere, quam viribus repellere, malebat. Quinetiam milites benigne appellando hac ratione mulcebat: Non debere illos[5] mirari si sanguinis eorum prodigus esse caveret, quos sibi fideles non modicis experimentis approbasset; impium essse, ut, ad regnum sibi parandum, eorum glorietur mortibus, qui vitam suam pro ejus salute ultroneis devoveant certaminibus: illos regni sui nutritos, pietatis alumpnos; quapropter boni principis se velle sequi exemplum, ut modestia sua eorum remoretur impetum, quos ita paratos pro se videat ad moriendum. Postremo, cum videret prudentiam suam sinistra interpretatione turbari et ignaviam vocari, in tantum ut Lodowicus prope Rotomagum quatuor miliariis ignes faceret, prædas ageret, majori fortitudine vim animi concussit, et procinctu parato vicit egregie, præteritas dissimulationes feroci puniens victoria. Veruntamen aliquanto post pax parta est; quia et rerum[6] omnium est vicissitudo, et nummi quaslibet injurias levant, ad

---

[1] *denotari*] devotari, Aa. Al. Bc. Cc.
[2] *diu*] om. Cc¹.
[3] *pro*] om. Cc¹.
[4] *ut*] om. Cc². Ag. At.; ad, Bc.
[5] *illos*] eos, Bc.
[6] *rerum*] om. Cc¹.

His son William does homage to Lewis and marries.

persuadendum quod intendunt potentes. Quare Wil- lelmus, filius regis nostri, homagium regi Francorum de Normannia fecit, jure legitimo de eo provinciam[1] cogniturus. Illud fuit tempus quo idem puer filiam Fulconis comitis Andegavensis despondit, et accepit; patris prudentia satagente, ut hinc pecunia, hinc affinitate mediante, nihil contra filium turbaretur.

Intercourse of Henry with Pope Calixtus. (A.D. 1119.)

§ 406. His diebus Calixtus papa, de quo posterius dicam plura, præsentiam suam prope Normanniam exhibuit: cujus colloquio potitus, rex Angliæ Romanos prudentiam Normannorum mirari et prædicare coegit. Namque ille, ut fertur, infesto venerat animo, ut cum asperius conveniret quare fratrem et sancti Sepulcri peregrinum in captione teneret; sed responso principis, quod erat simile veri, et probabilibus argumentis perstrictus, parum contra retulit. Possunt enim communes loci ad quamlibet partem inflecti pro facundia oratoris, præsertim cum non contempnatur eloquentia

A display of Norman cleverness before the cardinals.

quam pretiosa condiunt xenia. Et ut nihil cumulatæ pompæ deesset, adolescentulos clarissimi generis, filios comitis de Mellento, ut contra cardinales de dialectica disputarent, subornavit: quorum tortilibus sophismatibus cum[2] vivacitate rationum obsisti nequiret, non puduit cardinales confiteri, majori occiduas plagas florere litterarum peritia quam ipsi audissent vel putassent in patria. Itaque hæc collocutio hunc finem emeruit, ut pronuntiaret apostolicus nihil Anglorum regis causa justius, prudentia eminentius, facundia uberius.

Account of Robert of Beaumont count of Meulan.

§ 407. Horum puerorum pater erat comes de Mellento Robertus, ut dixi, filius Rogerii de Bello Monte qui Pratellum cœnobium Normanniæ construxit: homo antiquæ simplicitatis et fidei, qui, crebro a Willelmo primo invitatus ut Angliam veniret, largis ad voluntatem possessionibus munerandus, supersedit; pronuntians patrum suorum hereditatem se velle fovere, non

---

[1] *de eo provinciam*] om. Ce¹. | [2] *cum*] pro, ins. Aa. Al.

transmarinas et indebitas possessiones vel appetere vel invadere. Hic duos filios habuit: Robertum istum, et Henricum. Henricus comes Warwicensis, dulcis et quieti animi vir, congruo suis moribus studio vitam egit et clausit. Alter, astutior et pronioris ad versutiam cordis, præter paternam hereditatem in Normannia et ingentia prædia in Anglia, castellum, quod matris suæ frater Hugo filius Gualeranni tenuerat, Mellentum nomine, a rege Franciæn nundinatus est pecunia. Qui cum superiorum regum tempore, spe sensim pullulante, in gloriam procederet, hujus ætate summo provectu effloruit; habebaturque ejus consilium quasi quis divinum consuluisset sacrarium. Jamque non immerito assecutus æstimabatur quod esset ævi maturus ad consulendum, suasor concordiæ, dissuasor discordiæ, et prorsus ad quod intenderet, pro viribus eloquentiæ, citissimus persuasor. Ingentis in Anglia momenti, ut inveteratum vestiendi vel comedendi exemplo suo inverteret morem. Denique consuetudo semel prandendi in omnium optimatum curiis per eum frequentatur, quam ipse causa bonæ valitudinis acceptam nuntiis[1] a Constantinopolitano imperatore Alexio, suo, ut dixi, ceteris refudit exemplo. Quod tamen magis parcitate dapsilitatis fecisse et docuisse, quam timore cruditatis et indigeriei, immerito culpatur; quia nemo eo, ut fertur, in dapibus aliis sumptuosior, vel sibi moderatior fuit. In placitis propugnator justitiæ, in guerris provisor victoriæ: dominum regem ad severitatem legum custodiendam exacuens, ipse non eas sequens, sed proponens: expers in regem[2] perfidiæ, in ceteros ejus persecutor.

§ 408. Habebat præterea rex Henricus episcopum Salesberiensem Rogerium a secretis, cujus maxime nitebatur consilio, nam et ante regnum omnibus suis præfecerat rex; primum cancellarium, mox episcopum

---

[1] *nuntiis*] om. Ce¹.
[2] *regem*] reges, Aa. Al. Bc. By. Cc². Cs.; rege, Cd.

constituerat, prudentiam viri expertus. Sollerter administrati episcopatus officium spem infudit quod majori dignus haberetur munere; itaque totius regni moderamen illius delegavit justitiæ, sive ipse adesset Angliæ, sive moraretur Normanniæ. Refugit episcopus tantis se curis involvere, nisi tres archiepiscopi Cantuarienses, Anselmus, Radulfus, Willelmus, et postremo papa, injunxissent ei munus obedientiæ. Sategit ita fieri Henricus, non nescius quod fideliter sua tractaret commoda Rogerius: nec defuit ille spei regiæ; sed tanta integritate, tanta se agebat industria, ut nulla contra eum conflaretur invidia. Denique rex plerumque triennio, nonnunquam quadriennio, et eo amplius, in Normannia moratus, cum in regnum reverteretur, deputabat justitiarii modestiæ quod nihil aut parum inveniebat molestiæ. Inter hæc, ecclesiastica officia non negligere, sed cotidie mane omnia honeste persolvere, ut expeditius et tutius ceteris posset accedere. Pontifex magnanimus, et nullis unquam parcens sumptibus, dum quæ facienda proponeret, ædificia præsertim, consummaret: quod cum alias, tum maxime in Salesberia et Malmesberia[1] est videre. Fecit enim ibi ædificia spatio diffusa, numero pecuniarum sumptuosa, specie formosissima; ita juste composito ordine lapidum, ut junctura perstringat intuitum, et totam maceriam unum mentiatur esse saxum. Ecclesiam Salesberiensem et novam fecit et ornamentis excoluit, ut nulli in Anglia cedat, sed multas præcedat; ipseque non falso possit dicere Deo, "Domine dilexi Ps. xxvi. s. "decorem domus tuæ."

§ 409. Hibernensium regem Murcardum, et successores ejus, quorum nomina fama non extulit, ita devotos habuit noster Henricus, ut nihil nisi quod eum palparet scriberent, nihil nisi quod juberet agerent: quamvis feratur Murcardus, nescio qua de causa,

---

[1] *et Malmesberia*] om. Aa. Aah. Ag. Ap. At.

paucis diebus inflatius in Anglos egisse; sed mox, pro interdicto navigio et mercimonio navigantium, tumorem pectoris sedasse. Quanti enim valeret Hibernia si non adnavigarent merces ex Anglia? Ita pro penuria, immo pro inscientia cultorum, jejunum omnium bonorum solum, agrestem et squalidam multitudinem Hibernensium extra urbes producit: Angli vero et Franci, cultiori genere vitæ, urbes nundinarum commercio inhabitant. Paulus Orcadum comes, quamvis Noricorum regi hereditario jure subjectus, ita regis amicitias suspiciebat ut crebra ei munuscula missitaret: nam et ille prona voluptate exterarum terrarum miracula inhiabat, leones, leopardos, lynces, camelos, quorum fœtus Anglia est inops, grandi, ut dixi, jocunditate a regibus alienis expostulans: habebatque conseptum quod Wudestoche dicitur, in quo delicias talium rerum confovebat. Posueratque ibi animal quod hystrix[1] vocatur, missum sibi a Willelmo de Monte Pislerio; de quo animali Plinius secundus in octavo Naturalis Historiæ libro, et Isidorus de Etymologiis, memorant, esse animal in Affrica, quod Affri ericii genus dicunt, coopertum hispidis setis, quas in canes insectantes naturaliter emittat. Sunt enim[2] setæ,[3] ut vidi, palmo et plus longæ, in utraque summitate acutæ; similes pennis aucarum ubi desinunt plumæ, sed paulo plus grossæ; nigro et albo quasi intertinctæ.

§ 410. Illud præter cetera Henricum insigniebat, quod quamvis pro tumultibus Normannicis sæpe et diu regno suo deesset, ita timore suo rebelles frænabat, ut nihil pacis in Anglia desiderares; quocirca etiam exteræ gentes illuc, velut ad unicum tutæ quietis portum, libenter appellebant. Denique Siwardus rex Noricorum, primo ævi processu fortissimis conferendus,

---

[1] *hystrix*] strix, Ag. Al. Ap. Bc. Cc.; stryx, Aa.
[2] *enim*] vero, Aa. Al. Bc. By. Cd. Ce¹.
[3] *setæ*] illæ, ins. Cc².

Visit of Sigurd, king of Norway, on his way to the Crusade.

incepto itinere Jerosolimitano, rogataque regis pace, in Anglia tota resedit hyeme; plurimoque per ecclesias auro expenso, mox, ut Favonius ad serenitatem pelagi vernales portas aperuit, naves repetiit; provectusque in altum, Baleares[1] insulas, quæ Majorica et Minorica dicuntur, armis territas,[2] faciliores ad subigendum præfato Willelmo de Monte Pislerio reliquit. Inde pertendit Jerosolimam, navibus omnibus incolumibus præter unam; quæ, dum retinacula a portu solvere tardat, absorpta

Loss of one ship in the Race of Alderney.

est immani voragine quam inter Sequanica et Aquitanica littora esse Paulus historicus Longobardorum asseverat, tanto undarum impetu ut ad triginta miliaria garrulitas discernatur aquarum. Jerosolimam

Paul. Diac. Hist. Lang. l. c. 6.

Sigurd subdues the coast of Palestine.

veniens, Tyrum et Sidonem, urbes quas mare allambit, ad Christianitatis gratiam obsedit, effregit, subegit. Mutato itinere Constantinopolim ingressus, navem au-

His offering at S. Sophia, Constantinople.

reis rostratam draconibus fastigio sanctæ Sophiæ pro trophæo affixit. Hominibus suis in eadem urbe[3] catervatim morientibus remedium excogitavit, ut reliqui parcius et aqua mixtum vinum biberent: ingenii[4] acrimonia, ut, porcino jecore mero injecto, moxque pro

His medical practice.

asperitate liquoris resoluto, idem in hominibus fieri primo præsagiret; post etiam, quodam defuncto exenterato, visu addisceret. Quare contuitu prudentiæ et fortitudinis quæ grande quid pollicebantur, imperatore illum retinere temptante, spem ejus, qua jam aurum

He overreaches the emperor.

Noricum devorabat, pulchre cassavit; impetrata ad proximam urbem licentia, cistas thesaurorum, plumbo impletas et obsignatas, apud eum deponens, quasi citissimi reditus vades. Ita ille illusus est; alter pedes domum contendit.

§ 411. Sed enim ut ad Henricum regrediatur oratio. Erat ille in rebus suis providendo efficax, defendendo pertinax: bellorum quatenus posset cum honestate

Character of Henry I.

repressor; cum vero decrevisset non pati, impatiendus

---

[1] *Baleares*] Balcarum, Ce¹.
[2] *territas*] territans, Aa. Ap.
[3] *in eadem urbe*] om. Ce¹.
[4] *ingenii*] ingenti ingenii, Aa. Al.

injuriarum exactor, obvia pericula virtutis umbone decutiens. Odii et amicitiæ in quemlibet tenax; in altero nimio irarum æstui, in altero regiæ magnanimitati, satisfaciens; hostes videlicet ad miseriam deprimens, amicos et clientes ad invidiam efferens: nam et hanc curam vel primam vel maximam boni principis philosophia proponit, ut parcat subjectis, et debellet superbos. Justitiæ rigore inflexibilis, provinciales quiete, proceres dignanter continebat; fures et falsarios latentes maxima diligentia perscrutans, inventos puniens: parvarum quoque rerum non negligens. Cum nummos fractos, licet boni argenti, a venditoribus non recipi audisset, omnes vel frangi vel incidi præcepit. Mercatorum falsam ulnam castigavit; brachii sui mensura adhibita, omnibusque per Angliam proposita. Curialibus suis,[1] ubicunque villarum esset, quantum a rusticis gratis accipere, quantum et quoto pretio emere debuissent, edixit; transgressores vel gravi pecuniarum mulcta, vel vitæ dispendio, afficiens. Principio regni, ut terrore exempli reos inureret, ad membrorum detruncationem, post ad pecuniæ solutionem proclivior; pro morum prudentia, ut fere fert natura mortalium, optimatibus venerabilis, provincialibus amabilis habebatur. Quod si qui majorum, jurati sacramenti immemores, a fidei tramite exorbitarent, continuo et consiliorum efficacia et laborum perseverantia, erroneos revocabat ad lineam; per asperitatem vulnerum detrectantes reducens ad sanitatem animorum. Nec facile quam diuturnos sudores in talibus effuderit enumerem, dum nihil patitur inultum quod a delinquentibus commissum dignitati suæ non esset consentaneum. Pugnarum erat maxima causa Normannia, ut ante dixi, in qua ipse pariter multis annis degens, Angliæ quoque

---

[1] *suis*]. Here MS. A1. (Hardy's L.1), the Arundel MS. 35, breaks off abruptly. The text of the class which it represents, from this point is cited from MS. At. (Hardy's L.2), the MS. Trin. Coll., Camb., R. 7. 10.

prospiciebat; nullo audente caput erigere dum ille audaciam, ille suspiceret prudentiam. Nec vero propter rebellionem aliquorum procerum unquam suorum appetitus est insidiis, nisi semel: auctor earum fuit quidam cubicularius, plebeii generis patre, sed pro regiorum thesaurorum custodia famosi nominis homine natus: is deprehensus, et facile confessus, poenas perfidiæ acriter luit. Præter hoc tota vita securus, animos omnium timori, sermones amori obstrictos habebat.

§ 412. Statura minimos supergrediens, a maximis vincebatur: crine nigro et juxta frontem profugo, oculis dulce serenis, thoroso pectore, carnoso corpore. Facetiarum pro tempore plenus; nec pro mole negotiorum, cum se communioni dedisset, minus jocundus. Minus pugnacis famæ, Scipionis Africani dictum repræsentabat, "Imperatorem me mea mater, non bella-"torem, peperit." Quapropter sapientia nulli unquam [1] modernorum regum secundus, et pene dicam omnium antecessorum in Anglia facile [2] primus, libentius bellabat consilio quam gladio: vincebat, si poterat, sanguine nullo; si aliter non poterat, pauco. Omnium tota vita omnino obscoenitatum cupidinearum expers, quoniam, ut a consciis accepimus, non effræni voluptate, sed gignendæ prolis amore,[3] mulierum gremio infunderetur: nec dignaretur advenæ delectationi præbere assensum, nisi ubi regium semen procedere posset in effectum; effundens naturam ut dominus, non obtemperans libidini ut famulus. Cibis indifferenter utens, magisque explens esuriem, quam multis obsoniis urgens ingluviem; potui nunquam præter sitim indulgens. Continentiæ minimum excessum tum in suis tum in omnibus execrans. Sompni gravis, et quem frequens runcatio interrumperet. Facultatis in dicendo magis fortuitæ quam elaboratæ; nec præcipitis, sed maturæ.

---

[1] *nulli unquam*] nunquam, Ce¹.; nulli, Aa.; non nulli, At.

[2] *facile*] om. Ce¹.

[3] *amore*] amoris, Ce.

§ 413. Pietatis in Deum prædicandæ, monasteria in Anglia et Normannia construxit; quibus quia nondum supremam manum imposuit, ego quoque interim judicium meum differrem, nisi me Radingensium fratrum caritas tacere non sineret. Hoc ille cœnobium inter duo flumina Kenetam et Tamensem constituit, loco ubi pene omnium itinerantium ad populosiores urbes Angliæ posset esse diversorium; posuitque ibi monachos Cluniacenses, qui sunt hodie præclarum sanctitatis exemplum, hospitalitatis indefessæ et dulcis indicium:[1] videas ibi quod non alibi, ut plus hospites, totis horis venientes, quam inhabitantes insumant. Præproperum me et adulatorem fortasse quis dixerit, quod nunc primum nascentem religionem tanto efferam præconio, nesciens quid ventura pariat dies; sed ipsi, ut spero, cum Dei gratia enitentur ut in bono durent. Ego non erubesco si sanctis viris blandiar; et bonum quod in me non habeo, in aliis admirer. Investituras ecclesiarum Deo et sancto Petro remisit, post multas controversias inter eum et Anselmum archiepiscopum habitas; vix tandem ad consentiendum, pro ingenti Dei gratia, ingloriosa de fratre victoria inflexus. Sed harum causarum tenorem multo verborum circuitu egit dominus Edmerus: nos, pro pleniore notitia, Paschalis sæpe dicti apostolici scripta ad hanc rem pertinentia subnectemus.

Eadmer, Hist. Nov. ii., p. 74.

§ 414. "Paschalis episcopus Henrico regi salutem. In
" litteris quas nuper ad nos per familiarem tuum, nostræ
" dilectionis filium, clericum Willelmum transmisisti, et per-
" sonæ tuæ sospitatem cognovimus, et successus prosperos
" quos tibi, superatis regni adversariis, benignitas divina
" concessit: audivimus præterea optatam virilem sobolem ex
" ingenua te et religiosa conjuge suscepisse. Quod profecto
" cum nos lætificaverit, opportunum rati sumus nunc tibi
" præcepta et voluntatem Dei validius inculcare, cum am-
" plioribus beneficiis benignitati ejus te prospicis debitorem.
" Nos quoque divinis beneficiis benignitatem nostram penes

---

[1] *Hoc—indicium*]. Reproduced in the Gesta Pontificum, lib. ii., § 89.

"te sociare optamus; sed grave nobis est, quia id a nobis "videris expetere quod omnino[1] præstare non possumus. "Si enim consentiamus aut patiamur investituras a tua "excellentia fieri, et nostrum proculdubio et tuum erit im- "mane periculum. Qua in re contemplari te volumus quid "aut non faciendo perdas, aut faciendo conquiras: nos enim "in prohibitione hac nihil amplius obedientiæ, nihil liber- "alitatis, per ecclesias nanciscimur; nec tibi debitæ potes- "tatis aut juris subtrahere quicquam nitimur, nisi ut erga "te Dei ira minuatur, et sic tibi prospera cuncta con- "tingant. Ait enim Dominus, 'Honorificantes me honorifi- "'cabo; qui autem contempnunt me erunt ignobiles.' Dices "itaque 'Mei hoc juris est.' Non utique: non est im- "peratorium, non regium, sed divinum; solius illius est qui "dixit 'Ego sum ostium.' Unde pro ipso te rogo, cujus "hoc munus est, ut reddas hoc ipsi; ipsi dimittas, cujus "amori etiam quæ tua sunt debes. Nos autem cur tuæ "obniteremur voluntati, cur obsisteremus gratiæ, nisi Dei, "in hujus negotii consensu, sciremus nos voluntati obviare, "gratiam amittere? Cur tibi quicquam negaremus, quod "cuiquam esset mortalium concedendum, cum beneficia de "te ampliora sumpserimus? Prospice, fili carissime, utrum "decus an dedecus tibi sit, quod sapientissimus ac religio- "sissimus Gallicanorum episcoporum Anselmus propter hoc "tuo lateri adhærere, tuo veretur in regno consistere. Qui "tanta de te bona hactenus audierant, quid de te sentient? "quid loquentur, cum hoc fuerit in regionibus divulga- "tum? Ipsi qui coram te tuos excessus extollunt, cum "præsentia tua caruerint, hoc profecto validius infamabunt. "Redi ergo carissime fili, ad cor tuum, propter misericor- "diam Dei et propter amorem Unigeniti deprecamur: revoca "pastorem tuum, revoca patrem tuum; et si quid, quod "non opinamur, gravius adversus te gesserit, si investituras "aversatus fueris, nos juxta voluntatem tuam, quantum cum "Deo possumus, moderabimur: tu tamen talis repulsæ in- "famiam a persona tua et regno removens. Hæc si feceris, "et si gravia quælibet a nobis petieris, quæ cum Deo "præberi facultas sit, profecto consequeris, et pro te Do- "minum ipso adjuvante exorare curabimus; et de peccatis "tam tibi quam conjugi tuæ, sanctorum apostolorum meritis,

---

[1] *omnino*] om. Bc. Cd. Ce.

"indulgentiam et absolutionem faciemus. Filium autem
"tuum, quem ex spectabili et gloriosa conjuge suscepisti,
"quem, ut audivimus, egregii patris Willelmi nomine nomi-
"nasti, tanta tecum imminentia confovebimus, ut qui te vel
"illum læserit Romanam ecclesiam videatur læsisse. Datum
"Lateranis, nono kalendas Decembris."

§ 415. "Paschalis Anselmo. Suavissimas dilectionis tuæ
"accepimus litteras, caritatis calamo scriptas. In his re-
"verentiam devotionis tuæ complectimur; et perpendentes
"fidei tuæ robur, et piæ sollicitudinis instantiam, exulta-
"mus, quia, gratia Dei tibi præstante auxilium, te nec pro-
"missa sustollunt, nec minæ concutiunt. Dolemus autem
"quia, cum fratres nostros episcopos, legatos regis Anglorum,
"benigne susceperimus, quæ nec diximus iis, nec cogita-
"vimus, redeuntes ad propria retulerunt. Audivimus enim
"eos dixisse, quia, si rex in aliis bene ageret, nos investi-
"turas ecclesiarum nec prohibere, nec factas excommuni-
"care; et quod ideo nolebamus cartæ committere, ne sub
"occasione ea ceteri principes in nos inclamarent. Unde
"Jesum, qui corda et renes scrutatur, in animam nostram
"testem invocamus, si, ex quo hujus sanctæ sedis curam
"suscepimus gerere, hoc immane scelus vel descendit in
"mentem." Et infra. "Si ergo virgam pastoralitatis sig-
"num, si anulum signaculum fidei, tradit laica manus,
"quid in ecclesia pontifices agunt? Episcopos autem qui
"veritatem in mendacium commutarunt, ipsa veritate, quæ
"Deus est, in medium introducta, a beati Petri gratia et a
"nostra societate secernimus donec Romanæ ecclesiæ satis-
"faciant. Quicunque vero intra prædictas inducias investi-
"turas consecrationum [1] acceperunt a consortio nostro et
"ecclesiæ alienos habemus."

§ 416. "Paschalis Anselmo. Quod Anglici regis cor ad
"apostolicæ sedis obedientiam omnipotentis Dei dignatio
"inclinavit, eidem miserationum Domino gratias agimus, in
"cujus manu corda regum versantur. Hoc nimirum tuæ
"caritatis gratia, tuarumque orationum instantia, factum
"credimus, ut in hac parte populum illum, cui tua solli-
"citudo præsidet, miseratio superna respiceret. Quod autem
"et regi, et his qui obnoxii videntur, adeo condescendimus,

---

[1] *investituras consecrationum*] investituram seu consecrationem, Eadmer (ed. Rule, p. 151).

"eo affectu et compassione factum noveris, ut eos qui ja- *Eadmer,*
"cebant erigere valeamus : te autem, in Christo venerabilis *Hist. Nov.* iii. 87
"et carissime frater, ab illa prohibitione sive, ut tu credis,
"excommunicatione absolvimus, quam ab antecessore nostro
"sanctæ memoriæ Urbano papa adversus investituras ac
"hominia factam intelligis. Tu vero eos qui aut investi-
"turas accepere, aut investitos benedixere, aut hominia fecere,
"cum ea satisfactione quam tibi per communes legatos
"Willelmum ac Baldewinum, viros fideles et veridicos,
"significamus, Domino cooperante suscipito, et eos vice nos-
"træ auctoritatis absolvito ; quos vel ipse benedicas, vel a
"quibus volueris benedici præcipias, nisi in iis aliud forte
"reperias propter quod a sacratis honoribus sint repellendi.
"Si qui vero deinceps præter investituras ecclesiarum
"prælationes assumpserint, etiamsi regi hominia fecerint,
"nequaquam ob hoc a benedictionis munere arceantur, donec [1]
"omnipotentis Dei gratia [2] ad hoc omittendum cor regium
"tuæ prædicationis imbribus molliatur. Præterea super
"episcopis qui falsum, ut nosti, a nobis rumorem retulerunt,
"cor nostrum commotum est vehementius, quia non solum
"nos læserunt, sed multorum simplicium animas decepe-
"runt, et regem adversus caritatem sedis apostolicæ im-
"pulerunt ; unde et inultum eorum flagitium, Domino co-
"operante, non patimur : sed quia filii nostri regis instantia
"pro iis nos pulsat attentius, etiam ipsis communionis tuæ
"participium non negabis. Sane regem et conjugem, et
"proceres illos qui pro hoc negotio cum rege ex præcepto
"nostro laboraverunt, quorum nomina ex supradicti Wil-
"lelmi suggestione cognosces, juxta sponsionem nostram
"a peccatis et pœnitentiis absolves. Rotomagensis episcopi
"causam tuæ deliberationi committimus, et quod ei indul-
"seris indulgemus."

Names of the offending bishops.

§ 417. Hæc Paschalis summus papa, pro ecclesiarum Dei libertate, sollicitus agebat. Fuerunt autem episcopi quos mendacii arguit, Girardus archiepiscopus Eboracensis, et Herbertus Norwicensis ; quorum errata reprehenderunt veraciores legati, Willelmus postea Exoniensis episcopus, et Baldewinus Beccensis monachus.

Anselm at Lyons.

Eratque tunc Anselmus archiepiscopus iterum tempore istius regis Lugduni exul, apud Hugonem

---

[1] *donec*] per, ins. Aa. At.   [2] *gratia*] gratiam, Aa. At.

ejusdem civitatis archiepiscopum, quando epistola prima, quam apposui, emissa est; quia nec ipse ullo desiderio veniendi tenebatur, nec rex animositatem suam pro copia susurronum sedari patiebatur. Diu ergo et revocare illum, et monitionibus apostolicis obsecundare, distulit; non elationis ambitu, sed procerum, et maxime comitis de Mellento instinctu, qui, in hoc negotio magis antiqua consuetudine quam recti tenore rationem reverberans, allegabat multum regiæ majestati diminui, si, omittens morem antecessorum, non investiret electum per baculum et anulum. Veruntamen rex, diligentius inspecto quid vivida epistolarum ratio, quid divinorum munerum in se ubertim confluens admoneret largitio, investituram anuli et baculi indulsit in perpetuum; retento tantum electionis et regalium privilegio. Coacto ergo apud Londoniam magno episcoporum et procerum abbatumque concilio, multa ecclesiasticarum et secularium rerum ordinata negotia, decisa litigia. Nec multo post, uno die quinque sunt ordinati episcopi in Cantia ab Anselmo archiepiscopo : Willelmus ad Wintoniam, Rogerius ad Salesberiam, Willelmus ad Exoniam, Rainaldus ad Herefordum, Urbanus ad Glamorgan. Itaque contro versia frequentibus dissensionibus agitata, plurimo Anselmi ad Romam itu et reditu ventilata, laudabilem finem accepit.

The count of Meulan opposes his return.

The king determines the controversy in a council at London.

Anselm consecrates five bishops in a day.

§ 418. Uxor regis[1] ex antiqua et illustri regum stirpe descendit Matildis, filia regis Scottorum, ut prædixi. A teneris annis inter sanctimoniales apud Wiltoniam et Rumesium educata, litteris quoque fœmineum pectus exercuit. Unde ut ignobiles nuptias respueret, plusquam semel a patre oblatas, peplum sacratæ professionis index gestavit: quapropter, cum rex suscipere vellet[2] eam thalamo, res in disceptationem venit; nec nisi legitimis productis testibus,

History of queen Matilda.

Objection to her marriage.

---

[1] *regis*] ejus, Cd. ; regi, Ag. At. Cc¹.
[2] *suscipere vellet*] susciperet, Bc. By.

qui eam jurarent sine professione causa procorum velum gessisse, archiepiscopus adduci potuit ad consentiendum. Hæc igitur duobus partubus, altero alterius sexus, contenta, in posterum et parere et parturire destitit: æquanimiterque ferebat, rege alias intento, ipsa curiæ valedicere, Westmonasterio multis annis morata. Nec tamen quicquam ei regalis magnificentiæ deerat; sed indefessa frequentia, undæ salutantium, et totis apportantium temporibus, accipiebantur et vomebantur superbis ædibus: hoc regis jubebat liberalitas, hoc ipsius gratia et dulcis attrahebat benignitas. Sanctitudinis egregiæ, non usquequaque despicabilis formæ, maternæ pietatis æmula, nihil sinistrum quantum ad se moribus admittens; præter regium cubile pudoris integra, nulla etiam suspicione læsa. Cilicio sub regio cultu convoluta, nudipes diebus Quadragesimæ terebat ecclesiarum limina: nec horrebat pedes lavare morbidorum, ulcera sanie distillantia contrectare; postremo longa manibus oscula protelare, mensam apponere. Erat ei in audiendo servitio Dei voluptas unica ideoque[1] in clericos bene melodos inconsiderate provida;[2] blande quoscunque alloqui, multa largiri, plura polliceri. Inde, liberalitate ipsius per orbem sata, turmatim huc adventabant scholastici tum cantibus tum versibus famosi; felicemque se putabat qui carminis novitate aures mulceret dominæ. Nec in his solum expensas conferebat, sed etiam omni generi hominum, præsertim advenarum: qui, muneribus acceptis, famam ejus longe per terras venditarent. Est enim cupiditas gloriæ ita innata mentibus hominum, ut vix aliquis, bonæ conscientiæ pretiosis contentus fructibus, si quid bene fecerit, non dulce habeat efferri in vulgus: unde aiunt, et constat, dominæ esse surreptum, ut extraneos quos posset præmiis deliniret; ceteros promissis, aliquando efficacibus, aliquando et

---

[1] *ideoque*] ideo, Cc. [2] *provida*] prodiga, Aa. At. By.

sæpius inanibus, suspenderet. Eo effectum est ut prodige donantium non effugeret vitium, multimodas colonis suis deferens calumpnias, inferens injurias, auferens substantias; quo bonæ largitricis nacta famam, suorum parvi pensaret contumeliam. Sed hæc qui recte judicare volet, consiliis ministrorum imputabit; qui, more harpyiarum,[1] quicquid poterant corripere unguibus, vel infodiebant marsupiis vel insumebant conviviis: quorum fæculentis susurris aures oppleta, nævum honestissimæ menti contraxit: de reliquo factis omnibus approbanda et sancta. Inter hæc erepta est patriæ, magno provincialium dampno, suo nullo; nam et funus nobiliter curatum apud Westmonasterium, quietem accepit, et spiritus se cælum incolere non frivolis signis ostendit. Obiit, regno post septemdecim annos et sex menses libenter relicto; fatum parentum experta, qui pene omnes virente potissimum ævo excessere mundo. Successit thoro ejus, sed non ita cito, Adala filia ducis de Lovanio, quod est castellum caput Lotharingiæ.

§ 419. Filium habuit rex Henricus ex Matilde, nomine Willelmum, dulci spe et ingenti cura in successionem educatum et provectum; nam et ei, vix dum duodecim annorum esset, omnes liberi homines Angliæ et Normanniæ, cujuscunque ordinis et dignitatis, cujuscunque domini fideles, manibus et sacramento se dedere coacti sunt. Filiam quoque Fulconis comitis Andegavensis vix nubilem ipse etiam impubis despondit et accepit, dato sibi a socero comitatu Cenomannico pro munere sponsalitio: quin et Jerosolimam Fulco ire contendens, comitatum commendavit regi suum, si viveret;[2] futurum profecto generi, si non rediret. Plures ergo provinciæ spectabant nutum pueri, putabaturque regis Edwardi vaticinium in eo complendum; ferebaturque spes Angliæ, modo arboris succisa, in

---

[1] *harpyiarum*] arpiarum, MSS.   [2] *viveret*] veniret, At.

illo juvenculo iterum floribus pubescere, fructus protrudere, et ideo finem malorum sperari posse. Deo aliter visum; hujuscemodi enim opinionem tulerunt auræ, quod eum proxima dies urgebat fato satisfacere. Enimvero socero tunc annitente, simulque Thetbaldo filio Stephani et Adalæ amitæ, Lodowicus rex Franciæ Normanniam concessit puero, ut facto sibi hominio possideret eam jure legitimo: ordinabat hæc et efficiebat prudentissimi patris prudentia, ut hominium, quod ipse pro culmine imperii fastidiret facere, filius delicatus, et qui putabatur viam seculi ingressurus, non recusaret. His agitandis et placita concordia componendis quatuor annorum tempus rex impendit, in Normannia toto hoc tempore moratus. Veruntamen tam splendidæ et excogitatæ pacis serenum, tam omnium spes in speculam erectas, confudit humanæ sortis varietas. Namque indicto in Angliam reditu, rex sub ipso[1] crepusculo septimo kalendas Decembris apud Barbeflet naves solvit; eumque, qui impleverat carbasa, ventus feliciter regno et amplæ fortunæ invexit. At vero adolescentulus, jam septendecim annorum et paulo plus, cui nihil deliciarum præter nomen regis pro paterna indulgentia deesset, aliam sibi navem parari præcepit, omnibus pene adolescentulis procerum filiis, quasi pro colludio ætatis puerilis, eo accurrentibus; quin et remiges immodice mero ingurgitati, voluptate nautica quam potus ministrabat, mature illos qui præcesserant post tergum relinquendos clamitabant. Erat enim navis optima, tabulatis novis et clavis recenter compacta. Itaque cæca jam nocte, juventus sapientiæ indiga, simulque potu obruta, navem a littore impellunt. Volat illa pennata pernicior arundine; et, crispantia maris terga radens, imprudentia ebriorum impegit in scopulum non longe a littore supra pelagus exstantem. Consurgunt ergo miseri, et magno clamore

---

[1] *ipso*] noctis, ins. Aa.

ferratos contos expediunt, diu certantes ut navem a rupe propellerent; sed obsistebat fortuna, omnes eorum conatus in irritum deducens. Itaque et remi in saxum obnixi crepuere, concussaque prora pependit. Jamque alios undis exponebat, alios ingressa per rimas aqua enecabat, cum ejecta scafa filius regis excipitur; salvarique potuisset ad littus regressus, nisi soror ejus notha, comitissa Perticæ, in majori nave cum morte luctans, fœmineo ululatu fratris opem implorasset, ne tam impie se relinqueret. Ille, misericordia infractus, lembum carinæ applicari jussit, ut sororem exciperet; mortem misellus pro clementiæ teneritudine indeptus: continuo enim multitudine insilientium scafa victa subsedit, omnesque pariter fundo involvit. Evasit unus et ille agrestis, qui, tota nocte malo supernatans, mane totius tragœdiæ actum expressit. Nulla unquam fuit navis Angliæ tantæ miseriæ, nulla toti orbi tam patulæ famæ. Periit ibi cum Willelmo alter filius regis Ricardus, quem ante regnum ex provinciali fœmina susceperat, juvenis magnanimus et patri pro obsequio acceptus; Ricardus comes Cestræ, et frater ejus Otuelus, nutricius et magister filii regis; filia regis, comitissa Perticæ; et neptis ejus soror Thetbaldi, comitissa Cestræ: præterea quisquis erat in curia lectissimus miles vel capellanus, et optimatum filii ad militiam provehendi; accurrerant[1] enim undique, ut dixi, non leve gloriæ suæ numeraturi commodum si filio regis vel deferrent ludicrum vel conferrent obsequium. Accumulavitque calamitatem difficultas inveniendorum cadaverum, quia dispersis per littora quæsitoribus nullum facile repertum est; sed ierunt tam delicata corpora æquoreis crudelia pabula monstris Juvenculi ergo morte cognita res mirum in modum mutatæ. Parens enim cælibatui renuntiavit, cui post mortem Matildis studuerat, futuros heredes ex nova

---

[1] *accurrerant*] accurrerunt, Ce¹.

conjuge jamjamque operiens. Socer, ex Jerosolimis domum reversus, partibus Willelmi filii Roberti Normanni comitis improbus astitit, tradens ei alteram filiam nuptum et Cenomannicum comitatum: irarum stimulos in regem acuebat dos filiæ, post mortem filii in Anglia retenta.

§ 420. Filiam Matildem ex Mathilde susceptam, dedit rex Henricus Henrico imperatori Alemanniæ, filio Henrici de quo tertius liber memoriam fecit. Fuit hic Henricus quintus ejus nominis apud Teutonicos imperator: qui licet pro contumeliis apostolicæ sedis patri graviter succensuisset, ipse tamen ejusdem sententiæ sequax et propugnator suo tempore fuit infestus; namque cum Urbano papæ Paschalis successisset, vir nullo virtutis genere carens, rursus quæstio de investituris ecclesiarum, rursus bella, rursus lites agitari, neutris partibus loco cedentibus. Imperator omnes episcopos et abbates regni sui quod citra montes est fautores habebat; quia Carolus magnus, pro contundenda gentium illarum ferocia, omnes pene terras ecclesiis contulerat: consiliosissime perpendens, nolle sacri ordinis homines tam facile quam laicos fidelitatem domini rejicere; præterea, si laici rebellarent, illos posse et excommunicationis auctoritate et potentiæ severitate compescere. Papa ultramontanas ecclesias suæ rationi subjecerat; parumque suspiciebant[1] urbes Italiæ Henrici dominium, servitio se putantes exutas post Conradi fratris ejus interitum, qui, a patre relictus Longobardiæ in regem apud Aretium obierat diem: at vero Henricus, antiquis Cæsaribus in nullo virtute dejectior, post pacatum regnum Teutonicum præsumebat animo Italicum, rebellionem urbium subjugaturus, quæstionemque de investitura suo libito recisurus. Sed iter illud ad Romam magnis exercitationibus pectorum, magnis angoribus corporum, consummatum, David Scottus Bancornensis episcopus exposuit; magis in regis

---

[1] *suspiciebant*] suscipiebant, Bc.

gratiam quam historicum deceret acclinis: denique et inauditam violentiam, quod apostolicum cepit quamvis libere custodierit, laudi ducit, ab exemplo quod Jacob, angelum violenter tenens, benedictionem ab eo extorserit. Præter hæc, laborat asserere dictum apostoli, "Nemo, militans Deo, implicat se negotiis secularibus," non adversari cupiditatibus pontificum per laicos investitorum, quia non sit seculare negotium si clericus laico fecerit hominium: quæ quantum sint frivola, cujuslibet dijudicabit prudentia. Ego interim, ne bonum virum verbo videar premere, statuo indulgendum, quia non historiam sed panegyricum [1] scripsit. Nunc vero privilegium et conventionem, violenta trium septimanarum captione a papa extorta, veraciter inseram; et qualiter non multo post religiosiori consilio enervata sunt, subjiciam.

2 Tim. ii. 4.

He is a partial writer.

§ 421. "Dominus papa Paschalis non inquietabit dominum regem, nec ejus imperium vel regnum, de investitura episcopatuum et abbatiarum, neque de injuria sibi illata et suis, in persona et bonis; neque aliquod malum reddet sibi vel alicui personæ pro hac causa: et penitus in personam regis Henrici numquam anathema ponet; nec remanebit in domino papa quin coronet eum, sicut in ordine continetur; et regnum et imperium, officii sui auxilio, eum tenere adjuvabit pro posse suo. Et hæc adimplebit dominus papa sine fraude et malo ingenio. Hæc sunt nomina illorum [2] episcoporum et cardinalium qui, præcepto domini papæ Paschalis, privilegium et amicitiam domino Henrico imperatori sacramento confirmaverunt: Petrus Portuensis episcopus, Centius Sabinensis episcopus, Robertus cardinalis sancti Eusebii, Bonefacius cardinalis sancti Marci, Anastasius cardinalis sancti Clementis, Gregorius cardinalis apostolorum Petri et Pauli, item Gregorius cardinalis sancti Crisogoni, Johannes cardinalis sanctæ Potentianæ, Risus cardinalis sancti Laurentii, Reinerus cardinalis sanctorum Marcellini et Petri, Vitalis cardinalis sanctæ Balbinæ, Teuzo cardinalis sancti Marci, Thetbaldus cardinalis Johannis et Pauli, Johannes decanus in Schola Græca, Leo decanus sancti Vitalis, Albo decanus Sergii et Bachi."

Treaty between Paschal II. and Henry

Names of the witnesses.

---

[1] *panegyricum*] panagericum, MSS. | [2] *illorum*] om. Cc¹.

Oath of the emperor.

§ 422. Ipse etiam rex hoc sacramentum fecit: "'Ego
"'Henricus rex liberos dimittam, quarta vel quinta feria
"'proxima, et dominum papam et episcopos et cardinales,
"'et omnes captivos et obsides qui pro eo vel cum eo capti
"'sunt, et secure perduci faciam intra portas Transtiberinæ
"'civitatis; nec ulterius capiam, aut capi permittam, eos
"'qui in fidelitate domini papæ Paschalis permanent: et
"'populo Romano et Transtiberinæ civitati [1] pacem et se-
"'curitatem servabo, tam per me quam per meos, in per-
"'sonis, qui pacem mihi servaverint. Dominum papam
"'fideliter adjuvabo ut papatum suum quiete et secure teneat.
"'Patrimonia et possessiones Romanæ ecclesiæ quæ abstuli
"'restituam, et cuncta quæ habere debet more antecessorum
"'suorum recuperare et tenere adjuvabo, bona fide, sine fraude
"'et malo ingenio: et domino papæ Paschali obediam, salvo
"'honore regni et imperii, sicut catholici imperatores ca-
"'tholicis pontificibus Romanis.' Et isti sunt juratores ex
" parte ipsius regis: Fridericus Coloniensis archiepiscopus,
" Godebardus Tridentinus episcopus, Bruno Spirensis epi-
" scopus, Berengarius comes, Albertus cancellarius, Heriman-
" nus comes, Fridericus comes palatinus, Bonefacius marchio,
" Albertus comes de Blandriaco, Fridericus comes, Godefricus
" comes, Warnerius marchio."[2]

The pope receives the emperor to communion, April 10, A.D. 1111.

§ 423. Hac conventione expleta, et prædictorum episcoporum et cardinalium sacramento confirmata, osculo utrinque dato, dominus papa quarto idus Aprilis, Dominica Quasi modo geniti, missam celebravit; in qua, post communionem suam et ministrorum altaris, imperatori corpus et sanguinem Domini[3] dedit in hæc verba: "Hoc Dominicum corpus, quod sacrosancta tenet
" ecclesia, natum ex Maria virgine, elevatum in cruce
" pro redemptione humani generis, damus tibi, fili
" carissime, in remissionem peccatorum tuorum, et in
" conservationem confirmandæ pacis et veræ amicitiæ
" inter me et te, et regnum et sacerdotium." Altero vero die apostolicus et rex ad columpnas quæ sunt in

---

[1] *nec—civitati*] om. Aa. At. Ag. Aah. Ap.

[2] These documents are given likewise by Florence of Worcester (ed. Thorpe) ii. 62; in the Monumenta Hist. Germ. ed. Pertz, Leges, ii. 72; and elsewhere.

[3] *Domini*] om. Ce¹.

foro convenerunt; dispositis præsidiis loricatorum ubicunque videbatur opus esse, ne impediretur regis consecratio. Et in Argentea Porta receptus est rex ab episcopis, et cardinalibus, et toto clero Romano; et cœpta oratione quæ in ordine continetur ab Ostiensi episcopo, quoniam Albanus deerat, a quo debuisset dici si adesset, ad mediam rotam ductus est; et ibi recepit secundam orationem a Portuensi episcopo, sicut præcipit Romanus ordo. Deinde duxerunt eum cum letaniis usque ad confessionem Apostolorum; [1] et ibi unxit eum Hostiensis episcopus inter scapulas et in brachio dextro. Post hæc a domino apostolico ad altare eorundem apostolorum deductus [1]; et ibidem, imposita sibi corona ab ipso apostolico, in imperatorem est consecratus. Post impositam coronam missa de Resurrectione Domini est celebrata; in qua ante communionem dominus apostolicus [2] privilegium imperatori propria manu dedit, in quo sibi et regno suo quod hic scriptum est concessit et in eodem loco sub anathemate confirmavit.

Reception of the emperor at the Silver gate.

Orations on the occasion.

The emperor is anointed and crowned.

§ 424. "Paschalis episcopus, servus servorum Dei, carissimo in Christo filio, et per Dei omnipotentis gratiam Romanorum imperatori augusto, Henrico, salutes et apostolicam benedictionem. Regnum vestrum sanctæ Romanæ ecclesiæ cohærere divina dispositio constituit; prædecessores siquidem vestri, probitatis et prudentiæ amplioris gratia, Romanæ urbis coronam et imperium consecuti sunt: ad cujus videlicet coronæ et imperii dignitatem, tuam quoque personam, filii carissime Henrice, per nostri sacerdotii ministerium, majestas divina provexit. Illam [3] igitur dignitatis prærogativam, quam prædecessores nostri vestris prædecessoribus catholicis imperatoribus concesserunt, et privilegiorum paginis confirmaverunt, nos quoque tuæ dilectioni concedimus, et præsentis privilegii pagina confirmamus, ut regni tui episcopis vel abbatibus, libere,

The pope's recognition of the imperial right and dignity.

---

[1] *et ibi—deductus*] om. Bc.
[2] *apostolicus*] papa, At. Cd.

[3] *Illam igitur dignitatis prærogativam, quam*] Illud igitur dignitatis privilegium, quod, Bc.

"præter violentiam vel simoniam electis, investituram virgæ
"et anuli conferas; post investitionem vero canonice con-
"secrationem accipiant ab episcopo ad quem pertinuerit.
"Si quis autem a clero vel populo, præter assensum tuum,
"electus fuerit, nisi a te investiatur, a nemine consecretur;
"exceptis nimirum illis qui vel in archiepiscoporum vel in
"Romani pontificis solent dispositione consistere. Sane
"archiepiscopi vel episcopi libertatem habeant a te investitos
"episcopos vel abbates canonice consecrandi: prædecessores
"enim vestri ecclesias regni sui tantis regalium suorum
"beneficiis ampliarunt, ut regnum ipsum maxime[1] episco-
"porum vel abbatum præsidiis oporteat communiri, et popu-
"lares dissensiones, quæ in electis omnibus sæpe contingunt,
"regali oporteat majestate compesci. Quamobrem prudentiæ
"tuæ et potestati cura debet sollicitius imminere, ut Ro-
"manæ ecclesiæ magnitudo, et ceterarum salus, tuis, Do-
"mino præstante, beneficiis et servitiis conservetur. Si
"qua igitur[2] ecclesiastica vel secularis persona hanc nostræ
"concessionis paginam sciens, contra eam temerario ausu
"venire temptaverit, anathematis vinculo, nisi resipuerit, in-
"nodetur, honorisque ac dignitatis suæ periculum patiatur;
"observantes autem hæc misericordia divina custodiat, et
"personam potestatemque tuam ad honorem suum et gloriam
"feliciter imperare concedat."

Settlement of the point of investiture.

§ 425. Peracto itaque toto ipsius consecrationis officio, apostolicus et imperator, complexis invicem dextris, iverunt cum celebri pompa ad cameram quæ est ante confessionem sancti Gregorii, ut ibi deponerent apostolicus sua sacerdotalia, imperator autem sua regalia. Imperatori autem exeunti de camera, et suis regalibus exuto, occurrerunt Romani patricii cum aureo circulo, quem imposuerunt imperatori in capite, et per eum dederunt sibi summum patriciatum Romanæ urbis, communi consensu omnium et volenti animo.

The emperor made patrician of Rome.

§ 426. Omnem hanc ambitionem privilegiorum et consecrationis, verbo de scriptis præfati David transtuli, quæ ille, ut dixi, pronius quam deberet ad gratiam regis inflectit. Sequenti vero anno congregatum

David the authority for this story

---

[1] *maxime*] om. Ce¹.   [2] *igitur*] ergo, Ce¹.

est concilium Romæ, non tam præcipiente quam connivente papa, et privilegium illud irritum factum est. Auctores fuere hujusce mutationis archiepiscopus Viennensis, qui postea sedem apostolicam rexit, et episcopus Engolismensis, Girardus nomine, qui coepiscopos ad hæc exinanienda irritabant. Ejus ergo concilii actio hæc est :

§ 427. " Anno ab incarnatione Domini millesimo centesimo duodecimo, indictione quinta, anno pontificatus domini papæ Paschalis secundi tertiodecimo, mense Martio, quintodecimo kalendas Aprilis, celebratum est concilium Romæ Lateranis in basilica Constantiniana. In qua cum dominus papa Paschalis resedisset, cum archiepiscopis, et episcopis, et cardinalibus, et varia multitudine clericorum et laicorum, ultima die concilii, facta coram omnibus professione catholicæ fidei, ne quis de fide ipsius dubitaret, dixit: 'Amplector omnem divinam scripturam Veteris ac 'Novi Testamenti, legem a Moyse scriptam et a sanctis 'prophetis: amplector quatuor evangelia, septem canonicas 'epistolas, et epistolas gloriosi doctoris beati Pauli apos'toli, sanctos canones apostolorum, quatuor concilia uni'versalia sicut quatuor evangelia, Nicenum, Ephesinum, 'Constantinopolitanum, Chalcedonense; præterea Antio'chenum concilium, et decreta sanctorum patrum Roma'norum pontificum, et præcipue decreta domini mei 'papæ[1] Gregorii septimi, et beatæ memoriæ papæ Ur'bani. Quæ ipsi laudaverunt, laudo; quæ tenuerunt, 'teneo; quæ confirmaverunt, confirmo; quæ dampnaverunt, 'dampno; quæ repulerunt, repello; quæ interdixerunt, in'terdico; quæ prohibuerunt, prohibeo; in omnibus et per 'omnia in his semper perseverabo.' Quibus expletis, surrexit pro omnibus Girardus Engolismensis episcopus, legatus in Aquitania; et communi assensu domini papæ Paschalis, totiusque concilii, legit hanc scripturam :—

§ 428. " 'Privilegium illud, quod non est privilegium, 'sed vere[2] dici debet pravilegium,[3] pro liberatione capti'vorum et ecclesiæ, a domino papa Paschali per violen'tiam regis Henrici extortum, nos omnes, in hoc sancto

---

[1] papæ] om. Ce.¹
[2] vere] jure, At.
[3] pravilegium] privilegium, An.

"'concilio cum domino papa congregati, canonica censura
"'et ecclesiastica auctoritate judicio Sancti Spiritus dampna-
"'mus, et irritum esse judicamus, atque omnino quassamus,
"'et, ne quid auctoritatis et efficaciæ habeat penitus excom-
"'municamus. Et hoc ideo dampnatum est, quia in eo pra-
"'vilegio[1] continetur quod electus canonice a clero et
"'populo a nemine consecretur nisi prius a rege investia-
"'tur; quod est contra Spiritum Sanctum et canonicam
"'institutionem.' Perlecta vero hac carta, acclamatum
"ab omnibus et universo concilio, 'Amen, Amen! fiat,
"'fiat!'

Names of the prelates present.

"§ 429. Archiepiscopi, qui cum suis suffraganeis inter-
"fuerunt, hi sunt: Johannes patriarcha Veneticus, Semies[2]
"Capuanus, Landulfus Beneventanus, Amalfitanus, Regita-
"nus, Hidrontinus, Brundisinus, Capsanus, Girontinus; et
"Græci, Rosanus, et[3] archiepiscopus sanctæ Severinæ. Epi-
"scopi vero: Centius Sabinensis, Petrus Portuensis, Leo
"Hostiensis, Cono Prænestinus, Girardus Engolismensis,
"Galo Leonensis, legatus pro Bituricensi, et Viennensis
"archiepiscopus, Rogerius Vulturnensis, Gaufridus Senensis,
"Rollandus Populonensis, Gregorius Terracinensis, Willelmus
"Trojanus,[4] Willelmus Siracusanus, legatus pro omnibus
"Siculis; et alii fere centum episcopi. Siwinus, et Johan-
"nes Tusculanus episcopus, cum essent Romæ, illa die con-
"cilio non interfuerunt; qui postea, lecta dampnatione pri-
"vilegii, consenserunt et laudaverunt."

The emperor goes to Rome in 1117.

§ 430. Ferebantur ista per orbem, nec dissimulabat omnis Gallia imperatorem execrari, ecclesiastici zeli vigore[5] in eum intentato. His commotus Romam

Death of the pope.

septimodecimo anno Paschalis papæ contendit, acrius in illum ulturus; sed is felici transitu mundanas effugerat ærumpnas, ridebatque in requie positus ex alto

Gelasius II. and Maurice of Braga.

contumacis Cæsaris minas. Cujus morte accepta, alacrius imperator celerabat viam, ut Johanne Gaitano, superioris papæ cancellario, qui jam electus et Gelasius dictus fuerat, ejecto, Mauricium Bracarensem episcopum,

---

[1] *pravilegio*] privilegio, Aa. Cd.
[2] *Semies*] Sennes, Aa. At.
[3] *et*] om. Cd.
[4] *Trojanus*] om. Bc. Bk. By. Cd. Ce.
[5] *vigore*] rigore, Ce.¹

cognomento Burdinum, intruderet. Sed hæc epistola Gelasii certius proponet.

Eadmer, Hist. Nov., lib. v., p. 122.

"§ 431. Gelasius, servus servorum Dei, archiepiscopis, episcopis, abbatibus, clericis, principibus, et ceteris per Galliam fidelibus, salutem. Quia vos Romanæ ecclesiæ membra estis, quæ in ea nuper acta sunt dilectioni vestræ significare curamus. Siquidem post electionem nostram dominus imperator, furtive et inopinata velocitate Romam veniens, nos egredi compulit. Pacem postea et minis et terroribus postulavit, dicens, quæ posset se facturum, nisi nos ei juramento pacis certitudinem faceremus : ad quæ nos ista respondimus : ' de controversia quæ inter ecclesiam ' et regnum est, vel conventioni vel justitiæ libenter adquiescimus loco et tempore competenti, videlicet Mediolani vel Cremonæ in proxima beati Lucæ festivitate, ' fratrum nostrorum judicio, qui a Deo sunt judices constituti in ecclesia, et sine quibus hæc causa tractari non ' potest. Et quoniam dominus imperator a nobis securitatem quærit, nos verbo et scripto eam promittimus, ' nisi ipse interim impediat. Alias enim securitatem facere, nec honestas ecclesiæ nec consuetudo est.' Ille statim die post electionem nostram quadragesimo quarto [1] Bracarensem episcopum, anno præterito a domino prædecessore [2] nostro Paschali papa in concilio Beneventi excommunicatum, in matris ecclesiæ invasionem [3] ingessit ; qui etiam, cum per nostras olim manus pallium accepisset, eidem domino nostro, et catholicis successoribus, quorum primus ego sum, fidelitatem juravit. In hoc autem tanto facinore nullum de Romanis dominus imperator, Deo gratias! socium habuit ; sed Wibertini soli, Romanus de sancto Marcello, Centius qui dicebatur sancti Crisogoni, Teuzo qui multo per Daciam debacchatus est tempore, tam infamem gloriam celebrarunt. Vestræ igitur experientiæ, litterarum præsentium perceptione, mandamus ut, super his per Dei gratiam communi deliberatione tractantes, ad matris ecclesiæ ultionem, communibus præstante Deo auxiliis, sicut oportere cognoscitis, accingamini. Data Gaitæ, septimodecimo kalendas Februarii." [4]

---

[1] *quarto*] tertio, At.
[2] *prædecessore*] præcessore, At. Ce¹.
[3] *invasionem*] gremium, By. ; om. B.c.

[4] *Februarii.*] So the MSS. and Eadmer : the real date seems to be April 15, 1119. See Jaffé, Reg. Pontif., No. 4884.

§ 432. Expulsus autem Gelasius, Salerni navibus conscensis, inde venit Genuam; indeque itinere pedestri Cluniacum contendens, ibidem obiit.[1] Tunc, id est, anno Dominicæ incarnationis millesimo centesimo nonodecimo, cardinales qui cum Gelasio venerant, simulque omnis ecclesia Cisalpina, Guidonem archiepiscopum Viennensem in papam grandi paratu levantes, Calixtum vocarunt, religionis et efficaciæ ipsius contuitu,[2] sperantes se per illius potentiam, quod esset in auxiliando facultatis maximæ, imperatoris viribus obniti posse. Nec ille credulos[3] spei effectu exinaniens, mox concilio Remis celebrato investitos vel investiendos a laicis ab ecclesiis removit; pariter et imperatorem, nisi resipisceret, involvens. Ita tempore aliquanto in inferioribus plagis moratus, ut partes suas augeret, Romam, compositis in Gallia rebus, venit, libenterque a civibus, nam jam imperator discesserat, receptus est. Tum Burdinus, in medio relictus, Sutrium effugit, multis peregrinorum calamitatibus papatum suum fovere meditatus; sed, quo modo inde sit ejectus, sequenti epistola cognosces:

" § 433. Calixtus episcopus, servus servorum Dei, dilectis
" fratribus et filiis, archiepiscopis, episcopis, abbatibus, prioribus, et ceteris tam clericis quam laicis, beati Petri
" fidelibus, per Gallias constitutis, salutem et apostolicam
" benedictionem. Quia dereliquit populus legem Domini, et
" in judiciis ejus non ambulat, visitat Dominus virga iniquitates eorum et in verberibus peccata eorum: paternæ
" tamen conservans viscera pietatis, de sua confidentes
" misericordia non relinquit. Diu siquidem, peccatis exigentibus, per illud Teutonicorum regis idolum, Burdinum
" videlicet, fideles ecclesiæ conturbati sunt; et alii quidem
" capti, alii usque ad mortem carceris maceratione afflicti
" sunt. Nuper autem, festis Paschalibus celebratis, cum
" peregrinorum et pauperum clamores ferre penitus non

---

[1] *obiit*] diem, ins. Ce¹.
[2] *contuitu*] intuitu, Aa. At.
[3] Here MS. Ap. has a lacuna, beginning again with " municare inciperet," below, p. 510, line 24.

"possemus, cum ecclesiæ fidelibus ab urbe digressi sumus,
"et tamdiu Sutrium obsedimus, donec divina potentia et
"supradictum ecclesiæ inimicum Burdinum, qui diabolo
"nidum ibidem fecerat, et locum ipsum, omnino in nostram
"tradidit potestatem. Rogamus itaque caritatem vestram
"ut pro tantis beneficiis una nobiscum Regi regum gratias
"referatis, et in catholicæ ecclesiæ obedientia et servitio
"constantissime maneatis, retributionem debitam in præsenti
"et futuro ab omnipotente Domino per ejus gratiam recep-
". turi. Rogamus etiam ut has litteras alter alteri præsen-
"tari, omni remota negligentia, faciatis. Data Sutrii, quinto *Dated April 27, 1121.*
". kalendas Maii."

§ 434. Urbana omnino et excogitata facetia, ut eum, *Account of the anti-pope.* quem oderat, regis Teutonici vocaret idolum ; quod ille Mauritii peritiam, tum in litteris tum in civilibus negotiis, magni pensaret. Erat is, ut dixi, Bracarensis archiepiscopus, quæ est civitas Hispaniæ; quem multum quislibet revereri, et pene adorare, pro viva magnæ industriæ specie debuisset, nisi tam famoso facinore enitescere maluisset. Nec enim sanctissimam *He is sent to la Cava.* sedem nummis nundinari dubitasset, si tam desperatus inveniretur venditor quam paratus erat emptor. Tum autem captus, et monachus factus, in Caveam, monasterium enim[1] ita vocant,[2] directus est.

§ 435. Processit ulterius in augendo bono laudabilis *The pope's reforms and other wise measures.* papæ magnificentia, ut illam effrænem et ingenitam Romanorum cupiditatem cohiberet. Nullæ ipsius tempore viantibus circa Romam insidiæ, nullæ urbem ingressis injuriæ. Oblationes apud sanctum Petrum quas pro petulantia proque libidine potentes diripiebant, anteriores apostolicos, qui vel mutire auderent, indignis afficientes contumeliis, Calixtus revocavit ad medium, scilicet ad apostolicæ sedis rectoris publicum usum. Nec quicquam in ejus pectore pecuniarum vel *He discourages pilgrimages to Rome.* habendarum ambitus, vel habitarum amor, operari bono abhorrens potuit : adeo ut Anglos peregrinos magis ad sanctum David quam Romam pergere ad-

---

[1] *enim*] om. Aa. At. Bc. By. Cd. | [2] *vocant*] vocatum, By. Cd.

moneret, pro viæ longitudine; ad illum locum bis euntibus idem benedictionis refundendum commodum, quod haberent qui semel Romam irent. Quid quod illam inveteratam investituræ controversiam inter regnum et sacerdotium, quæ jam plus quam quinquaginta annis turbas fecerat, adeo ut, aliquo hæresis fautore morbo vel morte succiso, illico quasi hydræ capita plura pullularent, ipse sua industria abrasit, decidit, delevit;[1] Teutonicæ animositatis colla vigore securis apostolicæ decutiens. Quod et ejus[2] et apostolici professiones mundo his dictis ostendent.

Letter of Calixtus II. to Henry V. settling the investiture controversy.

§ 436. "Ego Calixtus episcopus, servus servorum Dei, tibi dilecto filio Henrico, Dei gratia Romanorum imperatori,[3] concedo electiones episcoporum et abbatum Teutonici regni qui ad regnum pertinent in præsentia tua fieri, absque simonia et absque ulla violentia; ut si qua inter partes discordia emerserit, metropolitani vel provincialium consilio vel judicio, saniori parti assensum et auxilium præbeas. Electus autem regalia a te recipiat, et quæ ex his jure tibi debet faciat: ex aliis vero partibus imperii consecratus infra sex menses regalia a te per sceptrum recipiat, et quæ ex his jure tibi debet faciat; exceptis omnibus quæ ad Romanam ecclesiam pertinere noscuntur. De quibus vero mihi querimoniam feceris et auxilium postulaveris, secundum officii mei debitum auxilium tibi præstabo. Do tibi veram pacem, et omnibus qui in tua parte sunt, vel fuerunt tempore hujus discordiæ. Vale!"

Pertz, *Mon. Hist., Legg.* ii. 75.

The emperor's acceptance of the settlement. (Sept. 23, 1122.)

§ 437. "In nomine sanctæ et individuæ Trinitatis. Ego Henricus, Dei gratia Romanorum imperator augustus, pro amore Dei, et sanctæ Romanæ ecclesiæ, et domini Calixti papæ, et pro remedio animæ meæ, dimitto Deo, et sanctis Dei apostolis Petro et Paulo, sanctæque catholicæ ecclesiæ, omnem investituram per anulum et baculum; et concedo in omnibus ecclesiis, quæ in regno vel imperio meo sunt,

---

[1] *delevit*] delevit, evellit, Aa.; delevit, interlined over evellit, Ag.; delevit vel evellit, At. Bq.; delevit, Cf. Bk.; dejecit, delevit, By.

[2] MS. Cf. omits all from *Quod et ejus* to the end of § 439, p. 512, below; reading here, "quod et ejus et apostolici in Dei fervet obsequio."

[3] *imperatori*] Augusto, ins. Aa. Ag. At. By.

"canonicam fieri electionem et liberam consecrationem.
"Possessiones et regalia beati Petri, quæ a principio hujus
"discordiæ usque ad hodiernum diem, sive tempore patris
"mei, sive etiam meo, ablata sunt, quæ habeo, eidem sanctæ
"Romanæ ecclesiæ restituo; quæ non habeo, ut restituantur
"fideliter juvabo. Possessiones etiam omnium aliarum ec-
"clesiarum, et principum, et omnium aliorum tam laicorum
"quam clericorum, quæ in guerra ista amissæ sunt, consilio
"principum vel justitia, quas habeo reddam; quas non ha-
"beo, fideliter ut reddantur juvabo. Et do veram pacem
"domino papæ Calixto, et sanctæ Romanæ ecclesiæ, et om-
"nibus qui in parte ipsius sunt vel fuerunt, et in quibus
"sancta Romana ecclesia auxilium postulaverit, fideliter
"juvabo; et de quibus mihi querimoniam fecerit, debitam *Names of the consenting princes.*
"sibi faciam justitiam." Hæc omnia acta sunt consensu
et consilio principum quorum nomina subscripta sunt: Albertus archiepiscopus Magontiæ, Fredericus Coloniensis archiepiscopus, Ratisbonensis episcopus, Babenbergensis episcopus,
Bruno Spirensis, Augustensis, Trajectensis, Constantiensis,
abbas Foldensis, Heremannus dux, Fredericus dux, Boncfa-
cius marchio, Thetbaldus marchio, Ernulfus comes palatinus,
Otbertus comes palatinus, Berengarius comes.

§ 438. Sedato itaque tam veterno morbo, qui eccle- *Henry V. subdues* siæ statum conturbaverat, magnum gaudium quisquis *Italy.* Christiane sapuit, accepit, quod is imperator, qui proxima fortitudinis gloria acriter Caroli magni invaderet vestigia, etiam a devotione ipsius in Deum non degeneraret; qui, præter Teutonici regni nobiliter sopitas rebelliones, etiam Italicum ita subegit ut nullus adeo. Ter enim in decennio Italiam ingressus urbium tumorem compescuit; primo adventu Novariam, Placentiam, Aretium, secundo et tertio Cremonam et Mantuam, incendio exterminans: sed et Ra- *His three visits.* vennæ motum paucorum obsidione dierum lenivit; namque Pisani et Papienses, cum Mediolanensibus, amicitiam ejus quam vim experiri malebant. Huic, *Above, § 420.* ut ante fatus sum, filia regis Angliæ nupta exhibebat patrem fortitudine, matrem religione; contendebat in ea pietas industriæ, nec quod magis probares discerneres facile.

§ 439. Erat tunc Willelmus comes Pictavorum fatuus et lubricus; qui, postquam de Jerosolima, ut superiori libro lectum est, rediit, ita omne vitiorum volutabrum premebat quasi crederet omnia fortuitu agi, non providentia regi. Nugas porro suas, falsa quadam venustate condiens, ad facetias revocabat, audientium rictus cachinno distendens. Denique apud castellum quoddam, Niort,[1] habitacula quædam, quasi monasteriola, construens, abbatiam pellicum ibi se positurum delirabat; nuncupatim illam et illam, quæcunque famosioris prostibuli esset, abbatissam vel priorem, ceterasve[2] officiales instituturum cantitans. Legitima quoque uxore depulsa, vicecomitis cujusdam conjugem surripuit, quam adeo ardebat ut clypeo suo simulacrum mulierculæ insereret; perinde dictitans se illam velle ferre in prælio, sicut illa portabat eum in triclinio. Unde increpitus et excommunicatus a Girardo Engolismorum episcopo, jussusque[3] illicitam venerem abjicere, "Antea," inquit, "crispabis pectine refugum a fronte "capillum quam ego vicecomitissæ indicam repu- "dium;" cavillatus in virum, cujus pertenuis cæsaries pectinem non desideraret. Nec minus, cum Petrus præclaræ sanctitatis Pictavorum episcopus eum liberius argueret, et detrectantem palam excommunicare inciperet, ille, præcipiti furore percitus, crinem antistitis involat, strictumque mucronem vibrans, "Jam," inquit, "morieris, nisi me absolveris." Tum vero præsul, timore simulato, inducias petens loquendi, quod reliquum fuerat excommunicationis fidenter peroravit; ita comitem a Christianitate[4] suspendens, ut nec cum aliquo convivari nec etiam loqui auderet, nisi mature resipisceret. Ita officio suo, ut sibi videbatur, peracto, martyriique trophæum sitiens, collum protendit;

Above, § 383.

---

[1] *Niort*] Niorth, Aa. By.; Nior, Bc. Cd. Ce.

[2] *ceterasve*] ceteras vero, Aa. At.

[3] *que*] om. Ce.¹

[4] *a Christianitate*] om. Ce.¹

"Feri!" inquiens, "feri!" At Willelmus, refractior, consuetum leporem intulit ut diceret, "Tantum certe "te odio, ut nec meo te digner odio, nec cælum un- "quam intrabis meæ manus ministerio." Veruntamen post modicum, viperio meretriculæ[1] infectus sibilo, incesti dissuasorem detrusit exilio; ubi beato fine conclusus, frequentibus et magnis miraculis innuit mundo quam gloriose vivat in cælo. Quibus auditis, comes dicacitate insolenti non abstinuit; professus palam, pœnitere se quod non ei jamdudum mortem accelerasset, ut ipsi anima sancta grates haberet potissimum, cujus furore cæleste mercatus esset commodum. Vitam Petri et mortem versus isti commendant. De vivo dictum est: *Exile and death of the bishop.*

Versus de Petro episcopo Pictavorum.

" Corpus—opes—studium—mores, cibus asper—egenus— *Verses written upon him.*
" Lectio—probra, domat—carpit—alit—fugiunt.
" Virtutes—culpas—fructum, colit—amputat—auget—
" Jus—litem—pacem, protegit—odit—amat.
" Fert misero—tribuit peccanti—servat amico,
" Auxilium—veniam—continuamque fidem.
" Mente Maria vacat, sed in actum Martha laborat;
" Est intenta gregi Martha, Maria Deo:
" Sic apud hunc regnat Deus intra, proximus extra;
" Hic desiderio, proximus obsequio.
" Diligit ille Rachel, nec Liam ferre recusat,
" Uxoremque novus duxit utramque Jacob:
" Hujus amat vultum, juvat hujus carpere fructum,
" Cum sit pulchra Rachel, fertiliorque Lia."

De mortuo dictum est:

Versus de eodem Petro mortuo.

" Exutus rebus, intentus, pulsus ab urbe,
" Præsul pauperiem, vincla, fugamque tulit.
" Nunc dives—liber—stabilis, sua præmia—Christum—
" Astra, capit—sequitur—possidet iste Petrus.

---

[1] *meretriculæ*] mulierculæ, An. At. Aah.

" Vitam religio, mentem discretio, famam
" Lux operum, studium lectio, verba modum,
" Judicium jus, justitiam rigor, ora venustas,
" Ornabant, pietas viscera, virga manum.
" Promovit—privavit eum—profugumque recepit,
" Papa—comes—Christus, ordine—sede—polo."

De auctoribus monasteriorum fontis Ebraldi et Tirunensis.

§ 440. Hujus Petri fuerunt contemporanei, et in religione socii, Robertus de Arbreisel et Bernardus abbas Tirunensis; quorum primus omnium hujus temporis sermocinatorum famosissimus et profusissimus. Tantum non spumea sed mellea viguit eloquentia, ut hominibus certatim opes congerentibus, illud egregium sanctimonialium monasterium apud Fontem Ebraldi construeret; in quo, tota seculi voluptate castrata, fœminarum Deo devotarum quanta nusquam multitudo in Dei fervet obsequio: nam præter ceterarum illecebrarum abdicationem, quantulum illud est, quod in nullo loco loquuntur nisi in capitulo; proposita a magistro perennis taciturnitatis regula, quia semel laxato silentio fœminæ pronæ sunt ad mussitandum frivola. Alter, famosus paupertatis amator, in saltuosum et desertum locum, relicto amplissimarum divitiarum cœnobio, cum paucis concessit; ibique, quia lucerna sub modio latere non potuit, undatim multis confluentibus monasterium fecit, magis insigne religione monachorum et numero, quam fulgore pecuniarum et cumulo.

De Serlone Abbate Gloecestræ.

§ 441. Et, ne Anglia expers boni putetur, quis possit præterire Serlonem abbatem Gloecestrensem, qui locum illum ex humili et pene nullo ad gloriosum provectum extulit? Nota est omnibus Anglis Gloecestrensis discreta religio, quam infirmus possit suspicere, nec possit fortis contempnere. Hoc illis signifer

Serlo intulit, ut ne quid nimis. Quamvis ut erat
bonis humilis, ita superbis minax ac terribilis.[1] Ad
quod firmandum versus de eo Godefridi prioris addu-
cam in medium.

Versus de eodem mortuo.

" Ecclesiæ murus cecidit, Serlone cadente :   Verses of
  " Virtutis gladius, buccina justitiæ,   Godfrey
" Vera loquens, et non vanis sermonibus utens,   about him.
  " Et, quos corripuit, principibus placuit.
" Judicium præceps, contrarius ordinis error,
  " Et levitas morum, non placuere sibi.
" Tertius a Jano mensis, lux tertia mensis,
  " Cum nece suppressum vita levavit eum."

De Lanzone priore Sancti Pancratii.

§ 442. Quis Lanzonem taceat, qui ea ætate nullo Lanzo,
inferius sanctitate floruit, monachus Cluniacensis, et S. Pancras
prior sancti Pancratii in Anglia? qui probitate sua ita at Lewes.
locum illum reverentiæ monachilis gratia nobilitavit,
ut unicum bonitatis pro vero asseratur esse domicilium. De cujus vita quia quicquid dixero infra
illius merita esse denuntio, solum illius obitum, verbis
quibus scriptum inveni, apponam, ut liquido pateat
quam gloriose vixerit qui tam gratiose obiit.

De morte ejusdem Lanzonis.

§ 443. "Pius Dominus, qui flagellat omnem filium quem Story of
" recipit, qui justos suæ socios passionis simul et consola- the death of
" tionis fore promittit, tam acerbo languore dominum prior Lanzo.
" Lanzonem triduo passionem suam prævenire permisit, ut
" si aliquis ex terrena conversatione mundissimæ menti
" ejus pulvis adhæsit, illa eum tribulatione excussum esse
" non sit ambiguum. Cum enim dicat tantus apostolus,

---

[1] *Nota—terribilis.*] Reproduced in the Gesta Pontificum, lib. iv.,
§ 155.

" qui super Dominicum recubuit pectus, 'Si dixerimus quia 1 S. John,
" 'peccatum non habemus, ipsi nos seducimus, et veritas in i. 8, 9.
" 'nobis non est:' cumque peccatum omne aut levius hic,
" aut in futuro gravius, judicet Christus, noluit ei aliquid
" offensionis post mortem occurrere, quem se toto corde
" sciebat amare; ideoque, si quid in eo examinandum
" judicabat, voluit in vivente[1] decoquere. Huic nempe
" assertioni fiducia morientis attestata est. Nam cum
" quinta feria ante Passionem Domini incolumis, dicto ex
" quotidiana Quadragesimæ consuetudine psalterio, se hora
" tertia missam celebraturus usque ad casulam induisset, et
" usque ad incipiendam missam quæquæ dicenda erant præ-
" dixisset, subito languore tam molesto corripitur, ut ipse,
" quæ induerat vestimenta exuens, etiam non plicata reli-
" querit: egressusque oratorio, sine intermissione per bi-
" duum, hoc est, usque ad Sabbatum, conteritur; non
" sedendo, non ambulando, non jacendo, non stando, neque
" dormiendo, ullam omnino requiem habens. Nunquam
" tamen noctibus locutus, rogantibus[2] ut silentium solveret
" non acquievit; rogans ne monachatus sui pudicitiam

The last days and death of prior Lanzo.

" libarent, quod nunquam, postquam monachicum habitum
" accepisset, a completorio exiens usque ad sequentis diei
" primam locutus fuisset. Sabbato autem sequente dum
" ita quassatus se putaret jam jamque defungi, surgentes
" ad matutinam synaxim fratres ad se inungendum venire
" præcepit; quos cum inunctus ex more osculari voluisset;
" nimio eorum compulsus amore, non jacendo, nec sedendo,
" sed, quamvis ad mortem anxiatus, inter brachia susten-
" tatus stando osculatus est. Die illucescente in capitulum
" ductus, cum sedisset, fratres ante se omnes venire ro-
" gavit; quibus paternam benedictionem et absolutionem
" impertiens, idem sibi ab iis voluit impertiri. Postea
" docuit quid, si obiret, eis esset agendum. Sicque regres-
" sus est unde venerat, reliquum diei cum sequenti Do-
" minica aliquanto quietius transigens: cum ecce post hæc,
" id est, post Dominicam, imminentis mortis indicia de-
" prehenduntur; et ipse manibus ablutis, pexo capite, mis-
" sam auditurus oratorium ingreditur, sumptoque corpore
" et sanguine Domini ad lectum regressus est. Post modi-
" cum obmutuit: fratres ante illum venientes singillatim

---

[1] *vivente*] juventute, Bc. Bk. | [2] *rogantibus*] fratribus, add. Aa. At.

" benedicebat, simili modo totum conventum; at vero,
" oculis in cælum erectis, utraque manu dominum abbatem
" cum omnibus sibi commissis benedicere nitebatur. Roga-
" tus autem a fratribus ut apud Deum, ad quem ibat,
" eorum memor esset, caput inclinando benignissime ad-
" quievit. Hæc et his similia cum fecisset, innuit sibi
" porrigi crucem; quam capite, immo toto corpore, inclinato
" adorans, manibus amplexans, læto ore salutare videbatur
" et jocundo affectu [1] deosculabatur; cum ilico astantes mi-
" grando percellit, raptusque in manibus eorum vivus adhuc
" in presbyterium ante altare sancti Pancratii defertur.
" Ubi aliquamdiu supervivens, roseo faciei rubore suavis,
" eadem diei hora qua purgandus infirmatus est, cariturus
" perenniter omni malo, purus migravit ad Christum. Et
" vide quam mirabiliter [2] in eo cuncta concurrerunt: passio
" servi cum passione Domini; hora incipientis infirmitatis,
" cum hora incipientis æternæ salutis; quinque dies quos
" sustinuit' ægritudinis, quinis corporis sensibus, quibus
" nemo vitat peccatum, emundandis. Porro quod quinto
" die needum transacto decessit, ut remur [3] innuit eum in
" ultimo sensu, qui tactus dicitur, non perfecisse peccatum.
" Tertia vero diei hora, qua et infirmatus est et moriendo
" in vitam ingressus est æternam, quid aliud insinuat quam
" eandem Spiritus Sancti gratiam, qua omnem ejus vitam
" gubernatam cognoscimus, et infirmato et obeunti eviden-
" ter affuisse? Ut etiam esse supparem illis patribus
" nostris, Odoni scilicet atque Odiloni, et merito et præ-
" mio, non ambigamus, insigne quiddam illis concessum
" huic quoque collatum est. Cum enim illis contulerit
" Dominus ut octavo die sollempnitatum quas præ ceteris
" diligebant transirent; nam et beatus Odo festivitatem
" beati Martini, et sanctus Odilo Nativitatem Domini præ-
" cipue amabant, in quorum octava die uterque decessit;
" domino Lanzoni, qui præ ceteris hujus ævi hominibus
" regulam sancti Benedicti observabat, et beatam Dei geni-
" tricem ejusque sollempnia singulari venerabatur affectu,
" contulit, ut solita sibi consuetudine, et in transitu sancti
" Benedicti, et in festivitate sanctæ Mariæ quæ Annun-

His death.

He is the equal of Odo and Odilo, the founders of Cluny.

---

[1] *affectu*] om. Bc. Bk. Cd. Ce.
[2] *mirabiliter*] mutabiliter, Bc. Ce.
[3] *remur*] reor, Aa. At.

" tiatio Dominica dicitur, majorem missam in conventu
" celebraret, et octavo [1] a prædicto sancti Benedicti tran-
" situ die præventus infirmitate, octavo nihilominus die ab
" Annuntiatione Dominica migraret ad Christum. Igitur,
" qui vitam domini Lanzonis ignorat, quam placens Deo
" fuerit ex fine colligat; nec usitato morientium more præ-
" dicta illi contigisse nobiscum credat, quem Spiritus
" Sancti charismatibus nemine hujus temporis inferius di-
" tatum sciat."

De Godefrido priore Wintoniæ.

Commemoration of Godfrey, prior of Winchester.

§ 444. Nec memoria Godefridi prioris Wintoniensis ire debet in perditum, qui temporibus his litteratura et religione insignis fuit. Litteraturam protestantur libri plures, et epistolæ familiari illo et dulci stilo editæ; maximeque epigrammata, quæ satirico modo absolvit, præterea versus de primatum Angliæ laudibus. Quid? omne divinum officium, quod agresti quadam vetustate obsoletum, per industriam suam nativa excultum venustate fecit enitescere. Religionis et hospitalitatis normam pulchre inchoatam deliniavit in monachos, qui hodieque ita in utrisque prioris terunt vestigium, ut aut nihil aut parum eis desit ad laudis cumulum. Denique est in ea domo hospitum terra marique venientium quantum libuerit diversorium, sumptu indeficienti, caritate indefatigata. Inter hæc inerat sancto viro morum humilitas, ut nihil ex illo unico philosophiæ promptuario redoleret nisi humile, procederet nisi dulce. Quantula vero potest videri hæc ejus laudatio? Quotus enim quisque est qui vel minimum litteris imbutus non alios infra dignitatem suam opinetur, tumido gestu et pompatico incessu præ se ferens conscientiam litterarum? Veruntamen, ne quid perfectionis sanctæ deesset animæ, multis ille annis grabatum fovit, camino diuturnæ tabis medullas et peccata excoctus.[2]

---

[1] *et octavo—infirmitate*] om. Bc. Bk. Bq. By. Cd. Ce. Cf.

[2] The whole of this section, from " Litteraturam " to " excoctus " is reproduced in the Gesta Pontificum, lib. ii., § 77.

De translatione Sancti Cutberti, et de Sancta Etheldritha, quorum corpora integra inventa sunt.

§ 445. Sed quid de talibus plura? Erant prorsus tunc in Anglia multi scientia illustres, religione celebres; quorum virtus eo probabilior, quo, seculo senescente, constantior et viridior. Laudabiliter igitur vivendo fidem præteritis faciebant historiis, ne vetera possint falsitatis argui, cum novorum exemplo probentur potuisse fieri. Quin etiam si qui essent ecclesiarum prælati qui viderentur ab antiquorum sanctitate degeneres, in mundialibus scilicet efficaces, in spiritualibus desides; tales inquam, si qui essent, sumptuosis locorum cultibus conabantur errata obumbrare. Erigebat quisque templa recentia, sanctorumque suorum argento et auro amiciebat corpora, nihil prætermittendo caritate sumptuum quod ad gratiam possit allicere oculos intuentium. Quorum est Rannulfus superius nominatus, qui, apud Dunelmum factus episcopus, in ædificiis monachorum novis, et beati Cuthberti veneratione, nonnullam gloriam nomini suo commentus est: cujus extulit famam sacrati corporis translatio, quod, e mausoleo levatum, cunctis volentibus fecit conspicuum. Tractavit illud ausu felici Radulfus tunc abbas Sagii, postea Cantuariæ archiepiscopus; et propalam illibatum protulit, quod quibusdam venisset in dubium utrum olim vulgatum adhuc de integritate compaginis duraret miraculum.[1] Eodemque fere tempore in Heliensi cœnobio, sub abbate Ricardo, virginales exuviæ beatæ Etheldrithæ integræ visæ videntibus stupori et plausui fuere. Monasterium illud, nuper a rege Henrico in episcopatum mutatum, primum Herveum accepit episcopum; qui, pro penuria victualium, Bancornensem, ubi intronizatus fuerat, deseruerat locum: et ne Lin-

---

[1] *in ædificiis—miraculum.*] Reproduced in the Gesta Pontificum, lib. iii., § 134.

coliensis pontifex mutilatam suam quereretur diocesim, ex rebus Heliensis coenobii dampnum rex sarcivit, querelam composuit.¹ Sane quid ejus tempore de primatu duorum metropolitanorum, Cantuariensis et Eboracensis, sit vel justitiæ surreptum, vel violentia præsumptum, dicam cum ad ordinem venero. Jam enim terminata serie regum, de successione totius Angliæ pontificum mihi video esse dicendum; in quo utinam afflueret uber dicendi copia, ne ulterius sub oblivione jaceant tam præclara patriæ lumina. Et quidem erunt multi fortassis, in diversis regionibus Angliæ, qui quædam aliter ac ego dixi² se dicant audisse vel legisse: veruntamen, si recto aguntur judicio, non ideo me censorio expungent stilo; ego enim, veram legem secutus historiæ, nihil unquam posui nisi quod a fidelibus relatoribus vel scriptoribus addidici. Porro, quoquo modo hæc se habeant, privatim ipse mihi sub ope Christi gratulor, quod continuam Anglorum historiam ordinaverim post Bedam vel solus vel primus: si quis ergo, sicut jam susurrari audio, post me scribendi de talibus³ munus attemptaverit, mihi debeat collectionis gratiam, sibi habeat electionis materiam.

§ 446. Hæc habui, domine venerabilis Comes, de gestis Anglorum quæ dicerem, ab adventu eorum in Angliam usque in annum vicesimum octavum⁴ feli-

---

¹ *composuit.*] Here MS. Cf. (Hardy's MS. F.) the MS. All Souls 33, ends, with the addition of the following verses, giving the name of the writer Ivo:

Scripserit hunc librum quis, lector forte requiret;
Exacuat sensus et metra legat, cito discet.
Illius nomen tria componunt elementa,
In numeris quorum primum satis indicat unum,
Ponunt et leges numeri pro quinque secundum,
Si Græcus scribat postremo collige finem.

Here also MS. Ap. (add. 23, 147) ends.

² *dixi*] om. Ce.¹
³ *de talibus*] om. Ce.¹
⁴ *octavum*] om. Aa, Ag. At. The date of 1127 for the closing of this section of this history rests on the authority of MSS. Bc. Bk. By. Cd. Ce., all of the later recensions.

cissimi regni patris vestri: cetera proprium occupabunt libellum, si benignum istis non negaveritis vultum. Hoc autem opus postquam absolvi, circumspectis plurimis, vobis potissimum delegandum credidi. Cum enim alios considero, in uno nobilitatem, in altero militiam, in isto litteraturam, in illo justitiam, in paucis munificentiam invenio; itaque in aliis aliqua, in singulis singula, in vobis admiror universa. Si quis enim unquam fuit nobilis, vos in ea re præcellitis; cujus genus a præcellentissimis regibus et comitibus lineam trahit, animus a moribus imitationem conducit. Habetis ergo a Normannis bellandi peritiam, a Flandrensibus[1] liniamentorum gratiam, a Francis generositatis eminentiam. De militiæ porro vestræ industria quis hæsitet, cum eam excellentissimus pater in vobis suspiciat? Cum enim aliqui motus in Normannia nuntiantur, vos præmittit, ut virtute vestra profligentur, suspecta sagacitate redintegretur concordia: cum redit in regnum, vos reducit, ut sitis ei foris tutelæ, domi lætitiæ, ornamento ubique.

§ 447. Litteras ita fovetis, ut cum sitis tantarum occupationum mole districti, horas tamen aliquas vobis surripiatis, quibus aut ipsi legere, aut legentes possitis audire. Digno itaque moderamine fortunæ vestræ celsitudinem componitis, dum nec militiam propter litteras postponitis, nec litteras propter militiam, ut quidam, conspuitis: in quo etiam scientiæ vestræ patescit miraculum, quia, dum libros diligitis, datis indicium quam avidis medullis fontem eorum combiberitis; multæ siquidem res, etiam cum non habentur, desiderantur, philosophiam nullus amabit qui eam extrema satietate non hauserit.

---

[1] *Flandrensibus*] The MS. Phillipps 26,641 (once 2777), Hardy's A.³, our Aa.³, ended originally with the middle of this word; it is continued by a later hand.

His justice.

§ 448. Justitiæ vestræ fama regiones etiam nostras attigit; a vobis siquidem pravum judicium nunquam extorsit vel personæ sublimitas vel fortunæ tenuitas. Nihil reperit in vestro pectore quod suis conducat artibus qui justitiam labefactare conatur, seu oblatione muneris, seu delinimento favoris.[1]

His munificence.

The happiness of a state under such a ruler.

§ 449. Munificentiæ vestræ pecuniæque contemptum prætendit Teochesbiriæ cœnobium; de quo, ut audio, non solum xenia non corraditis, sed etiam ultro missa remittitis.[2] Quantum hoc sit isto præsertim tempore, quantæ in seculo gloriæ, quantæ apud Deum gratiæ, ipsi certe intelligitis. Beata est igitur, secundum sententiam Platonis, respublica cujus rector est philosophus, cujus princeps non delectatur muneribus.

The writer does not flatter, but does the simple duty of a historian.

Plura de talibus dicerem, nisi et suspicio meæ adulationis, et laudanda modestia vestri pudoris dicturientem cohiberet. Sane quæ dixi non prætermittere fuit consilium, ut per officium linguæ meæ probitas vestra posteros non lateat, et ipsa de virtute in virtutem proficere contendat. Et quidem jamdudum, quibusdam persuadentibus, ferebat animus ut, quæ prætereunda non putarem, per succiduos semper annos huic operi apponerem; sed consultius videtur alium de talibus librum procudere, quam jam absoluto frequenter

He has another work in contemplation.

nova[3] insuere. Nec vero quisquam superfluam me operam dicat insumere, si clarissimi omnium sua ætate regum gesta propono: multa enim sublimitati ejus mea humilitas debet, et adhuc plura debebit, ut, si nihil aliud esset, quod se talem filium habere gaudet;[4] nam et olim felici sorte susceptum, non perfunctorie, ut hodie claret, litteris erudiri præcepit, post etiam amplissimarum possessionum fecit dominum, nunc postremo patrium[5] in vos reclinat affectum. Sit

---

[1] Here the 5th book in MS. Ce.[1] ends, the whole of the following section being omitted.

[2] *remittitis*] mittitis, Bc. Cd. Ce.[2]

[3] *nova*] om. Bc.

[4] *gaudet*] gauderet, Bc.

[5] *patrium*] paternum, Bc.; om. Ag.

ergo hic liber, ut est, vestræ gloriæ absolute consecratus; in altero erit idem vitæ, qui scripturæ, terminus. Quod superest, munus meum dignanter suscipite, ut gaudeam grato cognitoris arbitrio, qui non erravi eligendi judicio.[1]

This is dedicated to the earl's glory.

---

[1] MS. Bc[2]. adds, "Hæc habui domine venerabilis comes de gestis." Bk. has, "Explicit liber quintus de gestis Anglorum, incipit liber "sextus." MS. Aah. has, " Explicit gesta Guillelmi dignæ memoriæ " monachi Malmesberiensis coenobii de Anglorum regibus. Liber Jo- " hannis de Whytefeld monachi de Rouecestria." MSS. Cs. Bc.[2] By. Aa. Aa.[2] Aa.[3] Aah. Ar. and Harl. 528 end here.—Cd. Cm. have " Incipit " liber sextus." The MS. Claudius C. 9. (Aa.) has here the letter of Edward I. to the abbot of Battle, containing the submission of the candidates for Scotland, and dated Westminster, July 19, Anno xix°.

Note on § 397; above p. 473.

Non tamen—percussum] Here MS. Cs. reads as follows :

Neque tamen victoriam hanc sine sanguine consummavit; nam ex carissimis suis multos amisit, et inter eos egregium virum ac strenuissimum militem Rogerium de Gloecestra. Is, in obsidione Fallesii telo arcubalistæ graviter vulneratus in capite, donavit ecclesiæ sancti Petri de Gloecestra manerium quod appellatur Culna S. Andreæ, et in hoc assensum et concessionem regis, qui statim ad se videndum venerat, impetravit, ita quod manum ipsius cum eam hujus rei gratia deoscularetur, frontis sanguine cruentavit. Cujus donationis confirmationem et testimonium regis adversus Gilbertum de Mineriis ad majorem rei evidentiam operi huic inserere dignum duximus :—

" Henricus rex Anglorum Samsoni episcopo Wigornensi et Walterio " vicecomiti de Gloecestra, et omnibus baronibus suis Francis et Anglis " de Gloecestresira salutem. Notum sit vobis quod dedi et concessi " manerium de Culna ecclesiæ sancti Petri de Gloecestra ad communem " victum monachorum, sicut Rogerius de Gloecestra eis dedit et con- " cessit, et sicut melius tenuit, pro anima mea et uxoris meæ et pro " animabus antecessorum meorum; teste Girmundo abbate Winchel- " cumbæ et Rogerio de Gloecestra et Hugone parvo."

" Henricus rex Anglorum archiepiscopis, episcopis, abbatibus, comiti- " bus, baronibus, vicecomitibus et omnibus fidelibus suis Francis et " Anglis, totius Angliæ, salutem. Sciatis quia monachi de Gloecestra " et Gilebertus de Mineriis in curiam meam venerunt coram me ad " terminum inter eos positum, de placito manerii de Culna quod Gile- " bertus versus eos et abbatem suum clamabat, et Adam de Port de " Willelmus filius Odonis coram me testificati fuerunt, quod ipsi afflu- " erunt ubi Rogerius de Gloecestra manerium illud ecclesiæ sancti

Note on § 397—*continued.*

" Petri et monachis ibidem Deo servientibus in elemosinam dederat,
" et ubi ego requisitione ipsius Rogerii donationem illam eis concessi,
" et unde isdem Gilebertus judicium recusavit: testibus Willelmo
" archiepiscopo Cantuariæ, et Rogerio episcopo Salesberiæ, et Willelmo
" episcopo Wintoniæ, et Bernardo episcopo de Sancto David, et Willelmo
" episcopo Exoniæ et Urbano episcopo de Glamorgan, et Gaufrido can-
" cellario, et Roberto de Sigillo, et Milone de Gloccestra, et Henrico
" de Port, et Walterio de Amfrevilla et Willelmo de Folia, et Rogerio
" et Willelmo filiis Adam de Port; apud Wintoniam anno ab Incar-
" natione Domini M°C°XX°VII°. Porro Robertum," &c.

HISTORIA NOVELLA.

PROLOGUS.

Incipit Prologus Willelmi Malmesberiensis in libros novellæ historiæ, missos Roberto comiti Gloecestriæ.

DOMINO amantissimo Roberto, filio regis Henrici, et consuli Gloecestrensi, Willelmus bibliothecarius Malmesberiæ, post emerita trophæa in terris triumphare in cœlis. Pleraque gestorum præcellentis memoriæ patris vestri stilo apponere non neglexi, et in quinto libro regalium actuum,[1] et in tribus libellis quibus Chronica dedi vocabulum. Nunc ea quæ moderno tempore magno miraculo Dei acciderunt in Anglia, ut mandentur posteris, desiderat animus vestræ serenitatis: pulcherrimum plane[2] desiderium, et vestrorum omnium simile. Quid enim plus ad honestatis spectat commodum, quid conducibilius[3] æquitati, quam divinam agnoscere circa bonos indulgentiam, et erga perjuros[4] vindictam? Quid porro jocundius quam fortium facta[5] virorum monumentis tradere litterarum; quorum exemplo ceteri exuant ignaviam, et ad defendendam armentur patriam? Quod quia officio stili mei præceptum est fieri, ordinatius puto posse historiam transigi, si, paulo altius repetens, a reditu imperatricis in

William dedicates the continuation of his history to Earl Robert.

---

[1] *actuum*] om. Bc. Bk. Bq. Cd.
[2] *plane*] plene, Bc. Bk. Cd.
[3] *conducibilius*] magis conducit, Ag. At. Bc. Bk. Bq. Cd.
[4] *perjuros*] perversos, Bc. Cd. Cm.
[5] *facta*] factum, Ce¹.

Angliam post viri sui[1] decessum seriem annorum contexam. Itaque primo vocata, ut decet, in auxilium Divinitate, rerum veritatem scripturus, nihilque offensæ daturus aut gratiæ, ita incipiam.

Explicit prologus.

---

[1] *sui*] om. At. Bc. Bk. Cd.

WILLELMI MALMESBIRIENSIS
HISTORIÆ NOVELLÆ

Libri Tres.

Incipit liber primus novellæ Historiæ.

Quibus de causis imperatricem rex Henricus ab Alemannia revocaverit.

§ 450. Anno Henrici regis Anglorum vicesimo sexto, qui fuit incarnationis Dominicæ millesimus centesimus vicesimus sextus, Henricus imperator Alemannorum, cui præfati regis filia Matildis nupserat, in ipso ætatis et victoriarum flore obiit.[1] Morabatur eo tempore rex noster Normanniæ, ob[2] pacificandos, si qui in eis partibus fierent, motus; qui, ubi primum obitum generi accepit, non multo post honoratis viris a se missis filiam revocavit. Invita, ut aiunt, imperatrix rediit, quod dotalibus regionibus consueta esset, et multas ibidem possessiones haberet. Constat certe aliquos Lotharingorum et Longobardorum principes succedentibus annis plus quam semel Angliam venisse, ut eam sibi dominam requirerent; verumtamen[3] fructu laborum caruisse, cogitante rege ut filiæ connubio inter se et Andegavensem comitem pacem componeret. Mirum enim in modum vir ille, omnium regum quos nostra et etiam patrum nostrorum tenet memoria maximus, suspectam tamen semper habuit Andegavensium potentiam. Hinc est quod sponsalitia quæ

A.D. 1125. The death of the emperor Henry V.

Matilda returns to her father.

Her wooers.

Project for her marriage with Geoffrey of Anjou.

---

[1] *obiit*] obierat vel obiit, Ag. At.
[2] *ob*] ad, Ag. At. Bc. Cd.
[3] *verumtamen*] sed, Ag. At. Bc. Bk. Cd.

Willelmus nepos suus, comes postea Flandriæ, cum filia comitis Andegavensis Fulconis, postea regis Jerosolimorum, contracturus esse videbatur,[1] dissolvit et cassavit. Hinc est quod aliam ejusdem filiam filio suo Willelmo impubi vixdum adolescenti conjunxit. Hinc est quod hanc filiam suam, de qua incepimus loqui, post imperatorium thorum, ejusdem Fulconis filio nuptum collocavit, sicut sermo procedens dicere perget.

Policy of Angevin marriages.

De concilio habito Londoniis.

A.D. 1126.

§ 451. Anno vicesimo septimo regni sui[2] rex Henricus Angliam venit mense Septembri, adducens secum filiam suam. Proximo vero Natali Domini convocato apud Londoniam magno cleri et optimatum numero, uxori suæ, filiæ ducis Lovannensis, quam post obitum Matildis duxerat, comitatum Salopesberiæ dedit: quam videlicet fœminam dolens non concipere, dum et perpetuo sterilem fore timeret, de successore regni merito anxius cogitabat. De qua re antea multum diuque considerato[3] consilio, tunc in eodem concilio omnes totius Angliæ optimates, episcopos etiam et abbates, sacramento adegit et obstrinxit, ut, si ipse sine herede masculo decederet, Matildem filiam suam quondam imperatricem incunctanter et sine ulla retractatione dominam susciperent: præfatus quanto incommodo[4] patriæ fortuna Willelmum filium suum[5] sibi surripuisset, cui jure regnum competeret: nunc superesse filiam, cui soli legitima debeatur successio, ab avo, avunculo, et patre regibus; a[6] materno genere multis retro seculis. Siquidem ab Egbirto rege[7] West-Saxo-

Second marriage of the king.

Settlement of the succession.

Argument for the empress, and her descent from the native kings.

---

[1] *videbatur*] dicebatur, At. Bc. Cd.

[2] *regni sui*] om. Ce.

[3] *considerato*] deliberato, Bc. Bk.; desiderato, Cd.

[4] *incommodo*] dampno, Ag. At. Bc. Bk. Bq. Cd.

[5] *suum*] om. At. Cc.¹

[6] *a*] et a, Bc. Cd.

[7] *rege*] om. Bc. Cd.

num, qui primus ceteros insulæ reges vel expulit vel subegit, anno Dominicæ incarnationis octingentesimo, sub quatuordecim regibus, usque ad ejusdem incarnationis annum millesimum quadragesimum tertium, quo rex Edwardus[1] in regnum sullimatus est. Nec unquam ejusdem regalis sanguinis linea defecit, nec in successione regni claudicavit. Porro Edwardus illius progeniei ultimus, idemque et præclarissimus, proneptem suam Margaretam ex fratre Edmundo Ireneside, Malcolmi regis Scottorum nuptiis copulavit; quorum filiam fuisse Matildem, hujus imperatricis matrem, constat.[2]

De sacramento quod primates Angliæ fecerunt Imperatrici.

§ 452. Juraverunt ergo cuncti, quicunque in eodem concilio alicujus viderentur esse momenti; primo Willelmus Cantuariæ archiepiscopus, mox ceteri episcopi, nec minus abbates. Laicorum primus juravit David rex Scotiæ, ejusdem imperatricis avunculus; tunc Stephanus comes Moritonii et Bononiæ, nepos Henrici regis ex sorore Adala: mox Robertus regis filius, quem ante regnum susceperat, et comitem Gloecestræ fecerat; data ei in matrimonium Mabilia, spectabili et excellenti fœmina, domina tum viro morigera, tum etiam fœcunditate numerosæ et pulcherrimæ prolis beata.[3] Notabile, ut dicitur,[4] fuit certamen inter Robertum et Stephanum, dum æmula laude virtutum inter se contenderent quis eorum prior juraret; illo privilegium filii, isto dignitatem nepotis spectante. Ita obstrictis proceribus[5] omnibus fide et sacramento, tunc quidem

Fealty sworn to the empress.

Robert and Stephen contend with another about priority.

---

[1] *Edwardus*] qui apud Westmonasterium jacet, At. Bc. Cd.
[2] *filiam—constat*] filia Matildis hujus imperatricis mater extitit, Ag. At. Bc. Bk. Bq. Cd.
[3] *data—beata*] om. Ag. At. Bc. Bk. Cd.
[4] *dicitur*] fertur, Ag. At. Bc. Cd.
[5] *proceribus*] om. Ag. At. Bc. Bk. Cd.

a quoque in sua discessum est. Post Pentecosten vero misit rex[1] filiam suam[2] in Normanniam, jubens eam per Rothomagensem archiepiscopum desponsari filio prædicti Fulconis, adolescenti magnæ nobilitatis et prædicandi roboris: nec distulit quin ipse quoque Normanniam navigaret, eosque matrimonio conjungeret. Quo facto, quodam vaticinio omnes prædicabant ut post mortem ejus a sacramento desciscerent. Ego Rogerum Salesberiensem episcopum sæpe dicentem audivi, "Solutum se a[3] sacramento quod imperatrici " fecerat: eo enim pacto se jurasse, ne rex præter " consilium suum et ceterorum procerum filiam cui- " quam nuptum daret extra regnum. Ejus matrimonii " nullum auctorem, nullum fuisse conscium, nisi Ro- " bertum comitem Gloecestræ, et Brianum filium comi- " tis, et episcopum Luxoviensem." Nec vero hæc iccirco dixerim quod credam vera fuisse verba hominis, qui se unicuique tempori pro volubilitate fortunæ accommodare nosset; sed sicut verax historicus opinionem provincialium scriptis appono.

De obitu Honorii papæ, et de contentione eligendi apostolici.

§ 453. Reliquos annos vitæ et regni Henrici regis[4] breviter percensere libet; ut nec rerum cognitione fraudentur posteri, nec his quæ minus ad hanc historiam pertinent prolixius immorari videar. Anno vicesimo octavo rediit in Angliam rex a Normannia. Anno vicesimo nono quiddam accidit in Anglia quod mirum videatur crinitis nostris, qui, obliti quid[5] nati sunt, libenter se in muliebris sexus habitum transformant.[6]

---

[1] *rex*] om. Cc.[1]
[2] *suam*] om. Cc.
[3] *a*] om. Cc.
[4] *regis*] om. At. Bc. Cd.
[5] *quid*] quod, Ag.

[6] *libenter—transformant*] in muliebris sexus habitum capillorum longitudine se ipsos transformant, Ag. At. Bc. Bk. Cd.

Quidam provincialium militum, magno crinium luxu superbiens, conscientiaque stimulante perterritus, visus est sibi videre in sompniis quasi aliquis eum capillorum suorum criniculis suffocaret; quare, sompno excussus, quicquid superfluebat comarum cito abscidit. Cucurrit exemplum per Angliam, et, sicut recens pœna mentem movere solet, omnes pene milites ad justum modum crines suos recidi æquanimiter tulerunt. Sed non diu stetit hæc sanctitas; vix enim anno elapso, cuncti, qui sibi curiales esse videbantur, in prius vitium recide-runt: longitudine capillorum cum fœminis certabant, et, ubi crines deficiunt, involucra quædam innodabant; obliti vel potius ignari sententiæ apostolicæ, "Vir si "comam nutrierit, ignominia est illi."

Change of fashion in hair cutting.

1 Cor. xi. 14.

Anno tricesimo rex Henricus transiit in Norman-niam. Eo anno defuncto papa Honorio, magna contentione eligendi apostolici Romana fluctuavit ecclesia. Erant tunc in eadem urbe duo famosissimi cardinales, Gregorius diaconus sancti Angeli, et Petrus presbyter cardinalis, filius Leonis Romanorum principis: ambo litteris et industria insignes; nec erat facile discernere populo quisnam eorum justius eligeretur a clero. Prævenit tamen pars quæ favebat Gregorio ut pontifex ordinatus vocaretur Innocentius: sparsus est etiam rumor in plebem quod adhuc Honorius spiraret, et ita fieri præciperet. Auctores fuerunt hujus ordinationis Willelmus Prænestinus episcopus, Mathæus Albanensis, Conradus Sabinensis, Johannes Hostiensis, Petrus Cremensis de titulo sancti Crisogoni, Haimericus cancellarius. At vero pars altera, sepulto jam Honorio, annitentibus fratribus Petri, locupletissimis Romanorum et potentissimis, eum electum et sacratum vocavit Anacletum. Maximus hujus ordinationis hortator et auctor Petrus Portuensis episcopus fuit: cujus epistolam si posuero, ea omnem controversiam aperiet, pronior tamen in Anacletum.

Henry goes back to Normandy. Schism at Rome on the death of pope Honorius II., A.D. 1130.

Parties of the rival pontiffs.

Epistola Petri Portuensis de eadem contentione.

§ 454. "Petrus Portuensis episcopus, quatuor episcopis
" Willelmo Praenestino, Mathaeo Albanensi, Conrado Sabinensi,
" Johanni Ostiensi. Quanta sit pro vobis tribulatio cordis
" mei, ille solus novit qui omnia novit: vobis quoque meis
" litteris cognitum saltem jam ex parte fuisset, nisi ecclesiae
" sententia et communis auctoritas prohiberet. De commen-
" datione seu vituperatione personarum de quibus nunc ser-
" monum varietas agitatur, non est hujus temporis judicare:
" est qui quaerat et judicet. Si tamen quisquam praesto S. John viii.
" fuerit accusare, praesto erit et qui debeat respondere; 50.
" praesertim cum in vestro et meo, immo in totius ecclesiae
" conspectu, uterque sapienter vixerit et honeste, et quae
" officii sui erant plena hucusque exercuerit libertate. Abs-
" tinere vos potius convenit a sermonibus otiosis et verbis
" praecipitationis: si de rumoribus agitur, longe se aliter
" habent res quam vestrae apud me litterae protestantur. Ad
" haec, si verba quae posuistis, si ordinis rationem attenditis,
" ut salva reverentia vestra loquar, factionem illam vestram
" qua confidentia, qua fronte, electionem vocare praesumitis?
" Cur illum vestrum dicitis ordinatum, cum prorsus in causa
" ejus ordo non fuerit? Siccine didicistis papam eligere?
" in angulo, in abscondito, in tenebrosis et umbra mortis?
" Si mortuo papae vivum succedere volebatis,[1] cur mortuum
" vivere praedicabatis? multo melius erat mortuo humanita-
" tem impendere, et sic de vivi solatio cogitare. Sed ecce!
" dum[2] de mortuo solatium vivo requiritis, et vivum et
" mortuum pariter suffocastis. Postremo, nec vestrum, sicut
" nec meum, fuit eligere; sed potius electum a fratribus
" spernere vel approbare. Quod igitur, neglecto ordine, con-
" tempto canone, spreto etiam ipso a vobis condito anathe-
" mate, me inconsulto priore vestro, inconsultis etiam fratribus
" majoribus et prioribus, nec etiam vocatis aut expectatis,
" cum essetis novitii et in numero brevi paucissimi, facere
" praesumpsistis, pro infecto habendum esse, et nihil omnino
" existere, ex ipsa vestra aestimatione potestis advertere.
" Cito autem nobis Dominus affuit, et viam qua errori

---

[1] *volebatis*] voluistis, Cd.; voluistis vel volebatis, At.

[2] *dum*] om. Ce.¹

"vestro contraire possemus ostendit; fratres siquidem vestri
"cardinales, quorum præcipua est in electione potestas, cum
"clero, universo expetente populo, cum honoratorum con-
"sensu, in luce, in manifesto, unanimi voto et desiderio,
"elegerunt dominum Petrum cardinalem in Romanum ponti-
"ficem Anacletum. Hanc ego electionem canonice celebra-
"tam conspexi, et auctore Deo confirmavi. Hunc ecclesia
"suscipit et veneratur: hunc per Dei gratiam episcopi, ab-
"bates, principes, capitanei, et barones, quidam per se ipsos,
"quidam per nuntios suos, videntibus nobis frequentant. De-
"prædationem illam et crudelitatem, quam prætenditis, non
"videmus. Quicunque ad eum pro responsis seu negotiis
"suis veniunt benigne suscipiuntur, benignius revertuntur.
"Redite, jam redite ad cor: nolite schisma in ecclesia fa-
"cere; ad animarum subversionem nolite ulterius laborare:
"teneat vos timor Dei,[1] non pudor seculi. Nunquid qui
"dormit, non adjiciet ut resurgat? desistite jam mendaciis,
"in quibus impii spem suam ponere consuerunt. Dominus
"Tiburtius in scriptis suis cum juramento[2] testificatus est,
"dicens quod ego diaconum sancti Angeli solum idoneum
"judicavi ad pontificatus ordinem. Videat ipse quid dixerit:
"ego in occulto locutus sum nihil; non est aliquis qui hoc
"verbum ab ore meo unquam audierit. Hæc fuit senten-
"tia mea semper, ut non nisi sepulto papa de successoris
"persona mentio haberetur. Unitatem ecclesiæ tenui, et
"tenebo: veritati et justitiæ adhærere curabo, confidenter
"sperans quia justitia et veritas liberabit me."

Election of Anacletus II., in whose favour the writer is inclined.

Sic prædictus Petrus Portuensis,[3] Petro Leoni pronior, scripsit. Nec vero pars altera cessabat quin et ipsum Petrum catulum leonis diceret, et fautores ejus factionis complices nominaret. Et illi quidem varia inter se dubiis de rebus agebant. Innocentius vero exclusus Roma, transcensis Alpibus, Galliam contendit. Ibi ab omni citramontana ecclesia incunctanter susceptus est: quin etiam et rex Henricus, qui non leviter a sententia quam semel proposuisset dejici nosset,

Innocent goes to France.

Meeting the king and pope.

---

[1] *Dei*] Domini, Bc. Cd.
[2] *juramento*] sacramento, At. Bc. Cd.
[3] *Portuensis—Leoni*] Portuensis episcopus in Petrum Leonis filium, Ag. At. Bc. Cd.

illi apud Carnotum ultro manus dedit; et apud Rothomagum non modo suis, sed et optimatum et etiam Judæorum, muneribus eum¹ dignatus est. Nec vero Innocentius, quamvis ab Anglorum et Francorum regibus, simul et ab imperatore Alemannorum, valde juvaretur, nunquam tamen quiete potiri potuit, quod Anacletus Romanæ sedem teneret ecclesiæ. At vero ipso² Anacleto defuncto, octavo præsumpti ut dicebatur sui episcopatus anno, dominus Innocentius inconcussa ad hoc tempus pace apostolica fruitur dignitate.

§ 455. Anno tricesimo primo regni sui rediit rex³ in Angliam. Imperatrix quoque eodem anno natali⁴ solo adventum suum exhibuit; habitoque non parvo procerum conventu apud Northamtonam, priscam fidem apud eos qui dederant novavit, ab his qui non dederant accepit. Eodem anno Lodowicus rex Francorum, et in senium vergens et nimia corpulentia gravis, filium coronari jussit ut regni successorem: quo non multo post casu equi exanimato, alterum per manum pontificis Romani⁵ diademate insignivit. Is, ut ferunt,⁶ ab antiqua Francorum fortitudine non degenerans, etiam Aquitaniam juri suo per uxoris dotale fœdus adquisivit; quam post Lodowicum, Caroli magni filium, in proprio dominatu Francorum reges non habuisse noscuntur.

De lue pecorum.

§ 456. Anno tricesimo primo regni Henrici infesta lues domesticorum animalium totam pervagata est Angliam: plenæ porcorum haræ subito vacuabantur; integra boum præsæpia repente destituebantur. Duravit sequentibus annis eadem pestis, ut nulla omnino totius regni villa, hujus miseriæ immunis, alterius in-

---

¹ *eum*] suscipere, ins. Ce.²
² *ipso*] om. Ce.¹
³ *rex*] Henricus, add. At. Bc. Cd.
⁴ *natali*] Angliæ, ins. Ce.²
⁵ *Romani*] Remensis, Ce. Lewis VII. was crowned by the pope at Rheims.
⁶ *ferunt*] dicunt, Ce.²

commoda ridere posset. Tunc etiam contentio inter Bernardum episcopum Menevensem et Urbanum Landavensem de jure parochiarum, quas idem Urbanus illicite usurpaverat, æterno fine sopita est: tot enim ad curiam Romanam appellationibus, tot itinerum expensis, tot causidicorum conflictibus multis annis ventilata, tandem aliquando morte Urbani apud Romam soluta, vel potius decisa est; nam et apostolicus, æquitate rei perpensa, religioni et justitiæ Menevensis episcopi qua decebat sententia satisfecit. Eodem etiam anno Willelmus archiepiscopus Cantuariæ legationem in Anglia, Romanæ sedis indulgentia, personaliter impetravit.

De transitu Regis Henrici et de morte ejus.

§ 457. Anno tricesimo secundo regni pridie transacto, Henricus nonis Augusti, quo die quondam apud Westmonasterium coronæ culmen acceperat, Normanniam navigavit. Ultimus ille fatalisque regi transitus fuit. Mira tunc prorsus providentia Deitatis rebus allusit humanis, ut eo[1] die navem ascenderet, nunquam iterum[2] reversurus, quo dudum coronatus fuerat, tam diu et tam feliciter regnaturus. Erat tunc, ut dixi, nonæ Augusti; et feria quarta prosecuta sunt elementa dolore suo extremum tanti principis transitum. Nam et sol ipsa die, hora sexta, tetra ferrugine, ut poetæ solent dicere, nitidum caput obtexit, mentes hominum defectione sua terrens:[3] et feria sexta proxima, primo mane, tantus terræ motus fuit ut penitus subsidere videretur, horrifico sono sub terra[4] ante audito. Vidi ego et in eclipsi stellas circa solem; et in terræ motu parietem domus in qua sedebam, bifario impetu elevatum, tertio resedisse. Fuit ergo rex in Normannia triennio continuo, et tanto plus quantum est inter nonas Augusti, quo

---

[1] *Eo*] Eodem, Ce².
[2] *iterum*] vivus, At. Bc. Bk. Cd.
[3] *defectione—terrens*] eclipsi sua concutiens, Ag. At. Bc. Bk. Cd.
[4] *terra*] terris, At. Bc. Cd.

Henry's death, Dec. 1, 1135.

die, ut¹ dictum est, mare transivit, et kalendas Decembris, qua nocte decessit. Nec vero dubitandum, multa eum, quæ non immerito scribi deberent, in Normannia gessisse; sed consilium fuit præterire quæ ad nostram notitiam non integre pervenere. Opiniones reditus ejus in Angliam multæ; sive fato quodam, sive divina voluntate, omnes frustratæ. Regnavit ergo annis triginta quinque, et a nonis Augusti usque ad kalendas Decembris; id est, mensibus quatuor, diebus quatuor² minus.³ Apud Liuns⁴ exercitio venationis intentus, valitudine adversa correptus decubuit. Qua in deterius⁵ crescente, evocavit ad se Hugonem, quem primo ex priore de Lewis abbatem apud Radingas, mox Rothomagi archiepiscopum, fecerat; merito sibi, et heredibus suis, pro tantis beneficiis obnoxium. Optimates rumor suæ⁶ ægritudinis celeriter contraxit.

His son Robert was with him, and testified that he made his daughter his sole successor.

Affuit et Robertus filius ejus, comes Gloecestræ, qui, pro integritate fidei et virtutis eminentia, victuram in omne seculum memoriam sui nominatim promeruit. A quibus de successore interrogatus, filiæ omnem terram suam citra et ultra mare legitima et perenni successione adjudicavit; marito ejus subiratus, quod eum et minis et injuriis aliquantis irritaverat. Septimo incommodi die transacto, nocte jam intempesta naturæ cessit. Cujus magnanimos mores hic dicere supersedeo quia in quinto libro regalium gestorum plenissime illos contexui: quam Christiane autem⁷ obierit, hæc subsequens epistola supradicti Rothomagensis archiepiscopi docebit:

Above, § 411.

Epistola Rothomagensis Archiepiscopi de obitu Regis Henrici.

Letter of Hugh of Rouen.

§ 458. "Domino et patri suo Innocentio papæ, servus "Hugo Rothomagensis sacerdos, obedientiæ debitum. De

---

¹ *ut*] om. Ce¹.
² *quatuor*] om. Ce¹.; quinque, Ce².
³ *minus*] plus, Ce².
⁴ *Liuns*] Leonas, At. Cd; Leonibus, Bc.

⁵ *in deterius*] evidentius, Ce².
⁶ *suæ*] om. At. Bc. Cd.
⁷ *autem*] om. Cd.

" domino meo rege, non sine dolore memorando, piæ pater- *describing*
" nitati vestræ notificandum duximus; qui, subita præventus *the pious end of King*
" ægritudine, nos, missis quam citissime legatis suis, ægri- *Henry.*
" tudinis¹ solatiis voluit interesse. Venimus ad ipsum, et
" cum ipso plenum mæroribus confecimus triduum. Prout
" ei dicebamus, ipse ore proprio sua fatebatur peccata, et
" manu propria pectus suum percutiebat, et malam volun-
" tatem dimittebat. Consilio Dei, et nostro, et episcoporum,
" emendationem vitæ suæ observaturum sese promittebat.
" Sub ista promissione,² eo firmiter annuente, pro nostro
" officio tertio eum et per triduum absolvimus. Crucem
" Domini adoravit; corpus et sanguinem Domini devote sus-
" cepit; eleemosynam suam disposuit, ita dicendo: 'Solvan-
" ' tur debita mea, reddantur liberationes et solidatæ quibus ³
" ' debeo; reliqua indigentibus distribuantur.' Utinam sic
" fecissent qui thesauros ejus tenebant et tenent! Tandem
" illi auctoritatem de unctione infirmorum, quam ecclesia a
" beato Jacobo apostolo suscepit, studiose proposuimus; et
" ipsius pia petitione oleo sancto eum inunximus. Sic in
" pace quievit: pacem det ei Deus, quia pacem dilexit!"

Quomodo corpus Regis Henrici exinteratum est.

§ 459. Hæc præfatus Rothomagensis archiepiscopus *He is brought to Rouen.* de fide regis Henrici morientis vere contestatus est. Funus regaliter curatum, proceribusque vicissim portantibus Rotomagum usque delatum est. Illic in quodam recessu ecclesiæ majoris exinteratum est, ne diuturnitate corruptum nares assidentium vel astantium *His bowels buried there; his body brought to Caen.* exacerbaret: reliquiæ interaneorum in cœnobio sanctæ Mariæ de Pratis juxta urbem humatæ; quod ipse, ut audio, a matre sua inchoatum, non paucis compendiis honoraverat. Corpus Cadomi servatum, quousque serenas auras paulo clementior hyems inveheret, quæ tum aspera inhorrebat.

---

¹ *ægritudinis*] suæ, ins. At. Bc. Cd.
² *sub ista promissione*] ista ei, add. Cd.; sub ipsa promissione ista ei, At. Bc. Bk.
³ *quibus*] quæ, At. Bc. Cd.

De Stephano Rege in regnum promoto.

Stephen, Count of Mortain, hurries to England.

§ 460. Interea Stephanus comes Moritonii et Bononiæ, nepos regis Henrici, ut supra dixi, qui post regem Scottiæ primus laicorum fidem suam imperatrici obstrinxerat, in Angliam per Witsand maturavit adventum. Imperatrix certis ex causis, simul et frater ejus Robertus comes Gloecestræ, cum omnibus pene *The empress supported in Normandy.* proceribus, redire in regnum distulerunt. Quædam tamen[1] castella in Normannia, inter quæ præcipuum Danfrontum, partibus heredis se applicuere. Constat sane illo die quo Stephanus appulsus est Angliam, summo mane, contra naturam hyemis in regionibus nostris, terricrepum sonum tonitrui cum horrendo fulgure fuisse, ut paulo minus mundus solvi æstimaretur. *Stephen is received by London and Winchester.* Ille, ubi a Londoniensibus et Wintoniensibus in regem exceptus est, etiam Rogerum Salesberiensem episcopum et Willelmum de Ponte Arcus, custodes thesaurorum regalium, ad se transduxit. Ne tamen veritas celetur posteris, omnes ejus conatus irriti fuissent, nisi Henricus frater ejus, Wintoniensis episcopus, qui modo[2] apostolicæ sedis legatus est in Anglia, placidum ei commodasset assensum; spe scilicet captus amplissima *The bishop of Winchester supports him and stands surety for his oath.* quod Stephanus avi sui Willelmi in regni moderamine mores servaret, præcipueque in ecclesiastici vigoris disciplina. Quapropter districto sacramento, quod a Stephano Willelmus Cantuariensis archiepiscopus exegit de libertate reddenda ecclesiæ et conservanda, episcopus Wintoniensis se mediatorem et vadem apposuit. Cujus sacramenti tenorem, postea scripto inditum, loco suo non prætermittam.

Above, § 452.

Below, § 464.

De coronatione Regis Stephani, et de moribus ejus.

Stephen is crowned Dec. 22, 1135.

§ 461. Coronatus est ergo in regem Stephanus Angliæ undecimo kalendas Januarii, Dominica, tribus

---

[1] *tamen*] om. Ce¹.
[2] *modo*] om. Bc. Bk. Cd. The bishop was made legate in March 1189, and his legation ended on the death of pope Innocent II. in 1143.

episcopis præsentibus, archiepiscopo, Wintoniense, Salesberiense, nullis abbatibus, paucissimis optimatibus, vicesima secunda die post excessum avunculi, anno Dominicæ incarnationis millesimo centesimo tricesimo quinto. Vir quidem impiger sed minus prudens,[1] armis strenuus, immodici animi ad quælibet ardua inchoanda, lenis et exorabilis hostibus, affabilis omnibus: cujus cum dulcedinem in promissis suspiceres, veritatem tamen dictorum et promissorum efficaciam desiderares; unde fratris consilium non multo post lapso tempore postponebat, cujus, ut dixi, auxilio munitus, et adversantes summoverat, et ad regnum ascenderat.

His character.

De humatione regis Henrici.

§ 462. Anno Dominicæ incarnationis millesimo centesimo tricesimo sexto,[2] postea,[3] regis Henrici corpus, lenibus flabris spirantibus, statim post Natale Domini impositum navi Angliam devectum est; et apud Radingense cœnobium, quod et foris prædiorum magnitudine, et intus religiosorum monachorum ordine decoraverat, præsente regni successore, humatum est. Postea vero rex Stephanus in Northanhumbriam paulo ante Quadragesimam contendit, ut David regem Scottiæ, qui diversa sentire dicebatur, conveniret: nec vero difficulter[4] ab eo quod voluit impetravit, quia et ille morum lenitate, et propiori jam senectute infractus, libenter in otium vel veræ vel simulatæ pacis concessit.

A.D. 1136. King Henry buried at Reading.

Stephen goes into the north before Lent (Feb. 4), and makes terms with the Scots.

De adventu Roberti comitis Gloecestræ in Angliam.

§ 463. Eodem anno post Pascha Robertus comes Gloecestræ, cujus prudentiam rex Stephanus maxime

After Easter (March 22), earl Robert lands.

---

[1] *minus prudens*] imprudens, Bc. Cd.; prudens, At.
[2] *sexto*] quinto, Bc. Cd.
[3] *postea*] om. Bc. Cd.
[4] *vero difficulter*] difficile, At. Bc. Cd.

verebatur, venit in Angliam. Is, dum esset in Normannia, multa cogitatione fatigarat animum quidnam sibi super hoc negotio statuendum putaret : si enim regi Stephano subderetur, contra sacramentum quod sorori fecerat fore videbat ; si refragaretur, nihil sorori vel nepotibus profuturum, sibi certe immaniter nociturum, intelligebat. Habebat enim, ut supra tetigi, rex immensam vim thesaurorum, quos multis annis rex Henricus.[1] avunculus suus[2] aggesserat ; æstimabantur denarii, et hi exquisitissimi, fere ad centum milia libras : erant et vasa tam aurea quam argentea magni ponderis et inæstimabilis pretii, et antiquorum regum, et Henrici potissimum, prudentia[3] congesta. Hanc copiam gazarum habenti auxiliatores deesse non poterant ; præsertim cum esset ipse in dando diffusus, et, quod minime principem decet, prodigus. Currebatur ad eum ab omnium generum militibus, et a levis armaturæ hominibus, maximeque ex Flandria et Britannia. Erat genus hominum rapacissimum et violentissimum, qui nihil pensi haberent vel cimiteria frangere vel ecclesias exspoliare ;[4] religiosi quinetiam ordinis viros non solum equis proturbare, sed et in captionem abducere ; non solum advenæ, sed etiam indigenæ milites, qui pacem regis Henrici oderant, quod sub ea tenui victu vitam transigebant. Hi omnes gratanter principi assenserant, quem levi negotio ad sua commoda inflectere possent, provincialium dispendio suas fortunas urgentes. Erat præterea Stephanus, cum esset comes, facilitate morum, et communione jocandi, considendi, convescendi[5] etiam cum infimis, amorem tantum demeritus quantum vix mente aliquis concipere queat : et jam omnes proceres Angliæ in ejus assen-

---

[1] *rex Henricus*] om. At. Bc. Cd.
[2] *sius*] om. At. Bc. Cd.
[3] *prudentia*] magnanimitate, Ag. At. Bc. Bk. Cd.
[4] *exspoliare*] expilare, At. Bc. Bk. Cd.
[5] *convescendi*] om. Bc. Cd.

sum pronis mentibus transierant. Erat igitur[1] anxius prudentissimus comes ut illos delicti coargueret, et ad saniorem sententiam præsenti colloquio revocaret; nam viribus obviare nulla propter præfatas causas dabatur facultas: cui nimirum nec in Angliam venire liberum erat, nisi, quasi defectionis eorum particeps, mentis suæ arcanum ad tempus dissimularet. Itaque homagium regi fecit sub conditione quadam, scilicet, quamdiu ille dignitatem suam integre custodiret et sibi pacta servaret; spectato enim jamdudum regis ingenio, instabilitatem fidei ejus prævidebat.

Earl Robert does conditional homage to him.

De sacramento quod rex Stephanus fecit de servanda justitia et privilegiis et legibus regni.

§ 464. Eodem anno, non multo post adventum comitis, juraverunt episcopi fidelitatem regi quamdiu ille libertatem ecclesiæ et vigorem disciplinæ conservaret Ipse quoque juravit juxta tenorem scripti quod sic habetur in subditis: "Ego Stephanus, Dei gratia, assensu
" cleri et populi, in regem Angliæ electus, et a domino Wil-
" lelmo archiepiscopo Cantuariæ et sanctæ ecclesiæ Romanæ
" legato consecratus, et ab Innocentio sanctæ Romanæ sedis
" pontifice postmodum confirmatus, respectu et amore Dei
" sanctam ecclesiam liberam esse concedo, et debitam re-
" verentiam illi confirmo. Nihil me in ecclesia, vel in rebus
" ecclesiasticis, simoniace acturum vel permissurum esse
" promitto. Ecclesiasticarum personarum et omnium cleri-
" corum, et rerum eorum, justitiam et potestatem, et dis-
" tributionem bonorum ecclesiasticorum, in manu episcopo-
" rum esse perhibeo et confirmo. Dignitates ecclesiarum
" privilegiis earum confirmatas, et consuetudines earum an-
" tiquo tenore habitas, inviolate manere statuo et con-
" firmo.[2] Omnes ecclesiarum possessiones et tenuras, quas
" die illa habuerunt qua Willelmus rex avus meus fuit vivus
" et mortuus, sine omnium calumpniantium reclamatione, eis
" liberas et absolutas esse concedo. Si quid vero de habitis

The bishops swear fealty.

Stephen's charter of liberties:

to churches;

---

[1] *igitur*] quidem, At. Bc. Cd.
[2] *statuo et confirmo*] concedo et statuo, At. Bc. Bk. Cd.

"aut possessis ante mortem regis, quibus modo careat, ec"clesia deinceps repetierit, indulgentiæ et dispensationi meæ "vel discutiendum vel restituendum reservo. Quæcunque "vero post mortem regis, liberalitate regum, largitione prin"cipum, oblatione vel comparatione vel qualibet transmuta"tione fidelium, collata sunt, confirmo. Pacem me et justi"tiam in omnibus facturum, et pro posse meo conservaturum,

on the question of forests;

"promitto. Forestas quas Willelmus rex avus meus, et "Willelmus secundus avunculus meus, instituerunt et tenu"erunt, mihi reservo: ceteras omnes, quas Henricus rex "superaddidit, ecclesiis et regno quietas reddo et concedo. "Si quis autem episcopus vel abbas, vel alia ecclesiastica

on wills;

"persona[1] ante mortem suam rationabiliter suo distribuerit, "vel distribuenda statuerit, firmum manere concedo: si "vero morte præoccupatus fuerit, pro salute animæ ejus ec-

on vacancies;

"clesiæ consilio eadem fiat distributio. Dum vero sedes "propriis fuerint pastoribus vacuæ, et ipsæ et omnes earum "possessiones in manu et custodia[2] clericorum et proborum "hominum ejusdem ecclesiæ committantur, donec pastor can-

on the extortions of sheriffs.

"onice substituatur. Omnes exactiones, et meschenningas, "et injustitias, sive per vicecomites vel per alios quoslibet "male inductas, funditus exstirpo. Bonas leges, et antiquas

Promise of good laws.

"et justas consuetudines in murdris, et placitis, et aliis "causis observabo, et observari præcipio et constituo. Apud "Oxeneford, anno incarnationis Domini millesimo centesimo "tricesimo sexto, regni mei primo."

Quod rex Stephanus omnia hæc quæ juraverat perperam mutavit.

The king fails to keep his promises.

§ 465. Nomina testium, qui multi fuerunt, apponere fastidio; quia pene omnia ita perperam mutavit, quasi ad hoc tantum jurasset ut prævaricatorem sacramenti se regno toti ostenderet. Liceat enim mihi, pace mansuetissimi hominis, verum non occulere; qui, si legitime regnum ingressus fuisset, et in eo administrando credulas aures malivolorum susurris non exhibuisset, parum ei profecto ad regiæ personæ decorem defuisset.

---

[1] *alia ecclesiastica persona*] alius ecclesiasticus, Cc.
[2] *et custodia*] om. Cc¹.

Itaque sub eo aliquarum ecclesiarum thesauri direpti, possessiones terrarum laicis datæ; ecclesiæ clericorum alienis venditæ; episcopi capti, et[1] res suas abalienare coacti; abbatiæ, vel amicorum gratia, vel relaxatione debitorum, indignis concessæ. Sed hæc non tam illi, quam consiliariis ejus, ascribenda puto; qui persuadebant ei, nunquam eum debere carere denariis dum monasteria essent referta thesauris.

De transitu regis Stephani et Roberti comitis Gloecestræ in Normanniam, et de insidiis habitis a rege in comitem.

§ 466. Anno Dominicæ incarnationis millesimo centesimo tricesimo septimo,[2] rex, primo tempore Quadragesimæ, transiit mare. Comes etiam, pertemptatis illorum et cognitis animis quos datæ fidei tenaciores esse noverat, dispositoque quid deinceps agendum decerneret, ipso[3] die Paschæ mare ingressus, plenaque felicitate in terram evectus est. Nec multo post, malignitatem adversæ fortunæ paulo minus expertus est; rex enim eum, incentore quodam Willelmo de Ipre, insidiis intercipere conatus est. Comes autem eas per quendam insidiarum conscium præmunitus, paratos sibi evitavit dolos; et curia, quo sæpe invitabatur, aliquantis diebus abstinuit. Rex, consternatus animo quod insidiis parum profecisset, astutia agendum ratus, serenitate vultus et gratuita confessione magnitudinem culpæ attenuare studuit. Juravit tamen verbis pro placito comitis conceptis, se nunquam ulterius tanto sceleri affuturum; et ut magis in gratiam reciperetur, manu archiepiscopi Hugonis Rothomagensis in manum Roberti missa, sacramentum solidavit. Et hæc quidem

---

[1] *et*] vel, Bc. Cd.
[2] *septimo,* sexto, Ce.
[3] *ipso*] ipse, Bc. Cd.

egit ille; sed nunquam plenam ei exhibuit amicitiam, cujus semper suspectam habebat potentiam: itaque coram comite¹ pulchre jocundeque comitem illum² appellans, retro maledicis verbis mordebat, et quibus poterat possessionibus vellicabat. Robertus quoque, arte artem eludens, occultabat fronte animum; pacificeque regem in regnum redire dimittens, ipse commodis suis in Normannia manens intendit. Ita Stephano multis tumultibus in Anglia impedito, et nunc super hos,³ nunc super alios irruente, ut merito illi quod de Ismahele dictum est coaptari posset, "quia " manus omnium contra illum, et illius contra omnes," Robertus toto anno illo securum in Normannia egit otium. Rex prompte contra sibi resistentes crebro, ut ferebatur, dicere solebat, "Cum me in regem ele-" gerint, cur me destituunt? per nascentiam Dei, nun-" quam rex dejectus appellabor!" Robertus, quasi positus in specula,⁴ rerum providebat exitum; et ne de juramento, quod sorori fecerat, erga Deum et homines perfidiæ notaretur, sedulo cogitabat.

Gen. xvi. 12.

Quomodo et quibus de causis Robertus comes homagium regis abdicavit.

§ 467. Anno incarnationis Dominicæ millesimo centesimo tricesimo octavo, intestinis discidiis Anglia quatebatur: multi siquidem, quos nobilitas generis, vel magnitudo animi, vel potius viridioris⁵ ætatis audacia, ad illicita præcipitabat, a rege, hi prædia, hi castella, postremo quæcunque semel collibuisset, petere non verebantur; quæ cum ille dare differret, excusata mutilatione regni, vel quod eadem alii calumpniarentur aut etiam possiderent, illi continuo ira commoti castella

---

¹ *comite*]om. Ce.
² *illum*] om. Ce.
³ *hos*] unos, At. Bc. Bk. Cd.
⁴ *specula*] speculo, Ce².
⁵ *viridioris*, animi vel, ins. Ce².

contra eum obfirmabant, prædas ingentes ex ejus terris
agebant. Nec vero ille aliquorum defectione frange- His mis-
batur animo; sed modo hic, modo illic subitus aderat, ment.
semperque suo magis quam resistentium dampno rem
conficiebat: multis enim et magnis laboribus suis in
cassum effusis, datis vel honoribus vel castellis, simulatam ad tempus pacem ab illis promerebat. Denique The creation
multos etiam comites, qui ante non fuerant, instituit; of earls.
applicitis possessionibus et redditibus quæ proprio jure
regi competebant. Erant illi avidiores ad petendum,
et is profusior ad dandum; quia fama per Angliam
volitabat, quod comes Gloecestræ Robertus, qui erat
in Normannia, in proximo partes sororis foret adju- Alarm of
turus, rege tantum modo ante diffidato. Nec fides [1] invasion.
rerum famæ levitatem destituit: celeriter enim post Earl Robert
Pentecosten, missis a Normannia suis regi more ma- his homage
jorum amicitiam et fidem interdixit, homagio etiam Whitsun-
abdicato; rationem præferens quam id juste faceret, tide, May 22.
quia et rex illicite ad regnum aspiraverat, et omnem
fidem sibi juratam neglexerat, ne dicam mentitus fuerat;
ipsemet quin etiam contra legem egisset, qui, post sacramentum quod sorori dederat, alteri cuilibet ea vivente
se manus dare non erubuisset. Animabant nimirum Advice
mentem ejus multorum religiosorum responsa, quos given him.
super negotio consuluerat: Nullo modo eum posse sine
ignominia vitam præsentem transigere, vel mereri beati-
tudinem futuræ, si paternæ necessitudinis sacramentum
irritum haberet. Ad hæc [2] etiam apostolici decreti præ The pope
se tenorem ferebat, præcipientis ut sacramento, quod to keep the
præsente patre fecerat, obediens esset; cujus decreti oath taken
paginam posteriori libello indicare curabo. Hæc vir to Henry.
ille, qui plena satietate litterarum scientiam com-
biberat, magno fructu sibi fore in posterum sciebat

---

[1] *fides*] veritas, At. Bc. Bk. Cd.
[2] *Ad hæc*] Adde quod, Bc. Bk. Cd.; Addebant quod, At.

The king seizes his estates.

Ceterum, rex ægre ferens comitis magnanimitatem, omnibus eum possessionibus in Anglia quibus poterat¹ privavit, et quædam ejus castella complanavit. Solum Bristowia² remansit, ut non solum hostes expelleret, sed etiam crebris regem incursionibus fatigaret. Sed quia primum librum Novellæ Historiæ a reditu imperatricis, post mortem mariti, ad patrem hucusque protraxisse suffecerit, nunc secundum ordiemur, ab eo anno quo eadem virago in Angliam venit, jus suum contra Stephanum assertura.³

Explicit Liber Primus Novellæ Historiæ.

---

[1] *quibus poterat*] quantum in ipso fuit, At. Bc. Cd.
[2] *Bristowia*] Bristoye, Cd.

[3] The MSS. At. Bc. Bk. Cd. Cm. continue without break or rubric.

WILLELMI MALMESBIRIENSIS
HISTORIÆ NOVELLÆ.

LIBER SECUNDUS.

Incipit Liber Secundus.

§ 468. ANNO Dominicæ incarnationis millesimo centesimo tricesimo nono, venenum malitiæ, diu in animo regis Stephani nutritum, tandem erupit in publicum. Serebantur in Anglia rumores jam jamque adventurum e Normannia comitem Robertum cum sorore; qua spe cum multi a rege non solum animo, sed et facto, deficerent, ipse dispendia sua multorum injuriis [1] sarciebat. Plures etiam, pro sola suspicione diversarum contra se partium, in curia sua contra decus regium captos, et ad redditionem castellorum, et ad quascunque voluit conditiones, adduxit. Erant tunc duo in Anglia episcopi potentissimi, Rogerius Salesberiensis, et nepos ejus ex fratre, Alexander Lindocoliensis. Alexander ad tutamen, ut dicebat, et dignitatem episcopii, castellum de Niwewerche construxerat. Rogerius, qui ædificiorum constructione magnanimum se videri vellet, plura apud Scireburnam, et apud Divisas multum terrarum ædificiis amplexus, turritas moles erexerat. Apud Malmesberiam in ipso cimiterio, ab ecclesia principali vix jactu lapidis, castellum inchoaverat. Castellum Salesberiæ, quod cum [2] regii juris proprium esset, ab Henrico rege impetratum, muro cinctum custodiæ suæ attraxerat. His moti quidam potentes laici, qui se a clericis et opum congerie et municipiorum magnitudine

A.D. 1139. General mistrust on the alarm of the arrival of the empress.

The king compels the surrender of castles.

The castles of the bishops of Lincoln and Salisbury.

The castles of Sherborne, Devizes, Malmesbury, and Salisbury.

---

[1] *dispendia — injuriis*] injurias suas multorum dispendiis, Ag. At. Bc. Bk. Cd.

[2] *cum*] om. At. Cd.

superatum iri dolerent, cæcum intra pectora[1] vulnus alebant invidiæ. Itaque conceptas querimonias regi effundunt: Episcopos, oblitos ordinis, in castellis ædificandis insanire; nulli dubium esse debere quin hæc ad perniciem regis fierent omnia, dum illi, statim ut venisset imperatrix, cum traditione castellorum dominæ occurrerent, paternorum scilicet beneficiorum memoria inducti; præveniendos ergo citius, et ad deditionem munitionum arctandos; alioquin regem seram pœnitentiam acturum, cum in potestate hostium esse[2] videret quæ, si saperet, sibi apponere potuisset. Hæc optimates sæpius. Ille, quamvis eis nimio esset favore obnoxius, aliquamdiu auribus suis blandientes dissimulavit audire; molliens delationis[3] amaritudinem, vel religionis in episcopis gratia, vel, quod magis opinor, suæ detractionis invidia. Denique illorum, quæ proceres suaserant, effectum non distulit cum primum volenti se occasio ingessit. Ea fuit hujusmodi.

De captione episcoporum.

469. Apud Oxenefordum circa octavum kalendas Julii facto conventu magnatum, prædicti quoque pontifices advenerunt. Invitus valde Salesberiensis hanc expeditionem incepit. Audivi etenim[4] eum dicentem verba in hanc sententiam: "Per dominam meam sanc-
"tam Mariam, nescio quo pacto, reluctatur mens mea
"huic itineri! Hoc scio, quod ejus utilitatis ero in
"curia, cujus est equinus pullus in pugna." Ita præsagiebat animus mala futura. Tum, quasi fortuna videretur favere[5] voluntati regis, concitatus est tumultus inter homines episcoporum et Alani comitis Britanniæ pro vindicandis hospitiis: eventu miserabili ut homines episcopi Salesberiensis ecclesiæ,[6] mensæ

---

[1] *pectora*] pectus, At. Cd. Bk.
[2] *esse*] om. At. Cd.
[3] *delationis*] dilationis, Bc. Cd. Cm.
[4] *etenim*] om. At. Cd. Bk.
[5] *favere*] famulari At. Bk. Cd.
[6] *ecclesiæ*] om. At. Bk. Cd.

assidentes, semesis epulis ad pugnam prosilirent. Primo maledictis, mox gladiis res acta. Satellites Alani fugati, nepos ejus paulo minus occisus: victoria non incruenta episcopalibus cessit; multis sauciatis, uno etiam milite interfecto.[1] Rex, occasione accepta,[2] per antiquos incentores conveniri jussit episcopos ut curiæ suæ[3] satisfacerent de hoc, quod homines eorum pacem ipsius exturbassent: modus satisfactionis foret, ut claves castellorum suorum quasi fidei vades traderent. Illos ad satisfaciendum paratos, sed de deditione castellorum cunctantes, ne abirent arctius asservari præcepit. Ita Rogerium episcopum absque vinculis, cancellarium, qui nepos esse, vel plusquam nepos, ejusdem episcopi ferebatur, compeditum, duxit ad Divisas, si vel castellum recipere posset,[4] multis et vix numerabilibus sumptibus, non, ut ipse præsul dictabat, ad ornamentum, sed, ut se rei veritas habet, ad ecclesiæ detrimentum, ædificatum. In ipsa obsessione castella Salesberiæ, Sciresburniæ, Malmesberiæ regi data: ipsæ Divisæ post triduum redditæ, cum sibi ultroneum jejunium episcopus indixisset, ut hac angustia sua animum[5] episcopi Eliensis, qui eas occupaverat, flecteret. Nec Alexander[6] episcopus Lindocoliensis obstinatius egit, redditione castellorum Niwerh et Eslefford[7] liberationem mercatus.

§ 470. Hoc regis factum in diversas sententias solvit ora multorum. Quidam dicebant jure castellis alienatos episcopos videri, quæ præter scita canonum ædificassent: illos evangelistas pacis esse debere, non architectos domorum quæ auctoribus maleficii forent refugium. Hæc amplioribus rationibus et sermonibus

---

[1] *interfecto*] occiso, At. Bk. Cd.
[2] *occasione accepta*] occasionem aucupatus, At. Bk. Cd.
[3] *suæ*] om. Ce¹.
[4] *si—posset*] scilicet castellum, Bc. Ce². ; secundum castellum, At. ; simul castellum, Bk.
[5] *animum*] animositatem, At. Cd.
[6] *Alexander*] om. At. Bc. Bk. Cd.
[7] *castellorum—Eslefford*] castelli, At. Bk. Cd.

agebat Hugo archiepiscopus Rothomagi, quantum illa facundia poterat maximus regis propugnator. Alii contra, quorum partibus assistebat Henricus Wintoniensis episcopus, sedis apostolicæ in Anglia legatus, frater regis Stephani, ut ante dixi ; quem nec fraterna necessitudo, nec periculi metus, a vero tunc[1] exorbitare cogebat. Sic porro dicebat : "Si episcopi tra-
" mitem justitiæ in aliquo transgrederentur, non esse
" regis, sed canonum judicium ; sine publico et eccle-
" siastico concilio illos nulla possessione privari de-
" buisse : regem id non[2] rectitudinis zelo, sed commodi
" sui compendio fecisse; qui castella non ecclesiis, ex
" quarum sumptibus et in quarum terris constructa
" erant, reddiderit, sed laicis eisdemque parum reli-
" giosis contradiderit." Ista vir ille tum privatim, tum etiam publice coram rege affirmans, ejusdemque aures de liberatione et restitutione pontificum appellans, omnem consumpsit operam, in nullo auditus : quapropter, vigorem canonum experiendum ratus, concilio, quod quarto kalendas Septembris celebraturus erat Wintoniæ, fratrem incunctanter adesse præcepit.

De concilio habito pro captione episcoporum.

§ 471. Dicto die omnes fere episcopi Angliæ, cum Thetdbaldo archiepiscopo Cantuariæ qui Willelmo successerat, venerunt Wintoniam. Archiepiscopus Eboracensis Turstinus pro valitudine qua gravabatur, vix enim animi viribus corpus regebat, ceteri vero pro guerra, litteris absentiam suam excusarunt Lectum est primo in concilio decretum Innocentii papæ, quo jam a kalendis Martii, si bene commemini, partes sollicitudinis suæ idem apostolicus domino episcopo Wintoniensi jure legationis in Anglia injunxerat. Exceptum id summo favore, quod, diuturnitate tem-

---

[1] *tunc*] om. At. Cd.   [2] *non*] ex, ins. Cd.

poris temperantiam suam ostendens episcopus, non se præerupta legatum promulgasset jactantia. Processit deinceps in concilio sermo ejusdem Latialiter, ad litteratos habitus, de indignatione captionis episcoporum: quorum Salesberiensis in camera curiæ, Lindocoliensis in diversorio suo intercepti essent; Eliensis exemplum simile veritus, veloci profugio ad Divisas se calamitati exemisset. "Scelus miserabile, regem ab incentoribus ita fuisse
" seductum, ut hominibus suis, præsertim episcopis, in
" curiæ suæ pace manus injici jussisset. Adjecta esset
" regio dedecori cælestis injuria, ut, sub obtentu culpæ
" pontificum, ecclesiæ possessionibus suis spoliarentur.
" Sibi regis contra Dei legem excessum tanto dolori
" esse, ut mallet se multo dispendio et corporis et
" rerum suarum affici, quam episcopalem celsitudinem
" tanta indignitate dejici. Quin etiam regem de emen-
" datione peccati multoties commonitum;[1] postremo[2]
" concilii vocationem non abnuisse. Proinde archie-
" piscopus et ceteri consulerent in medium quid opus
" esset facto: se ad executionem concilii nec pro regis,
" qui sibi frater erat, amicitia, nec pro dampno posses-
" sionum, nec etiam pro capitis periculo, defuturum."

§ 472. Dum hæc ille sensim per amplificationem exponit, rex, causæ suæ non diffisus, comites in concilium misit, quærens cur vocatus esset. Responsum est a legato ex compendio: "Non debere illum, qui se
" Christi fidei subjectum meminisset, indignari si a
" ministris Christi ad satisfactionem vocatus esset,
" tanti reatus conscius quantum nostra secula nusquam
" vidissent. Gentilium quippe seculorum opus esset
" episcopos incarcerare, et possessionibus suis exuere.
" Dicerent ergo fratri, quod, si consilio suo placidum
" commodare dignaretur assensum, tale illi Deo auc-
" tore largiretur, cui nec ecclesia Romana, nec curia
" regis Franciæ, nec ipse comes Thetbaldus frater am-

---

[1] *commonitum*] admonitum, At. | [2] *postremo*] tunc, ins. At. Cd.

"borum, sapiens profecto vir et religiosus, ex ratione
"contraire posset, sed quod favorabiliter complecti de-
"berent. Consulte vero in præsentiarum rex faceret,
"si vel rationem facti sui redderet, vel canonicum
"judicium subiret. Ex debito etiam oportere ut ec-
"clesiæ faveret, cujus sinu exceptus, non manu mili-
"tum, in regnum promotus fuisset." Cum[1] dicto
comites egressi nec multo post cum[2] responso reversi
sunt. Comitabatur eos Albericus quidam de Ver, homo
causarum varietatibus exercitatus. Is responsum regis
retulit, et quantum potuit causam antistitis Rogerii,
episcopus enim Alexander aberat,[3] quem manutenuit,[4]
gravavit; modeste tamen, sine ulla verborum contumelia: quamvis quidam comitum, astantes juxta, crebro
loquelam ejus interrumperent, probra in episcopum
jacientes.

Aubrey's speech.

§ 473. Hæc ergo fuit summa dictorum Alberici:
"Multis injuriis Rogerium episcopum affecisse regem
"Stephanum: rarissime ad curiam[5] venisse, quin
"homines sui, de ejus potentia præsumentes, seditio-
"nes movissent. Qui cum sæpe[6] alias, tum nuper
"apud Oxenefordum fecissent impetum in homines et
"in ipsum nepotem comitis Alani; in homines etiam
"Hervei de Liuns, qui esset tantæ nobilitatis, tanti
"supercilii, ut nunquam regi Henrico petenti anim-
"um indulserit in Angliam venire. In injuriam ergo
"regis Stephani redundare, pro cujus amore venerit,
"quod ei[7] tanta vis illata sit. Episcopum Lindoco-
"liensem, ex veteri odio in Alanum, seditionis per
"homines suos auctorem fuisse. Episcopum Salesberi-
"ensem inimicis regis clam favere, dissimulata interim
"pro tempore versutia: id regem ex multis indubi-

---

[1] *Cum*] Sic cum, At. Cd.
[2] *cum*] proviso, At. Cd.
[3] *aberat*] abierat, At. Cd.
[4] *quem manutenuit*] om. At. Bk. Bq. Cd.
[5] *curiam*] regis, ins. At. Cd.
[6] *sæpe*] om. Cc¹.
[7] *ei*] ea, Cc.

" tanter comperisse; eoque potissimum, quod Rogerium *Other charges.*
" de Mortemer, cum militibus regiis quos ducebat,[1] in
" summo de Bristowiensibus metu, nec una nocte idem
" episcopus Malmesberiæ manere dimisisset. Omnibus
" esse in ore, quod, statim ut imperatrix venisset, ille
" ad eam cum nepotibus et castellis se conferret.
" Rogerius itaque captus sit non ut episcopus, sed ut *Roger was arrested not*
" regis serviens, qui et procurationes ejus administraret *as a bishop but as a*
" et solidatas acciperet. Castella non per violentiam *minister.*
" rex eripuerit, sed episcopi ambo gratanter reddider-
" int, ut calumpniam de tumultu quem in curia con-
" citaverant evaderent. Aliquantum[2] pecuniarum rex
" in castellis invenerit, quæ ipsius legitime essent;
" quia eas tempore regis Henrici, avunculi et anteces- *The money found in the*
" soris sui, ex fisci regii redditibus Rogerius episcopus *castles was the king's.*
" collegisset. Eis tamen, sicut et castellis, idem præsul
" pro timore commissorum in regem libens cesserit;
" inde non deesse testes regi. Ipsum proinde velle ut
" pacta inter se et episcopos rata permanerent."

§ 474. Reclamatum est ab episcopo Rogerio contra *Roger replies that he*
sermones Alberici, quod nunquam regis Stephani *had never been Ste-*
minister fuisset, nec ipsius solidatas accepisset: minæ *phen's minister.*
quinetiam ab animoso viro, et qui malis erubesceret
frangi, prolatæ, si justitiam de rebus sibi ablatis in
illo concilio non invenisset, eam in audientia majoris
curiæ quærendam. Leniter legatus, ut cetera: " Omnia *The legate directs the*
" quæ dicuntur contra episcopos prius in concilio *king to re-vest the*
" ecclesiastico et accusari et an vera essent decuisset *bishops in their rights*
" inquiri, quam in indempnes contra canonum decreta *until the case has*
" sententiam proferri. Rex itaque faciat, quod etiam *been ex-amined.*
" in forensibus judiciis legitimum est fieri, ut revestiat
" episcopos de rebus suis: alioquin jure gentium
" dissaisiti non placitabunt."

§ 475. Dictis in hunc modum utrobique multis,
causa petitu regis in posterum diem dilata; nec minus

---

[1] *ducebat*] ductitabat, Ag. At. Bk. By. Cd.
[2] *Aliquantum*] Aliquantulum, At. Cd.

in crastinum, ad adventum archiepiscopi Rothomagensis postridie prolongata. Is ubi venit, omnium suspensis animis quidnam afferret, dixit se concedere ut episcopi castella haberent si se jure habere debere per canones probare possent; quod quia non possent, extremæ improbitatis esse contra canones niti velle. "Et " esto," inquit, "justum sit ut habeant: certe, quia " suspectum est tempus, secundum morem aliarum " gentium, optimates omnes claves munitionum suarum " debent voluntati regis contradere, qui pro omnium " pace debet militare. Ita omnis controversia episco" porum infirmabitur:[1] aut enim secundum canonum " scita injustum est ut habeant castella; aut, si hoc " ex[2] indulgentia principali toleratur, ut tradant claves " necessitati temporis debent cedere."

§ 476. His prædictus subjecit[3] causidicus Albericus; Significatum esse regi quod murmurarent[4] inter se pontifices, pararentque aliquos ex suis contra eum Romam mittere. "Et hoc," ait, "laudat vobis rex, " ne quisquam vestrum præsumat facere; quia, si quis " contra voluntatem suam et regni dignitatem ab " Anglia quoquam iret, difficilis ei fortassis reditus " foret. Ipse quinetiam, quia se gravari videt, ultro " ad Romam appellat vos."

§ 477. Hæc postquam rex, partim quasi laudando, partim minando, mandasset, intellectum est quo tenderet. Quapropter ita discessum est, ut nec ipse censuram canonum pati vellet, nec episcopi in eum exserere consultum[5] ducerent: duplici ex causa, seu quia principem excommunicare sine apostolica conscientia temerarium esset; seu quoniam audirent, quidam etiam viderent, gladios circa se nudari. Non enim

---

[1] *infirmabitur*] infirmabatur, Ag. At. Cd.
[2] *ex*] pro, At. Cd. Ce².
[3] *subjecit*] addidit, At. Ag. Bk. Cd.
[4] *murmurarent*] minitarent, At.; minarentur, Cd.
[5] *in—consultum*] cum exccrare consultum, Cd.; cum exerere consultum, At. Ag.

jam ludicra erant verba, sed de vita et sanguine pene certabatur. Non omiserunt tamen legatus et archiepiscopus quin tenorem officii sui prosequerentur: suppliciter enim pedibus regis in cubiculo affusi, oraverunt ut misereretur ecclesiæ, misereretur animæ et famæ suæ, nec pateretur fieri discidium inter regnum et sacerdotium. Ille dignanter assurgens, quamvis a se facti eorum amoliretur invidiam, malorum tamen præventus consiliis, nullam bonarum promissionum exhibuit efficaciam.

De adventu imperatricis et Roberti comitis in Angliam.

§ 478. Kalendis Septembris solutum est concilium. Pridie vero kalendarum Octobrium comes Robertus, tandem nexus morarum eluctatus, cum sorore imperatrice invectus est Angliæ, fretus pietate Dei et fide legitimi sacramenti: ceterum, multo minore armorum apparatu quam quis alius tam periculosum bellum aggredi temptaret, non enim plusquam centum et quadraginta milites tunc secum adduxit. Testimonio veridicorum relatorum sermo meus nititur. Dicerem, nisi adulatio videretur, non imparem fuisse illum[1] Julio Cæsari duntaxat animo, quem Titus Livius commemorat quinque solum cohortes habuisse quando civile bellum inchoavit; cum quibus, inquiens, orbem terrarum adortus est. Quamvis iniqua comparatione Julius et Robertus conferantur: Julius enim, veræ fidei extorris, in fortuna sua, ut dicebat, et legionum virtute spem reclinabat: Robertus, Christiana pietate insignis, in Sancti Spiritus et dominæ sanctæ Mariæ patrocinio totus pendulus erat. Ille in tota Gallia, et partim in Germania et Britannia, fautores habens, omnem etiam Romanam plebem, excepto senatu, muneribus sibi devinxerat: iste, præter paucissimos qui fidei quondam

---

[1] *illum*] om. At. Cd.

juratæ non immemores erant, in Anglia optimates vel adversantes vel nihil adjuvantes expertus est. Appulit ergo Arundellum; ibique novercæ suæ, quam, amissa matre imperatricis, ut præfatus sum, Henricus rex quondam lecto copulaverat, tuta, ut putabat, custodia sororem interim delegavit. Ipse per tam confertam barbariem, vixdum, ut audivi, duodecim militibus comitatus, Bristou contendit; occurrente sibi medio itineris Briano filio comitis ex Walengeford. Nec multo post cognovit sororem ex Arundello profectam; noverca enim fœminea levitate fidem, totiens etiam missis in Normanniam nuntiis promissam, fefellerat. Dedit rex porro[1] imperatrici Wintoniensis episcopi Henrici et comitis Mellentensis Walleranni conductum; quem cuilibet, quamvis infestissimo inimico, negare laudabilium militum mos non est. Et Wallerannus quidem ultra Calnam tendere supersedit, episcopo in conductu perseverante. Contractis ergo comes celeriter copiis ad metas a rege datas advenit, sororemque Bristou ad tutiora[2] perduxit. Recepit illam postea in Gloecestram Milo, qui castellum ejusdem urbis sub comite habebat tempore regis Henrici, dato ei homagio et fidelitatis sacramento: nam eadem civitas caput est sui comitatus.

Quomodo rex ceperat Malmesberiam, et de obsidione Trohbrigiæ.

§ 479. [3] Nonis Octobris Robertus quidam, filius Huberti, immanis ac barbarus, castellum Malmesberiæ, quod Rogerius episcopus infausto auspicio inchoaverat, furtim noctu ingressus, combustoque vico, quasi magno triumpho gloriatus est. Veruntamen ante quindecim dies lætitia excidit, a rege fugatus. Castellum præ-

---

[1] *porro*] ergo, At. Cd.
[2] *tutiora*] tutior, Ce.

[3] This whole section is omitted in MSS. At. Ag. Bc. Bk. Bq. Cd. Cm.

cepit rex interim asservari, quoad, pace data, posset destrui. Ipse vero rex, antequam Malmesberiam venisset, quandam munitiunculam Milonis supernominati, Cernei nomine, occupaverat, ibique milites suos posuerat. Quapropter, sicut et ibi[1] et Malmesberiæ, alias sibi successurum existimans, castellum Hunfridi de Buhun, qui partibus imperatricis favebat, vocabulo Trobrigge, invasit, sed irritus abiit.

A.D. 1139.

Cerney occupied: and Trowbridge besieged by the king.

Quomodo Hereford cessit imperatrici.

§ 480. Tota itaque regio circa Gloecestram usque profundas Guallias, partim vi, partim benivolentia pedetemptim residuis illius anni mensibus, se dominæ imperatrici applicuit. Aliquanti castellanorum, intra munitiones suas se contutantes, exitum rerum speculabantur. Civitas Hereford sine difficultate recepta: pauci milites, in castello animis obstinatis se includentes, a foris[2] obsessi. Appropinquavit rex si forte laborantibus opem aliquam comminisci posset; sed frustratus voto, inglorius discessit: equitavit etiam juxta Bristou, superiusque contendens, villas quæ fuerunt in circuitu Dunestor combussit, nihil omnino, in quantum valebat, reliquum faciens quod posset inimicis suis esui vel alicui usui esse.

The progress of the empress in the west of England.

Stephen fails to relieve Hereford castle; and ravages Somerset.

De obitu et moribus Rogerii episcopi Salesberiæ.

§ 481. Tertio idus Decembris Rogerius episcopus Salesberiæ febrem quartanam, qua jamdudum quassabatur, beneficio[3] mortis evasit: dolore animi aiunt eum contraxisse valitudinem, utpote tantis et tam crebris a rege Stephano pulsatum incommodis. Eum mihi videtur Deus exemplum divitibus pro volubilitate rerum exhibuisse, ne sperent in incerto divitiarum;

Death of Roger bishop of Salisbury, Dec. 11.

1 Tim. vi. 17.

---

[1] *et ibi*] sibi, Ce².
[2] *foris*] foribus, Ce².
[3] *beneficio*] a beneficio, Ce.

A.D. 1139.

He had been steward to Henry before his accession.

He was made chancellor at the beginning of the reign, and afterwards bishop.

His aggrandizement.

His buildings.

The advancement of his nephews.

quas quidam, ut ait apostolus, appetentes a fide naufra-[1] gaverunt. Insinuatus est primo comiti Henrico, qui postmodum rex fuit, pro prudentia res domesticas administrandi, et luxum familiæ cohibendi. Fuit enim Henricus ante regnum in expensis parci animi et frugi, penuria scilicet rei familiaris astrictus, fratribus Willelmo et Roberto arroganter eum tractantibus. Cujus cognitis moribus, Rogerius ita eum tempore inopiæ demeruit, ut, cum ille solium regni ascendisset, nihil ei vel parum negaret quod ipse petendum putasset: largiri prædia, ecclesias, præbendas clericorum, abbatias integras monachorum, ipsum postremo regnum fidei ejus committere: cancellarium initio regni, nec multo post episcopum Salesberiæ, fecit. Rogerius ergo agebat causas, ipse moderabatur expensas; ipse servabat gazas; hoc quando rex erat in Anglia, hoc sine socio et teste quando, quod crebro et diu accidit, morabatur Normanniæ. Nec solum a rege, sed et ab optimatibus, ab his etiam quos felicitatis ejus invidia clam mordebat, maximeque a ministris et tunc[1] debitoribus regis, ei quæcunque pene cogitasset conferebantur. Si quid possessionibus ejus contiguum erat quod suis utilitatibus conduceret, continuo vel prece vel pretio, sin minus violentia, extorquebat. Ipse, singulari gloria, quantum nostra ætas reminisci potest, in domibus ædificandis, splendida per omnes possessiones suas construxit habitacula, in quibus solum tuendis successorum ejus frustra laborabit opera; sedem suam mirificis ornamentis et ædificiis, citra ullam expensarum parsimoniam, in immensum extulit. Erat prorsus mirum videre de homine illo, quanta eum in omni genere dignitatum opum sequebatur copia, et quasi ad manum affluebat: quantula illa gloria, qua quid posset accidere majus? quod duos nepotes, suæ educationis opera, honestæ litteraturæ et industriæ

[1] 1 Tim. i. 19.

---

[1] *tunc*] om. At. Cd. Bk.

viros, effecit episcopos; nec vero exilium episcopatuum, A.D. 1139. sed Lindocoliensis et Heliensis, quibus opulentiores nescio si habeat Anglia. Sentiebat ipse quantum posset, et, aliquanto durius quam talem virum deceret, Divinitatis abutebatur indulgentia. Denique, sicut poeta quidam de quodam¹ divite dicit,

Horace, Ep. l. i. 100.

" Diruit, ædificat, mutat quadrata rotundis:"

ita Rogerius abbatias in episcopatum, res episcopatus in abbatiam, alterare conatus est. Malmesberiense et Abbadesberiense, antiquissima coenobia, quantum in ipso fuit, episcopatui delegavit: Scireburnensem prioratum, qui proprius est episcopi Salesberiensis, in abbatiam mutavit; abbatia de Hortuna proinde destructa et adjecta. Hæc tempore regis Henrici, sub quo res ejus, ut dixi, magnis successibus floruerunt: sed enim sub Stephano rege,² sicut prædixi, retro sublapsæ sunt; nisi quod in initio regni ejus nepotibus suis, uni cancellariam, alteri thesaurariam, sibi burgum Malmesberiæ impetravit, subinde rege familiaribus suis ingeminante, "Per nascentiam Dei! medietatem Angliæ " darem ei, si peteret, donec tempus pertranseat: ante " deficiet ipse in petendo, quam ego in dando." Posterioribus annis fortuna, nimium et ante diu ei blandita, ad extremum scorpiacea crudeliter hominem cauda percussit. Quale fuit illud, quod ante ora sua vidit homines bene de se meritos sauciari, familiarissimum militem³ obtruncari: postero die seipsum, ut supra fatus sum, et nepotes suos potentissimos episcopos, unum fugari, alterum teneri, tertium, dilectissimum sibi adolescentem, compedibus vinciri: post redditionem castellorum thesauros suos diripi, et se postmodum in concilio foedissimis conviciis proscindi: ad ultimum, cum apud Salesberiam pene anhelaret in exitum, quicquid residuum erat nummorum et vasorum, quod scilicet ad

His modification of ecclesiastical foundations.

His early influence with Stephen.

Change of fortunes.

His fall, and accumulated misfortunes.

---

¹ *quodam*] quolibet, At. Cd.
² *rege*] om. At. Bk. Cd.
³ *militem*] militum, Ce¹.

A.D. 1139.
His death caused little sympathy.

perficiendam ecclesiam super altare posuerat, se invito asportari. Extremum puto calamitatis, cujus etiam me miseret, quod, cum multis miser videretur, paucissimis erat miserabilis; tantum livoris et odii ex nimia potentia contraxerat, et immerito apud quosdam quos etiam honoribus auxerat.

De institutione abbatiarum.

A.D. 1140.
Events at Malmesbury.

John elected abbot of Malmesbury.

§ 482. Anno incarnati Verbi millesimo centesimo quadragesimo monachi abbatiarum quas Rogerius episcopus contra fas tenuerat, rege adito, antiqua privilegia et abbates habere meruerunt. Electus est in abbatem Malmesberiæ a monachis, secundum tenorem privilegii quod beatus Aldelmus a Sergio papa jam ante quadringentos sexaginta et sex annos impetraverat, et a regibus West-Saxonum Ina, Merciorum Ethelredo, roborari fecerat, ejusdem loci monachus Johannes, vir benignitate morum et animi liberalitate apprime insignis. Probavit legatus causam, improbavit personam; nullo enim modo menti ejus persuaderi poterat regem præter dationem pecuniæ electioni consensisse. Et quidem aliquantum nummorum promissum fuerat, causa libertatis ecclesiæ, non electionis personæ. Itaque Johannes, quamvis immatura morte anno eodem præreptus fuerit, æternam tamen et laudabilem sui memoriam cunctis post se seculis dereliquit: nullus enim, vere fateor, ejus loci monachus tantæ magnanimitatis facto assisteret, nisi Johannes inchoasset. Itaque habeant successores ejus laudem si libertatem ecclesiæ tutati fuerint, ipse proculdubio eam a servitute vendicavit.

He dies the same year.

De confusione guerræ per Angliam.

Misery of the year 1140.

§ 483. Totus annus ille asperitate guerræ inhorruit. Castella erant crebra per totam Angliam; quæque suas partes defendentia, immo ut verius dicam, depopulantia. Milites castellorum abducebant ab agris et pecora et pecudes, nec ecclesiis nec cimiteriis parcentes. Vavassores, rusticos, quicunque pecuniosi putabantur, intercipientes, suppliciorum magnitudine ad quodvis promittendum cogebant.[1] Domibus miserorum ruricolarum usque ad stramen[2] expilatis, ipsos vinctos incarcerabant; nec, nisi omnibus quæcunque habebant, et quocunque modo adquirere poterant, in redemptionem consumptis, dimittebant. Plures in ipsis tormentis quibus ad se redimendum constringebantur dulces efflabant animas, quod solum poterant, Deo miserias suas applorantes. Et quidem, ex voluntate comitis, legatus cum episcopis omnes effractores cimiteriorum et violatores ecclesiarum, et qui sacri vel religiosi ordinis hominibus vel eorum famulis manus injecissent, multotiens excommunicavit; sed nihil propemodum hac profecit industria. Erat ergo videre calamitatem, Angliam, præclarissimam quondam pacis nutriculam, speciale domicilium quietis, ad hoc miseriæ devolutam esse, ut nec etiam episcopi nec monachi de villa in villam tuto possent progredi. Sub Henrico rege multi alienigenæ, qui genialis humi inquietationibus[3] exagitabantur, Angliam annavigabant, et sub ejus alis quietum otium agebant: sub Stephano plures ex Flandria et Britannia, rapto vivere assueti, spe magnarum prædarum Angliam involabant. Comes Gloecestræ Robertus[4] interea modeste se agere, nihil magis cavere quam ne vel parvo detrimento suorum vinceret. Magnates Anglorum, quos ad religionem jurisjurandi servandam flectere non posset, satis habebat in officio continere, ut qui nihil adjuvare vellent minus nocerent; secundum comicum, volens quod posset, dum non posset quod vellet. Ubicumque tamen commode

---

[1] *Vavassores—cogebant*] om. At. Ag. Bc. Bk. Bq. Cd.
[2] *stramen*] stratum, At. Cd. Bk.
[3] *inquietationibus*] turbellis, Bk. Bq. Cd.
[4] *Gloecestræ Robertus*] om. At. Cd. Bk. Bq.

fieri posse videbat, et militis et ducis probe officium exequebatur: denique munitiones, quæ potissimum partibus susceptis nocebant, strenue debellavit; scilicet Harpetreu, quam rex Stephanus a quibusdam militibus comitis, antequam in Angliam venisset, ceperat; et alias multas, Sudleie, Cernei, quam rex, ut dixi, militibus suis impleverat; et castellum quod idem rex contra Valengeford obfirmaverat, solo complanavit.[1] Fratrem etiam suum Reinaldum in tanta difficultate temporis comitem Cornubiæ creavit. Nec vero minor erat regi animus ad adeunda quæ sibi competebant munia, qui nullam occasionem prætermittebat quo minus sæpe et adversarios propulsaret et sua defenderet; sed frustrabatur successibus, vergebantque in pejus omnia pro justitiæ penuria: jamque caritas[2] annonæ paulatim crescebat; et pro falsitate difficultas[3] monetæ tanta erat, ut interdum ex decem et eo amplius solidis vix duodecim denarii reciperentur. Ferebatur ipse rex pondus denariorum, quod fuerat tempore Henrici regis, alleviari jussisse; quia, exhausto prædecessoris sui immenso illo thesauro, tot militum expensis nequiret sufficere. Erant igitur Angliæ cuncta venalia; et jam non clam, sed palam, ecclesiæ et abbatiæ venum distrahebantur.

De eclipsi solis.

§ 484. Eo anno in Quadragesima, tertiodecimo kalendas Aprilis, hora nona, feria quarta, fuit eclipsis, per totam Angliam ut accepi. Apud nos certe, et apud omnes vicinos nostros, ita notabiliter solis deliquium fuit, ut homines, quod tunc fere accidit, erat enim Quadragesima,[4] mensis assidentes, primo[5] antiquum

---

[1] *scilicet—complanavit*] om. Ag. At. Bk. Cd.
[2] *caritas*] raritas, Cd.
[3] *difficultas*] enim, ins. Ce.
[4] *erat—Quadragesima*] om. At. Cd.
[5] *primo*] om. Ce.; primum, At.

chaos timerent; mox, re cognita, progredientes, stellas circa solem cernerent. Cogitatum et dictum est a multis, non falso, regem non perannaturum in regno sine dispendio.[1]

De captione Roberti Filii Huberti.

§ 485. Sequenti hebdomada, ipso tempore Passionis, septimo kalendas Aprilis, præfatus barbarus Robertus filius Huberti,[2] ad furta belli peridoneus, castellum de Divisis clanculo intercepit. Homo cunctorum quos nostri seculi memoria complectitur immanissimus, in Deum etiam blasphemus; ultro quippe gloriari solebat se interfuisse ubi quater viginti monachi pariter cum ecclesia concremati fuerint: idem se in Anglia factitaturum et Deum contristaturum deprædatione Wiltoniensis ecclesiæ, etiam[3] subversione Malmesberiensis, cum monachorum illius loci omnium cæde; id se muneris eis repensurum, quod regem ad nocumentum sui admisissent. Hoc enim illis imponebat, sed falso. Hisce auribus audivi, quod si quando captivos, quod quidem rarissime fuit, immunes absque tortionibus dimittebat, et gratiæ ipsi de Dei parte agebantur, audivi, inquam, eum respondisse, "Nunquam mihi "Deus grates sciat!" Captivos melle litos flagrantissimo sole nudos sub divo[4] exponebat, muscas et id genus animalia ad eos compungendum irritans. Jam vero nactus Divisas, jactare non dubitavit se totam regionem a Wintonia usque Londoniam per id castellum occupaturum, et ad tuitionem sui pro militibus Flandriam missurum. Hæc facere meditantem ultio cælestis impedivit per Johannem filium Gildeberti,[5]

---

[1] *sine dispendio*] om. At. Cd.

[2] *præfatus—Huberti*] Robertus quidam, filius Huberti, immanis et barbarus, Ag. At. Bk. Cd.

[3] *etiam*] et, At. Cd.; jam, Cc².

[4] *sub divo*] sub acre, Cc².; aere, interl. Ce¹.

[5] *filium Gildeberti*] quendam, At. Ag. Bk. Cd. John the Castellan of Marlborough, the ancestor of the Marshalls.

A.D. 1140.
He is arrested by the Castellan of Marlborough, and executed.

magnæ versutiæ virum, qui apud Merleberge castellum habebat: ab eo siquidem vinculis innodatus, quia Divisas dominæ suæ imperatrici reddere detrectabat, patibulo appensus et exanimatus est.[1] Miro circa sacrilegum Dei judicio concitato, ut non a rege cui adversabatur, sed ab illis quibus favere videbatur, exitium tam turpe meruerit. Mortis illius auctores digno attollendi præconio, qui tanta peste patriam liberarint, ac intestinum hostem tam juste dampnarint.

De conventu legati et archiepiscopi et reginæ, et Roberti comitis Gloecestræ, pro fœdere pacis agendo inter regem et imperatricem.

§ 486. Eodem anno in Pentecoste resedit rex Londoniæ[2] in Turri, episcopo tantummodo Sagiensi præsente: ceteri vel fastidierunt vel timuerunt venire. Aliquanto post, mediante legato, colloquium indictum est inter imperatricem et regem, si forte Deo inspirante pax reformari posset. Conventum juxta Bathoniam: misso ex parte imperatricis Roberto fratre, et ceteris suis; ex parte regis, legato et archiepiscopo, simul et regina. Sed inaniter, inaniter inquam, triverunt et verba et tempora, infectaque pace discessum. Nec fuit ambarum partium æquum discidium; dum imperatrix, ad bonum pronior, ecclesiasticum non se vereri judicium mandasset; et regii illud quam maxime nollent, dum dominari ad utilitates suas valerent.[3] Postremo[4] Septembri legatus, qui nosset officii sui potissimum interesse ut pax conveniret, pro ea restituenda laborem itineris transmarini aggressus, in Galliam navi-

Court at London, at Whitsuntide, May 26.

Parley at Bath, ineffectual.

---

[1] *patibulo—est*] more latronum suspensus est, Ag. At. Cd.

[2] *Londoniæ in.*] Here is a lacuna in MS. Ag. ending at "fuisse ita," p. 574.

[3] *et regii—valerent*] et rex illud quam maxime caveret, consiliis illorum male credulus, qui nihil minus quam pacem vellent dum ei dominari ad utilitates suas valerent, At. Bc. Bk. Bq. Cd. Cm.

[4] *Postremo*] Proximo, Cc.

gare maturavit. Ibi a rege Franciæ et comite Thet- A.D. 1140.
baldo, multisque religiosi ordinis personis, magno et The legate goes abroad
sollicito tractatu de pace Angliæ habito, reversus est from September to
in fine pene¹ Novembris; salubria patriæ mandata November.
referens, si esset qui verba factis apponeret. Et plane
imperatrix et comes confestim consensere;² rex vero de
de die in diem producere, postremo in summa frustrari. The king
Tum demum legatus se intra se continuit, rerum delays decision on terms of
exitum, ut ceteri, speculaturus: quid enim attinet peace.
contra torrentem brachia tendere ? cum, laboribus non
nisi odium quærere, extremæ sit, ut quidam ait,
dementiæ.³

Explicit Liber Secundus Novellæ Historiæ.

---

¹ *pene*] om. Ce.¹
² *consensere*] assensere, At. Bk. Cd. Ce.²

³ MS. Cd. proceeds without break or rubric.

PROLOGUS
IN LIBRUM TERTIUM.

Incipit Prologus Libri Tertii.

ANNO incarnationis Dominicæ millesimo centesimo quadragesimo primo [1] inextricabilem labyrinthum rerum et negotiorum quæ acciderunt in Anglia, aggredior evolvere; ea causa, ne per nostram incuriam lateat posteros, cum sit operæ pretium, cognoscere volubilitatem fortunæ, statusque humani [2] mutabilitatem, Deo duntaxat permittente vel jubente. Itaque quia moderni non mediocriter et merito reprehendunt prædecessores nostros, qui nec sui nec suorum post Bedam ullam [3] reliquerunt memoriam, ego, qui a nobis hanc proposui summovere infamiam, debeo apud lectores bonam, si recte judicabunt, pacisci gratiam.[4]

Purport of the third book: the unravelling the complications of A.D. 1141.

---

[1] *primo*] secundo, At. Bk. Cd. Ce.[2] Cm. In Ce.[1] a figure is erased.
[2] *humani*] om. At. Bk. Cd.
[3] *ullam*] om. Ce.[1]
[4] *gratiam*] gloriam, Ce.

WILLELMI MALMESBIRIENSIS
HISTORIÆ NOVELLÆ.
Liber Tertius.

Liber Tertius.

Quomodo rex venerit ad obsidionem Lindcolniæ.

§ 487. Rex Stephanus, ante Natale, a Lindocolina provincia pacifice abscesserat; comitemque Cestrensem et ejus fratrem honoribus auxerat. Is comes filiam comitis Gloecestrensis jamdudum a tempore regis Henrici duxerat. Burgenses[1] interim Lindocolinæ civitatis, qui vellent apud regem grandem locare amicitiam, eum Londoniæ manentem per nuntios certiorem faciunt ambos fratres in castello ejusdem urbis securos resedisse: eos, nihil minus quam regis adventum opinantes, levi negotio posse circumveniri; se daturos operam ut quam occultissime rex castello potiatur. Ille, qui nullam occasionem ampliandæ potestatis omittere vellet, lætus eo contendit: ita fratres circumventi et obsessi sunt in ipsis Natalis Dominici feriis.

Iniquum id visum multis, quia, sicut dixi, nulla suspicione rancoris ab eis ante festum abscesserat, nec modo more majorum amicitiam suam eis interdixerat, quod "Diffidiare" dicunt. Porro comes Cestrensis, quamvis ancipiti periculo involutus, probe tamen castelli angustias evasit, non diffinio qua versutia; sive consensu aliquorum obsidentium; sive,

---

[1] *Burgenses*] Cives, At. Bc. Bk. Cd. Cm.

A.D. 1141.

The Earl escapes, obtains help from the Earl of Gloucester, and adheres to the empress.

quia virtus deprehensa solet multis modis quærere, et plerumque invenire, consilium. Itaque non contentus sua solum liberatione, de salute fratris et uxoris, quos in castello reliquerat, sollicitus, animum partes versabat in omnes. Sanior sententia visa flagitare a socero auxilium, quamvis animos ejus jamdudum nonnullis ex causis offendisset, maxime quia in neutro latere fidus videretur esse. Misit ergo perpetuam per nuntios pactus fidelitatem imperatrici, si, respectu pietatis magis quam ullius sui meriti, periclitantes, qui in ipsis captionis faucibus tenebantur, eximeret injuriæ.

Quomodo comes Gloecestræ Robertus ierit ad succurrendum obsessis.

Earl Robert marches to the relief of the castle of Lincoln.

§ 488. Non habuit comes Gloecestræ difficiles aures, indignitatem rei non ferens; simul etiam pertæsus moræ, quia præclarissima patria causa duorum hominum intestinis rapinis et cædibus vexabatur, maluit, si Deus permisisset, rem in extremos deducere casus. Sperabat etiam divinum in incepto favorem, quia rex generum suum nullis ejus culpis injuriaverat, filiam obsidebat, ecclesiam beatæ Dei genitricis de Lindocolino incastellaverat. Hæc quanti apud mentem principis esse debebant? Nonne præstaret mori et gloriose' occumbere, quam tam insignem contumeliam pati? Ulciscendi ergo causa Deum et sororem, simulque necessitudines suas liberandi, dedit se discrimini. Comitati sunt eum impigre suæ fautores partis, quorum erat major exheredatorum numerus, quos in martem

He keeps his errand a secret.

accendebat rerum amissarum dolor et conscia virtus: quamvis toto itinere, quod protenditur a Gloecestra in Lindocolinum, ipse callide intentionem dissimularet, quibusdam ambagibus totum exercitum præter paucissimos suspendens.

De pugna comitis Gloecestræ et captione regis.

§ 489. Ventum ad supremum ipso die Purificationis beatissimæ Mariæ, ad flumen quod inter duos exercitus præterfluebat, Trenta nomine, quod et ortu suo, et pluviarum profluvio, tam magnum fuerat ut nullatenus vado transitum præberet. Tum demum et genero, qui cum manu valida occurrerat, et ceteris quos ductaverat, detegens animum hoc sibi propositum jam dudum esse adjecit, quod nulla unquam necessitate terga verteret; vel moriendum vel capiendum esse, si non vicisset. Cunctis igitur bona spe ipsum implentibus, mirabile auditu, ilico belli discrimen initurus, prædicti rapacitatem fluminis cum omnibus suis nando transgressus est. Tantus erat comiti ardor finem malis[1] imponere, ut mallet ultima experiri quam regni calamitatem ulterius protendi: nam et rex cum comitibus quamplurimis, et non inerti militum copia, bello se animose, intermissa obsidione, obtulerat. Temptavere primo regii proludium pugnæ facere, quod Justam vocant, quia tali periti erant arte: at ubi viderunt quod consulares, ut ita dictum sit, non lanceis eminus, sed gladiis cominus rem gererent, et infestis viribus vexillisque aciem regalem perrumperent, fuga sibi omnes ad unum comites consuluere; sex enim cum rege comites bellum inierant; plures barones,[2] prædicandæ fidei et fortitudinis, qui regem nec in hac necessitate deserendum ducerent, capti. Rex ipse, quamvis ad se defensandum non ei defuisset animus, tandem a militibus comitis Gloecestræ circumquaque aggressus, ictu lapidis cujusdam, terræ procubuit; a quo autem id factum fuerit, ignoratur. Ita omnibus circa se vel captis vel fugatis, cedendum pro tempore, et teneri sustinuit. Prædicandus itaque comes Gloecestræ præcepit regem vivum et illæsum conservari,[3] non passus

---

[1] *malis*] om. Ce.
[2] *sex — barones*] pauci barones, At. Bk. Bq. Cd.
[3] *conservari*] reservari, At.; asservari, Bk. Cd.

etiam ullo exprobrationis convitio illum irretiri:[1] et quem iratus modo impugnabat regno fastigatum, placidus, ecce! protegit triumphatum; ut, compositis irae et laetitiae motibus, et consanguinitati impenderet humanitatem, et in captivo diadematis respiceret dignitatem. Vulgus vero burgensium[2] Lindocolinorum multa parte obtruncatum est, justa ira illorum qui vicissent, nullo dolore illorum qui victi essent, quod ipsi principium et fomes istius mali fuissent.

Quomodo rex imperatrici praesentatur.

§ 490. Rex vero,[3] juxta morem illius generis hominum quos captivos nominant, imperatrici a fratre praesentatus Gloecestrae: post etiam ad Bristou ductus, et ibi honorifice praeter progrediendi facultatem servatus est primo. Succedenti enim[4] tempore, propter insolentiam quorundam palam et probrose dictitantium non expedire comiti ut regem secus ac ipsi vellent servaret, simul et quia ipse ferebatur plus quam semel, vel elusis vel delinitis custodibus, extra statutam custodiam noctu praesertim inventus, anulis ferreis innodatus est.

Quomodo imperatrix, industria comitis Gloecestrae, a legato et quibusdam episcopis et primatibus Wintoniae recepta sit.

§ 491. Interim et imperatrix et comes apud legatum fratrem ejus nuntiis egerunt, ut ipsam, tanquam regis Henrici filiam, et cui omnis Anglia et Normannia jurata esset, incunctanter in ecclesiam et regnum reciperet. Quarto decimo kalendas Martii eo anno prima Dominica Quadragesimae fuit. Ita, mediantibus utro-

---

[1] *irretiri*] irritari, Ce.²; proscindi, At. Bk. Cd.
[2] *burgensium*] civium, At. Bk. Cd.
[3] *vero*] om. Bc. Cd.
[4] *enim*] vero, At. Cd.

bique nuntiis, ad hoc res expedita, ut ad colloquium in patenti planitie camporum citra Wintoniam conveniretur. Ventum ergo Dominica tertia Quadragesimæ, pluvioso et nebuloso die, quasi mæstam causæ vicissitudinem Fata portenderent. Juravit et affidavit imperatrix episcopo, quod omnia majora negotia in Anglia, præcipueque donationes episcopatuum et abbatiarum, ejus nutum spectarent, si eam ipse cum [1] sancta ecclesia in dominam reciperet, et perpetuam ei fidelitatem teneret. Idem juraverunt cum ea, et affidaverunt pro ea, Robertus frater ejus comes de Gloecestra, et Brianus filius comitis marchio de Walingeford, et Milo de Gloecestra, postea comes de Hereford, et nonnulli alii. Nec dubitavit episcopus imperatricem in dominam Angliæ recipere, et ei cum quibusdam suis affidare, quod, quamdiu ipsa pactum non infringeret, ipse quoque fidem ei custodiret. Crastino, quod fuit quinto nonas Martii, honorifica facta processione recepta est in ecclesia episcopatus Wintoniæ; episcopo, eodemque legato, eam ducente in dextro latere, Bernardo vero de sancto David episcopo in sinistro. Affuerunt præterea episcopi, Alexander de Lindocolino, Robertus de Hereford, Nigellus de Heli, Robertus de Bathonia: abbates etiam, Ingulfus de Abbenduna, Edwardus de Radinges, Petrus de Malmesberia, Gilebertus de Gloecestra, Rogerius de Theokesberia, et nonnulli alii. Paucis post diebus Thetbaldus Cantuariensis archiepiscopus venit ad imperatricem apud Wiltunam,[2] invitatus a legato: distulit sane fidelitatem dominæ facere; inconsulto rege alias divertere famæ personæque suæ indignum arbitratus. Itaque et ipse et plerique præsules, cum aliquantis laicis, permissi ad regem ire et colloqui, dignanterque impetrata venia ut in necessitatem temporis transirent, in sententiam legati concessere.[3] Pascha,

A.D. 1141.

Great assembly before Winchester, March 2.

The empress swears to abide by the legate's advice.

He receives her as lady of England.

She is received in Winchester cathedral, March 3, by the bishops and abbots.

Archbishop Theobald visits her at Wilton a few days later.

The king gives him leave to comply with the times.

---

[1] *cum*] in, Ce.
[2] *Wiltunam*] Wiltoniam, Bk.
[3] *concessere*] cessere, At. Bk. Cd. Ce.²

A.D. 1141.
Matilda at Oxford,
March 30.

quod tunc fuit tertio kalendas Aprilis, imperatrix apud Oxenefordum egit; a ceteris in sua discessum.

Quomodo sollempni concilio imperatricem in dominam Angliæ confirmaverint.

Great council at Winchester, April 7.

§ 492. Feria secunda post octavas Paschæ, concilium archiepiscopi Cantuariæ Thedbaldi, et omnium episcoporum Angliæ, multorumque abbatum, legato præsidente, Wintoniæ ingenti apparatu inceptum. Si qui defuerunt, legatis et litteris causas cur non venissent dederunt.[1] Cujus concilii actioni, quia interfui, integram rerum veritatem posteris non negabo. Egregie quippe memini. Ipsa die, post recitata scripta excusatoria quibus absentiam suam quidam tutati sunt, sevocavit in partem legatus episcopos, habuitque cum eis arcanum consilii sui; post[2] mox abbates, postremo archidiaconi convocati. Ex consilio nihil processit in publicum; volutabatur tamen per omnium mentes et ora quid foret agendum.

Our author tells what he saw there.

The clergy consulted in three bodies.

Quomodo legatus debitam et legitimam successionem imperatricis in regnum commendaverit.

April 8. Speech of the legate.

§ 493. Feria tertia hoc fere sensu legati cucurrit oratio: "Dignatione papæ se vices ejus in Anglia te-
" nere; ideoque per ejus auctoritatem clerum Angliæ
" ad hoc concilium congregatum, ut de pace patriæ,
" quæ grandi periculo naufragabatur, consuleretur in
" medium. Tempore regis Henrici avunculi sui sin-
" gulare domicilium pacis in Anglia[3] fuisse; ita ut,
" per vivacitatem, animositatem, industriam ejusdem
" præcellentissimi viri, non solum indigenæ, cujuscun-
" que potentiæ vel dignitatis essent, nihil turbare au-
" derent, sed etiam ejus exemplo finitimi quicunque

Sound government under Henry I.

---

[1] Here is a lacuna in MS. Ce.², ending at *impedimenta*, p. 592 below. The intervening matter is supplied in print.

[2] *post*] om. At. Bk. Cd.

[3] *Anglia*] Here MS. Ag. resumes.

" reges et principes in otium et ipsi concederent, et
" subjectos vel invitarent vel compellerent.¹ Qui vi-
" delicet rex, nonnullis ante obitum annis, filiæ suæ
" quondam imperatrici, quæ sola sibi proles ex des-
" ponsata quondam conjuge supererat, omne regnum
" Angliæ, simul et ducatum Normanniæ, jurari ab
" omnibus episcopis simulque baronibus fecerit, si suc-
" cessore masculo ex illa, quam ex Lotharingia duxe-
" rat, uxore careret. Et invidit," inquit, "atrox fortuna
" præcellentissimo avunculo meo, ut sine masculo he-
" rede in Normannia decederet. Itaque quia longum
" videbatur dominam expectare, quæ moras ad veni-
" endum in Angliam nectebat, in Normannia quippe
" residebat, provisum est paci patriæ, et regnare per-
" missus frater meus. Enimvero, quamvis ego vadem
" me apposuerim inter eum et Deum quod sanctam
" ecclesiam honoraret et exaltaret, et bonas leges
" manuteneret, malas vero abrogaret; piget memi-
" nisse, pudet narrare, qualem se in regno exhibuerit:
" quomodo in præsumptores nulla justitia exercita,²
" quomodo pax omnis statim ipso pene anno abolita;
" episcopi capti, et ad redditionem possessionum sua-
" rum coacti; abbatiæ venditæ, ecclesiæ thesauris de-
" pilatæ; consilia pravorum audita, bonorum vel sus-
" pensa vel omnino contempta. Scitis quotiens eum
" tum per me tum per episcopos convenerim, concilio
" præsertim anno prædicto³ ad hoc indicto, et nihil
" nisi odium adquisierim. Nec illud quenquam, qui
" recte pensare velit, latet, debere me fratrem meum
" mortalem diligere, sed causam Patris immortalis
" multo pluris facere. Itaque quia Deus judicium
" suum de fratre meo exercuit, ut eum, me nesciente,
" in potestatem potentium incidere permitteret; ne
" regnum vacillet, si regnante careat, omnes vos pro

A.D. 1141.
April 8.

He had had fealty sworn to the empress in all his States, in case he should die without a son.

The delay of the empress had caused the acceptance of Stephen.

He has belied his promises of good government.

He has rejected good advice.

Now God has given judgment against him.

---

¹ *compellerent*] impellerent, At. Bk. Cd.
² *exercita*] exercitata, At.
³ *prædicto*] præterito, Cd. Cm.

A.D. 1141.

"jure legationis meæ huc convenire invitavi. Ventilata est hesterno die causa secreto coram majori parte cleri Angliæ, ad cujus jus[1] potissimum spectat principem eligere, simulque ordinare. Invocata itaque primo, ut par est, in auxilium Divinitate, filiam pacifici regis, gloriosi regis, divitis regis, boni regis, et nostro tempore incomparabilis, in Angliæ Normanniæque dominam eligimus, et ei fidem et manutenementum promittimus."

We elect the empress to be lady of England and Normandy.

Quomodo Londonienses in concilio.

§ 494. Cumque omnes præsentes vel modeste acclamassent sententiæ, vel silentes non contradixissent, subjecit legatus:[2] "Londonienses, qui sunt quasi optimates, pro magnitudine civitatis, in Anglia, nuntiis nostris convenimus, et conductum ut tuto veniant misimus, eosque confido non ultra hunc diem moraturos: bona venia usque cras sustineamus."

He has summoned the Londoners.

§ 495. Feria quarta venerunt Londonienses, et, in concilium introducti, causam suam eatenus egerunt ut dicerent, missos se a communione quam vocant Londoniarum, non certamina sed preces offerre,[3] ut dominus suus rex de captione liberaretur. Hoc omnes barones, qui in eorum communionem jamdudum recepti fuerant, summopere flagitare a domino legato, et ab archiepiscopo, simulque ab omni clero qui præsens erat. Responsum est eis a legato ubertim et splendide; et, quo minus fieret quod rogabant, eadem oratio quæ pridie habita. Adjectum quinetiam, "Non decere ut Londonienses, qui præcipui habebantur in Anglia sicut proceres, illorum partes foverent qui dominum suum in bello reliquerant, quorum consilio idem sanctam ecclesiam exhonoraverat, qui

April 9. The Londoners pray for the king's release.

The barons who are in their "communio" join in the prayer.

The legate answers with a refusal.

---

[1] *jus*] om. Cc., which has *examen* in the margin.

[2] *legatus*] om. At. Bk. Cd.

[3] *offerre*] afferre, At. Bk. Cd.

" postremo non ob aliud ipsis Londoniensibus favere
" videbantur nisi ut eos pecuniis emungerent."

De clerico reginæ.

§ 496. Interea surrexit quidam, cujus nomen, si bene memini, Christianus, reginæ, ut audivi, clericus, porrexitque cartam legato; qua ille sub silentio lecta, voce quantum potuit exaltata dixit non esse legitimam, nec quæ deberet in tanto, præsertimque sublimium et religiosarum personarum, conventu recitari. Præter cetera enim quæ reprehensibilia et notabilia erant scripta, testem appositum qui præterito anno, in eodem quo tunc sedebant capitulo, venerabiles episcopos maxima verborum affecerit contumelia. Ita illo tricante, clericus legationi suæ non defuit, sed præclara fiducia litteras legit in audientia, quarum hæc erat summa: "Rogabat regina obnixe omnem clerum " congregatum, et nuncupatim episcopum Wintoniæ " fratrem domini sui, ut eundem dominum regno res- " tituerent, quem iniqui viri, qui etiam homines sui " essent, in vincula conjecissent." Huic suggestioni retulit legatus verba in eandem sententiam qua et Londoniensibus. Illi, communicato consilio, dixerunt se decretum concilii convicaneis suis relaturos, et favorem suum quantum possent præstituros. Feria quinta solutum est concilium, excommunicatis ante multis qui regiarum erant partium; nominatim Willelmo Martello, qui quondam pincerna regis Henrici, tunc dapifer Stephani. Iste immaniter exulceraverat legati animum, multis rebus ejus interceptis et surreptis.

Quomodo imperatrix a Londoniensibus recepta sit.

§ 497. Itaque multæ fuit molis Londoniensium animos permulcere posse, ut, cum hæc statim post Pascha, ut dixi, fuerint actitata, vix paucis ante Nativitatem

A.D. 1141.
June.

beati Johannis diebus imperatricem reciperent. Pleraque tunc pars Angliæ dignanter[1] dominatum ejus suspiciebat;[2] frater ejus Robertus assiduus circa eam omnibus quibus decebat modis ejus gloriam exaltare, proceres benigne appellando, multa pollicendo, diversas partes vel terrendo, vel etiam per internuntios ad pacem sollicitando, jam jamque in omnibus partibus imperatrici faventibus justitiam, et patrias leges, et pacem reformando. Satisque constat quod, si ejus moderationi et sapientiæ a suis esset creditum, non tam sinistrum postea sensissent aleæ casum. Aderat et dominus legatus sedula, ut videbatur, fide imperatricis commodis præsto. Sed ecce, dum ipsa putaretur omni Anglia statim posse potiri, mutata omnia. Londonienses, semper suspecti, et intra se frementes, tunc in aperti odii vocem eruperunt; insidiis etiam, ut fertur, dominam ejusque comites appetiverunt. Quibus illi præcognitis et vitatis, sensim sine tumultu quadam militari disciplina urbe cesserunt. Comitati sunt imperatricem legatus, et rex Scottiæ David avunculus ejusdem viraginis, et frater ejus Robertus, in omnibus ut semper, sic et tunc, fortunarum sororis socius, et, ut de compendio dicam, partium ejus omnes ad unum incolumes Londonienses, cognito eorum abscessu, in hospitia involant, quicquid rerum pro festinatione relictum erat abradentes.

Co-operation of Earl Robert and the legate.

The empress and her party, with the Earl, the legate, and the king of Scots, quit London.

De discordia imperatricis et legati.

Quarrel of the empress and legate.

The cause of the breach.

§ 498. Nec multis post diebus surrexit simultas inter legatum et imperatricem, quem casum vere possum dicere fomitem omnium malorum rursum in Anglia fuisse: quod qualiter[3] acciderit, expediam. Habebat rex Stephanus, Eustachium nomine, ex filia Eustachii

---

[1] *dignanter*] om. Ce¹.
[2] *suspiciebat*] suscipiebat, Cd.
[3] *qualiter*] quatinus, Ce.¹

comitis Bononiensis, susceptum filium. Rex enim Henricus, pater imperatricis, ut altius repetam, ne veritas gestorum lateat posteros, sororem uxoris suæ, matris istius dominæ, Mariam nomine, nuptum dederat prædicto comiti, quod esset is et amplis majoribus ortus, simulque prudentia et fortitudine juxta insignis. Ex Maria Eustachius nihil liberorum tulit præter filiam Matildem vocabulo. Hanc, patre defuncto, nubilem idem magnificentissimus rex Stephano nepoti legitimo matrimonio copulavit, et pariter Bononiensem comitatum industrie adquisivit; nam antea Moritoliensem in Normannia ex suo dederat. Hos comitatus nepoti suo quem nominavi, Eustachio, legatus jure dandos destinaverat dum pater in captione teneretur; imperatrice prorsus abnuente, incertum an aliis etiam promittente. Qua ille offensus injuria, multis diebus ab ejus abstinuit curia, et, quamvis sæpe revocaretur, negare perseveravit. Interea familiare apud Geldeford cum regina, fratris uxore, colloquium habuit, ejusque lacrymis et satisfactione infractus ad liberationem germani animum intendit; omnes etiam illius partis quos in concilio excommunicaverat, inconsultis episcopis, absolvit. Ferebantur et per Angliam ejus in imperatricem querelæ: quod eum capere voluerit; quod quicquid ei juraverat pro nihilo habuerit; omnes barones Angliæ fidem suam circa eam implesse, sed ipsam temerasse, quæ acquisitis uti modeste nesciret.

Quomodo comes Gloecestrensis legatum convenerit cum imperatrice et coadjutoribus suis.

§ 499. Ad hos motus, si posset, componendos comes Gloecestrensis non adeo denso comitatu Wintoniam contendit; sed re infecta ad Oxeneford rediit, ubi soror stativa mansione jamdudum se continuerat.[1] Ipsa itaque, ex his quæ continue audiebat et a fratre tunc cognovit, nihil legatum molle ad suas partes

---

[1] *continuerat*] continuaverat, Ce.

cogitare intelligens, Wintoniam cum quanto potuit apparatu venit. Illic intra castellum regium sine cunctatione recepta, bona forsitan mente per nuntios episcopum convenit, ut, quia ipsa præsens erat, non pigritaretur ad eam venire: ille, non integrum sibi fore arbitratus si veniret, ambiguo responso nuntios elusit hoc tantum[1] verbo, "Ego parabo me;" statimque propter omnes misit quos regi fauturos[2] sciebat. Venerunt ergo fere omnes comites Angliæ; erant enim juvenes et leves, et qui mallent equitationum discursus quam pacem. Præterea plures illorum, confusi quia regem bellantem, ut superius dictum est, deseruerant, conventu illo fugæ suæ obprobrium lenire conabantur. Pauci vero cum imperatrice venerant:[3] rex Scottiæ David, Robertus comes Gloecestræ, Milo de Hereford, et barones pauci; Reinnulfus[4] comes Cestriæ tarde et inutiliter advenit. Ut ergo magnam seriem rerum brevi verborum compendio explicem: a regina, et comitibus qui venerant, undique foras muros Wintoniæ observatæ sunt viæ, ne victualia imperatricis fidelibus inferrentur; Andevera etiam vicus incensus. Ab occidente itaque[5] raro et anguste importabantur necessaria, viatoribus nonnullis interceptis vel occisis, vel parte membrorum mutilatis: ab oriente vero toto tramite versus Londoniam constipabantur semitæ multitudine commeatuum,[6] episcopo et suis importandorum; Gaufrido de Mandevilla, qui jam iterum auxilio eorum cesserat, antea enim post captionem regis imperatrici fidelitatem juraverat,[7] et Londoniensibus maxime annitentibus, nihilque omnino quod possent prætermittentibus quo imperatricem contristarent. Wintonienses porro vel tacito ei favebant judicio, memores fidei quam ei pacti fuerant cum inviti propemodum ab

---

[1] *tantum*] tamen, Ce.
[2] *fauturos*] fautores, At. Cd.
[3] *venerant*] convenerant, Cd. Bk.
[4] *Reinnulfus*] enim, ins. Cd.
[5] *itaque*] om. Ag.
[6] *commeatuum*] commeantium, Ce.
[7] *Gaufrido—juraverat*] om. At. Ag. Bc. Bk. Bq. Cd. Cm.

episcopo ad hoc adacti essent. Interea ex turre ponti- A.D. 1141.
ficis jaculatum incendium in domos burgensium, qui, Hyde abbey burned.
ut dixi, proniores erant imperatricis felicitati quam
episcopi, comprehendit et combussit abbatiam totam
sanctimonialium intra urbem, simulque coenobium[1]
quod dicitur Ad Hidam extra. Erat ibi imago crucifixi Domini magna mole auri et argenti, simulque
gemmarum, dono[2] Cnutonis quondam regis operosa
devotione fabrefacta: hæc, igne tunc comprehensa et The crucifix
solo prostrata, post etiam jubente legato excrustata est. stripped of
Inventæ plusquam quingentæ argenti marcæ, auri tri- gems.
ginta, donativo militum profecere. Combusta est etiam Werewell
abbatia sanctimonialium de Warewella a quodam Wil- nunnery burned.
lelmo de Ipra, homine nefando, qui nec Deo nec
hominibus reverentiam observaret, quod in ea quidam
imperatricis fautores se contutati essent.

De discessu comitis Gloecestræ a Wintonia et captione sua.

§ 500. Comes Gloecestræ[3] interea, quamvis coti- Earl Robert
diano regiorum prælio cum suis afflictaretur, minusque retire.
quam cogitaret res ex sententia cederet, semper tamen ab incendio ecclesiarum temperandum putavit,
quamvis in vicino sancti Swithuni hospitatus esset.
Veruntamen indignitatem rei ultra non ferens, se su-
osque pene obsideri, et fortunam in alteros declinare,
cedendum tempori ratus, compositis ordinibus disces-
sionem paravit. Itaque in primo agmine ut libere He sends off
abiret sororem præmittens cum reliquis, ipse cum but is him-
paucis qui auderent animis multos non timere, lente tured.
progrediebatur. Quapropter comitibus regiis[4] confes- Sept. 14.
tim insecutis, dum et ipse fugere pudori et citra dignitatem suam æstimat, et solus ab omnibus præcipue

---

[1] coenobium] monachorum, ins. Ag. At. Cd.
[2] dono] ex dono, Cd.
[3] Gloecestræ] om. Ag. At. Bc. Bk. Cd. Cm.
[4] regiis] om. At. Bk. Cd.

A.D. 1141.
Sept. 14.

impetitur, captus est. Ceteri cœptum iter, proceres praesertim, continuare; summaque cum festinatione Divisas pervenerunt. Sic a Wintonia die sanctae Crucis Exaltationis, quae tunc habebatur in Dominica, discessum; cum illuc paucis ante Assumptionem beatae Dei genitricis[1] diebus ventum fuisset. Nonnullique miraculi exemplum et multorum materia sermonum fuit in Anglia, quod sicut rex Dominica in dominae nostrae Purificatione, ita comes Dominica in vivificae Crucis Exaltatione,[2] unam eandemque sortem experti sunt. Illud vero percelebre magnificumque fuit, quod pro isto eventu nemo comitem Gloecestrae vel infractum mente, vel etiam tristem vultu, viderit; ita conscientiam altae nobilitatis spirabat, ne se fortunae ludibrio subjiceret. Quamvis enim primo blanditiis invitatus, post etiam minis lacesseretur, nunquam tamen inflexus est ut de liberatione sua praeter consensum[3] sororis tractaretur. Ad ultimum eo modo res ventilata, ut aequis conditionibus et rex et ipse absolverentur; nullo pacto alio interveniente, nisi ut quisque partes suas pro posse, sicut et[4] prius,[5] tutaretur. Haec ab Exaltatione sanctae Crucis usque ad festum Omnium Sanctorum plurimo verborum agmine saepe versata, tunc demum debito fine conclusa; ea enim die rex eluctatus captionem. In eadem apud Bristou reginam suam et filium cum duobus magnatibus reliquit, vades liberandi comitis continuo cum festinato itinere rex Wintoniam venisset; ibi enim asservabatur comes, reductus a Rovecestra, quo prius abductus fuerat. Tertio die, mox ut rex Wintoniam venit, comes abscessit; dimisso ibi, quousque regina absolveretur, in eodem[6] obsidatu filio suo Willelmo. Celeriter igitur permensa via, Bristou veniens reginam absolvit;

Coincidence of the days of capture in the cases of king and earl.

Magnanimity of Earl Robert.

Release of the king Nov. 1:

and of the earl Nov. 3.

---

[1] *genitricis*] Mariae, ins. Cd.
[2] *ita—Exaltatione*] om. Ce.
[3] *consensum*] conscientiam, At. Bk. Cd.
[4] *et*] om. At. Bk. Cd.
[5] *prius*] superius, Bk. Cd.
[6] *eodem*] die, ins. Cd.

cujus reditu Willelmus filius comitis ab obsidatu liberatur. Satis autem constat, toto tempore captionis, sequentibusque mensibus usque ad Natale, multis et magnis pollicitationibus sollicitatum ut a sorore desciceret, pluris semper pietatem germanitatis quam quaslibet[1] promissiones fecisse: nam et relictis rebus castellisque suis, quibus commode frui posset, circa germanam sedulo apud Oxeneford mansitabat; quo loco, ut præfatus sum, illa sedem sibi constituens, curiam fecerat.

De concilio quo legatus temptavit lenire causam receptionis imperatricis in dominam.

§ 501. Interea legatus, immodici animi pontifex, qui quod semel proposuisset non ineffectum relinquere vellet, concilium pro jure legationis suæ apud Westmonasterium die octavarum sancti Andreæ coegit. Ejus concilii actionem non ita exacta fide pronuntio ut superioris, quia non interfui. Auditum est lectas in eo litteras domini apostolici, quibus modeste legatum argueret quod liberare fratrem suum dissimulasset; delicti tamen superioris gratiam facere; et magnopere cohortari, ut quocunque modo, vel ecclesiastico vel seculari, posset, ad germani liberationem accingeretur. Regem ipsum in concilium introisse, et apud sanctum conventum querimoniam deposuisse, quod homines sui et eum ceperint, et afflictione contumeliarum paulo minus exstinxerint, qui justitiam eis nunquam negasset. Ipsum legatum magnis eloquentiæ viribus factorum suorum invidiam temptasse alleviare: "quod scilicet im-
" peratricem non voluntate sed necessitate recepisset,
" quippe cum recenti adhuc fratris sui clade, omnibus
" comitibus vel fugatis, vel eventum rei suspecta mente
" præstolantibus, ipsa cum suis muros Wintoniæ circum-
" sonasset; ipsam quæcunque pepigerat ad ecclesiarum

---

[1] *quam quaslibet*] quas qualibet, Cd.

584   HISTORIA NOVELLA.   [LIB. III.

A.D. 1141.
Dec. 7.

He orders all men to obey the king.

He describes the empress as comitissa of Anjou.

"jus pertinentia obstinate fregisse. Quin etiam certis
"auctoribus ad se delatum eam et suos non solum dig-
"nitati suæ, sed et vitæ, struxisse insidias: ceterum,
"Deum pro sua clementia secus quam ipsa sperasset
"vertisse negotia, ut et ipse perniciem vitaret, et fratrem
"suum vinculis eximeret. Itaque jubere se de parte
"Dei et apostolici, ut regem, voluntate populi et assensu
"sedis apostolicæ inunctum, quantis possent viribus
"enixe juvarent; turbatores vero pacis, qui comitissæ
"Andegavensi faverent ad excommunicationem vocan-
"dos, præter eam quæ Andegavorum domina esset."

Quomodo quidam fautor imperatricis locutus fuit pro imperatrice.

Protest on the part of the empress, made by a layman.

§ 502. Hæc ejus[1] verba non dico quod omnes[2] gratis animis exceperint, certe nullus expugnavit; omnes clerici[3] vel[4] metu vel reverentia frœnarunt ora. Unus fuit laicus, imperatricis nuntius, qui palam legato interdixit, ne, per fidem quam ei pactus fuerat quicquam in illo concilio statueret quod ejus honori adversum foret: fidem ab eo hanc[5] imperatrici factam, ne fratrem suum ullo auxilio juvaret,[6] nisi forte viginti ei[7] milites, nec plures, mitteret. Quod in Angliam ipsa venisset, frequentibus epistolis ejus factum: quod regem cepisset, quod in captione tenuisset, ipso potissimum connivente actum. Dixit[8] hæc et alia pleraque magna verborum austeritate, nihil omnino legato blanditus: nec vero ullo sermonum pondere ille moveri potuit ut iram proderet, semel incepti, ut prius dixi, sui non segnis executor. Fuit ergo hic annus, cujus tragœdias compendio digessi, fatalis et pene perniciosus Angliæ; in quo cum aliquo modo sibi ad libertatem respi-

An unfortunate year, 1141.

---

[1] *ejus*] cras, Cd. Cm.
[2] *omnes*] clerici, ins. At. Cd. Cm.
[3] *clerici*] om. At. Bk. Cd. Cm.
[4] *vel*] om. Cd.
[5] *hanc*] om. Ce.
[6] *juvaret*] adjuvaret, Bk. Cd.
[7] *ei*] om. Ce.
[8] *Dixit*] nuntius, ins. At. Bk. Cd.

randam putasset, rursum in ærumpnam recidit, et, nisi Dei misericordia mature occurrat, diu hærebit.

Recapitulatio de comite Gloecestræ.

§ 503. Principia gestorum hujus anni, qui est incarnationis Dominicæ millesimus centesimus quadragesimus tertius, ex reliquis superioris anni successit animo resarcire; simulque summam rerum quæ de Roberto filio regis Henrici comite Gloecestræ sparsim dictæ sunt, quasi in fasciculum collectam, lectoris æstimationi per recapitulationem proponere. Ipse quippe sicut primus ad partes sororis suæ juste defendendas initium suscepit, ita semper invicto animo in incepto gratis perseveravit: gratis dico, quia nonnulli fautorum ejus vel, fortunam sequentes, cum ejus volubilitate mutantur, vel, multa jam emolumenta consecuti, spe ampliorum præmiorum pro justitia pugnant. Solus vel pene solus Robertus, in neutram partem pronior, nec spe compendii, nec dispendii timore, unquam flexus est, sicut ex sequentibus liquebit. Non ergo alicui, si hæc integre scribo, adulationis surrepat suspicio; nihil enim a me dabitur gratiæ, sed sola veritas historiæ sine ullo fuco mendacii posterorum producetur notitiæ.

§ 504. Dictum est de comite quo modo primus omnium primatum[1] post David regem Scottiæ, præsente patre Henrico, fidelitatem sorori suæ imperatrici de regno Angliæ et ducatu Normanniæ sacramento firmavit: nonnulla, ut dixi, contentione inter eum et Stephanum tunc Bononiæ comitem, postmodum Angliæ regem, quisnam prior sacramentum faceret; Roberto excellentiam filii, Stephano dignitatem nepotis, defendentibus.

§ 505. Dictum est etiam quam rationabiles eum causæ a Decembri, quo pater defunctus est, usque post

---

[1] *primatum*] om. Cc.

sequens Pascha, in Normannia continuerint, ne statim in Angliam veniens sororis injurias vindicaret. Postremo veniens, quam prudenti consilio et qua exceptione ad hominium regis se inclinaverit, et quam juste idem sequenti anno et deinceps abjecerit.

§ 506. Nec est prætermissus secundus ejus post mortem patris a Normannia in Angliam cum sorore adventus; in quam se sicut in quandam sylvam frementium beluarum immersit, Dei quidem gratia et animi confidentia fretus, sed vix centum et quadraginta militibus stipatus. Sed nec illud tacitum, quod in tanto motu bellorum, cum sollicitæ ubique prætenderentur excubiæ, cum solis duodecim militibus impigre ad Bristou venit; sorore interim apud Arundellum fida, ut putabat, custodia commissa. Qua prudentia et tunc sororem suam e mediis hostibus ad se receperit, et postmodum in omnibus pro posse provexerit; semper circa eam conversatus, ipsius commoda procurans, sua postponens, cum quidam abutentes ejus absentia terras ipsius undique vellicarent. Ad postremum, qua necessitate adductus, ut generum suum, quem rex incluserat, periculo eximeret, bello gravi se dederit regemque ceperit. Sed tam felicem eventum captio ejus[1] apud Wintoniam, ut in superioris anni gestis perstrinxi, paulo minus decoloravit;[2] quanquam ea captione non tam miserandum quam laudandum se ipse per Dei gratiam exhibuerit: cum enim videret regios comites ita obstinatos ad persequendum ut sine suorum detrimento res transigi nequiret, omnes quibus timebat, nominatimque imperatricem, præmisit; quibus prægressis,[3] ut jam tuto possent evadere, ipse sensim equitans, ne similis fugæ profectio putaretur, admisit in se persequentium manus, amicorum liberationem impedimento suo mercatus. Jam vero in ipsa captione

---

[1] *ejus*] om. At. Cd.
[2] *decoloravit*] declinavit, Cc.
[3] *prægressis*] prætergressis, Cc.

nemo eum, ut ante dixi, vel sensit dejectum animo, A.D. 1141.
vel audivit humilem in verbo: adeo supra fortunam
eminere videbatur, ut persecutores suos, nolo enim
dicere hostes, ad reverentiam sui excitaret. Itaque
regina, quæ licet meminisset virum suum ejus jussu
fuisse compeditum, nihil ei unquam vinculorum inferri
permisit, nec quicquam inhonestum de sua majestate
præsumpsit: denique apud Rovecestram, illuc quippe *He is honourably treated by the queen.*
ductus fuit, libere ad ecclesias infra castellum quo
libebat ibat; et quibus libebat loquebatur, ipsa duntaxat regina præsente: nam post profectionem ejus in
turrim sub libera custodia ductus est, adeo præsenti
et securo animo ut ab hominibus suis de Cantia
accepta pecunia equos non parvi pretii compararet,
qui ei post aliquanto tempore et usui et commodo
fuere.

De liberatione regis.

§ 507. Temptavere primo comites, et hi quorum in- *Negotiations for the liberation of Stephen.*
tererat de talibus loqui, si forte regem et se sineret
æquis conditionibus liberari. Hoc quamvis Mabilla
comitissa præ desiderio viri sui dilecti[1] statim amplexa nuntiis acceptis esset, in ejus liberationem conjugali caritate propensior, ille profundiori consilio
contradixit, regem et comitem non æqualis ponderis *Conduct of the countess Mabilia.*
esse asseverans: ceterum, si permitterent omnes qui
vel secum vel sui causa capti essent liberari, id se
posse pati. Sed noluerunt assentiri comites, et alii qui
regalium partium erant; regem quidem liberari cupientes, sed citra suas in pecuniæ amissione jacturas: *Prudent economy of the earls.*
nam et Gillebertus comes Willelmum de Salesberia,
Willelmus de Ipra Hunfridum de Bohun, et nonnulli[2]
alii quos potuerant, Wintoniæ ceperant, multis in
eorum redemptione marcis inhiantes.

---

[1] *dilecti*] om. At. Bk. Cd. | [2] *et nonnulli*] nonnullique,

Quomodo temptatum est comitem Gloecestræ posse inflecti in partes regis.

§ 508. Itaque alia via comitem adorsi, promissis ingentibus, si forte possent, illicere cupiebant. Concederet, sorore dimissa, in partes regis, habiturus proinde totius terræ dominatum, ut ad ipsius arbitrium penderent omnia; essetque in sola corona rege inferior, ceteris omnibus pro velle principaturus. Repulit comes immensas promissiones memorabili responso, quod posteritas audiat et miretur volo: "Non sum," inquit, "meus sed alieni juris: cum meæ potestatis me videro, "quicquid ratio de re quam allegatis dictaverit, fac- "turum me respondeo."

§ 509. Tum illi concitatiores et nonnihil moti, cum blanditiis nihil promoverent, minas intentare cœperunt, quod eum ultra mare in Bononiam mitterent, perpetuis vinculis usque ad mortem innodandum. Enimvero ille, minas sereno vultu dissolvens, nihil minus se timere protestatus est constanter et vere: confidebat enim in magnanimitate comitissæ, uxoris suæ scilicet,[1] et animositate suorum, qui statim regem in Hiberniam mitterent, si quid perperam in comitem factum audissent.

§ 510. Transiit in his mensis, tantæ molis erat liberari posse principes quos fortuna sua innexuisset catena. Tandem porro communicato consilio, quicunque imperatrici favebant crebris legationibus comitem conveniunt, ut quia non posset quod vellet, secundum comici dictum, vellet quod posset: pateretur ergo regem et se liberari mutuis conditionibus; "alioquin "timemus," aiebant, "ne comites facti sui maximi et "præclarissimi, quo te ceperunt, erecti conscientia, "unos et unos ex nobis invadant, castella expugnent,[2] "ipsam sororem tuam obsideant."[3]

Terence, *Andria*, II. 1. 5.

---

[1] *scilicet*] om. Ag. At. Bk. Cd.
[2] *expugnent*] oppugnent, Ce.
[3] *obsideant*] oppugnent, At. Bk. Cd. Cm.

§ 511. Tum demum Robertus mollitus legato et archiepiscopo assensit; ita tamen, ne quicquam castellorum vel terrarum redderetur quod post regis captionem in jus imperatricis vel quorumque fidelium ejus transierat. Illud sane nullo potuit obtinere modo quatenus sui secum liberarentur; offensis videlicet aliis, quod tantas eorum promissiones de principatu totius regni, quodam quasi fastu fastidiens, repudiaverat. Et quia maxime annitebantur ut, propter regiam dignitatem, primo rex liberaretur, deinceps[1] comes; cum id ille dubitaret concedere, firmaverunt jurejurando legatus et archiepiscopus, quod, si rex post liberationem suam detrectaret comitem liberare, ipsi se in captionem comitis incunctanter injicerent, quocunque ipsi libuisset abducendi.

§ 512. Nec adhuc quievit, sed, præter hæc, quo sibi provideret sagax animus invenit: posset nempe fieri ut rex, malorum, quod sæpe fit, præventus consilio, captionem fratris sui et archiepiscopi parvi duceret dummodo ipse liber in pluma jaceret. Exegit ergo ab utroque singillatim brevia et sigilla sua ad apostolicum in hunc sensum; "Sciret dominus apostolicus eos
" ob regis liberationem et regni pacem hoc se pacto
" comiti astrinxisse, quod, si eum rex post suam ipsius
" liberationem liberare dissimularet, ipsi ultro se in
" captionem ipsius immitterent. Quapropter, si ad hoc
" infortunium perventum foret, obnixe rogare, quod
" apostolicæ humanitatis esset sponte facere, ut et eos
" qui suffraganei ipsius erant, et comitem pariter, ab
" indebitis nexibus exueret;" et quædam talia.

§ 513. Hæc scripta Robertus ab utrisque pontificibus recepta tuto loco deposuit; et Wintoniam cum eisdem, simulque magna baronum copia, venit. Rex quoque, ut in præteritis dictum est, non multo post eodem veniens, familiare colloquium cum comite communicavit:

---

[1] *deinceps*] deinde, Ag. At. Bk. Cd.

A.D. 1141. sed quamvis et ipse rex, et cuncti principes qui aderant, magno annisu satagerent comitem in sua vota traducere, ille, "velut pelagi rupes immota resistens," omnes eorum conatus vel irritos fecit, vel rationabiliter compescuit: "Non esse rationis," dicens, "sed nec " humanitatis, ut sororem suam desereret, cujus partes " juste defendendas suscepisset: nullius commodi causa, " nec tam regis odio quam sacramenti sui respectu, " quod violare nefas esse ipsi quoque deberent atten- " dere, præsertim cum ab apostolico sibi mandatum " meminisset ut sacramento quod sorori, præsente pa- " tre, fecerat, obedientiam exhiberet." Ita infecta pace ab utrisque discessum.

Robert resists all attempts to persuade him to desert the empress.

The matters recorded were beyond our author's cognizance.

§ 514. Hæc ideo sic[1] in superioris anni gestis non apposui, quia clam conscientia mea erant: semper quippe horrori habui aliquid ad posteros transmittendum stilo committere, quod nescirem solida veritate subsistere. Ea porro, quæ de præsenti anno dicenda sunt, hoc habebunt principium.

Tractatus ut pro comite Andegavense mitteretur.

A.D. 1142. *From Christmas to Lent there is intermission of hostilities;*

§ 515. Utræque partes, imperatricis et regis, se cum quietis modestia egerunt a Natali usque ad Quadragesimam, magis sua custodire quam aliena incursare studentes: rex in superiores regiones abscessit, nescio quæ compositurus. Superveniens Quadragesima omnibus vacaturam[2] bellorum indixit; qua mediante, imperatrix cum suis ad Divisas venit, illic mysterium consilii cum suis habitura[3]: quod tamen eatenus exiit in vulgus, ut sciretur omnibus fautoribus ejus[4] complacitum quatenus pro comite Andegavensi mitteretur, qui conjugis et filiorum hereditatem in Anglia jure

the empress comes to Devizes in Lent; the count of Anjou sent for.

---

[1] *sic*] om. Ag. At. Bk. Cd.
[2] *vacaturam*] vacationem, At. Bk. Cd.; vel cessationem, interl. Ce.
[3] *cum suis habitura*] sui habitura, Bk. Cd.; sui habitum, At.
[4] *ejus*] om. Cd.

defensitare deberet. Missi sunt ergo spectabiles viri, A.D. 1142. et qui merito tantæ rei curam exequerentur.

De infirmitate regis.

§ 516. Non multo post, in ipsis pene¹ Paschalibus feriis, regem, quædam, ut aiunt, dura meditantem, gravis incommodum morbi apud Norhamptunam detinuit, adeo ut in tota propemodum Anglia sicut mortuus² conclamaretur. Duravit improspera valitudo usque post Pentecosten; tunc enim sensim refusus salutis vigor eum in pedes erexit.

§ 517. Interim nuntii ex Andegavis redeuntes, iterato apud Divisas in ipsis octavis Pentecostes coacto concilio, imperatrici et principibus audita reportant: "Comitem Andegavensem legationibus procerum non"nulla ex parte favere; ceterum, solum ex omnibus "comitem Gloecestrensem recognoscere,³ ejusque pru"dentiam ac fidem, magnanimitatem et industriam, "probatam jam olim habuisse. Is si ad se transito "mari adveniat,⁴ voluntati ejus se pro posse non "defuturum; alioquin ceteros in eundo et redeundo "frustra laborem consumpturos."

Quomodo comes Gloecestræ ad comitem Andegavensem ierit.

§ 518. Ita omnium audientium spebus erectis, ad comitem preces versæ, ut hunc laborem pro sororis et nepotum hereditate dignaretur. Dissimulavit ille primo, difficilem rem prætendens: susceptum per confertissimos hostes iter citra et ultra mare; periculosum sorori, quam in absentia ejus alii ægre tuerentur, qui eam in captione sua pene reliquerant, rebus ipsi suis diffisi. Favens tandem omnium unanimi volun-

---

¹ *pene*] om. Ce.
² *mortuus*] moriturus, Savile.
³ *recognoscere*] cognoscere, At. Ce.
⁴ *adveniat*] veniat, Ce.

A.D. 1142.

tati, obsides poposcit singillatim ab his qui optimates videbantur, secum in Normanniam ducendos, vadesque futuros tam comiti Andegavensi quam etiam[1] imperatrici, quod omnes junctis umbonibus ab ea, dum ipse abesset, injurias propulsarent, vicibus suis apud Oxenefordum manentes. Acclamatum est sententiæ, datique obsides Normanniam ducendi.

The empress stays at Oxford.

Quomodo comes Andegavensis auxilio comitis Gloecestræ decem castella in Normannia ceperit.

The earl commits Wareham to his eldest son, and soon after Midsummer sails.

§ 519. Robertus ergo valefaciens sorori, ductis secum obsidibus, cum expeditis militibus per tuta hospitia ad Waram profectus est, quem vicum cum castello jamdudum commiserat filio suo primogenito Willelmo. Ibi aliquanto post festum sancti Johannis alto se per Dei gratiam committens, naves quas tunc habebat solvit. Quæ fere in medium mare delatæ, omnes præter duas tempestate coorta in diversa jactatæ; quædamque retro versæ, quædam ultra destinatum propulsæ sunt: duæ solummodo, in quarum una comes cum fidissimis erat, rectum cursum tenentes, in idoneam stationem appulerunt. Veniens itaque Cadomum, comitem Andegavensem per nuntios accersivit. Venit ille non aspernanter, sed auditæ legationi sua impedimenta,[2] et ea multa, objecit: inter quæ, quod rebellione multorum castellorum in Normannia detineretur quo minus in Angliam veniret. Ea res moras redeundi comiti Gloecestrensi ultra placitum innexuit: nam ut Andegavensem omni occasione nudaret, cum eo decem castella expugnavit in Normannia, quorum hæc sunt vocabula, Tenerchebrai, Seithilaret, Brichesart, Alnai,[3] Bastonborg, Triveres, Castel de Vira, Plaisciz, Vilers, Moretoin.[4] Sed propemodum nihil quantum ad lega-

He summons the Count of Anjou to Caen.

He is detained in Normandy taking castles.

---

[1] *etiam*] om. Ce.
[2] *impedimenta*] Here MS. Ce.[2] resumes.
[3] *Alnai*] Alani, Cc[1].
[4] *quorum—Moretoin*] om. Ag. At. Bc. Bk. Bq. Cd. Cm.

tionem hac promovit industria; Andegavensis enim comes et alias occasiones, prioribus solutis, substituit, quibus in Angliam adventum excusaret suum. Magni sane loco beneficii filium suum ex imperatrice primogenitum avunculo concessit in Angliam deducendum, cujus intuitu proceres justi heredis partes propugnare animarentur. Henricus vocatur puer, nomen avi referens, utinam felicitatem et potentiam quandoque relaturus.

Quomodo rex cepit Waram, absente comite.

§ 520. Interea rex in Anglia, comitis absentiam aucupatus, subito ad Waram veniens, et non bene munitum[1] propugnatoribus offendens, succensa et depraedata villa,[2] statim etiam castello potitus est. Nec eo contentus, qui fortunam sibi aspirare videret, tribus diebus ante festum sancti Michaelis inopinato casu Oxeneford civitatem concremavit, et castellum, in quo cum domesticis militibus imperatrix erat, obsedit; ita scilicet offirmato animo, ut nullius spe commodi, nullius timore detrimenti, discedendum pronuntiaret, nisi castello reddito, et imperatrice in ditionem suam redacta. Mox igitur[3] optimates quidem[4] omnes imperatricis, confusi quia a domina sua praeter statutum abfuerant, confertis cuneis ad Walengeford convenerunt, eo proposito ut regem bello impeterent si ipse in aperto campo martem experiri vellet,[5] sed eum intra civitatem aggredi consilium non fuit, quam ita comes Gloecestrae fossatis munierat, ut inexpugnabilis praeter incendium videretur.

---

[1] *non bene munitum*] vacuum, At. Bk. Cd. Cm.
[2] *succensa—villa*] succenso et depraedato vico, At. Bk. Cd. Cm.
[3] *igitur*] om. At. Bk. Cd. Cm.
[4] *quidem*] om. At. Bk. Cd. Cm.
[5] *vellet*] voluisset, At. Bk. Cd. Cm.

De reditu comitis Gloecestrœ in Angliam.

<small>A.D. 1142.
The earl of Gloucester returns home.</small>

§ 521. His rumoribus in Anglia[1] disseminatis, comes Gloecestrœ[2] Robertus reditum maturavit. Trecentos itaque milites et aliquanto plures, quorum tamen numerus ad quadringentos non pervenit, navibus quinquaginta duabus imposuit; his duas, quas redeundo in pelago expugnavit, adjunxit. Itaque piœ voluntati Deus per gratiam sui[3] egregie favit, ut nulla e tanto numero navium longius evagaretur; sed omnes, vel pariter junctis lateribus, vel leniter unœ ante alias progressœ, placida sulcarent maria. Nec vero violentia fluctuum navigia impetebat, sed quodam famulatu prosequebatur; sicut aspectus maris solet esse gratissimus, cum placidis allisa lapsibus alludit unda littoribus.

<small>He lands at Wareham.</small>

In portum ergo Waram delatœ, comitem[4] et omnes socios desideriis suorum felices carinœ restituere.

Quomodo comes Gloecestrœ reditu suo Waram ceperit.

<small>He is dissuaded from landing at Southampton by the influence of the "Calves" or "Seals."</small>

§ 522. Cogitaverat primo ad Hamtunam appellere, ut dispendio burgensium[5] simul et domini eorum injurias suas ulcisceretur; sed flexerunt ejus impetum precibus multis Vituli, qui arctissimarum necessitudinum parentes, quos apud Hamtunam habebant, œrumpnis ceterorum involvi timerent. Genus hominum nauticorum est quos Vitulos[6] vocant; qui quia fidi clientes comitis sunt, preces eorum non negligendas arbitratus, cœpto destitit; simul et honoratius visum, ut in locum de quo egressus fuerat reverteretur, quod per violentiam

---

[1] *Anglia*] Normannia, Ag. At. Bk. Cd. Cm.
[2] *Gloecestrœ*] om. At. Bk. Cd.
[3] *sui*] suam, At. Bk. Cd.
[4] *comitem*] comites, At. Bk. Cd.
[5] *burgensium*] civium, Ag. At. Bk. Cd.

[6] William and Ralph Vituli were the leaders of the Southampton men in the second crusade. Osb. *Exp. Lyxbon.*; Mem. Rich. i. p. clvii.

amiserat vi recuperaturus. Statim ergo portu et vico in potestatem subactis, castellum obsedit, quod lectissimorum militum quos ibi rex locaverat munitione sua confirmarat[1] animositatem, ne dicam contumaciam. At enim paulo post milites, machinis comitis labefactati et consternati, petiverunt inducias ut, sicut moris est illorum hominum, efflagitarent a rege suppetias; die dicta, si forte venire negaret, castellum reddituri. Id, spe regem ab obsidione sororis abducendi, acceptissimum comiti fuit, quamvis impatienti desiderio castelli habendi teneretur; qua putamus animi confidentia, ut nullo ex Anglia fultus adhuc auxilio, cum trecentis et paulo plus militibus regem intrepidus operiretur, qui mille milites et eo amplius habere ferebatur; multi enim non tam imperatricis odio quam aviditate prædæ ad obsidendum convolaverant.

Quomodo comes Gloecestræ congregato exercitu tetendit ad liberandam imperatricem.

§ 523. Veruntamen, cum relatum esset quod obsessis apud Waram a rege negaretur auxilium, ea scilicet obstinatione qua prædixi castellum recepit; eodemque impetu insulam Portland, quam incastellaverant, subegit; nec minus et tertium, cujus nomen Lulleworda, quod Willelmi de Glastonia, cujusdam cubicularii, fuerat, qui nuper a fide imperatricis desciverat.[2] Inde omnes fautores imperatricis ad Cirecestram convocavit, jam ingresso Domini[3] adventu. Ibi igitur ad dominæ suæ succurrendum omnibus suis[4] viribus conspirati, profectionem ad Oxenefordum meditabantur; infensis mentibus cum rege, nisi abscederet, præliatum[5] iri. Enimvero jam progressis plausibile nuntium allatum est, egressam imperatricem ab obsesso castello

---

[1] *confirmarat*] confirmabat, At. Bk. Cd.

[2] *quod—desciverat*] armis perdomuit, Ag. At. Bc. Bk. Cd.

[3] *Domini*] om. Ce.

[4] *suis*] om. Bk. Cd.

[5] *præliatum*] præliaturum, Ce.

596　　　　　HISTORIA NOVELLA.　　　　[LIB. III.

A.D. 1142.
The empress's escape to Wallingford.

Oxeneford, et apud Walengeford tuto manere. Illic ergo divertentes, ejusdem dominæ suæ[1] consilio, quia et milites qui ea exeunte remanserant, castello reddito, indempnes abierant, et sancti dies quiescere vel parum admonebant, bello abstinendum rati, ad sua quique sunt reversi.[2]

Explicit Liber Tertius Novellæ Historiæ.

Conclusion.

§ 524. Modum sane liberationis imperatricis gratanter apponerem, si pro certo compertum haberem. Est enim evidens Dei miraculum. Illud satis constat, quod, metu adventantis[3] comitis, obsessoribus plurimis apud Oxeneford, quo quisque poterat, dilapsis, reliqui laxiores custodias et remissiores excubias fecere; magis, si ad bellum veniretur, saluti suæ solliciti, quam aliorum exitio infesti. Qua re ab oppidanis animadversa, imperatrix cum solis quatuor militibus per posterulam egressa amnem transiit. Mox, ut nonnunquam, et fere semper, necessitas et remedium excogitat et audaciam subministrat, pede Abbenduniam profecta, hinc ad Walingeford equo subvecta est. Quæ tamen latius persequi fert animus si unquam, dante Deo, ab his qui interfuere veritatem accepero.[4] Sed hæc in volumine sequenti, Deo volente, latius expedientur.[5]

---

[1] *suæ*] om. At. Bk. Cd.
[2] *reversi.*] This is the end of the third book in MS. Ce.¹
[3] *adventantis*] advenientis, At. Bk. Cd.
[4] *Qua re—accepero*] omitted in Cc¹, and written over an erasure in Ce². The sentence occurs in MSS. Ag. At. Ao. Bc. Bk. Bq. Cd. Cd². Cm., all which end with the word *accepero.*
[5] *Sed—expedientur*] only in MSS. Cc¹. Ce².

INDEX.

INDEX.

A.

Aaron, church dedicated in honour of, near the Dead Sea, 442.
Abacuc, S., remains of, near the Cornelian gate at Rome, 404.
Abbotsbury, appropriated by bishop Roger to Salisbury, 559.
Abdon, S., burial place of, 408.
Abingdon, Ethelstan receives an embassy from France at, 150; escape of the empress Matilda to, 596.
——— Ethelwold, abbot of, 166.
——— Siward, abbot of, 239.
——— Adelelm, abbot of, 352.
——— Ingulf, abbot of, 573.
Abraham, burial place of, visited by Baldwin, 441.
Abundius, S., the martyr, burial place of, 406.
Acca (Acha), sister of Edwin and wife of Ethelfrith of Northumbria, 48.
Acca, bishop of Hexham, story preserved by, 261.
Accaron (Acre), passed by the Crusaders on the way to Jerusalem, 421; men of, send supplies to Baldwin, 440; occupied by him, 447.
Achilleus, S., burial place of, 407.
Achim (Hakem), the calif, seizes Jerusalem, 425; nephew of the patriarch, ib.
Adam, the beginning of the genealogy drawn by S. Luke, 120.
Adauctus, S., burial place of, 405.

Adela, daughter of the Conqueror, and wife of Stephen of Blois, became a nun, 333; her son Theobald, 480, 496; her son Stephen, 529.
Adela, of Louvain, second wife of Henry I., 495, 556, 528, 575; the county of Shrewsbury given to her, 528; the empress badly received by her at Arundel, 556.
Adelard, a subregulus of Wessex, benefactor of Glastonbury, 36, 37.
Adelbold, bishop of Utrecht, 195.
Adelelm, bishop, see Wells: abbot, see Abingdon.
Adelstan, bishop, see Ramsbury.
Adhemar, bishop of Puy, leader of the Crusaders, 398, 400; commands at Antioch, 420; his death, 421.
Adrian, the emperor, his treatment of Jerusalem, 422.
Adrian, abbot of St. Augustine's, Canterbury, comes to England, 16; succeeds Benedict Biscop, 59.
Adrian, the martyr, his burial place, 407.
Adrian I., pope, invites Charles the Great to Rome, 71; authorises the division of the province of Canterbury, 85; succeeded by Leo III., 86, 87; recognised the royal right of investiture, 250.
Adulf, count of Flanders. See Flanders.
Adultery, punishment of, among the old Saxons, 80.
Ae, Anglo Saxon names beginning with Aelf-, Aethel- are indexed under E.
Aesc, ancestor of the kings of Kent. See Kent.
Africa ravaged by the Vandals, 9; conquered by the Saracens, 92, 395, 424.

Agapetus the Martyr, church of, 406; remains of, 407.
Agareni, Saracens so called by Alcuin, 92, 276.
Agatha, S., relics of, at Constantinople, 413.
Agatha, sister of the queen of Sweden, marries Edward, son of Edmund Ironside, 218.
Agilbert, bishop. *See* Dorchester.
Agnes, S., church of, at Rome, 405.
Agrippa, son-in-law of Augustus, 204.
Agrippina, Cologne so named from Agrippa, 204.
Aidan, bishop. *See* Lindisfarne.
Alan, count of Brittany, imprisons his uncle Eudes, and has to submit to duke William, 294.
Alan, Fergant, count of Brittany, marries Constance, daughter of the Conqueror, 338.
Alan, count; his men quarrel with bishop Roger's men at Oxford, 548, 549, 552.
Alandreus, an astronomical authority, 194.
Alani, conquered by the Franks, 69.
Alban, relics of, discovered by Offa, 85; church built in his honour, *ib.*
Albano, the bishop of, has the duty of making an oration on the reception of the emperor, 501.
Albano, Matthew, bishop of, takes part in the election of Innocent II., 531.
Alberic, abbot of Citeaux, 384.
Alberic de Vere. *See* Vere.
Albert, the chancellor of Henry V., 500.
Albert, count de Blandriaco, 500.
Albert, archbishop of Mainz, 509.
Albo, dean of SS. Sergius and Bacchus, 499.
Alcred, king of Northumbria, 74. *See* Northumbria.
Alcuin, described the library at York, 68; extracts from his letters to Eanbald, 68; to Charles the Great, 68; his learning and literary position, 68, 69; set by Charles over the monastery at Tours, 72; his letter to the monks of Wearmouth, 73; to the clergy of York, 73; to king Offa,

Alcuin—*cont.*
73, 75; to king Ethelred, 73; to Osbert, 73, 94; to archbishop Ethelheard, 74, 82, 86; his mention of Ethelred's restoration, 75; he mentions the ravages of the Danes, 73, 75; his anticipation of later troubles, 80; his notices of the conquests of Charles, 91, 92.
Alderia, William de, his treason, confession, and execution, 372.
Aldfrith, king of Northumbria. *See* Northumbria.
Aldgitha, sister of Ethelstan, married to a duke near the Alps, 117.
Aldhelm, bishop of Sherborne. *See* Sherborne.
Aldred, Ealdred, archbishop. *See* York.
Aldulf, rebellion of, against Ethelstan in Northumbria, 142.
Aldulf, bishop of Lichfield. *See* Lichfield.
Alemannia, 72, 110.
Alençon, castle of, seized by Geoffrey Martel, 288; surrendered to duke William, 289.
Alexander, patriarch of Jerusalem, 424.
Alexander, emperor of Constantinople, 412.
Alexander I., pope, his burial place, 405.
Alexander II., pope, supports the cause of the Conqueror, 299; promotes Hildebrand, 322; dies, 325; his letter to the Conqueror, 347, 348; his direction as to the decision between York and Canterbury, 350, 354; his mission of the legate Hubert, 351.
Alexander, king of Scots, 278, 309, 476; removed his father's body to Dunfermline, 309; married to an illegitimate daughter of Henry I., 476.
Alexander the Great, William Rufus compared with, 364, 365.
Alexander, S., the martyr, his burial place, 405.
Alexandria, patriarchate of, translated to Babylon, 425; the spoils of Rome and Syracuse carried by the Saracens to, 412; position of, among the great cities of the world, 416.

Alexius, emperor of Constantinople, 276; attacked by Robert Wiscard, 321, 390; attacks Bohemond, 321; his cunning and humiliation, 381, 322; he poisons Wiscard, 321, 453; his treatment of the Crusaders, 400, 401; drove his predecessor Michael into Apulia, 413; has the surrender of Nice, 413; dismisses the Crusaders, 414; connives at the attack of Soliman on the Crusaders, 447; attacked by Bohemond, 454; sets the example of moderation at meals, 483.

Alfonso, king of Gallicia, translated S. Isidore to Toledo, 193; betrothed to a daughter of the Conqueror, 333; his success against the Moors, 337.

Alfred, king of the West Saxons. *See* West Saxons.

Alfred, son of king Ethelred, 191; lives in Normandy during the reign of Canute, 218; is brought to England, imprisoned, and blinded, and dies, 229; connexion of Godwin with the tragedy, 240.

Alfwold, king of Northumbria. *See* Northumbria.

Alfwold, father of Leofstan, 192.

Alheard, bishop of Elmham, 85.

Alla, king of Northumbria, 50. *See* Northumbria.

Almodis, the wife of count William of Toulouse, 455; her marriages, 456.

Alnai, castle of, in Normandy, taken by earl Robert of Gloucester, 572.

Alpheus, father of S. James, 424.

Alps, the, 71, 400, 402; a duke near, marries Aldgitha, 117; crossed by Urban II., 390, 456.

Alric, king of Kent. *See* Kent.

Aluric. *See* Elfric.

Alstan, bishop of Sherborne. *See* Sherborne.

Alwius, brother of Penda, 79.

Amalfi, archbishop of, 504.

Ambrose, pious saying of, 65; his use of chants and hymns at Milan, 383; his eloquence, 413; history ascribed to, 415.

Ambrosius, Aurelius, exploits of, 11.

Anacletus II. (Pier Leoni) elected pope

Anacletus II.—*cont.*
by a party on the death of Honorius II., 531; his partizans, 531; letter of the bishop of Portus on this, 532, 533; struggles for eight years against Innocent II., 534; dies, 534.

Anastasius, emperors of Constantinople, named, 412.

Anastasius, the martyr, 408; his head, 408.

Andover, Edgar's sin at, 179; the town burned by queen Matilda, 580.

Andrew, S., relics of, at Constantinople, 413.

Angles, invited from Germany, 5; their conquests in Britain, 8, 9–12.

Anglesey, conquered by Edwin, 50; landing of the Norwegians in, 318, 376; conquered by the Welsh, 376.

Anglia, Vetus, in Germany, 121.

Angoulême, Gerard, bishop of, 503, 504; frustrates the peace of 1112, 503; excommunicates William of Poictou, 510.

Anjou, history of the counts of, 291, 292; their power always dangerous to Normandy, 527.

————— Fulk, count of, draws the count of Maine into his power, 292; resigns his county to his son, 292; reduces him to obedience, goes to Jerusalem, *ib.*; returns home and dies, 293.

————— Geoffrey Martel, count of, takes up arms against his father, and has to submit with great humiliation, 292; succeeds to the county, 293; captures the count of Poictou, 287; marries the count's stepmother, 288; captures count Theobald of Blois, and compels him to surrender Tours, 288; is attacked by duke William and king Henry, 287; occupies Alençon, 288; William sends spies to reconnoitre him, *ib.*; leaves his county to his sister's son, 293; Le Mans burned by, 294.

————— Geoffrey, count of, nephew of Geoffrey Martel, succeeds, 293; his piety and weakness, *ib.*

————— Fulk Rechin, count of, supplants his brother Geoffrey, 293; his wife commits adultery with king Philip, *ib.*, 315, 480.

Anjou, Geoffrey Martel II., count of, his good government, 293 ; murdered, *ib.*
—————— Fulk, count of, the brother of Geoffrey, succeeds, 293 ; his daughter betrothed to William, son of Henry I., 482, 495 ; another daughter given to William, son of Robert, 498 ; goes to Jerusalem, 495 ; policy of the marriages, 528, 530; king of Jerusalem, 528.
—————— Geoffrey, count of, son of Fulk, project of marrying him to the empress Matilda, 527 ; married, 530; sent for to defend the rights of his wife and son, 590 ; declines to listen to any one but earl Robert, 591 ; visited by him, 591, 592 ; still delays, and takes castles in Normandy, 592; allows his son Henry to visit England, 593.
Anlaf, son of Sihtric, 147, 151; his flight to Ireland, 147 ; his alliance with the Scots against Ethelstan, 142; his adventure before the battle of Brunanburh, 143 ; set up as king by the Northumbrians, 157; accepts Christianity, but relapses and is sent into exile, 158 ; Elwin and Ethelwin killed in the war against, 151.
Anna, king of the East Angles. *See* East Angles, 76.
Ansbert, the senator, ancestor of Charles the Great, 71.
Anschetil, son of Riulf, opposes duke William, 160 ; murdered at Pavia, 161.
Anschisus, an ancestor of Charles the Great, 71.
Ansegis, son of Anschisus, and father of Pipin, 70, 71.
Anselm, archbishop. *See* Canterbury :— Eadmer's history down to his death, 2.
Anselm of Lucca, pope Alexander II., 299.
Anteros, pope, burial place of, 407.
Antioch, council of, 503 ; expedition of the Crusaders against, 390 ; position of, among the great cities of the world, 415, 416 ; description of, 415, 416 ; besieged by the Crusaders, 416 ; Aoxian, the governor of, 416 ; churches at, 416 ;

Antioch—*cont.*
famine among the besiegers at, 418 ; Bohemond intrigues for the surrender of, 418, 419 ; Kerbogha attempts to relieve, 419 ; the city taken, 420 ; Bohemond stays to secure, 421 ; Odo of Bayeux dies at, 334 ; siege of, referred to, 433, 460; distance of Tarsus from, 434 ; Bohemond, prince of, 436, 438 ; *See* Bohemond;- distance of Edessa from, 435 ; Tancred undertakes the government of, 443 ; Bohemond returns to, 454 ; Tancred succeeds him at, 455 ; claim of Raymond to, 457 ; held by Baldwin II., and given by him to Roger, son of Richard, 452, 455 ; Bohemond II., prince of, 452, 455.
Antioch in Pisidia, passed by the Crusaders, 415.
Antiochus, father of Seleucus, gives his name to Antioch, 416.
Antonius, patriarch of Jerusalem, 424.
Antony, visit of Herod to, 436.
Aoxian, governor of Antioch at the time of the siege, 416 ; sends for aid to the sultan of Persia, 417 ; is killed by a Syrian rustic, 419.
Apollinaris, S., his head preserved at Glastonbury, 181.
Appia, Via, at Rome, 407.
Apulia, conquest of, by Robert Wiscard, 320 ; he gives it to his son Roger, 321, 391 ; returns to, 321 ; he is buried in, 322 ; the body of duke Robert of Normandy buried in, 333 ; Guimund, a bishop in, 339 ; crossed by the Crusaders, 409 ; the emperor Michael was driven by Alexius into, 413 ; Bohemond returns to, 454 ; Robert of Normandy marries in, 461.
Aqua Salina (Salvia ?), at Rome, 408.
Araxes, the river, 403.
Arbrissel, Robert of, founder of the order of Fontevraud, 512.
Arcadius, emperor of Constantinople, 412.
Archadius, the governor of Cæsarea, 445.
Ardeatina, Via, at Rome, 407.

INDEX.

Ardenna, policy of Cæsar in clearing the forest of, 312.
Arezzo, Conrad, son of Henry IV., dies at, 343, 498; subdued by Henry V., 509.
Argentiæ (Argences), village in Normandy, 210.
Arians, continuity of, in Spain, 193.
Arles, the count of, husband of Almodis, 455; Raymond, her son, acquires, 456.
Armenia, conquered by the Saracens, 394; offers itself to Baldwin, 435.
Armenians, the Turks avenge themselves on, 417.
Arnold, son of Ansbert, ancestor of the Karolings, 71.
Arnulf, saint, son of Arnold, and bishop of Metz, 71; his sons, ib.
Arnulf, the emperor, his reign, 116, 117; drives the pirates out of Gaul, 128.
Arnulf, Ernulf, grandson of Alfred, ancestor of the counts of Flanders, 133; his enmity with duke William of Normandy, 161.
Arnulf, son of Baldwin of Flanders, 315; receives fealty as count of Flanders, and is killed by Robert Friso, 315.
Arques, count of, rebels against duke William, is besieged, succoured by the king of France, and surrenders, 289, 290; Baldwin, count of Flanders, wounded at, 479.
Arragon, the king of, his daughter marries Raymond of S. Giles, 456.
Arthemius, burial place of, 408.
Arthur, king of Britain, his exploits, 11; his nephew Walwen, 342.
Arundel, fortified by Robert of Belesme against Henry I., 472; surrendered, 472; the empress sent to her step-mother at, 556; she leaves, ib.; this visit referred to, 586.
Ascalon, the Ethiopian garrison of the Tower of David, sent to, 427, 428; the Crusaders march on, 429; battle of, 429, 430; the Egyptian fleet comes to, 445; the land forces at, 446; negotiations of Raymond of S. Giles at, 457, 458.

Ashdown, Escendune, battle of, 122.
Asia, ravages of the Saracens in, 92, 394, 395, 415; Seleucus was king of, 415, 416.
Assandun, battle of, 216, 217; church founded by Canute at, 220.
Assenarica, the gate of S. John at Rome called, 407.
Asser, of St. David's, friend and counsellor of Alfred, 131, 133; bishop of Sherborne, 131.
Athanasius, patriarch of Jerusalem, 425.
Athelingi, meaning of the name, 70.
Athelm, archbishop of Canterbury. See Canterbury.
Athelney, S. Cuthbert appears to Alfred in, 125; Alfred visits after his victory, 126; his foundation of a monastery at, 130; John, the Old Saxon, abbot of, 130, 133.
Audifax, remains of, near the Cornelian gate at Rome, 404.
Augsburg, bishop of, 509.
Augustine, Saint, his arm brought from Pavia to Coventry, 224.
Augustine. See Canterbury, archbishops of.
Augustus, the name of, offered to Charles the Great, 72; equivalent of Soldanus, 417.
Aumâle, acquired by William Rufus, 363.
Aurelia, Via, at Rome, 408.
Austrasia, pedigree of the mayors of the palace of, 70, 71; under Lewis of Bavaria, 110, 111.
Auvergne, Clermont in, 391.
Auxerre, S. German, bishop of, 26; Fontenay in the district of, 111; translation of S. Martin at, 127; miraculous events at, 127.
Avars, or Huns, ravages of, 92.
Aventine, the Mount, at Rome, 408.
Aversa, Guimund, bishop of, 339.
Avranches, occupied by Henry against Robert and William, 469.
Azarias, the high priest, 252.
Azotus, passed by Baldwin, on his march to Joppa, 441; besieged by Baldwin,

Azotus—*cont.*
444; surrendered, 444; he escapes from the battle of Ramlah to, 450.

B.

Babylon (Cairo), built by Cambyses in Egypt, 429; the patriarchate of Alexandria removed to, 425; Robert, son of Godwin, suffers martyrdom in, 310; the desert reaches to, 442.
Babylon, king of, 425.
Babylon, the sultan of, 428; his war with Godfrey, 429, 433; sends a fleet to Ascalon, against Baldwin, 446.
Badonicus, mons, battle at, 11.
Baldac, the garrison of, attacks the Crusaders, 437.
Baldred, king of Kent. *See* Kent.
Baldred, a subregulus of the West Saxons, benefactor of Glastonbury, 36, 37.
Baldwin, count, of Flanders. *See* Flanders.
Baldwin, abbot of S. Edmunds, 352.
Baldwin, envoy of Anselm, to the pope, 492; a monk of Bec, *ib.*
Baldwin I., king of Jerusalem, 241; brother of Godfrey, 432; and his successor, 434; acquires Tarsus, Turbessel and Edessa, 434, 435; frees Armenia from the Turks, 435, 436; is summoned to Jerusalem and reaches Laodicea, 436, 437; Godfrey meets him at the gate of Jerusalem, 437; returns to Edessa, 438; fails to rescue Bohemond, and takes Malatia, 438; goes to Antioch, 438; his difficult march on Joppa, 439, 440; reaches Jerusalem, 441; marches on Ascalon, 441; visits the eastern parts of Palestine, and is crowned at Bethlehem, 442; spends Easter at Jerusalem, 444; his bargain

Baldwin I.—*cont.*
with the Genoese and Pisans, 444; takes Azotus and Cæsarea, 444, 445; defeats the Egyptian army, 446; takes other cities, 447; attacks the Turks besieging Ramlah, 448; his defeat and narrow escape, 448, 449; fights another great battle some years after, 451; marries the countess of Sicily, separates from her, and dies, 451; his character, 451, 452.
Baldwin II. succeeds his cousin Baldwin I. at Edessa, 438; and at Jerusalem, 452; had governed Antioch, 452; sketch of his reign, captivity and deliverance, 452; acts as guardian of Antioch for Bohemond II., 455.
Balearic Isles, occupied by the Saracens, 92, 395, 424, 425; visited by Sigurd of Norway, 486; conquered by William of Montpellier, 486.
Balzo, the murderer of duke William of Normandy, 161.
Bamberg, bishop of, 509.
Bamborough, Bebbanburg, shrine of S. Oswald at, 53.
Bancor, massacre of the monks of, 47, 48.
Bangor, bishopric of, 48.
————— Hervey, bishop of, translated to Ely, 517.
————— David the Scot, bishop of, writes an account of the struggle between Henry V. and the pope, 498, 502.
Bantomp, a name on one of the pyramids at Glastonbury, 25.
Barcelona, story of a citizen's son of, 198; the count of, marries Almodis, 456.
Bardney, translation of S. Oswald to, 53; king Ethelred receives the tonsure at, 54; he becomes abbot at, 78; translation of S. Oswald from, to Gloucester, 136.
Bardulf, Hugh. *See* Pardulf.
Barfleur, Henry I. and his court embark at, 496.
Barking, abbey; Hildelida, abbess of, 35.
Basil, saint, his relics at Constantinople, 413.

Basil, emperors of Constantinople named, 412.
Basilides, patriarch of Jerusalem, 425.
Bastonborg, castle in Normandy taken by earl Robert of Gloucester, 592.
Bate, a name on one of the pyramids at Glastonbury, 25.
Bath, the Britons take refuge at, 21; see of, 100; Edgar crowned at, 180.
Bath, Sweyn takes, 208; Elfege was abbot of, 225; ravaged by Geoffrey of Coutances, 361; see of Wells fixed at, 358, 385, 387, 388; negotiations for peace held at, 564.
Bath, Robert, bishop of, 573.
Battle, abbey of, founded, 326.
Baugaria, overrun by the Saracens, 92.
Bavaria, under Lewis, grandson of Charles the Great, 110, 111.
Bayeux, Rannulf, viscount of, rebels against duke William in his minority, 286.
Bayeux, Odo, bishop of, 334; earl of Kent, *ib*, 360; his quarrels with his brother and nephew, and his death at Antioch, 334; attests the synodal decree on the claims of Canterbury, 351; his rebellion at the beginning of the reign of William Rufus, 360, 361; taken prisoner, rescued and banished, 362; his succession withheld from his nephew, 473.
Bayeux, burned by Henry I., 475.
Bearn, a name on one of the pyramids at Glastonbury, 25.
Beaumont, Henry of, earl of Warwick, faithful to Henry I., 471, 493; son of Roger, 493.
Beaumont, Roger of, founded the monastery of Preaux, 482; his character, 492.
Beaumont, Robert of, count of Meulan, 482. *See* Mellent.
Bec, Baldwin, a monk of, envoy of Anselm to the pope, 492.
Beda, the first writer of English history, 1, 2; his dates for the reign of Ethelbert, 13; his account of Ethelbert's conversion, 14; his mention of Agilbert, 30; his description of the reign of Ethel-

Beda—*cont.*
frith, 46; his testimony about S. Oswald, 53; his lives of the abbots, 57; his translation of the gospel of S. John, 65; account of his life, 58; and works, 59, 60, 63; his reported invitation to Rome, 62, 63; his last illness, 64, 65; and death, 65, 66; his epitaph, 67; his literary position, 66, 67, 69, 389, 518, 567; mentioned by Alcuin, 73; his account of Sebbi, 99; of Selsey, 100; of Jerusalem, 422; his history translated under Alfred, 132; on the East Angles, 264, 266.
Bedfordshire, included in Mercia, 101.
Bedwigius, in the mythical pedigree of the West Saxon kings, 121.
Beldegius, son of Woden, 45, 121.
Belesme, Robert of Montgomery, lord of, 472; fortifies his castles against Henry I., 472; is banished from England, 473; renews his rebellion in Normandy, 473; escapes from the battle of Tenchebrai, but is taken prisoner and confined for life, 475; his character, 475, 476.
Benedict I., pope, gives S. Gregory leave to attempt the conversion of Britain, 46.
Benedict X. gives a pall to Stigand, 244.
Benedict, S., rule of, 381.
Benedict, Biscop, his foundations on the Wear, 59; account of him, 60.
Benedicta, burial place of, 408.
Benignus succeeds Patrick at Glastonbury, 27; his epitaph under the name of Beonna, *ib.*
Beneventum, Landulf, archbishop of, 504.
Bensington, Offa defeats Cynewulf at, 41.
Beocheric, or Little Ireland, an estate of Glastonbury, 171.
Beonna, abbot. *See* Benignus.
Beorhtwald, abbot of Glastonbury, 29; his legendary history, 29, 37.
Beorhtwald, archbishop of Canterbury. *See* Canterbury.
Beorn (Bruno) cousin of Sweyn, killed by him, 245.
Beorna, king of the East Angles. *See* East Angles.

Beornred, king of the Mercians. See Mercia.

Beornulf, king of the Mercians. See Mercia.

Beorward, abbot of Glastonbury, 26.

Beowius, son of Sceld, 121.

Berengar, the heresiarch of Tours, his controversy on the Eucharist, 338; his character and the poem of Hildebert about him, 339, 340; prophecy of Fulbert about, 341.

Berengar, count, swears on behalf of the emperor, 500; consents to the peace, 509.

Berferth, the murder of Saint Wistan, 263.

Berhtulf, king of the Mercians. See Mercia.]

Berkeley, story of the witch of, 253, 254; the neighbourhood of, ravaged by Geoffrey of Coutances, 361.

Berkshire, included in Wessex, 100; a fountain of blood springs up in, 376.

Bernard, the pilgrim, his visit to Jerusalem, 423, 425.

Bernard, abbot, founder of the order of Tiron, 512.

Bernege, bishop of Selsey. See Selsey.

Bernicia, a division of Northumbria, 50, 54.

Bertha, wife of Ethelbert of Kent, 13.

Bertram, son of Raymond of S. Giles, his birth and marriage, 456; completes the conquest of Tripoli, 459; and leaves it to his son Pontius, 459.

Berytus, passage of the Crusaders by, 421; description of the pass between Tripoli and, 439; the emir of, sends provisions to Baldwin, 440.

Bethlehem, church of, built by Cyril, 424; arrival of Tancred with the Crusaders at, 422; Godfrey keeps Christmas at, 437; Baldwin crowned at, 442.

Beverstane, Godwin and his sons bring an armed force to, 242.

Bigot, Roger, joins in the first rising against William Rufus at Norwich, 361;

Bigot, Roger—*cont.*
adheres to Henry I. in his quarrel with Robert, 471.

Birine, messenger of the King Kenulf to the pope, 89.

Birinus, bishop of Dorchester. See Dorchester.

Bistonia, a name for Thrace, 411.

Bithynia, duke Robert of Normandy dies in, 211; in the hands of the Saracens, 394; Nice in, 401; crossed by the Crusaders, 414; the Turks quit, 414.

Bladon, charter granted at, 31.

Blandrinco, Albert, count de, 500.

Blastus, a martyr, his burial place at Rome, 405.

Bleddanhide, estate of Glastonbury at, 37.

Blegent, brother of Griffin, king of the Welsh, 280.

Bliswerh, a name on one of the Glastonbury pyramids, 25.

Blithildis, the wife of Ansbert, ancestor of the Karolings, 71.

Blois, Theobald, count of, compelled to surrender Tours to Geoffrey Martel, 288.

——— Stephen, count of, marries Adela, the Conqueror's daughter, 333; joins the first crusade, 402; spends the winter in Italy, 409; does homage to Alexius, 413; after returning to Europe, joins William of Poictou in his crusade, 447; is killed at the battle of Ramlah, 449, 480; his daughter, the countess of Chester, 497.

——— Theobald, count of, son of Stephen and Adela, causes a quarrel between Henry I. and Lewis VI., 480, 481; assists in securing Normandy to the king's son, William, 496; his sister lost in the shipwreck, 497; appealed to by his brother Henry against Stephen, 551; negotiates for peace, 565.

Bocard, Godfrey of Lorraine, surnamed, 431.

Boetius, translated by Alfred, 131, 132; quotation from, 195.

Bohemond I., son of Robert Wiscard, 321, 452; goes with his father against the emperor Alexius and defeats the Greeks, ib; his brother Roger preferred as heir of Apulia, 391, 453; is at the council of Clermont, 453; leads the Crusaders from Brundusium to Dyrrachium, 400; attempt of Alexius to entrap him, 401; negotiates for the betrayal of Antioch, 418; takes the principal tower, 418, 419; stays at Antioch after the capture, 421; summons Baldwin from Edessa to Jerusalem, 436; is taken prisoner by Danischemend, 438, 454; returns to Antioch, 454; occupies Laodicea, 454; returns to Europe and offers his chains to S. Leonard, 454; goes into Apulia, and renews his attack on Alexius, ib; sets out for Antioch, and dies, 454, 455; his successors there, 455.

Bohemond II., prince of Antioch, son of Bohemond I., 452, 455; succeeds on the death of Roger, son of Richard, under the tutelage of Baldwin II., 452, 455; betrothed to his daughter, 455.

Bohun, Humfrey de, lord of the castle of Trowbridge, 557; taken prisoner at Winchester, 587.

Boniface V., pope, his letter to archbishop Justus, 347.

Boniface, Saint, archbishop of Mainz, writes to Ethelbald, king of Mercia, 79, 80–82; succeeded by Lullus, also an Englishman, 84; his letter to archbishop Cuthbert mentioned, 82; his oath to Gregory III., 82.

Boniface, the marquess, negotiation of Robert Curthose for marriage with the daughter of, 332; one of the jurors for Henry V., 500; consents to the peace, 509.

Boniface, a martyr, his burial place at Rome, 405.

Boniface, burial place of, on the Aventine, 408.

Boniface, cardinal of S. Mark, 499.

Bouillon, Godfrey of, king of Jerusalem, 400; attacked by the Turks in Asia Bouillon, Godfrey of—*cont.*

Minor, 414; commands a division at Antioch, 420; advances on Jerusalem, 421; takes the city, 427; chosen king, 428; wins the battle of Ascalon, 429, 430; sketch of his descent and earlier career, 431–433; his death, 433; buried on Golgotha, 434; mentioned, 437, 438, 444, 451, 453, 457.

Boulogne, family of the counts of, descended from Alfred, 134.

——— Adulf, count of, son of Baldwin of Flanders, 133, 150; heads an embassy to Ethelstan, 150.

——— Eustace, count of, brother-in-law of Edward the Confessor, quarrels with Godwin and the Kentish men, 244; his sons, kings of Jerusalem, 431.

——— Eustace II., count of, marries Mary of Scotland, 278, 579; holds Rochester against William Rufus, 362; is with Godfrey and Baldwin at Jerusalem, 437; his daughter the wife of king Stephen, 578, 579; his inheritance refused by the empress to Eustace, son of Stephen, 579.

——— Stephen, count of. *See* Stephen King.

Boulogne, threats to imprison the earl of Gloucester at, 588.

Bourdeaux, surrendered to Geoffrey Martel, 288.

Bourdin, Maurice, archbishop of Braga, anti-pope, 504, 506; flies to Sutri, 506; captured by Calixtus II., 506, 507; imprisoned at La Cava, 507.

Braga. *See* Bourdin.

Bregden, a name on one of the Glastonbury pyramids, 25.

Bregercie, estate of Glastonbury at, 37.

Bregored, abbot of Glastonbury, 26, 29.

Brent, estate of Glastonbury at, 37, 38, 172.

Brentcnol, Brent Knoll, 26.

Brentford, battle at, 216.

Brentmeirs, belonging to Glastonbury, 26.

Brian, Fitz Count, advises the marriage of Geoffrey and Matilda, 530; lord of

Brian, Fitz Count—*cont.*
Wallingford, meets Robert of Gloucester on his way to, 556; swears on behalf of the empress to accept the advice of the legate, 573.
Bridget, S., at Glastonbury, 27.
Bridgnorth, fortified by Robert of Belesme against Henry I., 472.
Brie, S. Ethelburga, abbess of, 266.
Brichesart, castle of, in Normandy, taken by earl Robert of Gloucester, 592.
Brihthelm, bishop of Wells. *See* Wells.
Brihtric, king of the West Saxons. *See* West Saxons.
Brihtwald, archbishop. *See* Canterbury.
Brihtwold, bishop of Wiltshire. *See* Ramsbury.
Brionne, given to Guy of Burgundy, 286; he flies to, 287.
Bristol, the headquarters of Geoffrey of Coutances, in his rebellion against William Rufus, 361; the only possession left by Stephen to earl Robert, 546; the men of, alarm the king's party, 552; earl Robert visits, 556; the empress Matilda brought to, 556, 586; Stephen threatens, 557; Stephen is brought to the empress and kept in custody at, 572; on his liberation he leaves his wife and son as sureties at, 582; arrival of the earl at, 582.
Britain, under the Romans, 6, 7, 8; conquered by the Germans, 9, 10, 11; massacre of the nobles of, 12.
Brittany, the Danes expelled by the emperor Arnulf from, 128; letter to Ethelstan on the saints of, 155; relics brought from, 157; origin of the claim of the Norman dukes on, 294; Henry, son of the Conqueror, retires to, 468; more connected with Normandy than with France, 480.
Brittany, Alan, count of, 294. *See* Alan.
Brittany, Alan Fergant, count of, 333. *See* Alan.
Brittany, Conan of. *See* Conan.
Brittany, men of, undertake service under Henry I., 478; and under Stephen, 540.

Brondius, in the West Saxon pedigree, 121.
Brunanburh, battle of, 143, 144.
Brundusium, passage of the Crusaders from, 400.
Brunefeld. *See* Brunanburh.
Bruno, bishop of Speyer, a juror for Henry V., 500.
Bruno, the name of Leo IX., called bishop of Speyer, 286.
Bruno (Beorn), cousin of Sweyn, killed by him, 245.
Bucinacius, emperor of Constantinople, 276.
Buckinghamshire, included in Mercia, 101.
Budecalech, estate of Glastonbury at, 37, 171, 172.
Burgred, Burhred, king of Mercia. *See* Mercia.
Burgundy, the people of, punished for their sins by the Saracens, 81; S. Felix, of East Anglia, a native of, 97; assigned to Charles the Bald, 110.
————— Guy of, insurrection of, against duke William in his minority, 286; flight of, 287.
————— Stephen of, joins in the crusade of 1102, 447; and is killed at the battle of Ramlah; 449.
Byzantium, the precursor of Constantinople, 410; mentioned, 458.

C.

Caedwalla, king of the West Saxons. *See* West Saxons.
Caen, church of S. Stephen built by the Conqueror at, 326, 327; foundation of the church of the Trinity at, 327; queen Matilda buried at, 332; her daughter Cecilia, abbess at, 333; the Conqueror buried at, 337; remains faithful to Robert, 462; but at last surrenders to Henry, *ib.*; the body of Henry kept at, before his funeral, 537; the earl of Gloucester summons Geoffrey of Anjou to, 592.

Cæsarea, in Palestine, passed by the Crusaders, 421; advances money to Baldwin, 437; visited by him on his way to Jerusalem, 441; battle and siege at, 445.
Cæsarea Philippi, visited by the Crusaders, 437.
Cahors, the bishop of, invites Bohemond to the council of Clermont, 453; the district of, assigned to Raymond of S. Giles, by his father, 456; enmity of the bishop to him, 456.
Caipha (Haifa), passed by the Crusaders, 421; occupied by Tancred, 440; garrisoned, 443.
Cala (Chelles), S. Ercongota, a nun at, 16.
Calabria, Robert Wiscard makes himself duke of, 321; passage of the Crusaders through, 409.
Calepodius, burial place of, 408.
Calixtus, Saint, his burial place, 408.
Calixtus II., pope, his struggle with Henry V., 343; was Guy, archbishop of Vienne, 504; elected pope, 506; his letter announcing the capture of Sutri and the anti-pope, 506, 507; his visit to Normandy, 482; his reforms at Rome, 507; letter to Henry V., 508; concludes the peace with him, 508, 509.
Calne, miraculous event in the synod of, 182; the empress goes to Bristol by, 556.
Cambridgeshire (Grantebrigensis pagus), included in East Anglia, 101.
Cambyses, built Babylon in Egypt, 429.
Campania, crossed by the Crusaders, 409.
Campus Martius, at Rome, 196.
Candida Casa, Whithern, see of, 131.
Candida, S., burial place of, 408.
Canterbury, foundation of S. Augustine's monastery at, 14; conduct of Benedict Biscop at, 59; S. Mildred buried at, 78, 267; Scotland, abbot of, 351; city of, burned, 18; ransomed from the Danes, 122.
Canterbury, province of, divided under king Offa, 85; restored to its former

Canterbury, province of—*cont.*
dignity, 94; archbishopric of, 100; controversy with York, 346; documents and decision upon this, 347–352.
Canterbury, Augustine, archbishop of, converts king Ethelbert, 13, 14; date of his arrival, 22, 28; has instructions from S. Gregory about the arrangement of the church, 88; called the *syncellus* of S. Gregory, 91; his feast day kept, 159; letter of S. Gregory to, 347.
——— Laurentius, archbishop of, contemplates flight, but is miraculously prevented, 14; consecrated the church of S. Augustine, 88.
——— Mellitus, archbishop of, bishop of London. *See* London.
——— Justus, archbishop of, letter of pope Boniface to, 347.
——— Theodore, archbishop of, comes to Canterbury in the reign of Egbert, and founds schools, 16; his influence with Kenwalch of Wessex, 29; in connexion with Glastonbury, 37; his authority respected by Benedict Biscop, 59; his organisation of the church, 55; negotiates the wer-gild of Elfwin, 78.
——— Beorhtwald, archbishop of, succeeds Theodore, 29; his legendary history, 29; in connexion with Glastonbury, 29, 36, 224.
——— Cuthbert, archbishop of, letter of Boniface to, on the clothing of religious, 82; holds a great synod, 83.
——— Jaenbert, archbishop of, loses his dignity on the creation of the archbishoprick of Lichfield, 85, 88; retains four suffragan sees, 85, 86; succeeded by Ethelheard, 86.
——— Ethelheard, archbishop of, letter of Alcuin to, 74; on the dress of the clergy, 82, 83; his visits to Rome, 86, 90; his synodal letter sent by Kenulf to the pope, 89; carries letters from Kenulf to Rome, 89; his reception there, 90; his character, *ib.*; privilege granted to him, 91; his influence with Egfrith, 94.

Canterbury, Plegmund, archbishop of, literary friend and assistant of Alfred, 133; consecrates seven bishops, 140, 141.
——— Athelm, archbishop of, bishop of Wells and monk of Glastonbury, 224.
——— Odo, archbishop of, divorces Edwy from his mistress, 163; his nephew Oswald, 167.
——— Dunstan, archbishop of; abbot of Glastonbury, has a warning of the murder of King Edmund, 160; of the birth of Edgar, 164; and of the death of Edred, 162; devotion of king Edred to, 162; separates king Edwy from his mistress, 163; exiled to Flanders, ib.; intercedes for the soul of Edwy, 164; bishop of Worcester, 165; made archbishop, 166; his greatness and ability, 166; his biography by Osbern, 166; mentioned in charters of Edgar, 169, 170; promotes the succession of Edward, 181; his miraculous escape at Calne, 182; his prophecy about Ethelred, 185, 186, 187; about S. Eadgitha, 270; appears to S. Wulfstan, 355; mentioned, 187, 224.
——— Ethelgar, archbishop of, abbot of New Minster and bishop of Selsey, a monk of Glastonbury, 224.
——— Sigeric (Siricius), archbishop of, the second successor of Dunstan, 187; his advice about bribing the Danes, 187; a monk of Glastonbury, 224.
——— Elfege, archbishop of, 260; his martyrdom by the Danes, 188, 207, 219; buried at London, 188, 207; translated by Ethelnoth to Canterbury, 224; had been abbot of Bath and bishop of Winchester, 225.
——— Living, archbishop of, appointed in the place of Elfege, 207.
——— Ethelnoth, archbishop of, a monk of Glastonbury, 224, 225; dean, ib.; translated S. Elfege, 224; letter of Canute to, 221.
——— Eadsin, archbishop of, crowns Edward the Confessor, 239; appoints

Canterbury, Eadsin—cont.
Siward, abbot of Abingdon, as his coadjutor, ib.
——— Robert, archbishop of, a monk of Jumiéges, bishop of London, appointed to Canterbury by Edward the Confessor, 239; opinions of the English about him, 240; sentence passed against him as a disturber of the realm, 244; goes to Rome, settles at Jumiéges, dies and is buried there, 244.
——— Stigand, archbishop of, his promotions, 244; bishop of Winchester, ib.; made archbishop in the place of Robert, 244; has the pall from Benedict X., ib.; derides the dreams of the Confessor, 277; his deposition and successors, 244, 328; appealed to by William as a witness to Edward's concession, 302; William avoids being crowned by, 307; submits, 309.
——— Lanfranc, archbishop of, compared to Cato, 326; made abbot of Caen, 326; archbishop, 329; abolishes the slave trade, 329; his dealings with Waltheof, 314; his controversy with Berengar, 338; his share in the controversy with York, 350-354; consents to the determination, 351; receives the profession of archbishop Thomas, 352; knighted and educated William Rufus, 360; enmity of Odo of Bayeux to, 360; his good influence on William Rufus,367.
——— Anselm, archbishop of, Eadmer's history ends at his death, 2; the light of England, 376; persecuted by William Rufus, 370; in exile, 376; has a vision and warning of the king's death, 377; recalled by Henry I., 470; sustains the cause of the king, 471, 472; allowed bishop Roger of Salisbury to undertake secular office, 484; his controversy with the king on investiture, 489, 490; letters of Paschal II. to, 491, 492; is in exile at Lyons, 492, 493; returns and consecrates five bishops, 493; makes peace with the king, 493.

Canterbury, Ralph, archbishop of, end of Eadmer's history at, 2; abbot of Seez, 472; presents the keys of Shrewsbury to Henry I., 472; present at the translation of S. Cuthbert, 517; allowed bishop Roger of Salisbury to undertake secular office, 484.

—————— William, archbishop of, attests a charter of Henry I., 522; takes the oath of fealty to the empress, 529; obtains the office of legate, 535; demands from Stephen an oath to support the church, 538; crowns Stephen, 539, 541; succeeded by Theobald, 550; allowed bishop Roger of Salisbury to undertake secular office, 484.

—————— Theobald, archbishop of, succeeds William, 550; attends a great council at Winchester, 550; comes to visit the empress at Wilton, but postpones doing fealty to her, 573; is allowed by the king to comply for the time, 573; attends a great council at Winchester on the deposition of Stephen, 574, 576; surety for Stephen, 589.

Canute, king. *See* English, kings of.

Canute, king of Denmark, son of Sweyn, threatens to invade England, 308, 317, 337; marries a daughter of Robert Friso, 315; his descent, 317–319; his brother Olaf banished, 319; he is killed in a church and canonized, 320.

Capet, Hugh, ancestor of the modern kings of France, 72.

Capito, patriarch of Jerusalem, 424.

Capsa, the archbishop of, 504.

Capua, Richard prince of, 321; the archbishop of, 504.

Caria, in the hands of the Saracens, 394.

Caritas, S., burial place of, 408.

Carmentis, the mother of Evander, 259.

Cassianus, patriarch of Jerusalem, 424.

Castellum Peregrinorum, built by Raymund as check on Tripoli, 458.

Catigis, son of Vortigern, killed, 11.

Cato, quoted by Seneca, 64; Lanfranc compared to, 326; the pride of, 355; his definition of an orator, 64.

Cavea (la Cava), the anti-pope Maurice Bourdin, sent in confinement to, 507.

Ceadwalla, king of the Britons, assists Penda against Edwin, 50, 77; overthrows Eanfrid and Osric and is overthrown by Oswald, 51.

Ceaulin, Cheaulin, king of the West Saxons. *See* West Saxons.

Cecilia, S., the martyr, her church at Rome, 407.

Cecilia, daughter of the Conqueror, abbess of Caen, 333.

Cedd, bishop of London. *See* London.

Cedron, the brook, 426.

Celestine, I., pope, his mission of St. Patrick, 26.

Celestine, the martyr, his burial place, 405.

Ceola, the vessel used by the invaders of Britain, 8, 19.

Ceolbert, messenger of king Kenulf to the pope, 89.

Ceolfrith, abbot of Wearmouth, 56, 60; he sets out for Rome and dies at Langres, 60; letter of pope Sergius to, 62, 63.

Ceolred, Cheorred, king of Mercia. *See* Mercia.

Ceolric, king of the West Saxons. *See* West Saxons.

Ceolwulf, king of the West Saxons. *See* West Saxons.

Ceolwulf, king of Northumbria. *See* Northumbria.

Ceolwulf, king of Mercia. *See* Mercia.

Cerdic, king of the West Saxons. *See* West Saxons.

Cerney, castle of, belonging to Miles of Hereford, occupied by Stephen, 557; garrisoned by Earl Robert, 562.

Chalcedon, council of, 503.

Charles, Martel, Tudites, drives the Saracens out of Gaul, 71; his family, *ib*; question of his punishment after death, 81, 82, 255.

Charles the Great, 68, 69, 82, 509, 534; his descent traced, 71; son of Pipin, *ib.*; his reign, *ib.*; he goes to Rome and

Charles the Great—*cont.*
becomes emperor, 72; his patronage of Alcuin, 72, 73; his mission to Offa, 75; his interest in books, 68; his friendship with Offa, 91; his victories over the infidels, 91, 92; a letter from him to Offa, 93; his quarrel with Offa, 96; lives 12 years after the accession of Egbert, 106; his adventure with Eadburga, 118; extinction of his posterity, 139; Lewis of Aquitaine the survivor of it, 149; his lance presented to Ethelstan, 150; his recovery of Spain, 193, 424, 425; has a grant of investiture from Adrian I., 250, 251; his descendant Godfrey of Bouillon, 400, 431; his relations with the popes, 498.

Charles the Bald, son of Lewis the Pious, 110; and Judith, 110; his share of the dominions, 110; Ethelwulf marries his daughter Judith, 109, 117, 136; sends his nephew Pipin into exile, 110; wars with his brother Lothar, 111; and defeats him, *ib.*; becomes emperor, *ib.*; crowned at Rome, 112; his expeditions to Italy, 112; crosses Mont Cenis, and dies, 112; the hierarchy of Dionysius translated for, 131; his son Lewis, 111, 136, 138; brought the robe of the Blessed Virgin from Constantinople, 138.

Charles III., son of Lewis of Bavaria, king of Alemannia, 111; or Swabia, 112; becomes emperor, 112; his vision, 112-116.

Charles the Simple, succeeds to France, 116; marries a daughter of king Edward, *ib.*, 136, 137; gives his daughter Gisela with Normandy to Rollo, 116; his son Lewis, 139.

Charles, son of the emperor Lothar, king of Provence, 111; reigns eight years, 111.

Charles, son of S. Canute, count of Flanders, 315.

Chartres, siege of, by Rollo, 138; Henry I. and Innocent II. meet at, 534.

Chartres, Fulbert, bishop of, his correspondence with Canute, 226; his prophecy about Berengar, 341.

Chartres, Fulcher of, historian of the crusade, 434.

Chenulf, Kenulf, king of Mercia. *See* Mercia.

Chenulf, bishop of Dorchester. *See* Dorchester.

Chertsey, Wulfnoth, abbot of, 351.

Cheshire, included in Mercia, 100; ravaged by the Welsh, 376.

Chester, defeat of the Britons near, 47; burial of St. Werburga at, 78, 267; called the city of legions and seat of the bishop, 100; taken by king Edward just before his death, 144; Edgar is rowed by kings at, 165.

Chester, bishopric of Lichfield migrates to, 353, 385, 388; and thence to Coventry, 385, 388.

Chester, Robert, bishop of, 388, 389.

Chester, earls of, Repton belonged to, 264.

——— Hugh, earl of, 267; has a battle with the returning exiles, 318, 376.

——— Richard, earl of, son of Hugh, a ward of Henry I., attacked by William of Mortain, 473, 474; his brother Otuel, 497; his wife the sister of Theobald of Blois, 497; perishes with them in the great shipwreck, 497.

——— Ranulf, earl of, his honours increased by Stephen, 569; marries a daughter of the Earl of Gloucester, *ib.*; his castle at Lincoln, *ib.*; Stephen attacks him without warning, 569; he escapes from Lincoln and asks the aid of earl Robert, 570; arrives late in support of the empress at Winchester, 580.

Chichester, see of, 100; removed from Selsey, 100, 353; Ethelgar called bishop of, 224.

——— Ailric, Ethelric, bishop of, 347.

——— Stigand, bishop of, 351.

Chinric, Cynric. *See* West Saxons, kings of.

Chosdroes, king of the Persians, takes Jerusalem, 424.
Christianus, the clerk who pleaded for Stephen at the council of Winchester, 577.
Christina, sister of Edgar Atheling, a nun at Romsey, 278.
Christodolus, patriarch of Jerusalem, 425.
Chrysantus, burial place of, 405.
Chrysogonus, Grisogonus, S.; Centius, cardinal of, 505; Gregory, cardinal of, 499; Peter, cardinal of, 531.
Chrysostom, S. John, relics of, at Constantinople, 413.
Cicero, his words referred to, 65, 129, 144, 462, 465.
Cilicia, in the hands of the Saracens, 394; Tarsus in, 434; adheres to Baldwin, 435.
Cirencester, the Britons take refuge in, 21; attempt of Penda on, 21; meeting of the empress's party at, 595.
Ciriacus, patriarch of Jerusalem, 424.
Cistercians, origin of the order of, 380-385.
Citeaux, early history of the monastery of, 380; Alberic, abbot of, 384; Stephen Harding, abbot of, 384.
Claudia, mother of St. Eugenia, her burial place, 407.
Clement, S., pope, appointed by St. Peter, 325.
Cleopas, father of Simeon, the cousin of Christ, 424.
Clermont, council of, for promoting the crusade, 391-398, 453, 456.
Clovesho, council at, under archbishop Cuthbert, 83.
Cluny, Gelasius II., dies at, 506; Odo and Odilo of, 515.
Cluny, Hugh, abbot of; his stories about Hildebrand, 322, 323; his story about Anselm, 377.
Cluny, Odo, prior of, pope Urban II., 326.
Cluny, monks of, settled at Thetford, 387; and at Reading, 489; and at Lewes,

Cluny, monks of—*cont.*
513; commemoration of the abbots of, 515.
Coloceros, burial place of, 407.
Cologne, story of a bishop of, 204, 205; Herbert and Piligrinus, archbishops of, 204.
Cologne, Frederick, archbishop of, 500, 509.
Compiegne, Lewis, son of Charles the Bald, dies at, 112, 116.
Conan, count of Brittany, his daughter Judith, 211.
Conan the traitor, thrown from the tower at Rouen, 469.
Coneneie, an estate of Glastonbury at, 37.
Concordia, burial place of, 406.
Conrad, king of the Germans, carries the empire from the Karolings, 72; succeeded by Henry, 117, 149.
Conrad the Salic, emperor, crowned at Rome, 222; story of his son Henry, 234.
Conrad, son of Henry IV., dies at Arezzo, 343, 498.
Constance, daughter of the Conqueror, marries Alan Fergant, 333.
Constance, bishop of, 509.
Constans, emperor of Constantinople, 412.
Constantine, the emperor, son of Constantius and Helena, 5; draws the Britons into Gaul, 6; his sword presented to Ethelstan, 150; his vision of the future of Byzantium, 410, 411.
Constantine, several emperors of Constantinople, named, 412, 413.
Constantine, king of Scots, his war with Ethelstan, 142, 147; defeated at Brunanburh, 144.
Constantine, the pretender to empire in Britain, put down by Honorius, 6.
Constantine, abbot of S. Maximin, at Orleans, 195.
Constantinople, emperors of, list of, 412, 413, 483.
Constantinople, council of, 503.
Constantinople, Charles the Great takes the title of emperor and defends it

Constantinople—*cont.*
against the emperors of, 72; their degeneracy, 71, 92; relics brought by Charles the Bald from, 138; the emperor of (Maniches), informs Edward the Confessor about the seven sleepers, 275; names of his successors, 276; arrival of the Crusaders at, 400, 409; legend of the foundation of, 410, 411; William of Poictiers at, 401, 447; Bohemond visits, 458; visit of Sigurd of Norway to, 486; his offerings and cleverness there, 486.

Constantius I., the emperor, husband of Helena and father of Constantine, 5; buried in Britain, 5.

Constantius II., emperor, son of Constantine the Great, 412.

Conteville, Herlewin of, husband of the Conqueror's mother, 333; his sons, 334.

Conversana, William of, Robert of Normandy marries his daughter, 461.

Corbaguath (Kerbogha) attempts to relieve Antioch, 419; refuses to negotiate with the Crusaders, 419, 420; killed by Robert of Normandy, 460.

Cornelia, a gate of Rome, 404.

Cornubiensis (a mistake for Corvinensis), 145.

Cornwall, S. Patrick sails on his altar to, 26; conquered by Egbert, 106; visited by Ethelstan, 148; see of, 352, 353.

Cornwall, earldom of, given by William the Conqueror to Robert of Mortain, held by his son William, 473.

Cornwall, Reginald, brother of Earl Robert, made Earl of, 562.

Corsica, recovered from the Saracens by the Pisans, 92.

Cosham, illness of Ethelred at, 214.

Côtentin, Nigel viscount of the, joins the rebellion against duke William 286; submits, 287.

Coutances, Geoffrey, Gosfrid, bishop of, 351; his rebellion against William Rufus, 360; uncle of Robert Mowbray, 360; his head quarters at Bristol, 361.

Coventry, see of, 100; migrates from Chester, 385.

Coventry, relics brought from Italy to, 224; ecclesiastical foundations of Leofric at, 237, 388; bishop Robert buried at, 389.

Crediton, see of, 100, 352; removed to Exeter, 100, 353; bishop of, consecrated, 141; Living, bishop of, 221, 229.

Crema, Peter of, cardinal of S. Chrysogonus, 531.

Cremona, arrangement for a conference at, 505; subdued by Henry V. 509.

Crescentianus, his burial place at Rome, 405, 406.

Crete, not yet occupied by the Saracens, 92.

Crispin, his burial place at Rome, 408.

Crispinian, his burial place at Rome, 408.

Crispus, his burial place at Rome, 405.

Crowland, Waltheof, buried at, 312; miracles at, *ib.*

Cucumeris, burial place at Rome, 404.

Cuda, brother of Cinegisl, king of the West Saxons; his death and sons, 21; his descendant Caedwalla, 32.

Cuda, son of Cudwin, 120.

Cudwin, in the West Saxon pedigree, 120.

Culna, grant of an estate at, to Gloucester Abbey, 521, 522.

Cumbran, murdered by Sigebert, king of Wessex, 41.

Cumbria, Eugen, king of, 147; intrusted to Malcolm, 158, 165; Malcolm, son of the king of, made king of Scots by Siward, 237.

Curwala (Cornu-Galliæ) given to Charles, a son of Lewis the German, 111.

Cuthbald, ancestor of Ine, 34.

Cuthbert, archbishop. *See* Canterbury.

Cuthbert, abbot of Malmesbury. *See* Malmesbury.

Cuthbert, S., bishop of Lindisfarne. *See* Lindisfarne.

Cuthburga, a sister of Ine, wife of Aldfrith of Northumbria, 35.

Cuthgils, brother of Cinegisl, 32.

Cuthred, king of Kent, *see* Kent; king of West Saxons, *see* West Saxons.

Cynegils. *See* West Saxons, kings of.
Cynewise, wife of Penda, 77.
Cynewulf. *See* West Saxons.
Cynric. *See* West Saxons, kings of.
Cyprus, not yet overrun by the Saracens, 92.
Cyriaca, burial place of, at Rome, 406.
Cyrilla, burial place of, at Rome, 406.
Cyrus, father of Cambyses, 429.

D.

Dacor, the Scots submit to Ethelstan at, 147.
Dædalus, maker of the Labyrinth, 199, 276.
Dagobert, king of the Franks; his sister Blithildis, 71.
Daimbert, of Pisa, lands at Laodicea, 436; elected patriarch of Jerusalem, 437; crowns Baldwin, 442.
Dalmatia, passage of the Crusaders through, 400.
Damasus, saint, burial place of, 407.
Damian, Peter, an authority on witchcraft, 202.
Danes, the, invasion by, in Brihtric's reign, 43, 75, 76; their first landing, 107; conquer Mercia in the reign of Berhtulf, 96; make Ceolwulf king, 96; they ravage Kent and London, 108; they winter in Thanet, 122; defeated by Ethelred and Alfred, 123; struggle of Alfred with, 124-126; their return, 128; libraries burned by, 132; their castle in York burned by Ethelstan, 147.
——— renew their visits to England under Edgar, 165; invade England in the reign of Ethelred, 187; bribed to depart, *ib.*; Elfric deserts to, 187; murder of Elfege by, 188; failure of Ethelred against, 188; massacre of, 191; the revenge of Sweyn for, 207; in East

Danes—*cont.*
Anglia, *ib.*; land at Sandwich, 207; drive Ethelred into the Isle of Wight, 208; elect Canute king, 212; fly into East Anglia, 216; gain the battle of Assandun, 216, 217; reconciled by Canute with the English, 219; they join in the crusade, 399.
Daniel, the prophet, relics of, at Constantinople, 413.
Danisman, Danischemend, takes Bohemond captive, 438; and liberates him, 454.
Daria, S., burial place of, at Rome, 405.
David, S., at Glastonbury, 27; his vision, *ib.*; bishop of Menevia, *ib.*, 36.
David, king of Scots, son of Malcolm and Margaret, 476; helps to overthrow king Donald, *ib.*; succeeds his brother Alexander, *ib.*; his character and policy, 477; swears fealty to the empress, 529, 538; makes terms with Stephen, 539; accompanies the empress on her entrance into London, 578; is with her at Winchester, 580; was the first of the barons of England, 585.
David, king of Judah, his tomb plundered by Hyrcanus, 198.
David, bishop of Bangor. *See* Bangor.
Decius, his wife Trifena, 406.
Dee, Edgar rowed by kings on the river, 165.
Degsastan, battle at, 47.
Deiri, people of Northumbria, 45, 54.
Delphi, tripods of, brought to Constantinople, 411.
Demetrius, S., appears with S. George at the battle of Antioch, 420.
Denebert, bishop of Worcester. *See* Worcester.
Denmark, arrival of Sweyn from, 207; Canute arranges affairs in, 214; return of Turkill and Iric to, 219; expedition of Canute to, 223; Hardicanute in, 227; history of the kings of, 312, 317-320.
Denys, S. (Dionysius), near Paris, Charles Martel buried at, 255.

Denys, S. near Southampton, consecration of the church of, 270.
Derbyshire, included in Mercia, 100.
Desiderius, king of the Lombards, subdued by Pipin, 71.
Desiderius, abbot of Monte Cassino, 325; pope as Victor III., 326.
Devizes, the castle of, built and embellished by bishop Roger of Salisbury, 547; the keys of, demanded by Stephen and surrendered, 549; flight of the bishop of Ely to, 551; seized by Robert Fitz-Hubert, 563; visit of the empress to, 590; council at, 591.
Devon, Domnonia, king of, grants lands to Glastonbury, 28, 29.
Devonshire, Domnonia, part of Wessex, 100; Ordgar ealdorman of, 178, 180.
Digera, the surname of Siward, 312.
Dijon, William, abbot of, at Fecamp, 191.
Diogenes, the emperor, 276.
Diogenes, the martyr, his burial place at Rome, 405.
Dionysius, the Areopagite, his hierarchia translated by John Scotus, 131.
Dionysius, Exiguus, his cycle, 345.
Dionysius, the pope, his burial place at Rome, 407.
Dius, patriarch of Jerusalem, 424.
Dive, the river, 291.
Docilianus, patriarch of Jerusalem, 424.
Dol, in Brittany, letter of Rohbod, prior of, 154, 155; losses of duke William at, 316.
Domfront, the castle of the count of Anjou at, besieged by duke William, 288; surrenders, 289; belonged to Henry I. in his younger days, 478; adheres to the empress, 538.
Dominanda, saint, her burial place at Rome, 405.
Donald. See Dufnal.
Donald, king of Scots, kills Duncan, and is overthrown by William Rufus, 476; misleads Edmund, 477.
Donata, saint, her burial place at Rome, 405.
Dorchester, ancient see of, 101.
——— Birinus, bishop of, apostle of the West Saxons, 22.

Dorchester, Agilbert, bishop of, 3 defends the Roman Easter, 55.
——— Leutherius, bishop of, neph to Agilbert, 30; his grant to Aldhel 30, 31.
Dorchester, Mercian see, removed to L coln, 352, 353; claims of York on, 3 354.
Dorchester, Mercian see of, bishops Ceolwulf, consecrated, 145.
——— Remigius, bishop of. Lincoln.
Dorsetshire, included in Wessex, 100.
Dover, straits of, 156; quarrel of Eust of Boulogne with the men of, 2 Godwin refuses to punish, ib.; Har agrees to deliver the castle of, to V liam, 279.
Ducah, king of Damascus, blocks the p of Tripoli against Baldwin, 439; stratagems, 439.
Dufnal (Donald), king of the Welsh, r Edgar on the Dee, 165.
Dulting, property of Glastonbury at, 37
Duncan, illegitimate son of Malcolm I knighted and made king in succes to his father, 476; killed by his u Donald, ib.
Dunfermline, Malcolm III., buried at, 3
Dunstan. See Canterbury.
Dunster, burned by Stephen, 557.
Dunwich, Felix, apostle of the Angles, bishop of, 97.
Dunwich, Tidfrith, bishop of, 85.
Dunwich, see of, now extinct, 86, 352.
Durazzo (Dyracchium), taken by Rol Wiscard, 321, 453; the limit of his quests, 390; passage of the Crusa from Brundusium to, 400.
Durham, relics of S. Oswald at, 53.
Durham, see of Lindisfarne translate 101; its subjection to York, 350, translation of the relics of S. Cuth at, 517.
Durham, bishop of, conducts queen E to Normandy, 209.
Durham, Walcher, bishop of, his tr history and death, 330, 331.

Durham, bishop of—*cont.*
——— William of S. Calais, succeeds Walcher and introduces monks into the cathedral, 321; his share in the rebellion against William Rufus, 360; his flight and return, 362.
——— Rannulf Flambard, his administration under William Rufus, 368, 369; Henry I. abolishes his customs and imprisons him, 470; his escape, 471; his eminence, 517.

E.

Eadbald, king of Kent. *See* Kent.
Eadbert, king of Kent. *See* Kent.
Eadbert, king of Northumbria. *See* Northumbria.
Eadbert, Præn. *See* Kent.
Eadburga, daughter of Offa, wife of Brihtric, 43, 105; called Edelburga, 91; her adventure at the court of Charles, 118.
Eadburga, daughter of Edward and Edgiva, a nun at Winchester, 137, 268; stories of her sanctity, 268, 269.
Eadfleda, daughter of Edward and Elfleda, buried at Wilton, 137.
Eadgar, Edgar, king. *See* English, kings of. Eadmer's history begins from, 1.
Eadgar, Atheling, son of Edward, 278; his old age in obscurity, *ib.*; a candidate for throne on the death of the Confessor, 297, 307; attaches himself to the Scots, 308, 309; his character, 309; his crusade and return, 310; still alive, 278, 310.
Eadgar, king of Scots, 278, 366, 476.
Eadgaring, explained, 70.
Eadgitha, Edgitha, daughter of king Edward, married to Otto of Saxony, 117, 137.
Eadgitha, daughter of Edgar and Wulfrida, 180; her story, 269, 270; buried at Wilton, 269.

Eadgitha, daughter of Godwin and wife of Edward the Confessor, 239; her matrimonial relations and troubles, 239; confined at Werewell, 243; her saying about bishop Walcher, 331; is buried at Westminster, 332.
Eadgiva, wife of Edward, her children, 137, 268.
Eadgiva, daughter of Edward and Elfleda, wife of Charles the Simple, 137.
Eadgiva, daughter of Edward and Eadgiva, married to Lewis of Aquitaine, 137.
Eadmer, character and scope of his history, 1, 2, 3; the authority for the history of Anselm, 370, 377, 489.
Eadmund, Edmund, king of the East Angles. *See* East Angles.
Eadmund, Edmund, king of the English. *See* English.
Eadmund, son of Malcolm III., misled by his uncle Donald, 477.
Eadmunding, explained, 70.
Eadnoth, Ednoth, the staller, killed in defence against the returning exiles, 318; was the father of Herding, 318.
Eadred, Edred, king of the English. *See* English.
Eadric, Edric, king of Kent. *See* Kent.
Eadric, Edric, king of the South Saxons. *See* South Saxons.
Eadric, Streone, his treachery to Ethelred, 189; his share in the murder of Gunhildis, 207; informs against Sigeferth and Morcar, 213; procures the banishment of Edwy, brother of Edmund Ironside, 217; deserts Edmund Ironside, 214; his behaviour at the battle of Sherstone, 215; punished by Canute, 219.
Eadsin, Edsin, archbishop. *See* Canterbury.
Eadulf, Edulf, bishop of Sidnacester, 85.
Eadward, Edward, son of Edmund Ironside, 218; sent to Sweden, takes refuge with the king of Hungary, *ib.*; marries Agatha, 218; summoned by Edward the Confessor to England, arrives and

Eadward, Edward—*cont.*
dies, 278; buried at S. Paul's, *ib.*; his descendants, *ib.*, 470.
Eadward, Edward, son of Malcolm and Margaret, 278; killed in battle, *ib.*
Eadward, Edward, abbot of Reading, 573.
Eadwin, Edwin, king of Northumbria. *See* Northumbria.
Eadwin, Edwin, brother of Ethelstan, son of Edward and Elfleda, 137; his legendary story, 156.
Eadwin, Edwin, son of Elfgar, defends Northumbria against Tostig, 281; retires to Northumbria after the Conquest, 307, 310; rebels, and is slain, 311.
Eadwig, Edwius, brother of Edmund Ironside, exiled by the influence of Eadric Streone, 217; buried at Tavistock, 218.
Eadwig, Edwius, son of Edmund Ironside, sent to Sweden and protected by the king of Hungary, 218.
Eafa, ancestor of Egbert, 120.
Ealhstan, Alstan. *See* Sherborne, bishops of.
Eanbald, archbishop. *See* York.
Eanfrith, king of Northumbria. *See* Northumbria.
Eanulf, Enulf, ealdorman of Somerset, tries to divide Wessex, 117.
East Angles, extent of the kingdom of the, 100.
East Angles, kings of the;
——— Redwald, receives Edwin of Northumbria on his exile, 48; his son Reiner killed, *ib.*; defeats Ethelforth, 48; his death, 49; his son has the empty title, 49; he was the first and greatest king of the nation, 96; drives Sigebert into exile, 97; his baptism and relapse, 97.
——— Eorpwald, baptized and killed, 97.
——— Sigebert, his piety and institution of schools, 97; becomes a monk, *ib.*; slain by Penda, 76, 97.
——— Egric succeeds, 97; slain by Penda, 76.

East Angles, kings of—*cont.*
——— Anna succeeds Egric, killed by Penda, 76, 97; his family, 266.
——— Ethelhere, his reign and fate, 97; his sons, *ib.*
——— Ethelwald, 97.
——— Adulf and Elewold, 97.
——— Beorna, 97.
——— Ethelred, 97.
——— Ethelbert, 98; killed, by Offa, king of Mercia, 84, 98; his church at Hereford, 262.
——— S. Edmund, killed by Hinguar after reigning sixteen years, 98, 124; his vengeance on Sweyn, 212; his sanctity, 260, 264–266.
——— Guthrum, the Dane, succeeds after nine years, 98; is baptized and receives territory from Alfred, 126, 146, 158.
——— Eohric succeeds Guthrum, 98.
East Angles, end of the dynasty, 98.
East Saxons, extent of the kingdom of the, 600.
East Saxons, kings of the;
——— Sledda the first king, 98; marries Ricula, sister of Ethelbert, *ib.*
——— Sebert, 98; becomes a Christian, *ib.*
——— Sexred and Seward, banish the bishop, 98; slain, *ib.*
——— Sigebert the Little, son of Seward, 99; his son Sighere, 99.
——— Sigebert, son of Sigebald, 99; baptized by Finan, *ib.*
——— Swithelm, baptized by Cedd, 99.
——— Sighere, son of Sigebert the Little, 99.
——— Sebbi, son of Seward, 99.
——— Sigehard and Senfred, 99.
——— Offa, son of Sighere, 99; goes to Rome, becomes a monk, and dies, 99.
——— Selred, son of Sigebert the Good, 99.
——— Swithed, 99; conquered by Egbert, *ib.*

INDEX. 619

Ebroin, mayor of the palace, kills Martin, 71.
Ebusa, nephew of Hengest, sent to North Britain, 44.
Ecgbert, Egbert, king. *See* Kent, Northumbria.
Ecgbert, Egbert, king of the West Saxons, importance of his reign as a date, 2; conquers Kent, 18, 19; succeeds in Wessex, 43. *See* West Saxons.
Ecgfrith, Egfrith, king of Northumbria. *See* Northumbria.
Ecgfrith, Egfrith, king of Mercia. *See* Mercia.
Ecgric, Egric, king of the East Angles. *See* East Angles.
Ecgwin, Egwin, bishop. *See* Worcester.
Ecgwinna, mother of Ethelstan, 136.
Ed. *See* Ead.
Edan, king of the Scots, his war with Ethelfrith, 47.
Edessa, the chieftain of, adopts Baldwin as his heir, 435; called Rohasia, 435; occupied by Baldwin, 436; he returns from Jerusalem to, 438; entrusted to his cousin Baldwin, 438; who succeeds him there, 452.
Edredescie, estate of Glastonbury at, 37, 171.
Effrem, patriarch of Jerusalem, 424.
Egel. *See* Ethel.
Eiglaf, king of the Swedes, subjugated by Canute, 220.
Eilmer, a monk of Malmesbury, attempts to fly, 276, 277.
Eilward, abbot of Glastonbury, 180.
Elbert, the martyr, 16, 261.
Elewold, king of the East Angles, 97.
Elesius, ancestor of Egbert, 121.
Eleutherius, pope, his mission to Britain, 23.
Elfege, Elfbeah, bishop. *See* Canterbury.
Elferius, Elfhere, the ealdorman, overthrows the monasteries under Edward, 182; translates Edward to Shaftesbury, 184; his son Elfric, 189.
Elfgar, the earl, son of Leofric, 243; earl of Mercia, 243; his son Morcar, 246; and Edwin, 310.

Elfgiva, daughter of Alfred, a virgin, 129; abbess of Shaftesbury, 131.
Elfgiva, daughter of Edward and Elfleda, her marriage, 137.
Elfgiva, wife of Edmund, mother of Edgar, explains his vision, 175.
Elfhelm, earl, father of Canute's first wife, 227.
Elfleda, wife of Edward, and daughter of Ethelm, 137; her children, *ib.*
Elfnoth, abbot of Glastonbury, 351.
Elfred, opposes Ethelstan at his accession, 141, 142; he tried to seize and blind him, 153; sent to Rome, 153; his death and the dispute about his burial, 152, 153.
Elfreda, daughter of Afred, a virgin, 129.
Elfric, ealdorman, son of Elfhere, deserts Ethelred, 187, 189; papal letter to, 172, 173.
Elfric, abbot of Malmesbury, 154.
Elfthritha, Elfrida, wife of Edgar, story of her marriage, 178, 180; her son Ethelred, 185; murders Edward, 183; legends about her and her penance, 183, 184.
Elfwin, Elwin, brother of Egfrith, king of Northumbria, his wergild, 78.
Elfwin, abbot of Ramsey, 351.
Elfwin, abbot of Evesham, 352.
Elisha, relics of, at Constantinople, 415.
Elmham, see of, detached from Canterbury, 85; removed to Thetford and Norwich, 101, 352, 353, 386.
——— Alheard, bishop of, 85.
——— Herfast, bishop of, 351.
Elmund, father of Egbert, 120.
Elwin, son of Ethelwerd, buried at Malmesbury, 151; killed in the war against Anlaf, 151.
Ely, see of, 101; monastery at, 166; imprisonment of Alfred the brother of Edward the Confessor at, 229; abbesses at, 267; erection of the see of, 517, 518.
Ely, Turstan, abbot of, 351.
Ely, Richard, abbot of, 517.
Ely, bishop of, Hervey, translated from Bangor, 517, 518.

U 15113. Y

Ely, Nigel, bishop of, flies to Devizes, 551; nephew of bishop Roger of Salisbury, 558; defends Devizes against the king, 549; has one of the richest sees in England, 558, 559; is at the reception of the empress Matilda at Winchester, 573.

Emerentiana, burial place of, at Rome, 405.

Emma, wife of Eadbald of Kent, 15.

Emma, wife of Ethelred, daughter of duke Richard of Normandy, 213, 278; her treatment by her husband, and her sons, 191, 213; is sent to her brother Richard, 209, 210; remains in Normandy, 218; marries Canute, 218, 219; induces him to be liberal to Winchester, 220; put in charge of earl Godwin during the reign of Harold, 227; driven into Flanders, 228; her dislike of her son Edward, 238; was mother of Hardicanute, 229.

English, kings of;
———— Edward, son of Alfred, 129; succeeds his father, 135; reunites the kingdom, 96, 135; subdues the Scots and Britons, 135; rebellion of Ethelwold against him, 135; his children, 116, 117, 136, 137; institution of new bishoprics under him, 140, 141; takes Chester, 144; he dies, 141, at Farringdon, 145, and is buried at Winchester, 141, 145; a benefactor to Glastonbury, 159, 225; his saintly daughter, Eadburga, 268, 269.

———— Ethelstan, son of Edward and Egwinna, 136; knighted by his grandfather, 145; educated by Ethered and Ethelfleda, 145; succeeds his father at the age of 30, 141, 145; crowned at Kingston, 141, 145; opposed by Elfred on account of his birth, 141, 142; he gives his sister to Sihtric, and afterwards annexes Northumbria, 142; 146, 147; receives the submission of the Scots, 142, 147; destroys the Danish castle at York, 147; receives the submission of the Welsh at Hereford, 148; visits Cornwall and fortifies Exeter, 148, 149; defeats the Scots and their allies

English, kings of—cont.
at Brunanburh, 143, 144; negotiations for the marriage of his sisters, 116, 117, 149, 150; subdues the East Anglian Danes, 126; his grand reception of envoys at Abingdon, 150; his treasures, 150, 151; his treatment of Elfred, and its consequences, 153, 154; legend of his birth, 155; of his brother Edwin, 156; ancient biography of him, 145; poetical extracts from it, 145, 146, 151, 152; he dies at Gloucester, 157; and is buried at Malmesbury, 157; mentioned, 225.

———— Edmund, son of Edward, 137; succeeds Ethelstan, 157; takes all the towns south of the Humber from the Danes, 158; grants a charter to Glastonbury, 158, 159; murdered at Pucklechurch, 159, 160; mentioned, 225.

———— Edred, son of Edward, 137; succeeds Edmund, 162; conquers Northumbria, imprisons Wulfstan, 162; his devotion to Dunstan, ib.; dies and is buried at Winchester, ib.

———— Edwy, son of Edmund, succeeds Edred, 163; his foolish behaviour, oppression of Dunstan and the monasteries, ib.; dies and is buried at Winchester, 164.

———— Edgar, brother of Edwy, succeeds, 164; prophecy at his birth, ib.; rowed by kings on the Dee, 165; the saints of his reign, 165; his benefactions to Glastonbury, 167-172; to Malmesbury, 173, 174; his vision, 174 -176; his virtues, 176, 177; anecdotes of him, 177, 178; legends of his vices, 178-180; his seven years' penance, 179; his coronation at Bath, 180; dies and is buried at Glastonbury, 180, 181; his wife Elfrida, 179, 183, 185; mentioned, 225, 238, 261; his daughter Eadgitha, 180, 269.

———— Edward, son of Edgar, elected under the influence of Dunstan, 181; murdered, 183; buried at Wareham, ib.; translated to Shaftesbury, 184, 185.

English, kings of the—*cont.*

——— Ethelred succeeds Edward, 185; stories of his childhood, *ib.*; prophecy of Dunstan about him, 185, 186, 187; his behaviour at Rochester, 187; his dealings with the Danes, *ib.*; bribes them away, 187, 188; his indecision and failure, 189; massacres the Danes, 191; letter of the pope on his quarrel with Normandy, 191-193; makes Living archbishop, 207; shut up by the Danes in London, 208; goes to the isle of Wight, 208; consults his advisers and sends his wife and children to Normandy, 209; goes to Normandy, 210; is recalled by the English, 212; executes Sigeferth and Morcar, 213; shuts himself up in London, 214; dies and is buried at S. Pauls, 215; mentioned, 227, 236.

——— Edmund II., Ironside, son of Ethelred, 213; marries the widow of Sigeferth, 213; his character, 214; and policy, 214; he is driven into London and chosen king there on his father's death, 215; his battles, *ib.*; returns to London, 216; wins a battle at Brentford, but is defeated at Assandun, 216; flies to Gloucester, challenges Canute, divides the realm with him and dies, 217; his children, 218, 470, 529; buried at Glastonbury, 217, 224, 225.

——— Canute, son of Sweyn, chosen king by the Danes, 212; is driven out of Lindsey, and goes to Denmark, 213; returns and ravages Kent and Wessex, 214; also Northumbria, 215; besieges London, 216; is victorious at Assandun, 216, 217; refuses to meet Edmund, but divides England with him, 217; succeeds to the whole kingdom and marries Emma, 218, 219; divides England into four and punishes Eadric Streone, 219; builds churches, goes to Sweden, 220; conquers Norway, 221; writes an account of his pilgrimage to Rome, 221-224; gains privileges for his people, 222; directs the payment of money to

English, kings of the—*cont.*

churches, 223; re-enacts the old laws, 224; his charter to Glastonbury, 225, 226; his correspondence with Fulbert of Chartres, 226; his sons, 227; his first wife, 227; his daughter Gunhildis, 229, 230; his death and burial at Winchester, 227; his sister, 245; his successors in Denmark, 317; his crucifix at Hyde Abbey, 581.

——— Harold, son of Canute, succeeds, 227, 317; banishes queen Emma, 228; dies at Oxford, *ib.*; treatment of his body, *ib.*

——— Hardicanute; his claim put forward on his father's death, 227; succeeds, sends for Edward, insults Harold's corpse, and dies, 227; gives his sister to the emperor Henry, 229; his successors in Denmark, 317.

——— Edward III., the Confessor, son of Ethelred and Emma, sent by his father to England, 212; remains in Normandy during the reign of Canute, 218; sent for by Hardicanute and succeeds him, 228; his reign, 236; crowned by Eadsin, 239; his character, 236, 237; disliked by his mother, 237; Godwin's advice to, 238; his marriage, 239; promotes archbishop Robert and the Normans, 239; Godwin's last words to him, 240; origin of Godwin's quarrel with him in the matter of Eustace of Boulogne, 241; banishes Godwin and his sons, 243; sends a fleet against them, 243; pardons them, 243, 244; appoints Tostig earl of Northumbria, 245; his character, 271, 272; dream of bishop Brihtwold concerning him, 272; his miracles of healing, 272, 273, 274; his vision of the seven sleepers, 275; his vision of the succession of kings, 277, 495; sends for his nephew Edward, 278; on his death makes duke William his heir, 278; orders the consecration of Westminster, and dies 280, 297; mentioned, 431, 529.

English, kings of the—*cont.*

———— Harold, son of Earl Godwin, 245; summoned to Gloucester, 242; exiled to Ireland, 243; deposes Tostig from his earldom, 246; is at Westminster when Edward sees the seven sleepers, 274, 275; is driven to Ponthieu, 279; surrendered to William, *ib.*; his visit to Normandy, 294; agrees to support his claim to the crown, 279, 280; conquers the Welsh, 280; crowned, 280, 297; fights the battle of Stamford Bridge, 281; argues about the succession in reply to William, 298; advances from the north, 300; refuses the proposals of William, 301; fights on foot, 302, at the battle of Hastings, 282, 303; is killed there, 282, 383, and buried at Waltham, 306; was betrothed to one of William's daughters, 280, 333; attempt of his son to invade England, 318, 376.

English, comparison of the Normans and, 304, 305.

Eni, father of king Anna, 97.

Ennius, the poet, 259.

Eohric, king of the East Angles. *See* East Angles.

Eoppa, ancestor of Egbert, 120.

Eorcombert, Earcombert, Ercombert. *See* Kent, kings of.

Eorcongota, daughter of Ercombert, a nun at Chelles, 15, 16, 267.

Eormenburga, wife of Merewald, son of Penda, 78.

Eormenfred, bishop of Sion, legate to England, 328.

Eormengard, wife of Lewis the pious, 110.

Eormengard, wife of the emperor Lothar, 111.

Eormenhild, daughter of Ercombert, king of Kent, and wife of Wulfhere, 78, 267.

Eormenred, brother of Ercombert, king of Kent, father of Eormenburga, 78, 267.

Eorpwald, king of the East Angles. *See* East Angles.

Ephesus, the council of, 503.

Epimachus and Gordius, burial place of, 406.

Eric, king of Denmark, 320.

Ermon, patriarch of Jerusalem, 424.

Ernulf, the emperor. *See* Arnulf.

Ernulf, the count Palatine, 509.

Escendune, battle of, 122.

Eslius, ancestor of Egbert, 121.

Essex, kingdom of the East Saxons, 101; county of, included in the diocese of London, 101.

Ethelbald, king of Mercia. *See* Mercia.

Ethelbert, king of Kent. *See* Kent.

Ethelbert, king of the West Saxons. *See* West Saxons.

Ethelbert (Aegelbert), the martyr, 16, 261, 267.

Ethelburga, wife of Ine, persuades him to renounce the world, 35, 36.

Ethelburga, wife of Edwin, of Northumbria, 49.

Ethelburga, wife of Brihtric. *See* Eadburga.

Ethelburga, daughter of Anna, and abbess of Brie, 266.

Etheldreda, wife of Ecgfrith, of Northumbria, 56; daughter of Anna, 266; her sanctity, 261, 266; abbess of Ely, 517.

Ethelfleda, daughter of Edwin, and abbess of Whitby, 56.

Ethelfleda, daughter of Ceolwulf, and mother of Wistan, 263.

Ethelfleda, daughter of Alfred, governs Mercia with her husband, Ethered, 128, 129; she educates Ethelstan, 145; dies and is buried at Gloucester, 144; her great ability and services, 136.

Ethelfleda, Egelfleda, wife of Edgar, and mother of Edward, 180.

Ethelfrith, king of Northumbria. *See* Northumbria.

Ethelheard, archbishop. *See* Canterbury.

Ethelheard, king of the West Saxons. *See* West Saxons.

Ethelhere, king of the East Angles. *See* East Angles.

INDEX. 623

Ethelm, father of Elfieda, wife of king Edward, 137.
Ethelmer, ealdorman of the West, submits to Sweyn, 208.
Ethelnod, son of Wistan, 192.
Ethelnoth, archbishop of Canterbury. *See* Canterbury.
Ethelred, ealdorman, father-in-law of Alfred, 129.
Ethelred, king of Mercia. *See* Mercia.
Ethelred, the martyr, 16, 261, 267.
Ethelric, king of Northumbria. *See* Northumbria.
Ethelsin. *See* Sherborne.
Ethelstan, son of Ethelwulf, has the conquests of Egbert entrusted to him, 108; uncertainty of his history, 108.
Ethelwalch, king of the South Saxons. *See* South Saxons.
Ethelswitha, daughter of Ethelwulf, wife of king Burhred,; follows her husband on pilgrimage and dies at Pavia, 96.
Ethelswitha, wife of Alfred, her children, 129.
Ethelswitha, daughter of Alfred, her marriage, 129, 133.
Ethelward (Elward, Elfward), his history, a translation from the English Chronicles, 1, 2; his style, 3.
Ethelward, son of Alfred, a learned person, 129; died four years before Edward, 141; his sons buried at Malmesbury, 151.
Ethelward (Elward), son of Edward, 136; dies soon after his father, 141, 156.
Ethelwin, son of Ethelward, buried at Malmesbury, 151.
Ethelwold, cousin of king Edward, his rebellion crushed, 135.
Ethelwold the ealdorman, and his wife Elfrida, story of, 178, 179.
Ethelwulf, king. *See* West Saxons.
Ethered, duke or ealdorman of the Mercians, husband of Ethelfleda, 128, 136, 145.
Ethilda, daughter of Edward and Elfleda, married to count Hugh, 137.
Ethiopians, garrison the Tower of David, 427, 428.

Eu, Robert, count of, a chief captain of duke William, 290.
Eu, William of, his treason and punishment, 372.
Eucherius, his account of Jerusalem, referred to, 422.
Eucherius, S., bishop of Orleans, 256, note.
Eudes, of Brittany, imprisoned by his nephew Alan, 294.
Eugenia, the heroine of the story of Palumbus, 256.
Eugenia, saint, her burial place at Rome, 407.
Eugenius, king of Cumbria, wars against Ethelstan, 147.
Euphorbus, the soul of, passed into Pythagoras, 374.
Euphrates, crossed by the Turks, 414; Samosata beyond, 435.
Euripus, the Greek word for a spring tide, 213.
Eusebius, burial place of, at Rome, 407.
Eusebius, the historian, 436.
Eusebius Saint, the cardinal of, 499.
Eustace, count of Boulogne. *See* Boulogne.
Eustace, son of king Stephen, his claim to the county of Boulogne, through his mother, disregarded by the empress, 578.
Euthimius, patriarch of Jerusalem, 435.
Euticianus, burial place of, at Rome, 407.
Evander, the father of Pallas, 258; his mother Carmentis, 259.
Eventius, burial place of, at Rome, 405.
Evesham, S. Wistan buried at, 264; Elfwin, abbot of, 352.
Evreux, county of, 290.
Ewellinus, saltus, Karloman dies in, 112.
Exeter, see of, 100, 352, 353; visited by Ethelstan, 148; memorials of him at, 149; burned by the Danes, 188; captured by the Conqueror, 307.
———— Osbern, bishop of, 351.
———— William, bishop of 492, 522.

F.

Falaise, remains in the hands of Robert of of Normandy until his downfall, 462; Roger of Gloucester shot at the siege of, 475, 521.

Falernian wine, Godfrey of Bouillon said to have been poisoned with, 432.

Faramond, first leader of the Franks, and ancestor of the Merovingians, 70.

Farringdon, king Edward dies at, 145.

Faustinian, story of, 202.

Fecamp (Fiscamnum), monastery of, adorned by duke Richard, who is buried there, 191; enriched by Richard II., 210; an adventure of the duke at, 210, 211; William, abbot of, 211; council of, in which oaths are taken to the child William, 285; Maurilius, a monk of, 327; surrendered to William Rufus, 363.

Felicianus, burial place of, at Rome, 408.

Felicissimus, burial place of, at Rome, 407.

Felicitas, saint, burial place of, at Rome, 405.

Felix, bishop of Dunwich, 97.

Felix, several saints, buried at Rome, 405, 408.

Fernus, name of the Orontes, 416.

Ferramere, given to Glastonbury, 29, 37, 171.

Festus, burial place of, at Rome, 404.

Fides, S., burial place of, at Rome, 408.

Fildas, messenger of Kenulf to Leo III., 89.

Finan, bishop of Lindisfarne, baptizes Sigebert of Essex, 99.

Finn, ancestor of Egbert, 121.

Firmicus, Julius, an astrologist, 194.

FitzGilbert, John, Castellan of Marlborough, overcomes and executes Robert FitzHubert, 563, 564.

FitzHamon, Robert, 286; a faithful supporter of Henry I., 471; taken prisoner

FitzHamon, Robert—*cont.*
at the siege of Falaise, 475; his daughter, wife of earl of Gloucester, 529.

FitzHubert, Robert, seizes the castle of Malmesbury, but is expelled by Stephen, 556; occupies Devizes, 563; his cruelty, *ib.*; is overthrown by John FitzGilbert, 563; and executed, 564.

FitzOsbern, William, chief minister of William the Conqueror, sent to spy out the resources of Geoffrey Martel, 288, 384; his wooing of the countess of Flanders, wars in Flanders and death, 314, 315; his administration of the law in Herefordshire, 314; conspiracy of his son Roger, 313; marriage of his daughter to Ralph Guader, 313.

Flambard, Rannulf. *See* Durham.

Flaminia, porta, at Rome, 404.

Flanders, Baldwin, count of, son-in-law of Alfred, 133, 150.

————— Arnulf, count of, son of Baldwin, 133; his enmity with William, duke of Normandy, 161.

————— Baldwin V., count of, entertains queen Emma during the reign of Harold, 228; is guardian to Philip I., 228, 291; marriage of his daughter to duke William, 291; helps the Conqueror, and has a pension from him, 478; which is continued to his son, *ib.*

————— Baldwin VI., count of, son of Baldwin, and brother of Matilda, 314, 315; his wife Richildis, 315; his sons Arnulf and Baldwin, *ib.*

————— Arnulf, count of, succeeds his father, and is killed by his uncle Robert Friso, 315.

————— Robert Friso, count of, son of the elder Baldwin, 314; marries the countess of Friesland, 314, 431; returns and usurps Flanders, 315; gives his daughter in marriage to Philip I., 315; another to Canute of Denmark, *ib.*, 317; he goes on pilgrimage, 316; ceases to have the pension from William, 478.

————— Robert, count of, the Crusader, 316; accompanies Robert of Normandy

Flanders, Robert, count of—*cont.*
402; sails over the Adriatic alone, 409; refused homage to Alexius, 413; commands a force at Antioch, 420; neglects to send help to Robert of Normandy, 463; obtains the renewal of his pension, 479; but loses it when Henry becomes king, 479.

——— Baldwin, count of, son of Robert, 316; offends Henry I., 472; dies of a wound received at Arques, 479.

——— Charles, count of, son of S. Canute, 315, 316; is friendly with Henry I., 479.

——— William, count of, son of Robert of Normandy, 479. *See* William.

Flanders, Dunstan exiled to, 163; men of, visit Edgar's court, 165; queen Emma banished to, 228; Godwin and Sweyn banished to, 248; Tostig retires to, 246; he returns from, 280; war of William FitzOsbern in, 314, 315; men of, planted in Wales by Henry I., 365, 366, 477; descent of Robert of Gloucester from the counts of, 519; men of, become mercenaries under Stephen, 540, 561.

Fleury, Oswald the archbishop educated at, 167; Gerbert educated at, 193; Philip I., takes the habit of a monk at, 480.

Flodulf, son of S. Arnulf, 71.

Florence, the bishop of, made pope, as Nicolas II., 244.

Florentius, count of Friesland dies, 431.

Fontanetum, Fontenay, peace of, 111.

Fontevraud, order of, founded, 512.

Fontevraud, the adulterous countess of Anjou becomes a nun at, 480.

Fontinetum (Wells), mentioned in a charter of Ine, 38.

Formosus, pope, his action in regard to the vacant sees, 140, 141.

France, early history of, 69–72.

France, Hugh, duke of, called king, 150.

France, kings of. *See* Charles, Lewis, Philip, Hugh Capet, Henry.

Franks, the, early history of, 69–72.

Franks, Ethelbert's marriage with a daughter of the king of, 13; Eadbald

Franks—*cont.*
marries Emma, a daughter of the king of, 15.

Frea, the wife of Woden, Friday sacred to, 9.

Freculf, the historian quoted, 24.

Frederick, the count Palatine, 500; another count, 500.

Frelaf, ancestor of Egbert, 121.

Frewin, ancestor of Egbert, 121.

Frideric, abbot of S. Alban's, 351.

Frideswide, S., her church at Oxford, 213.

Fridewald, ancestor of Egbert, 121.

Fridestan, bishop. *See* Winchester.

Fridgar, ancestor of Egbert, 121.

Friesland, Gertrude, countess of, marries Robert of Flanders, 314, 431; Florence, count of, her husband, 431; Theoderic count of, 431.

Frigia, Phrygia, in the hands of the Saracens, 394.

Frisians, join in the crusade, 400.

Friso, Robert. *See* Flanders, counts of.

Fulbert, bishop of Chartres, corresponds with Canute, 226; his prophecy about Berengar, 341.

Fulcher, of Chartres, historian of the first crusade, 434.

Fulda, curious story about, 233, 234; Marianus Scotus, a monk at, 345; another strange story about, 345, 346.

Fulda, the abbot of, 509.

Fulk. *See* Anjou, counts of.

G.

Gaetanus, John, chancellor to pope Paschal II.; becomes pope as Gelasius II., 504.

Gaius, patriarch of Jerusalem, 424.

Galatia, in the hands of the Saracens, 394

INDEX.

Gallicia, Alfonso, king of, translates S. Isidore, 193. *See* Alfonso.
Galwalas, ancient name for the French, 70.
Garganus, Mount, mentioned by Canute in his letter, 222.
Gargara, harvests of, 411.
Garonne, the river, 290, 400.
Gascony, Pipin rules in, 110; transferred to Charles the Bald, 111.
Gauls, their style of writing, 81.
Gelasius II., pope, John Gaetanus, 504; his letter of protest against the antipope, 505; sails from Salerno to Genoa, and dies at Cluny, 506.
Geldeford, Guildford, conference between the legate and empress at, 579.
Genoa, Gelasius lands at, 506.
Genoese, their bargain for a share of the conquests of Baldwin, 444; assist in the conquest of Tripoli, 459.
Genuinus, burial place of, at Rome, 406.
Geoffrey. *See* Anjou, counts of.
Geoffrey, the chancellor (Rufus), 522.
George, S., with S. Demetrius, appears at the battle of Antioch, 420; church of, at Ramlah, 421.
Georgius, patriarch of Jerusalem, 425.
Gerard, bishop of Angoulême, 503; legate in Aquitaine, 503, 504.
Gerberoi (Gibboracum), battle of, 317.
Gerbert (pope Silvester II.), his origin, 193; educated at Fleury, studies in Spain, *ib.*; legends about him, 194, 195; his pupils, 195, 196; is made archbishop of Rheims, archbishop of Ravenna, and pope, 196; he finds the treasures of Octavian, 196-198; his magical head, 202; legend of his death and self condemnation, 195, 203.
Germanio, patriarch of Jerusalem, 424.
Germans, migrations of the, 8, 9.
Germanus, S., his visit to Britain, 26; his church in Cornwall, 100; his relics translated to Tours, 127; miracle of, *ib.*
Germany, origin of the name, 8; migrations from, 8, 9; under the rule of the Franks, 69, 70; dynasties of the rulers,

Germany—*cont.*
69–72, 110–112; a miracle which took place in, 341.
Gertrude, widow of Florence of Friesland, marries Robert of Flanders, 314, 431.
Getius, ancestor of Egbert, 121.
Gibell, passed by Baldwin on his way to Tripoli, 438.
Giferth, king, rows Edgar on the Dee, 165.
Gilbert, earl of Hertfordshire, detains prisoners for ransom, 587.
Gilbert, count, guardian of king William, 285; murdered, 286.
Gilbert, counsellor of bishop Walcher, slain, 330.
Gilbert, John, son of. *See* FitzGilbert.
Gildas, the British writer, 24; at Glastonbury, *ib.*; his work cited by Alcuin, 74.
Gillingham (Dorset), battle at Penn, near, 215.
Gillingham (Kent), Alfred, son of Ethelred, arrested at, 229; council assembled, at, 238.
Girontinus, archbishop, 504.
Gisla, daughter of Charles the Simple, given to Rollo, 116, 294.
Giwius, ancestor of Egbert, 121.
Glamorgan, Urban bishop of (Llandaff), consecrated, 493, 522.
Glaston, William de, lord of Lulworth castle, 595.
Glastonbury, called Ineswitrin, 29; foundation of the abbey at, 23; the old church at, 24; the burial pyramids at, 25; visit of S. Patrick, S. Bridget, and other saints to, 26; visit of S. David to, 27; of S. Paulinus, 28; grant of the king of Devon to, 28, 29; grant of Coinwalch to, 29; charter of Ine to, 36–39; charter of Cuthred to, 40; our author's book on the antiquities of, 56; relics of S. Hilda at, 56, 60; charter of king Edmund to, 158, 159; Dunstan, abbot of, 160; Edmund buried at, 160; benefactions of Edgar to, 165–172; papal letter in defence of, 172, 173; Edgar buried at, 180; Edmund Ironside buried at, 217; seven archbishops of Canterbury were

Glastonbury—*cont.*
monks at, 224 ; charter of Canute to, 225, 226 ; dream of bishop Brihtwold at, 272 ; struggle between the abbot and monks at, 329, 330 ; abbots of ; *see* Elfnoth, Bregored, Beorward, Beorhtwald.

Gloucester, the Britons take refuge in, 20 ; translation of S. Oswald's relics to, 54, 136; Ethelfleda buried at, 136 ; Ethelstan dies at, 157 ; Edmund Ironside at, 217 ; Witenagemot at, 242 ; William the Conqueror held his Christmas court at, 335; Malcolm, king of Scots, visits William Rufus at, 366.

Gloucester, Robert, earl of. *See* Robert.

Gloucester, Miles, constable of, 522 ; receives the empress at, 556 ; his castle of Cerney taken by Stephen, 557 ; takes the oath for the empress, 573 ; earl of Hereford, 573 ; is with the empress at Winchester, 580.

Gloucester, Roger of, killed at the siege of Falaise, 475 ; his benefactions to the abbey, 521, 522.

Gloucester, Serlo, abbot of, 512, 513.

—————— Gilbert, abbot of, in attendance on the empress, 573.

Gloucestershire, included in Mercia, 100.

—————— Walter, sheriff of, 521.

Goar, S., life of, quoted, 84.

Goda, sister of Edward the Confessor, married to Walter of Nantes and to Eustace of Boulogne, 241.

Godebard, bishop of Trent, 500.

Godefricus, count, 500.

Godeneie, property of Glastonbury at, 171.

Godfrey, son of Sihtric, flies to Scotland, 147 ; returns and besieges York, submits and is banished, *ib.*

Godfrey, prior of Winchester, 513, 516.

Godfrey, Bocard, duke of Lorraine, 431.

Godfrey, duke of Lorraine, 431.

Godfrey, nephew of Godfrey of Bouillon, killed, 451.

Godiva, the wife of Leofric, 237, 388 ; the name given to Queen Matilda, 471.

Godric, the nickname given to Henry I., 471.

Godulf, ancestor of Egbert, 121.

Godwin, earl, his rise under Canute, 220 ; his policy with regard to the succession, 227 ; has charge of queen Emma, 227 ; implicated in the murder of Alfred, 229, 240 ; his advice to Edward, 238 ; his rivalry with Edward's ministers and the violence of his sons, 237 ; marries the king to his daughter, 239 ; dies and is buried at Winchester, 240 ; his quarrel with the king on his refusal to punish the men of Kent, 241, 242 ; his banishment and return, 243 ; his wives and children, 245, 287 ; his authority alleged for William's claim to the throne, 302.

Godwin, Robert, son of, his prowess and martyrdom, 310, 318.

Golgotha, Godfrey of Bouillon buried on, 434.

Gomorrah, visited by Baldwin, 442.

Gordian, burial place of, at Rome, 406.

Gordius, patriarch of Jerusalem, 424.

Gorgonius, burial place of, at Rome, 406.

Goscelin, a monk of S. Bertin, brought to England by bishop Herman of Sherborne, writes the lives of the saints, 389.

Gosfrid, of Anjou. *See* Anjou.

Gosfrid, abbot of Westminster, 351.

Gothia, part of the dominion of Charles the Bald, 110.

Goths, migrations of, 9 ; in Spain, *ib.* ; in North Germany, 121 ; their conversion from Arianism, 193.

Goths, join in the crusade, 400.

Gournay, Hugh of, a chief captain under duke William, 290.

Grantmesnil, Hugh of, joins in the rebellion against William Rufus, 361 ; his headquarters at Leicester, 361.

Gratian, the name of pope Gregory VI., 246.

Greece, put for England, 356, note.

Greeks, style of the, 81 ; Greek origin of the name of Franks, 69.

Greeks, school of the, at Rome ; John, dean of, 499.

Gregory I., pope, sends Augustine to Britain, 28; had himself intended to conduct the mission under the licence of pope Benedict, 46; story of his interview with the English slaves at Rome, 45, 46; his instructions to Augustine, 88, 91; mentioned in a charter of Ethelwulf, 120; his pastoral translated, 132; his dialogues also, 131; conversion of the Goths in his time, 193; stories in his dialogues, 255; miracle under, 341; letter of, to Augustine, 347; his burial place, 502.

Gregory III., pope, oath of St. Boniface to, 82.

Gregory VI., traditional story of, 246–253.

Gregory VII. (Hildebrand), history of his rise, 322; expelled from Rome, 321; stories about, 322–325; he humiliates Henry IV., 325; suggests a successor, and dies, 325, 326, 343.

Gregory, Nazianzen, his relics at Constantinople, 413.

Gregory, cardinal of SS. Peter and Paul, 499.

Gregory, cardinal of St. Chrysogonus, 499.

Gregory, cardinal of St. Angelus (Innocent II.), 531.

Griffin, king of the Welsh, defeated by Harold, 237, 280; his brothers, 280.

Grimbald, abbot of Winchester, friend of Alfred, 130, 133.

Guildford. See Geldeford.

Guimund, bishop of Aversa, his controversy with Berengar, 338, 339.

Guiscard, Wiscard, Robert, his origin and progress, 320; conquers Apulia, and crosses the Adriatic, 321; restores pope Gregory VII., 321; his son Bohemond, ib., 391; he defeats the Venetians, 321; is poisoned at the instigation of Alexius, 322, 401; buried at Venosa, 322; his epitaph, 322; his conquests, 413, 453.

Gunhildis, the sister of Sweyn, perishes in the massacre of the Danes, 207; her husband Palling, 207.

Gunhildis, daughter of Canute and wife of the emperor Henry III., her history, 229, 230.

Guorongus, name of the ruler of Kent under the Briton king, 10.

Gurmund, Guthrum, king. See East Angles.

Gurth, son of Godwin, 245; his advice to Harold, 301.

Guthrum, king over the East Angles, 98; called Gurmund, 126, 146, 158.

Guy (Wido), count of Ponthieu, captures Harold and surrenders him to duke William, 279; taken prisoner by William, 290.

Guy, of Burgundy. See Burgundy.

Guy, brother of the count of Poictou, 290.

Guy, brother of Bohemond, 401.

Gwala, ancestor of Egbert, 121.

H.

Hacco, commands a fleet sent by Sweyn to England, 319.

Hadra, an ancestor of Egbert, 121.

Haimeric, chancellor of Rome, 531.

Haimo, dentatus, rebels against duke William, 286; unhorses the king of France at Val-es-dunes, 287; is killed, 287.

Hainault, Baldwin, count of; 316.

Hampshire, assigned to king Sigebert on his deposition, 41; adheres to Alfred in his troubles, 125.

Hamstede, in Berkshire, a fountain of blood breaks out at, 376.

Hardicanute, king of the English. See English, kings of.

Harding, Stephen, founder of the order of Cîteaux, his origin and education at Sherborne, 380; his conversion, 381; becomes abbot, 384; his character and administration, 384, 385.

Harold, king of Norway, sends ambassadors to Ethelstan, 149.

Harold, son of Harold of England, invades England, 318, 376.
Harold, king of Denmark, son of Sweyn and brother of S. Canute, 319.
Harptree, occupied by Stephen, and afterwards by Robert, 562.
Harvagra, Harold, his invasion of England and death at Stamford Bridge, 281; his adventures at Constantinople, 318; his ancestry, 317; 318.
Hasten, the Danish leader, 126, 127, 138, 162.
Hasten, son of Magnus, king of Norway, 318.
Hastings, battle of, 245, 281, 282, 300, 326, 475.
Hathaby, the ancient name of Sleswick, 121.
Hebron, visited by Baldwin, 441.
Hebrus, the river of Thrace, 411.
Hedde, a name on one of the Glastonbury pyramids, 25.
Hegesippus, the pseudo-Ambrosian history of, 415.
Helena, mother of Constantine, 5, 406, 410; her church at Rome, 406; her explanation of Constantine's dream, 410; she brought the holy cross from Jerusalem, 413.
Helgrim, ambassador of Norway to Ethelstan, 149.
Helias, the sailor who mutinied against William Rufus, 373, 374.
Hellendune, battle at, 106.
Helmham. *See* Elmham.
Hemgisl, abbot of Glastonbury, 40.
Hengest. *See* Kent, kings of, 342.
Henry I., king of the Germans, 117; his son Otto, *ib.*; he finds husbands for Ethelstan's sisters, *ib.*, 137, 149.
Henry III., emperor, stories about, 205, 206; other legends about him, 230-236; his death, 276; his son Henry IV., 276; his marriage with Gunhildis, 229, 230; his epitaph at Speyer, 235.
Henry IV., emperor, 276; his struggle with Hildebrand, 321, 325; his fate, 325, 342; his struggles with his sons,

Henry IV., emperor—*cont.*
343; the good points in his character, 343, 344; excommunicated at the council of Clermont, 393; helped by Godfrey of Bouillon in his wars, gives him Lorraine, 438.
Henry V., emperor, 72; his rebellion against his father, 325, 326, 343, 498; is still alive, 343; his controversy with the successive popes, 343, 498 *seq.*; marries Matilda, daughter of Henry I., 498; invades Italy, 498; makes a treaty with Paschal II., 499; his oath, 500; received to communion, 500; anointed and crowned, 501; his dignity recognised, 501; made patrician of Rome, 502; the engagement with him repudiated, 503, 504; he returns to Rome, 504; sets up Maurice of Braga as antipope, 504, 505; makes peace with Calixtus II., 508, 509; his death, 527; his three visits to Italy, 509.
Henry I., king of France, 140; succeeds his father Robert, 226, 227; with the aid of duke Robert of Normandy, 227; is poisoned, 276; undertakes the protection of Normandy, 285; is dismounted by Haimo at Val-es-dunes, 287; threatens duke William, 289; retires, 289, 290; invades Normandy, 290; again retires and makes peace, 291; dies, *ib.*
Henry (Eric), king of Denmark, 320.
Henry I., king of England, his reign to be included in the history, 284, 293; difficulty of writing it, 465, 466; his laws, 348, *notes*; son of William the Conqueror, 332; born in 1068, 467; his sound education in England, 467; knighted at Westminster, 468; his father's prophecy about him, 468; his affection for his brother Robert, 468; pays for his father's grave and attends his funeral, 337, 338, 468; is oppressed by both his brothers, 468; is imprisoned at Rouen, 468; occupies Avranches, 469; besieged by his brothers at Mont S. Michel, 363, 364, 365, 460; throws the traitor Conan from the tower of Rouen,

Henry I., king of England—*cont.*
469 ; is elected king on William's death, 470 ; good hopes of his succession, 370 ; claims of Robert in conflict with his, 461, 471 ; recalls Anselm and imprisons Rannulf, 470 ; crowned, 470 ; marries Matilda of Scotland, 470, 493 ; they are nicknamed Godric and Godiva, 471 ; is supported by the clergy and people, 472 ; subdues Robert of Belesme, 472, 473 ; and William of Mortain, 473–475 ; interferes to save Normandy, 462 ; defeats Robert at Tenchebrai, 475 ; imprisons Robert for life, 462, 463 ; plants Flemings in Wales, 366, 477 ; returns to England and makes laws against forgery, 476 ; his relations with the Bretons, 478 ; with Flanders, 478, 479 ; with the Irish, 484 ; and Orkney, 485 ; with Philip of France, 479 ; and his son Lewis, 480, 481 ; defeats Lewis and makes peace, 481, 482 ; entertains Calixtus II. with the dialectic performances of the sons of the count of Meulan, 482 ; his chief ministers Robert of Meulan, 483 ; and Roger bishop of Salisbury, 483, 484 ; his menagerie at Woodstock, 485 ; the peace of England during his reign, 485 ; his character in detail, 486, 487, 488 ; and personal appearance, 488 ; founds an abbey at Reading, 489 ; correspondence of, with Paschal II., 489, 490, 491, 492 ; reconciliation with Anselm, and the terms of it, 493 ; his son William, 491, 495 ; loses his first wife, 495 ; returns from Normandy, 496 ; loses his son in the shipwreck off Barfleur, 497 ; his second marriage, 495 ; marries his daughter to the emperor, 498 ; makes the abbey of Ely an episcopal see, 517 ; his confirmation of the grant of Roger of Gloucester, 521, 522 ; projects the marriage of Matilda with Geoffrey of Anjou, 527 ; gives Shrewsbury to queen Adela, 528 ; has fealty sworn to Matilda, 529 ; returns to England, 530 ; goes back to Normandy, 531 ; joins pope Innocent II. at Chartres,

Henry I., king of England—*cont.*
533, 534 ; again in England, has fealty sworn to Matilda, 534, 585 ; his last voyage to Normandy, 535 ; dies, 536 ; account of his death by the archbishop of Rouen, 536, 537 ; his body disembowelled at Rouen and brought to Caen, 537 ; is buried at Reading, 539 ; seizure and expenditure of his treasures, 540 ; disforesting of his forests, 542 ; reference to his times, 553 ; and contrast of them with those of Stephen, 561, 574 ; reception of the empress as his daughter, 573.

Henry II. (of Anjou), son of Geoffrey and the empress, allowed by his father to come to England, 593.

Heracleonas, emperor of Constantinople, 412.

Heraclius, emperor of Constantinople, 412 ; his son Constantine, *ib.*

Herbert, archbishop of Cologne, 204.

Herbert, count of Maine, captured by Fulk of Anjou at Saintes, 292 ; his son Hugh, 294.

Herbert, son of Hugh, count of Maine, makes duke William his heir, 294.

Herbert, abbot, bishop of the Pilgrims' Castle, 458.

Herculanus, burial place of, at Rome, 405.

Herding, son of Eadnoth the Staller, 313.

Hereford, the princes of North Wales submit to Ethelstan at, 148 ; the city of, occupied by the empress, 557.

Hereford, see of, 352 ; withdrawn from the obedience of Canterbury, 85 ; diocese of, 101 ; church of S. Ethelbert at, 262.

——— Wulfhard, bishop of, 85.

——— Walter, bishop of, 351.

——— Reiner, bishop of, consecrated by S. Anselm, 493.

Hereford, Miles, earl of. *See* Gloucester.

Herefordshire, included in Mercia, 101 ; Leofric, ealdorman of, 237.

Herefordshire, Ralph, earl of, son of Walter of Mantes, 241.
Herefordshire, William FitzOsbern, his government of, 314; his son's conspiracy, 313, 314.
Heremod, ancestor of Egbert, 121.
Heriman, count, one of the jurors for Henry V., 500; consents to the peace of the church, 509.
Herman, bishop of Salisbury. *See* Salisbury.
Hermengild, S., martyrdom of, 193.
Hermes, burial place of, at Rome, 405.
Herod, attempted to plunder David's tomb, 198; his visit to Antony, 436.
Hersexi, a name on one of the Glastonbury pyramids, 25.
Hertfordshire, included in Mercia and partly in the kingdom of the East Saxons, 101.
Hexham, Alfwold, king of Northumbria, buried at, 74; ancient see of, 101, 353.
Hilaria, burial place of, at Rome, 405.
Hilarina, burial place of, at Rome, 405.
Hilda, abbess of Whitby, 56, 60; her connexion with Glastonbury, 36; her relics there, 56, 60.
Hildebert, bishop of le Mans, and archbishop of Tours, his poem on Berengar, 338-340; his verses on Rome, 402, 403.
Hildebrand. *See* Gregory VII., pope.
Hildelida, abbess of Barking, 35.
Hinguar, puts S. Edmund to death, 98, 264.
Hippolytus, S., church of at Rome, 407.
Hister, the river Danube, 411.
Hiwingendes, a name on one of the Glastonbury pyramids, 25.
Hlotheri, king of Kent. *See* Kent.
Honorius, the emperor, overthrows Constantius, 6; Spain won by the Goths from, 198.
Honorius I., pope, sends the pall to Paulinus, 68.
Honorius II., pope, dies, 530; schism following his death, 531, 532, 533.
Horace, quoted, 84, 559.
Hors, brother of Hengest, 6; killed in battle, 11.

Horton, abbey of, suppressed by bishop Roger of Salisbury, 559.
Hubba, murderer of S. Edmund, 264.
Hubert, legate of Rome to William the Conqueror, 351.
Hugh, abbot of Cluny. *See* Cluny.
Hugh, Rodulf, son of, 192.
Hugh, earl of Chester. *See* Chester.
Hugh, Capet, 72; confused account of his rise, 139, 140; his son Robert, 196.
Hugh, count, son of count Robert, husband of Ethilda, daughter of Edward, 187; confused account of him, 139; called king, 150.
Hugh, the Great, brother of Philip I., 320; on crusade, 400; is at the siege of Antioch, 420; attacked in Asia Minor, 414; returns to Europe, 413; comes on a second expedition, 447; and dies at Tarsus, 448.
Hugh, count of Alsace, father of the empress Ermengard, 111.
Hugh, earl of Shrewsbury. *See* Shrewsbury.
Humber, the river, 97, 101, 158, 280, 352, 354.
Huwal, king, rows Edgar on the Dee, 165.
Hyde, Abbey of, at Winchester; Canute's crucifix at, 581. *See* Winchester.
Hyde, Ruald, abbot of, 352.
Hydromel, described, 230.
Hyrcanus, plunders the tomb of David, 198.

I.

Ida, ancestor of the kings of Northumbria, 11. *See* Northumbria.
Ida, mother of Godfrey of Bouillon, 431, 432.
Ilia, two patriarchs of Jerusalem, named, 425.
Illyricum, plan of the Crusaders for crossing, 390; ravaged by the Saracens, 394.

Ina. *See* West Saxons, kings of.
India, mission of Alfred to, 130.
Indract, S., a Glastonbury saint, 27, 35.
Ineswitrin, a name of Glastonbury, 29.
Ingild, ancestor of Egbert, 105, 120.
Innocent II. (Gregory, cardinal of S. Angelo), elected pope on the death of Honorius II., 531; his opponents set up Anacletus II., 531, 532; and the schism continues for eight years, 533; visits France and makes agreement with Henry II. at Chartres, 534.
Innocentia, burial place of, at Rome, 408.
Ireland, Little, an estate of Glastonbury, 171.
Ireland, S. Patrick and S. Benignus come from, 26, 27; exile of Aldfrith in, 57; flight of Anlaf to, 147; his return from, 157; Harold banished to, 243; the countess of Gloucester threatens to send king Stephen to, 588.
Ireland, Murchard, king of, 484, 485.
Irene, S., church of, at Byzantium, 411.
Iricius, a Danish king of Northumbria in the time of Edred, 162.
Iricius, earl of Northumbria under Canute, 215, 218; sent to Denmark, 219.
Irish, beaten by Ecgfrith, 57; their custom about Easter, 55.
Irmeneus, patriarch of Jerusalem, 424.
Isaac, the patriarch, his burial place visited by Baldwin, 441.
Isaac, Sachius, emperor of Constantinople, 412.
Isambard, killed by count Hugh, 139.
Isambard, count of Ponthieu, killed at Arques, 289; his brother Guy, 290. *See* Guy.
Isauria, in the hands of the Saracens, 394.
Isidore, saint, his body translated to Toledo, 293; his etymologies, 485.
Italy, rule of the Karolings in, 72; attacked by the Avars, 92; Robert of Normandy intrigues in, 332; three visits of Henry V. to, 509.
Italy, the duke of, 161.

J.

Jacinctus, S., his burial place at Rome, 405.
Jacob, the patriarch, his burial place, 441.
Jacob, king, rows Edgar on the Dee, 165.
Jaenbert (Lambriht), archbishop. *See* Canterbury.
Januarius, S., his burial place at Rome, 407.
James, S., patriarch of Jerusalem, 424.
Jason, burial place of, at Rome, 405.
Jebusites, at Jerusalem, 422.
Jericho, the Crusaders furnish themselves with palms at, 437.
Jerome, saint, quoted, 230, 358, 387.
Jerusalem, kings of. *See* Bouillon, Godfrey of; Baldwin, Anjou Fulk of.
Jerusalem, recovered by the Franks from the Saracens in our author's time, 92; the Statio ad Jerusalem in Rome, 202, 203; pilgrimage of duke Robert of Normandy to, 211, 218, 227, 283; pilgrimage of Fulk of Anjou to, 292; of Edgar Atheling to 310; of Robert of Flanders to, 316, of Sigurd of Norway to, 319; of Henry (Eric) to, 320; vision of, 328; list of the patriarchs of, 424, 425; crusade to, 358, 371, 390, 399, 401, 432; description of, 422–424.
Jerusalem, advance of the Crusaders on, 421; siege of, 425; water supply of, 426; escalade of, 426; final assault on, 426, 427; taken, 427, 428; Godfrey chosen king of, 428, 433; the Crusaders return after the battle of Ascalon to, 430; Baldwin was at Edessa whilst the siege was going on, 436; he is summoned to, and Godfrey meets him, 437; Daimbert chosen patriarch of, 437; Baldwin returns to, after Godfrey's

Jerusalem—*cont.*
death, 441; he is crowned king of, 442; miracle of the sacred fire at, 443, 444; expedition of William of Poictou to, 447, 510; he arrives at, 448; flight from the defeat at Ramlah to, 450; burial of Baldwin I. at, 451; Baldwin II. captured near, 452; expedition of Fulk of Anjou to, 495, 528.

Jews, treatment of, by William Rufus, 371.

John, patriarch of Jerusalem, 424.

John, emperor of Constantinople, 412.

John, saint, his gate, at Rome, 406.

John, saint, and Paul, church of, at Rome, 408.

John, the martyr, burial place of, 404.

John VIII., pope, consecrates Charles the Bald as emperor, 112; has a second visit from him, *ib.*

John XI., pope, authorises the action of Ethelstan in disposing of the property of Elfred, 153.

John XIII., confirms the rights of Glastonbury, 168, 169, 172.

John XV., writes to the Ealdorman Elfric, about Glastonbury, 172, 173; and tries to make peace between Ethelred and duke Richard, 191-193.

John XVI., pope, 193.

John, the Old Saxon, abbot of Athelney, 130.

John, Scotus, translates the hierarchy of Dionysius, 131; tradition of his death at Malmesbury, 131, 132.

Joppa, Baldwin forces his way to, 441; the men of, conduct him to Jerusalem, 441; battles in the neighbourhood of, 443, 446, 448, 450.

Jordan, the river, 328.

Jordanes, the historian, quoted, 121.

Joseph, the patriarch, buried at Nablous, 441.

Joseph, patriarch of Jerusalem, 425; Cleophas, brother of, 424.

Josephus, quoted, 198, 422, 436, 441.

Jovenianus, archbishop of Dol, 154.

Jovian, Jovinianus, the emperor, 412.

Judas, patriarch of Jerusalem, 424.

Judethil, king, rows Edgar on the Dee, 165.

Judith, wife of Lewis the Pious, 110.

Judith, wife of Ethelwulf, daughter of Charles the Bald, 109; the troubles that arose from her marriage, 117; Ethelbald wishes to marry her, 122.

Judith, wife of duke Richard of Normandy, 211.

Judith, niece of the Conqueror, wife of earl Waltheof, 312.

Judwal, king of the Welsh, at war with Ethelstan, 142.

Julian, two patriarchs of Jerusalem named, 424.

Julian, emperor, the apostate, 412.

Julian, saint, his burial place at Rome, 407.

Julius Cæsar conquers Britain, 5; clears the Ardennes with Gallic troops, 312; his account of the ancient Britons, 301; William Rufus compared to, 374; his soul transmigrated into him, 374; earl Robert of Gloucester compared with him, 555; began his conquests with five cohorts, 555.

Jumiéges, devastated by Hasteng and restored by duke William, 162; Robert, a monk of, archbishop of Canterbury, 239; he dies and is buried at, 244.

Justin the Greater, emperor of Constantinople, 412.

Justin the Less, emperor, 412.

Justin, saint, burial place of, 406.

Justinian I., emperor, builds the church of S. Sophia at Constantinople, 412.

Justinian II., emperor, 412.

Justinian III., emperor, 412.

Justus, two patriarchs of Jerusalem named, 424.

Justus, archbishop. *See* Canterbury.

Juvenal, quoted, 53, 57, 326, 380, 446.

Juvenalis, patriarch of Jerusalem, 424.

Jutes, settlement of, in Britain, 9.

K.

Karloman, son of Charles Martel, tonsured at Monte Cassino, 71.
Karloman, son of Pipin, and brother of Charles the Great, his short reign, 71.
Karloman, son of Lewis the German, king of Bavaria, 111.
Karloman, son of Lewis III., shares the kingdom with his brother Lewis, 112.
Kedwalla, king of the West Saxons. *See* West Saxons.
Kenelm. *See* Mercia, kings of.
Kennet, the river in Berkshire, 489.
Kenred, king of Northumbria. *See* Northumbria.
Kent, handed over to Hengest, 12; its continuance as a kingdom, 19; invaded by Ethelred of Mercia, 178; ravaged by the Danes, 108; ravaged by Canute, 214; Odo of Bayeux made earl of, 334, 351, 360; *see* Bayeux. William of Mortain is refused the succession to, 473.
Kent, Hengest, king of, leads the Saxons into Britain, 9; receives the isle of Thanet for a settlement, 9; invites his countrymen, 10; gives his daughter to Vortigern, 10; his battles, 11; murders the British nobles, 12; dies 39 years after his arrival, 12; date of his death, 19, 76; his brother and nephew conquer the north, 44, 342.
——— Eisc, king of, succeeds Hengest, character and length of his reign, 12.
——— Oht, king of, succeeds Eisc, 12.
——— Yrmenric, king of, son of Oht and father of Ethelbert, 12, 13.
——— Ethelbert, king of, succeeds, 13; his reign, marriage, and conversion, *ib.*; contrasted with Eadbald, 14; his struggle with the West Saxons, 20, 21; his sister Ricula, 98.
——— Eadbald, king of, succeeds Ethelbert, 14, his incestuous marriage, *ib.*;

Kent, Eadbald, king of—*cont.*
contrasted with his father, *ib.*; his repentance, 15; his marriage with Emma, *ib.*; his daughter Ethelburga, 49.
——— Ercombert, king of, succeeds, 15; his policy and laws, 15; his daughter Ercongota, 15, 16, 78; his daughter Ermenhilda, 78; his brother Ermenred, 78, 261, 266, 267.
——— Egbert, king of, succeeds and reigns nine years, 16; arrival of archbishop Theodore during his reign, 16, 56; his cruelty to his cousins, 16, 261, 267; his son Wihtred, 17.
——— Lothar (Hlothere), king of, brother of Egbert, succeeds, 16; derides the martyrs, his kinsmen, 16; his struggle with Edric, *ib.*
——— Edric, king of, son of Egbert, succeeds, 16; his short reign, 16; his kingdom invaded by Ceadwalla and Mollo, 17.
——— Wihtred, king of, son of Egbert, succeeds, 17; his long and successful reign, 17, 18; his three sons, 18.
——— Eadbert, king of, son of Wihtred, his reign, 18.
——— Ethelbert, king of, son of Wihtred, his reign, 18.
——— Alric, king of, son of Wihtred, his reign, 18; defeated by the Mercians, 18.
——— Edelbert (Eadbert) Præn, king of, rules for two years, 18; imprisoned by Kenulf of Mercia, 94; released and present at the consecration at Winchcomb, 95.
——— Cuthred, king of, reigns eight years, 18; is at the consecration of Winchcomb abbey, 95.
——— Baldred, king of, conquered by the West Saxon Egbert, 18, 19, 106, 107.
Kenulf, king of Mercia. *See* Mercia.
Kenwalch, king of the West Saxons. *See* West Saxons.
Kenwalch, brother of Penda, ancestor of Kenulf, 94.
Kerbogha. *See* Corbaguath.

Kinad, king of the Scots, rows Edgar on the Dee, 165; insults him and is rebuked, 177.

Kineburga, daughter of Penda, wife of Aldfrith, and a nun, 77, 78.

Kinehard, banished from Wessex, 41; kills Cynewulf, 42; killed and buried at Repton, 43, 44.

Kineswitha, wife of Penda, her children, 77.

Kineswitha, daughter of Penda, 77; connected with the pilgrimage of Offa, 99.

Kinethritha, Quendreda, sister of S. Kenelm, 95, 262.

Kingston, Ethelstan crowned at, 140, 145.

L.

Lademund, abbot of Glastonbury, 29.

Lambeth, Hardicanute dies at, 228.

Lanfranc, archbishop. *See* Canterbury.

Langres, death of abbot Ceolfrith at, 60.

Lantocal, estate of Glastonbury at, 37.

Lanzo, prior of Lewes, account of his life and death, 513, 514, 515, 516.

Laodicea, gathering of the Crusaders at, 438; Daimbert of Pisa lands at, 436; occupied by Tancred, 454, 458; given up by Raymond, 458; occupied by Bohemond, 454; the Italian fleets anchor at, 444.

Lateran, council of, under Paschal II., 503; letters dated at, 491.

Latina, Via, at Rome, 406.

Laurentius, archbishop. *See* Canterbury.

Laurentius, saint, his gate at Rome, 406.

Lavicana, Via, at Rome, 406.

Leah, burial place of, 441.

Leander, archbishop of Seville, 193.

Ledon, answering to the Greek Euripus, 213.

Leicester, see of, now extinct, 86, 352, 353.
——— Werenbert, bishop of, 85.

Leicester, town of, headquarters of Hugh Grentmesnil, 361.

Leicestershire, included in Mercia, 101.

Le Mans, burned by Geoffrey Martel, 294; William Rufus agrees to conquer it for Robert, 363, 364; besieged, 373; Hildebert, bishop of. *See* Hildebert.

Lemannus, lacus; the lake of Geneva, 322.

Leo, several emperors of Constantinople named, 412.

Leo III., pope, crowns Charles the Great, 72; succeeds pope Adrian, 86; letter of Kenulf to, 86; letter of, to Kenulf, 89, 90.

Leo IV., pope, anointed Alfred when a child, 109, 124; receives the English tribute, *ib.*

Leo. IX., pope, convinced of a miraculous event by Peter Damian, 202; named Bruno, 236; his death, 235, 236; holds a council at Vercelli, 338.

Leo, called bishop of Treves, 191, 192.

Leo, dean of S. Vitalis, 499.

Leobwin, tragic history of, 330.

Leof, the murderer of king Edmund, 159.

Leofric, the earl of Mercia, a great minister of Edward the Confessor, his benefactions to churches, 237, 388; attends a royal council at Gloucester, 242; his son Elfgar, 243, 310; his wife Godiva, 388.

Leofstan, son of Alfwold, 192.

Leofstan, his punishment for desecrating the grave of S. Edmund, 266.

Leominster, in Herefordshire, founded by Leofric, 237.

Leofwin, son of earl Godwin, 245.

Leonard, S., Bohemond offers his chains to, 454.

Leonensis, bishop, 504.

Leonthos, patriarch of Jerusalem, 425.

Leopards, curious story about, 344.

Lesignan, Hugh of, joins the crusade of, 1102, 447; escapes from the battle of Ramlah, 449, 460.

Letard, bishop, his moral influence on the Kentish court, 13.
Leufred, saint, monastery of, in Normandy, 338.
Leutherius, bishop of the West Saxons. *See* Winchester.
Leuticii, conquered by the emperor Henry III., 230.
Levi, patriarch of Jerusalem, 424.
Lewes, priory of Cluniac monks at S. Pancras, in, 513.
─────── Lanzo, prior of, 513–516.
─────── Hugh, prior of, abbot of Reading and archbishop of Rouen, 536.
Lewis I., the Pious, son of Charles the Great, succeeds him, 72; his wife Ermengard, 110; his four sons, *ib.*; his second wife Judith, *ib.*; deposed by his son Lothar, *ib.*; possessed Aquitaine, 584.
Lewis, the German, son of Lewis the Pious, 110; his dominions and his children, 111; dies 111; seen in purgatory, 114, 115.
Lewis II., the son of Lothar, emperor, 111; in glory, 115.
Lewis III., the son of Charles the Bald, 112, 136.
Lewis, son of Lewis III., reigns conjointly with Karloman, 112.
Lewis, king of the Saxons, son of Lewis, the German, 112; his son Charles, 112.
Lewis, the Child, 116, 117.
Lewis of Aquitaine, marries a daughter of Edward, 137; the survivor of the house of Charles the Great, 149.
Lewis VI., king when Malmesbury wrote, 72, 140, 315; succeeds Philip I., 480; his relations with Henry I., 480; invades Normandy, 481; makes peace and invests William with the duchy, 482, 496; has his son Philip crowned, 534; and his son Lewis, *ib.*; dies, *ib.*
Lewis VII., marries the heiress of Aquitaine, 584; mentioned, 551; tries to make peace in England, 565.
Liberalis, burial place of, at Rome, 406.

Lichfield, Ceolred buried at, 79.
Lichfield, see of, made an archbishopric, 85; reduced to its former rank, 86; diocese of, in Mercia, 100; see of, removed to Chester, 352, 353.
─────── Aldulf, bishop of, 85.
─────── Robert, bishop of, removes the see to Coventry, 385; account of him, his oppression of the monks and burial, 388, 389.
Lillebonne, council of, 299.
Limousin, county of, acquired by Raymond of S. Giles, 456.
Lincoln, Bardney abbey is near, 53; a blind man of, healed by Edward the Confessor, 273; besieged by Stephen, 569, 570; succoured by the earl of Gloucester, 570; battle of, 571; massacre of the citizens of, 572.
Lincoln, see of, in Mercia, removed from Dorchester, 101, 351. *See* Dorchester.
─────── Remigius, bishop of, 351.
─────── [Robert], bishop of, his claims on Ely, 518.
─────── Alexander, bishop of, nephew of bishop Roger of Salisbury, 547, 559; has one of the richest sees in England, 559; builds a fine castle at Newark, 547; summoned to surrender Newark and Sleaford, 549; arrested and compelled to surrender, *ib.*, 551; his enmity towards Alan of Brittany, 552; attends the empress at the council of Winchester, 573.
Lindisfarne, 67, 101; ancient see of, 350, 353.
─────── Aidan, bishop of, relics of, 56; Oswald interprets his sermons, 52.
─────── Cuthbert, bishop of, promoted by Ecgfrith, 56; sees Ecgfrith's spirit, 57; his tomb and relics at Durham, 53, 66, 67; appears to Alfred in his troubles, 125, 126; his sanctity, 260; his translation to Durham, 517.
Lindsey, Canute driven out of, 212.

Lisieux, bishop of, advises the marriage of Matilda and Geoffrey, 530.
Liulf, tragedy of, 330.
Liuns, Hervey of, 552.
Liuns, death of Henry I. at, 536.
Living, archbishop. *See* Canterbury.
Living, bishop. *See* Crediton, Worcester.
Livy, quoted on the history of Julius Cæsar, 555.
Llandaff, Urban, bishop of, consecrated, 493, 522, 535; his struggle with the bishop of S. David's, 535; dies at Rome, 535.
Logor, a name on the Glastonbury pyramid, 25.
Logweresburh, the ancient name of Montacute, 26.
Loire, the river, 127, 155.
Lombards, migrations of, from Germany, 9; conquered by Charles the Great, 71.
Lombardy, Bertram of S. Giles marries in, 456, 459; princes come from, to woo the empress in her widowhood, 527.
London, Wulfred sells the bishopric of, to Wina, 78; see of, continued under the obedience of Canterbury when the archbishopric of Lichfield was founded, 85; diocese of, 101; the city belongs to Mercia, 101; entrusted to Ethered, 128; besieged by the Danes, 187; ransomed, 187, 188; Elfege's body translated to, 188; Ethelred at, 208; besieged by the Danes, 208; Ethelred stays in, 214; he is buried at S. Paul's, 215; besieged by Canute, 216; S. Elfege removed from, 220; Lambeth, near, 228; Edward the Confessor summons a council to, 242; Godwin asks pardon at, 243; Harold crowned at, 280; negotiations after his death at, 307; Edwin and Morcar at, 311; Westminster, near, 352; William Rufus argues with the Jews at, 371; his great house built at, 374; great storm in which S. Mary-le-Bow is wrecked at, 375; Henry I. crowned at, 470; great council held by Anselm

London—*cont.*
at, 493; fealty sworn to the empress at, 528; receives Stephen as king, 538; ———— project of Robert FitzHubert for a march on, 568; Stephen keeps court in the Tower, 564; the men of Lincoln send to him at, 569; the citizens send to the council of Winchester on behalf of Stephen, 576; their communio, 576; the legate's answer to them, 576, 577; they receive the empress, 577, 578; they rise against her, 578; she leaves the city, 578; the way to, blocked by the forces of the queen, 580.
London, bishops of;
———— Mellitus, the first bishop, preaches to the East Saxons, 98, 99.
———— Cedd recovers Sigebert to the faith and baptizes Swithelm, 99.
———— Wina, 78; buys the see from Wulfhere, 78.
———— Theodred examines the body of S. Edmund, 265; buried at S. Paul's, 265.
———— Robert of Jumieges, made archbishop of Canterbury, 239, 240.
———— William, 351.
Lorraine, Lotharingia, origin of the name, 110; Godfrey of Bouillon, duke of, 400; Godfrey Bocard, his uncle, 431; given to Godfrey of Bouillon by Henry IV., 432; Louvain, the capital of the duchy of, 495, 528; princes of, come to court the empress in her widowhood, 527; queen Adela came from, 495, 528, 575.
Losinga, Herbert. *See* Norwich, bishops of.
Losinga, Robert, father of Herbert, abbot of Hyde, 385, 386.
Lothar, king of Kent. *See* Kent.
Lothar, father of Dagobert, king of the Franks, 71.
Lothar, son of Lewis the Pious, 110; shares the empire and displaces his father, *ib.*; divides the dominion with his brothers, 111; his wife, Ermengard, *ib.*; his sons, *ib.*; is seen in the vision of Charles, in glory, 115.

Lothar II., son of Lothar I., divides Provence with his brother, Lewis III.
Lotharingi, the branch of the Franks called, 70.
Louvain, Godfrey, duke of, father of queen Adela, 495, 528.
Lucan, quoted, 220, 374, 387, 395, 417, 418, 419, 446.
Lucca, oath by the Face of, 364, 373.
Lucca, pope Urban visited by the Crusaders at, 402.
Lucia, saint, relics of, at Constantinople, 413.
Lucian, the hero of the story of Palumbus, 256.
Lucina, burial place of, at Rome, 405.
Lucius, king of Britain, legend of, 23.
Lucius, saint, burial place of, at Rome, 407.
Ludecan, king. *See* Mercia.
Luke, S., quoted as an example to genealogists, 120; relics of, at Constantinople, 413.
Lullus, successor of S. Boniface, his epitaph, 84; he was an Englishman, *ib.*
Lulworth, castle of, belonging to William of Glaston, revolts from the empress, 595; taken by the earl of Gloucester, 595.
Lusitania, recovered from the Saracens, 193.
Lycia, in the hands of the Saracens, 394.
Lydia, in the hands of the Saracens, 394.
Lyons, Anselm in exile at, 492.
——— Hugh, archbishop of, 492.

Maccabees, appearance of angels to the, 420.
Maccabeus, patriarch of Jerusalem, 424.
Macedonia, to be crossed by the Crusaders, 390.
Macharius, patriarch of Jerusalem, 424.
Macotis, the lake, marshes of, 69.
Magnus, king of Norway, ejects Sweyn of Denmark, 317, 318; other kings of Norway of the line of, 318, 319.
Magnus, king of Norway, invades Anglesey, 318, 376.
Magnus, S., in Saxony, wonderful event at his church, 204.
Mahomet, worshipped not as God but as a prophet, 230; image of, 423.
Maine, Herbert, count of, 292; Hugh, count of, 294; Herbert, son of Hugh, 294; right of succession in, 294; the Conqueror sends English forces into, 316; Tanea, a castle in, 460; promised to William, son of duke Robert, 498.
Mainz, S. Boniface archbishop of, 79; Lullus archbishop of, 84; story about, 233; Marianus Scotus at, 345; Albert, archbishop of, 509.
Majorca, visited by Sigurd of Norway, 486.
Malcolm, king of Scots, Cumbria given in charge to, 158; king of Cumbria rows Edgar on the Dee, 165.
Malcolm II., king of Scots, subdued by Canute, 221.
Malcolm III., son of the king of Cumbria, placed on the throne of the Scots by Siward, 237; marries Margaret, 278; their children, 278, 366; his protection of the English exiles, 308; submission, revolt and death, 309; buried at Dunfermline, 369; his visit to William Rufus at Gloucester, 366; his wife's mourning for him, 366; his family, 470, 471, 493, 528.
Malger, archbishop of Rouen, his deposition, 327.
Malmesbury, founded by Meildulf, 30; and Aldhelm, *ib.*; grant of Leutherius to, 30, 31; plundered by Offa, 86; restored

M.

Mabilia, Mabilla, daughter of Robert Fitz-Hamon, wife of Robert of Gloucester, 529; negotiates for the exchange of the earl for the king, 587; threatens to send Stephen a prisoner to Ireland, 588.
Macbeth, king of Scots, overthrown by Siward, 237.

Malmesbury—*cont.*
by Egfrith, 94; appropriated by bishop Alhstan, 109; and afterwards by bishop Roger, *ib.*; benefaction of Ethelwulf to, 119, 120; tragedy of John Scotus traditional at, 131, 132; Ethelstan buries his cousins at, 151, 152; his grant of Elfred's property to, 153; relics placed by Ethelstan at, 154, 155; burial of Ethelstan at, 157; clerks introduced into, under Edwy, 168; charter of Edgar to, 173, 174; the wife of Sigeferth confined at, 213; buildings of bishop Roger at, 484; Roger of Salisbury begins a castle at 547; it is given up to Stephen, 549; seized by Robert FitzHubert, 556, 563; recovered by Stephen, 556, 557; the abbey is appropriated by Roger, 559; the borough of, given to one of his nephews, 559; the monastery restored to its independence, 560; the bishop refuses to let Roger Mortimer stay at, 553.
———— Cuthbert, abbot of, 94.
———— Elfric, abbot of, 154.
———— John, abbot of, elected by the monks, 560; dies the same year, *ib.*
———— Peter, abbot of, attends the empress at Winchester, 573.
Malmesbury, William of, his account of his education, 103; the plan of his work, 103, 104, 283, 284; akin to both Englishman and Norman, 283; his opinion about the doctrine of Berengarius, 341, 342; his motives for writing, 355, 356; was librarian at Malmesbury, 525.
Malvern, Walcher, prior of, 346.
Mandeville, Geoffrey de, swears fealty to the empress after the capture of Stephen, changes sides and joins the Londoners against her, 580.
Maniches, emperor of Constantinople, 275.
Mantes, Walter of, brother-in-law of the Confessor, and father of earl Ralph, 241; marries the sister of count Hugh of Maine, 294.
Mantes, town of, burned by the Conqueror, 336.

Mantua, subdued by Henry V., 509.
Marcellinus, burial place of, at Rome, 406.
Marcellinus S., cardinal of, 499.
Marcellus, burial place of, at Rome, 407.
Marcellus, S., cardinal of, 499.
Marcenniacum, the countess Adela, a nun at, 333; story of S. Anselm's vision at, 377.
Marcian, the emperor of Constantinople, 412.
Marcus, pope, his burial place at Rome, 407.
Marcus, patriarch of Jerusalem, 424.
Margaret, sister of Edgar Atheling, queen of Scots, 278; her piety and mortification, 366; mother of queen Matilda, 477, 493, 528.
Marianus, Scotus, account of, 345.
Marinus, pope, sends a piece of the true cross to Alfred, 130.
Mark, S., cardinal of, 499.
Marius, S., burial place of, at Rome, 404.
Marlborough, castle of, in the hands of John FitzGilbert, 564.
Martel, William, steward of king Stephen, 577.
Martha, burial place of, at Rome, 404, 407.
Martial, S., burial place of, at Rome, 405.
Martin, the duke, killed by Ebroin, 71.
Martin, S., of Tours, miraculous story of his relics, 127.
Martinianus, and Processus, relics of, at Rome, 408.
Martinseie, estate of Glastonbury at, 37, 171.
Mary, of Scotland, marries Eustace the younger, count of Boulogne, 278, 519.
Mary and Martha, burial place of, at Rome, 407.
Mascusius, the pirate, rows Edgar on the Dee, 165.
Matilda, wife of William the Conqueror, daughter of Baldwin of Flanders, 291, 314; her consanguinity with William, 327; is buried at Caen, 332; her husband's grief for, 331; false stories about his treatment of her, 331; attests the

Matilda—*cont.*
  synodal decree about the relations of York and Canterbury, 351.
Matilda, daughter of Malcolm and Margaret, marries Henry I., 470; called Godiva, 471; educated at Romsey, 493; her family and court, 494; her death and burial at Westminster 495, 497.
Matilda, the Marchioness, ally of Gregory VII., 348, 402, 432; wife of Godfrey of Lorraine, 432; her niece married to Bertram of S. Giles, 456.
Matilda, the empress, daughter of Henry I., 498; marries the emperor Henry V., 498; is left a widow and wooed by the princes of Lorraine and Lombardy, 527; a marriage with Geoffrey of Anjou proposed for, 527, 528; fealty sworn to her, 528, 529; married, 530; fealty again sworn to her, 534; her claims to the succession set aside in England, 538; supported in Normandy, 538, 545, 546; especially by her brother, earl Robert, 545, 546, 570; she arrives in England, 555; is sent to Arundel, and then to Bristol and Gloucester, 556; at Hereford, 557; conferences for peace between her party and Stephen's, 564, 565; Stephen brought to her as a prisoner, 572; she attends a great council at Winchester and is received as lady of England, 573; visited by the archbishop at Wilton, 573; received in London, 577; is disliked by the citizens and leaves, 578; refuses to grant Boulogne and Mortain to Stephen's sons, and so quarrels with the legate, 579; goes to Winchester, 580; is sent off by her brother, 581; keeps her court at Oxford, 583; the legate describes her as countess of Anjou, and threatens to excommunicate her party, 584; argument on her behalf, 584, 585; faithfulness of earl Robert to her, 585, 586; recapitulation of his merits towards her, 586; he refuses to desert her, 589; she comes to Devizes, 590; besieged at Oxford, 593; her forces at Wallingford, 593;

Matilda—*cont.*
  at Cirencester, 595; her escape from Oxford to Wallingford, 596.
Matilda, wife of king Stephen, daughter of Eustace of Boulogne and Mary of Scotland, 578, 579; her clerk Christian pleads for the king in the council of Winchester, 577; is kept at Bristol as a surety on the king's release, 582; her honourable treatment of Robert when in her power, 587.
Matthias, saint, relics of, at Constantinople, 413.
Maurice, his banner, among Ethelstan's treasures, 150.
Maurice, emperor of Constantinople, 412.
Maurilius, archbishop of Rouen, 527.
Maurus, S., burial place of, at Rome, 405.
Maworn, an unknown bishop who attests a Glastonbury charter, 27.
Maxilianus, burial place of, at Rome, 405.
Maximin, saint, his monastery at Orleans, 195.
Maximus, pretender to the empire in Britain, crushed by Theodosius, 6.
Maximus, two patriarchs of Jerusalem named, 424.
Maximus, saint, burial place of, at Rome, 407.
Mazabanus, patriarch of Jerusalem, 424.
Medantum (Mantes). See Mantes.
Medard, S., Pipin tonsured in the monastery of, 110.
Medway, river, 216.
Meildulf, founder of Malmesbury, 30.
Melanius, saint, monastery of, at Rennes, 296, 297.
Melchizedek, king of Salem, 422.
Mellent, Meulan, castle of, bought by Hugh, the son of Waleran, 482.
Mellent, Meulan, Robert of Beaumont, count of, faithful to Henry I., 471; account of his father and family, 482, 483; his economic reforms in meals, 483; his power as a minister, judge, and warrior, 483; opposes the return of S. Anselm, 493; cleverness of his sons exhibited to Pope Calixtus II., 482.

INDEX.   641

Mellent, Meulan, Waleran, count of, conducts the empress from Arundel to Calne, 556.
Mellentinia, Malatia, taken by Baldwin, 438.
Mellitus, archbishop. *See* Canterbury.
Menevia, 27. *See* S. David's.
Mercelm, Mercelin, son of Penda, 77.
Mercia, Penda, king of, 21, 22, 50, 52, 55, 57; the first who took the name of king, 76; he destroys five kings, 76; his war with Kenwalch, 21, 76, 77; with Edwin, 50, 76; with Oswald, 52, 76; with the East Angles, 76, 97; slain by Oswy, 55, 57, 77; his wife and children, 77, 78; relationship of Offa to, 84; of Kenulf, 94; his daughter Kineswitha, 99.
——— Peada, Weda, king of, succeeds Penda, 77; his conversion, reign, and death, *ib.*
——— Wulfhere, king of, succeeds, 77; restores the Mercian power, 77; his war with the West Saxons, 23, 78; conquers the Isle of Wight, 78; sells London to Wina, 78; his wife and family, 78, 267.
——— Ethelred, king of, son of Penda, 77; succeeds Wulfhere, and goes to war with Kent, 78; is successful against Northumbria, 57; confirmed the privileges of Malmesbury, 560; his wife Osthritha or Ostgitha, 53, 78; he becomes a monk and abbot of Bardney, 53, 78.
——— Kenred, king of, son of Wulfhere, succeeds Ethelred and goes to Rome, 78, 79, 99.
——— Ceolred, Chelred, king of, son of Ethelred, succeeds Kenred, wars against Ine, dies, and is buried at Lichfield, 79; his evil life, 81.
——— Ethelbald, king of, succeeds Ceolred, 79; mentioned in a Glastonbury charter, 40; killed by Beornred, 79; letter of S. Boniface to, 79, 80–82; council held by him and archbishop Cuthbert, 83; his charter freeing the

Mercia, Ethelbald, king of—*cont.*
monasteries, 83, 84; succeeded by Offa, 84.
——— Beornred, king of, kills Ethelbald, 79; killed by Offa, *ib.*
——— Offa, king of, succeeds, 79, 84; his character, 84; his cruelty to Ethelbert, king of the East Angles, 84, 98, 262; his foundation at S. Albans, 85; he institutes an archbishopric at Lichfield, 85, 88; he plunders Malmesbury, 86; marries his daughter to Brihtric, 43, 91, 118, *see* Eadburga; his friendship with Charles the Great, 91; his quarrel with him, 92; letter from Charles to, 93; makes his son Egfrith king, 93; East Anglia subject to him, 95; his treatment of Egbert, 105; founded the English school at Rome, 109.
——— Egfrith, king of, made king by his father during his life, 93; his piety, 93, 94; restores the property of Malmesbury, 94; dies early on account of his father's sins, 94; reigns four months, *ib.*
——— Kenulf, king of, succeeds, 94; his letter to Leo III. on the dignity of Canterbury, 86–88; letter of the pope to, 88–91; restores the dignity of Canterbury, 94; captures Eadbert Præn, releases him, and takes him to Winchcomb, 95; dies and is buried at Winchcomb, 95, 262.
——— Kenelm, king of, murdered by his sister, 95, 262, 263; decline of the kingdom from that time, *ib.*
——— Ceolwulf, king of, brother of Kenulf, reigns one year, 95; Ethelfleda, his daughter, 263.
——— Bernulf, king of, supplants Ceolwulf, and is conquered by Egbert, 95; killed by the East Angles, 95, 107.
——— Ludecan, king of, reigns two years, and is overthrown by the East Angles, 95, 96, 107.
——— Wihtlaf (Withlacus), king of, reigns 13 years, tributary to Egbert, 96, 107; grandfather of S. Wistan, 263.

Mercia, Berhtulf, king of, reigns 13 years, expelled by the Danes, 96.
—— Burhred, king of, marries Ethelswitha and goes on pilgrimage to Rome, 96; dies there and is buried at the school of the English, 96.
—— Ceolwulf, king of, set up by the Danes, 96.
Merefin, son of Merewald, 78.
Merelinch, estate of Glastonbury at, 38, 171, 172.
Merewald, son of Penda, father of S. Mildred, 78, 267.
Merovæus, ancestor of the Frank kings, 70.
Mesopotamia, Edessa in, 432; adheres to Baldwin, 432.
Metrosi, porta, at Rome, 406.
Metz, S. Arnulf, bishop of, 71.
Mevania (Anglesey), 318, 376.
Mice, curious story about, 344.
Michael, patriarch of Alexandria, 425.
Michael, several emperors of Constantinople named, 276, 412, 413.
Milan, the Ambrosian rite at, 383; conference proposed at, 505; hostility of Henry V. to, 509.
Milburga, S., of Wenlock, daughter of Merewald, 78, 267.
Mildritha, S., the abbess, buried at S. Augustine's, 78, 267.
Milex, burial place of, at Rome, 408.
Milo, of Gloucester, earl of Hereford. See Hereford.
Milton, Mideltun, abbey, relics deposited by Ethelstan at, 155.
Mineriis, Gilbert de, contests the rights of the abbey of Gloucester, 521, 522.
Minorca, visited by Sigurd of Norway, 486.
Modestus, patriarch of Jerusalem, 424.
Molbius, pons, the Milvian bridge at Rome, 404.
Molendinis, castle of, 290.
Molendinum Herle, 287.
Molesme, Stephen Harding becomes a monk at, 381; conduct of the monks of, 384.

Mons Aericus, Karloman dies at, 112.
Mollo, brother of Caedwalla, burned in Kent, 17; his Wer-gild, 17, 34.
Mollo, king of Northumbria. See Northumbria.
Mons Celius, the seven sleepers on, 275.
Mont Cenis, Charles the Bald crosses the pass, 112.
Montdidier, Robert, count of, 139.
Monte Cassino, Karloman tonsured at, 71; Desiderius, abbot of, 325, 326.
Montfort, Hugh of, chief captain of duke William, 290.
Montgomery, Ernulf of, banished with Robert of Belesme, 473.
Montgomery, Robert of. See Belesme.
Montgomery, Roger of, spies out the force of Geoffrey Martel, 288.
Montgomery, Roger of, joins in the rebellion against William Rufus, 360; his head-quarters at Shrewsbury, 361; submits, 361; his sons, 460, 472, 473.
Montgomery, Philip of, a clerk, prowess of, 460, 461.
Montpellier, William of, a nobleman of the province of Toulouse, promotes the succession of the child William, son of Raymond, 458, 459; sends a porcupine to Henry I., 485; conquers the Balearic isles, 486.
Montpellier, merchants from, come to Ascalon, 457.
Mont S. Michel, William and Robert besiege their brother Henry in, 364, 365; the castle belonged to Henry in his earlier years, 478.
Morcar, put to death by Ethelred at Oxford, 213.
Morcar, son of Elfgar, 246, 281; defends Northumbria against Tostig, 281; comes to London after the battle of Stamford Bridge, 307, 310, 311; his fate, 311.
—— Robert, count of, brother of the Conqueror, 334.
—— William, count of, inherits Cornwall, but rebels because he is refused the earldom of Kent, 473; taken prisoner

Mortain, William, count of *cont.*
at Tenchebrai, 475 ; and imprisoned for life, 475.
———— Stephen, count of. *See* Stephen, king of England.
Mortain, the county refused by the empress to Stephen's children, 579 ; the castle of, taken by Earl Robert, 592.
Mortimer, castle of, defeat of the French by the Normans at, 290.
Mortimer, Roger, the bishop of Salisbury refuses to allow him to stay at Malmesbury, 553.
Moses, the rock struck by, visited by Baldwin, 442.
Mowbray, Robert, kills king Malcolm, 309 ; joins in the first rebellion against William Rufus, 360, 366 ; rebels a second time, and is imprisoned for life, 372.
Mowinus, Ralph, servant of duke Robert of Normandy, 212.
Murchard, king of Ireland, his relations with Henry I., 484, 485.

N.

Nantes, curious story of two clerks of, 294, 295.
Narbonne, acquired by Raymond of S. Giles, 456.
Narcissus, patriarch of Jerusalem, 424.
Neapolis, Nablous, the patriarch Joseph buried at, 441.
Nemesius, burial place of, at Rome, 407, 408.
Nemetum, the ancient name of Speyer, 235.
Nereus, and Achilleus, their burial place at Rome, 407.
Newark, castle of, fortified by bishop Alexander of Lincoln, 547 ; extorted from him by Stephen, 549.

New-forest, creation of the, 332 ; fatal accidents to the royal house in, 332, 333.
Nicea, duke Robert of Normandy dies at, 211, 333, 425 ; the Crusaders approach, 401 ; besieged, 413 ; surrendered to Alexius, 413, 414 ; capture of, 425.
Nicea, the council of, 503.
Nicephorus, patriarch of Jerusalem, 425.
Nicephorus, emperor of Constantinople, 412.
Nicephorus, Phocas, emperor of Constantinople, 412.
Nicephorus, Botaniates, emperor of Constantinople, 413.
Nicolas II., pope, bishop of Florence, 244, 276.
Nicolas II., king of Denmark, 320.
Nicomedes, burial place of, at Rome, 405.
Nigel, viscount of the Côtentin, 286, 287.
Nimrod, founder of the Assyrian Babylon, 428.
Noah, West Saxon pedigree traced to, 121 ; his son born in the ark, *ib.*
Nola, mount, burial place of S. Tatiana, on, 408.
Norfolk, included in East Anglia, 101.
Normandy, given to Rollo, 116, 137 ; dukes of ; *see* William, Richard, Robert.
Normandy, a double bodied woman seen in, 259.
Normandy, question about the royal touch in, 273.
Northampton, fealty sworn to the empress Matilda at, 534 ; illness of Stephen at, 591.
Northamptonshire, included in Mercia, 101.
Northumberland, earl of. *See* Mowbray, Tostig, Siward.
Northumbria, Ida, king of, first of the Northumbrian kings who is known, 10, 11 ; establishes his kingdom, 44 ; his character and descent, 44, 45 ; his son Ethelric, 46 ; he was ancestor of the house of Deira, 50.
———— Alla, king of, succeeds Ida, 45 ; connexion of, with the story of S.

Northumbria, Alla, king of—*cont.*
Gregory, *ib.*; of different descent from Ida, 46; his son Edwin, 48; he was ancestor of the Bernician dynasty, 50.

——— Ethelric, king of, succeeds Alla, 46.

——— Ethelfrith, king of, son of Ethelric, 46; his reign described by Bede, 46, 47; conquers Edan, king of Scots, at Degsastan, 47; and the Britons at Chester, 47; massacres the monks of Bangor, 47; defeated by Redwald, 48, 97; banishes Edwin, 48; his death, marriage, and family, *ib.*

——— Edwin, king of, son of Alla, takes refuge with Redwald in East Anglia, 48; his life attempted by Cwichelm, 22; he succeeds Ethelfrith, and governs East Anglia and all Britain except Kent, 49; marries Ethelburga, daughter of Eadbald, and becomes a Christian, *ib.*; his wise government, defeat by Penda, and death, 50, 76; he persuaded the king of the East Angles to be baptized, 97.

——— Eanfrith, king of, son of Ethelfrith, succeeds in Bernicia, 50; and Osric in Deira, 50; overthrown by Chedwalla, the British king, 51; their apostasy, 51.

——— Oswald, king of, son of Ethelfrith, 48, 50; succeeds, 51; defeats Chedwalla, *ib.*; destroys idolatry, 51; his piety, 52; he interprets S. Aidan's sermons, 52; his other virtues, *ib.*; his miracles and relics, 53; his incorruptible arm, 52; translated to Bardney, 53; and to Gloucester, 54, 136; his sanctity, 260.

——— Oswy, king of, son of Ethelfrith, 48, 50; rules in Bernicia, Oswin in Deira, 54; Oswin slain by Oswy, 55; Oswy overcomes Penda, 55, 97; the saints of his reign, 56; makes Peada king of the Southern Mercians, 177; persuades the king of the East Saxons to be baptized, 99.

Northumbria, Egfrith, king of, the younger son of Oswy, succeeds, 56; his dealings with Wilfrid, 56; conquers the Irish, and falls in battle with the Picts, 57.

——— Aldfrith, king of, succeeds Ecgfrith, 57; his illegitimacy, *ib.*; his studies in Ireland, *ib.*; his dealings with Wilfrid, *ib.*; his kingdom limited by the Picts, 58; his wife Kineburga, 78.

——— Osred, king of, son of Aldfrith, succeeds, and is killed, 58; his vicious life noted by Alcuin, 81.

——— Kenred, king of, succeeds Osred, 58.

——— Osric, king of, succeeds Kenred, 58.

——— Ceolwulf, Chelwulf, king of, succeeds Kenred, 58; to him Bede dedicated his history, 58; he becomes a monk at Lindisfarne and is buried near S. Cuthbert, 67.

——— Eadbert (Egbert), king of, succeeds, 67; he governs with the help of his brother the archbishop, *ib.*; becomes a monk, 74.

——— Osulf, Oswulf, king of, son of Eadbert, succeeds, and is slain, 74.

——— Mollo, king of, reigns eleven years and is slain, 74.

——— Alcred, king of, reigns ten years and is deposed, 74.

——— Ethelbert or Ethelred, king of, son of Mollo, succeeds, 74; and is deposed, 74; is restored, 74, 75; mentioned by Alcuin in his letters, 75; the last powerful king, 75; letter of Alcuin to, 73.

——— Alfwold, king of, succeeds on Ethelred's deposition, 74; slain and buried at Hexham, 74.

——— Osbert, king of, contemporary with Alfred, expelled and restored, 124.

——— Sihtric, king of, son-in-law of king Edward, 136, 142; dies, 142; Anlaf, his son, *ib.*, 146, 147.

Norway, Harold, king of, sends an embassy to Ethelstan, 149.

Norway, history of the kings of, 317–320; men of, join the crusade, 399.
Norwich, see of, removed from Thetford, 101, 353, 385, 386; earl Ralph takes ship at, 314; the headquarters of Roger Bigot, 361.
Norwich, bishop of, Herbert Losinga, his offences and repentance, 385, 386; removes his see to Norwich, 353, 385, 386; accused of falsehood by the pope, 492.
Nottinghamshire, included in Mercia, 101.
Novara, reduced by Henry V., 509.
Numentana, the fifth gate of Rome, 405.
Nutegareshalle, Wulfmar of, 273.

O.

Octavian, the pope, 168.
Octavian, the emperor, treasures of, 198, 199.
Odilo, of Cluny, 515.
Odo, archbishop of Canterbury. *See* Canterbury.
Odo, son of king Robert of France, 226, 227; put in command of an army to invade Normandy, 290.
Odo, the earl, kinsman of the Confessor, placed at the head of his fleet, 243.
Odo, bishop of Ostia, pope Urban II., 325, 326.
Odo, bishop of Bayeux. *See* Bayeux.
Odo, abbot of Cluny, 515.
Offa, king of Mercia. *See* Mercia.
Oht (Octa), king of Kent. *See* Kent.
Oht (Octa), brother of Hengest, 44.
Olaf (Analafus), baptism of, 188; driven out of Norway by Canute and slain, 221.
Olaf (Analafus), kings of Norway named, 318; and of Denmark, 319, 320.
Optatius, S., his burial place at Rome, 407.

Ordgar, father of queen Elfrida, 178, 180; ealdorman of Devon, 179.
Ordmer, father of Egelfleda the Fair, 180.
Orestes, patriarch of Jerusalem, 425; uncle of the calif Hakem, *ib.*
Orkney islands, visited by the German invaders of Britain, 10; subject to Edwin, 50; subdued by Magnus of Norway, 318, 376.
Orkney, Paul, earl of, sends wild animals to Henry's menagerie at Woodstock, 485.
Orleans, monastery of S. Maximin at, 195; vision of the bishop of, 256.
Orne, river (Olna), 287.
Orontes, the river of Antioch, 416.
Orosius, translated by Alfred, 132.
Osbern, biographer of Dunstan, 166; his skill in music, 389.
Osbern, brother of Sweyn, king of Denmark, 319.
Osbert, ealdorman of the Mercians, addressed by Alcuin, 73; extract from a letter to, 94.
Osceg, a Danish king, killed at Ashendown, 123.
Osfrith, ambassador from Norway to Ethelstan, 149.
Osred, king of Northumbria. *See* Northumbria.
Osric, a West Saxon leader, avenges Cynewulf, 42.
Osric, king of Northumbria. *See* Northumbria.
Ostensa, Ostiensis, a gate and road at Rome, 407, 408.
Ostgitha, Osthritha, wife of Ethelred of Mercia, 53, 79; translates S. Oswald, 53.
Ostia, Odo, bishop of, pope Urban II. 325, 326.
Ostia, Leo, bishop of, 504.
Ostia, John, bishop of, 531, 532.
Oswald, king of Northumbria. *See* Northumbria.

Oswald, a West Saxon prince, opposed to Ethelhard, 39.
Oswald, archbishop of York. See York.
Oswen, her piety towards S. Edmund, 265.
Oswin, king. See Northumbria.
Oswulf, king of Northumbria. See Northumbria.
Otbert, his story of the miracle at S. Magnus' in Saxony, 203, 204.
Otbert, count Palatine, 509.
Otranto (Hydruntinus), bishop of, 504.
Otto I., emperor, 72; marries a sister of Ethelstan, 117, 137, 149.
Otto III., emperor, promotes Gerbert, 196.
Otuel, brother of the earl of Chester, 497.
Ovid, quoted, 48, 194, 293.
Oxford, assembly of witan under Ethelred at, 213; church of S. Frideswide at, 213; Harold dies at, 228; council held by Stephen at, in which the bishops are arrested, 548, 552; the empress at, 574; visited by earl Robert at, 579; she keeps her court at, 583; town of, burned, 593; the empress besieged in, 593; her forces set out to rescue her, 595; she escapes from, to Wallingford, 596.
Oxfordshire, a part of Mercia, 101; subdued by Sweyn, 208.
Oximensis, pagus (Hiesmes), 291.
Ozias, king of Judah, 252.

P.

Pallas, son of Evander, discovery of his body, 258, 259.
Palling, the husband of Gunhildis, sister of Sweyn, 207.
Palumbus, wonderful story of the priest, 257, 258.
Pamphilus, burial place of, at Rome, 405.
Pamphylia, in the hands of the Saracens, 394.
Pancras, S., gate of, at Rome, 408.
Pancras, S., church of, at Lewes, 513.
Papias, burial place of, at Rome, 405.
Pardulf, Hugh, taken prisoner at Arques, 289.
Paris, devastated by the Danes, 127; legendary trial of duke William at, 161.
Parthenius, S., burial place of, at Rome, 407.
Paschal II., pope, his struggle with Henry IV., 343; encourages Henry I. in his interference in Normandy, 474; letters of, on the question of investitures, 489, 490, 491, 492; his controversy with the emperor Henry V., 498, seq.; letters on this controversy, 499, 500, 501; crowns the emperor, 501; recognises his dignity and repudiates the act, 501, 503; dies 504.
Paschasius, Radbert, stories on the Eucharist from, 341, 342.
Paternus, relics of, obtained by Ethelstan, 154, 155.
Patheneberge, property of Glastonbury at, 171.
Patrick, legend of his visit to Cornwall and Glastonbury, 26, 27.
Paul, burial place of, at Rome, 405, 408.
Paul, saint, at Antioch, 416.
Paul, of Samosata, 435.
Paulina, burial place of, at Rome, 405.
Paulinus, legend of his visit to Glastonbury, 28; archbishop of York. See York.
Paulinus, burial place of, at Rome, 408.
Paulus, burial place of, at Rome, 405, 408.
Paulus, diaconus, his history of the Lombards, 486.
Pavia, Ethelswitha dies at, 96; murder of Anschetil at, 161; relics brought to Coventry from, 224; men of, oppose the emperor Henry V., 509.

INDEX. 647

Peada, king of Mercia. *See* Mercia.
Penda, king of Mercia. *See* Mercia.
Penn, battle against the Britons at, 22.
Penn, near Gillingham, battle at, 215.
Perche, the countess of, lost in the great shipwreck, 497.
Peregrinus, archbishop of Cologne, 204.
Pershore, miracles of S. Eadburga at, 269.
Persia, Chosdroes, king of, 424.
Persia, the sultan of, sends aid to the Turks at Antioch, 419.
Peter, Saint, his chair at, Antioch, 416.
Peter, Damian, 202.
Peter, burial place of, at Rome, 406.
Peter, the hermit, leader of a crusade, 401; attempts to negotiate with Kerbogha 419.
Peter, cardinal of S. Chrysogonus, 531, 533.
Peterborough, monastery of, 166; abbot of, 209.
Peterborough, Turold, abbot of, 351.
Petronilla, burial place of, at Rome, 407.
Petronius, burial place of, at Rome, 407.
Pevensey, castle of, taken by William Rufus, 362.
Philip, Saint, legend of his visit to Britain, 24.
Philip, patriarch of Jerusalem, 424.
Philip I., king of France, 140; succeeds under the guardianship of Baldwin of Flanders, 228, 291; his adultery, 293; his wife a daughter of Robert Friso, 315; intrigues with Robert Curthose, 332, 363; insults the Conqueror, 336; excommunicated at the council of Clermont, 393; his brother joins the crusade, 400; his penitence and death, 479; an unseemly pun of his, 479.
Philip, a saint, his burial place at Rome, 405.
Philip, the clerk, son of Roger of Montgomery, 460, 461.
Philippicus, emperor of Constantinople, 412.
Phocas, emperor of Constantinople, 412.

Piacenza, subdued by Henry V., 509.
Picts, subject to Edwin, 50; Ecgfrith killed in battle against them in Northumbria, 58.
Pilton, estate of Glastonbury at, 37, 38, 172.
Pipin, son of Ansegis, mayor of the palace of Austrasia, rules in the name of king Theoderic, 70, 71; his pedigree, 71; his son Charles Martel, 71.
Pipin, son of Charles Martel, crowned at S. Denys, 71; compels Desiderius to do justice to the pope, *ib*. his sons, *ib*.
Pipin, son of Lewis the Pious, 110.
Pipin, son of Pipin, deprived of his dominions and tonsured, 170; escapes and takes part in the war of his uncles, 111; betrayed and exiled, 110.
Pisa, men of, recover Corsica and Sardinia from the Saracens, 92; compact of, with Baldwin of Jerusalem, 444; assist in the conquest of Tripoli, 459; resist Henry V. in Italy, 509.
———— Daimbert of, becomes patriarch of Jerusalem, 436, 437.
Pisidia, Antioch in, 415.
Plato, quotation from, 467, 520.
Plaiseiz, castle of, in Normandy, taken by earl Robert, 592.
Plegild, the priest, has a vision of the Eucharist, 341.
Plegmund, archbishop of. *See* Canterbury.
Pliny, his description of the Porcupine, 485.
Poelt, estate of Glastonbury at, 37.
Poictiers, William Rufus proposes to keep Christmas at, 379; and to get a mortgage on the county, 379.
Poictiers, Peter, bishop of, persecuted by William VII., 510, 511; verses on, 511, 512.
Poictou, William V., count of, captured by Geoffrey Martel, 287; who marries his step mother, 288; his brother, Guy, 290.
———— William VII., the Crusader, 379; ruined by the craft of Alexius, 401; his crusade of 1102, 447, 448, 458, 510; his follies and vices, 510, 511.

Policamus, burial place of, at Rome, 407.
Polion, burial place in, at Rome, 408.
Ponthieu, war of Lewis IV. of, 139; adventures of Harold in, 279.
Ponthieu, counts of. *See* Isambard, Guy.
Pontianus, burial place of, at Rome, 407.
Pontius, son of Bertram of Toulouse, count of Tripoli, 459.
Pont l'Arche, William of, treasurer of Henry I., adheres to Stephen, 538.
Populonia, bishop of, 504.
Porciniana, the Pincian gate at Rome, 404.
Port, Adam de, 521; H. de, 522.
Portland, castle of, taken by earl Robert, 595.
Portsmouth, Robert of Normandy lands at, 471.
Portus, gate of, at Rome, 408.
Portus, cardinal bishop of, 501, 504, 531, 532.
Potentiana, S., her burial place at Rome, 405.
Præneste, cardinal bishop of, 504, 531, 532.
Prailius, patriarch of Jerusalem, 424.
Pratellum (Preaux), founded by Roger of Beaumont, 482.
Praxedes, saint, burial place of, at Rome, 405.
Primus, burial place of, at Rome, 408.
Prisca, burial place of, at Rome, 405.
Processus, burial place of, at Rome, 408.
Protus, S., his burial place at Rome, 405.
Provence, Raymond, count of, invites Bohemond to the council of Clermont, 453.
Ptolemais, Accaron, Acre, 440, 447.
Ptolemy, the astronomer, 194.
Publius, patriarch of Jerusalem, 424.
Pucklechurch, murder of king Edmund at, 159.
Puy, Adhemar, bishop of, 398, 400, 420, 421.
Pybba, father of Penda, king of Mercia, 76.
Pythagoras, 193; the soul of Euphorbus migrated into, 374.

Q.

Quartus, burial place of, at Rome, 407.
Quenburga, sister of Ine, 35, note.
Quendreda, sister and murderer of S. Kenelm, 95, 262.
Quercy. *See* Cahors.
Quintinus, burial place of, at Rome, 407.
Quintus, burial place of, at Rome, 407.
Quirinus, burial place of, at Rome, 405, 407.

R.

Raculf, Berhtwald, abbot of, 29.
Ralph, archbishop. *See* Canterbury.
Ralph, Mowinus, servant of duke Robert of Normandy, 212.
Ralph, earl of Hereford, 241, 243.
Ralph, the murderer of count Gilbert, 286, 287.
Ramsbury, an ancient see of, in Wiltshire, 100; bishop of, consecrated, 140; Brihtwold, bishop of, his dream, 272.
Ramsey, Felix, the apostle of the East Angles, buried at, 97; monastery of, restored by S. Oswald, 167; the Kentish martyrs translated to, 262.
Ramsey, Elfwin, abbot of, 351; Herbert Losinga, abbot of, 385, 386.
Ramula, description of, 421; arrival of the Crusaders at, 421; battles at, 443, 445, 447, 448, 480; garrison kept at, 443.
Rannulf, "præfectus," betrays Pipin, 110.
Rannulf, viscount of Bayeux, 286, 287.
Rannulf, Flambard. *See* Durham, bishops of.
Ratisbon, bishop of, 509.
Ravenna, Gerbert, archbishop of, 196.
——— Wibert, archbishop of, 323, 343, 380, 390, 393.

INDEX.

Ravenna, the gate of Rome leading to, 404.
Ravenna, submits to Henry V., 509.
Raymond, count of S. Giles, goes on crusade, 400; refuses to do homage to Alexius, 401; crosses Asia Minor, 414; remains in Antioch during the battle, 420; his forces left at Antioch are expelled by Bohemond, 421; besieges the Tower of David at Jerusalem, 426; spares the Ethiopian guards at the tower, 427, 428; has command at Laodicea, 436; furnishes Baldwin with supplies, 436; his brother, Hugh of Lesignan, 447; sketch of his life, 455–459; his parents, William and Almodis, 455; his son, Bertram, 456; his failures to obtain a principality at Antioch or Jerusalem, 457; or Ascalon, 457, 458; at Laodicea, 458; he builds the Pilgrims' castle, 458; attempts the conquest of Tripoli and dies, 458; his successors, 459.
Reading, Cluniac monastery founded by Henry I. at, 489; Hugh, abbot of, archbishop of Rouen, 536, 543, 558; Edward, abbot of, in attendance on the empress, 573.
Reading, burial of king Henry I. at, 539.
Rebecca, burial place of, 441.
Recared, king of the Goths in Spain, 193.
Redvers, Richard of, is faithful to Henry I., 471.
Redwald, king of the East Angles. See East Angles.
Reggio, bishop of, 504.
Reinold, son of Gurmund, 158.
Reginald, son of Henry I. made earl of Cornwall, 562.
Reiner, son of Redwald, killed, 48.
Reiner, cardinal, 499.
Reiner, bishop of Hereford, consecrated, 493.
Remigius, S., power of his prayers, 115.
Rennes, monastery of S. Melanius at, 297.
Repton, Kineberd buried at, 48.
Rheims, archbishop of, sends Grimbald to Alfred, 130; Gerbert made archbishop of, 196.
Rhine, the river, 400.

Rhodes, not yet conquered by the Saracens, 92.
Riebert, a heathen, kills king Eorpwald, 97.
Richard I., duke of the Normans, his quarrel with Ethelred, 191, 192, 193; his daughter Emma, 191; his benefactions to Fecamp, 191.
Richard II., duke of the Normans, Ethelred asks his aid, 209; he entertains Emma and her sons, 210; his character and connexion with Fecamp, 210, 211; his brother Robert, ib.; his wife Judith, 211; marries Emma to Canute, 218, 219; his son Robert, 211, 278; his grandson Guy of Burgundy, 286.
Richard III., duke of the Normans, reigns one year, 211.
Richard, son of the Conqueror, killed in the New Forest, 332.
Richard, son of Robert Curthose, killed in the New Forest, 333.
Richard, son of Henry I., lost in the great shipwreck, 497.
Richildis, wife of Baldwin of Flanders, 315; offered in marriage to William Fitz-Osbern, 315.
Ripon, ancient see of, 101, 353.
Ris, king of the Welsh, subdued by Harold, 237.
Risus, cardinal, 499.
Riulf, story of, 160, 161.
Riwallo, brother of Griffin, king of Wales, 280.
Robert, count of Montdidier, ancestor of the kings of France, 139.
Robert FitzHaimon, 286; story told him by a monk before the death of William Rufus, 377, 378.
Robert, king of France, 140, 196; dies, 226; contest about the succession, 226, 227.
Robert, Friso, count of Flanders. See Flanders.
Robert, count of Mortain. See Mortain.
Robert, son of Godwin, his crusade and martyrdom, 310, 318, 449.

Robert, duke of Normandy, succeeds Richard III. with some suspicion of poison, 211; goes on pilgrimage, 211, 285; and dies at Nicea, 211; intended to place Emma's children on the throne, 218; father of William the Conqueror, 212, 278; aided Henry of France in obtaining the crown, 227.

Robert, Curthose, son of William I., 316, 331; his intrigues against his father in Italy, 332; death of his son in the New Forest, 333; has Normandy by his father's bequest, 337; absent from his father's funeral, 338; his mortgage of of Normandy, 332, 371; his claims on England asserted by the rebels against William Rufus, 360; William attacks him in revenge, 363; he seeks the aid of the king of France, but makes peace and joins Rufus in attacking Henry, 363, 364; story of his good nature, 365; negotiated peace between William and the Scots, 366; starts on the crusade, 402; spends the winter in Italy, 409; does homage to Alexius, 413; attacked in Asia Minor, 414; commands a division at the battle of Antioch, 420; advances on Jerusalem, 421; takes part in the capture, 427; is at the battle of Ascalon, 429; sketch of his youth, and account of his nickname, 459; his prowess at Antioch, 460; kills Kerbogha, 460; refuses the kingdom of Jerusalem, 461; returns to Europe, *ib.*; his marriage, the death of his wife, and fate of his son, 461; his character, 461, 462; his wars with Henry I., 461; his early treatment of him, 468, 558; he imprisons him at Rouen, 468; besieges him at Mont. S. Michel, 469; returns home and forms a party against him, 471; lands at Portsmouth and sells peace, 471, 472; his misgovernment, 474; taken at Tenchebrai, 475; his imprisonment for life, 463; his son William, 479.

Robert, earl of Gloucester, son of Henry I., dedicatory letter of our author to, 355;

Robert, Earl of Gloucester—*cont.* his character, 356; another address to him, 518–520; a further dedication, 525; his marriage with Mabilia, 529; swears fealty to Matilda, 529, 530; present at his father's death, 536; continues in Normandy, 538; arrives in England, 539; does conditional homage to Stephen, 541; returns to Normandy and escapes the snares of Stephen, 543; Stephen swears not to molest him, 543, 544; his plans against him, 544; renounces his homage, 545; is ordered by the pope to keep his oath to Henry, 545; his property seized, 546; he comes with Matilda to England, 555; sends her to Arundel and then to Bristol, 555; his attitude at the opening of the war, 561; makes his brother earl of Cornwall, 562; has a conference on peace at Bath, 564; is summoned to the aid of the earl of Chester, his son-in-law, 569, 570; wins the battle of Lincoln and takes the king prisoner, 571, 572; acts as surety for the empress, 573; attends her at London, 578; acts as mediator between her and the legate, 579, 580; sends his sister away from Winchester, but is himself captured, 581, 582; negotiations for their exchange, 583; his son William, 583; recapitulation of his acts and merits, 585, 586; honourably treated by the queen, 587; activity of his wife, 587, 588; he resists all attempts to bring him to the king's side, 589, 590; he goes to France to invite the count of Anjou to England, 591; he assists in the capture of the Norman castles, 592; brings the boy Henry to England, 593; returns home, 594; takes Wareham and other castles and proposes to relieve Oxford, 595, 596.

Rochester, see of, continues under the obedience of Canterbury, 86, 100, 352; attack of Ethelred upon, 186, 187.
——— Paulinus, bishop of, 28, 67.
——— Siward, bishop of, 351.

Rochester, on the Medway, 216; castle of, besieged and taken by William Rufus, 360–362; the earl of Gloucester brought from, to Bristol, 583; having been honourably treated by the queen at, 587.

Rodulf, son of Hugh, 192.

Rogantina S., her burial place at Rome, 405.

Roger, earl of Hereford, son of William Fitz Osbern, conspires against the Conqueror, 313.

Roger, of Apulia, son of Robert Guiscard, called Marsupium, 452, 453.

Roger, son of Richard, governor of Antioch, 452, 455; slain, 452, 455.

Roger, the Poictevin, son of Roger Montgomery, banished, 473.

Roger, the chancellor, son of bishop Roger of Salisbury, 549.

Rohbod, prior of Dol, his letter to Ethelstan, 155.

Roland, the song of, sung before the battle of Hastings, 302.

Rollo, besieges Chartres, 138; occupies Rouen before the death of Charles the Bald, 138; receives Normandy and the hand of Gisela from Charles the Simple, 116, 137, 138; insults the king, 139; returns to Rouen and dies, 139; his son William, 160.

Romania, part of Asia Minor, so called, 414.

Romanus, saint, his burial place at Rome, 406.

Romanus, emperors of Constantinople named, 412.

Romanus, Diogenes, emperor of Constantinople, 413.

Rome, pilgrimage of Caedwalla to, 33; and of Ine, 39; Ceolfrith sets out for, 60; invitation to Bede from, 62, 63; pilgrimage of Kenred to, 79; coronation of Charles at, 72; Aldhelm brings a charter from, 79; pilgrimage of Burhred and Ethelswitha to, 96; the school of the English at, 96, 109, 153; visit of archbishop Ethelbeard to, 86,

Rome—*cont.*
89; Alfred anointed at, 109, 124; visit of Ethelwulf to, 109; his benefactions to, 118, 136; Alfred sends alms to, 130; transactions about the burial of Elfred at, 153; proceedings on the rights of Glastonbury at, 172; and on the quarrel of Ethelred and Richard, 191; legendary stories about, 196, 201, 202, 203.
———— visit of Canute to, 221–224.
———— grief of, for Henry III., 235.
———— legendary stories about, 246, 256; condition of, under Gregory VI., 246, 247.
———— martyrdom of S. Kenelm revealed at, 263.
———— Gregory VII., expelled from, 325; miracles of the Eucharist at, 341.
———— Urban II. expelled from, 390.
———— verses of Hildebert of le Mans about, 402, 403.
———— description of the gates and sanctuaries of, 404–408.
———— the treasures of, carried by Constans to Syracuse, 411, 412.
———— the first city in the world, 416.
———— adventure of Godfrey of Bouillon at, 432.
———— struggles of the pope and emperor about investitures, 498, *seq.*
———— Henry V. crowned at, 501.
———— reforms by Calixtus II. at, 507, 508.
———— schism at, on the death of Honorius II., 530, 531–533.
———— Stephen forbids the bishops to go to, 554.

Romsey, Christina, a nun at, 278; queen Matilda brought up at, 493.

Romulus, founded the Asylum at Rome, 203.

Ros, Gawain's grave discovered in, 342; Flemings planted by Henry I. in, 477.

Rosanus, Greek bishop, 504.

Rothasia, Rohasia, the name of Edessa, 435.

Rouen, act done at, 102; the remains of duke Robert's ships still to be seen at, 217; illness of the Conqueror at, 336;

Rouen—*cont.*
 his death at, 337; negotiation of William Rufus with the Jews at, 371; Henry imprisoned at, 468; murder of Conan the traitor at, 469; continues faithful to Robert, 462; ravaged by Lewis VI., 481.
——— Robert, archbishop of, his character, 211.
——— Malger, archbishop of, 327.
——— Maurilius, archbishop of, 327.
——— William, archbishop of, 480, 492.
——— Hugh, archbishop of, 536; was prior of Lewes and abbot of Reading, *ib.*; his letter on the death of Henry I., 536, 537; marries the empress to Geoffrey of Anjou, 530; acts as Stephen's surety to earl Robert, 543; takes the king's part against the bishops, 550; his advice, 554.

Ruald, abbot of Hyde, Winchester, 352.

Rudolf, king of Burgundy, negotiates with Canute, 222.

Rudolf of Swabia, anti-Cæsar to Henry IV., 325.

Rufina, saint, her burial place at Rome, 404.

S.

S. Albans, monastery founded by Offa, 85; Frideric, abbot of, 352.

S. Carilef (S. Calais), William of. *See* Durham.

S. David's, pilgrimages to, 507.

S. David's, Menevia, S. David, bishop of, 27.
——— Bernard, bishop of, 522; his struggle with the bishop of Llandaff, 534; attends the empress at Winchester, 573.

S. Denys, Pipin crowned at, 71; Charles Martel buried at, 255.

S. Denys, near Southampton, 270.

S. Edmund's, Canute's foundation at, 220. *See* East Angles.
——— Baldwin, abbot of, 352.

S. George, arm of, the Archipelago, 394.

S. George of Ramlah, 421.

S. German's, see of, in Cornwall, 100.

S. Giles, Count Raymond of. *See* Raymond.

S. Hilary, Seithilaret, castle of, in Normandy, taken by earl Robert of Gloucester, 592.

S. Leufred, monastery of, in Normandy, 338.

S. Pancras. *See* Lewes.

S. Valery, William the Conqueror sails from, 299, 300; acquired by William Rufus from Robert, 363.

Sabina, Centius, cardinal bishop of, 499, 504.
——— Conrad, cardinal bishop of, 582.

Sachius (Isaac), emperor of Constantinople, 412.

Salaria, porta and Via, at Rome, 404, 405.

Salerno, Gelasius II. sails from, to Genoa, 506.

Salina, Aqua (Salvia?), at Rome, 408.

Salisbury, see of, 100, 352, 353.

Salisbury, Herman, bishop of, 352, 389.
——— Osmund, bishop of, 372, 375.
——— Roger, bishop of, his rise and character, 483; allowed by three archbishops to undertake secular office, 484; consecrated by S. Anselm, 493; his statement about Matilda's marriage, 530; joins the party of Stephen against Matilda, 538; is at Stephen's coronation, 539; his great influence and promotion of his nephews, 547, 559; his castles at Devizes and Sherborne, 547; he is arrested at Oxford and obliged to surrender them, 548, 549; accused in the council at Winchester, 552; his defence, 553; his death, 557; review of his ecclesiastical career, 558, 559, 560.

Salisbury, Wulfnoth, son of Godwin, imprisoned at, 245; the tower of the cathedral struck by lightning, 375; buildings of bishop Roger at, 484; royal castle at, fortified by bishop Roger, 547.

Salisbury, William of, a prisoner of earl Gilbert of Hertford, 587.
Salomontos, patriarch of Jerusalem, 425.
Samosata, joins Baldwin of Edessa, 435, 436; Paul of, 435.
Sampson, S., of Dol, 154.
Samuel, the prophet, relics of, at Constantinople, 413.
Sandwich, Canute lands at, 213; he devastates Kent from, 214.
Sansadolem, son of the governor of Antioch, sent to ask succours from the sultan, 417, 419.
Sapientia, S., burial place of, at Rome, 408.
Sapwic, estate of Glastonbury at, 38, 171, 172.
Saracens, driven from France by Charles Martel, 71, 255; their threatening attitude in the days of Boniface, 81; their conquests in the time of Alcuin, 92; their losses since, 92; war of Charles the Great with, 150; lose Spain, 193; Gerbert studies among them, 194; beset the way to Jerusalem, 211; their religion, 230; Sweyn, son of Godwin, killed by, 245; repressed in Spain, 337; their progress before the crusade, 395; carried the treasures of Rome to Alexandria after the capture of Syracuse, 412.
Sardinia, recovered from the Saracens by the Pisans, 92.
Saturnina, burial place of, at Rome, 405.
Saturninus, burial place of, at Rome, 405.
Saxons, foreigners visit the court of Edgar, 165.
Saxony, assigned to Lewis, son of Lewis of Bavaria, 111.
―――― miracle at the church of S. Magnus in, 203, 204.
Scandza, spoken of by Jordanes, 121.
Sceaf, ancestor of Egbert, 121.
Sceapwic, estate of Glastonbury at, 171, 172.
Sceldius, ancestor of Egbert, 121.
Sceorstan, battle at, 215.
Scipio Africanus, saying of, 488.

Scotland, under the Northumbrian kings, 101.
Scotland, ambassadors from, at the court of Charles the Great, 75; Stephen Harding studies in, 380.
―――― Edan, king of, defeated by Ethelfrith, 47.
―――― Constantine, king of, 147.
―――― Malcolm, king of, 158.
―――― Malcolm II., king of, 221.
―――― Kinad, king of, 165, 177.
―――― Malcolm III., king of. See Malcolm.
Scotlandus, abbot of S. Augustine's, 351.
Scots, oppressions of the Britons by the, 6, 7; defeated by Ethelstan at Brunanburh, 142, 143; failure of William Rufus in his attack on, 365; their zeal for the crusade, 399.
Scubilio, S., relics of, 154.
Sebbi, king. See East Saxons.
Sebert, king. See East Saxons.
Sebastian, saint, his burial place at Rome, 407.
Secunda, saint, her burial place at Rome, 404.
Seez, Ralph, abbot of, afterwards archbishop of Canterbury, 472, 517.
Seez, the bishop of, alone attends Stephen's court at London, 564.
Segor, or Zoar, visited by Baldwin, 442.
Seine, river, 127, 161, 290, 337, 400, 469.
Seleucus, king of Asia, founder of Antioch, 415.
Selred, king. See East Saxons.
Selsey, see of, continues under the obedience of Canterbury, 86; removed to Chichester, 100, 352, 353; monastery built by Wilfrid at, 100, 261.
Selsey, Bernege, bishop of, consecrated, 140.
―――― Alric, bishop of, 347.
―――― Stigand, bishop of, 244, note. See Chichester.
Semetrius, saint, his burial place at Rome, 405.
Semiramis, her extension of the Assyrian Babylon, 428.

A A 2

Senator, S., relics of, 154.
Seneca, quoted, 64.
Seneca, patriarch of Jerusalem, 424.
Sennes, burial place of, at Rome, 407.
Serantina, burial place of, at Rome, 405.
Sergius I., pope, baptizes Caedwalla, 33; his patronage of Aldhelm, 35, 560; his invitation of Bede to Rome, 62, 63.
Sergius, patriarch of Jerusalem, 425; another, ib.
Severus, the emperor, buried in Britain, 5; his wall, ib.
Seville, Leander and Isidore, archbishops of, 193; capital of the Saracens, 194.
Seward, king. See East Saxons.
Sewei e, estate of Glastonbury at, 36, 38.
Sexburga, queen of the West Saxons. See West Saxons.
Sexburga, abbess, 266.
Sexred, king of the East Saxons. See East Saxons.
Shaftesbury, nunnery founded by Alfred at, 131; Elfgiva, abbess of, 131; Edward buried at, 184, 185.
Sherborne, see of, removed to Salisbury, 100, 352, 353; Ethelbald buried at, 122; and Ethelbert, 122; Stephen Harding educated at, 380; castle of, built by Roger, 547; and extorted from him by Stephen, 549; abbey of, 559.
Sherborne, Aldhelm, bishop of, a monk of Malmesbury, 30; charter of Leutherius to, 30, 31; his character, books, and Latinity, 31, 35; his influence with Ine, 35; obtained a privilege for Malmesbury, 560; his eminence as a scholar, 68; brings a charter from Rome, 79; his book on Virginity, 35, 410; invoked by Ethelstan, 144; he buries his relations near the tomb of, 152, 163, 174.
———— Alhstan, bishop of, assists Ethelwulf in the conquest of Kent, 106; is one of his chief counsellors, 108; he appropriates Malmesbury to his see, 109; conspires against Ethelwulf, 117; mentioned in Ethelwulf's charter, 119.

Sherborne, Asser, bishop of, 131, 133.
———— Sigelm, bishop of, 130. See note 1.
———— Werstan, bishop of, consecrated, 140.
———— Edelsin, bishop of, 192.
———— Herman, bishop of, 351.
Shrewsbury, Hugh, earl of, killed in repelling invasion, 318, 376; castle of, fortified by Robert of Belesme, 472; surrendered, 472.
Shropshire, included in Mercia, 100; earldom of, given to queen Adela, 528.
Sichem, the patriarch Joseph buried at, 441.
Sicily, overrun by the Saracens, 92, 412; the countess of, marries king Baldwin, 451.
Sidon, siege of, 319; passed by the Crusaders, 421; men of, furnish Baldwin with provisions, 440; captured by Baldwin, 447; by Sigurd, 486.
Sidnacester, see of, 85, 86, 352; Eadulf, bishop of, 85.
Sidonius, Apollinaris, verse of, on S. Martin, 127.
Sienna, Geoffrey, bishop of, 504.
Sigebald, brother of king Sebert, 99.
Sigebert, king of the East Saxons. See East Saxons.
Sigebert, king of the East Angles. See East Angles.
Sigeferth, earl of Northumbria put to death by Ethelred; his widow marries Edmund Ironside, 213, 214.
Sigelm, called bishop of Sherborne, 130.
Sigeric, archbishop. See Canterbury.
Sighere, king of the East Saxons. See East Saxons.
Sigurd, king of Norway, goes on crusade, 319, 485; spends the winter in England, alarms the Balearic isles, loses a ship on the voyage, subdues the coast of Palestine, returns by Constantinople, and disappoints the emperor of his spoil, 486.
Sihtric. See Northumbria, kings of.
Silanus, S., burial place of, at Rome, 405.
Silvester I., pope, his basilica at Rome, 405.

INDEX. 655

Silvester II., pope. *See* Gerbert.
Simacas, patriarch of Jerusalem, 424.
Simeon, patriarch of Jerusalem, 424; another, 425.
Simeon, saint, his burial place at Rome, 408.
Simon, Magus, story of, 202.
Sion, Ermenfred, bishop of, legate in England, 328.
Sircurana, porta, a gate at Rome, 406.
Siward, earl of Northumbria, 237; puts down Macbeth, 237; attends a council at London, 242; his death, 245; his surname, 312; his son Waltheof, 311; was witness of the Confessor's grant to duke William, 302.
Siward, abbot of Abingdon, coadjutor of archbishop Eadsin, 239.
Siwinus, archbishop, 504.
Sixtus, saint, burial place of, at Rome, 407.
Sleaford, castle of, extorted by Stephen from bishop Alexander of Lincoln, 549.
Sledda, first king of the East Saxons, 98.
Sleswick, in the Anglia Vetus, 121.
Sodom, the site of, visited by Baldwin, 442.
Sofronius, two patriarchs of Jerusalem named, 424, 425.
Soldanus, explanation of the title, 417.
Soliman, defeats the Poictevin Crusaders in Asia Minor, 447, 448.
Solomon, quoted, 81; the Temple of, 422; gave the name to Jerusalem, 422.
Somerset, included in Wessex, 100; Eanulf, caldorman of, 117.
Sophia, saint, burial place of, at Rome, 407.
Sotheris, saint, burial place of, at Rome, 407.
Southampton, county of, in Wessex, 100; landing of Danes at, 122; again in the reign of Ethelred, 186; Ethelred sails from, for the Isle of Wight, 208; earl Robert of Gloucester proposes to land at, 594; faction of the "Vituli" at, 594, 595.

South Saxons, Ethelwalch, king of, defeated by Caedwalla, 83; receives the Isle of Wight from Wulfhere, 78.
———— Edric, king of, successor of Ethelwalch, 83.
Soweie, estate of Glastonbury at, 171, 172.
Spain, occupied by the Goths, 9; over-run by the Saracens, 81; recovered to some extent under Charles the Great, 92; condition of, in the time of Gerbert, 193, 194; victories of Alfonso of Gallicia in, 337; still in danger from the Saracens, 395.
Spes, saint, burial place of, at Rome, 408.
Speyer, Henry III., buried at, 235; Leo IX., called bishop of, 236.
Speyer, Bruno, bishop of, 500, 509.
Spiridion, relics of, at Constantinople, 413.
Stamford-bridge, battle of, 281.
Staffordshire, part of Mercia, 101.
Stauracius, emperor of Constantinople, 412,
Stephen, king of England, son of Stephen of Blois and Adela, 529; swears fealty to Matilda, 529, 538; claims the crown, is received at London and Winchester, obtains the king's treasures, 538; is crowned, 538, 539; his oath to the church, 538; goes into Northumberland to meet king David, 539; wastes the treasures of his uncle, 540; admits earl Robert's conditional homage, 541; his charter of liberties, 541, 542; ill kept by his ministers, 543; goes to Normandy, fails to catch earl Robert, and swears not to molest him, 543; returns home, 544; makes lavish grants, 544; Robert renounces his homage to him, 545; makes new earls, 545; orders the surrender of castles, 547; arrests the two bishops at Oxford, and compels them to surrender theirs, 548, 549; is summoned by the legate to a council at Winchester, 550; questions the right, and makes his answer by Aubrey de Vere, 551, 552; forbids the bishops to go to Rome, 554;

Stephen, king of England—*cont.*
occupies Malmesbury and besieges Trowbridge, 556, 557; fails to relieve Hereford, 557; his saying about bishop Roger, 559; the miseries of his reign, 561; refuses to make peace, 564; is induced to attack the earl of Chester without warning, 569; besieges Lincoln, 569, 570; is defeated and taken prisoner, 571, 572; delivered to the empress at Bristol, 572; declared by the legate to be a usurper and deposed, 575; the Londoners intercede for, 576, 577; exchanged for the earl, 582; complains to the prelates, 583; negotiations for his release, 587, 588; is ill at Northampton, 591; takes Wareham, burns Oxford, and besieges the empress in the castle there, 593; he refuses to relieve Wareham, 595.

Stephen, S., church of, at Rome, 408.
Stephen, prior of Cîteaux, 384.
Stephen III., pope, crowns Pipin at S. Denys, 71.
Stephen X., pope, 276.
Stermonius, ancestor of Egbert, 121.
Stigand, archbishop. *See* Canterbury.
Stow Maries, ecclesiastical foundation of Leofric at, 237.
Street, estate of Glastonbury at, 38, 171, 172.
Streneshall, or Whitby, S. Hilda at, 56; Ethelfleda at, 56.
Strephius, ancestor of Egbert, 121.
Sudeley, castle of, occupied by earl Robert, 562.
Suffolk, part of the kingdom of the East Angles, 101.
Sulpicius, S., his burial place at Rome, 407.
Surrey, part of Wessex, 100; subdued by Egbert, 107.
Sussex, a portion of Wessex, 100; subdued by Egbert, 107.
Sutri, the anti-pope Maurice flies to, and is captured at, 506, 507.
Swabia, Charles, king of, emperor, 112.

Sweden, Agatha, sister of the queen of, 218.
Sweden, subdued by Canute, 220, 221; by Magnus of Norway, 317.
Swelwes, a name on one of the Glastonbury pyramids, 25.
Sweyn, king of Denmark, invades England in revenge for Gunhildis, 207; beats Ethelred, 208, 209; his tyranny and death, 212.
Sweyn, son of Godwin, 245; commander in Herefordshire, 242; exiled to Flanders, 243; turns pirate, 245; killed by the Saracens, 245.
Sweyn, king of Denmark, his reign and successors, 317, 318; threatens England, 308.
Swithelm, king of the East Saxons. *See* East Saxons.
Swithred, king. *See* East Saxons.
Swithun, bishop of Winchester. *See* Winchester.
Syracuse, the emperor Constantine (Constans II.), dies at, 412; plundered by the Saracens, 412.
Syracuse, archbishop of, 504.

T.

Tambra, the river Tamar, 148.
Tancred, the nephew of Bohemond, 421; reaches Bethlehem, *ib.*; plunders Solomon's Temple, but surrenders his spoils, 427, 428; remains in Palestine when the other Crusaders leave, 430; joins in the election of Baldwin as king, 434; suggested by him as prince of Antioch, 438; his men at Haifa, 441; sets out for Antioch, 443; false intelligence sent from Joppa to, 446; entertains the Poictevin Crusaders at Antioch, 448; is lord

Tancred—*cont.*
of Laodicea, 454, 458; ruled Antioch after Bohemond, 455; dies soon after, 455; his widow marries Pontius of Tripoli, 459.
Tanea, Warin de, is at the battle of Antioch, 460; killed there, 461.
Tarsicius, saint, his burial place at Rome, 407.
Tarsus, the city of S. Paul, in Cilicia, secured by Baldwin, 434, 435; death of Hugh the Great at, 448.
Tatiana, saint, her burial place at Rome, 408.
Tavistock, Edwy, brother of Edmund Ironside, buried at, 218; Living, bishop of Crediton, abbot of, 221.
Tecla, saint, her burial place at Rome, 408.
Temple, of Solomon, 422, 443.
Tenchebrai, battle of, 475, 592; date of, 475.
Tenzo, cardinal, 499.
Terence, quoted, 295, 481, 561.
Terracina, 504.
Tetbald, brother of Ethelfrith, killed in battle, 47.
Tetius, ancestor of Egbert, 121.
Tewkesbury, Robert FitzHamon, a benefactor of, 475; Robert of Gloucester, also a benefactor of, 520.
————, Roger, abbot of, 573.
Thames, the river, 106, 216, 219, 228, 376, 489.
Thanet, assigned to the Saxons for habitation, 9; monastery founded in honour of the martyrs in, 16; occupied by the Danes, 122; monastery of S. Mildred in, 267.
Thaphnis, Zoan in Egypt, 429.
Theban legion, standard of, among Ethelstan's treasures, 150.
Theobald, count of Blois. *See* Blois.
Theoderic, king of the Franks under the tutelage of Pipin, 70.
Theodolus, S., his burial place at Rome, 405.

Theodora, empress of Constantinople, 412.
Theodorus, archbishop of Canterbury. *See* Canterbury.
Theodorus, patriarch of Jerusalem, 425.
Theodosius, the emperor, 412; crushes the pretender Maximus, 6.
Theodosius II., emperor of Constantinople, 412.
Theodosius III., emperor, 412.
Theodosius, patriarch of Jerusalem, 423, 425.
Theodred, bishop of London. *See* London.
Theophilus, patriarch of Jerusalem, 425.
Theophilus, emperor of Constantinople, 412.
Thessalonica, one limit of Robert Wiscard's conquests, 390; metropolis of Thessaly, 409.
Thessaly, crossed by the Crusaders, 409.
Thetbald, cardinal, 499.
Thetbald, the margrave, 509.
Thetford, see of, removed to Norwich, 101, 353, 385, 386, 387.
Thomas, saint, his churches in India, 130.
Thomas, two patriarchs of Jerusalem named, 425.
Thorney, monastery of, 166.
Thrace, crossed by the Crusaders, 409; described, 411.
Thunre, executioner of the Kentish martyrs, 261.
Thuringia, included in the dominions of Lewis the German, 111.
Tiber, river, 432.
Tiberias, visited by the Crusaders, 437; acquired by Baldwin I., 447; Hugh, lord of, sends succours to Joppa, 450.
Tiberius, emperors of Constantinople named, 412.
Tiburtina porta, at Rome, 406.
Tiburtius, saint, his burial place at Rome, 406.
Tiburtius, attests the election of Innocent II., as approved by the Bishop of Portus·

Tiburtius —*cont.*
533; the bishop's comment on him, *ib.*
Tidferth, bishop of Dunwich, 85.
Timotheus, burial place of, at Rome, 408.
Tiron, the order of, instituted by abbot Bernard, 512.
Tithings, institution of, ascribed to Alfred, 129.
Tobias, patriarch of Jerusalem, 424.
Toledo, the capital of Christian Spain, 193.
Tortosa, Tortuosa, plundered by the Crusaders in 1102, 448; taken by Raymond, 458.
Tosti, Tostig, son of Godwin, 245; earl of Northumbria, 245; deposed by Harold, 246; attempts to recover his earldom, 280, 281; killed at Stamford Bridge, 281, 310, 311; buried at York, 311.
Toulouse, Raymond of. *See* Raymond.
Toulouse, William, count of, father of Raymond, 455; his wife Almodis, 455; leaves Toulouse to his son William, 456.
Tours, Hildebert, archbishop of, 338, 402, 403.
——— John of, bishop of Bath and Wells, 387.
Tours, settlement of Alcuin at, 68; translation of S. Martin from, 127, 128; surrendered to Geoffrey Martel, 288.
Trajan, the emperor, 205, 409.
Transrhenani, the Austrasian Franks, 70.
Trent, bishop of, 500.
Trent, the river, 571.
Treves, Leo, bishop of, 191, 192.
Trifena, burial place of, at Rome, 406.
Trifenus, burial place of, at Rome, 407.
Tripoli, passed by the Crusaders, 421; furnishes supplies to Baldwin, 437; he comes from Laodicea to, 438; fights through the pass between Berytus and, 439; Raymond builds the castle of pilgrims as a check on, 458; the conquest of, nearly accomplished, 458; completed by his son Bertram, 459; his son Pontius succeeds him, 459.

Triveres, castle of, in Normandy, taken by earl Robert of Gloucester, 592.
Troja, in Italy, 504.
Trowbridge, castle of, besieged by Stephen, 556, 557.
Tudites, name of Charles Martel, 71.
Tunbridge, castle of bishop Odo at, taken by William Rufus, 362.
Turbessel, given up to Baldwin of Edessa, 435.
Turbessel, Jocelin of, ransoms Baldwin II., 452.
Turfrith, accompanies Godfrey, son of Sihtric, in his flight, 147.
Turgis, Turstene, son of, 192.
Turkill, the earl, one of the murderers of S. Elfege, 207; invites Sweyn to England, 207; has the earldom of East Anglia, 218; returns to Denmark, 219.
Turks, worship God, and Mahomet as his prophet, 230.
Turnus, Pallas killed by, 258.
Turstene, son of Turgis, 192.
Tusculum, bishop of, 504.
Tynemouth, Malcolm, king of Scots, buried at, 309; removed from, *ib.*
Tyre, passed by the Crusaders, 421; supplies Baldwin with provisions on his march, 440; reduced by Sigurd, 486.
Tyrrel, Tirel, Walter, his share in the murder of William Rufus, 378.
Tyrrhene Sea, 127, 138, 400.

U.

Uhtred, the earl of Northumbria, joins the Danes, 208; is an ally of Edmund Ironside, 214; beheaded by Canute, 215.
Ulf, king of Sweden, submits to Canute, 220.
Ulfkill, earl of the East Anglian Danes, his death, 190.

INDEX. 659

Urban, saint, his burial place at Rome, 407.
Urban, bishop of Llandaff. *See* Llandaff.
Urban II., pope, Odo, bishop of Ostia, 325, 326; his struggles with the emperor, 343; urges the crusade, 371; holds the council of Clermont, 391–398; at the instigation of Raymond, 456; meets the Crusaders at Lucca, 462; his contest with the anti-pope, 380, 453; Anselm declares his obedience to, 380; his consent required for the appointment of a patriarch of Jerusalem, 437.
Utrecht, bishop of, 509.

V.

Valenciennes, castle of Baldwin of Hainault, 316.
Valens, patriarch of Jerusalem, 424.
Valens, the Emperor, 412.
Valens, saint, his burial place at Rome, 407.
Valentine, saint, his burial place at Rome, 404.
Valentinian, rise of the Franks in the reign of, 69.
Valeria, her burial place at Rome, 407.
Valerian, burial place of, at Rome, 407.
Valesdunes, battle of, 287.
Vandals, conquer Africa, 9.
Vasella, burial place of, at Rome, 405.
Vendome, Geoffrey of, narrow escape of, at the battle of Ramlah, 450.
Venice, attacked by Robert Wiscard and Bohemond, 321, 322; the patriarch of, 504.
Venosa, Robert Wiscard, buried at, 322.
Vercelli, council held by Leo IX. at, 338.
Vere, Aubrey de, acts as Stephen's counsel against the bishops in the council of Winchester, 552, 553, 554.
Vernon, castle of, given to Guy of Burgundy, 286.

Victor II., pope, 276.
Victor III., pope, 326.
Vienne, Guy, archbishop of, 504; pope Calixtus II., 382, 506.
Vilers, castle of, in Normandy, taken by earl Robert of Gloucester, 592.
Vimniacus, pagus, 112.
Vincent, saint, his burial place at Rome, 408.
Vindelici, conquered by Henry III., 230, 251.
Vire, castle of, in Normandy, taken by earl Robert of Gloucester, 592.
Virgil, quoted, 3, 135, 150, 184, 255, 258, 266, 402, 411, 465, 487, 497.
Vitalis, saint, his burial place at Rome, 405.
Vortigern, king of Britain, a bad ruler, 7; consults his nobles before inviting succour from Germany, 7, 8; gives Thanet to Hengest, 9; marries his daughter, 10; gives him Kent, 10; had been ruler of the whole island, 10.
Vortimer, son of Vortigern, heads the resistance to the invaders, 11; his battles and death, *ib.*

W.

Wada, abbot, envoy of Kenulf to the pope, 89.
Waher, Ralph de, conspiracy and escape of, 312, 313, 314.
Walcher, bishop. *See* Durham.
Walcher, prior of Malvern, story told by, 346.
Waleran, his son Hugh, brother of the mother of Robert of Beaumont, 483.
Wales, kings of, row Edgar on the Dee, 165.
Wales, conquered by Harold, 237; relations of William I. with, 316; Flemings settled by Henry I. in, 366, 477; he is wounded in an expedition to, 477.

Walkelin, bishop of Winchester. See Winchester.

Wallingford, blockaded by Stephen with a new castle, 562; the empress's forces at, 593; she escapes from Oxford to, 595, 596.

———— Brian FitzCount, lord of, 556; attends the empress at Winchester, 573.

Waltchis, son of S. Arnulf, 71.

Walter, of Mantes, brother-in-law of Edward the Confessor, 241; marries a sister of the count of Maine, 294.

Walter, the people of Moulins persuaded to join king Henry against duke William by, 290.

Walter, commander of the crusade of Peter the Hermit, 401.

Waltham, Harold buried at, 306.

Waltheof, earl, son of Siward, his share in the conspiracy against the Conqueror, 311, 312, 313; his death, burial, and miracles, 314.

Walweitha, the demesne of Walwen, 342.

Walwen (Gawain), nephew of king Arthur, his grave discovered, 342.

Wandregesil, the abbot, son of Waltchis, 71.

Wareham, Brihtric buried at, 43; Edward the Martyr buried at, 183.

———— castle of, committed by the earl of Gloucester to his son William, 592; taken by Stephen, 593; besieged by the earl's forces, 594; the king refuses to relieve, 595; taken by the earl, 595.

Warner, the margrave, 500.

Warwick, Henry de Beaumont, earl of, 471, 488, 493; chief supporter of Henry I.'s succession, 470.

Warwickshire, included in Mercia, 100, 101.

Wear, Benedict Biscop's foundations on the, 59, 60, 61.

Wearmouth, monastery at, 61; letter of Alcuin to the monks of, 73.

Weaslicas, a name on a Glastonbury pyramid, 25.

Weda, Peada, king of Mercia. See Mercia.

Weldegius, son of Woden, 45.

Wells, called Fontinetum, seat of a bishop, 38, 352; removed to Bath, 353; in Somerset, 100; his rights at Glastonbury, 171, 172.

———— bishops of:

———— Ethelhelm consecrated first bishop, 141, 224.

———— Brihthelm, 170.

———— Giso, 351.

———— John of Tours, acquires and removes to Bath, 353, 385, 387.

Welsh, failure of William Rufus in attacking the, 365; they conquer Anglesey, 376; their zeal for the crusade, 399.

Wencrest, a name on a Glastonbury pyramid, 25.

Wenlock, S. Milburga of, 78, 267, 268, benefactions of Leofric at, 237.

Werburga, S., daughter of Wulfhere, buried at Chester, 78, 267.

Werefrith, bishop of Worcester. See Worcester.

Werenbert, bishop of Worcester. See Worcester.

Werewell, murder of Ethelwold at, 179; monastery at, ib.; penance of Elfrida at, 184; queen Eadgith imprisoned at, 243; the abbey of, burned by William of Ypres, 581.

Werstan, bishop of Sherborne. See Sherborne.

Westminster, Harold buried at, 228; residence of Edward the Confessor at, 274; consecration of the abbey of, 280; queen Eadgitha buried at, 332; the Conqueror's Whitsuntide courts at, 335; Henry I. knighted at, 468; crowned at, 585; queen Matilda keeps her court at, 494; is buried at, 495; great council at, 583.

Westminster, Gosfrid, abbot of, 352.

West Saxons, Cerdic, king of, 19; lands with five keels, 19; becomes king and reigns 15 years, 20; ancestor of the royal race, 19, 43, 121, 280.

———— Cenric (Cynric), king of, accompanies his father, 19; succeeds

West Saxons, kings of—*cont.*
and reigns 26 years, 20; his place in the pedigree, 121.
———— Ceaulin, king of, succeeds and reigns 30 years, 20, 21; his success against Kent and the Britons, 21; defeated at Wodensdie, 21; his exile and death, 21; mentioned, 121.
———— Ceolric (Celric), king of, reigns 5 years, 21.
———— Ceolwulf, king of, reigns 14 years, 21.
———— Cinegisl, king of, succeeds with Cwichelm, 21; his wars against the Britons and Penda, 21; baptized, 22; survives his brother six years, *ib.*; his brother Cuthgils and nephew Escwin, 32; his son Kentwin, 32; Ine descended from, 34.
———— Cwichelm, king of, his reign, 21; his delayed baptism, and death, 22.
———— Kenwalk, king of, succeeds, is attacked by Penda, 22, 76; apostatizes, and is driven into East Anglia, 22; his victories over the Britons, 23; foundation of Glastonbury in his time, 23; and Winchester, *ib.*; his endowment of Glastonbury, 29, 37, 40; his munificence, 29, 30; foundation of Malmesbury in his reign, 30; his death, 32.
———— Sexburga, queen, wife of Kenwalk, rules for a year, 32; mentioned in a charter of Ine, 36.
———— Escuin, king of, great nephew of Cinegisl, succeeds, 32; his struggle with Mercia, *ib.*
———— Chentwin (Kentwin), king of, succeeds, 32; his struggle with the Britons, 32; benefactor of Glastonbury, 37, 40, 159, 168, 225.
———— Kedwalla (Caedwalla), king of, succeeds, 32; his wars with the South Saxons, 33; and with Kent, 17, 32; demands compensation for the burning of Mollo, 17; he gives tithe of his spoils, 33; he goes to Rome, and is

West Saxons, kings of—*cont.*
baptized, *ib.*; dies, 34; benefactor of Glastonbury, 40.
————, Ine, king of, succeeds, 34; obtains compensation for the murder of Mollo, 17, 34; his war with the East Angles, 34; his laws, 34; his benefactions to Glastonbury, 35, 40; his charter to Glastonbury, 36-39; his renunciation of the world, 35, note; he goes to Rome and dies there, 39; mentioned, 43, 78, 79, 120, 159, 168, 172, 225.
———— Ethelheard, king of, succeeds, 39; opposed by Oswald, *ib.*; reigns 14 years, 40; benefactor of Glastonbury, 40, 168.
———— Cuthred (Cudred), king of, succeeds, 40; his grant to Glastonbury, 40, 159, 168, 225; his victories, 41.
———— Sigebert, king of, 41; his short reign and deposition, 41; killed by a swine herd, 41.
———— Cynewulf, king of, succeeds, 41; defeated by Offa at Bensington, *ib.*, 84; banishes Kinehard, 42; is murdered and buried at Winchester, 42.
———— Brihtric, king of, 43; marries a daughter of Offa, *ib.*, 91; banishes Egbert, 43; invasion of the Danes in his reign, *ib.*; buried at Wareham, *ib.*
———— Egbert, king of, succeeds, 43; conquers Kent, 18, 106, 107; and Mercia, 95, 96, 106, 107; obtains the superiority of Northumbria, 76; and of Essex, 98; our author begins his second book with the reign, 2, 105; his descent, 105; his exile under Brihtric, 43, 105; learns government in France, 105; his war with the Cornish Britons, 106; his dominions invaded by the Danes, 107; length of his reign, 107, 108; buried at Winchester, 108; mentioned, 528.
———— Ethelwulf, king of, son of Egbert, 96, 108; succeeds, and reigns 25 years, 108; gives up his father's conquests to Ethelstan, 108; his daughter Ethels-

West Saxons, kings of—*cont.*
witha, 96, 108; his chief advisers, 108, 109; his donation to monasteries, 109; sends Alfred to Rome and goes thither, 109; repairs the school of the English, 109; marries Judith, daughter of Charles the Bald, 109, 117; gives offence and loses half his kingdom, 117; makes his will and sends benefactions to Rome, 118; his charter to Malmesbury, 119, 120; his pedigree, 120, 121; dies and is buried at Winchester, 118.

——— Ethelbald, king of the, divides the kingdom with his father, 117; succeeds him in Wessex, 121; marries Judith, 122; dies and is buried at Sherborne, 122.

——— Ethelbert, king of the, succeeds his father in Kent, 121, 122; dies and is buried at Sherborne, 122.

——— Ethelred, king of the, succeeds Ethelbert, 122; defeats the Danes at Ashendown, 122, 123; dies and is buried at Wimborne, 123.

——— Alfred, king of the, sent to Rome and anointed by Leo IV., 109, 124; assists Ethelred in his wars, 123; commands against the Danish dukes at Ashendown, 123; succeeds his brother, 124; struggles for nine years, 124, 125; takes refuge in Athelney, where he has a vision of S. Cuthbert, 125; wins a battle and returns to Athelney, 126; has Guthrum baptized and yields East Anglia and Northumbria to him, 98, 126; sets the kingdom in order, 128; perseveres against the renewed attacks of the Danes, 128; his rule over Mercia, 96; his adventure in the Danish camp, 126; his wife and children, 129; his social reforms and reformed institutions, 129, 130; his mission to India, 130; his literary labours, 130, 131-133; his literary friends, 131, 132, 133; his administration of finance, 133; his descendants in Flanders, 133, 134; he dies and is buried at Winchester, 134; legends

West Saxons, Alfred, king of the—*cont.*
about him, 134, 185; his enchiridion, 132; mentioned, 159, 166, 168, 225.
Whitby, or Streneshall, 56. *See* Streneshall.
Whithern, ancient see of (Candida Casa), 101, 853.
Wibert, of Ravenna, the anti-pope, 323, 343, 380, 390, 393, 402, 453.
Wiburga, saint, 260.
Wight, isle of, conquest of, 19; given to Wihtgar, *ib.*; given by Wulfhere to Ethelwalch, 78; recovered from Mercia by Caedwalla, 83; Ethelred sails to, 208.
Wigius, ancestor of Egbert, 121.
Wihtgar, has the isle of Wight, 19.
Wihtlaf, king of Mercia. *See* Mercia.
Wihtred, king of Kent. *See* Kent.
Wilfrid. *See* York.
William the Conqueror, king of England, son of duke Robert of Normandy, 212, 227, 239, 244, 283, 284; left by his father under the tutelage of count Gilbert and king Henry, 285; troubles of his minority, 286, *seq.*; defeats the rebels at Val-es-dunes 287; his gratitude to King Henry, 287; his war with Geoffrey Martel of Anjou, 288, 289; rebellion of the count of Arques, 290; he defends Normandy against king Henry, 290, 291; his marriage with Matilda of Flanders, 291; makes good his claim on Maine and Brittany, 293; obtains the surrender of Harold from the count of Ponthieu, 279; plans with him the acquisition of the crown of England, 279, 280; named as heir by Edward the Confessor, 278; claims England on Edward's death, 282, 297, 298, 299; holds council at Lillebonne, 299; sails from S. Valery, 299, 300; wins the battle of Hastings, 282, 300-302; his accident at landing, 300; punishes a knight who stabbed Harold when down, 303; is received in London and crowned, 307; takes Exeter, 307; punishes York, 307, 308; his treatment

William the Conqueror—*cont.*
of Edwin and Morcar, 311; is exasperated against the English and forbids the promotion of native clergy, 312, 313; his treatment of Waltheof, 314; his relations with Wales, 316; dismounted by his son at Gerberoi, 317; compiles Domesday, 317; threatened by the Danes, 317, 319, 320; his religious foundations, 326, 327; his treatment of Malger, archbishop of Rouen, 327; question of his marriage, 327; procures the deposition of Stigand, 328, 329; abolishes the slave trade, 329; portents before his death, 331; stories of his treatment of his wife, 331; his sons, 332; his daughters, 333; his mother, step father, and brothers, 333, 334; his creation of the New Forest, 332, 333; his appearance, customs and character, 335, 336; his quarrel with Philip, 336; he burns Mantes, 336; dies at Rouen, 337; division of his dominions, *ib.*; his burial at Caen, 337, 338; his grave paid for by Henry, 337; his treasures seized by William Rufus, 338; his synodal meetings on the claims of York, 347–352; his jest when Robert demanded Normandy, 459; his laws confirmed, 541, 542; his forests retained by Stephen, 541, 542.

William II., Rufus, son of the Conqueror, 332, 333; has England by his father's bequest, 337; goes to England immediately, 338; seizes his treasures, 338; has the mortgage of Normandy, 332, 371; enmity of his uncle Odo to, 334; his birth and education, 359; his career before his accession, 359; crowned, 360; rebellion of his uncle Odo and the Norman lords, 360; he brings the native English to his side, 361; captures Odo, and reduces the rebels to submission, 362; invades Normandy, wins several places from Robert, makes peace and joins in attacking Henry, 363, 364, 468, 469, 558; stories of his magnanimity and contempt for

William II.—*cont.*
Robert, 365; makes Edgar king of Scots, 366; his regard for Lanfranc, 367; his manners and character, 367, 368; his minister Rannulf, 368; his treatment of the church, 369; of the Jews, 371; his extortions, 372; his presence of mind and contempt of danger, 373; the soul of Julius Cæsar passed into him, 374; his buildings in London, 374; portents of his reign, 374, 375, 376; miraculous warnings of his death, 376, 377, 378; details of his last days, 378, 379; his death, 378, 379, 470; refused payment to Rome, 380; his treatment of his brother Henry, 468; his dealings with Flanders, 478; his forests retained by Stephen, 542.

William, son of Henry I., his birth, congratulations on, 491; receives homage, 495; does homage for Normandy, 482, 495; betrothed to a daughter of Fulk of Anjou, 482; perishes in the great shipwreck, 496, 497.

William of Normandy, son of duke Robert, 461; supported by Fulk of Anjou, 498; his claims on Flanders, 479; married to a daughter of Fulk, 498, 528.

William, son of earl Robert of Gloucester, surety for his father, 583; has charge of the castle of Wareham, 592.

William, duke of the Normans, murdered, 160; various accounts of the matter, 161; his intention to become a monk at Jumiéges, 162; his son Richard, 191.

William, Crispin, 290.

William, FitzOsbern. *See* FitzOsbern.

Wilthegius, son of Woden, 45.

Wilton, Elfleda, and two of her daughters buried at, 137; S. Eadgitha of, 269; Matilda, wife of Henry I., educated at, 493; church of, devastated by Robert FitzHubert, 563; the empress visited by the archbishop at, 573.

Wiltshire, part of Wessex, 100.

Wimburne, Cuthburga, sister of Ine, abbess at, 35; Ethelred buried at, 124.
Wimund, father of S. Wistan, 263.
Wina, buys the see of London, 78.
Winchcomb, consecration of the monastery of, 94, 95; king Kenulf buried at, 95; a great storm at, 374, 375; Girmund, abbot of, 521.
Winchester, Cynewulf buried at, 42; Egbert buried at, 108; charter of Ethelwulf dated at, 120; Ethelwulf buried at, 118; sacked by the Danes, 122; the New Minster founded at, 130; Alfred buried in it, 134; also Edward and his brother and son, 141, 145; attempt to blind Ethelstan at, 153; Edred buried at, 162; also Edwy, 164; occupied by Sweyn, 208; enriched by Canute, 220; Canute buried at, 225; Hardicanute also, 228; Edward the Confessor crowned at, 239; the treasures of Emma at, 237, 238; miracles of S. Eadburga at, 269; the Conqueror's Easter courts at, 335; consecration of Walcher of Durham at, 331; the Conqueror's treasures at, seized by William Rufus, 338; he is buried at, 379; Andover, near, 179; synod at, under Dunstan, 182; Southampton, near, 186; council at, 550; another, 572; Stephen comes to, after his release, 582.
Winchester, see of, remains under the obedience of Canterbury, 85, 100, 352.
Winchester, bishops of. *See* Dorchester.
—————— Swithun, bishop of, a chief counsellor of king Ethelwulf, 108, 109; mentioned in his charter, 119; his church, 581.
—————— Fridestan, bishop of, consecrated, 141.
—————— Ethelwold, bishop of, abbot of Abingdon, restorer of monasteries, 166, 167; expels secular clerks from, 167; rebukes S. Eadgitha, 269.
—————— Stigand, bishop of, 244; archbishop of Canterbury. *See* Canterbury.
—————— Walkelin, bishop of, appointed to succeed Stigand, 329, 351.

Winchester, bishops of—*cont.*
—————— William Giffard, bishop of, consecrated by Anselm, 493.
—————— Henry of Blois, bishop of, grandson of the Conqueror, and brother of king Stephen, supports his claim, 538; is at his coronation, 539; is legate in England, 538; holds a council at Winchester, 550; summons the king to it, 551; bids him revest the bishops in their rights, 553; mediates for peace, 564; goes abroad to negotiate, 565; holds a council at Winchester in which the empress is received as lady of England, 572-577; his speech there, 574-576; co-operates with Earl Robert, 578; quarrels with the empress on account of his nephew's inheritance, 579; negotiates with the earl, 579, 580; is attacked by the empress, 580; his answer to Stephen, 583, 584.
Winchester, Godfrey, prior of, his literary ability and sanctity, 516.
Winchester, Wulfstan, chantor of, his works, 167.
Winchester, the New Minster at, Ethelgar, abbot of, 224; Canute's crucifix at, 581.
—————— Ruald, abbot of, 352.
—————— Robert Losinga abbot of, 385.
Windsor, Wulfwin Spillecorn, warder at, 274; council held at, 351.
Winethegn, a name on one of the Glastonbury pyramids, 25.
Winziburg, Wiltaburg, Adelbold, bishop of, 195.
Wirtgernesburg, battle of, 23.
Wistan, Edelnod, son of, 192.
Wistan, saint, legend of, 263.
Witsand, divided by a narrow sea from Dover, 156; Eustace of Boulogne sails from, 241; Stephen embarks at, for England, 538.
Woden, ancestor of the kings of the English, 9, 19, 44, 45, 76, 96, 98, 121; Wednesday called from him, 9; his descent from Noah, 121.
Woodstock, Henry I. has a menagerie at, 485.

Worcester, men of, kill the tax gatherers of Hardicanute, 228 ; their punishment, 229.
Worcester, see of, withdrawn by Offa from the obedience of Canterbury, 85, 100; claims of York on, 347, 354.
Worcester, bishop of, Egwin, his visit to Rome, 99.
———— Werenbert, bishop of, 85.
———— Werefrith, bishop of, literary adviser of Alfred, 131.
———— Dunstan, bishop of, 165. *See* Canterbury.
———— Oswald, bishop of, 167 ; translates the Kentish martyrs to Ramsey, 262. *See* York.
———— Wulfstan, bishop of, suppresses the slave trade, 329 ; attests the decision about York and Canterbury, 351 ; miraculous story about, 354, 355 ; supports the cause of William Rufus during the rebellion, 361.
———— Sampson, bishop of, 521
Worgret, an unknown abbot of Glastonbury, 28, 29.
Wulfhard, bishop of Hereford, 85.
Wulfhere, king of Mercia. *See* Mercia.
Wulfnoth, outlawed by Ethelred, 189 ; destroys the fleet, 189.
Wulfnoth, son of earl Godwin, his history, 245.
Wulfnoth, abbot of Chertsey, 351.
Wulfred, a name on one of the Glastonbury pyramids, 23.
Wulfrida, mother of S. Eadgitha, 180.
Wulfstan, bishop. *See* Worcester.
Wulfwin, Spillecorn, miracle wrought upon, 273, 274.
Wye, the river (Waia), 148.

X.

Xeno, saint, his burial place at Rome, 407.

Y.

York, famous library at, 68 ; lettter of Alcuin to the clergy at, 78 ; the head of Northumbria, 73 ; dignity of the see of 88, 346, 518 ; burned by the Northumbrians, 124 ; besieged by Godfrey, 147 ; the Danish castle at, burned by Ethelstan, *ib.* ; Norwegian ambassadors received at, 149 ; severely punished by the Conqueror, 308 ; Tostig buried at, 311.
York, archbishops of;
———— Paulinus, archbishop of, his connexion with Glastonbury, 28 ; preaches in Northumbria, 49 ; has the pall from pope Honorius, 68 ; retires and dies at Rochester, 67, 73.
———— Wilfrid, archbishop of, defends the Roman Easter, 55 ; ill-treated by Ecgfrith, 56, 57, and by Aldfrith, 57 ; built a monastery at Selsey, 100, 260.
———— Egbert, archbishop of, brother of the king of Northumbria, 67 ; collected the library at York, 68.
———— Eanbald, archbishop of, the third after Egbert, 68 ; letter of Alcuin to, 68.
———— Wulfstan, archbishop of, imprisoned and released by king Edred, 162.
———— Oswald, archbishop of, restorer of monachism, 167 ; educated at Fleury, bishop of Worcester and founder of Ramsey, *ib.* ; mentioned in a Glastonbury charter, 170 ; translated SS. Ethelbert and Ethelred to Ramsey, 262 ; mentioned, 355.
———— Elfric, archbishop of, letter of Canute addressed to, 221 ; he obeys Hardicanute in disinterring the body of Harold, 228.

York, Ealdred, Aldred, archbishop of, at London after the battle of Stamford Bridge, 307; submits to the Conqueror, 309; crowns him, 309; was the restorer of the church of S. Oswald at Gloucester, 136.

——— Thomas, archbishop of, claims the obedience of Worcester and Dorchester, 347, 354; decision of his dispute with Lanfranc, 349-352; make profession to Lanfranc, 352.

——— Girard, archbishop of, accused of falsehood by Paschal II., 492.

——— Thurstan, archbishop of, excuses himself on the ground of health from attending the council at Winchester, 550.

Ypres, William of, incites Stephen to attempt treachery against earl Robert,

Ypres, William of —*cont.*
543; burns Werewell abbey, 581; takes Humfrey de Bohun prisoner, 587.

Yrmenric, king of Kent. *See* Kent.

Z.

Zabdas, patriarch of Jerusalem, 424.
Zacheus, patriarch of Jerusalem, 424.
Zacharias, patriarch of Jerusalem, 424.
Zachary, pope, 71.
Zeno, emperor of Constantinople, 412.
Zephyrinus, S., his burial place at Rome, 407.

CATALOGUE

OF

ENGLISH, SCOTCH, AND IRISH RECORD PUBLICATIONS,

REPORTS OF THE HISTORICAL MANUSCRIPTS COMMISSION,

AND

ANNUAL REPORTS OF THE DEPUTY KEEPERS OF THE PUBLIC RECORDS, ENGLAND AND IRELAND,

Printed for

HER MAJESTY'S STATIONERY OFFICE,

And to be purchased,
Either directly or through any Bookseller, from
EYRE AND SPOTTISWOODE, EAST HARDING STREET, FLEET STREET, E.C.; or
ADAM AND CHARLES BLACK, 6, NORTH BRIDGE, EDINBURGH; or
HODGES, FIGGIS, & Co., 104, GRAFTON STREET, DUBLIN.

CONTENTS.

	Page
CALENDARS OF STATE PAPERS, &c.	3
CHRONICLES AND MEMORIALS OF GREAT BRITAIN AND IRELAND DURING THE MIDDLE AGES	9
PUBLICATIONS OF THE RECORD COMMISSIONERS, &c.	23
WORKS PUBLISHED IN PHOTOZINCOGRAPHY	25
HISTORICAL MANUSCRIPTS COMMISSION	27
REPORTS OF THE DEPUTY KEEPER OF THE PUBLIC RECORDS	31
SCOTCH RECORD PUBLICATIONS	36
IRISH RECORD PUBLICATIONS	37
REPORTS OF THE DEPUTY KEEPER OF THE PUBLIC RECORDS, IRELAND	38

ENGLAND.

CALENDARS OF STATE PAPERS, &c.

[IMPERIAL 8vo., boards. *Price* 15s. each Volume or Part.]

As far back as the year 1800, a Committee of the House of Commons recommended that Indexes and Calendars should be made to the Public Records, and thirty-six years afterwards another Committee of the House of Commons reiterated that recommendation in more forcible words; but it was not until the incorporation of the State Paper Office with the Public Record Office that the Master of the Rolls found himself in a position to take the necessary steps for carrying out the wishes of the House of Commons.

On 7 December 1855, he stated to the Lords of the Treasury that although "the Records, State Papers, and Documents in his charge constitute the most "complete and perfect series of their kind in the civilized world," and although "they are of the greatest value in a historical and constitutional point of view, "yet they are comparatively useless to the public, from the want of proper "Calendars and Indexes." Acting upon the recommendations of the Committees of the House of Commons above referred to, he suggested to the Lords of the Treasury that to effect the object he had in view it would be necessary for him to employ a few Persons fully qualified to perform the work which he contemplated.

Their Lordships assented to the necessity of having Calendars prepared and printed, and empowered the Master of the Rolls to take such steps as might be necessary for this purpose.

The following Works have been already published in this Series:—

CALENDARIUM GENEALOGICUM; for the Reigns of Henry III. and Edward I. *Edited by* CHARLES ROBERTS, Esq., Secretary of the Public Record Office. 2 Vols. 1865.

    This is a work of great value for elucidating the early history of our nobility and landed gentry.

CALENDAR OF STATE PAPERS, DOMESTIC SERIES, OF THE REIGNS OF EDWARD VI., MARY, ELIZABETH, and JAMES I., preserved in Her Majesty's Public Record Office. *Edited by* ROBERT LEMON, Esq., F.S.A. (Vols. I. and II.), *and by* MARY ANNE EVERETT GREEN, (Vols. III.–XII.). 1856–1872.

Vol. I.— 1547–1580.	Vol. VII.— Addenda, 1566–1579.
Vol. II.— 1581–1590.	Vol. VIII.—1603–1610.
Vol. III.—1591–1594.	Vol. IX.— 1611–1618.
Vol. IV.—1595–1597.	Vol. X.— 1619–1623.
Vol. V.— 1598–1601.	Vol. XI.— 1623–1625, with
Vol. VI.—1601–1603. with	Addenda, 1603–1625.
Addenda, 1547–1565.	Vol. XII.— Addenda, 1580–1625.

    These Calendars render accessible to investigation a large and important mass of historical materials concerning the Northern Rebellion of 1566–67; the plots of the Catholic fugitives in the Low Countries; numerous designs against Queen Elizabeth and in favour of a Catholic succession; the Gunpowder-plot; the rise and fall of Somerset; the Overbury murder; the disgrace of Sir Edward Coke; the rise of the Duke of Buckingham, and numerous other subjects.

CALENDAR OF STATE PAPERS, DOMESTIC SERIES, OF THE REIGN OF CHARLES I., preserved in Her Majesty's Public Record Office. *Edited by* JOHN BRUCE, Esq., F.S.A., (Vols. I.–XII.); *by* JOHN BRUCE, Esq., F.S.A , and WILLIAM DOUGLAS HAMILTON, Esq., F.S.A., (Vol. XIII.); and *by* WILLIAM DOUGLAS HAMILTON, Esq., F.S.A., (Vols. XIV.–XVII.). 1858–1888.

Vol. I.— 1625–1626.	Vol. XI.— 1637.
Vol. II.— 1627–1628.	Vol. XII.— 1637–1638.
Vol. III.— 1628–1629.	Vol. XIII.— 1638–1639.
Vol. IV.— 1629–1631.	Vol. XIV.— 1639.
Vol. V.— 1631–1633.	Vol. XV.— 1639–1640.
Vol. VI.— 1633–1634.	Vol. XVI.— 1640.
Vol. VII.— 1634–1635.	Vol. XVII.— 1640–41.
Vol. VIII.—1635.	Vol. XVIII.—1641–43.
Vol. IX.— 1635–1636.	Vol. XIX.— 1644.
Vol. X.— 1636–1637.	

This Calendar presents notices of a large number of original documents of great value to all inquirers relative to the history of the period to which it refers, many hitherto unknown.

CALENDAR OF STATE PAPERS, DOMESTIC SERIES, DURING THE COMMONWEALTH, preserved in Her Majesty's Public Record Office. *Edited by* MARY ANNE EVERETT GREEN. 1875–1885.

Vol. I.— 1649–1649.	Vol. VIII.—1655.
Vol. II.— 1650.	Vol. IX.— 1655–1656.
Vol. III.—1651.	Vol. X.— 1656–1657.
Vol. IV.— 1651–1652.	Vol. XI.— 1657–1658.
Vol. V.— 1652–1653.	Vol. XII.— 1658–1659.
Vol. VI.— 1653–1654.	Vol. XIII.— 1659–1660.
Vol. VII.—1654.	

This Calendar is in continuation of those during the reigns from Edward VI. to Charles I.

CALENDAR OF STATE PAPERS:—COMMITTEE FOR THE ADVANCE OF MONEY, 1642–1656. *Edited by* MARY ANNE EVERETT GREEN. In three Parts. 1888.

CALENDAR OF STATE PAPERS:—COMMITTEE FOR COMPOUNDING, &c., 1643–1660. *Edited by* MARY ANNE EVERETT GREEN. Part I., 1889.

CALENDAR OF STATE PAPERS, DOMESTIC SERIES, OF THE REIGN OF CHARLES II., preserved in Her Majesty's Public Record Office. *Edited by* MARY ANNE EVERETT GREEN. 1860–1866.

Vol. I.— 1660–1661.	Vol. V.— 1665–1666.
Vol. II.— 1661–1662.	Vol. VI.— 1666–1667.
Vol. III.—1663–1664.	Vol. VII.—1667.
Vol. IV.—1664–1665.	

CALENDAR OF HOME OFFICE PAPERS OF THE REIGN OF GEORGE III., preserved in Her Majesty's Public Record Office. Vols. I. and II. *Edited by* JOSEPH REDINGTON, Esq. 1878–1879. Vol. III. *Edited by* RICHARD ARTHUR ROBERTS, Esq., Barrister-at-Law. 1881.

Vol. I.—1760 (25 Oct.)–1765.	Vol. III.—1770–1772.
Vol. II.—1766–1769.	

These are the first three volumes of the modern series of Domestic Papers, commencing with the accession of George III.

CALENDAR OF STATE PAPERS relating to SCOTLAND, preserved in Her Majesty's Public Record Office. *Edited by* MARKHAM JOHN THORPE, Esq., of St. Edmund Hall, Oxford. 1858.

Vol. I., the Scottish Series, of the Reigns of Henry VIII., Edward VI., Mary, and Elizabeth, 1509–1589.
Vol. II., the Scottish Series, of the Reign of Elizabeth, 1589–1603; an Appendix to the Scottish Series, 1543–1592; and the State Papers relating to Mary Queen of Scots.

CALENDAR OF DOCUMENTS relating to IRELAND, in Her Majesty's Public Record Office, London. *Edited by* HENRY SAVAGE SWEETMAN, Esq., B.A., Trinity College, Dublin, Barrister-at-Law (Ireland); *continued by* GUSTAVUS FREDERICK HANDCOCK, ESQ. 1875–1886.

    Vol. I.— 1171–1251. | Vol. IV.—1293–1301.
    Vol. II.— 1252–1284. | Vol. V.— 1302–1307.
    Vol. III.—1285–1292.

CALENDAR OF STATE PAPERS relating to IRELAND, OF THE REIGNS OF HENRY VIII., EDWARD VI., MARY, AND ELIZABETH, preserved in Her Majesty's Public Record Office. *Edited by* HANS CLAUDE HAMILTON, Esq., F.S.A. 1860–1885.

    Vol. I.— 1509–1573. | Vol. III.—1586–1588.
    Vol. II.—1574–1585. | Vol. IV.— 1588–1592.

CALENDAR OF STATE PAPERS relating to IRELAND, OF THE REIGN OF JAMES I., preserved in Her Majesty's Public Record Office, and elsewhere. *Edited by* the Rev. C. W. RUSSELL, D.D., and JOHN P. PRENDERGAST, Esq., Barrister-at-Law. 1872–1880.

    Vol. I.— 1603–1606. | Vol. IV.—1611–1614.
    Vol. II.— 1606–1608. | Vol. V.— 1615–1625.
    Vol. III.—1608–1610.

    This series is in continuation of the Irish State Papers commencing with the reign of Henry VIII.; but for the reign of James I., the Papers are not confined to those in the Public Record Office, London.

CALENDAR OF STATE PAPERS, COLONIAL SERIES, preserved in Her Majesty's Public Record Office, and elsewhere. *Edited by* W. NOEL SAINSBURY, Esq. 1860–1884.

    Vol. I.—America and West Indies, 1574–1660.
    Vol. II.—East Indies, China, and Japan, 1513–1616.
    Vol. III.—East Indies, China, and Japan 1617–1621.
    Vol. IV.—East Indies, China, and Japan, 1622–1624.
    Vol. V.—America and West Indies, 1661–1668.
    Vol. VI.—East Indies, 1625–1629.
    Vol. VII.—America and West Indies, 1669–1674.

    These volumes include an analysis of early Colonial Papers in the Public Record Office, the India Office, and the British Museum.

CALENDAR OF LETTERS AND PAPERS, FOREIGN AND DOMESTIC, OF THE REIGN OF HENRY VIII., preserved in Her Majesty's Public Record Office, the British Museum, &c. *Edited by* J. S. BREWER, M.A., Professor of English Literature, King's College, London (Vols. I.–IV.); and *by* JAMES GAIRDNER, Esq., (Vols. V.–XI.) 1862–1888.

    Vol. I.—1509–1514. | Vol. IV., Part 3.—1529–1530.
    Vol. II. (in two Parts)—1515–1518. | Vol. V.— 1531–1532.
        | Vol. VI.— 1533.
    Vol. III. (in two Parts)—1519–1523. | Vol. VII.— 1534.
        | Vol. VIII.—1535, to July.
    Vol. IV.—Introduction. | Vol. IX.— 1535, Aug. to Dec.
    Vol. IV., Part 1.—1524–1526. | Vol. X.— 1536, Jan. to June.
    Vol. IV., Part 2.—1526–1528. | Vol. XI.— 1536, July to Dec.

    These volumes contain summaries of all State Papers and Correspondence relating to the reign of Henry VIII., in the Public Record Office, of those formerly in the State Paper Office, in the British Museum, the Libraries of Oxford and Cambridge, and other Public Libraries; and of all letters that have appeared in print in the works of Burnet, Strype, and others. Whatever authentic original material exists in England relative to the religious, political, parliamentary, or social history of the country during the reign of Henry VIII., whether despatches of ambassadors, or proceedings of the army, navy, treasury, or ordnance, or records of Parliament, appointments of officers, grants from the Crown, &c., will be found calendared in these volumes.

CALENDAR OF STATE PAPERS, FOREIGN SERIES, OF THE REIGN OF EDWARD VI., preserved in Her Majesty's Public Record Office. 1547–1553. *Edited by* W. R. TURNBULL, Esq., of Lincoln's Inn, Barrister-at-Law, &c., 1861.

CALENDAR OF STATE PAPERS, FOREIGN SERIES, OF THE REIGN OF MARY, preserved in Her Majesty's Public Record Office. 1553–1558. *Edited by* W. B. TURNBULL, Esq., of Lincoln's Inn, Barrister-at-Law, &c. 1861.

> The two preceding volumes exhibit the negotiations of the English ambassadors with the courts of the Emperor Charles V. of Germany, of Henry II. of France, and of Philip II. of Spain. The affairs of several of the minor continental states also find various incidental illustrations of much interest. The Papers descriptive of the circumstances which attended the loss of Calais merit a special notice; while the progress of the wars in the north of France, into which England was dragged by her union with Spain, is narrated at some length. These volumes treat only of the relations of England with foreign powers.

CALENDAR OF STATE PAPERS, FOREIGN SERIES, OF THE REIGN OF ELIZABETH, preserved in Her Majesty's Public Record Office, &c. *Edited by* the Rev. JOSEPH STEVENSON, M.A., of University College, Durham, (Vols. I.–VII.), and ALLAN JAMES CROSBY, Esq., M.A., Barrister-at-Law, (Vols. VIII.–XI.) 1863–1880.

Vol. I.— 1558–1559.
Vol. II.— 1559–1560.
Vol. III.— 1560–1561.
Vol. IV.— 1561–1562.
Vol. V.— 1562.
Vol. VI.— 1563.
Vol. VII.— 1564–1565.
Vol. VIII.— 1566–1568.
Vol. IX.— 1569–1571.
Vol. X.— 1572–1574.
Vol. XI.— 1575–1577.

> These volumes contain a Calendar of the Foreign Correspondence during the early portion of the reign of Elizabeth. They illustrate not only the external but also the domestic affairs of Foreign Countries during that period.

CALENDAR OF TREASURY PAPERS, preserved in Her Majesty's Public Record Office. *Edited by* JOSEPH REDINGTON, Esq. 1868–1889.

Vol. I.— 1557–1696.
Vol. II.— 1697–1702.
Vol. III.—1702–1707.
Vol. IV.—1708–1714.
Vol. V.— 1714–1719.
Vol. VI.—1720–1728.

> The above Papers connected with the affairs of the Treasury comprise, petitions, reports, and other documents relating to services rendered to the State, grants of money and pensions, appointments to offices, remissions of fines and duties, &c. They illustrate civil and military events, finance, the administration in Ireland and the Colonies, &c., and afford information nowhere else recorded.

CALENDAR OF THE CAREW PAPERS, preserved in the Lambeth Library. *Edited by* J. S. BREWER, M.A., Professor of English Literature, King's College, London; and WILLIAM BULLEN, Esq. 1867–1873.

Vol. I.— 1515–1574.
Vol. II.— 1575–1588.
Vol. III.—1589–1600.
Vol. IV.—1601–1603.
Vol. V.—Book of Howth; Miscellaneous.
Vol. VI.—1603–1624.

> The Carew Papers relating to Ireland, in the Lambeth Library, are unique and of great importance to all students of Irish history.

CALENDAR OF LETTERS, DESPATCHES, AND STATE PAPERS, relating to the Negotiations between England and Spain, preserved in the Archives at Simancas, and elsewhere. *Edited by* G. A. BERGENROTH, (Vols. I. and II.) 1862–1868, *and* DON PASCUAL DE GAYANGOS (Vols. III. to V.) 1873–1888.

Vol. I.—Hen. VII.—1485–1509.
Vol. II.—Hen. VIII.—1509–1525.
Supplement to Vol. I. and Vol. II.
Vol. III., Part 1.—Hen. VIII.— 1525–1526.
Vol. III., Part 2.—Hen. VIII.— 1527–1529.
Vol. IV., Part 1.—Hen. VIII.—1529–1530.
Vol. IV., Part 2.— Hen. VIII.—1531–1533.
Vol. IV., Part 2.—*continued*.— 1531–1533.
Vol. V., Part 1.— Hen. VIII.— 1534–1536.
Vol. V., Part 2.— Hen. VIII.— 1536–1538.

> Mr. Bergenroth was engaged in compiling a Calendar of the Papers relating to England preserved in the archives of Spain. The Supplement contains new

information relating to the private life of Queen Katherine of England; and to the projected marriage of Henry VII. with Queen Juana, widow of King Philip of Castile, and mother of the Emperor Charles V.

Upon the death of Mr. Bergenroth, Don Pascual de Gayangos was appointed to continue the Calendar, and he has been able to add much valuable matter from Brussels and Vienna, with which Mr. Bergenroth was unacquainted.

CALENDAR OF STATE PAPERS AND MANUSCRIPTS, relating to ENGLISH AFFAIRS, preserved in the Archives of Venice, &c. *Edited by* RAWDON BROWN, Esq, 1864-1884.

Vol. I.— 1202-1509.	Vol. V.— 1534-1554.
Vol. II.— 1509-1519.	Vol. VI., Part I.— 1555-1556.
Vol. III.—1520-1526.	Vol. VI., Part II.— 1556-1557.
Vol. IV.—1527-1533.	Vol. VI., Part III.—1557-1558.

Mr. Rawdon Brown's researches have brought to light a number of valuable documents relating to various periods of English history; his contributions to historical literature are of the most interesting and important character.

SYLLABUS, IN ENGLISH, OF RYMER'S FŒDERA. *By* Sir THOMAS DUFFUS HARDY, D.C.L., Deputy Keeper of the Public Records. Vol. I.—Will. I.-Edw. III. 1066-1377. Vol. II.—Ric. II.-Chas. II. 1377-1654. Vol. III., Appendix and Index. 1869-1885.

Rymer's "Fœdera," is a collection of miscellaneous documents illustrative of the History of Great Britain and Ireland, from the Norman Conquest to the reign of Charles II. Several editions of the "Fœdera" have been published, and the present Syllabus was undertaken to make the contents of this great national work more generally known.

REPORT OF THE DEPUTY KEEPER OF THE PUBLIC RECORDS AND THE REV. J. S. BREWER TO THE MASTER OF THE ROLLS, upon the Carte and Carew Papers in the Bodleian and Lambeth Libraries. 1864. *Price* 2s. 6d.

REPORT OF THE DEPUTY KEEPER OF THE PUBLIC RECORDS TO THE MASTER OF THE ROLLS, upon the Documents in the Archives and Public Libraries of Venice. 1866. *Price* 2s. 6d.

In the Press.

CALENDAR OF STATE PAPERS AND MANUSCRIPTS, relating to ENGLISH AFFAIRS, preserved in the Archives of Venice, &c. Vol. VII.—1559–1580.

CALENDAR OF LETTERS, DESPATCHES, AND STATE PAPERS, relating to the Negotiations between England and Spain, preserved in the Archives at Simancas, and elsewhere. *Edited by* DON PASCUAL DE GAYANGOS. Vol VI.—1539–1542.

CALENDAR OF STATE PAPERS:—COMMITTEE FOR COMPOUNDING, &c. *Edited by* MARY ANNE EVERETT GREEN. Part II.

CALENDAR OF STATE PAPERS relating to IRELAND, OF THE REIGN OF ELIZABETH, preserved in Her Majesty's Public Record Office. *Edited by* HANS CLAUDE HAMILTON, Esq., F.S.A. Vol. V.—1592–1596.

DESCRIPTIVE CATALOGUE OF ANCIENT DEEDS, preserved in Her Majesty's Public Record Office. Vol. I.

CALENDAR OF STATE PAPERS, DOMESTIC SERIES, OF THE REIGN OF CHARLES I., preserved in Her Majesty's Public Record Office. *Edited by* WILLIAM DOUGLAS HAMILTON, Esq., F.S.A. Vol. XX. 1645, &c.

CALENDAR OF THE PATENT ROLLS OF THE REIGN OF EDWARD III. *Prepared by Officers of the Public Record Department.*

CALENDAR OF LETTERS AND PAPERS, FOREIGN AND DOMESTIC, OF THE REIGN OF HENRY VIII., preserved in Her Majesty's Public Record Office, the British Museum, &c. *Edited by* JAMES GAIRDNER, Esq. Vol. XII.—1537.

In Progress.

CALENDAR OF STATE PAPERS, COLONIAL SERIES, preserved in Her Majesty's Public Record Office, and elsewhere. *Edited by* W. NOEL SAINSBURY, Esq. Vol. VIII.—East Indies, 1630, &c.

CALENDAR OF TREASURY PAPERS, preserved in Her Majesty's Public Record Office. *Edited by* JOSEPH REDINGTON, Esq. Vol. VII.

CALENDAR OF THE PATENT ROLLS OF THE REIGN OF EDWARD II. *Prepared by Officers of the Public Record Department.*

CALENDAR OF ANCIENT CORRESPONDENCE, Diplomatic Documents, Papal Bulls, and the like, preserved in Her Majesty's Public Record Office.

THE CHRONICLES AND MEMORIALS OF GREAT BRITAIN AND IRELAND DURING THE MIDDLE AGES.

[ROYAL 8vo. *Price* 10*s*. each Volume or Part.]

On 25 July 1822, the House of Commons presented an address to the Crown, stating that the editions of the works of our ancient historians were inconvenient and defective; that many of their writings still remained in manuscript, and, in some cases, in a single copy only. They added, "that an uniform and con-
" venient edition of the whole, published under His Majesty's royal sanction,
" would be an undertaking honourable to His Majesty's reign, and conducive to
" the advancement of historical and constitutional knowledge; that the House
" therefore humbly besought His Majesty, that He would be graciously pleased
" to give such directions as His Majesty, in His wisdom, might think fit, for
" the publication of a complete edition of the ancient historians of this realm,
" and assured His Majesty that whatever expense might be necessary for this
" purpose would be made good."

The Master of the Rolls, being very desirous that effect should be given to the resolution of the House of Commons, submitted to Her Majesty's Treasury in 1857 a plan for the publication of the ancient chronicles and memorials of the United Kingdom, and it was adopted accordingly. In selecting these works, it was considered right, in the first instance, to give preference to those of which the manuscripts were unique, or the materials of which would help to fill up blanks in English history for which no satisfactory and authentic information hitherto existed in any accessible form. One great object the Master of the Rolls had in view was to form a *corpus historicum* within reasonable limits, and which should be as complete as possible. In a subject of so vast a range, it was important that the historical student should be able to select such volumes as conformed with his own peculiar tastes and studies, and not be put to the expense of purchasing the whole collection; an inconvenience inseparable from any other plan than that which has been in this instance adopted.

Of the Chronicles and Memorials, the following volumes have been published. They embrace the period from the earliest time of British history down to the end of the reign of Henry VII.

---

1. THE CHRONICLE OF ENGLAND, by JOHN CAPGRAVE. *Edited by* the Rev. F. C. HINGESTON, M.A., of Exeter College, Oxford. 1858.

    Capgrave was prior of Lynn, in Norfolk, and provincial of the order of the Friars Hermits of England shortly before the year 1464. His Chronicle extends from the creation of the world to the year 1417. As a record of the language spoken in Norfolk (being written in English), it is of considerable value.

2. CHRONICON MONASTERII DE ABINGDON. Vols. I. and II. *Edited by* the Rev. JOSEPH STEVENSON, M.A., of University College, Durham, and Vicar of Leighton Buzzard. 1858.

    This Chronicle traces the history of the great Benedictine monastery of Abingdon in Berkshire, from its foundation by King Ina of Wessex, to the reign of Richard I., shortly after which period the present narrative was drawn up by an inmate of the establishment. The author had access to the title-deeds of the house; and incorporates into his history various charters of the Saxon kings, of great importance as illustrating not only the history of the locality but that of the kingdom. The work is printed for the first time.

3. LIVES OF EDWARD THE CONFESSOR. I.—La Estoire de Seint Aedward le Rei II.—Vita Beati Edvardi Regis et Confessoris. III.—Vita Æduuardi Regis qui apud Westmonasterium requiescit. *Edited by* HENRY RICHARDS LUARD, M.A., Fellow and Assistant Tutor of Trinity College, Cambridge. 1858.

    The first is a poem in Norman French, containing 4,686 lines, addressed to Alianor, Queen of Henry III., probably written in 1245, on the restoration of the church of Westminster. Nothing is known of the author. The second is an anonymous poem, containing 536 lines, written between 1440 and 1450, by command of Henry VI., to whom it is dedicated. It does not throw any new light on the reign of Edward the Confessor, but is valuable as a specimen of the Latin poetry of the time. The third, also by an anonymous author, was apparently written for Queen Edith, between 1066 and 1074, during the pressure of the suffering brought on the Saxons by the Norman conquest. It notices many acts not found in other writers, and some which differ considerably from the usual accounts.

4. MONUMENTA FRANCISCANA. Vol. I.—Thomas de Eccleston de Adventu Fratrum Minorum in Angliam. Adæ de Marisco Epistolæ. Registrum Fratrum Minorum Londoniæ. *Edited by* J. S. BREWER, M.A., Professor of English Literature, King's College, London. Vol. II.—De Adventu Minorum; re-edited, with additions. Chronicle of the Grey Friars. The ancient English version of the Rule of St. Francis. Abbreviatio Statutorum, 1451, &c. *Edited by* RICHARD HOWLETT, Esq., of the Middle Temple, Barrister-at-Law. 1858, 1882.

The first volume contains original materials for the history of the settlement of the order of Saint Francis in England, the letters of Adam de Marisco, and other papers connected with the foundation and diffusion of this great body. None of these have been before printed. The second volume contains materials found, since the first volume was published, among the MSS. of Sir Charles Isham, and in various libraries.

5. FASCICULI ZIZANIORUM MAGISTRI JOHANNIS WYCLIF CUM TRITICO. Ascribed to THOMAS NETTER, of WALDEN, Provincial of the Carmelite Order in England, and Confessor to King Henry the Fifth. *Edited by* the Rev. W. W. SHIRLEY, M.A., Tutor and late Fellow of Wadham College, Oxford. 1858.

This work derives its principal value from being the only contemporaneous account of the rise of the Lollards. When written, the disputes of the schoolmen had been extended to the field of theology, and they appear both in the writings of Wycliff and in those of his adversaries. Wycliff's little bundles of tares are not less metaphysical than theological, and the conflict between Nominalists and Realists rages side by side with the conflict between the different interpreters of Scripture. The work gives a good idea of the controversies at the end of the 14th and the beginning of the 15th centuries.

6. THE BUIK OF THE CRONICLIS OF SCOTLAND; or, A Metrical Version of the History of Hector Boece; by WILLIAM STEWART. Vols. I., II., and III. *Edited by* W. B. TURNBULL, Esq., of Lincoln's Inn, Barrister-at-Law, 1858.

This is a metrical translation of a Latin Prose Chronicle, written in the first half of the 16th century. The narrative begins with the earliest legends and ends with the death of James I. of Scotland, and the "evil ending of the traitors that slew him." Strict accuracy of statement is not to be looked for; but the stories of the colonization of Spain, Ireland, and Scotland are interesting if not true; and the chronicle reflects the manners, sentiments, and character of the age in which it was composed. The peculiarities of the Scottish dialect are well illustrated in this version, and the student of language will find ample materials for comparison with the English dialects of the same period, and with modern lowland Scotch.

7. JOHANNIS CAPGRAVE LIBER DE ILLUSTRIBUS HENRICIS. *Edited by* the Rev. F. C. HINGESTON, M.A., of Exeter College, Oxford. 1858.

This work is dedicated to Henry VI. of England, who appears to have been, in the author's estimation, the greatest of all the Henries. It is divided into three parts, each having a separate dedication. The first part relates only to the history of the Empire, from the election of Henry I. the Fowler, to the end of the reign of the Emperor Henry VI. The second part is devoted to English history, from the accession of Henry I. in 1100, to 1446, which was the twenty-fourth year of the reign of Henry VI. The third part contains the lives of illustrious men who have borne the name of Henry in various parts of the world. Capgrave was born in 1393, in the reign of Richard II., and lived during the Wars of the Roses, for which period his work is of some value.

8. HISTORIA MONASTERII S. AUGUSTINI CANTUARIENSIS, by THOMAS OF ELMHAM. formerly Monk and Treasurer of that Foundation. *Edited by* CHARLES HARDWICK, M.A., Fellow of St. Catharine's Hall, and Christian Advocate in the University of Cambridge. 1858.

This history extends from the arrival of St. Augustine in Kent until 1191. Prefixed is a chronology as far as 1418, which shows in outline what was to have been the character of the work when completed. The author was connected with Norfolk, and most probably with Elmham.

9. EULOGIUM (HISTORIARUM SIVE TEMPORIS): Chronicon ab Orbe condito usque ad Annum Domini 1366; a Monacho quodam Malmesbiriensi exaratum. Vols. I., II., and III. *Edited by* F. S. HAYDON, Esq., B.A. 1858–1863.

This is a Latin Chronicle extending from the Creation to the latter part of the reign of Edward III., and written by a monk of the Abbey of Malmesbury, in Wiltshire, about the year 1367. A continuation, carrying the history of England down to the year 1413, was added in the former half of the fifteenth century by an author whose name is not known. The original Chronicle contains a history of the world generally, but more especially of England to the year 1366. The continuation extends the history down to the coronation of Henry V. The Eulogium itself is chiefly valuable as containing a history, by a contemporary, of the period between 1356 and 1366. Among other interesting matter, the Chronicle contains a diary of the Poitiers campaign, evidently furnished by some person who accompanied the army of the Black Prince. The continuation of the Chronicle is also the work of a contemporary, and gives a very interesting account of the reigns of Richard II. and Henry IV.

10. MEMORIALS OF HENRY THE SEVENTH: Bernardi Andreæ Tholosatis Vita Regis Henrici Septimi; necnon alia quædam ad eundem Regem spectantia. *Edited by* JAMES GAIRDNER, Esq. 1858.

The contents of this volume are—(1) a life of Henry VII., by his poet laureate and historiographer, Bernard André, of Toulouse, with some compositions in verse, of which he is supposed to have been the author; (2) the journals of Roger Machado during certain embassies on which he was sent by Henry VII. to Spain and Brittany, the first of which had reference to the marriage of the King's son, Arthur, with Catharine of Arragon; (3) two curious reports by envoys sent to Spain in 1505 touching the succession to the Crown of Castile, and a project of marriage between Henry VII. and the Queen of Naples; and (4) an account of Philip of Castile's reception in England in 1506. Other documents of interest are given in an appendix.

11. MEMORIALS OF HENRY THE FIFTH. I.—Vita Henrici Quinti, Roberto Redmanno auctore. II.—Versus Rhythmici in laudem Regis Henrici Quinti. III.—Elmhami Liber Metricus de Henrico V. *Edited by* CHARLES A. COLE, Esq. 1858.

This volume contains three treatises which more or less illustrate the history of the reign of Henry V., viz.: A life by Robert Redman; a Metrical Chronicle by Thomas Elmham, prior of Lenton, a contemporary author; Versus Rhythmici, written apparently by a monk of Westminster Abbey, who was also a contemporary of Henry V. These works are printed for the first time.

12. MUNIMENTA GILDHALLÆ LONDONIENSIS; Liber Albus, Liber Custumarum, et Liber Horn, in archivis Gildhallæ asservati. Vol. I., Liber Albus. Vol. II. (in Two Parts), Liber Custumarum. Vol. III., Translation of the Anglo-Norman Passages in Liber Albus, Glossaries, Appendices, and Index. *Edited by* HENRY THOMAS RILEY, Esq., M.A., Barrister-at-Law. 1859-1862.

The manuscript of the *Liber Albus*, compiled by John Carpenter, Common Clerk of the City of London in the year 1419, gives an account of the laws, regulations, and institutions of that City in the 12th, 13th, 14th, and early part of the 15th centuries. The *Liber Custumarum* was compiled probably by various hands in the early part of the 14th century during the reign of Edward II. The manuscript, a folio volume, is preserved in the Record Room of the City of London, though some portion in its original state, borrowed from the City in the reign of Queen Elizabeth and never returned, forms part of the Cottonian MS. Claudius D. II. in the British Museum. It also gives an account of the laws, regulations, and institutions of the City of London in the 12th, 13th, and early part of the 14th centuries.

13. CHRONICA JOHANNIS DE OXENEDES. *Edited by* Sir HENRY ELLIS, K.H. 1859.

Although this Chronicle tells of the arrival of Hengist and Horsa in England in 449, yet it substantially begins with the reign of King Alfred, and comes down to 1292, where it ends abruptly. The history is particularly valuable for notices of events in the eastern portions of the Kingdom, not to be elsewhere obtained. Some curious facts are mentioned relative to the floods in that part of England, which are confirmed in the Friesland Chronicle of Anthony Heinrich, pastor of the Island of Mohr.

14. A COLLECTION OF POLITICAL POEMS AND SONGS RELATING TO ENGLISH HISTORY, FROM THE ACCESSION OF EDWARD III. TO THE REIGN OF HENRY VIII. Vols. I. and II. *Edited by* THOMAS WRIGHT, Esq., M.A. 1859-1861.

These Poems are perhaps the most interesting of all the historical writings of the period, though they cannot be relied on for accuracy of statement. They are various in character; some are upon religious subjects, some may be called satires, and some give no more than a court scandal; but as a whole they present a very fair picture of society, and of the relations of the different classes to one another. The period comprised is in itself interesting, and brings us through the decline of the feudal system, to the beginning of our modern history. The songs in old English are of considerable value to the philologist.

15. The "OPUS TERTIUM," "OPUS MINUS," &c., of ROGER BACON. *Edited by* J. S. BREWER, M.A., Professor of English Literature, King's College, London. 1859.

This is the celebrated treatise—never before printed—so frequently referred to by the great philosopher in his works. It contains the fullest details we possess of the life and labours of Roger Bacon: also a fragment by the same author, supposed to be unique, the "*Compendium Studii Theologiæ*."

16. BARTHOLOMÆI DE COTTON, MONACHI NORWICENSIS, HISTORIA ANGLICANA; 449-1298: necnon ejusdem Liber de Achiepiscopis et Episcopis Angliæ. *Edited by* HENRY RICHARDS LUARD, M.A., Fellow and Assistant Tutor of Trinity College, Cambridge. 1859.

The author, a monk of Norwich, has here given us a Chronicle of England from the arrival of the Saxons in 449 to the year 1298, in or about which year it appears that he died. The latter portion of this history (the whole of the reign of Edward I. more especially) is of great value, as the writer was contemporary with the events which he records. An Appendix contains several illustrative documents connected with the previous narrative.

17. BRUT Y TYWYSOGION; or, The Chronicle of the Princes of Wales. *Edited by* the Rev. JOHN WILLIAMS AB ITHEL, M.A. 1860.

This work, also known as "The Chronicle of the Princes of Wales," has been attributed to Caradoc of Llancarvan, who flourished about the middle of the twelfth century. It is written in the ancient Welsh language, begins with the abdication and death of Caedwala at Rome, in the year 681, and continues the history down to the subjugation of Wales by Edward I., about the year 1282.

18. A COLLECTION OF ROYAL AND HISTORICAL LETTERS DURING THE REIGN OF HENRY IV. 1399-1404. *Edited by* the Rev. F. C. HINGESTON, M.A., of Exeter College, Oxford. 1860.

This volume, like all the others in the series containing a miscellaneous selection of letters, is valuable on account of the light it throws upon biographical history, and the familiar view it presents of characters, manners, and events.

19. THE REPRESSOR OF OVER MUCH BLAMING OF THE CLERGY. By REGINALD PECOCK, sometime Bishop of Chichester. Vols. I. and II. *Edited by* CHURCHILL BABINGTON, B.D., Fellow of St. John's College, Cambridge. 1860.

The "Repressor" may be considered the earliest piece of sound theological disquisition of which our English prose literature can boast. The author was born about the end of the fourteenth century, consecrated Bishop of St. Asaph in the year 1444, and translated to the see of Chichester in 1450. While Bishop of St. Asaph, he zealously defended his brother prelates from the attacks of those who censured the bishops for their neglect of duty. He maintained that it was no part of a bishop's functions to appear in the pulpit, and that his time might be more profitably spent, and his dignity better maintained, in the performance of works of a higher character. Among those who thought differently were the Lollards, and against their general doctrines the "Repressor" is directed. Pecock took up a position midway between that of the Roman Church and that of the modern Anglican Church; but his work is interesting chiefly because it gives a full account of the views of the Lollards and of the arguments by which they were supported, and because it assists us to ascertain the state of feeling which ultimately led to the Reformation. Apart from religious matters, the light thrown upon contemporaneous history is very small, but the "Repressor" has great value for the philologist, as it tells us what were the characteristics of the language in use among the cultivated Englishmen of the fifteenth century.

20. ANNALES CAMBRIÆ. *Edited by* the Rev. JOHN WILLIAMS AB ITHEL, M.A. 1860.

These annals, which are in Latin, commence in 447, and come down to 1288. The earlier portion appears to be taken from an Irish Chronicle used by Tigernach, and by the compiler of the Annals of Ulster. During its first century it contains scarcely anything relating to Britain, the earliest direct concurrence with English history is relative to the mission of Augustine. Its notices throughout, though brief, are valuable. The annals were probably written at St. Davids, by Blegewryd, Archdeacon of Llandaff, the most learned man in his day in all Cymru.

21. THE WORKS OF GIRALDUS CAMBRENSIS. Vols. I., II., III., and IV. *Edited by* J. S. BREWER, M.A., Professor of English Literature, King's College, London. Vols. V., VI., and VII. *Edited by* the Rev. JAMES F. DIMOCK, M.A., Rector of Barnburgh, Yorkshire. 1861–1877.

These volumes contain the historical works of Gerald du Barry, who lived in the reigns of Henry II., Richard I., and John, and attempted to re-establish the independence of Wales by restoring the see of St. Davids to its ancient primacy. His works are of a very miscellaneous nature, both in prose and verse, and are remarkable chiefly for the racy and original anecdotes which they contain relating to contemporaries. He is the only Welsh writer of any importance who has contributed so much to the mediæval literature of this country, or assumed, in consequence of his nationality, so free and independent a tone. His frequent travels in Italy, in France, in Ireland, and in Wales, gave him opportunities for observation which did not generally fall to the lot of mediæval writers in the twelfth and thirteenth centuries, and of these observations Giraldus has made due use. Only extracts from these treatises have been printed before and almost all of them are taken from unique manuscripts.

The Topographia Hibernica (in Vol. V.) is the result of Giraldus' two visits to Ireland. The first in 1183, the second in 1185–6, when he accompanied Prince John into that country. A very interesting portion of this treatise is devoted to the animals of Ireland. It shows that he was a very accurate and acute observer, and his descriptions are given in a way that a scientific naturalist of the present day could hardly improve upon. The Expugnatio Hibernica was written about 1188 and may be regarded rather as a great epic than a sober relation of acts occurring in his own days. Vol. VI. contains the Itinerarium Kambriæ et Descriptio Kambriæ: and Vol. VII., the lives of S. Remigius and S. Hugh.

22. LETTERS AND PAPERS ILLUSTRATIVE OF THE WARS OF THE ENGLISH IN FRANCE DURING THE REIGN OF HENRY THE SIXTH, KING OF ENGLAND. Vol. I., and Vol. II. (in Two Parts). *Edited by* the Rev. JOSEPH STEVENSON, M.A., of University College, Durham, and Vicar of Leighton Buzzard. 1861–1864.

These letters and papers are derived chiefly from originals or contemporary copies extant in the Bibliothèque Impériale, and the Depôt des Archives, in Paris. They illustrate the policy adopted by John Duke of Bedford and his successors during their government of Normandy, and other provinces of France acquired by Henry V. Here may be traced, step by step, the gradual declension of the English power, until we are prepared for its final overthrow.

23. THE ANGLO-SAXON CHRONICLE, ACCORDING TO THE SEVERAL ORIGINAL AUTHORITIES. Vol. I., Original Texts. Vol II., Translation. *Edited and translated by* BENJAMIN THORPE, Esq., Member of the Royal Academy of Sciences at Munich, and of the Society of Netherlandish Literature at Leyden. 1861.

This chronicle, extending from the earliest history of Britain to 1154, is justly the boast of England; no other nation can produce any history, written in its own vernacular, at all approaching it, in antiquity, truthfulness, or extent, the historical books of the Bible alone excepted. There are at present six independent manuscripts of the Saxon Chronicle, ending in different years, and written in different parts of the country. In this edition, the text of each manuscript is printed in columns on the same page, so that the student may see at a glance the various changes which occur in orthography, whether arising from locality or age.

24. LETTERS AND PAPERS ILLUSTRATIVE OF THE REIGNS OF RICHARD III. AND HENRY VII. Vols. I. and II. *Edited by* JAMES GAIRDNER, Esq. 1861–1863.

The papers are derived from the MSS. in Public Record Office, the British Museum, and other repositories. The period to which they refer is unusually destitute of chronicles and other sources of historical information, so that the light obtained from them is of special importance. The principal contents of the volumes are some diplomatic Papers of Richard III.; correspondence between Henry VII. and Ferdinand and Isabella of Spain; documents relating to Edmund de la Pole, Earl of Suffolk; and a portion of the correspondence of James IV. of Scotland.

25. LETTERS OF BISHOP GROSSETESTE, illustrative of the Social Condition of his Time. *Edited by* HENRY RICHARDS LUARD, M.A., Fellow and Assistant Tutor of Trinity College, Cambridge. 1861.

The Letters of Robert Grosseteste (131 in number) are here collected from various sources, and a large portion of them is printed for the first time. They range in date from about 1210 to 1253, and relate to various matters connected not only with the political history of England during the reign of Henry III. but with its ecclesiastical condition. They refer especially to the diocese of Lincoln, of which Grosseteste was bishop.

26. DESCRIPTIVE CATALOGUE OF MANUSCRIPTS RELATING TO THE HISTORY OF GREAT BRITAIN AND IRELAND. Vol. I. (in Two Parts); Anterior to the Norman Invasion. Vol. II.; 1066–1200. Vol. III.; 1200–1327. *By* Sir THOMAS DUFFUS HARDY, D.C.L., Deputy Keeper of the Public Records. 1862–1871.

The object of this work is to publish notices of all known sources of British history, both printed and unprinted, in one continued sequence. The materials, when historical (as distinguished from biographical), are arranged under the year in which the latest event is recorded in the chronicle or history, and not under the period in which its author, real or supposed, flourished. Biographies are enumerated under the year in which the person commemorated died, and not under the year in which the life was written. A brief analysis of each work has been added when deserving it, in which original portions are distinguished from more compilations. If possible, the sources are indicated from which compilations have been derived. A biographical sketch of the author of each piece has been added, and a brief notice of such British authors as have written on historical subjects.

27. ROYAL AND OTHER HISTORICAL LETTERS ILLUSTRATIVE OF THE REIGN OF HENRY III. Vol. I., 1216–1235. Vol. II., 1236–1272. *Selected and edited by* the Rev. W. W. SHIRLEY, D.D., Regius Professor of Ecclesiastical History, and Canon of Christ Church, Oxford. 1862–1866.

The letters contained in these volumes are derived chiefly from the ancient correspondence formerly in the Tower of London, and now in the Public Record Office. They illustrate the political history of England during the growth of its liberties, and throw considerable light upon the personal history of Simon de Montfort. The affairs of France form the subject of many of them, especially in regard to the province of Gascony. The entire collection consists of nearly 700 documents, the greater portion of which is printed for the first time.

28. CHRONICA MONASTERII S. ALBANI.—1. THOMÆ WALSINGHAM HISTORIA ANGLICANA; Vol. I., 1272–1381 : Vol. II., 1381–1422. 2. WILLELMI RISHANGER CHRONICA ET ANNALES, 1259–1307. 3. JOHANNIS DE TROKELOWE ET HENRICI DE BLANEFORDE CHRONICA ET ANNALES, 1259–1296; 1307–1324; 1392–1406. 4. GESTA ABBATUM MONASTERII S. ALBANI, A THOMA WALSINGHAM, REGNANTE RICARDO SECUNDO, EJUSDEM ECCLESIÆ PRÆCENTORE, COMPILATA; Vol. I., 793–1290: Vol. II., 1290–1349: Vol. III., 1349–1411. 5. JOHANNIS AMUNDESHAM, MONACHI MONASTERII S. ALBANI, UT VIDETUR, ANNALES; Vols. I. and II. 6. REGISTRA QUORUNDAM ABBATUM MONASTERII S. ALBANI, QUI SÆCULO XV^{mo} FLORUERE; Vol. I., REGISTRUM ABBATIÆ JOHANNIS WHETHAMSTEDE, ABBATIS MONASTERII SANCTI ALBANI, ITERUM SUSCEPTÆ; ROBERTO BLAKENEY, CAPELLANO, QUONDAM ADSCRIPTUM: Vol. II., REGISTRA JOHANNIS WHETHAMSTEDE, WILLELMI ALBON, ET WILLELMI WALINGFORDE, ABBATUM MONASTERII SANCTI ALBANI, CUM APPENDICE, CONTINENTE QUASDAM EPISTOLAS, A JOHANNE WHETHAMSTEDE CONSCRIPTAS. 7. YPODIGMA NEUSTRIÆ A THOMA WALSINGHAM, QUONDAM MONACHO MONASTERII S. ALBANI, CONSCRIPTUM. *Edited by* HENRY THOMAS RILEY, Esq., M.A., Cambridge and Oxford; and of the Inner Temple, Barrister-at-Law. 1863–1876.

In the first two volumes is a History of England, from the death of Henry III. to the death of Henry V., by Thomas Walsingham, Precentor of St. Albans.
In the 3rd volume is a Chronicle of English History, attributed to William Rishanger, who lived in the reign of Edward I.: an account of transactions attending the award of the kingdom of Scotland to John Balliol, 1291–1292, also attributed to William Rishanger, but on no sufficient ground: a short Chronicle of English History, 1292 to 1300, by an unknown hand: a short Chronicle Willelmi Rishanger Gesta Edwardi Primi, Regis Angliæ, with Annales Regum Angliæ, probably by the same hand: and fragments of three Chronicles of English History, 1285 to 1307.
In the 4th volume is a Chronicle of English History, 1259 to 1296: Annals of Edward II., 1307 to 1323, by John de Trokelowe, a monk of St. Albans, and a continuation of Trokelowe's Annals, 1323, 1324, by Henry de Blaneforde: a full Chronicle of English History, 1392 to 1406; and an account of the Benefactors of St. Albans, written in the early part of the 15th century.
The 5th, 6th, and 7th volumes contain a history of the Abbots of St. Albans, 793 to 1411, mainly compiled by Thomas Walsingham: with a Continuation, from the closing pages of Parker MS. VII., in the Library of Corpus Christi College, Cambridge.
The 8th and 9th volumes, in continuation of the Annals, contain a Chronicle, probably by John Amundesham, a monk of St. Albans.
The 10th and 11th volumes relate especially to the acts and proceedings of Abbots Whethamstede, Albon, and Wallingford, and may be considered as a memorial of the chief historical and domestic events during those periods.
The 12th volume contains a compendious History of England to the reign of Henry V., and of Normandy in early times, also by Thomas Walsingham, and dedicated to Henry V. The compiler has often substituted other authorities in place of those consulted in the preparation of his larger work.

29. CHRONICON ABBATIÆ EVESHAMENSIS, AUCTORIBUS DOMINICO PRIORE EVESHAMIÆ ET THOMA DE MARLEBERGE ABBATE, A FUNDATIONE AD ANNUM 1213, UNA CUM CONTINUATIONE AD ANNUM 1418. *Edited by* the Rev. W. D. MACRAY, Bodleian Library, Oxford. 1863.

The Chronicle of Evesham illustrates the history of that important monastery from its foundation by Egwin, about 690, to the year 1418. Its chief feature is an autobiography, which makes us acquainted with the inner daily life of a great abbey, such as but rarely has been recorded. Interspersed are many notices of general, personal, and local history which will be read with much interest. This work exists in a single MS., and is for the first time printed.

30. RICARDI DE CIRENCESTRIA SPECULUM HISTORIALE DE GESTIS REGUM ANGLIÆ. Vol. I., 447-871. Vol. II., 872-1066. *Edited by* JOHN E. B. MAYOR, M.A., Fellow of St. John's College, Cambridge. 1863-1869.

The compiler, Richard of Cirencester, was a monk of Westminster, 1355-1400. In 1391 he obtained a licence to make a pilgrimage to Rome. His history, in four books, extends from 447 to 1066. He announces his intention of continuing it, but there is no evidence that he completed any more. This chronicle gives many charters in favour of Edward the Confessor, whose reign occupies the fourth book. A treatise on the Coronation, by William of Sudbury, a monk of Westminster, fills book ii. c. 3. It was on this author that C. J. Bertram fathered his forgery, *De Situ Brittaniæ* in 1747.

31. YEAR BOOKS OF THE REIGN OF EDWARD THE FIRST. Years 20-21, 21-22, 30-31, 32-33, and 33-35 Edw. I.; and 11-12 Edw. III. *Edited and translated by* ALFRED JOHN HORWOOD, Esq., of the Middle Temple Barrister-at-Law. Years 12-13, 13-14, 14, and 14-15 Edward III. *Edited and translated by* LUKE OWEN PIKE, Esq., M.A., of Lincoln's Inn, Barrister-at-Law. 1863-1886.

The "Year Books" are the earliest of our Law Reports. They contain matter not only of practical utility to lawyers in the present day, but also illustrative of almost every branch of history, while for certain philological purposes they hold a position absolutely unique. The history of the constitution and of the law, of procedure, and of practice, the jurisdiction of the various Courts, and their relation to one another, as well as to the Sovereign and Council, cannot be known without the aid of the Year Books.

32. NARRATIVES OF THE EXPULSION OF THE ENGLISH FROM NORMANDY 1449-1450. —Robertus Blondelli de Reductione Normanniæ : Le Recouvrement de Normendie, par Berry, Hérault du Roy : Conferences between the Ambassadors of France and England. *Edited, from MSS. in the Imperial Library at Paris, by* the Rev. JOSEPH STEVENSON, M.A., of University College, Durham. 1863.

This volume contains the narrative of an eye-witness who details with considerable power and minuteness the circumstances which attended the final expulsion of the English from Normandy in 1450. Commencing with the infringement of the truce by the capture of Fougères, and ending with the battle of Formigny and the embarkation of the Duke of Somerset. The period embraced is less than two years.

33. HISTORIA ET CARTULARIUM MONASTERII S. PETRI GLOUCESTRIÆ. Vols. I., II., and III. *Edited by* W. H. HART, Esq., F.S.A., Membre correspondant de la Société des Antiquaires de Normandie. 1863-1867.

This work consists of two parts, the History and the Cartulary of the Monastery of St. Peter, Gloucester. The history furnishes an account of the monastery from its foundation, in the year 681, to the early part of the reign of Richard II., together with a calendar of donations and benefactions. It treats principally of the affairs of the monastery, but occasionally matters of general history are introduced. Its authorship has generally been assigned to Walter Froucester the twentieth abbot, but without any foundation.

34. ALEXANDRI NECKAM DE NATURIS RERUM LIBRI DUO; with NECKAM'S POEM, DE LAUDIBUS DIVINÆ SAPIENTIÆ. *Edited by* THOMAS WRIGHT, Esq., M.A., 1863.

Neckam was a man who devoted himself to science, such as it was in the twelfth century. In the "De Naturis Rerum" are to be found what may be called the rudiments of many sciences mixed up with much error and ignorance. Neckam was not thought infallible, even by his contemporaries, for Roger Bacon remarks of him, "This Alexander in many things wrote what was "true and useful; but he neither can nor ought by just title to be reckoned among authorities." Neckam, however, had sufficient independence of thought to differ from some of the schoolmen who in his time considered themselves the only judges of literature. He had his own views in morals, and in giving us a glimpse of them, as well as of his other opinions, he throws much light upon the manners, customs, and general tone of thought prevalent in the twelfth century. The poem entitled "De Laudibus Divinæ Sapientiæ" appears to be a metrical paraphrase or abridgment of the "De Naturis Rerum." It is written in the elegiac metre, and it is, as a whole, above the ordinary standard of mediæval Latin.

35. LEECHDOMS, WORTCUNNING, AND STARCRAFT OF EARLY ENGLAND; being a Collection of Documents illustrating the History of Science in this Country before the Norman Conquest. Vols. I., II., and III. *Collected and edited*

by the Rev. T. OSWALD COCKAYNE, M.A., of St. John's College, Cambridge, 1864–1866.

This work illustrates not only the history of science, but the history of superstition. In addition to the information bearing directly upon the medical skill and medical faith of the times, there are many passages which incidentally throw light upon the general mode of life and ordinary diet. The volumes are interesting not only in their scientific, but also in their social aspect.

36. ANNALES MONASTICI. Vol. I.:—Annales de Margan, 1066–1232; Annales de Theokesberia, 1066–1263; Annales de Burton, 1004–1263. Vol. II.:—Annales Monasterii de Wintonia. 519–1277; Annales Monasterii de Waverleia, 1–1291. Vol. III.:—Annales Prioratus de Dunstaplia, 1–1297. Annales Monasterii de Bermundeseia, 1042–1432. Vol. IV.:—Annales Monasterii de Oseneia, 1016–1347; Chronicon vulgo dictum Chronicon Thomæ Wykes, 1066–1289; Annales Prioratus de Wigornia, 1–1377. Vol. V.:—Index and Glossary. *Edited by* HENRY RICHARDS LUARD, M.A., Fellow and Assistant Tutor of Trinity College, and Registrary of the University, Cambridge. 1864–1869.

The present collection of Monastic Annals embraces all the more important chronicles compiled in religious houses in England during the thirteenth century. These distinct works are ten in number. The extreme period which they embrace ranges from the year 1 to 1432, although they refer more especially to the reigns of John, Henry III., and Edward I. Some of these narratives have already appeared in print, but others are printed for the first time.

37. MAGNA VITA S. HUGONIS EPISCOPI LINCOLNIENSIS. From MSS. in the Bodleian Library, Oxford, and the Imperial Library, Paris. *Edited by* the Rev. JAMES F. DIMOCK, M.A., Rector of Barnburgh, Yorkshire. 1864.

This work contains a number of very curious and interesting incidents, and being the work of a contemporary, is very valuable, not only as a truthful biography of a celebrated ecclesiastic but as the work of a man, who, from personal knowledge, gives notices of passing events, as well as of individuals who were then taking active part in public affairs. The author, in all probability, was Adam Abbot of Evesham. He was domestic chaplain and private confessor of Bishop Hugh, and in these capacities was admitted to the closest intimacy. Bishop Hugh was Prior of Witham for 11 years before he became Bishop of Lincoln. His consecration took place on the 21st September 1186; he died on the 16th of November 1200; and was canonized in 1220.

38. CHRONICLES AND MEMORIALS OF THE REIGN OF RICHARD THE FIRST. Vol. I.:—ITINERARIUM PEREGRINORUM ET GESTA REGIS RICARDI. Vol. II.:—EPISTOLÆ CANTUARIENSES; the Letters of the Prior and Convent of Christ Church, Canterbury; 1187 to 1199. *Edited by* WILLIAM STUBBS, M.A., Vicar of Navestock, Essex, and Lambeth Librarian. 1864–1865.

The authorship of the Chronicle in Vol. I., hitherto ascribed to Geoffrey Vinesauf, is now more correctly ascribed to Richard, Canon of the Holy Trinity of London. The narrative extends from 1187 to 1199; but its chief interest consists in the minute and authentic narrative which it furnishes of the exploits of Richard I., from his departure from England in December 1189 to his death in 1199. The author states in his prologue that he was an eye-witness of much that he records; and various incidental circumstances which occur in the course of the narrative confirm this assertion.

The letters in Vol. II., written between 1187 and 1199, are of value as furnishing authentic materials for the history of the ecclesiastical condition of England during the reign of Richard I. They had their origin in a dispute which arose from the attempts of Baldwin and Hubert, archbishops of Canterbury, to found a college of secular canons, a project which gave great umbrage to the monks of Canterbury, who saw in it a design to supplant them in their function of metropolitan chapter. These letters are printed, for the first time, from a MS. belonging to the archiepiscopal library at Lambeth.

39. RECUEIL DES CRONIQUES ET ANCHIENNES ISTORIES DE LA GRANT BRETAIGNEA PRESENT NOMME ENGLETERRE, par JEHAN DE WAURIN. Vol. I. Albina to 688. Vol. II., 1399–1422. Vol. III., 1422–1431. *Edited by* Sir WILLIAM HARDY, F.S.A. 1864–1879. Vol. IV. 1431–1443. *Edited by* Sir WILLIAM HARDY, F.S.A., and EDWARD L. C. P. HARDY, Esq., F.S.A. 1884.

40. A COLLECTION OF THE CHRONICLES AND ANCIENT HISTORIES OF GREAT BRITAIN, NOW CALLED ENGLAND, by JOHN DE WAVRIN. Albina to 688. (Translation of the preceding Vols. I. and II.) *Edited and translated by* Sir WILLIAM HARDY, F.S.A., and EDWARD L. C. P. HARDY, Esq., F.S.A. 1864–1887.

This curious chronicle extends from the fabulous period of history down to the return of Edward IV. to England in the year 1471 after the second deposition of Henry VI. The manuscript from which the text of the work is taken is preserved in the Imperial Library at Paris, and is believed to be the only complete and nearly contemporary copy in existence. It is illustrated with exquisite miniatures, vignettes, and initial letters. It was written towards the end of the fifteenth century, having been expressly executed for Louis de Bruges, Seigneur de la Gruthuyse and Earl of Winchester, from whose cabinet it passed into the library of Louis XII. at Blois.

41. POLYCHRONICON RANULPHI HIGDEN, with Trevisa's Translation. Vols. I. and II. *Edited by* CHURCHILL BABINGTON, B.D., Senior Fellow of St. John's College, Cambridge. Vols. III., IV., V., VI., VII., VIII., and IX. *Edited by* the Rev. JOSEPH RAWSON LUMBY, D.D., Norrisian Professor of Divinity, Vicar of St. Edward's, Fellow of St. Catharine's College, and late Fellow of Magdalene College, Cambridge. 1865-1886.

This is one of the many mediæval chronicles which assume the character of a history of the world. It begins with the creation, and is brought down to the author's own time, the reign of Edward III. Prefixed to the historical portion, is a chapter devoted to geography, in which is given a description of every known land. To say that the Polychronicon was written in the fourteenth century is to say that it is not free from inaccuracies. It has, however, a value apart from its intrinsic merits. It enables us to form a very fair estimate of the knowledge of history and geography which well-informed readers of the fourteenth and fifteenth centuries possessed, for it was then the standard work on general history.

The two English translations, which are printed with the original Latin, afford interesting illustrations of the gradual change of our language, for one was made in the fourteenth century, the other in the fifteenth. The differences between Trevisa's version and that of the unknown writer are often considerable.

42. LE LIVERE DE REIS DE BRITTANIE E LE LIVERE DE REIS DE ENGLETERE. *Edited by* JOHN GLOVER, M.A., Vicar of Brading, Isle of Wight, formerly Librarian of Trinity College, Cambridge. 1865.

These two treatises, though they cannot rank as independent narratives, are nevertheless valuable as careful abstracts of previous historians, especially "Le Livere de Reis de Engletere." Some various readings are given which are interesting to the philologist as instances of semi-Saxonized French. It is supposed that Peter of Ickham was the supposed author

43. CHRONICA MONASTERII DE MELSA AB ANNO 1150 USQUE AD ANNUM 1406. Vols. I., II., and III. *Edited by* EDWARD AUGUSTUS BOND, Esq., Assistant-Keeper of Manuscripts, and Egerton Librarian, British Museum. 1866-1868.

The Abbey of Meaux was a Cistercian house, and the work of its abbot is both curious and valuable. It is a faithful and often minute record of the establishment of a religious community, of its progress in forming an ample revenue, of its struggles to maintain its acquisitions, and of its relations to the governing institutions of the country. In addition to the private affairs of the monastery, some light is thrown upon the public events of the time, which are however kept distinct, and appear at the end of the history of each abbot's administration. The text has been printed from what is said to be the autograph of the original compiler, Thomas de Burton, the nineteenth abbot.

44. MATTHÆI PARISIENSIS HISTORIA ANGLORUM, SIVE, UT VULGO DICITUR, HISTORIA MINOR. Vols. I., II., and III. 1067-1253. *Edited by* Sir FREDERIC MADDEN, K.H., Keeper of the Manuscript Department of British Museum. 1866-1869.

The exact date at which this work was written is, according to the chronicler, 1250. The history is of considerable value as an illustration of the period during which the author lived, and contains a good summary of the events which followed the Conquest. This minor chronicle is, however, based on another work (also written by Matthew Paris) giving fuller details, which has been called the "Historia Major." The chronicle here published, nevertheless, gives some information not to be found in the greater history.

45. LIBER MONASTERII DE HYDA: A CHRONICLE AND CHARTULARY OF HYDE ABBEY, WINCHESTER, 455-1023. *Edited, from a Manuscript in the Library of the Earl of Macclesfield, by* EDWARD EDWARDS, Esq. 1866.

The "Book of Hyde" is a compilation from much earlier sources which are usually indicated with considerable care and precision. In many cases, however, the Hyde Chronicler appears to correct, to qualify, or to amplify—either from tradition or from sources of information not now discoverable—the statements, which, in substance, he adopts. He also mentions, and frequently quotes from writers whose works are either entirely lost or at present known only by fragments.

There is to be found, in the "Book of Hyde," much information relating to the reign of King Alfred which is not known to exist elsewhere. The volume contains some curious specimens of Anglo-Saxon and Mediæval English.

46. CHRONICON SCOTORUM: A CHRONICLE OF IRISH AFFAIRS, from the EARLIEST TIMES to 1135; and SUPPLEMENT, containing the Events from 1141 to 1150. *Edited, with Translation, by* WILLIAM MAUNSELL HENNESSY, Esq., M.R.I.A. 1866.

There is, in this volume, a legendary account of the peopling of Ireland and of the adventures which befell the various heroes who are said to have been connected with Irish history. The details are, however, very meagre both for this period and for the time when history becomes more authentic. The plan adopted in the chronicle gives the appearance of an accuracy to which the earlier portions of the work cannot have any claim. The succession of events is marked year by year, from A.M. 1599 to A.D. 1150. The principal events narrated in the later portion of the work are, the invasions of foreigners, and the wars of the Irish among themselves. The text has been printed from a MS. preserved in the library of Trinity College, Dublin, written partly in Latin, partly in Irish.

47. THE CHRONICLE OF PIERRE DE LANGTOFT, IN FRENCH VERSE, FROM THE EARLIEST PERIOD TO THE DEATH OF EDWARD I. Vols. I. and II. *Edited by* THOMAS WRIGHT, Esq., M.A. 1866–1868.

> It is probable that Pierre de Langtoft was a canon of Bridlington, in Yorkshire, and lived in the reign of Edward I., and during a portion of the reign of Edward II. This chronicle is divided into three parts; in the first, is an abridgment of Geoffrey of Monmouth's "Historia Britonum;" in the second, a history of the Anglo-Saxon and Norman kings, to the death of Henry III.; in the third, a history of the reign of Edward I. The principal object of the work was apparently to show the justice of Edward's Scottish wars. The language is singularly corrupt, and a curious specimen of the French of Yorkshire.

48. THE WAR OF THE GAEDHIL WITH THE GAILL, or THE INVASIONS OF IRELAND BY THE DANES AND OTHER NORSEMEN. *Edited, with a Translation, by* JAMES HENTHORN TODD, D.D., Senior Fellow of Trinity College, and Regius Professor of Hebrew in the University, Dublin. 1867.

> The work in its present form, in the editor's opinion, is a comparatively modern version of an undoubtedly ancient original. That it was compiled from contemporary materials has been proved by curious incidental evidence. It is stated in the account given of the battle of Clontarf that the full tide in Dublin Bay on the day of the battle (23 April 1014) coincided with sunrise; and that the returning tide in the evening aided considerably in the defeat of the Danes. The fact has been verified by astronomical calculations, and the inference is that the author of the chronicle, if not an eye-witness, must have derived his information from eye-witnesses. The contents of the work are sufficiently described in its title. The story is told after the manner of the Scandinavian Sagas, with poems and fragments of poems introduced into the prose narrative.

49. GESTA REGIS HENRICI SECUNDI BENEDICTI ABBATIS. CHRONICLE OF THE REIGNS OF HENRY II. AND RICHARD I., 1169–1192, known under the name of BENEDICT OF PETERBOROUGH. Vols. I. and II. *Edited by* WILLIAM STUBBS, M.A., Regius Professor of Modern History, Oxford, and Lambeth Librarian. 1867.

> This chronicle of the reigns of Henry II. and Richard I., known commonly under the name of Benedict of Peterborough, is one of the best existing specimens of a class of historical compositions of the first importance to the student.

50. MUNIMENTA ACADEMICA, OR, DOCUMENTS ILLUSTRATIVE OF ACADEMICAL LIFE AND STUDIES AT OXFORD (in Two Parts). *Edited by* the Rev. HENRY ANSTEY, M.A., Vicar of St. Wendron, Cornwall, and lately Vice-Principal of St. Mary Hall, Oxford. 1868.

> This work will supply materials for a History of Academical Life and Studies in the University of Oxford during the 13th, 14th, and 15th centuries.

51. CHRONICA MAGISTRI ROGERI DE HOUEDENE. Vols. I., II., III., and IV. *Edited by* WILLIAM STUBBS, M.A., Regius Professor of Modern History, and Fellow of Oriel College, Oxford. 1868–1871.

> This work has long been justly celebrated, but not thoroughly understood until Mr. Stubbs' edition. The earlier portion, extending from 732 to 1148, appears to be a copy of a compilation made in Northumbria about 1161, to which Hoveden added little. From 1148 to 1169—a very valuable portion of this work—the matter is derived from another source, to which Hoveden appears to have supplied little, and not always judiciously. From 1170 to 1192 is the portion which corresponds with the Chronicle known under the name of Benedict of Peterborough (see No. 49); but it is not a copy, being sometimes an abridgment, at others a paraphrase; occasionally the two works entirely agree; showing that both writers had access to the same materials, but dealt with them differently. From 1192 to 1201 may be said to be wholly Hoveden's work; it is extremely valuable, and an authority of the first importance.

52. WILLELMI MALMESBIRIENSIS MONACHI DE GESTIS PONTIFICUM ANGLORUM DIBBI QUINQUE. *Edited by* N. E. S. A. HAMILTON, Esq., of the Department of Manuscripts, British Museum. 1870.

> William of Malmesbury's "Gesta Pontificum" is the principal foundation of English Ecclesiastical Biography, down to the year 1122. The manuscript which has been followed in this Edition is supposed by Mr. Hamilton to be the author's autograph, containing his latest additions and amendments.

53. HISTORIC AND MUNICIPAL DOCUMENTS OF IRELAND, FROM THE ARCHIVES OF THE CITY OF DUBLIN, &c. 1172–1320. *Edited by* JOHN T. GILBERT, Esq., F.S.A., Secretary of the Public Record Office of Ireland. 1870.

> A collection of original documents, elucidating mainly the history and condition of the municipal, middle, and trading classes under or in relation with the rule of England in Ireland,—a subject hitherto in almost total obscurity. Extending over the first hundred and fifty years of the Anglo-Norman settlement, the series includes charters, municipal laws and regulations, rolls of names of citizens and members of merchant-guilds, lists of commodities with their rates, correspondence, illustrations of relations between ecclesiastics and laity; together with many documents exhibiting the state of Ireland during the presence there of the Scots under Robert and Edward Bruce.

54. THE ANNALS OF LOCH CÉ. A CHRONICLE OF IRISH AFFAIRS, FROM 1041 to 1590. Vols. I. and II. *Edited, with a Translation, by* WILLIAM MAUNSELL HENNESSY, Esq., M.R.I.A. 1871.

The original of this chronicle has passed under various names. The title of "Annals of Loch Cé" was given to it by Professor O'Curry, on the ground that it was transcribed for Brian Mac Dermot, an Irish chieftain, who resided on the island in Loch Cé, in the county of Roscommon. It adds much to the materials for the civil and ecclesiastical history of Ireland; and contains many curious references to English and foreign affairs, not noticed in any other chronicle.

55. MONUMENTA JURIDICA. THE BLACK BOOK OF THE ADMIRALTY, WITH APPENDICES. Vols. I., II., III., and IV. *Edited by* SIR TRAVERS TWISS, Q.C., D.C.L. 1871–1876.

This book contains the ancient ordinances and laws relating to the navy, and was probably compiled for the use of the Lord High Admiral of England. Selden calls it the "jewel of the Admiralty Records." Prynne ascribes to the Black Book the same authority in the Admiralty as the Black and Red Books have in the Court of Exchequer, and most English writers on maritime law recognize its importance.

56. MEMORIALS OF THE REIGN OF HENRY VI.:—OFFICIAL CORRESPONDENCE OF THOMAS BEKYNTON, SECRETARY TO HENRY VI., AND BISHOP OF BATH AND WELLS. *Edited, from a MS. in the Archiepiscopal Library at Lambeth, with an Appendix of Illustrative Documents, by* the Rev. GEORGE WILLIAMS, B.D., Vicar of Ringwood, late Fellow of King's College, Cambridge. Vols. I. and II. 1872.

These curious volumes are of a miscellaneous character, and were probably compiled under the immediate direction of Beokynton before he had attained to the Episcopate. They contain many of the Bishop's own letters, and several written by him in the King's name; also letters to himself while Royal Secretary, and others addressed to the King.

57. MATTHÆI PARISIENSIS, MONACHI SANCTI ALBANI, CHRONICA MAJORA. Vol. I. The Creation to A.D. 1066. Vol. II. A.D. 1067 to A.D. 1216. Vol. III. A.D. 1216 to A.D. 1239. Vol. IV. A.D. 1240 to A.D. 1247. Vol. V. A.D. 1248 to A.D. 1259. Vol. VI. Additamenta. Vol. VII. Index. *Edited by* HENRY RICHARDS LUARD, D.D., Fellow of Trinity College, Registrary of the University, and Vicar of Great St. Mary's, Cambridge. 1872–1884.

This work contains the "Chronica Majora" of Matthew Paris, one of the most valuable and frequently consulted of the ancient English Chronicles. It is published from its commencement, for the first time. The editions by Archbishop Parker, and William Watts, severally begin at the Norman Conquest.

58. MEMORIALE FRATRIS WALTERI DE COVENTRIA.—THE HISTORICAL COLLECTIONS OF WALTER OF COVENTRY. Vols. I. and II. *Edited, from the MS. in the Library of Corpus Christi College, Cambridge, by* WILLIAM STUBBS, M.A., Regius Professor of Modern History, and Fellow of Oriel College, Oxford. 1872–1873.

This work, now printed in full for the first time, has long been a desideratum by Historical Scholars. The first portion, however, is not of much importance, being only a compilation from earlier writers. The part relating to the first quarter of the thirteenth century is the most valuable and interesting.

59. THE ANGLO-LATIN SATIRICAL POETS AND EPIGRAMMATISTS OF THE TWELFTH CENTURY. Vols. I. and II. *Collected and edited by* THOMAS WRIGHT, Esq., M.A., Corresponding Member of the National Institute of France (Académie des Inscriptions et Belles-Lettres). 1872.

The Poems contained in these volumes have long been known and appreciated as the best satires of the age in which their authors flourished, and were deservedly popular during the 13th and 14th centuries.

60. MATERIALS FOR A HISTORY OF THE REIGN OF HENRY VII., FROM ORIGINAL DOCUMENTS PRESERVED IN THE PUBLIC RECORD OFFICE. Vols. I. and II. *Edited by* the Rev. WILLIAM CAMPBELL, M.A., one of Her Majesty's Inspectors of Schools. 1873–1877.

These volumes are valuable as illustrating the acts and proceedings of Henry VII. on ascending the throne, and shadow out the policy he afterwards adopted.

61. HISTORICAL PAPERS AND LETTERS FROM THE NORTHERN REGISTERS. *Edited by* JAMES RAINE, M.A., Canon of York, and Secretary of the Surtees Society. 1873.

The documents in this volume illustrate, for the most part, the general history of the north of England, particularly in its relation to Scotland.

62. REGISTRUM PALATINUM DUNELMENSE. THE REGISTER OF RICHARD DE KELLAWE, LORD PALATINE AND BISHOP OF DURHAM; 1311–1316. Vols. I., II., III., and IV. *Edited by* Sir THOMAS DUFFUS HARDY, D.C.L., Deputy Keeper of the Public Records. 1873–1878.

Bishop Kellawe's Register contains the proceedings of his prelacy, both lay and ecclesiastical and is the earliest Register of the Palatinate of Durham.

63. MEMORIALS OF SAINT DUNSTAN, ARCHBISHOP OF CANTERBURY. *Edited by* WILLIAM STUBBS, M.A., Regius Professor of Modern History, and Fellow of Oriel College, Oxford. 1874.

This volume contains several lives of Archbishop Dunstan, opening various points of Historical and Literary interest.

64. CHRONICON ANGLIÆ, AB ANNO DOMINI 1328 USQUE AD ANNUM 1388, AUCTORE MONACHO QUODAM SANCTI ALBANI. *Edited by* EDWARD MAUNDE THOMPSON, Esq., Barrister-at-Law, and Assistant-Keeper of the Manuscripts in the British Museum. 1874.

This chronicle gives a circumstantial history of the close of the reign of Edward III.

65. THÓMAS SAGA ERKIBYSKUPS. A LIFE OF ARCHBISHOP THOMAS BECKET, IN ICELANDIC. Vols. I. and II. *Edited, with English Translation, Notes, and Glossary* by M. EIRÍKR MAGNÚSSON, M.A., Sub-Librarian of the University Library, Cambridge. 1875–1884.

This work is derived from the Life of Becket written by Benedict of Peterborough, and apparently supplies the missing portions in Benedict's biography.

66. RADULPHI DE COGGESHALL CHRONICON ANGLICANUM. *Edited by* the Rev. JOSEPH STEVENSON, M.A. 1875.

This volume contains the "Chronicon Anglicanum," by Ralph of Coggleshall, the "Libellus de Expugnatione Terræ Sanctæ per Saladinum," usually ascribed to the same author, and other pieces of an interesting character.

67. MATERIALS FOR THE HISTORY OF THOMAS BECKET, ARCHBISHOP OF CANTERBURY. Vols. I., II., III., IV., V., and VI. *Edited by* the Rev. JAMES CRAIGIE ROBERTSON, M.A., Canon of Canterbury. 1875–1883. Vol. VII. *Edited* by JOSEPH BRIGSTOCKE SHEPPARD, Esq., LL.D. 1885.

This publication comprises all contemporary materials for the history of Archbishop Thomas Becket. The first volume contains the life of that celebrated man, and the miracles after his death, by William, a monk of Canterbury. The second, the life by Benedict of Peterborough; John of Salisbury; Alan of Tewkesbury; and Edward Grim. The third, the life by William Fitzstephen; and Herbert of Bosham. The fourth, anonymous lives, Quadrilogus, &c. The fifth, sixth, and seventh, the Epistles, and known letters.

68. RADULFI DE DICETO DECANI LUNDONIENSIS OPERA HISTORICA. THE HISTORICAL WORKS OF MASTER RALPH DE DICETO, DEAN OF LONDON. Vols. I. and II. *Edited, from the Original Manuscripts,* by WILLIAM STUBBS, M.A., Regius Professor of Modern History, and Fellow of Oriel College, Oxford. 1876.

The Historical Works of Ralph de Diceto are some of the most valuable materials for British History. The Abbreviationes Chronicorum extend from the Creation to 1147, and the Ymagines Historiarum to 1201.

69. ROLL OF THE PROCEEDINGS OF THE KING'S COUNCIL IN IRELAND, FOR A PORTION OF THE 16TH YEAR OF THE REIGN OF RICHARD II. 1392–93. *Edited by* the Rev. JAMES GRAVES, A.B. 1877.

This Roll throws considerable light on the History of Ireland at a period little known. It seems the only document of the kind extant.

70. HENRICI DE BRACTON DE LEGIBUS ET CONSUETUDINIBUS ANGLIÆ LIBRI QUINQUE IN VARIOS TRACTATUS DISTINCTI. AD DIVERSORUM ET VETUSTISSIMORUM CODICUM COLLATIONEM TYPIS VULGATI. Vols. I., II., III., IV., V., and VI. *Edited* by SIR TRAVERS TWISS, Q.C., D.C.L. 1878–1883.

This is a new edition of Bracton's celebrated work, collated with MSS. in the British Museum; the Libraries of Lincoln's Inn, Middle Temple, and Gray's Inn; Bodleian Library, Oxford; the Bibliothèque Nationale, Paris; &c.

71. THE HISTORIANS OF THE CHURCH OF YORK, AND ITS ARCHBISHOPS. Vols. I. and II. *Edited by* JAMES RAINE, M.A., Canon of York, and Secretary of the Surtees Society. 1879–1886.

This will form a complete "Corpus Historicum Eboracense," a work very much needed.

72. REGISTRUM MALMESBURIENSE. THE REGISTER OF MALMESBURY ABBEY; PRESERVED IN THE PUBLIC RECORD OFFICE. Vols. I. and II. *Edited by* J S BREWER, M.A., Preacher at the Rolls, and Rector of Toppesfield; *and* CHARLES TRICE MARTIN, Esq., B.A. 1879, 1880.

This work illustrates many curious points of history, the growth of society, the distribution of land, the relations of landlord and tenant, national customs, &c.

73. HISTORICAL WORKS OF GERVASE OF CANTERBURY. Vols. I. and II. THE CHRONICLE OF THE REIGNS OF STEPHEN, HENRY II., and RICHARD I., BY GERVASE, THE MONK OF CANTERBURY. *Edited by* WILLIAM STUBBS, D.D.; Canon Residentiary of St. Paul's, London; Regius Professor of Modern History and Fellow of Oriel College, Oxford; &c. 1879, 1880.

    The Historical Works of Gervase of Canterbury are of great importance as regards the questions of Church and State, during the period in which he wrote. This work was printed by Twysden, in the "Historiæ Anglicanæ Scriptores X.," more than two centuries ago.

74. HENRICI ARCHIDIACONI HUNTENDUNENSIS HISTORIA ANGLORUM. THE HISTORY OF THE ENGLISH, BY HENRY, ARCHDEACON OF HUNTINGDON, from A.D. 55 to A.D. 1154, in Eight Books. *Edited by* THOMAS ARNOLD, ESQ., M.A. 1879.

    Henry of Huntingdon's work was first printed by Sir Henry Savile, in 1596, in his "Scriptores post Bedam," and reprinted at Frankfort in 1601. Both editions are very rare and inaccurate. The first five books of the History were published in 1848 in the "Monumenta Historica Britannica," which is out of print. The present volume contains the whole of the manuscript of Huntingdon's History in eight books, collated with a manuscript lately discovered at Paris.

75. THE HISTORICAL WORKS OF SYMEON OF DURHAM. Vols. I. and II. *Edited by* THOMAS ARNOLD, ESQ., M.A. 1882–1885.

    The first volume of this edition of the Historical Works of Symeon of Durham, contains the "Historia Dunelmensis Ecclesiæ," and other Works. The second volume contains the "Historia Regum," &c.

76. CHRONICLES OF THE REIGNS OF EDWARD I. AND EDWARD II. Vols. I. and II. *Edited by* WILLIAM STUBBS, D.D., Canon Residentiary of St. Paul's, London; Regius Professor of Modern History, and Fellow of Oriel College, Oxford, &c. 1882, 1883.

    The first volume of these Chronicles contains the "Annales Londonienses" and the "Annales Paulini:" the second, I.—Commendatio Lamentabilis in Transitu magni Regis Edwardi. II.—Gesta Edwardi de Carnarvan Auctore Canonico Bridlingtoniensi. III.—Monachi cujusdam Malmesberiensis Vita, Edwardi II. IV.—Vita et Mors Edwardi II. Conscripta a Thoma de la Moore.

77. REGISTRUM EPISTOLARUM FRATRIS JOHANNIS PECKHAM, ARCHIEPISCOPI CANTUARIENSIS. Vols. I., II., and III. *Edited by* CHARLES TRICE MARTIN, ESQ., B.A., F.S.A., 1882–1886.

    These Letters are of great value for illustrating English Ecclesiastical History.

78. REGISTER OF S. OSMUND. *Edited by* the Rev. W. H. RICH JONES, M.A., F.S.A., Canon of Salisbury, Vicar of Bradford-on-Avon. Vols. I. and II. 1883, 1884.

    This Register, of which a complete copy is here printed for the first time, is among the most ancient of the muniments of the Bishops of Salisbury. It derives its name from containing the statutes, rules, and orders made or compiled by S. Osmund, to be observed in the Cathedral and diocese of Salisbury. The first 19 folios contain the "Consuetudinary," the exposition, as regards ritual, of the "Use of Sarum."

79. CHARTULARY OF THE ABBEY OF RAMSEY. Vols. I. and II. *Edited by* WILLIAM HENRY HART, Esq., F.S.A., and the Rev. PONSONBY ANNESLEY LYONS. 1884, 1886.

    This Chartulary of the Ancient Benedictine Monastery of Ramsey, Huntingdonshire, came to the Crown on the Dissolution of Monasteries, was afterwards preserved in the Stone Tower Westminster Hall, and thence transferred to the Public Record Office.

80. CHARTULARIES OF ST. MARY'S ABBEY, DUBLIN, WITH THE REGISTER OF ITS HOUSE AT DUNBRODY, COUNTY OF WEXFORD, AND ANNALS OF IRELAND, 1162–1370. *Edited by* JOHN THOMAS GILBERT, Esq., F.S.A., M.R.I.A. Vols. I. & II. 1884, 1885.

    The Chartularies and register, here printed for the first time, are the only surviving manuscripts of their class in connexion with the Cistercians in Ireland. With them are included accounts of the other establishments of the Cistercian Order in Ireland, together with the earliest body of Anglo-Irish Annals extant.

81. EADMERI HISTORIA NOVORUM IN ANGLIA, ET OPUSCULA DUO DE VITA SANCTI ANSELMI ET QUIBUSDAM MIRACULIS EJUS. *Edited by* the Rev. MARTIN RULE, M.A. 1884.

    This volume contains the "Historiæ Novorum in Anglia," of Eadmer; his treatise "De Vita et conversatione Anselmi Archiepiscopi Cantuariensis," and a Tract entitled "Quaedam Parva Descriptio Miraculorum gloriosi Patris Anselmi Cantuariensis."

82. CHRONICLES OF THE REIGNS OF STEPHEN, HENRY II., AND RICHARD I. Vols. I. II., and III., *Edited by* RICHARD HOWLETT, Esq., of the Middle Temple, Barrister-at-law. 1884–1886.

Vol. I. contains Books I.-IV. of the "Historia Rerum Anglicarum" of William of Newburgh.
Vol. II. contains Book V. of that work, the continuation of the same to A.D. 1298, and the "Draco Normannicus" of Etienne de Rouen.
Vol. III. contains the "Gesta Stephani Regis," the Chronicle of Richard of Hexham, the "Relatio de Standardo" of St. Aelred of Rievaulx, the poem of Jordan Fantosme, and the Chronicle of Richard of Devizes.

83. CHRONICLE OF THE ABBEY OF RAMSEY. *Edited by* the Rev. WILLIAM DUNN MACRAY, M.A., F.S.A., Rector of Ducklington, Oxon. 1886.

This Chronicle forms part of the Chartulary of the Abbey of Ramsey, preserved in the Public Record Office (*see* No. 79).

84. CHRONICA ROGERI DE WENDOVER, SIVE FLORES HISTORIARUM. Vols. I., II., and III. *Edited by* HENRY GAY HEWLETT, Esq., Keeper of the Records of the Land Revenue. 1886-1889.

This edition gives that portion only of Roger of Wendover's Chronicle which can be accounted an original authority.

85. THE LETTER BOOKS OF THE MONASTERY OF CHRIST CHURCH, CANTERBURY. *Edited by* JOSEPH BRIGSTOCKE SHEPPARD, Esq., LL.D. Vols. I., II., and III., 1887-1889.

The Letters printed in these volumes were chiefly written between the years 1296 and 1333. Among the most notable writers were Prior Henry of Eastry, Prior Richard Oxenden, and the Archbishops Raynold and Meopham.

86. THE METRICAL CHRONICLE OF ROBERT OF GLOUCESTER. *Edited by* WILLIAM ALDIS WRIGHT, Esq., M.A. Parts I. and II., 1887.

The date of the composition of this Chronicle is placed about the year 1300. The writer appears to have been an eye witness of many events which he describes. The language in which it is written was the dialect of Gloucestershire at that time.

87. CHRONICLE OF ROBERT OF BRUNNE. *Edited by* FREDERICK JAMES FURNIVALL, Esq., M.A., Barrister-at-Law. Parts I. and II. 1887.

Robert of Brunne, or Bourne, co. Lincoln, was a member of the Gilbertine Order established at Sempringham. His Chronicle is described by its editor as a work of fiction, a contribution not to English history, but to the history of English.

88. ICELANDIC SAGAS AND OTHER HISTORICAL DOCUMENTS relating to the Settlements and Descents of the Northmen on the British Isles. Vol. 1. Orkneyinga Saga, and Magnus Saga. Vol. II. Hakonar Saga, and Magnus Saga. *Edited by* M. GUDBRAND VIGFUSSON, M.A. 1887.

89. THE TRIPARTITE LIFE OF ST. PATRICK, with other documents relating to that Saint. *Edited by* WHITLEY STOKES, Esq., LL.D., D.C.L., Honorary Fellow of Jesus College, Oxford; and Corresponding Member of the Institute of France. Parts I. and II. 1887.

90. WILLELMI MONACHI MALMESBIRIENSIS DE REGUM GESTIS ANGLORUM, LIBRI V.; ET HISTORIÆ NOVELLÆ, LIBRI III. *Edited by* WILLIAM STUBBS, D.D., Bishop of Oxford. Vols. I. and II. 1887-1889.

91. LESTORIE DES ENGLES SOLUM GEFFREI GAIMAR. *Edited by* the late Sir THOMAS DUFFUS HARDY, D.C.L., Deputy Keeper of the Public Records; *continued and translated by* CHARLES TRICE MARTIN, Esq., B.A., F.S.A. Vols. I. and II. 1888, 1889.

92. CHRONICLE OF HENRY KNIGHTON, Canon of Leicester. *Edited by* the Rev. JOSEPH RAWSON LUMBY, D.D., Norrisian Professor of Divinity. Vol. I. 1889.

93. CHRONICLE OF ADAM MURIMUTH, with the CHRONICLE OF ROBERT OF AVESBURY. *Edited by* EDWARD MAUNDE THOMPSON, Esq., LL.D., F.S.A., Principal Librarian and Secretary of the British Museum.

94. CHARTULARY OF THE ABBEY OF ST. THOMAS THE MARTYR, DUBLIN. *Edited by* JOHN THOMAS GILBERT, Esq., F.S.A., M.I.R.A.

In the Press.

ICELANDIC SAGAS, AND OTHER HISTORICAL DOCUMENTS relating to the Settlements and Descents of the Northmen on the British Isles. Vols. III.—IV. *Translated by* Sir GEORGE WEBBE DASENT, D.C.L.

CHARTULARY OF THE ANCIENT BENEDICTINE ABBEY OF RAMSEY, from the MS. in the Public Record Office. Vol. III. *Edited by* the late WILLIAM HENRY HART, Esq., F.S.A., and the Rev. PONSONBY ANNESLEY LYONS.

CHARTERS AND DOCUMENTS, ILLUSTRATING THE HISTORY OF THE CATHEDRAL AND CITY OF SARUM, 1100–1300; forming an Appendix to the Register of S. Osmund. Vol. III. *Edited by* the late Rev. W. H. RICH JONES, M.A., F.S.A., *and* the Rev. W. D. MACRAY, M.A., F.S.A., Rector of Ducklington.

FLORES HISTORIARUM, PER MATTHÆUM WESTMONASTERIENSEM COLLECTI. *Edited by* HENRY RICHARDS LUARD, D.D., Fellow of Trinity College, Registrary of the University, and Vicar of Great St. Mary's, Cambridge. Vol. I., II., and III.

RANULF DE GLANVILL; TRACTATUS DE LEGIBUS ET CONSUETUDINIBUS ANGLIÆ, &c. *Edited and translated by* Sir TRAVERS TWISS, Q.C., D.C.L.

YEAR BOOKS OF THE REIGN OF EDWARD III. *Edited and translated by* LUKE OWEN PIKE, Esq., M.A., of Lincoln's Inn, Barrister-at-Law.

CHRONICLE OF HENRY KNIGHTON, Canon of Leicester, to the death of RICHARD II. *Edited by* the Rev. JOSEPH RAWSON LUMBY, D.D. Vol. II.

ANNALS AND MEMORIALS OF ST. EDMUNDS ABBEY. *Edited by* THOMAS ARNOLD, Esq., M.A.

RECUEIL DES CRONIQUES ET ANCHIENNES ISTORIES DE LA GRANT BRETAIGNE A PRESENT NOMME ENGLETERRE, par JEHAN DE WAURIN. Vol. V. 1443–1461. *Edited by* the late Sir WILLIAM HARDY, F.S.A., and EDWARD L. C. P. HARDY, Esq., F.S.A., of Lincoln's Inn, Barrister-at-Law.

CHRONICLES OF THE REIGNS OF STEPHEN, HENRY II., AND RICHARD I. Vol. IV. *Edited by* RICHARD HOWLETT, Esq., of the Middle Temple, Barrister-at-Law.

In Progress.

DESCRIPTIVE CATALOGUE OF MANUSCRIPTS RELATING TO THE HISTORY OF GREAT BRITAIN AND IRELAND. Vol. IV.; 1327, &c. *Edited by* the late Sir THOMAS DUFFUS HARDY, D.C.L., Deputy Keeper of the Records, and C. TRICE MARTIN, Esq., B.A., F.S.A.

THE TREATISE "DE PRINCIPUM INSTRUCTIONE," of GIRALDUS CAMBRENSIS; with an Index to the first four volumes of the "Works of Giraldus Cambrensis," edited by the Rev. J. S. Brewer. *Edited by* GEORGE F. WARNER, Esq., of the Department of MSS., British Museum.

THE HISTORIANS OF THE CHURCH OF YORK AND ITS ARCHBISHOPS, Vol. III. *Edited by* JAMES RAINE, M.A., Canon of York, and Secretary of the Surtees Society.

PUBLICATIONS OF THE RECORD COMMISSIONERS, &c.
[In boards or cloth.]

ROTULORUM ORIGINALIUM IN CURIÂ SCACCARII ABBREVIATIO. Hen. III.—Edw. III. *Edited by* HENRY PLAYFORD, Esq. 2 Vols. folio (1805—1810). 12s. 6d. each.

CALENDARIUM INQUISITIONUM POST MORTEM SIVE ESCAETARUM. Hen. III.—Ric. III. *Edited by* JOHN CALEY and JOHN BAYLEY, Esqrs. Folio (1821—1828): Vol. 3, 21s.; Vol. 4, 24s.

LIBRORUM MANUSCRIPTORUM BIBLIOTHECÆ HARLEIANÆ CATALOGUS. Vol. 4. *Edited* by the Rev. T. HARTWELL HORNE. Folio (1812), 18s.

ABBREVIATIO PLACITORUM. Richard I.—Edward II. *Edited by* the Right Hon. GEORGE ROSE and W. ILLINGWORTH, Esq. 1 Vol. folio (1811), 18s.

LIBRI CENSUALIS vocati DOMESDAY-BOOK, INDICES. *Edited by* Sir HENRY ELLIS. Folio (1816), (Domesday-Book, Vol. 3). 21s.

LIBRI CENSUALIS vocati DOMESDAY-BOOK, ADDITAMENTA EX CODIC. ANTIQUISS. *Edited by* Sir HENRY ELLIS. Folio (1816), (Domesday-Book, Vol. 4). 21s.

STATUTES OF THE REALM. *Edited by* Sir T. E. TOMLINS, JOHN RAITHBY, JOHN CALEY, and WM. ELLIOTT, Esqrs. Vols. 7, 8, 9, 10, and 11, folio (1819—1828). 31s. 6d. each; Indices, 30s. each.

VALOR ECCLESIASTICUS, temp. Hen. VIII., Auctoritate Regia institutus. *Edited by* JOHN CALEY, Esq., and the Rev. JOSEPH HUNTER. Vols. 3 to 6, folio (1817—1834). 25s. each. The Introduction, separately, 8vo. 2s. 6d.

ROTULI SCOTIÆ IN TURRI LONDINENSI ET IN DOMO CAPITULARI WESTMONASTERIENS ASSERVATI. 19 Edw. I.—Hen. VIII. *Edited by* D. MACPHERSON, J. CALEY, W. ILLINGWORTH, Esqrs., and Rev. T. H. HORNE. Vol. 2. folio (1818). 21s.

FŒDERA, CONVENTIONES, LITTERÆ, &c.; or, RYMER'S FŒDERA, New Edition, folio Vol. 3, Part 2. 1361—1377 (1830): Vol. 4, 1377—1383 (1869). *Edited by* JOHN CALEY and FRED. HOLBROOKE, Esqrs. Vol. 3, Part 2, 21s.; Vol. 4. 6s.

DUCATUS LANCASTRIÆ CALENDARIUM INQUISITIONUM POST MORTEM, &c. Part 3, Calendar to Pleadings, &c., Hen. VII.—13 Eliz. Part 4, Calendar to Pleadings, to end of Eliz. (1827—1834). *Edited by* R. J. HARPER, JOHN CALEY, and WM. MINCHIN, Esqrs. Folio. Part 3 (or Vol. 2), 31s. 6d.; Part 4 (or Vol. 3), 21s.

CALENDARS OF THE PROCEEDINGS IN CHANCERY, ELIZ.; with Examples of Proceedings from Ric. II. *Edited by* JOHN BAYLEY, Esq. Vol. 3 (1832), folio, 21s.

PARLIAMENTARY WRITS AND WRITS OF MILITARY SUMMONS, with Records and Muniments relating to Suit and Service to Parliament, &c. *Edited by* SIR FRANCIS PALGRAVE. (1830—1834.) Folio. Vol. 2, Div. 1, Edw. II., 21s.; Vol. 2, Div. 2, 21s.; Vol. 2, Div. 3, 42s.

ROTULI LITTERARUM CLAUSARUM IN TURRI LONDINENSI ASSERVATI. 2 Vols. folio (1833, 1844). Vol. 1, 1204—1224. Vol. 2, 1224—1227. *Edited by* THOMAS DUFFUS HARDY, Esq. Vol. 1, 63s.; Vol. 2, 18s.

PROCEEDINGS AND ORDINANCES OF THE PRIVY COUNCIL OF ENGLAND. 10 Ric. II.—33 Hen. VIII. *Edited by* Sir NICHOLAS HARRIS NICOLAS. 7 Vols. royal 8vo. (1834—1837). 14s. each.

ROTULI LITTERARUM PATENTIUM IN TURRI LOND. ASSERVATI. 1201—1216. *Edited by* T. DUFFUS HARDY, Esq. 1 Vol. folio (1835), 31s. 6d. The Introduction, separately, 8vo. 9s.

ROTULI CURIÆ REGIS. Rolls and Records of the Court held before the King's Justiciars or Justices. 6 Richard I.—1 John. *Edited by* Sir FRANCIS PALGRAVE. 2 Vols. royal 8vo. (1835). 28s.

ROTULI NORMANNIÆ IN TURRI LOND. ASSERVATI. 1200—1205; 1417—1418. *Edited* by THOMAS DUFFUS HARDY, Esq. 1 Vol. royal 8vo. (1835). 12s. 6d.

ROTULI DE OBLATIS ET FINIBUS IN TURRI LOND. ASSERVATI, temp. Regis Johannis. *Edited by* THOMAS DUFFUS HARDY, Esq. 1 Vol. royal 8vo. (1835). 18s.

EXCERPTA E ROTULIS FINIUM IN TURRI LONDINENSI ASSERVATIS. Henry III., 1216—1272. *Edited by* CHARLES ROBERTS, Esq. 2 Vols. royal 8vo. (1835, 1836); Vol. 1, 14s.; Vol. 2, 18s.

FINES, SIVE PEDES FINIUM; SIVE FINALES CONCORDIÆ IN CURIÂ DOMINI REGIS. 7 Richard I.—16 John, 1195—1214. *Edited by* the Rev. JOSEPH HUNTER. In Counties. 2 vols. royal 8vo. (1835—1844); Vol. 1, 8s. 6d.; Vol. 2, 2s. 6d.

ANCIENT KALENDARS AND INVENTORIES OF THE TREASURY OF HIS MAJESTY'S EXCHEQUER; with Documents illustrating its History. *Edited by* Sir FRANCIS PALGRAVE. 3 Vols. royal 8vo. (1836). 42s.

DOCUMENTS AND RECORDS illustrating the History of Scotland, and Transactions between Scotland and England; preserved in the Treasury of Her Majesty's Exchequer. Edited by Sir FRANCIS PALGRAVE. 1 Vol. royal 8vo. (1837). 18s.

ROTULI CHARTARUM IN TURRI LONDINENSI ASSERVATI. 1199—1216. Edited by THOMAS DUFFUS HARDY, Esq. 1 Vol. folio (1837). 30s.

REPORT OF THE PROCEEDINGS OF THE RECORD COMMISSIONERS, 1831—1837. 1 Vol. fol. (1837). 8s.

REGISTRUM vulgariter nuncupatum "The Record of Caernarvon," e codice MS. Harleiano, 696, descriptum. Edited by Sir HENRY ELLIS. 1 Vol. folio (1838), 31s. 6d.

ANCIENT LAWS AND INSTITUTES OF ENGLAND; comprising Laws enacted under the Anglo-Saxon Kings, with Translation of the Saxon; the Laws called Edward the Confessor's; the Laws of William the Conqueror, and those ascribed to Henry I.; Monumenta Ecclesiastica Anglicana, from 7th to 10th century; and Ancient Latin Version of the Anglo-Saxon Laws. Edited by BENJAMIN THORPE, Esq. 1 Vol. folio (1840), 40s. 2 Vols. royal 8vo., 30s.

ANCIENT LAWS AND INSTITUTES OF WALES; comprising Laws supposed to be enacted by Howel the Good, modified by Regulations prior to the Conquest by Edward I.; and anomalous Laws, principally of Institutions which continued in force. With translation. Also, Latin Transcripts, containing Digests of Laws, principally of the Dimetian Code. Edited by ANEURIN OWEN, Esq. 1 Vol. folio (1841), 44s. 2 vols. royal 8vo., 36s.

ROTULI DE LIBERATE AC DE MISIS ET PRÆSTITIS, Regnante Johanne. Edited by THOMAS DUFFUS HARDY, Esq. 1 Vol. royal 8vo. (1844). 6s.

THE GREAT ROLLS OF THE PIPE, 2, 3, 4 HEN. II., 1155—1158. Edited by the Rev. JOSEPH HUNTER. 1 Vol. royal 8vo. (1844). 4s. 6d.

THE GREAT ROLL OF THE PIPE, 1 RIC. I., 1189—1190. Edited by the Rev. JOSEPH HUNTER. 1 Vol. royal 8vo. (1844). 6s.

DOCUMENTS ILLUSTRATIVE OF ENGLISH HISTORY in the 13th and 14th centuries, from the Records of the Queen's Remembrancer in the Exchequer. Edited by HENRY COLE, Esq. 1 Vol. fcp. folio (1844). 45s. 6d.

MODUS TENENDI PARLIAMENTUM. An Ancient Treatise on the Mode of holding the Parliament in England. Edited by THOMAS DUFFUS HARDY, Esq. 1 Vol. 8vo. (1846). 2s. 6d.

REGISTRUM MAGNI SIGILLI REG. SCOT. in Archivis Publicis asservatum. Vol. 1. 1306— 1424. (For continuation see p. 36.) Edited by THOMAS THOMSON, Esq. Folio (1814). 10s. 6d.

ACTS OF THE PARLIAMENTS OF SCOTLAND. Folio (1814—1875). Edited by THOMAS THOMSON and COSMO INNES, Esqrs. Vol. 1, 42s. Vols. 5 and 6 (in three Parts), 21s. each Part; Vols. 4, 7, 8, 9, 10, and 11, 10s. 6d. each; Vol. 12 (Index), 63s. Or, 12 Volumes in 13, 12l. 12s.

ACTS OF THE LORDS AUDITORS OF CAUSES AND COMPLAINTS (ACTA DOMINORUM AUDITORUM). 1466—1494. Edited by THOMAS THOMSON, Esq. Fol. (1839). 10s. 6d.

ACTS OF THE LORDS OF COUNCIL IN CIVIL CAUSES (ACTA DOMINORUM CONCILII), 1478— 1495. Edited by THOMAS THOMSON, Esq. Folio (1839). 10s. 6d.

ISSUE ROLL OF THOMAS DE BRANTINGHAM, Bishop of Exeter, Lord High Treasurer, containing Payments out of the Revenue, 44 Edw. III., 1370. Edited by FREDERICK DEVON, Esq. 1 Vol. 4to. (1835), 35s. Or, royal 8vo., 25s.

ISSUES OF THE EXCHEQUER, James I.; from the Pell Records. Edited by FREDERICK DEVON, Esq. 1 Vol. 4to. (1836), 30s. Or, royal 8vo., 21s.

ISSUES OF THE EXCHEQUER, Henry III.—Henry VI.; from the Pell Records. Edited by FREDERICK DEVON, Esq. 1 Vol. 4to. (1837), 40s. Or, royal 8vo., 30s.

HANDBOOK TO THE PUBLIC RECORDS. By F. S. THOMAS, Esq., Secretary of the Public Record Office. 1 Vol. royal 8vo. (1853). 12s.

HISTORICAL NOTES RELATIVE TO THE HISTORY OF ENGLAND. Henry VIII.—Anne (1509-1714). A Book of Reference for ascertaining the Dates of Events. By F. S. THOMAS, Esq. 3 Vols. 8vo. (1856). 40s.

STATE PAPERS, DURING THE REIGN OF HENRY THE EIGHTH : with Indices of Persons and Places. 11 Vols. 4to. (1830—1852), 10s. 6d. each.
Vol. I.—Domestic Correspondence.
Vols. II. & III.—Correspondence relating to Ireland.
Vols. IV. & V.—Correspondence relating to Scotland.
Vols. VI. to XI. Correspondence between England and Foreign Courts.

WORKS PUBLISHED IN PHOTOZINCOGRAPHY.

DOMESDAY BOOK, or the GREAT SURVEY OF ENGLAND OF WILLIAM THE CONQUEROR, 1086; fac-simile of the Part relating to each county, separately (with a few exceptions of double counties). Photozincographed, by Her Majesty's Command, at the Ordnance Survey Office, Southampton, Colonel Sir HENRY JAMES, R.E., F.R.S., &c., DIRECTOR-GENERAL of the ORDNANCE SURVEY, under the Superintendence of W. BASĒVI SANDERS, Esq., Assistant Keeper of Her Majesty's Records. 35 Parts, imperial quarto and demy quarto (1861–1863), boards. Price 8s. to 1l. 3s. each Part, according to size; or, bound in 2 Vols., 20l. (The edition in two volumes is out of print.)

>This important and unique survey of the greater portion of England[*] is the oldest and most valuable record in the national archives. It was commenced about the year 1084 and finished in 1086. Its compilation was determined upon at Gloucester by William the Conqueror, in council, in order that he might know what was due to him, in the way of tax, from his subjects, and that each at the same time might know what he had to pay. It was compiled as much for their protection as for the benefit of the sovereign. The nobility and people had been grievously distressed at the time by the king bringing over large numbers of French and Bretons, and quartering them on his subjects, "each "according to the measure of his land," for the purpose of resisting the invasion of Cnut, King of Denmark, which was apprehended. The Commissioners appointed to make the survey were to inquire the name of each place; who held it in the time of King Edward the Confessor; the present possessor; how many hides were in the manor; how many ploughs were in the demesne; how many homagers; how many villeins; how many cottars; how many serving men; how many free tenants; how many tenants in soccage; how much wood, meadow, and pasture; the number of mills and fish ponds; what had been added or taken away from the place; what was the gross value in the time of Edward the Confessor; the present value; and how much each free man or soc-man had, and whether any advance could be made in the value. Thus could be ascertained who held the estate in the time of King Edward; who then held it; its value in the time of the late King; and its value as it stood at the formation of the survey. So minute was the survey, that the writer of the contemporary portion of the Saxon Chronicle records, with some asperity—"So very narrowly he caused it to be "traced out, that there was not a single hide, nor one virgate of land, nor even, "it is shame to tell, though it seemed to him no shame to do, an ox, nor a cow, "nor a swine was left, that was not set down."
>
>Domesday Survey is in two parts or volumes. The first, in folio, contains the counties of Bedford, Berks, Bucks, Cambridge, Chester, and Lancaster, Cornwall, Derby, Devon, Dorset, Gloucester, Hants, Hereford, Herts, Huntingdon, Kent, Leicester and Rutland, Lincoln, Middlesex, Northampton, Nottingham, Oxford, Salop, Somerset, Stafford, Surrey, Sussex, Warwick, Wilts, Worcester, and York. The second volume, in quarto, contains the counties of Essex, Norfolk and Suffolk.
>
>Domesday Book was printed *verbatim et literatim* during the last century, in consequence of an address of the House of Lords to King George III. in 1767. It was not, however, commenced until 1773, and was completed early in 1783. In 1860, Her Majesty's Government, with the concurrence of the Master of the Rolls, determined to apply the art of photozincography to the production of a fac-simile of Domesday Book, under the superintendence of Colonel Sir Henry James, R.E., Director-General of the Ordnance Survey, Southampton.

FAC-SIMILES OF NATIONAL MANUSCRIPTS, from WILLIAM THE CONQUEROR to QUEEN ANNE, selected under the direction of the Master of the Rolls, and Photozincographed, by Command of Her Majesty, by Colonel Sir HENRY JAMES, R.E., F.R.S., DIRECTOR-GENERAL of the ORDNANCE SURVEY, and edited by

---

[*] For some reason left unexplained, many parts were left unsurveyed; Northumberland, Cumberland, Westmoreland, and Durham, are not described in the survey; nor does Lancashire appear under its proper name; but Furness, and the northern part of Lancashire, as well as the south of Westmoreland, with a part of Cumberland, are included within the West Riding of Yorkshire. That part of Lancashire which lies between the Ribble and Mersey, and which at the time of the survey comprehended 688 manors, is joined to Cheshire. Part of Rutland is described in the counties of Northampton and Lincoln.

W. BASEVI SANDERS, Assistant Keeper of Her Majesty's Records. *Price, each Part, with translations and notes, double foolscap folio, 16s.*
Part I. (William the Conqueror to Henry VII.). 1865. (*Out of print.*)
Part II. (Henry VIII. and Edward VI.) 1866.
Part III. (Mary and Elizabeth). 1867.
Part IV. (James I. to Anne). 1868.
 The first Part extends from William the Conqueror to Henry VII., and contains autographs of the kings of England, as well as of many other illustrious personages famous in history, and some interesting charters, letters patent, and state papers. The second Part, for the reigns of Henry VIII. and Edward VI., consists principally of holograph letters, and autographs of kings, princes, statesmen, and other persons of great historical interest, who lived during those reigns. The third Part contains similar documents for the reigns of Mary and Elizabeth, including a signed bill of Lady Jane Grey. The fourth Part concludes the series, and comprises a number of documents taken from the originals belonging to the Constable of the Tower of London; also several records illustrative of the Gunpowder Plot, and a woodcut containing portraits of Mary Queen of Scots and James VI., circulated by their adherents in England, 1580–3.

FAC-SIMILES OF ANGLO-SAXON MANUSCRIPTS. Photozincographed, by Command of Her Majesty, upon the recommendation of the Master of the Rolls, by the DIRECTOR-GENERAL of the ORDNANCE SURVEY, Lieut.-General J. CAMERON, R.E., C.B., F.R.S., and edited by W. BASEVI SANDERS, Assistant Keeper of Her Majesty's Records. Part I. *Price 2l. 10s.*
 The Anglo-Saxon MSS. represented in this volume form the earlier portions of the collection of archives belonging to the Dean and Chapter of Canterbury, and consist of a series of 25 charters, deeds, and wills, commencing with a record of proceedings at the first Synodal Council of Clovestho in 742, and terminating with the first part of a tripartite cheirograph, whereby Thurston conveyed to the Church of Canterbury land at Wimbish in Essex, in 1049, the sixth year of the reign of Edward the Confessor.

FAC-SIMILES OF ANGLO-SAXON MANUSCRIPTS. Photozincographed, by Command of Her Majesty, upon the recommendation of the Master of the Rolls, by the DIRECTOR-GENERAL of the ORDNANCE SURVEY, Major-General A. COOKE, R.E., C.B., and collected and edited by W. BASEVI SANDERS, Assistant Keeper of Her Majesty's Records. Part II. *Price 3l. 10s.*
(Also, separately. Edward the Confessor's Charter. *Price 2s.*)
 The originals of the Fac-similes contained in this volume belong to the Deans and Chapters of Westminster, Exeter, Wells, Winchester, and Worcester; the Marquis of Bath, the Earl of Ilchester, Winchester College, Her Majesty's Public Record Office, Bodleian Library, Somersetshire Archæological and National History Society's Museum in Taunton Castle, and William Salt Library at Stafford. They consist of charters and other documents granted by, or during the reigns of, Baldred, Æthelred, Offa, and Burgred, Kings of Mercia; Uhtred of the Huiccas, Ceadwalla and Ini of Wessex; Æthelwulf, Eadward the Elder, Æthelstan, Eadmund the First, Eadred, Eadwig, Eadgar, Eadward the Second, Æthelred the Second, Cnut, Eadward the Confessor, and William the Conqueror, embracing altogether a period of nearly four hundred years.

FAC-SIMILES OF ANGLO-SAXON MANUSCRIPTS. Photozincographed, by Command of Her Majesty, upon the recommendation of the Master of the Rolls, by the DIRECTOR-GENERAL of the ORDNANCE SURVEY, Colonel R. H. STOTHERD, R.E., C.B., and collected and edited by W. BASEVI SANDERS, Assistant Keeper of Her Majesty's Records. Part III. Price 6l. 6s.
 This volume contains fac-similes of the Ashburnham collection of Anglo-Saxon Charters, &c., including King Alfred's Will. The MSS. represented in it, range from A.D. 697 to A.D. 1161, being charters, wills, deeds, and reports of Synodal transactions during the reigns of Kings Wihtred of Kent, Offa, Eardwulf, Coenwulf, Cuthred, Beornwulf, Æthelwulf, Ælfred, Eadward the Elder, Eadmund, Eadred, Queen Eadgifu, and Kings Eadgar, Æthelred the Second, Cnut, Henry the First, and Henry the Second. In addition to these are two belonging to the Marquis of Anglesey, one of them being the Foundation Charter of Burton Abbey by Æthelred the Second with the testament of its great benefactor Wulfric.

Public Record Office,
 November 1889.

HISTORICAL MANUSCRIPTS COMMISSION.

REPORTS OF THE ROYAL COMMISSIONERS APPOINTED TO INQUIRE WHAT PAPERS AND MANUSCRIPTS BELONGING TO PRIVATE FAMILIES AND INSTITUTIONS ARE EXTANT WHICH WOULD BE OF UTILITY IN THE ILLUSTRATION OF HISTORY, CONSTITUTIONAL LAW, SCIENCE, AND GENERAL LITERATURE.

Date.		Size.	Sessional Paper.	Price.
1870 (Reprinted 1874.)	FIRST REPORT, WITH APPENDIX - Contents :— ENGLAND. House of Lords; Cambridge Colleges; Abingdon, and other Corporations, &c. SCOTLAND. Advocates' Library, Glasgow Corporation, &c. IRELAND. Dublin, Cork, and other Corporations, &c.	f'cap	[C. 55]	s. d. 1 6
1871	SECOND REPORT, WITH APPENDIX, AND INDEX TO THE FIRST AND SECOND REPORTS - - - - - Contents :— ENGLAND. House of Lords; Cambridge Colleges; Oxford Colleges; Monastery of Dominican Friars at Woodchester, Duke of Bedford, Earl Spencer, &c. SCOTLAND. Aberdeen and St. Andrew's Universities, &c. IRELAND. Marquis of Ormonde; Dr. Lyons, &c.	,,	[C. 441]	3 10
1872	THIRD REPORT, WITH APPENDIX AND INDEX - - - - - Contents :— ENGLAND. House of Lords; Cambridge Colleges; Stonyhurst College; Bridgewater and other Corporations; Duke of Northumberland, Marquis of Lansdowne, Marquis of Bath, &c. SCOTLAND. University of Glasgow; Duke of Montrose, &c. IRELAND. Marquis of Ormonde; Black Book of Limerick, &c.	,,	[C. 673]	6 0

Date.		Size.	Sessional Paper.	Price.

1878	FOURTH REPORT, WITH APPENDIX. PART I. - - - - -
	 Contents :—
	    ENGLAND. House of Lords; Westminster Abbey; Cambridge and Oxford Colleges; Cinque Ports, Hythe, and other Corporations, Marquis of Bath, Earl of Denbigh, &c.
	    SCOTLAND. Duke of Argyll, &c.
	    IRELAND. Trinity College, Dublin; Marquis of Ormonde.
		f'cap	[C. 857]	s. d.
				 6 8

,,	DITTO. PART II. INDEX - - -	,,	[C.857i.]	2 6

1876	FIFTH REPORT, WITH APPENDIX. PART I. -
	 Contents :—
	    ENGLAND. House of Lords; Oxford and Cambridge Colleges; Dean and Chapter of Canterbury; Rye, Lydd, and other Corporations, Duke of Sutherland, Marquis of Lansdowne, Reginald Cholmondeley, Esq., &c.
	    SCOTLAND. Earl of Aberdeen, &c.
		,,	[C.1432]	7 0

,,	DITTO. PART II. INDEX - - -	,,	[C.1432 i.]	3 6

1877	SIXTH REPORT, WITH APPENDIX. PART I. -
	 Contents :—
	    ENGLAND. House of Lords; Oxford and Cambridge Colleges; Lambeth Palace; Black Book of the Archdeacon of Canterbury; Bridport, Wallingford, and other Corporations; Lord Leconfield, Sir Reginald Graham, Sir Henry Ingilby, &c.
	    SCOTLAND. Duke of Argyll, Earl of Moray, &c.
	    IRELAND. Marquis of Ormonde.
		,,	C. 1745	8 6

,,	DITTO. PART II. INDEX - - -	,,	[C.2102]	1 10
1879	SEVENTH REPORT, WITH APPENDIX. PART I. - - - - - Contents :— House of Lords; County of Somerset; Earl of Egmont, Sir Frederick Graham, Sir Harry Verney, &c.	,,	[C.2340]	7 6
	DITTO. PART II. APPENDIX AND INDEX - Contents :— Duke of Athole, Marquis of Ormonde, S. F. Livingstone, Esq., &c.	,,	[C. 2340 i.]	3 6

1881	EIGHTH REPORT, WITH APPENDIX AND INDEX. PART I. - - -
	 Contents :—
	    List of collections examined, 1869–1880.
	    ENGLAND. House of Lords; Duke of Marlborough; Magdalen College, Oxford; Royal College of Physicians; Queen Anne's Bounty Office; Corporations of Chester, Leicester, &c.
	    IRELAND. Marquis of Ormonde, Lord Emly, The O'Conor Don, Trinity College, Dublin, &c.
		,,	[C.3040]	8 6

Date.		Size.	Sessional Paper.	Price.
				s. d.
1881	DITTO. PART II. APPENDIX AND INDEX - Contents :— Duke of Manchester.	f'cap	[C.3040 i.]	1 9
1881	DITTO. PART III. APPENDIX AND INDEX - Contents :— Earl of Ashburnham.	,,	[C.3040 ii.]	1 4
1883	NINTH REPORT, WITH APPENDIX AND INDEX. PART I. Contents :— St. Paul's and Canterbury Cathedrals; Eton College ; Carlisle, Yarmouth, Canterbury, and Barnstaple Corporations, &c.	,,	[C.3773]	5 2
1884	DITTO. PART II. APPENDIX AND INDEX - Contents :— ENGLAND. House of Lords; Earl of Leicester; C. Pole Gell, Alfred Morrison, Esquires, &c. SCOTLAND. Lord Elphinstone, H. C. Maxwell Stuart, Esq., &c. IRELAND. Duke of Leinster, Marquis of Drogheda, &c.	,,	[C.3773 i.]	6 3
1884	DITTO. PART III. APPENDIX AND INDEX - Contents :— Mrs. Stopford Sackville.	,,	[C.3773 ii.]	1 7
1883	CALENDAR OF THE MANUSCRIPTS OF THE MARQUIS OF SALISBURY, K.G. (OR CECIL MSS.). PART I. -	8vo.	[C.3777]	3 5
1885	TENTH REPORT - This is introductory to the following :—	,,	[C.4548]	0 3½
1885	(1.) APPENDIX AND INDEX - Earl of Eglinton, Sir J. S. Maxwell, Bart., and C. S. H. D. Moray, C. F. Weston Underwood, G. W. Digby, Esquires.	,,	[C.4575]	3 7
1885	(2.) APPENDIX AND INDEX - The Family of Gawdy, formerly of Norfolk.	,,	[C.4576 iii.]	1 4
1885	(3.) APPENDIX AND INDEX - Wells Cathedral.	,,	[C.4576 ii.]	2 0
1885	(4.) APPENDIX AND INDEX - Earl of Westmorland ; Captain Stewart ; Lord Stafford ; Sir N. W. Throckmorton, Bart., Stonyhurst College ; Sir P. T. Mainwaring, Bart., Misses Boycott, Lord Muncaster, M.P., Captain J. F. Bagot, Earl of Kilmorey, Earl of Powis, Revs. T. S. Hill, C. R. Manning, and others, the Corporations of Kendal, Wenlock, Bridgnorth, Eye, Plymouth, and the County of Essex.	,,	[C.4576]	3 6
1885	(5.) APPENDIX AND INDEX - The Marquis of Ormonde, Earl of Fingall, Corporations of Galway, Waterford, the Sees of Dublin and of Ossory, the Jesuits in Ireland.	,,	[4576 i.]	2 10

Date.		Size.	Sessional Paper.	Price.
				s. d.
1887	(6.) APPENDIX AND INDEX - Marquis of Abergavenny, Lord Braye, G. F. Luttrell, P. P. Bouverie, W. B. Davenport, M.P., R. T. Balfour, Esquires.	8vo.	[C.5242]	1 7
1887	ELEVENTH REPORT - This is introductory to the following :—	,,	[C.5060 vi.]	0 3
1887	(1.) APPENDIX AND INDEX - H. D. Skrine, Esq., Salvetti Correspondence.	,,	[C.5060]	1 1
1887	(2.) APPENDIX AND INDEX - House of Lords. 1678-1688.	,,	[C.5060 i.]	2 0
1887	(3.) APPENDIX AND INDEX - Corporations of Southampton and Lynn.	,,	[C.5060 ii.]	1 8
1887	(4.) APPENDIX AND INDEX - Marquess Townshend.	,,	[C.5060 iii.]	2 6
1887	(5.) APPENDIX AND INDEX - Earl of Dartmouth.	,,	[C.5060 iv.]	2 8
1887	(6.) APPENDIX AND INDEX - Duke of Hamilton.	,,	[C.5060 v.]	1 6
1888	(7.) APPENDIX AND INDEX - Duke of Leeds, Marchioness of Waterford, Lord Hothfield, F. Darwon, Hamon le Strange, A. W. Savile, Esquires; Bridgwater Trust Office, Reading Corporation Inner Temple Library.	,,	[C.5612]	2 0
1888	CALENDAR OF THE MANUSCRIPTS OF THE MARQUIS OF SALISBURY, K.G. (or CECIL MSS.). Part II. -	,,	[C.5463]	3 5
1889	TWELFTH REPORT. This will be introductory to the following :—		In the Press.	
1888	(1.) APPENDIX. Earl Cowper, K.G. (Coke MSS., at Melbourne Hall, Derby) Vol. I.	,,	[C.5472]	2 7
1888	(2.) APPENDIX Ditto. Vol. II.	,,	[C.5613]	2 5
1888	(3.) APPENDIX AND INDEX - Ditto. Vol. III.		In the Press.	
1888	(4.) APPENDIX Duke of Rutland, G.C.B. Vol. I.	,,	[C.5614]	3 2
	(5.) APPENDIX AND INDEX - Ditto. Vol. II.		In the Press.	
	(6.) APPENDIX. House of Lords, 1689, &c.		In the Press.	
	(7.) APPENDIX. S. H. le Fleming, Esq., of Rydal.		In the Press.	

Stationery Office,
   November 1889.

ANNUAL REPORTS OF THE DEPUTY KEEPER OF THE PUBLIC RECORDS.

REPORTS Nos. 1-22, IN FOLIO, PUBLISHED BETWEEN 1840 AND 1861, ARE NO LONGER ON SALE. SUBSEQUENT REPORTS ARE IN OCTAVO.

Date.	Number of Report.	Chief Contents of Appendices.	Sessional No.	Price.
				s. d.
1862	23	Subjects of Research by Literary Inquirers, 1852-1861.—Attendances at the various Record Offices, previously to the passing of the Public Record Act.	C. 2970	0 4
1863	24	List of Calendars, Indexes, &c., in the Public Record Office.	C. 3142	0 7½
1864	25	Calendar of Crown Leases, 33-38 Hen. VIII.—Calendar of Bills and Answers, &c., Hen. VIII.-Ph. & Mary, for Cheshire and Flintshire.—List of Lords High Treasurers and Chief Commissioners of the Treasury, from Hen. VII.	C. 3318	0 8
1865	26	List of Plans annexed to Inclosure Awards, 31 Geo. II.-7 Will. IV.—Calendar of Privy Seals, &c., Hen. VI.-Eliz., for Cheshire and Flintshire.—Calendar of Writs of General Livery, &c., for Cheshire, Eliz.-Charles I.—Calendar of Deeds, &c., on the Chester Plea Rolls, Hen. III. and Edw. I.—List of Documents photozincographed, Will. I.-Hen. VII.	C. 3492	0 7
1866	27	List of Awards of Inclosure Commissioners.—References to Charters in the Cartæ Antiquæ and the Confirmation Rolls of Chancery, Ethelbert of Kent-James I.—Calendar of Deeds, &c., on the Chester Plea Rolls, Edw. II.—List of Documents photozincographed, Hen. VIII. and Edw. VI.	C. 3717	1 6
1867	28	Fees in the Public Record Office.—Calendar of Fines, Cheshire and Flintshire, Edw. I.—Calendar of Deeds, &c., on the Chester Plea Rolls, Edw. III.—List of Documents photozincographed,	C. 3839	0 10½

Date.	Number of Report.	Chief Contents of Appendices.	Sessional No.	Price
				s.
		Mary and Eliz., and Scottish, Part I.—Table of Law Terms, from the Norman Conquest to 1 Will IV.		
1868	29	Calendar of Royal Charters.—Calendar of Deeds, &c., on the Chester Plea Rolls, Richard II.-Hen. VII.—Durham Records, Letter and Report.	C. 4012	0
1869	30	Duchy of Lancaster Records, Inventory.—Durham Records, Inventory, Indexes to Kellawe's Register. — Calendar of Deeds, &c., on the Chester Plea Rolls, Hen. VIII.—Calendar of Decrees of Court of General Surveyors, 34-38 Hen. VIII.—Calendar of Royal Charters.—State Paper Office, Calendar of Documents relating to the History of, to 1800.—List of Documents photozincographed, Eliz.-Anne.—Tower of London. Index to Documents in custody of the Constable of.—Calendar of Dockets, &c., for Privy Seals, 1634-1711, in the British Museum. Report of the Commissioners on Carte Papers.—Venetian Ciphers.	C. 4165	3 0
1870	31	Duchy of Lancaster Records, Calendar of Royal Charters, Will. II.-Ric. II.—Durham Records, Calendar of Chancery Enrolments; Cursitor's Records.—List of Officers of Palatinate of Chester, in Cheshire and Flintshire, and North Wales.—List of Sheriffs of England, 31 Hen. I. to 4 Edw. III.—List of Documents photozincographed, Scottish, Part II.	[C. 187]	2 3
1871	32	Part I.—Report of the Commissioners on Carte Papers. — Calendarium Genealogicum, 1 & 2 Edw. II.—Durham Records, Calendar of Cursitor's Records, Chancery Enrolments.—Duchy of Lancaster Records, Calendar of Rolls of the Chancery of the County Palatine.	[C. 374]	2 2
1871	--	Part II.—Charities; Calendar of Trust Deeds enrolled on the Close Rolls of Chancery, subsequent to 9 Geo. II. c. xxxvi.	[C. 374] I.	5 6
1872	33	Duchy of Lancaster Records, Calendar of Rolls of the Chancery of the County Palatine.—Durham Records, Calendar of the Cursitor's Records, Chancery Enrolments.—Report on the Shaftesbury Papers.—Venetian Transcripts.—Greek copies of the Athanasian Creed.	[C. 620]	1 10
1873	34	Parliamentary Petitions; Index to the Petitions to the King in Council.—	[C. 728]	1 9

Date.	Number of Report.	Chief Contents of Appendices.	Sessional No.	Price.
				s. d.
		Durham Records, Calendar of the Cursitor's Records, Chancery Enrolments.—List of Documents photozincographed, Scottish, Part III.—Supplementary Report on the Shaftesbury Papers.		
1874	35	Duchy of Lancaster Records, Calendar of Ancient Charters or Grants.—Palatinate of Lancaster; Inventory and Lists of Documents transferred to the Public Record Office. — Durham Records, Calendar of Cursitor's Records, Chancery Enrolments.—List of Documents photozincographed, Irish, Part I.—Second Supplementary Report on the Shaftesbury Papers.	[C. 1043]	1 6
1875	36	Durham Records, Calendar of the Cursitor's Records, Chancery Enrolments.—Duchy of Lancaster Records; Calendar of Ancient Charters or Grants.—List of Documents photozincographed; Irish, Part II.—M. Armand Baschet's Report upon Documents in French Archives relating to British History.—Calendar of Recognizance Rolls of the Palatinate of Chester, to end of reign of Hen. IV.	[C. 1301]	4 4
1876	37	Part I.—Durham Records, Calendar of the Cursitor's Records, Chancery Enrolments.—Duchy of Lancaster Records, Calendar of Ancient Rolls of the Chancery of the County Palatine.—M. Baschet's list of French Ambassadors, &c., in England, 1509-1714.	[C. 1544]	1 2
1876	—	Part II.—Calendar of Recognizance Rolls of the Palatinate of Chester; Hen. V.-Hen. VII.	[C. 1544] I.	4 4
1877	38	Exchequer Records, Catalogue of Special Commissions, 1 Eliz. to 10 Vict., Calendar of Depositions taken by Commission, 1 Eliz. to end of James I.—List of Representative Peers for Scotland and Ireland.	[C. 1747]	4 3
1878	39	Calendar of Recognizance Rolls of the Palatinate of Chester, 1 Hen. VIII.-11 Geo. IV. — Exchequer Records, Calendar of Depositions taken by Commission, Charles I.—Duchy of Lancaster Records; Calendar of Lancashire Inquisitions post Mortem, &c.—Third Supplementary Report on the Shaftesbury Papers.—Anglo-Saxon Charters photozincographed.—M. Baschet's List of Despatches of French Ambassadors to England, 1509-1714.	[C. 2123]	4 6

Date.	Number of Report.	Chief Contents of Appendices.	Sessional No.	Price.
				s. d.
1879	40	Calendar of Depositions taken by Commission, Commonwealth–James II.—Miscellaneous Records of Queen's Remembrancer in the Exchequer.—Durham Records, Calendar of the Cursitor's Records, Chancery Enrolments.—Duchy of Lancaster Records, Calendar of Patent Rolls, 5 Ric. II.-21 Hen. VII.—Rules and Regulations respecting the public use of the Records.	[C. 2377]	3 0
1880	41	Calendar of Depositions taken by Commission, William and Mary to George I.—Calendar of Norman Rolls, Hen. V., Part I.—Anglo-Saxon Charters photozincographed.—Report from Rome.—List of Calendars, Indexes, &c. in the Public Record Office on 31st December 1879.	[C. 2658]	4 8
1881	42	Calendar of Depositions taken by Commission, George II.—Calendar of Norman Rolls, Hen. V., Part II. and Glossary.—Calendar of Patent Rolls, 1 Edw. I.—Anglo-Saxon Charters photozincographed.—Transcripts from Paris.	[C. 2972]	4 0
1882	43	Calendar of Privy Seals, &c., 1-7 Charles I.—Duchy of Lancaster Records, Inventory of Court Rolls, Hen. III.-Geo. IV., Calendar of Privy Seals, Ric. II.—Calendar of Patent Rolls, 2 Edw. I.—Anglo-Saxon Charters photozincographed.—Fourth Supplementary Report on the Shaftesbury Papers.—Transcripts from Paris.—Report on Libraries in Sweden.—Report on Papers relating to English History in the State Archives, Stockholm.—Report on Canadian Archives.	[C. 3425]	3 10
1883	44	Calendar of Patent Rolls, 3 Edw. I.—Durham Records, Cursitor's Records, Inquisitions post Mortem, &c.—Calendar of French Rolls, 1-10 Hen. V.—Anglo-Saxon Charters photozincographed.—Report from Venice.—Transcripts from Paris.—Report from Rome.	[C. 3771]	3 6
1884	45	Duchy of Lancaster Records, Inventory of Ministers' and Receivers' Accounts, Edw. I.-Geo. III.—Durham Records, Cursitor's Records, Inquisitions post Mortem, &c.—Treasury of the Receipt of the Exchequer, Calendar of Diplomatic Documents. — Anglo-Saxon Charters photozincographed. — Transcripts from Paris. — Reports from Rome and Stockholm. — Report on	[C. 4425]	4 3

Date.	Number of Report.	Chief Contents of Appendices.	Sessional No.	Price.
				s. d.
1885	46	Archives of Denmark, &c.—Transcripts from Venice.—Calendar of Patent Rolls, 4 Edw. I. Presentations to Offices on the Patent Rolls, Charles II.—Anglo-Saxon Charters, &c., photozincographed.—Transcripts from Paris.—Reports from Rome.—Second Report on Archives of Denmark, &c.—Calendar of Patent Rolls, 5 Edw. I.—Catalogue of Venetian Manuscripts bequeathed by Mr. Rawdon Brown to the Public Record Office.	[C. 4746]	2 10
1886	47	Transcripts from Paris.—Reports from Rome.—Third Report on Archives of Denmark, &c.—List of Creations of Peers and Baronets, 1483–1646.—Calendar of Patent Rolls, 6 Edw. I.	[C. 4888]	2 2
1887	48	Calendar of Patent Rolls, 7 Edw. I.—Calendar of French Rolls, Henry VI.—Calendar of Privy Seals, &c., 8–11 Charles I.—Calendar of Diplomatic Documents.—Schedules of Valueless Documents.	[C. 5234]	3 0
1888	49	Calendar of Patent Rolls, 8 Edw. I.—Calendar of Early Chancery Proceedings.—Index to Leases and Pensions (Augmentation Office).—Calendar of Star Chamber Proceedings.	[C. 5596]	3 0
1889	50	Calendar of Patent Rolls, 9 Edw. I.	[C. 5847]	1 2
		Indexes to Printed Reports, viz.: Reports 1–22 (1840–1861) - „ 23–39 (1862–1878) -	— —	4 0 2 0

Public Record Office,
   November 1889.

SCOTLAND.

CATALOGUE OF SCOTCH RECORD PUBLICATIONS

PUBLISHED UNDER THE DIRECTION OF

THE LORD CLERK REGISTER OF SCOTLAND.

[OTHER WORKS RELATING TO SCOTLAND WILL BE FOUND AMONG THE PUBLICATIONS OF THE RECORD COMMISSIONERS, see pp. 26-28.]

1. CHRONICLES OF THE PICTS AND SCOTS, AND OTHER EARLY MEMORIALS OF SCOTTISH HISTORY. Royal 8vo., half bound (1867). *Edited by* WILLIAM F. SKENE, LL.D. Price 10s. *Out of print.*
2. LEDGER OF ANDREW HALYBURTON, CONSERVATOR OF THE PRIVILEGES OF THE SCOTCH NATION IN THE NETHERLANDS (1492-1503); TOGETHER WITH THE BOOKS OF CUSTOMS AND VALUATION OF MERCHANDISES IN SCOTLAND. *Edited by* COSMO INNES. Royal 8vo., half bound (1867). Price 10s.
3. DOCUMENTS ILLUSTRATIVE OF THE HISTORY OF SCOTLAND FROM THE DEATH OF KING ALEXANDER THE THIRD TO THE ACCESSION OF ROBERT BRUCE, from original and authentic copies in London, Paris, Brussels, Lille, and Ghent. In 2 Vols. royal 8vo., half bound (1870). *Edited by* Rev. JOSEPH STEVENSON. Price 10s. each.
4. ACCOUNTS OF THE LORD HIGH TREASURER OF SCOTLAND. Vol. 1, A.D. 1473-1498. *Edited by* THOMAS DICKSON. 1877. Price 10s.
5. REGISTER OF THE PRIVY COUNCIL OF SCOTLAND. *Edited and arranged by* J. H. BURTON, LL.D. Vol. 1, 1545-1569. Vol. 2, 1569-1578. Vol. 3, A.D. 1578-1585. Vol. 4, A.D. 1585-1592. Vol. 5, 1592-1599. Vol. 6, 1599-1604. Vol. 7, 1604-1607. Vol. 8, 1607-1610. Vol. 9 in progress. *Edited by* DAVID MASSON, LL.D. 1877-1887. Price 15s. each.
6. ROTULI SCACCARII REGUM SCOTORUM. THE EXCHEQUER ROLLS OF SCOTLAND Vol. 1, A.D. 1264-1359. Vol. 2, A.D. 1359-1379. *Edited by* JOHN STUART, LL.D., and GEORGE BURNETT, Lyon King of Arms. 1878-1880. Vol. 3, A.D. 1379-1406. Vol. 4, A.D. 1406-1436 (1880). Vol. 5, A.D. 1437-1454 (1882). Vol. 6, 1455-1460 (1883). Vol. 7, 1460-1469 (1884). Vol. 8, A.D. 1470-1479 (1885). Vol. 9, 1480-1487. Addenda, 1437-1487 (1886) Vol. 10, 1488-1496 (1887). Vol. 11, 1497-1591 (1888). Vol. 12, 1502-1507. *Edited by* GEORGE BURNETT. Price 10s. each.
   Vol. 13 (in progress). Vol. 14 (in progress).
7. CALENDAR OF DOCUMENTS RELATING TO SCOTLAND. *Edited by* JOSEPH BAIN. Vol. 1 (1881). Vol. II. 1272-1307 (1884). Vol. III. 1307-1357 (1887). Vol. IV., 1357-1509 (1888). Price 15s. each.
8. REGISTER OF THE GREAT SEAL OF SCOTLAND. (*Vol.* 1, *A.D.* 1306-1424, *see p.* 24). Vol. 2, A.D. 1424-1513 (1882). Vol. 3, A.D. 1513-1546 (1883). Vol. 4, A.D. 1546-1580 (1886). Vol. 5, A.D. 1580-1593 (1888). Vol. 6, A.D. 1593-1609. (In the press.) *Edited by* JAMES BALFOUR PAUL and J. M. THOMSON. Price 15s. each.
9. THE HAMILTON PAPERS. Vol. 1. In the press.

FAC-SIMILES OF THE NATIONAL MSS. OF SCOTLAND. (*Out of print.*)
   Parts I., II., and III. Price 21s. each.

Stationery Office,
   October 1889.

IRELAND.

CATALOGUE OF IRISH RECORD PUBLICATIONS.

1. CALENDAR OF THE PATENT AND CLOSE ROLLS OF CHANCERY IN IRELAND. HENRY VIII., EDWARD VI., MARY, AND ELIZABETH, AND FOR THE 1ST TO THE 7TH YEAR OF CHARLES I. *Edited by* JAMES MORRIN, Royal 8vo. (1861–3). Vols. 1, 2, and 3. *Price* 11s. each.
2. ANCIENT LAWS AND INSTITUTES OF IRELAND.
Senchus Mor. (1865–1880.) Vols. 1, 2, 3, and 4. *Price* 10s. each. Vol. 5 in progress.
4. Abstracts of the Irish Patent Rolls of James I. Unbound. *Price* 25s.
Abstracts of the Irish Patent Rolls of James 1. With Supplement. *Price* 35s.
5. ULSTER, ANNALS OF. Otherwise Annals of Senat; a Chronicle of Irish Affairs from A.D. 431 to A.D. 1540. With a translation and Notes. Vol. 1, A.D. 431–1056. 600 pp. Half morocco. *Price* 10s.
6. CHARTÆ, PRIVILEGIA EL IMMUNITATES, being transcripts of Charters and Privileges to Cities Towns Abbeys and other Bodies Corporate. 18 Henry II. to 18 Richard II. (1171 to 1395.) Printed by the Irish Record Commission, 1820–1830. Folio. 92 pp. Boards (1889). *Price* 5s.

FAC-SIMILES of NATIONAL MANUSCRIPTS of IRELAND, FROM THE EARLIEST EXTANT SPECIMENS TO A.D. 1719. *Edited by* JOHN T. GILBERT, F.S.A., M.R.I.A. *Part 1 is out of print.* Parts II. and III. *Price* 42s. each. *Part IV.* 1. *Price* 5l. 5s. *Part IV.* 2. *Price* 4l. 10s.

    This work forms a comprehensive Palæographic Series for Ireland. It furnishes characteristic specimens of the documents which have come down from each of the classes which, in past ages, formed principal elements in the population of Ireland, or exercised an influence in her affairs. With these reproductions are combined fac-similes of writings connected with eminent personages or transactions of importance in the annals of the country to the early part of the eighteenth century.

    The specimens have been reproduced as nearly as possible in accordance with the originals, in dimensions, colouring, and general appearance. Characteristic examples of styles of writing and caligraphic ornamentation are, so far as practicable, associated with subjects of historic and linguistic interest. Descriptions of the various manuscripts are given by the Editor in the Introduction. The contents of the specimens are fully elucidated and printed in the original languages, opposite to the Fac-similes—line for line—without contractions—thus facilitating reference and aiding effectively those interested in palæographic studies.

    In the work are also printed in full, for the first time, many original and important historical documents.

    Part I. commences with the earliest Irish MSS. extant.
    Part II.: From the Twelfth Century to A.D. 1299.
    Part III.: From A.D. 1300 to end of reign of Henry VIII.
    Part IV. 1.: From reign of Edward VI. to that of James I.
    In Part IV. 2.—the work is carried down to the early part of the eighteenth century, with Index to the entire publication.

ACCOUNT OF FAC-SIMILES OF NATIONAL MANUSCRIPTS OF IRELAND. IN ONE VOLUME; 8vo., WITH INDEX. *Price* 10s. Parts I. and II. together. *Price* 2s. 6d. Part II. *Price* 1s. 6d. Part III. *Price* 1s. Part IV. 1. *Price* 2s. Part IV. 2. *Price* 2s. 6d.

Stationery Office,
    October 1889.

ANNUAL REPORTS OF THE DEPUTY KEEPER OF THE PUBLIC RECORDS, IRELAND.

Date.	Number of Report.	Chief Contents of Appendices.	Sessional No.	Price. s. d.
1869	1	Contents of the principal Record Repositories of Ireland in 1864.—Notices of Records transferred from Chancery Offices.—Irish State Papers presented by Philadelphia Library Company.	[C. 4157]	2 3
1870	2	Notices of Records transferred from Chancery, Queen's Bench, and Exchequer Offices.—Index to Original Deeds received from Master Litton's Office.	[C. 137]	1 0
1871	3	Notices of Records transferred from Queen's Bench, Common Pleas, and Exchequer Offices.—Report on J. F. Ferguson's MSS.—Exchequer Indices, &c.	[C. 329]	2 0
1872	4	Records of Probate Registries	[C. 515]	0 2½
1873	5	Notices of Records from Queen's Bench Calendar of Fines and Recoveries of the Palatinate of Tipperary, 1664–1715.—Index to Reports to date.	[C. 760]	0 8
1874	6	Notices of Records transferred from Chancery, Queen's Bench, and Common Pleas Offices.—Report respecting "Facsimiles of National MSS. of Ireland."—List of Chancery Pleadings (1662–1690) and Calendar to Chancery Rolls (1662–1713) of Palatinate of Tipperary.	[C. 963]	0 7½
1875	7	Notices of Records from Exchequer and Admiralty Offices.—Calendar and Index to Fiants of Henry VIII.	[C. 1175]	0 7
1876	8	Calendar and Index to Fiants of Edward VI.	[C. 1469]	1 3
1877	9	Index to the Liber Munerum Publicorum Hiberniæ.—Calendar and Index to Fiants of Philip and Mary.	[C. 1702]	0 8
1878	10	Schedule of Parochial Registers deposited.—Index to Deputy Keeper's 6th, 7th, 8th, 9th, and 10th Reports.	[C. 2034]	0 3½
1879	11	Calendar to Fiants of Elizabeth (1558–1570)	[C. 2311]	1 4
1880	12	Calendar to Fiants of Elizabeth, continued (1570–1576).—Schedule of Parish Registers of Ireland.	[C. 2583]	1 3

Date.	Number of Report.	Chief Contents of Appendices.	Sessional No.	Price.
				s. d.
1881	13	Calendar to Fiants of Elizabeth, continued (1576–1583).	[C. 2929]	1 5
1882	14	Report of Keeper of State Papers containing Catalogue of Commonwealth Books transferred from Bermingham Tower.	[C. 3215]	0 6½
1883	15	Calendar to Fiants of Elizabeth, continued (1583–1586).—Index to Deputy Keeper's 11th, 12th, 13th, 14th, and 15th Reports.	[C. 3676]	1 0
1884	16	Calendar to Fiants of Elizabeth, continued (1586–1595).	[C. 4062]	1 6
1885	17	Report on Iron Chest of attainders following after 1641 and 1688.—Queen's Bench Calendar to Fiants of Elizabeth, continued (1596–1601).	[C. 4487]	1 6
1886	18	Calendar to Fiants of Elizabeth, continued (1601–1603).—Memorandum on Statements (1702) and Declarations (1713–14) of Huguenot Pensioners.—Schedule of present places of custody of Parish Registers.	[C. 4755]	1 1
1887	19	Notice of Records of Incumbered and Landed Estates Courts.—Report of Keeper of State Papers, containing Table of Abstracts of Decrees of Innocence (1663), with Index.	[C. 5185]	0 6
1888	20	Calendar to Christ Church Deeds in Novum Registrum, 1174–1684. Index to Deputy Keeper's 16th, 17th, 18th, 19th, and 20th Reports.	[C. 5535]	0 8½
1889	21	Index to Calendars of Fiants of the reign of Queen Elizabeth. Letters A—C.	[C. 5835]	1 0

Public Record Office of Ireland.
  October 1889.

www.ingramcontent.com/pod-product-compliance
Lightning Source LLC
Chambersburg PA
CBHW060750230426
43667CB00010B/1517